Essays in International Economic Theory

INTERNATIONAL FACTOR MOBILITY

Essays in International Economic Theory

Volume 2

Jagdish Bhagwati

Edited by Robert C. Feenstra

The MIT Press
Cambridge, Massachusetts
London, England

Printed and bound in the United States of America.

Library of Congress Cataloging in Publication Data
Bhagwati, Jagdish N., 1934–
International factor mobility.
(Essays in international economic theory; v. 2)
Includes bibliographies and index.
1. Commerce—Addresses, essays, lectures.
2. Brain drain—Addresses, essays, lectures.
3. Investments, Foreign—Addresses, essays, lectures.
4. Labor mobility—Addresses, essays, lectures.
I. Feenstra, Robert C. II. Title. III. Series:
Bhagwati, Jagdish N., 1934– . Essays in international economic theory; v. 2.
HF1411.B466 1983 vol. 2 337s [331.12'791] 83-859
ISBN 0-262-02197-8

MIT Press
0262021978
BHAGWATI
ECON TH FACTR V2

For
ANURADHA KRISTINA and PALLAVI

Contents

Volume 2
International Factor Mobility

V
Surveys and Controversies in International Trade and Comparative Advantage

VI
Aid, Trade, and Payments

Author's Preface

These two volumes contain a selection of my major writings in the theory of international trade since my first note on the theory of immiserizing growth appeared a little over two decades ago in the *Review of Economic Studies* in June 1958.

I have had the pleasure of collaborating with a number of teachers, students, and colleagues over a number of years. My debt to them is considerable. Harry Johnson, with whom I wrote two papers (both in volume 1), and T. N. Srinivasan, with whom I have written several (in both volumes), deserve particular thanks. The former seduced me into international trade at Cambridge, England, where I studied for the Economics Tripos during 1954–1956; the latter has been a close friend and collaborator ever since his return to Delhi in 1964 from his PhD at Yale. In addition, I must list among my colleagues and friends the following coauthors as well: Padma Desai, Koichi Hamada, Bent Hansen, Murray Kemp, V. K. Ramaswami, and Henry Wan, Jr. And my collaborating students have included Richard Brecher, Robert Feenstra, and Earl Grinols.

I am particularly thankful to Robert Feenstra for editing these two volumes with great care and attention to detail. MIT produced in the mid-1950s, when I had the good fortune to spend a year (1956–1957) there, a major generation of trade theorists, among whom were Ronald Jones, Robert Mundell, Jaroslav Vanek, Egon Sohmen, Ronald Findlay, and other important scholars, such as Stephen Hymer and Carlos Diaz Alejandro. I had the additional good fortune during my years at MIT (1968–1980) to oversee a new wave: Richard Brecher (cross-registering from Harvard), Paul Krugman, Gene Grossman, Robert Feenstra, and Earl Grinols, to name several of the leading young trade-theorists today. To have one of them edit these volumes is a great pleasure indeed.

Editor's Preface

These two volumes of Jagdish Bhagwati's essays in the theory of international trade are arranged into broad areas: first, commercial policy; and second, factor mobility. Each volume begins with essays of general interest and is then divided into specific topics. Earlier reprinted articles from *Trade, Tariffs and Growth,* including Bhagwati's widely read survey of international trade, have also been included. Editorial notes and errata are provided at the ends of the essays, where appropriate.

I had the pleasure of reading many of these essays while studying international economics with T. N. Srinivasan and Jagdish Bhagwati at the Massachusetts Institute of Technology. A substantial number of the essays in volume 1 are the result of their fruitful collaboration. Editing these volumes has filled out the gaps in my own reading, and increased my admiration for Bhagwati's significant contribution to trade theory over the past twenty-five years.

I
INTERNATIONAL FACTOR MOBILITY: SYNTHESES

International Factor Movements and National Advantage*

JAGDISH N. BHAGWATI

Massachusetts Institute of Technology, U.S.A.

Introductory Remarks

I am particularly touched by the invitation to give the V.K. Ramaswami Lecture this year. We were close personally and our friendship was enriched by a considerable body of joint theoretical work that was conceived and executed during his visits to Oxford and mine to Delhi over a period of many years.

Ramaswami's distinction lay, not in creating dazzling but irrelevant logical constructs, but rather in the uncanny instinct with which he sensed an interesting analytical problem in issues of practical policy. Thus many of his most interesting trade-theoretic papers had a direct policy relevance, in the best tradition of economic science. And, despite the many claims on his time – it is remarkable that he was an overworked bureaucrat – he found the energy and the inclination to turn his analytical gifts on a wide range of problems.

For example, he wrote two seminal papers on subjects that have been at the centre of active trade-theoretic research subsequently: the celebrated [1963] paper on distortions that stimulated and defined the framework of the recent, voluminous literature on the theory of policy intervention in an open economy; and his famous [1971] construction of an example designed to show the impossibility of devising an effective-rate-of-protection (ERP) index in the presence of generalized substitution, which was to generate sufficient controversy to provide the impetus for other theorists to analyse the ERP index in general-equilibrium models.

He wrote much else. Indeed, the subject-matter of this Lecture was immediately evident to me when, in the course of recently formulating the analytical problems raised by the international movements of labour, I thought of a new policy-suggested problem only to have my memory jogged that Ramaswami probably had formulated the same problem many years ago. On consulting his posthumously collected *Essays*, I was delighted to find that my memory had served me right. Indeed, here was a beautiful little piece, of five terse and economical paragraphs

*Thanks are due to National Science Foundation Grant No. SOC77-07188 for financial support of the research underlying this lecture. Pranab Bardhan, Koichi Hamada, and T.N. Srinivasan made helpful suggestions on an earlier draft of the lecture (The 9th V.K. Ramaswami Memorial Lecture).

so characteristic of Ramaswami, on the very same problem of international factor mobility and national advantage! As I shall argue presently, this neglected piece poses an interesting problem of considerable originality: and one that has some relevance today.

Nothing would be more appropriate, therefore, than the present occasion to rescue this contribution of Ramaswami's from oblivion. And, in doing this, I have decided to set it in the perspective of the modern policy-related, welfare theory of international factor flows.

I. Asymmetries and Philosophical Contrasts

I shall proceed initially to analyse international capital mobility, focusing on its interaction with national advantage, and will consider labour mobility across countries only later.[1] It should suffice to say here that consideration of international labour mobility can be treated symmetrically with the analysis of capital mobility, except for two critical questions: *first*, the simultaneous consideration of mobility by both factors opens up, as will be evident below, policy and analytical questions that consideration of only one of them precludes; and *second*, there *is* a fundamental asymmetry between the two types of factor mobility across countries, when one considers the impact of such mobility on "national" advantage.

This fundamental asymmetry in the treatment of international mobility of capital and of labour is to be traced to the fact that, in the latter case, one has an ambiguous definition of the population over which welfare is to be defined.

Thus, the investment of capital abroad does not affect, in principle, the group over which "national" welfare will be defined. By contrast, the "migration" of human beings raises the question: are the migrants part of this group? There is no universal answer to this question. Migrants who are temporary, because of explicit rules in that regard as with *gastarbeiters* in Western Europe and imported workers in the oil-rich Middle East, evidently will classify as part of the "national" population. But what of permanently emigrating nationals? If they do "go away" for good, as with emigration from Soviet Russia, there is a convincing case for treating "national" welfare as defined only over "those left behind".[2] On the other hand, as seems to be the case today with a large fraction of the highly skilled migration from the LDCs (less developed countries) to the DCs (developed countries), if this migrant population is characterized by retention of ethnic ties to the country of origin, a high frequency of visits and even continuation of citizenship status in many cases, the fact of permanent migration (embodied in the holding

1. I shall abstain from discussing recent analytical work on international transfer of technology, including that which is pertinent to discussing *direct* foreign investment. My analysis is primarily focused on capital and labour flows.
2. These issues have been raised in Bhagwati and Rodriguez [1975].

of immigrant visas) is thoroughly compatible with the analyst including such migrants in the definition of "national" welfare for the country of origin.

The critical nature of this issue will become apparent from a single example. Suppose that the migration leaves those left behind marginally impoverished, while the migrants improve themselves (as would be the presumption with voluntary migration). If the immigration is to be treated as justifying the definition of national welfare only over those left behind, migration evidently has worsened national welfare. However, if the migrants are to be treated as a part of the national population, social welfare functions could easily be imagined that would enable one to judge the migration to be welfare-improving.

Having thus forewarned you against drawing unwarranted parallels between the analyses of capital and labour mobility, let me now draw your attention to a sharp distinction between two different questions that may be raised to advantage in the welfare-theoretic analysis of international factor mobility.

These two questions may be posed, while formulating our analysis (without loss of generality) from the viewpoint of a capital-importing rather than capital-exporting country. The classic question is whether capital inflow, *left to itself*, is to national advantage; and the companion question relates to the nature of *policy intervention* to regulate the inflow to secure national advantage.

The former question has traditionally divided economists into two major ideological camps which I have described elsewhere (Bhagwati [1976]) as the "benign neglect" and the "malign neglect" schools. The "benign neglect" school is where the liberal economists have traditionally gravitated, since it ties in with their customary tendency to look for the positive-sum-game (i.e. every party to a transaction gains) aspects of an economic transaction; the Invisible Hand caresses each and all. By contrast, the economists in the "malign neglect" school have focused rather on the zero(or even negative)-sum-game dimensions of such transactions: the Invisible Hand strokes some and strangulates others. These diverse viewpoints are nowhere more pronounced than in the ever-expanding literature on the impact of foreign investments on national advantage.

Related, but not identical, philosophical differences divide economists on the companion question of optimal policy intervention. Thus, most economists are inclined to proceed by assuming that, since the foreign investment inflow possibility necessarily augments the set of opportunities available to a country, optimal policy intervention can only improve welfare. However, this view implicitly disregards the possibility, central to writings from the Chicago school as also predictably from the other end of the political spectrum, that governments do not function so as to pursue the public interest but are rather the creatures of special interests, so that the politically *feasible* outcomes when foreign investment was available may well be dominated by those obtaining in its absence. The greatest contrast therefore follows between those who, focusing on optimal interventions by host governments, unconsciously transit to the extreme view that foreign capital inflow will occur in the presence of welfare-maximizing policies, and those who, following after a fashion in the Marxist tradition, go to the other extreme and consider the inflow to be occurring in the context of local policies designed to serve the interests of domestic elite groups (often sharing the spoils with the foreign elites in darker versions where the bourgeoisie of the world unites).

II. The Welfare Impact of Capital Inflow

It will serve us well to keep these political-philosophical contrasts in view as I proceed with, and frankly concentrate on, the more technical analysis of the issues at hand. I proceed immediately, however, to the *first* of the two questions that I posed above: namely, the impact of foreign capital inflow, left to itself, on national advantage.

A. Basic Proposition : No Impact

The simplest and most insightful way to address this question is to build the analysis around the central proposition that, in the absence of distortions, a "small" inflow of foreign capital will neither harm nor benefit the recipient nation. For, the rental on such capital (γ) will then equal the value of its private marginal product (PMP) which, in turn, will equal the social marginal product (SMP):

$$\gamma = \text{PMP} = \text{SMP}$$

The rental represents the cost, and the social marginal product the gross gain, to the recipient country: and their equality ensures the absence of gain or loss.

B. Gain from "Large" Inflow

This paradoxical outcome, that the inflow of capital or its absence is a matter of indifference to the recipient country, reflects of course the assumption that the influx is small. When it is "large", the presence of diminishing returns and the ensuing decline in the rental on foreign capital leaves the economy with a surplus: the rental equals the private marginal product for the marginal inflow but the total return to all capital is less than its contribution to national product, the difference accruing to the economy as a gain in income and hence in welfare. This is seen readily for a one-sector economy where the standard measure of the gain to the economy from a large inflow of foreign capital is the area under the marginal product curve net of the return to the capital. This is the striped area in Figure 1 where K_f is the magnitude of the inflow, γ is its competitive rental, OSRT is the total increase in product from the capital inflow, and OQRT is the total return to foreign capital, with SR being the marginal product curve as foreign capital inflow is varied.[3]

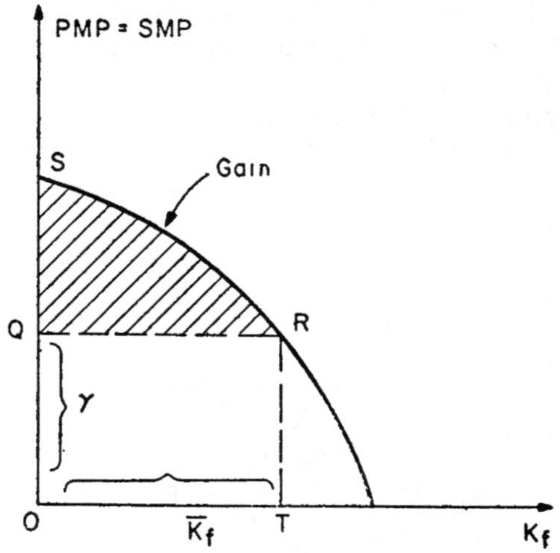

FIG. 1: K_f is the amount of foreign capital. Rental (γ) is OQ and total return to foreign capital is OQRT. SR is the marginal product curve. SQR is therefore the measure of the gain to the economy from the capital inflow.

The role of diminishing returns in this welfare-improving outcome is critical. For, it will be evident that if the capital inflow can be absorbed *without* diminishing returns, the no-impact proposition will resurrect itself even though the inflow is not small. Thus, consider a typical 2 × 2 model. With given commodity prices, it follows that factor prices and therefore factor proportions in the two commodities will remain unchanged, provided complete specialization or factor intensity reversal does not occur. The inflow and the resulting change in the factor endowment ratio will then produce a change only in relative outputs of the two commodities, with the relative and absolute output of the labour-intensive commodity falling and of the capital-intensive commodity rising (*a la* Rybczynski [1955]). The capital inflow therefore will *not* cause a decline in the reward to capital: diminishing returns will have been frustrated. More generally, as long as the economy remains within the McKenzie-Chipman diversification cone, defined on the pre-inflow factor prices, rewards to factors will *not* change, *no matter how large is the capital inflow*: and correspondingly the no-impact proposition will

3. For an extension of this argument to a dynamic framework of a growing economy, see Bardhan [1970] and Hamada [1966].

hold. This is illustrated in Figure 2. At the pre-inflow factor price-ratio AB, the factor proportions in *X* and *Y* production are given by OQ and OR respectively. The overall factor endowment ratio $\bar{K}/\bar{L}$ is only a weighted sum of the factor proportions in *X* and *Y*, given full employment. Any increase in the total endowment ratio via a capital inflow which leaves the economy still in the diversification cone QOR, as does the inflow raising the endowment ratio to $\bar{K}'/\bar{L}$, will permit the economy to remain at factor price-ratio AB, with factor proportions in *X* and *Y* unchanged.

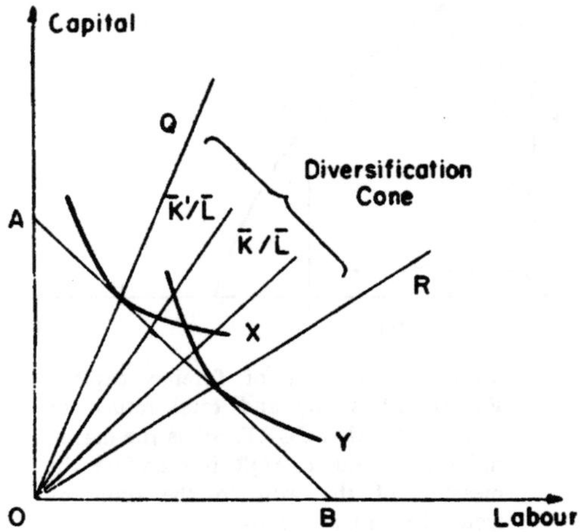

FIG. 2: OQ and OR are the factor proportions in *X* and *Y* respectively. QOR is the diversification cone. As long as the overall endowment ratio lies in this cone, diversification will obtain at factor price-ratio AB. A shift in endowment, for example from $\bar{K}/\bar{L}$ to $\bar{K}'/\bar{L}$, will *not* change factor prices and factor proportions. Diminishing returns are therefore frustrated within the cone QOR.

C. Distortions : Exogenous and Endogenous to the Capital Inflow

The presumption that follows, from the postulates of large flows and absence of distortions, is that capital inflows will be welfare-improving, with the limiting case of zero-impact if diminishing returns are frustrated. However, the interesting and important qualifications to this presumption follow precisely from the recognition and analysis of a number of distortions, whether in the nature of market imperfections or policy-imposed. In essence, they lead to an inequality between private and social marginal products to foreign capital, so that the situation is characterized by:

$$\gamma = \text{PMP} \neq \text{SMP}$$

Analytically, it is useful to distinguish here between cases where the capital inflow occurs subject to a given *exogenous* distortion and where the distortion is *endogenous* to, and therefore varies with, the capital inflow. I shall therefore develop initially a number of policy-relevant general-equilibrium arguments based on given, exogenous distortions and then discuss a model of a distortion-changing capital inflow that captures an oft-discussed implication of foreign investment.

1. Exogenous Distortions

(a) The simplest example of a distortion-caused inequality between private and social marginal products in general-equilibrium analysis, which reinforces the presumption of gain from such inflow, is provided by the factor market distortion *a la* Arthur Lewis [1954]. Here, labour is available in elastic supply at a constant real wage. If we graft this argument onto a two-factor, one-commodity model, it is easy to see that a pre-specified real wage pre-fixes the choice of technique, and the incremental capital resulting from the capital inflow leads to incremental employment and hence to incremental national product that *exceeds* the private marginal product to capital. Thus, in Figure 3, let the fixed real wage lead to fixed choice of capital-labour ratio along OQS. As capital flows in from initial equilibrium at Q, in amount QR, the increment in national output for given labour OT will be $(X^1 - X^0)$ and will accrue, for a small inflow, to the foreign capital. However, the actual increment in output will be $(X^2 - X^0) > (X^1 - X^0)$, since labour employment will *also* increase from OT to OW, given the assumption of elastic labour supply at the given real wage. Therefore SMP > PMP for the capital inflow. The Lewis model, should you think that it captures the essence of the economy, leads therefore to an optimistic assessment of the welfare impact of foreign investment.

(b) On the other hand, a distortion that *can* lead to a contrary outcome is where foreign investment occurs in the presence of unexploited, or inadequately exploited, monopoly power in trade: a situation that results in what I have called elsewhere [1971] a foreign distortion. As some of us showed in the 1950s (Bhagwati [1958], Johnson [1955]), even domestic accumulation of capital can result in a welfare loss for such an economy: a phenomenon now known as immiserizing growth. When the capital accumulation is due to inflow of foreign capital, we must also subtract from national gain the competitive return to foreign capital, so that the conditions for welfare loss resulting from the capital inflow can be shown to be less restrictive than those which have been established for immiseri-

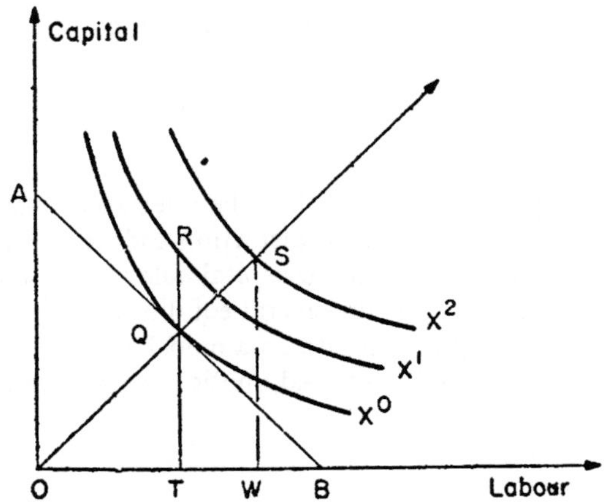

FIG. 3: In this one-sector, Lewis type model, the pre-specified real wage pre-fixes technique along OQS. Augmenting capital from QT to RT increases output, *not* to X^1 but, to X^2 since TW amount of additional labour will be forthcoming. Therefore, for a small augmentation of capital, the rental to capital will be (X^1-X^0) but the contribution to national income will be larger: (X^2-X^0).

zation from domestic accumulation. In the 2 × 2 model, it still remains true that either inelastic foreign demand for imports or capital-intensity of the importable good will increase the likelihood of such immiserization from the capital inflow; however, these conditions are no longer critical to such a paradoxical outcome in view of the added source of loss from the earnings of foreign capital and the fact that the capital inflow implies a capital outflow from the rest of the world which, in turn, *could* contract the external offer curve, faced by the recipient country, and thus be an external source of welfare loss.

(c) Finally, let me draw on yet another, still more policy-relevant, manner in which the influx of capital may immiserize the recipient country. Suppose that the capital inflow occurs in the presence of a tariff. This may occur due to a deliberate policy of the government which aims at inducing a tariff-jumping investment and indeed the analysis that I present here has relevance to determining the desirability of such a policy. But the postulated inflow may occur *exogenously* to the tariff. Assume then that, in the 2 × 2 model, foreign capital is introduced into a small economy with a tariff in place. With other distortions assumed away, the tariff is then the only (policy-imposed) distortion in the system and entails a loss for this small economy for *any* level of factor endowments. A small inflow can then be shown to be *necessarily* immiserizing when the importable is capital-intensive and necessarily welfare-improving when it is labour-intensive: in the former case, γ = PMP < SMP and in the latter case, γ = PMP > SMP.

This *is* a strong conclusion. For, what we know from the theory of immiserizing growth is that, in a tariff-distorted small economy, domestic capital accumulation *can* be, but is *not* necessarily, immiserizing when the importable is capital-intensive. When capital accumulates through influx of foreign capital, however, the competitive return to foreign capital is an added source of national loss and makes immiserization a *necessary* outcome.[4]

While this is true for small inflows, the effect of large flows is somewhat more complex. As the flow increases, the fact that factor proportions are fixed due to given commodity (and hence factor) prices ensures that what happens for a small inflow will hold for large inflows: the economy's welfare will continue to decline. However, the production of capital-intensive importables will continue to increase relative to their consumption with increasing capital inflow, thus eventually resulting in autarky. Further inflow will therefore begin reducing the relative price of the importable below its tariff-inclusive price, while keeping it above the external price. This reduction in the relative price of the capital-intensive importable will then be a source of welfare gain since it will successively reduce the rental on foreign capital *a la* the celebrated Stolper-Samuelson [1941] analysis. Therefore, beyond autarky, successive capital inflows will improve welfare until the process is halted by the domestic relative price of the importable falling so far below the tariff-inclusive price as to equal the external price. This restores the free trade situation and correspondingly the free-trade welfare level: this being the familiar Mundell [1957] result. As more capital flows in, it is absorbed by a relative and absolute decline in the importable output: the economy is operating in the diversification cone and welfare remains unchanged. Eventually, the economy reaches complete specialization on the importable good and then classical diminishing returns set in as more capital comes in, resulting again therefore in welfare improvement *a la* MacDougall [1960] and Jasay [1960]. These successive outcomes are illustrated in Figure 4. The decline in utility as the economy imposes a tariff is from F to T. The inflow of capital, K_f leads to successive decline in social utility down to A where autarky is reached. Utility then increases monotonically until the free trade level is reached and the Mundell equilibrium is established at M. Utility stays constant thereafter until Q, when complete specialization in production of the importable is reached. Further inflows of capital then lead to increasing welfare, along QR, owing to classical diminishing returns in the importable industry.

4. This remarkable conclusion has been arrived at by Brecher and Diaz-Alejandro [1978], building on the earlier work of Johnson [1967] and Bhagwati [1973], and independently by Hamada [1974] and Minabe [1974] who built on an earlier piece in Japanese by Uzawa [1969].

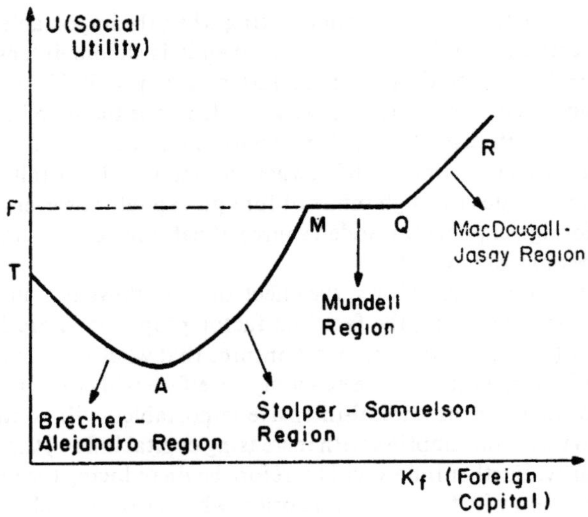

FIG. 4: For a small economy without domestic distortions, a tariff will bring social utility down to T from F (at free trade). Influx of capital, in this economy with importable capital-intensive, will successively reduce welfare down till autarky obtains at A. Thereafter, utility will increase due to Stolper-Samuelson effect until the free trade goods price-ratio is reached at M. At M, and as long as diversification obtains along MQ, the utility will therefore be at free trade level. At Q, complete specialization will occur on the importable. Diminishing returns thereafter will bring gains along QR.

This analysis has direct relevance to the important issues that have been raised recently by trade and developmental economists concerning the appropriate foreign trade strategy for developing countries. It is now indisputable that countries that have pursued an export promoting strategy have done remarkably better than those that have persisted with inward-looking, import-substituting strategy. Among the reasons for this superior performance, we must surely reckon the social efficiency of foreign investment in the export promoting countries and its inefficiency in the import replacing countries. For, the latter group of countries would appear to be characterized by the conditions favourable to immiserizing capital inflow that I have already sketched: protective policies combined with capital-intensity of the importable activities. On the other hand, the foreign investments in the export promoting countries, far from being of the tariff-jumping, local-market-oriented variety, have been essentially to exploit local cost conditions *a la* the Heckscher-Ohlin model, thus coming much closer to the welfare-improving set of conditions sketched by me earlier.[5] The distortionary policies that reduce the productivity of domestic investments in the import-substituting regimes thus also adversely affect the gains from foreign investments, suggesting strongly therefore the wisdom of Ian Little's observation that foreign investment is as good or bad for you as your own policies.

2. Endogenous Distortions

My analysis so far related to the welfare impact of foreign capital inflow in the presence of *given* distortions in general equilibrium, and I drew on three such distortions of interest: the Lewis-type factor market distortion, the foreign distortion represented by unexploited monopoly power in trade, and the foreign distortion constituted by a tariff in a small economy.

But distortions can themselves be endogenous to the policy or parametric change being considered. Those of you who are familiar with the theory of distortions and commercial policy will recall that a production distortion resulting from monopoly in production is not invariant to commercial policy: the introduction of free trade by a small country eliminates the distortion by destroying the domestic monopoly. Hence free trade continues to be the optimal policy in this case whereas a production distortion resulting alternatively from an externality which is invariant to commercial policy requires a production tax-cum-subsidy to achieve optimality! One does not have to go far to find analyses of the welfare impact of foreign investment that reflect analogously its effect on the distortions present in the recipient economy.

An apt illustration of such a distortion-changing analysis of foreign investment is readily built on the empirical observation that foreign firms typically tend to become islands of high wages which then tend to spread to local firms in a leap-frogging process. The consequences of the influx of foreign firms can then be analysed, where this wage-augmenting effect operates, in terms of as ticky-wage model of the Harris-Todaro [1970] type wherein the inflow both adds to the availability of capital in the modern sector and raises the sticky wage therein. The effect of the influx of capital in such a sticky-wage model would generally lead to an inequality between private and social marginal products in any event because the sticky wage is evidently distortionary; however, the outcome is influenced also by the fact that the level of the sticky wage is itself endogenous to the inflow of capital. The divergence between private and social marginal products arises simply

5. For a detailed empirically-based analysis of these issues, see Bhagwati [1978, Chapter 8].

because the model will generally yield a solution characterized by unemployment in the modern sector, so that the influx of capital, with the added wage raising effect in the modern sector, may well reduce welfare below the pre-inflow level.[6] This possibility, which can be readily demonstrated, is evidently of relevance to policies of host governments which often impose on foreign firms, on grounds of equity and indigenization, the obligation to pay to nationals the high salaries that foreigners earn in similar jobs: such policies may well be a source of welfare loss as modelled above.

On the other hand, the impact of the foreign firms may well be benign in influencing domestic distortions: as when unduly low salaries set by governmental fiat may be pulled up to desirable levels as a result of the stress arising from the entry of foreign firms with higher salary levels.

D. Two Distortion-Related Arguments in Developmental Policy

I should like to turn next to an analysis of two distortion-related arguments concerning foreign investment which are standard fare in developmental policy discussions and which, while influential, are somewhat less tractable to formal analysis than the neat arguments developed by me so far. They relate to the impact of foreign investments in the "grey" areas of entrepreneurship and of domestic and foreign savings.

1. Entrepreneurship

Among the more persistent worries relating to foreign investment has been the fear that its entry would deter the domestic growth of entrepreneurship. For those who consider the growth of such entrepreneurship to be the key to sustained development, the deterrent effect could be a serious source of inequality between the private and social marginal products of foreign investment.

There is no systematic analytical work, to my knowledge, that establishes this deterrent effect, though its presence cannot be ruled out. It stands, of course, in contrast to the generally favourable effect on efficiency that the presence of competitive firms is supposed to have in more traditional arguments.

The remedies suggested or practised to minimize this deterrent effect have been diverse. They include the celebrated but unimplemented Hirschman [1969] suggestion that a special institution be set up to buy up foreign firms at fair prices at future dates so that foreign investment in certain sectors, when introduced owing to necessity, would self-destruct on schedule. The policy of forced joint ventures such that foreign firms must seek local equity participation is yet another,

6. A formal, general-equilibrium analysis of brain drain along similar lines is deployed by Bhagwati and Hamada [1974].

rather common policy. However, if the domestic environment is protective and conducive to creation of a rentier rather than a Schumpeterian situation, then the result is going to be the sharing of the rents between local groups and the foreign firms, and the creation of a rentier rather than a genuine entrepreneurial class.

It is worth remarking that these entrepreneurial concerns do suggest selective restriction of foreign investment rather than generalized restriction of the kind I will presently discuss. Moreover, mention needs to be made of the role of capital market imperfections in the general area. Thus one of the important arguments produced in favour of selective restriction is that often local firms in the poor countries, owing to inadequate access to short-term liquidity, may be taken over by foreign firms for a song – the foreign firms being able to do this because they have much better access to funds – and therefore the government ought to prevent such take-overs (Kindleberger [1973]). This contention implicitly assumes of course that competition among foreign firms will not impute the correct social valuation to the local firms being taken over *and* that the local government will be able to identify such a situation with reasonable accuracy.

A related argument for selective control on foreign investment, based rather on imperfections arising from governmental policy, is that if QRs, licensing and other such barriers to competition create rents in specific activities, foreign investment should be barred from such activities as its PMP will exceed its SMP, ceteris paribus, by the amount of the rents.

2. Savings : Domestic and Foreign

Yet another source of distortion in the host economy may follow from the induced impact of the foreign inflow on domestic savings and on *other* foreign inflows.

A clearly distortionary situation can for example be identified if MNCs are a lobby against foreign aid and hence reduce the free resources available to the economy. On the other hand, as always with such arguments, we must also reckon with the reverse, more agreeable distortion: i.e. once MNCs are *in* the country, they often champion the local causes, including the aid-seeking efforts of their host countries.

The adverse impact on domestic savings from foreign capital inflows is statistically well established in innumerable works.[7] But the evidence remains essentially anchored on simple regressions, with minor exceptions, and alternative formulations of this substitution hypothesis, (e.g., that one would expect the adverse effect to register itself in public sector, rather than overall, savings, as in Bhagwati and Srinivasan [1977 : 234-35]) are not exactly supportive of the hypothesis.

7. These have been reviewed extensively in Bhagwati [1978, Chapter 6].

The contention that such an adverse effect on domestic savings, if any, necessitates restriction of such foreign capital inflows, however, presupposes that this adjustment in the domestic savings effort is not a Fisherian response to augmented resources and that one is dealing with an inherently distorted situation with a sub-optimal savings decision process.

E. Arguments Involving Inapplicability of Social Utility Function

There are also influential arguments, often raised against the free inflow (or outflow) of foreign capital, which essentially involve the inapplicability of analysis based on a well-defined social utility function. I will deal with two major types of argumentation here: (1) taste formation and income distribution; and (2) political objectives.

1. Taste Formation and Income Distribution

An important argument advanced against MNCs has been the contention in Latin American circles that the postwar MNCs in these countries have been responsible for "distorting" the domestic tastes in favour of elitist consumption, shifting resource allocation to industries providing such consumption, and producing a distorted development that is income-distributionally undesirable.

Fundamentally, this objection to MNCs departs from the distortionary arguments predicated on a social utility function in raising the issue of changing values in a fashion that is considered to be undesirable. At the same time, I think that it confuses cause with effect. The highly unequal income distribution predates the arrival of modern MNCs; the tastes for modern goods are formed as these new goods arrive on the DC stage and spread through the world economy, *quite independently* of local investment by the MNCs; and it is because these goods were imported, thanks to such income distribution and taste formation, that the process of import substitution inevitably implied the induced entry of MNCs to produce these goods. The local presence of MNCs is therefore a consequence, *not* a cause, of the unequal income distributional structures and the diffusion of consumption pattern from the DC to LDC elites.

That the foreign elites and the local elites *then* transit to a symbiotic relationship that reinforces such taste distortion and constrains the policy options towards the support of undesirable political and economic policies is a different issue: but it is also an issue that dominates the thinking of many intellectuals concerned with MNCs. While the argument just analysed interweaves the issue of taste formation with the issue of income distribution, the effect of foreign investment on either by itself has also been raised in the policy literature.

MNCs have been criticised, for instance, for influencing tastes of consumers in products, and of producers in technological choice, in "undesirable" directions.

In regard to consumer taste in products, one needs to distinguish between arguments that are built on the intransitive notion that my tastes are better than yours and those that reflect *disexternalities* from specific new products. That tastes do get conditioned to *some* degree by producers of differentiated products in a dynamic, capitalist economy is evident, though the Galbraithian vulgarization that they are so determined fully will impress only the illiterate. But I can see no philosophically convincing way of resolving disputes based on conflicting assertions of desirable tastes. The fact does remain that, for economies emerging from the Ricardian world of basic needs. perhaps the important economic-philosophical problem *is* one that we economists cannot resolve: whether to let tastes, and therefore consumption and availabilities, develop in response to market forces or whether any intervention in this process can be justified on deeper grounds than those based on the evident belief that one's lifestyle is so fetching that it must be forced on others who are unable to see its advantages.

The argument about disexternalities from new products, however, is more tractable though, in practice, extremely difficult to assess. A classic example is provided by the widespread condemnation of Nestlé for propagating formula food for babies in the less developed countries (LDCs): the charge being that this had bamboozled mothers into giving up nutritious breastfeeding and resulting in malnutrition additionally because LDC mothers often failed to use boiled water and sterilized utensils for formula preparation. If the few empirical studies on these issues were not extremely tenuous while also being conceptually confused, the argument against Nestlé would appear decisive. However, it is not. For example, how does one reckon with a mother – and, of these, there are many, if not most – who uses formula during the day so that she can go out to work rather than be confined to home to breastfeed her child? How is one to assess the externality of such "freeing" of the women for greater participation in economic life against the alleged disexternality of malnutrition? Thus, even with the question of externalities from the introduction of new products for old needs, the contentions can rapidly descend into the grey region where the dictates of one's prejudices and preferences are to be pitted against those of one's opponents.

As for income distributional implications, perhaps the politically most potent criticism of MNCs has come from the *outflow* end, with DC trade unions charging recently that MNCs were transferring jobs abroad and/or worsening labour's share in national income.

These concerns of trade unions can be formalized in models which build in distortionary sticky wages associated with unemployment; and the effects of international capital mobility can be readily grafted onto a traditional trade-theoretic model with sticky wages as in Brecher [1974a, 1974b] and Lefeber [1971]. This type of model would create a wedge between SMP and PMP, thanks to the sticky wage distortion, quite regardless of income distributional issues, of course.

Alternatively, one could choose to work with a non-distortionary, flexible-wage, full-employment model of the standard trade-theoretic variety, in which case the effects on factor shares follow from the effects of the capital flows on resource allocation and hence on factor rewards. The simulations by Thurow [1976] of the effects of capital outflow on U.S. labour incomes, built on a one-product economy, are only the simplest version of the kind of analysis that opens up in this area; whereas the familiar Stolper-Samuelson analysis of income distributional impact of alternative trade policies can be obviously extended to the analysis of income distributional implications of alternative levels of capital in the economy as in Thurow and White [1976].[8]

2. Political Objectives

Next, there are numerous arguments which are really based on the introduction of "non-economic" objectives into the social utility function. Thus, the total volume of foreign investment inflows is often sought to be restrained so as to avoid "dependence". Similarly, foreign investment in specific sectors is occasionally ruled out or regulated because they are considered politically "sensitive" and hence in the exclusive domain of domestic financing and control. The activities of MNCs in local politics, ranging from the financing of politicians or parties favourable to their interests to encouraging and fomenting foreign subversion *a la* ITT in Chile to the virtual military involvement of the Union Meuniere in Katanga, are all possibilities which cannot be taken lightly and suggest that the host country concerns with the domestic consequences of foreign firms are not exactly the results of a deranged imagination.

But there are also arguments that reduce in essence to a simple divergence between PMP and SMP because of political factors leading to economic externalities. A good illustration is provided by the exercise of political muscle by the U.S. on its MNCs to implement economic embargos against Cuba and Vietnam. This led to Canadian subsidiaries of U.S. MNCs also being subjected to this arbitrary restriction of Canadian trading opportunities purely in U.S., rather than Canadian, interests.

III. Optimal Policy Intervention

Having indicated to you the nature of these arguments concerning the welfare impact of capital inflow, let me now turn to the problem of optimal policy intervention: the second of the two welfare-theoretic questions that I distinguished at the outset.

8. For a dynamic analysis of the income distributional consequences of capital inflow combined with influx of capital-intensive technology, see Bardhan and Lapan [1973].

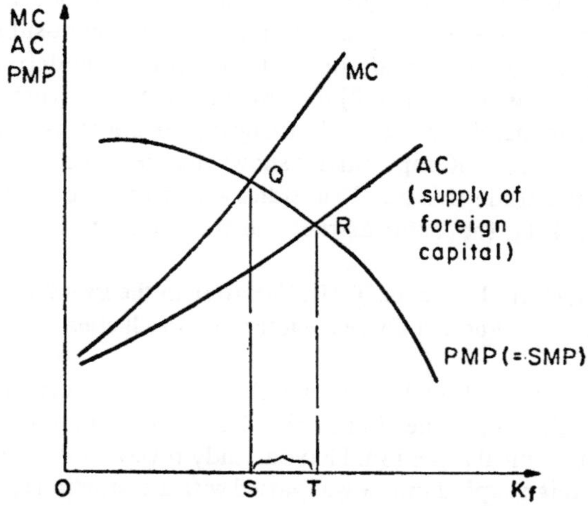

FIG. 5: This variation on Figure 1 draws in the supply curve of foreign capital (AC) and the marginal curve to it (MC). Free inflow of capital will imply inflow of OT capital. Optimal inflow however is OS where the marginal cost of capital and its PMP (= SMP) are equal. ST is the amount of restriction required: by a suitable tax on capital inflow that takes the tax-inclusive AC curve through Q.

I will make briefly three formal arguments, straying back now to the formal models where my comparative advantage lies.

(1) For a one-product economy, as portrayed in Figure 1, assume that capital flows in at a fixed rental: i.e., QR in Figure 1 is the supply curve of foreign capital. It is also then the marginal cost curve for foreign capital and the free trade inflow OT is evidently optimal. No intervention is necessary.

(2) Where, however, the foreign supply of capital is subject to a rising cost, it is plain that the host country will profit from restricting the inflow. In Figure 5, unrestricted inflow, given the rising supply price of foreign capital, will overshoot to OT whereas the optimal level of inflow is OS, given by the intersection of the marginal product and the marginal cost curves at Q. Optimal restriction then requires that the inflow be reduced by amount ST by imposing a tax that takes the tax-inclusive average curve through Q.

(3) Kemp [1966] and Jones [1967], in two classic articles, have generalized this analysis to the 2 × 2 model where capital mobility cannot be interfered with without influencing also the goods market. Their analysis thus integrates two

diametrically opposed problems: the levy of an optimal goods tariff when factors do not move and the levy of an optimal factor tax-cum-subsidy when the traded goods aspect does not obtain (as in a one-product model). As you would expect, either from Tinbergen [1952] and Meade [1951] or from the theory of distortions and commercial policy *a la* Bhagwati and Ramaswami [1963] and Johnson [1965], the Jones-Kemp analysis shows that generally two policy instruments – capital and trade taxes and subsidies – will be necessary to handle the impact in two markets: the factor market and the goods market.

IV. Welfare Impact on Tariff Variation in the Presence of Foreign-Owned Factors of Production

Before I address international labour mobility, let me now turn to yet a different, policy-relevant second-best question arising from capital mobility which has recently attracted analytical attention. I have already reviewed the welfare-theoretic analysis where foreign capital inflow was varied with a distortionary tariff in place. Suppose now that we turn this question on its head and ask what happens if, with foreign capital present in the economy, it is the external *tariff* which is varied. This is not a matter of playing analytical games: the question has been the focal point of concern in Latin American discussions where it has been feared that the effect of regional trade liberalization, as with the now-defunct Andean Common Market, would be to benefit the multinationals and to leave the member-countries with little gain and possibly even a welfare loss.

This novel and important problem lends itself to analysis fairly readily and it is easy to show, Bhagwati and Tironi [1978], that trade liberalization may be welfare-worsening in the presence of foreign-owned factors in the economy even though it would be welfare-improving in their absence. This can be demonstrated with a simple example. Thus, take the case of a small economy with none of the customary distortions. For such an economy, with all factors domestically-owned, free trade is the optimal policy and *any* tariff reduction is welfare-improving. However, assume now that, in a 2×2 model, all capital is foreign-owned and all labour is domestically-owned. Let Y be the importable good and X the exportable good, the former being labour-intensive and the latter being capital-intensive. To avoid tariff revenue problems, let me then compare free trade with autarky in such an economy. Clearly then, starting from autarky, the move to free trade will reduce the relative price of the labour-intensive importable good Y and hence result in a decline in the real wage of labour and a rise in the real rental of capital. Since labour is in fixed supply, it is clear therefore that it is unambiguously hurt and, since all capital is foreign-owned, this is tantamount to net welfare for the country having declined.

This paradoxical demonstration of immiserization following a tariff reduction builds on the simplifying assumptions of absence of tariff revenue and the exclusive identification of each factor as either foreign-owned or nationally-owned. These simplifications can be readily relaxed, of course.

Thus the analysis of tariff change has been extended to incorporate the more general case where each factor set embraces both foreign-owned and national factors of production (Bhagwati and Brecher [1978]). Moreover, as for tariff revenue effects, note that what underlies the paradox evidently is the redistribution of income towards foreign factors that occurs with the relative goods price change that follows upon the tariff change.[9] It follows therefore that the paradox may arise equally from the redistributive effect operating via tariff revenue distribution.

This is demonstrated neatly by Bhagwati and Tironi [1978] in their analysis of a trade diverting customs union in the Viner-Lipsey model of complete domestic specialization on the production of the exportable, which therefore altogether rules out any redistributive effect from production change. This model clearly has a tariff revenue effect since the tariff revenue is lost as imports are switched from the non-union country before the union to the partner country after the union. If the tariff revenue was entirely distributed by the government to domestic labour, and capital is wholly foreign, we then can get a redistributive effect *against* domestic factors. Thus, even a "large" consumption gain and "small" terms of trade loss may be compatible with welfare loss if this "redistributive" effect from the tariff revenue is large enough in a pure trade diverting union. And, if we were to assume that some or all revenue goes to foreign factors, then clearly a trade diverting union, with no substitution in consumption and hence no consumption gain, may still result in improved welfare because of the "redistributive" effect related to the tariff revenue: creating another paradox vis-a-vis the traditional conclusion that a trade diverting union, in the absence of a consumption gain, must necessarily be harmful!

Figure 6 illustrates the case where such improvement in welfare takes place in a pure trade diverting union with zero consumption gain. Assume there that consumption takes place in the fixed proportion along the ray $OC_1C_2C_3$. Let Q be the endowment of *Y*-goods, with these being divided between foreign capital and domestic labour in the ratio QQ_L/Q_LO. Prior to the customs union, trade takes place from Q to C_3 at the non-union country's foreign price-ratio QM and the domestic price-ratio is RS. The tariff revenue generated is QR and is redistributed to foreign capital. The tariff-revenue-inclusive income of *foreign capital* is therefore Q_LR (QQ_L of earnings plus QR of revenue) whereas the income of *labour* is Q_LO. With consumption of each factor group lying along the same ray $OC_1C_2C_3$, the pre-union consumption point for labour is C_1 on its budget line Q_LS_L whereas

9. See, however, Bhagwati and Brecher [1978] where it is noted that a *differential trade pattern* between the national and the foreign-owned factors is essential if such redistribution is to result in immiserization of the national factors.

the difference between C_3 and C_1 constitutes the bundle consumed by foreign capital. The union then eliminates trade with the outside country and diverts it to the partner country at its price-line $Q_L S_L'$. Since $Q_L S_L'$ is steeper than QM, the country's terms of trade have deteriorated: as necessary for a trade diverting union. However, the loss and more is absorbed by foreign capital; and domestic labour improves its welfare because its new budget line is $Q_L S_L'$ and therefore, the shift from C_1 to C_2 implies a corresponding *improvement* in national welfare. The trade diverting union has clearly been beneficial, therefore, even though there is no consumption gain (nor production gain, i.e., decline in domestic production of protected importable in favour of imports from the partner country, or Viner's "trade creation" in production). This is evidently an outcome attributable to the assumption made regarding the distribution of tariff revenue to foreign capital alone.

In conclusion, it should no longer puzzle you now that the presence of foreign-owned factors in the economy, with its consequent possibility of income redistribution in favour of foreign-owned factors, undermines the logical necessity of a number of other welfare-theoretic propositions. Thus, for example, whereas for a small non-distortionary country, exogenous improvements in the terms of trade will monotonically improve welfare under free trade, given the pattern of trade, this will no longer be so in the presence of foreign-owned factors of production (Bhagwati and Brecher [1978]). Again, the traditional conclusion that a transferee country cannot be immiserized by the transfer if market stability obtains (Samuelson [1952, 1954] and Mundell [1960]) must yield now to the paradox that such immiserization is compatible with market stability and the added paradox that it is compatible even with the transferee country's terms of trade improving (Brecher and Bhagwati [1979]).

V. International Labour Mobility

Finally, let me turn to the consideration of international labour mobility. This introduces in the analysis certain asymmetries vis-a-vis the analysis of international capital mobility. At the same time, it enables us to consider analytical problems which arise from the simultaneous presence of *both* capital and labour mobility across countries. I will address each of these aspects, in turn.

A. Asymmetries

Labour mobility across countries indeed has many parallels to capital mobility. Thus, the fundamental proposition that a small capital inflow in an economy without distortions will not harm or help the host country resurrects itself in the well-known argument in the theory of the brain drain that a small emigration will not harm or help those left behind because the emigrant will have been earning

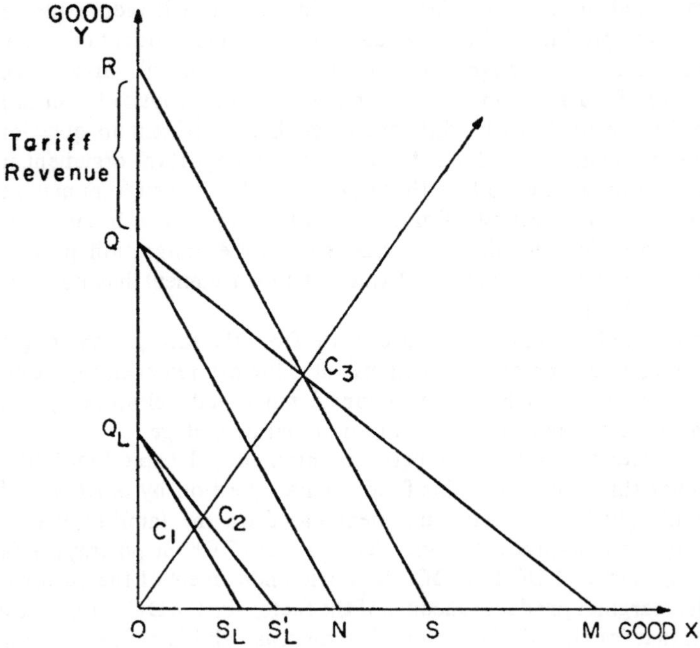

FIG. 6: This illustrates a welfare-improving trade diverting union in the Viner-Lipsey model. The gain arises entirely through the "redistribution effect", related to tariff revenue redistribution, arising in the presence of foreign-owned factors of production in the economy. All labour is assumed domestic and all capital is foreign-owned. Tariff revenue is redistributed to capital. QM is pre-union terms of trade and $Q_LS'_L$ the after-union terms of trade. Before union, labour share of income is OQ_L since tariff revenue QR accrues entirely to capital. $Q_LS'_L$ dominates Q_LS_L. Consumption is along $OC_1C_2C_3$, with fixed coefficients, so that consumption gain cannot arise. The gain to labour, and hence improvement in national welfare, follows *despite* the deterioration in terms of trade following on the trade-diverting shift to partner-country imports and without any consumption gain.

his social marginal product and therefore his departure will reduce his contribution to national product and his own earned share in it by identical amounts.

The rather elementary, though not unimportant, asymmetries arise of course in so far as some of the distortions that are relevant to the analysis of international labour mobility are likely to be different from those pertinent to questions of international capital mobility. Thus, for example, an important argument in the brain drain literature relates to how the wage earned by the emigrant may be less than his PMP (= SMP) because of monopsonistic hiring: as with doctors in the United Kingdom under socialized medicine, so that the emigration prima facie imposes a loss on those left behind. Evidently this argument has no plausible relevance to capital flows.[10]

But the more fundamental asymmetries arise from the fact that the migration raises the question, as I noted earlier in my introductory remarks, regarding the appropriate manner in which we are to consider national welfare, i.e., how the migrants are to be treated in considering national advantage.

Let me illustrate the differences between international capital mobility and labour mobility that arise from this fundamental question by borrowing from Koichi Hamada [1977] a brilliant argument based on the familiar analysis of factor flows in a single-product model. Take Figure 7 which portrays a factor flow occurring from an LDC to a DC, the world endowment of the factor being O_1O_2 and the marginal product schedule of the factor for the DC being measured from O_1 and that for the LDC from O_2. Assume away all distortions so that one can legitimately concentrate on gains and losses within the framework of Figure 7.

Let O_1A and AO_2 then be the national endowments of the factor in the DC and in the LDC *before* migration, respectively. Assume now that the factor in question is labour. When migration is allowed, an amount AB of labour will migrate from the LDC to the DC. Therefore, the domestic product of the LDC will reduce by the area QRAB, and the income received by those left behind will diminish by the area of the triangle QRT, reflecting the "large"-flow effect which I already discussed in relation to capital mobility. The domestic product of the DC will increase by PABQ, and the income received by those originally living in the DC will increase by PSQ. The gain obtained by the emigrants themselves is clearly equal to SRTQ.

Now, if we were considering capital instead on the horizontal axis, then the welfare gain due to the movement of capital, amounting to the triangle PQR, would be distributed to the two countries in amounts PSQ and SRQ. Thus *both* countries gain by the free movement of capital. On the other hand, in the case of labour migration, not only is this total gain PQR distributed to the pre-migration population of the DC and the migrants who constitute the new residents there,

10. The only weak parallel is provided by the possibility of artificially low interest rates maintained for lending by governments.

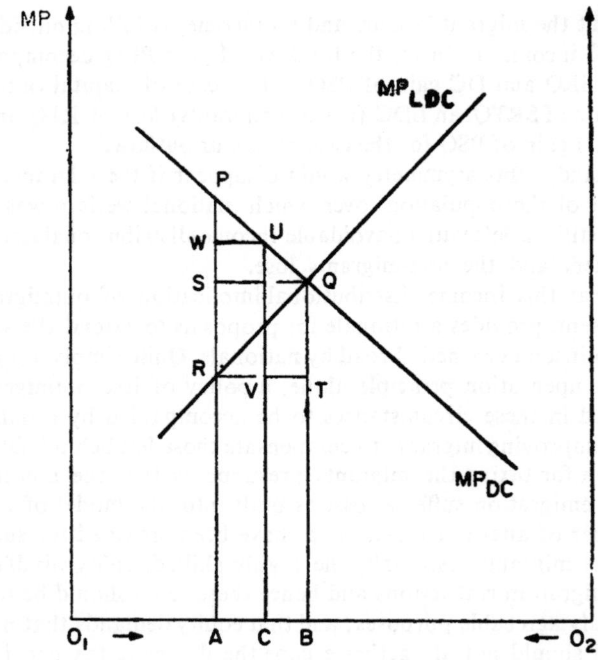

FIG. 7: O_1O_2 is the world supply of the factor. LDC and DC marginal product schedules are sketched. O_1A and O_2A are the initial endowments for the DC and LDC respectively. Introduction of migration leads to outmigration from the LDC of AB.

For Capital: Total Gain = PRQ
LDC Gain = SRQ
DC Gain = PSQ

For Labour: Total Gain = PRQ
Emigrants' Gain = SRTQ
LDC (excluding emigrants) Loss = RTQ
DC (excluding immigrants) Gain = PSQ

but there is actually a *loss* of an amount equal to the area QRT suffered by the non-migrants in the LDC.

Thus we have an asymmetry between the case of foreign capital outflow and the case of labour emigration, arising obviously from the fact that the income earned on capital invested abroad is part of national income whereas we are assuming here that the migrant labour, and its income, is falling outside of the definition of LDC income. In brief, the total world gain PRQ decomposes into an LDC gain of SRQ and DC gain of PSQ in the case of capital outflow and into emigrants' gain of SRTQ, an LDC (net of emigrants) *loss* of RTQ and a DC (net of immigrants) gain of PSQ for the case of labour outflow.

On the other hand, this asymmetry would disappear if the migrants were to be treated as part of the population over which national welfare was defined, though we could still be left with unavoidable income-distributional issues since the migrants benefit and the non-migrants lose.

I might add that this income distributional implication of outmigration of labour, when present, provides a rationale for proposals to extend the domestic tax jurisdiction to incomes earned abroad by nationals. Quite simply, on grounds of the familiar compensation principle alone, a policy of free outmigration of labour would need in these circumstances to be accompanied by a policy that taxes the welfare-improving migrants to compensate those left behind. Of course, this argumentation for taxing the migrants presupposes that the non-migrants in the country of emigration suffer a loss, as built into the model of Figure 7. However, a number of alternative rationales have been provided for such taxation: e.g., that the migrants, especially the highly skilled, enjoy windfall gains due to severe immigration restrictions and hence these rents should be taxed for spending on socially agreeable purposes; and that equity demands that nationals who work abroad should not altogether escape the domestic tax net, i.e., that the United States practice of taxing U.S. citizens no matter where they reside, under Internal Revenue Code Section 911, ought to be adopted since there should be no "representation without taxation".[11]

B. Optimal Choice Between Capital and Labour Mobility

In conclusion, let me turn to the problem that Ramaswami had addressed nearly two decades ago and which, as I remarked earlier, has become pertinent today. The problem is best illustrated with regard to the migration of labour to the United States. As you are doubtless aware, the U.S.A. has an enormous inflow of illegal migrants who come in principally from Latin America and, in turn, mostly from Mexico. The immigration barriers have not been successful in stemming this inflow which is variously estimated as having led to a stock of close to 10 million illegal immigrants. In response to this inflow, and as a result of the growing and effective trade union pressures, the Carter administration has had to take cognizance of the problem in its social, legal and economic dimensions. In this context, it has occasionally been suggested that the United States ought to encourage

11. For a comprehensive statement of these rationales, and the economic and ethical arguments involved, see Bhagwati [1979] and the earlier studies of Bhagwati and Partington [1976].

the flow of funds, both private and public, in order to create more prosperity in Mexico to reduce the economic disparities that fuel the illegal exodus.

With regard to the deployment of public funds, in the form of foreign assistance, towards this end, it is of course possible to think of this as a bribe to the countries of illegal emigration to use *their* control machinery more effectively to stem the illegal migration. For, democracies such as the United States, with their strong civil-libertarian and liberal lobbies, are not in a position to start shooting happily at the illegal migrants and the effectiveness of controls on migration may be enhanced from the emigration end by offering suitable incentives to these countries of emigration.

But, even if this is true, the fact remains that the principal motivation behind such a policy remains the creation of more job opportunities and improved standards of living in the poorer countries of emigration.

But this immediately suggests a related and interesting question. Suppose that we have a capital-rich country, the United States, and a capital-poor country, Mexico. Assume that the United States can unilaterally decide on two alternative courses of action, *both* assumed to be feasible: i.e., that it allows its capital to migrate to Mexico, while *effectively* closing the border to immigration; or *alternatively* that it prohibits *capital* outflow but permits immigration of Mexican labour. If then the United States can *also* choose optimal taxes and subsidies on such factor flows, so that we wind up comparing *optimal* ways of choosing between the two forms of mobility, which would be to greater national advantage?

As it happens, this is precisely the analytical problem to which Ramaswami [1968] gave a neat solution in a one-sector model. Starting from a position where the United States has no prohibitions, it is evident that if capital mobility is considered, the United States will maximize its welfare by imposing an optimal tax on capital outflow: for, diminishing returns abroad to the capital inflow creates a divergence between average and marginal return to United States capital abroad and since the market equates only the average rental abroad to domestic rental, laissez-faire leads to excessive investment in Mexico. Ramaswami then showed very neatly that the United States would do yet better if it permitted immigration of Mexican labour instead, while levying an optimal tax on its earnings. Thus, consider the notional argument that the United States, having invested optimally abroad, withdraws its capital and permits immigration of the Mexican workers who are using United States capital in Mexico. As the per capita capital stock in Mexico is left unchanged by this notional withdrawal, the Mexican immigrants need only be paid the wage they received hitherto; and if they continued to work with the same amount of capital per head as was previously employed in Mexico, the United States population is no better or worse off. However, this situation implies two unequal sets of capital-labour ratios in the United States, and evidently the adoption of a *uniform* capital-labour ratio for all production will improve income and enable the United States to increase welfare if it taxes the earnings of immigrants so as to keep their net wages constant at the Mexican level and distributes the tax proceeds to the United States population. Thus, *some* tax rate on immigrant earnings obviously exists which secures higher welfare for the United States than would be achieved under the alternative policy of optimal restriction of foreign investment.

A neat way to understand this outcome is to see that it implies that optimal taxation of the import of the scarce factor is preferable to optimal restriction of the export of the abundant factor. In either case, of course, the optimal restriction ensures equality of the foreign marginal cost or return from the country's viewpoint with the domestic return or cost. When a country exports its abundant factor, however, it winds up using that factor more intensively abroad than at home; and import of the scarce factor eliminates the loss on that account.

It is easy to imagine interesting extensions of this strand of argumentation. Evidently, the 2 × 2 Jones-Kemp analysis of the optimal combination of taxes and subsidies on trade and capital mobility could be extended to gain insight into the conditions under which a capital-rich country may find it profitable to permit the mobility of one factor rather than another. That this and other extensions will follow is beyond doubt. And they will constitute yet fresh evidence of the originality and strength of Ramaswami's theoretical contributions to international economics.

References

Bardhan, Pranab, 1970, *Economic Growth, Development and Foreign Trade*, John Wiley and Sons, U.S.A.

Bardhan, Pranab and Harvey Lapan, 1973, "Localized Technical Progress and Transfer of Technology and Economic Development", *Journal of Economic Theory*, December.

Bhagwati, Jagdish, 1958, "Immiserizing Growth : A Geometrical Note", *Review of Economic Studies*, June.

Bhagwati, Jagdish and V.K. Ramaswami, 1963, "Domestic Distortions, Tariffs and the Theory of Optimum Subsidy", *Journal of Political Economy*, February.

Bhagwati, Jagdish, 1971, "The Generalized Theory of Distortions and Welfare", in J. Bhagwati, *et al.* (ed.), *Trade, Balance of Payments and Growth*, Kindleberger Festschrift, North-Holland: Amsterdam.

Bhagwati, Jagdish, Ronald Jones, Robert Mundell, and Jaroslav Vanek (eds.), 1971, *Trade, Balance of Payments and Growth*, North-Holland: Amsterdam.

Bhagwati, Jagdish, 1973, "The Theory of Immiserizing Growth: Further Applications", in M. Connolly and A. Swoboda (eds.), *International Trade and Money*, George Allen and Unwin: London.

Bhagwati, Jagdish and Koichi Hamada, 1974, "The Brain Drain, International Integration of Markets for Professionals and Unemployment", *Journal of Development Economics*, Volume 1 (1).

Bhagwati, Jagdish and Carlos Rodriguez, 1975, "Welfare-Theoretical Analyses of the Brain Drain", *Journal of Development Economics*, Volume 2 (3).

Bhagwati, Jagdish and Martin Partington (eds.), 1976, *Taxing the Brain Drain: A Proposal*, North-Holland: Amsterdam.

Bhagwati, Jagdish (ed.), 1976, *The Brain Drain and Taxation: Theory and Empirical Analysis*, North-Holland: Amsterdam.

Bhagwati, Jagdish, 1976, "The Developing Countries", in *A Symposium in the World Economy* in *The Great Ideas Today*, Encyclopaedia Britannica, Inc., Chicago.

Bhagwati, Jagdish and T.N. Srinivasan, 1977, *Foreign Trade Regimes and Economic Development: India*, N.B.E.R., Ballinger Co.: Cambridge, Massachusetts.

Bhagwati, Jagdish (ed.), 1977, *The New International Economic Order : The North-South Debate*, M.I.T. Press: Cambridge, Massachusetts.

Bhagwati, Jagdish and Ernesto Tironi, 1978, "Tariff Change, Foreign Capital and Immiserization : A Theoretical Analysis", *M.I.T. Mimeo.*, August; forthcoming in: *Journal of Development Economics.*

Bhagwati, Jagdish and Richard Brecher, 1978, "National Welfare in an Open Economy in the Presence of Foreign-Owned Factors of Production", *M.I.T. Working Paper No. 224*, October.

Bhagwati, Jagdish, 1978, *The Anatomy and Consequences of Exchange Control Regimes*, N.B.E.R., Ballinger Co.: Cambridge, Massachusetts.

Bhagwati, Jagdish, 1978, "International Migration of the Highly Skilled : Economics, Ethics and Tax Arrangements", *Third World Quarterly*, June.

Brecher, Richard, 1974a, "Minimum Wage Rates and the Pure Theory of International Trade", *Quarterly Journal of Economics*, February.

Brecher, Richard, 1974b, "Optimum Commercial Policy for a Minimum Wage Economy", *Journal of International Economics*, May.

Brecher, Richard and Carlos Diaz Alejandro, 1977, "Tariffs, Foreign Capital and Immiserizing Growth", *Journal of International Economics*, November.

Brecher, Richard and Jagdish Bhagwati, 1979, "Foreign Ownership and the Theory of Trade and Welfare", *M.I.T. Mimeo.*, March; and *Carleton Economic Papers.*

Hamada, Koichi, 1966, "Economic Growth and Long-Term Capital Movements", *Yale Economic Essays*, Volume 6, Spring.

Hamada, Koichi, 1974, "An Economic Analysis of the Duty Free Zone", *Journal of International Economics*, November.

Hamada, Koichi, 1977, "Taxing the Brain Drain : A Global Point of View", in Bhagwati (ed.), *The New International Economic Order*, M.I.T. Press, Cambridge, Massachusetts.

Harris, John and Michael Todaro, 1970, "Migration, Unemployment and Development: A Two-Sector Analysis", *American Economic Review*, March.

Hirschman, Albert, 1969, *How to Divest in Latin America and Why*, Princeton Essays in International Finance, No. 76, November.

Jasay, Anthony, 1960, "The Choice Between Home and Foreign Investment", *Economic Journal*, March.

Johnson, Harry, 1955, "Economic Expansion and International Trade", *Manchester School*, May.

Johnson, Harry, 1965, "Optimal Trade Intervention in the Presence of Domestic Distortions", in R.E. Caves, *et al.* (ed.), *Trade, Growth and the Balance of Payments*, Rand-McNally: New York.

Johnson, Harry, 1967, "The Possibility of Income Losses from Increased Efficiency or Factor Accumulation in the Presence of Tariffs", *Economic Journal*, March.

Jones, R.W., 1967, "International Capital Movements and the Theory of Tariffs and Trade", *Quarterly Journal of Economics*, February.

Kemp, Murray, 1966, "The Gain from International Trade and Investment : A Neo-Heckscher-Ohlin Approach", *American Economic Review*, September.

Kindleberger, Charles, 1973, "Restrictions on Direct Foreign Investment in LDCs", in J. Bhagwati and R.S. Eckaus (eds.), *Development and Planning*, M.I.T. Press, Cambridge, Massachusetts.

Lefeber, Louis, 1971, "Trade and Minimum Wage Rates", in Bhagwati, *et al.* (ed.), *Trade, Balance of Payments and Growth*, North-Holland: Amsterdam.

Lewis, W. Arthur, 1954, "Economic Development with Unlimited Supplies of Labor", *Manchester School*, Volume 22, 139-191.

MacDougall, G. Donald A., 1960, "The Benefits and Costs of Private Investment from Abroad : A Theoretical Approach", *Economic Record*, Volume 36, 13-35.

Meade, James, 1951, *The Balance of Payments*, R.I.I.A., Oxford University Press.

Minabe, Noburo, 1974, "Capital and Technology Movements and Economic Welfare", *American Economic Review*, December.

Mundell, Robert, 1957, "International Trade and Factor Mobility", *American Economic Review*, Volume 47, 321-335.

Mundell, Robert, 1960, "The Pure Theory of International Trade", *American Economic Review*, March.

Ramaswami, V.K., 1968, "International Factor Movements and the National Advantage", *Economica*, August.

Ramaswami, V.K., 1970, "International Factor Movements and the National Advantage: Reply", *Economica*, February.

Ramaswami, V.K. and T.N. Srinivasan, 1971, "Tariff Structure and Resource Allocation in the Presence of Factor Substitution", in Bhagwati, *et al.* (ed.), *Trade, Balance of Payments and Growth*, North-Holland: Amsterdam.

Ramaswami, V.K., 1971, *Trade and Development: Essays in Economics*, (edited by J. Bhagwati, H.G. Johnson and T.N. Srinivasan), Allen and Unwin: London.

Rybczynski, T.N., 1955, "Factor Endowment and Relative Commodity Prices", *Economica*, November.

Samuelson, Paul, 1952, "The Transfer Problem and Transport Costs", *Economic Journal*, June.

Samuelson, Paul, 1954, "The Transfer Problem and Transport Costs", *Economic Journal*, June.

Stolper, Wolfgang and Paul Samuelson, 1941, "Protection and Real Wages", *Review of Economic Studies*, November.

Thurow, Lester, 1976, "International Factor Movements and the American Distribution of Income", *Intermountain Economic Review*, Spring.

Thurow, Lester and Halbert White, 1976, "Optimum Trade Restrictions and their Consequences", *Econometrica*, July.

Tinbergen, Jan, 1952, *On the Theory of Economic Policy*, Contributions to Economic Analysis Series, North-Holland: Amsterdam.

Errata

Page 76, line 3 from bottom: "K_f" should read "$\overline{K}_f$".

Page 77, caption to figure 1: "K_f" should read "$\overline{K}_f$".

Page 83, line 8 from bottom: "ticky" should read "sticky".

Editor's Note

A theoretical analysis of the Ramaswami problem bearing the same title as this essay and discussed in the introduction and concluding section is given in essay 43 in this volume.

ON THE CHOICE BETWEEN CAPITAL AND LABOUR MOBILITY

Jagdish N. Bhagwati
and
T. N. Srinivasan

I. Introduction

Trade theorists, since the pioneering work of Kemp (1966), have considered the question of national advantage from international factor mobility by considering only one factor to be so mobile.

Kemp analyzed elegantly the question of optimal policies in a $2 \times 2 \times 2$ model and showed that, since monopoly power could exist in both the goods and factor markets in consequence of international capital mobility, the optimal policy intervention would generally involve two policy instruments: tariffs(-cum-subsidies) on goods and duties(-cum-subsidies) on international capital flows. Jones (1967) subsequently extended Kemp's argument to the second-best context, by examining the optimal level of one of these instruments when the other was arbitrarily set at zero. Brecher (1982) has recently shown, in an elegant and original contribution, that the Jones policy problem is, in fact, a third-best, rather than a second-best, problem as generally believed; and that if only one of the tariff and capital mobility taxes(-cum-subsidies) can be used, it is generally possible to improve welfare further by admitting an altogether different, domestic policy instrument, *viz.* a production or consumption tax-cum-subsidy, as the case may be.[1]

Interesting as this line of analysis is, it is based on two critical assumptions:

(1) that the other country is passive in face of policymaking by one country, exactly as in the orthodox analysis of optimal policy intervention which assumes that the foreign offer curve facing a country is given exogenously; and

(2) that the other factor of production (labour, in the usual $2 \times 2 \times 2$ analysis of international capital mobility) is internationally immobile.

The former assumption is traditional in the international-economic-theoretic literature on optimal policies for open economies, with such classic exceptions as the theory of optimum tariffs with retaliation as developed by Scitovsky (1942), Johnson (1953–4) and later writers.

But the latter assumption is more crippling in ruling out of consideration the fact of international labour mobility and, indeed, its systematic regulation by the policy instrument of immigration restrictions by nation states since the beginning of the 20th century. As it happens, an important and novel question that has appeared in the policy context is precisely whether it would be to the national advantage of a capital-abundant country to export capital (*à la* the Marxist-Leninist prediction of monopoly capitalism) or to import labour (as countries such as West Germany did through their *Gastarbeiter* programs in the postwar period). Bhagwati (1979) raised this question in the Ramaswami Memorial Lecture as follows:

> The problem is best illustrated with regard to the migration of labor to the United States. As you are doubtless aware, the U.S.A. has an enormous inflow of illegal migrants who come in principally from Latin America and, in turn, mostly from Mexico. The immigration barriers have not been successful in stemming this inflow which is variously estimated as having led to a stock of close to 10 million illegal immigrants. In response to this inflow, and as a result of the growing and effective trade union pressures, the Carter administration has had to take cognizance of the problem in its social, legal and economic dimensions. In this context, it has occasionally been suggested that the United States ought to encourage the flow of funds, both private and public, in order to create more prosperity in Mexico to reduce the economic disparities that fuel the illegal exodus.
>
> With regard to the deployment of public funds, in the form of foreign assistance, towards this end, it is of course possible to think of this as a bribe to the countries of illegal emigration to use *their* control machinery more effectively to stem the illegal migration. For, democracies such as the United States, with their strong civil-libertarian and liberal lobbies, are not in a position to start shooting happily at the illegal migrants and the effectiveness of controls of migration may be enhanced from the emigration end by offering suitable incentives to these countries of emigration.
>
> But, even if this is true, the fact remains that the principal motivation behind such a policy remains the creation of more job opportunities and improved standards of living in the poorer countries of emigration.
>
> But this immediately suggests a related and interesting question. Suppose that we have a capital-rich country, the United States, and a capital-poor country, Mexico. Assume that the United States can unilaterally decide on two alternative courses of action, *both* assumed to be feasible: i.e., that it allows its capital to migrate to Mexico, while *effectively* closing the border to immigration; or *alternatively* that it prohibits *capital* outflow but permits immigration of Mexican labor. If then the United States can *also* choose optimal taxes and subsidies on such factor flows,

so that we wind up comparing *optimal* ways of choosing between the two forms of mobility, which would be to greater national advantage?

This precise formulation of the analytical question, which Ramaswami (1968) happened to pose in a neglected and ingenious contribution utilizing a one-good model, is however by analogy with the Kemp-Jones-Brecher analysis in that it treats international labour mobility as symmetric in its implications with international capital mobility, the only difference being that one may yield higher welfare to the policymaking country. However, the two types of international mobility are asymmetric in two important respects.

First, while it is generally possible to tax capital outflows from a country, the reverse taxation of labour coming into a country by the country of "immigration" is not such a straightforward matter. As the discussion of the proposal of Bhagwati's (1979) to "tax the brain drain" made manifest, the (discriminatory) taxation by the country of residence of foreign labour is fraught with numerous difficulties from legal, constitutional, human-rights and political standpoints.[2] Therefore, the economic theorist must rank-order, as in Ramaswami's (1968) classic paper, not just the optimal taxation of outflowing capital by the capital-rich country with the optimal taxation of incoming (foreign) labour by the capital-rich country. A realistic policy comparison must augment the policy set to include therefore the rank-ordering of policies where the discriminatory taxation of incoming foreign labour is *not* allowed: thus permitting an asymmetry in the tax-jurisdictional scope in regard to taxation of one's capital outflow and taxation of the other's labour outflow into one's country.

Second, international labour mobility raises the added difficulty that, once labour crosses national borders, we have to worry about which country's welfare it ought to be included in. As Bhagwati (1979) has argued, the investment of capital abroad does not affect, in principle, the group over which "national" welfare will be defined. By contrast, the "migration" of human beings raises the question: which national group do the migrants belong to? There is no universal answer to this question. Migrants who are temporary, because of explicit rules in that regard as with *Gastarbeiters* in Western Europe and imported workers in the oil-rich Middle East, evidently will classify as part of the "national" population in the country of origin. But what of permanently emigrating nationals? If they do "go away" for good, there is a convincing case for treating "national" welfare as defined only over "those left behind." On the other hand, as seems to be the case today with a large fraction of the highly skilled migration from the less developed countries to the developed countries, if this migrant population is characterized by retention of ethnic ties to the country of origin, a high frequency of visits and even continuation of citizenship status in many cases, the fact of permanent migration (embodied in the holding of immigrant visas) is thoroughly compatible with the analyst including such migrants in the definition of "national" welfare for the country of origin. When we rank-order the optimal taxation of capital outflow with the optimal taxation of labour inflow, as in Ramaswami (1968), we are treating the foreign labour as part of the *foreign* country's welfare function. But then we need also to consider the possibility that it may be regarded, after immigration, to be part of one's own welfare.

In the analysis below of the choice between capital and labour mobility from the viewpoint of national advantage, therefore, we will be mindful of these important asymmetries introduced by international labour, as against capital, mobility. We will utilize Ramaswami's one-good model, which eliminates the necessity to look simultaneously at the implications in the goods market that lead to the complexity of the Kemp-Jones-Brecher analysis. Using this model, we will consider the welfare-effects in a 2-country model where the capital-rich country uses (1) a free international factor mobility policy, (2) a quota policy in regard to capital outflow and labour inflow, (3) an optimal capital-outflow tax policy and (4) alternative discriminatory tax policies on inflow of labour. Evidently, Policies (1)–(3) do not, but Policies (4) do, require having to differentially tax "immigrant" labour; and where the differential taxation of foreign labour is inadmissible, the rank-ordering of policies will have to exclude Policies (4). We will principally consider, in Section II, the case where welfare of the immigrant labour is considered part of only foreign welfare.[3] In Section III, however, we will briefly indicate the complexities introduced in case this cannot be assumed.

II. Immigrants' Welfare Part of Only Foreign Welfare

Consider now a one-good model with 2 countries, America (A) and Mexico (M), with two factors of production (K and L), where A has initially a higher endowment ratio of capital such that $(K_A/L_A) > (K_M/L_M)$. The technology is moreover considered, as in Ramaswami, to be identical between A and M and characterised by the usual restrictions such as constant returns to scale and the Inada conditions.

Given this specification, turn now to Figure 1. The overall capital and labour endowment of America and Mexico determines the size of the box diagram. E represents the initial endowment point, such that O_AN and O_AZ are the capital and labour endowments respectively of America, and PN and ZQ of Mexico. The diagonal represents, given identical technology, the contract curve for the world endowment. *Any* point of

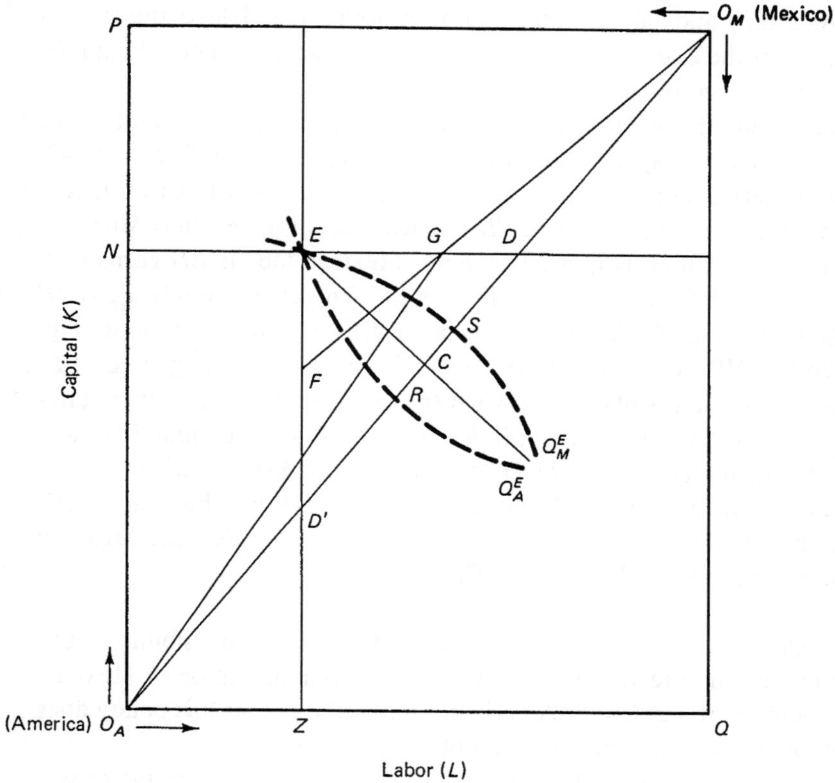

Figure 1

allocation of world factor supply on this contract curve is evidently Pareto-efficient; and along the diagonal, the wage-rental ratio is invariant. E, on the other hand, is off the contract curve and yields, in an initial autarkic, (i.e. no international factor mobility) situation, Q_A^E output for America and Q_M^E output for Mexico. Since we have constant returns to scale and identical world technology, we can equally measure the outputs along the diagonal and read the output of America as O_AR and of Mexico as O_MS. Finally, consider throughout that America is the policymaking country and that Mexico can take no policy action at all.

(1) *Free Factor Mobility:* Suppose now that America allows free factor mobility. It is evident then that the triangle EDD' defines the range of possible equilibrium outcomes for factor distribution among the two countries. Thus, ED' of capital could flow out of capital-rich America and that would equalize wage-rental ratios in the two countries at D'; or ED Mexican labour could flow into America and again wage-rental ratios would be equalized identically at D; or combinations of such capital

outflow from, and labour inflow into, America could lead the world-allocation of the overall factor supply to equilibrium anywhere along DD' at the same wage-rental ratio.

What about the welfare impact? It is immediately clear that, in all cases, America goes from O_AR to O_AC and Mexico from O_MS to O_MC, so that America gains RC, Mexico gains CS, and the world's gain is RS. To see this, take the case where ED Mexican labour moves into America. America's *GDP* then is O_AD. However, Mexican labour ED earns CD, since the equilibrium wage-rental ratio is EC. Therefore, America's *GNP* is $(O_AD\text{-}CD) = O_AC$, implying a gain of RC. By identical reasoning, Mexico's *GNP* goes from O_MS to O_MC, representing a gain of CS. Identically, these results follow when the factor reallocation settles anywhere else on DD′. Especially, if American capital of amount ED' flow out, American *GDP* will be O_AD', the earnings of ED' American capital in Mexico will be $D'C$; and hence American *GNP* will be again O_AC; American gain from the autarkic position will be again RC; and Mexican gain can similarly be shown to be CS.

(2) *Quotas on Factor Mobility:* Consider next the possibility of utilizing quantitative restrictions by America on (i) immigration of Mexican labour and on (ii) outflow of American capital. [Note that this policy does *not* involve discriminatory taxation of either factor.]

Of course, if only one of these policies is utilized, the other factor will move internationally until the world equilibrium winds up along DD', creating the same outcome as under free factor mobility. Suppose, however, that *both* quotas are utilized simultaneously. Take then two polar cases: (i) no capital outflow is permitted and labour inflow is restricted below ED; and (ii) no labour inflow is permitted and capital outflow is restricted below ED'.

In the former case, it is readily seen that, given the capital immobility, the restriction of labour inflow below ED is welfare-worsening for America. For, if more Mexican labour comes in, it produces increasing gain to America by driving down its own reward due to diminishing returns: and this continues until the inflow is stopped by wage equalization between both countries at D. Therefore, any immigration restriction that restricts the Mexican labour inflow below ED will reduce American gain below RC and reduce world gain below RS by pushing the world allocation off the contract curve O_AO_M. As for Mexico, it will also gain from the restricted outflow of its labour to America and its gain may be less or greater than or equal to CS (which is the gain from unrestricted outflow up to ED).

Consider now the latter case, where the labour flow is eliminated but America does not allow full outflow of American capital by amount ED'

to reach the contract curve. We then have an asymmetric result for America. For, from the American standpoint, it will pay America to restrict the outflow of capital to the point where the *marginal* return abroad equals its marginal product at home. This *optimal* export restriction on capital outflow, say *EF*, will then produce for America a gain *exceeding RC*; the world will gain less than *RS*; and Mexico will gain less than *CS*.

Thus, we have the asymmetrical result that, if only labour inflow is to be permitted, capital-rich America ought to allow it to the free-immigration level whereas, if only capital outflow is to be permitted, America ought to restrict it. This asymmetry, of course, follows from the fact that American capital is essentially driving down its reward in Mexico and hence its marginal return is below its average return there so that restriction of capital outflow below free-outflow level is desirable; whereas when Mexican labour is coming into America, it is Mexico that is correspondingly losing (part of its) gains from the labour outflow to higher-wage America and America that is gaining therefore, so that American advantage (though not Mexican advantage, of course) is best pursued by America letting Mexican labour come in freely!

The welfare outcomes under these alternative policies are readily illustrated by reference to the familiar marginal-product curves in Figures 2 and 3 for the capital-flow and the labour-flow cases respectively. In Figure 2, the marginal product curves for Mexico and America are drawn as *WY* and *NY*, with equalization of the marginal products and corresponding rentals at outflow *ED'* from America to Mexico. Optimal capital export from America's standpoint is, however, *EH* and derived by taking the curve *WT* marginal to *WY* and its intersection with *NY*, in the usual manner. Then, recalling the measures of gains in Figure 1 for the different policies as *RS*, *CS*, *RC*, etc., and examining Figure 2, we can infer Table 1. Similarly, for the labour immigration case, using Figure 3, we readily see that American advantage is maximized at *Y*, at which *ED* level of free-immigration labour inflow yields gain to America worth *WMY*: a gain that can only be reduced if the labour inflow is reduced by an arbitrary quota such as *EG*, which then yields American gain worth only *WXV*. Thus, we can infer Table 2.

But the rank-ordering of policies just derived depends critically on the assumption that America cannot levy discriminatory taxation on foreign labour as an instrument of policy. This yields an advantage, as we have just seen, to capital-outflow vis-a-vis the labour-inflow policies in America when it maximizes its national advantage. But as soon as we admit the possibility of levying taxation on immigrant (but not on national) labour, this advantage gets reversed, as we note immediately below.

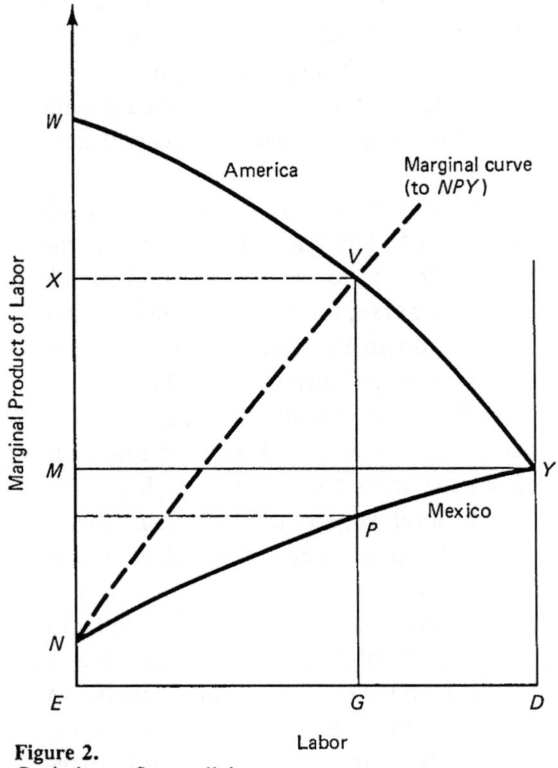

Figure 2.
Capital—outflow policies.

Table 1 Capital outflow policies

	World-efficient capital outflow (*ED*′)		Optimal-for-America capital outflow (*EH*)	
Gain	Figure 2	Figure 1	Figure 2	Figure 1
1. World gain	*WNYV*	(= *RS*)	*WVTN*	(<*RS*)
2. American gain	*MNY*	(= *RC*)	*XVTN*	(>*RC*)
3. Mexican gain	*WMY*	(= *CS*)	*WVX*	(<*CS*)

Table 2 Optimal labor inflow policy

	World-efficient *and* optimal-for-America labor inflow (*ED*)	
Gain	Figure 3	Figure 1
1. World gain	*WNY*	(= *RS*)
2. American gain	*WMY*	(= *RC*)
3. Mexican gain	*MNY*	(= *CS*)

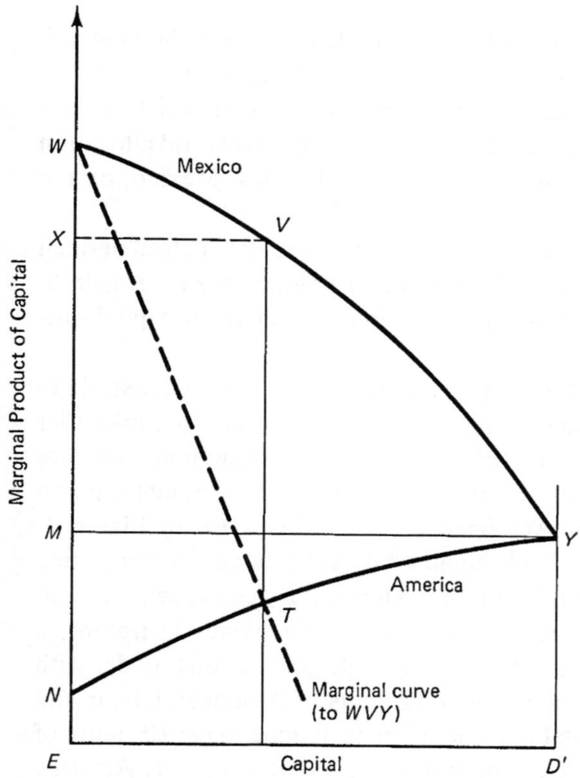

Figure 3.
Labor—inflow policies.

(3) *Discriminatory Taxation of Foreign Labour:* First, we should note that discriminatory taxation of American capital outflow by America produces an identical result as the American restriction of such outflow which we just discussed.

(i) *Optimal Tax on Labour Inflow:* On the other hand, the discriminatory taxation of Mexican labour by America enables America to gain more than it would simply by restricting Mexican labour inflow to a level identical to that produced by the tax policy. E.g. in Figure 3, if Mexican labour inflow is restricted to *EG* by a quota, it will yield gain *WXV* to America. But if this inflow is achieved by a tax on Mexican labour that effectively shifts the Mexican supply curve *NPY* up to cut *WVY* at *V*, the American gain will be *WVPQ* ($>$*WVX* by *XVPQ*, the tax revenues from the Mexican inflow of *EG* at tax rate *VP*/*PG*). And, for an *optimal* tax policy by America, this gain for America will *exceed* that under free immigration (i.e. *WMY*). I.e. if *V* were obtained, and the corresponding optimal tax rate was set by taking the marginal curve to *NPY* and intersecting it with *WVY*, we would be equating the *marginal* cost of Mexican labour supply to its marginal product in America and thus showing *VP/PG* as the welfare-maximizing American tax on Mexican labour.

Such an optimal labour-inflow tax policy by America will therefore yield a gain exceeding *RC* in Figure 1, while it will get the world allocation off the contract curve and reduce world gain below *RS*. Mexico, on the other hand, will find its gain reduced below *CS*.

Ramaswami (1968) ingeniously showed, moreover, that such an optimal tax policy on inflowing Mexican labour would produce a *greater* gain to America than the optimal tax-cum-restriction on American capital outflow.

The policies being compared appear, at first blush, to be impossible to compare analytically. Ramaswami, however, managed to rank-order them with the following remarkable argument. Following him, consider the hypothetical experiment where, starting from the optimal capital-export policy of export of American capital at level *EF* in Figure 1, America brings this capital back home while simultaneously permitting *only EG* amounts of Mexican labour into America. By construction, then, the Mexican capital-labour ratio at *F* and *G* is the same. Therefore, if we now envisage America producing the single good in this model with *two* techniques, one technique using O_AZ units of American labour and *ZF* units of American capital and the other technique using *EF* units of American capital with *EG* units of immigrant Mexican labour, America will earn the *same* income as with the optimal export of *EF* units of capital. For, the earnings of these *EF* units of capital will be identical at *F* and *G*, by construction. Equally, the identity of capital-labour ratios at *F* and *G* implies that the hypothesised withdrawal of *EF* units of American capital and importation of *EG* units of Mexican labour is a feasible immigration policy for America since it leaves American capital at its original endowment while paying Mexican labour its marginal product in Mexico. Therefore, an immigration policy, which produces the single good with *one* technique and the same factors of production while paying Mexican labour the same amount as in the two-technique solution just discussed, should do better for America. And, if Mexican labour import is varied optimally around *EG* (which was not optimally chosen, of course), there should be still further gain. Hence, it is evident that the policy of optimal taxation of labour inflow dominates the policy of optimal taxation-cum-restriction of capital outflow by capital-rich America.

(ii) *Perfectly-Discriminating Tax Policy:* Yet another policy may be considered, which taxes away all the gains from Mexican labour inflow by taxing in a "perfectly-discriminatory" fashion. Thus, in Figure 3, assume that America can tax each Mexican labourer to extract the full

Table 3 Discriminatory tax policies on labor inflow

Gain	Optimal-for-America tax on labor inflow (<*ED*)		World-efficient, perfectly discriminatory tax on labor inflow (*ED*)	
	Figure 3	Figure 1	Figure 3	Figure 1
1. World gain	*WVPN*	(<*RS*)	*WNY*	(= *RS*)
2. American gain	*WVPQ*	(>*RC*)	*WNY*	(= *RS*)
3. Mexican gain	*PQN*	(<*CS*)	Zero	(= zero)

difference between his American marginal product (= wage) and his Mexican marginal product (= wage forgone).

In that case, the entire world gain *WYN* from the Mexican labour inflow will accrue to America and the Mexican non-migrant population will suffer a loss equal to wages earned in America by the migrants. By reference to Figure 1, we can readily see that the world resource allocation will shift from *E* to (Pareto-efficient) *D*, the world gain will be *RS*, the American gain will also be *RS* and the Mexican gain will be zero.

The results of these two types of discriminatory-taxation policies are presented in Table 3.

(4) *Rank-ordering of Alternative Policies:* From the viewpoint of American advantage, therefore, we get a remarkable and strong rank-ordering of policies: Perfectly-discriminatory tax on labour inflow > Optimal tax on labour inflow > Optimal tax-cum-restriction on capital outflow > free factor mobility > restriction on labour inflow. Of this rank-ordering, it is the dominance of the optimal tax on labour outflow over the optimal tax on capital inflow that Ramaswami (1968) established.

III. Immigrants' Welfare Not Necessarily Part of Only Foreign Welfare

The analysis so far has assumed that Mexican migrants' welfare continues to be part of only Mexican welfare. We must however address a few pertinent remarks to the possibility where this is not the case. Thus the Mexican migrants' welfare may be regarded as part of American welfare. [We should also reckon with the possibilities that the migrants' welfare is not counted in either Mexican or American welfare, and that alternatively (in a benign world) it is considered by American and Mexican policymakers to be part of both rather than neither!]. Simply to illustrate the differences in conclusions that can arise, once these considerations are introduced, we focus here on the case where the Mexican migrant labour becomes part of American welfare (as indeed it unambiguously would if, after the 5-year residence requirement, naturalization ensued).

The basic difficulty that this change of assumptions about the national characterisation of initially Mexican labour makes is that the different policy rankings that we considered in the preceding Section are no longer welfare-comparable, without added assumptions, since the population over which they are defined will generally differ. Thus, the capital export policies will involve the initial American population; whereas the labour quota and taxation policies will each result in different levels of immigration of Mexican labour and hence of the American population. Given this problem, the analyst has no option except to settle for welfare criteria such as the resulting per capita income level under alternative policies, or some explicit cardinal weighting of the different individuals under the different policy options.

Thus, consider per capita income criterion and focus on American advantage to see how the rank-ordering of our policies can change from that derived in Section II. Turning to Figure 1, it is then easy to see that free factor mobility, to any point on the diagonal stretch DD', will yield an identical per capita income level so that all points on DD' continue to be weakly-ranked. However, the *optimum optimorum* perfectly-discriminating tax policy on Mexican labour inflow is no longer superior to the policy of free factor mobility since the fact that it transfers the gains from the Mexican migrants to pre-migration American natives is no longer an advantage!

The research of Bhagwati was supported by the German Marshall Fund Grant No. 1-34015. The problems analyzed in the paper were posed in Bhagwati (1979), and an early ingenious and neglected analysis in Ramaswami (1968) was noted by Bhagwati. We have profited greatly from these contributions, as also from reading Webb (1970), Ramaswami (1970), and a recent paper of Calvo and Wellisz (1983) on this problem.

1. This result is in consonance with the results of Bhagwati, Ramaswami, and Srinivasan (1969) for the case without international capital mobility; but the consonance is "intuitive" only after the result was established for the case with international capital mobility.

2. Many of these difficulties are discussed in Bhagwati and Partington (1976). However, they do not extend to the country of *nationality* exercising income tax jurisdiction over its citizens resident abroad. What we are discussing in the text is the country of *residence* exercising its own tax jurisdiction in an overtly discriminatory fashion on foreign residents: e.g. by levying a 10 percent surcharge on the incomes of foreigners resident in the country. The economics of the former question has been explored in a Symposium in the *Journal of Public Economics*, Vol. 18(3), 1982, by Bhagwati (1982), Bhagwati and Hamada (1982), Baumol (1982), Mirrlees (1982), and Wilson (1982a, 1982b).

3. Also see the analysis in Calvo and Wellisz (1981), which considers these issues utilizing the Ramaswami one-good model as well. Of interest also is the exchange between Ramaswami (1970) and Webb (1970).

References

1. Baumol, William, 1982, "The Income Distribution Frontier and the Taxation of Migrants", *Journal of Public Economics*, 18 (3).

2. Bhagwati, Jagdish N., 1979, "International Factor Movements and National Advantage", The 9th Ramaswami Lecture, *Indian Economic Review*, October, Vol. 14 (N.S.), pp. 73–100.

3. Bhagwati, Jagdish, 1978, "International Migration of the Highly Skilled: Economics, Ethics and Tax Arrangements", *Third World Quarterly*, June.

4. Bhagwati, Jagdish N., 1982, "Introduction: Symposium on Income Taxation in the Presence of International Personal Mobility", *Journal of Public Economics*, 18 (3).

5. Bhagwati, Jagdish N. and Koichi Hamada, 1982, "Tax Policy in the Presence of Emigration", *Journal of Public Economics*, Vol. 18 (3).

6. Bhagwati, Jagdish and Martin Partington (eds.), 1976, *Taxing the Brain Drain: A Proposal*, North-Holland: Amsterdam.

7. Bhagwati, Jagdish, V. K. Ramaswami, and T. N. Srinivasan, 1969, "Domestic Distortions, Tariffs, and the Theory of Optimum Subsidy: Some Further Results", *Journal of Political Economy*, 77, 1005–1010.

8. Brecher, Richard, 1982, "Second-Best Policy for International Trade and Investment", *Journal of International Economics*, November.

9. Calvo, Guillermo and Stanislaw Wellisz, 1983, "International Factor Mobility and National Advantage", *Journal of International Economics*, February.

10. Johnson, Harry, 1953–54, "Optimum Tariffs and Retaliation", *Review of Economic Studies*, XXI (2), No. 55, pp. 142–53.

11. Jones, R. W., 1967, "International Capital Movements and the Theory of Tariffs and Trade", *Quarterly Journal of Economics*, February, pp. 1–38.

12. Kemp, Murray, 1966, "The Gain from International Trade and Investment: A Neo-Heckscher-Ohlin Approach", *American Economic Review*, September.

13. Mirrlees, James A., 1982, "A Theory of Taxation and Migration", *Journal of Public Economics*, Vol. 18 (3).

14. Ramaswami, V. K., 1968, "International Factor Movements and the National Advantage", *Economica*, August, Vol. XXXV, pp. 309–310.

15. Ramaswami, V. K., 1970, "International Factor Movements and the National Advantage: Reply", *Economica*, February, Vol. XXXVII.

16. Scitovsky, Tibor de, 1942, "A Reconsideration of the Theory of Tariffs", *Review of Economic Studies*, Summer, IX (2), pp. 89–110.

17. Webb, L. R., 1970, "International Factor Movement and National Advantage: Comment", *Economica*, Vol. XXXVII, pp. 81–4.

18. Wilson, John D., 1982a, "Optimal Linear Income Taxation in the Presence of Emigration", *Journal of Public Economics*, 18 (3).

19. Wilson, John D., 1982b, "Optimal Income Taxation and Migration: A World Welfare Point of View," *Journal of Public Economics*, 18 (3).

The Economic Analysis of International Migration

It is an honour to be asked to address this Nordic Seminar on Migration. It is surely presumptuous of me to be sharing my thoughts on the subject with this distinguished group of experts in the field.

I Introduction

My own interest in the field of migration has been primarily confined to one, though admittedly significant, aspect of the phenomenon of migration today. In particular, I have been concerned in recent years, both from a public-policy viewpoint as also from an economic-theoretical perspective, with the international migration of highly skilled manpower from the poor to the rich nations: a migration flow once called the "brain drain" and now described in typical international bureaucratese, but not without some objective economic and psychological justification, as the "reverse transfer of technology." In the rather impressionistic classification of *international* migration flows given in table 1, my research has thus focused on cell D.

And, aside from extensive theoretical modeling of different types of skilled labor migrations and their consequences for countries of origin, I have come to be interested in the implication of international migration, mainly of the highly skilled but more exactly of all migrants, whether temporary or to-and-fro or permanent, for such issues as the tax policies of the nation states among which migrants circulate. While these issues can be approached at narrowly economic-theoretical levels, and indeed theoretical work along these lines is in progress, they also raise a whole host of questions to which answers can be yielded only by addressing issues that are the subject matter of fields as diverse as political science, psychology, ethics, international tax and human rights laws, and sociology. I *am* mindful of these wider ramifications of my economic research and towards the end of this lecture, I shall indeed address them in the context of the recent developments in the economic analysis of public finance policy in the presence of international migration.

Table 1 Patterns of international migration flows: a classification

From	To: Poor countries	Rich countries
Poor Countries	(A) Unskilled Relatively rare except for refugee migrations	(B) Unskilled (i) *Gastarbeiters*; (ii) OPEC area inflows; (iii) illegal migration; (iv) historical migration of indentured labor from East to West; early Central European migration to UK, US, etc.
	(C) Skilled (i) Intergovernmental and (ii) international agency programs in the main	(D) Skilled (i) Brain drain and (ii) OPEC area inflows in the main
Rich Countries	(E) Unskilled (i) Classical European outmigration; (ii) relatively rare (political protests, etc.) otherwise	(F) Unskilled Relatively unimportant
	(G) Skilled Mostly (i) technical assistance programs and (ii) *MNC*-related outflows	(H) Skilled Mostly brain drain from Europe and Canada to US

II International Migration versus Interregional Migration: Immigration Quotas

However, I wish to take as the main theme of my lecture, not the public-finance implications of international migration, but rather the fact of immigration quotas, which I regard as the one principal and dominant characteristic of international migration as distinguished from intranational, or what the Swedish Nobel laureate economist Bertil Ohlin called interregional, migration. Let me begin, then, with this one qualitative difference that currently exists between these two principal forms of migration. But let me also enter at the outset the caveat that such differences may dissolve in specific historical instances; as the economists among you must doubtless know, attempts to distinugish international from interregional *trade* in economic theorizing, based on notions such as that factors are immobile across but not within nations, have run into simply too many empirical contradictions. Besides, for migration, what Joan Robinson said of India once is almost equally applicable: Whatever you say about it, the opposite is also true!

With that caveat on the floor let me now argue that the most compelling difference between interregional and international migration today is that while (except in communist countries) the former is free, the latter is strictly regulated and controlled. The apparatus of immigration restrictions is now so widespread among twentieth-century nation states that it is easy to forget that the nineteenth century was not burdened with these restrictions to anywhere near the same degree. Indeed, the ethical and moral-philosophical viewpoint that human beings should be free to locate where they want to on this planet would appear today to be a utopian position. But it was not always so. Of course, restrictions on international mobility had surfaced in the form of passports, so that the word had entered common usage by the sixteenth century and been graced by Shakespeare in *Henry V* in his lines "Let him depart; his passport shall be made and crowns for convoy put into his purse," and the summary expulsion of aliens had also occasionally been undertaken. However, the persistent and strict regulation by legislation of the inflow of foreign nationals was not the hallmark of centuries earlier than the twentieth. Some of you may recall the universalist, single-planetary philosophical position on international mobility formulated during the sixteenth century and expressed by Franciscus a Vittoria in his *Reflectiones Theologicae*. Asserting what he graphically termed the "Right of Natural Society and Communication," he sought to provide the ethical rationale for the Spaniards proceeding to the Indies to settle there by arguing that "it has been the custom from the beginning of the world for anyone to go into whatever country he chooses and prohibition of entrance is a violent measure not removed from war."

Today the migration of both skilled and unskilled people, whether temporary or permanent in intention, is surrounded by restrictions on entry that have developed from legislation that was enacted in various developed countries in the early part of the twentieth century.

Let me consider the US situation in some detail. In the United States, which was a splendid example of open immigration up to the end of the nineteenth century, there had been occasional agitations against immigrants or free immigration, as when the aptly titled Know-Nothing Party arose in response to Irish immigration and even managed to elect six governors and seventy-five Congressmen in 1854; Chinese immigration was made illegal in 1882 under the Chinese Exclusion Act; and in 1907, as the economist observer of today's practices in regard to VERs on Japanese and other exports of goods will be amused to hear, President Theodore Roosevelt had even entered into a so-called Gentlemen's Agreement with Japan to limit immigration of Japanese laborers! But the truly restrictive, comprehensive legislation enacting immigration restrictions came with the 1921 Emergency Quota Law, which ended the era of essentially unrestricted immigration, and the 1924 National Origins Act, under which discriminatory national and racial quotas were adopted. This initiated the phase of "*ethnic screening with numerical limits*," which was to yield with the 1950s to the current phase, described as "*familial screening with numerical limits,*" as a result of the 1965 act that eliminated the racial and origin quotas and permitted open access to all races within quotas set by functional and familial considerations.

In brief, the modern experience even in the United States, the traditionally open-door country built on immigration, underscores the unwillingness of modern nation states to permit unregulated immigration. It is ironic indeed to contrast Jan Troell's film *The Emigrants,* with its sensitive portrayal of the harsh but optimistic Swedish emigration to the United States in the mid-nineteenth century, with the Charlie Chaplin film of an earlier vintage but on the later migration, *The Immigrant,* where the scene changes quickly from the cheerful and joyous throng of immigrants sailing past the Statue of Liberty to one where these immigrants find themselves being shoved and kicked unceremoniously by the uniformed immigration inspectors!

Why do I claim that the present-day restrictions on international, but not on interregional migration, matter, and that too for the economic theory and analysis of migration? First, because they bear rather directly on the question of the economic analysis of the factors that *lead to* migration. Second, because the *consequences* of migration across national frontiers, when nations are not embarrassed to use immigration restrictions, can be qualitatively different than when such restrictions are not utilized. Let me deal with each in turn.

A Demand-Determined Migration Models

The fact that international migration is controlled has meant, both for skilled and for semi- and unskilled labor, that the simple but powerful economic models of internal migration have limited applicability to any explanation of this phenomenon. For the best-known of these models take the *migrant's* decision to move as the central focus of analysis and then explain the movement in terms of a permanent move that reflects an improvement in expected income that would materialize from the migration. There are various alternative formulations of this basic notion, with economic theorists varying the formulation of the economic costs and returns to allow, for example, for costs of movement, for unemployment in the destination region implying that the expected wage is the actual wage times the probability of finding a job at that wage, and risk aversion. Perhaps the most influential such model of internal migration is the one developed by John Harris, my erstwhile colleague at MIT, with Michael Todaro, which envisages migration from the agricultural sector to the manufacturing sector and assumes that the potential migrant equates his actual wage in the former sector to the *expected* wage in the latter sector. The expected wage is taken as fixed by union bargaining or by legislation, weighted by the probability of finding a job in the manufacturing sector. Notationally, therefore, the critical labour allocational equation is

$$W_A = \overline{W}_M \cdot \left\{\frac{\overline{L}_M}{\overline{L}_M + L_U}\right\}$$

where W_A is the actual agricultural wage, $\overline{W}_M$ is the fixed manufacturing wage, $\overline{L}_M$ denotes the corresponding number of jobs that are available at the fixed manufacturing wage, and L_U is the labor unemployment in the manufacturing sector so that $(\overline{L}_M + L_U)$ is the laborforce looking for jobs in the manufacturing sector, whereas the number of jobs is only $\overline{L}_M$. When there is unemployment, the bracketed expression is less than unity and represents the ratio of jobs to people looking for these jobs. Multiplying this into the actual manufacturing wage yields the *expected* wage if we can assume that everyone has an equal chance of finding a job, so that everyone is *under*employed; and in a model of population change where some retire and others take their place, we can think of this underemployment as taking the form of waiting until the old retire and their places are available to be taken by those waiting in the queue.

I shall return to this precise model later, when I seek to contrast its differential implications for *QR*-restricted international immigration and for free internal migration. For the present, however, let me stress instead that this model, and indeed all variations by economists of this basic approach, ultimately turn on migration materializing when the cost-benefit ratio on migration turns in favor of the act of migration, with virtually no interaction between the sectors of origin and destination except through the goods market and the specified wage mechanism. The regressional evidence that has been turned up in countless econometric studies of *internal* migration across the world only underlines the inherent plausibility of this approach to analyzing free migration within a country: a typical such regression employing cross-sectional evidence on relative migration from different regions within a country to common areas of destination. I might add that *given* the countries of emigration, similar regressions have been successfully estimated even on post-1965 US immigration of highly skilled immigrants (the *PTK*s). For with the 1965 act, the United States essentially abolished origin quotas and opened up, among others, *PTK* quotas on a "first come, first served" basis, so that there *is* a theoretical basis, from the equal-access assumption, that countries of origin with more unemployment, lower wage rates, and other such economic variations would have correspondingly more applications in line for the *PTK* immigration quotas and hence, *ceteris paribus*, a higher ex post migration rate to the United States.

However, I do believe that this analysis, both theoretical and econometric, is seriously incomplete. And here I do *not* mean that noneconomic variables are left out. Economists are indeed prone to consider only the economic variables and, of course, when the data do yield high R^2 values, they feel that this focus is justified and that noneconomic factors, interesting as they appear, are only so much "noise" that theory, being an abstraction, must necessarily disregard. This elevation of greed to the principal position among the virtues and vices that afflict mankind must sit ill with some; but it has worked wonders at providing explanations of changes in human behavior and indeed even social institutions since Adam Smith invented the Invisible Hand to provide ethical legitimacy to private greed as but the handmaiden of public good.

What worries me, rather, is that neither this economic model, nor the conceptual framework encompassing sociological factors that was developed so brilliantly by Hoffman-Nowotny (in a companion lecture to the *Nordisk Migrasjonsforskerseminar*—see the note at the end of this lecture), comes to grips with the central fact that (at least for the *Gastarbeiter* type) international migration is largely *initiated* from the country of immigration where immigration quotas are combined with labor certification procedures aimed at filling domestically "unfillable" jobs.

As my colleague Michael Piore has reminded me, firms and intermediaries actively contract for *Gastarbeiters,* moving into one region after another *sequentially,* opening up new sources of labor supply that was "there," with its low wages, unemployment, or the Merton-Hoffmann-Nowotny anomy, but was unable to move freely into the *Gastarbeiter* region to increase its income or reduce its anomy. Thus France went from importing labor from Eastern Europe in the prewar period to North Africa, Italy, and Spain when the predominantly Polish supply was cut off by the war and the Iron Curtain. Then it shifted to Portugal and Yugoslavia when Spain and Italy became tighter labor markets with their own development. And so with West Germany. And in both cases, it appears that the employers were able to find workers quickly and easily when they needed it—and the labor, which responded so readily when actively recruited, exhibited so little tendency to move spontaneously on its own initiative before the initial recruitment efforts were made.

In the presence of immigration restrictions, therefore, one gets a *demand-determined* migration flow, and the analyst must *first* have a theory that explains the incremental demand for labor that makes the recruiting, immigration-law-clearance and related investment efforts by firms economically worthwhile. The simplest neoclassical model of this kind would, of course, be one in which a growing economy runs into rising wage costs, given the natural growth of the native labor force (whether from reproduction or internal migration of underemployed labor, as with black migration from the South to the expanding North in the interwar period); and this makes recruitment of foreign labor economical for private firms. Alternatively, one could visualize, as I prefer to do, a job-ladder economy in which the growing demand for labor leads to the higher-wage jobs, with more status, being filled with existing labor supply and the bottom-of-the-ladder, unskilled, lower-wage jobs resulting in "unfilled" vacancies that are filled by the recruitment of migrants. Either way, the immigration does not appear as impinging upon native labor's economic interests and is rather associated with increasing real wages on old jobs or with upward job mobility as the foreign labor is brought in. I might add, however, that the job-ladder model seems to fit the *Gastarbeiter* facts rather better, as they *are* brought often into the lower-level, "menial," low-wage jobs from which natives seem to be fleeing for higher wages and/or status as the economy expands.

But this harmony of proletarian interests has been short-lived for three major unanticipated reasons, recalling to mind Max Weber's famous concept of the "paradox of consequences," designed to characterize the unintended outcome of social action. First, these immigrants, while brought in for short periods and often expressing the intention to return home, have often stayed on much longer and quickly acquired the ambitions and aspirations of those further up the ladder, seeking better jobs by entering those labor markets. Second, the second-generation immigrants, the offspring of these first-generation immigrants, have entered to compete in these same markets, since they have grown up in the immigrant culture and both generations expect them to do better than their parents. Third, and perhaps most important, the migration process, once initiated, has failed in countries such as the United States to be controlled as intended. The long border with Mexico, in particular, has made illegal immigration, estimated at anywhere from 3 to 9 million, an ugly reality, turning a whole mass of humanity into a subterranean, deprived society of second-class American residents with little of the civil and criminal protections and employer-related rights that the legal immigrants enjoy. Simultaneously, it has implied a serious pressure on wages and adverse impact on unionization and observance of minimum-wage legislation, thus creating, as would *free* migration (to which it begins to approximate), the intralabor conflicts that demand-determined legal migration mostly avoids. And it has brought into sharp focus the potentiality of conflicts between the countries of origin and destination that migration can entail, with great acuteness, in a world of immigration restrictions.

B Quota-Related Conflicts between Sending and Receiving Countries

I should like now to analyze some such quota-related conflicts, as observed in the context of skilled *and* unskilled migration. Few of you need to be reminded of the tendency of European countries during recessions to protect the jobs of citizens and to dump the *Gastarbeiters* back onto the countries of origin, thus compounding the economic difficulties that the recession would probably cause directly through its adverse impact on world trade via the resulting shrinkage in import demands. Again, the contrast with the world of free internal migration is obvious. There is really little likelihood that a nontotalitarian government will pick up the rural immigrants from the urban centers during a recession and dump them back into the rural sector to fend for themselves while reserving the available jobs for the nonmigrant population.

Moreover, a subtle, malignly symbiotic relationship can exist between the immigration quotas and the *creation* of unemployment among the skilled classes in sending countries. The traditional, benign view was to argue that the migration of skilled nurses, engineers, and so forth was desirable because many underdeveloped countries had overproduced these kinds of professionals and that the "brain drain" was therefore a safety valve, a spillover phenomenon. This contention is particularly facile as it rests on the view that the employment in the sending country is exogenous to the quota-regulated immigration process. But this is hardly likely to be the case! When 100 Filipino nurses, who are currently unemployed, emigrate to the United States under an effective quota of 100, they set up an expectation that more can go. Even if the prospective nurse takes her expected wage in the United States as the actual wage times the probability of getting to the United States, the wage differential between the United States and the Philippines is so high that it may lead to training schools being set up (under purely private incentives) to produce 600 more nurses annually! But given the annual quota of 100, only 100 can migrate, and the Philippines will have 500 unemployed nurses on hand!

What the immigration quota does, aside from maintaining high wage differentials across countries, is to localize this induced unemployment in the Philippines. A similarly induced unemployment in, say, a high-wage urban sector would, by contrast, have led to the unemployment being localized in the urban sector itself if we were considering free, rural-urban migration within a country!

III Other Systemic Interactions between Sending and Receiving Countries

While these quota-related conflicts between sending and receiving countries are important, I should also mention a further phenomenon of significance bearing on the economic relation between the two sets of countries. It happens that a not insignificant fraction of the immigrant, unskilled labor flow, including the illegals in the United States, goes into the declining, unprogressive, senescent industries. This is itself not unrelated to the fact that the immigration restrictions occasionally tend to preselect and channel the *Gastarbeiters* into these low-productivity industries, where only lower wages can be afforded due to stiff overseas competition and therefore native workers are not readily available. But these industries are often in import competition precisely with the manufactured exports of other developing countries! I have heard Sol Chaikin, colorful head of the International Garment Workers' Union, argue passionately for protection for his largely immigrant, largely female, constituents—protection that would hurt the poor workers in the *exporting* underdeveloped countries! This is an interesting example of the potential for intrapoor, migrant versus nonmigrant conflicts that arise from international migration in the growing world capitalist system!

It is also interesting to observe that since civil-libertarian countries such as the United States are quite unlikely to be able to handle the problem of illegal, de facto free immigration from developing countries such as Mexico, one may confidently expect that this is likely to prompt a reverse flow of capital. This may be undertaken as foreign aid, simply as a bribe to these countries to assist in effectively restricting emigration from *their* side. Moreover, it may be also conceived as a way of creating added jobs, higher wages, and so forth, to make the opportunity cost of migration higher to the potential, illegal migrants. One may therefore see *both* foreign aid programs revive *and* (sending-country-) job-creating trade and investment initiatives undertaken by countries, such as the United States, that feel especially vulnerable to illegal migration.

Indeed, it is ironic that the capitalist countries, in turning to the reserve armies of labor in the developing countries after the war to sustain their economies, thought that they could draw from this in a regulated, fine-tuned fashion, utilizing immigration quotas to that effect. What they did in effect was to open up vast streams of labor inflow that, as I remarked earlier, have also encouraged in the end illegal immigration. For the illegals blend with the legals of identical ethnic origin, who provide the protective coloring; catching and prosecuting them tends to violate the civil liberties of the legal immigrants and naturalized citizens of identical origin; and the legal immigrants at times provide the political lobbies for better treatment of the illegals of similar origin. The controlled, legal immigration has therefore spawned the uncontrollable illegal one; a pandora's box has been opened. In retrospect, the evolution of the capitalist system, in a world of nation states zealous to prevent immigration, might have done better by going exclusively the traditional Marxist-Leninist route of exporting industry to the poor countries rather than importing their labor.

IV Migrants and Taxation by Nation States

Let me turn finally to the rather different set of economic-theoretic and policy-related issues that I have recently raised concerning international migration and its implication for income taxation by nation states. These issues center on two questions: (i) When people move across national boundaries, which country's income tax should be applied to them? (ii) How should the tax proceeds from taxing these individuals be allocated between the countries of origin and destination?

My interest in these questions originally led me to propose that there be a "tax on the brain drain." This would be an income tax to be levied on the earnings in the rich countries of the highly skilled migrants from the poor countries; this tax would be additional to the normal income tax they would pay in the rich countries; and the proceeds would be used to finance developmental spending in the poor countries of origin or in poor countries *en bloc*. You may have noticed that this proposal focused on taxing the migrants themselves, not at the point of migration, but after exit and on their actual earnings after the exit. The incidence of the tax would therefore not be on the rich countries of immigration, which would continue to levy their normal taxes on these aliens in their midst. What led me to make this startling proposal?

As it happens, I came to it while contemplating the process of migration of the highly skilled in the context of severe immigration restrictions. I started from the central fact that those, like myself, who managed to get past the rich countries' immigration barriers were earning what economists call "rents" and what others would call "windfall profits." The earning by migrants of these rents amounts to substantial improvements in incomes, reflecting the wide disparities in remunerations that the immigration quotas help maintain, and corresponds in principle exactly to the rents that are earned, when imports of goods are controlled and therefore fetch a scarcity premium, by those who are lucky or well connected enough to get the scarce and valuable import licenses.

This image of successful, welfare-improving migrants, earning substantial incremental incomes in the rich countries of immigration, of course fits reasonably well the facts on the voluntary migration of the highly skilled from the poor to the rich countries. It also conforms to the economist's usual assumption that any voluntary immigrant must axiomatically be welfare improving and "happier," or else he would return to his country of origin—an assumption that, however, fits poorly with the *Gastarbeiter* type of unskilled immigration, for which, as Brusati's poignant film *Bread and Chocolate* underlines, the migrant may well feel hopelessly trapped in a tragic situation in the country of immigration.

If these highly skilled migrants earn rents by successfully getting past the immigration restrictions, why not tax these rents and utilize the resulting tax revenues for developmental spending in the poor countries of their origin or in poor countries *en bloc*? Taxation of rents is just about the oldest, most respectable idea in the economic theory of taxation; and here would be an added source of tax revenues for poor countries' developmental programs. Besides, I also felt that free migration was no longer, in the twentieth century, considered an inviolable human right; witness the severe immigration restrictions, for example. If, then, migrants were freely allowed to emigrate and earned substantial rents, it seemed morally defensive for countries of origin to say, "We could restrict your emigration just as the symmetric right to immigrate is curtailed today; but we don't, and therefore in today's world of imperfect mobility accepted by nation states, we consider it ethically right to propose that part of your gains from permitted emigration be shared with 'those left behind.'" Finally, if this migration imposed any difficulties or economic losses on those left behind, as is arguable for certain classes of highly skilled migration and is probably true for most such classes to the minimal extent that the sending country has subsidized their educational costs, then the argument for sharing the rents of these migrants with their countries of origin, strong as it is if the two earlier arguments are accepted, becomes morally stronger indeed.

While these arguments implied that there was a case for levying a tax on the incomes of migrants in the countries of immigration, for the benefit of the countries of emigration, I also felt that the rich countries of immigration, given their selective quotas, could be presumed to have profited from such immigration, and therefore there was a separate case for the poor countries of emigration to share in the gains that the rich countries of immigration obtained from the migration of the nationals of the poor countries. This line of argumentation naturally leads to notions such as "revenue-sharing" whereby the "normal" taxes paid by the migrants in the countries of immigration are shared between the countries of immigration and emigration; this constitutes one convenient way in which the sharing of migration-caused gains to the countries of immigration could be carried out.

These two proposals, whereby the migrants themselves would be carrying a supplementary income tax burden and the countries of immigration would be undertaking "revenue sharing" and thus assuming a tax burden on themselves, have attracted considerable attention recently, while also drawing many scholars from different disciplines and also policymakers into the resulting debate. This is hardly the occasion to recount to you the history of the developments; they have been excellently surveyed in a splendid recent paper of Oliver Oldman and Richard Pomp in the *Harvard International Law Review* (1979) on the subject of tax measures in response to the brain drain; and I have myself traced the main developments in a paper in the new *Third World Quarterly* (July 1979) on ecomonics, ethics, and taxes as they pertain to international migration of the highly skilled. I should only add to those papers the fact that the recent Manila Conference on the UNCTAD did proceed so far as to adopt a unanimous resolution [No. 102(V)] to urge member countries to examine tax policies in the context of international migration, thus elevating for the first time this area of analysis to international policy discussions beyond the expert group level.

I should like to conclude by noting that while I came to propose the tax on the brain drain, the first of the two proposals described earlier, while considering the migration of the *highly skilled*, I now see the matter in a rather broader framework of *all* migration. My discussions of the brain-drain tax with international legal and human-rights lawyers led to the accidental discovery that it was well within traditional international law for a country to exercise its income tax jurisdiction on its citizens working abroad as long as they retained citizenship. This seems quite sensible, since there is really no reason why an egalitarian society should automatically exempt from its tax net those citizens who work abroad. And indeed, that is exactly what the United States has been doing from the beginning of its income tax legislation! Once, therefore, you see the logic of this way of bringing all citizens into the tax net, admittedly with due provisions to avoid double taxation, it is easy to see that my proposal to tax the brain drain can be generalized into the proposal that poor countries of emigration, which have nearly all (excepting the Philippines, which does have the US tax system) inherited the tax systems of their excolonial powers and hence have routinely let off their citizens working abroad by using residence as the tax criterion, should adopt the "global" tax system, based on citizenship, that the United States has been practicing. If this were done, it would be seen as ethically defensible (since it applies the principle of the income tax to all citzens) and nondiscriminatory (since, for example, citizens of India in the United States would be taxed at identical rates as Americans by the United States, but would be paying, if any, added taxes as Indian citizens, to India) and hence compatible with human-rights conventions. In this format the taxation of the migrants would also be more politically viable, since it would, in principle, extend to all citizens working abroad, regardless of their skill status; income alone would become the valid criterion for taxability and the rate of assessment. It would also become, unlike my earlier proposal, entirely a matter of self-help by the poor countries, thus being fully consonant with the philosophy of self-reliant intra-South actions currently fashionable in the poor countries.

I should emphasize that the moral basis for this generalized version of my original proposal to tax the brain drain is strictly egalitarian. There should be no "representation without taxation"; citizenship carries the obligation to be taxed, with no convenient escape from assuming one's share of the country's tax burden just because one happens to be abroad—and for many of the highly skilled in particular, even very successfully abroad. This ethical justification is somewhat distinct from the ones that I outlined as having led me to the original proposal; but it is one that can indeed be supplemented by them to make the case for adoption of the US "global" tax system by the poor countries yet stronger.

In conclusion, I might add that the mirror image of the anomaly of "representation without taxation" is the anomaly of "taxation without representation" in most countries of immigration today. Even resident aliens with permanent immigrant status in the United States are deprived altogether of any voting rights although they pay identical taxes as Americans. It is only recently, as Tomas Hammar has reminded us, that Sweden has granted voting rights in local elections to foreign workers; and Norway is considering the adoption of similar legislation. That in pluralistic democracies, the vote is a necessary condition for securing economic, civil, and other rights is fairly evident; that it follows that the migrant workers in one's midst ought to be allowed these rights, however, is an issue that has only recently come into the field of international discussion.

The grant of the vote in Sweden to foreign citizens in its midst should act as the kind of catalyst in moving the rich countries of immigration into removing the anomaly of "taxation without representation" that, I believe, the United States practice of taxing citizens abroad, and increasing appreciation of this fact and the ethical and economic principles underlying it, will have on the reverse anomaly of "representation without taxation." The traditionally inherited accidents of practice and prejudice in these two fields of politics and economics, and related disciplines, are increasingly being questioned in a world of migration and international mobility, however controlled and imperfect.

This is the text of a plenary lecture delivered to *Nordisk Migrasjonsforskerseminar*, Nordic Council of Ministers, Oslo, Norway, October 1979. Support by the National Science Foundation, Grant No. SOC79-07541, is acknowledged.

INTERNATIONAL MIGRATION OF THE HIGHLY SKILLED: ECONOMICS, ETHICS AND TAXES

Jagdish N Bhagwati

The analysis of the consequences of highly skilled migration across countries has recently moved into novel economic, legal and social areas of intellectual inquiry.

However, progress in the scientific pursuit of these questions, and their possible implications has been handicapped partly by the rigid mental and emotional reflexes of some of the economists who actively participated in the early postwar debate on the consequences of 'brain drain' and who evidently seem to fear that the newly burgeoning interest in the subject somehow breathes life into a public policy issue that they had hoped to have successfully buried. However, part of the explanation lies also in the fact that the new developments have resulted almost entirely as a result of 'advocacy economics' in the form of a proposal advanced by the author to tax brain drain in the shape of a supplementary income tax to be paid by the highly skilled migrants from the poor countries on their incomes in the developed countries.[1] This proposal has economic, ethical, tax-legal, human rights, sociological and political implications and has, therefore, proved to be a powerful stimulus in opening up afresh what was until recently a rather moribund field of inquiry. But it has also correspondingly tended to provoke more heat than light.

The Postwar Debate

The earliest economic analyses of the international migration of highly skilled manpower were almost wholly stimulated by the concerns of policymakers in the countries that were experiencing a net emigration of professional personnel such as doctors, engineers and academics. The emigration was therefore described typically as 'brain drain': a persuasive phrase that predisposed one to see the phenomenon in an unfavourable light.

The late Harry Johnson, writing first in *Minerva* in 1956 and often elsewhere thereafter, was to lead the 'counter-revolution', noting that brain drain could be

Originally mentioned in an article of mine in *Daedalus* (1972) on 'United States in the Nixon Era: the end of innocence', the idea was developed in other writings at greater length and was the subject of an international conference at Bellagio whose deliberations led to the two volumes: *Taxing the Brain Drain: a proposal* (Vol I) edited by J Bhagwati & M Partington. Amsterdam: North Holland Publishing. 1976; and *The Brain Drain and Taxation: theory and empirical analysis* (Vol II) edited by J Bhagwati. Amsterdam: North-Holland Publishing. 1976.

beneficial to the countries of emigration and arguing passionately that it often was.

The ensuing debate paralleled the classic division of economists into two different philosophical traditions which the author once described as the 'benign neglect' and the 'malign neglect' schools. The orthodox, professional economists typically tended to follow Adam Smith in looking for the non-zero-sum-game (i.e. every party to a transaction gains) aspects of an economic phenomenon. The resulting 'benign neglect' view of these economists contrasted sharply with the concerns of the economists whose 'malign neglect' analysis focused instead on the harmful aspects of the same economic phenomena for specific groups, and therefore raised more pointedly questions of desirable policy intervention on grounds of both efficiency and distributive justice.

Thus, while the economists led by Johnson tended to emphasise the advantages to the skilled migrants themselves and to the countries of origin and destination, the economists and policymakers arrayed on the other side emphasised the losses to 'those left behind' from such emigration, whether permanent, or of a to and fro variety.

Unfortunately, however, it became fashionable to consider the complacent, everyone-gains viewpoint as an 'internationalist' or 'cosmopolitan' position, whereas the group of economists more impressed by the possibility of the adverse impact of highly skilled migration on countries of origin came to be described as 'nationalist'. The very same economists who had brilliantly debunked the phrase 'brain drain' by noting that one had to draw a distinction between the brain drain phenomenon and the brain drain problem and that migration of the highly skilled could be beneficial to those left behind, were now to be guilty of describing their own position in self-congratulatory terms that equally prejudiced the ethical demerits of their opponents' position.

As it happens, there is nothing ethically reprehensible in worrying about specific groups within a social entity. Indeed, Rawls' *maximin* principle requires us to put a decisive weight on the impact of a policy change on the welfare of the least privileged, so that if highly skilled migration does affect those left behind adversely, and the incidence of such losses is on the underprivileged, the principles of Rawlsian distributive justice would indeed make it morally obtuse not to worry about the migration. Indeed, on more traditional utilitarian ethics as well, if the migrants are earning more than those left behind, one could argue that the migration, if it imposes losses on those left behind, will be an ethically undesirable phenomenon.

Evidently, therefore, the moral basis of those concerned with the impact of emigration of highly skilled manpower, especially from poor countries of origin, was more than defensible. And the description of these intellectuals as 'nationalists' was somewhat propagandistic.

Who Loses?

When we have abandoned the fetching but foolish term 'brain drain' and the 'internationalist' and 'nationalist' positions, we are left with the enhanced awareness that migration need not worsen the welfare, however defined, of the non-migrating population in the countries of origin.

However, the arguments on this question have remained primarily qualitative, as always. For, even when economists are agreed on the criteria by which they judge policies as desirable or otherwise, they can and will often disagree because several relevant variables will be quantifiable only with a generous input of imagination and goodwill, qualities that vary from individual to individual.

Thus, does the permanent emigration of a talented professor from India to the US hurt Indian education? The optimist will argue that his research output will be available to other Indians, that his research will be of significantly higher quality in better conditions and thus will inspire other Indians at home to better work; and that his knowledge will also be available on frequent summer visits to Indian institutions, to take only some of the more obvious and persuasive arguments in favour of the Johnsonesque position. On the other hand, the pessimists can equally well argue that his research output may be constrained by patents or by CIA secrecy requirements; that his research may then turn to fields where India derives no real economic advantage; that his success in research abroad may serve only to reinforce the feeling that it is not possible to work at home; and that success requires emigration abroad, and that the summer visits will often serve to create resentments among those not so fortunate as to leave and succeed abroad.

Several such questions do not lend themselves to easy quantification. The field is thus left open to the immediacy of one's own experience in these matters. It has, therefore, been customary for the pessimists to come from the poor countries where institution building and retention of professional manpower in several fields are important problems in the face of superior working conditions and enormously improved incomes abroad; and for the optimists to come from countries where this is not so because the countries of emigration and immigration are much closer to each other in working conditions and salary levels.

But while economists are divided, in the main, on what the empirical reality is, the optimist economists and the pessimist policymakers are divided rather on their assessment of the costs and benefits of the empirical reality. Typically, the policymakers have leaned to the pessimist view because they are concerned with shorter time horizons than the economists who write academically about the issues at hand. Thus, for example, economists will say that the emigrating scientist will probably return some years later, better informed and more experienced, and will be of greater value to the country than when he left it. After all, the Chinese nuclear capability was built by Chinese scientists who had returned to the mainland from American universities where they had earlier settled for long periods. This argument, however, makes little sense to politicians and planners who have to struggle with the problem of adapting their economy to the immediately disruptive exodus of highly skilled manpower. In economic jargon, therefore, the difference in assessment of the policymakers and the economists is to be attributed to a great extent to different time horizons over which they make their welfare judgment concerning the emigration of highly skilled manpower.

These differences are further compounded by the tendency of most economists to underplay the importance of the 'non-economic' objectives that people often have. Welfare is not simply a function of the availability of goods and services. If migration of the highly skilled raises the incomes of the unskilled left behind, the economist will rejoice, but politicians will probably regret the technological backwardness of the society that follows.

Recent Analytical Arguments

It is therefore easier now for the objective intellectual to see that categorical assertions affirming or denying the presence of a brain drain problem are without merit. Recent analytical developments have further suggested that the 'benign neglect' view, which had many adherents among economists, may have been oversold.

Thus, a principal argument advanced by the proponents of this view was that the migration of the highly skilled was a reflection of domestic unemployment; that it was a 'spillover', or 'safety valve', or 'vent-for-surplus' phenomenon. Thus, if a doctor was driving a taxicab in Manila, and was, therefore, virtually unemployed, how could his migration to New York hurt the Philippines? Persuasive as this argument is, it reflects an implicit economic model which is quite unrealistic. Why not think instead of the Filipino doctor as driving a taxicab precisely because he is waiting to pass his US examination for foreign medical graduates and that if this opportunity were not available, he would have to start practice in the outskirts of Manila or even further away if Manila is getting overcrowded with doctors. In short, the external migration possibility, the brain drain opportunity, actually inhibits the 'internal diffusion' process which carries, however slowly, these professional skills to where they will create greater social impact.[2]

Let us also examine the alternative model where the migration at high salaries abroad of one hundred nurses in the Philippines, in an initial situation of a hundred currently unemployed nurses, leads to a greatly enhanced expectation reward for becoming a nurse and hence to the private expansion of training facilities so that annually one thousand rather than one hundred nurses are turned out. Since, given immigration restrictions, no more than one hundred nurses can go abroad annually, the Philippines is going to be faced with the problem of contending with nine hundred unemployed nurses annually, at least

[2] K Hamada & J Bhagwati, 'Domestic Distortions, Imperfect Information and the Brain Drain', in Bhagwati (ed), 1976, *op cit*.

for some time.[3] This is not a fanciful example. It reflects empirical reality better than the one where the one hundred nurses, initially unemployed, leave for gainful foreign employment and the Philippines can rejoice at the outcome.

Again, if one presses this 'explosive expectations' argument home, it is easy to see that one does not need 'large' outflows to get the resulting expansion of unemployment and associated economic waste and political disruption. The mere integration of a professional market across countries, in the sense of expectations about earnings taking into account the probability of finding jobs in every national market, is enough to make the 'explosive expectations' effect possible. Moreover, if such integration also leads to an upward pressure in domestic salaries of such professionals in the poor countries, this will only accentuate the problem. In either case, the oft cited statistics about the 'smallness' of outflows of specific professionals in relation to total annual output or stock are really beside the point and do not invalidate the argument.

Moreover, these analytical developments indicate that the 'vent-for-surplus spillover' argument reaches optimistic results by incorrectly assuming that the unemployment is due to domestic reasons and emigration is exogenously superimposed on this situation with evident relief. Actually, it makes more sense to consider migration, actual and potential, as an integral part of the economic system and as itself being responsible for the unemployment phenomenon.

These and related new developments have left us with a keener awareness that losses to countries of origin cannot be ruled out and that, contrary to occasional assertions about the insanity or non-educability of policymakers in the poor countries that sometimes raise their voices in pleas for redress, there can be real problems here.

At the same time, it should be equally evident now that these problems will not generally apply to all professional categories in any one country of origin or to all countries in any one profession. There is considerable diversity of national objectives, the time horizon over which these objectives are sought, and the conditions in different professions concerning wage formation and employment. This makes it naive to make categorical assertions about the presence or absence of losses to countries of emigration.

Shift of Focus

While recent developments in economic analysis have served to lend more respectability to the contention that migration of the highly skilled can impose difficulties or losses on the countries of origin, other developments have served to undercut the relevance of this issue and to focus on quite different aspects of the migration process. These developments have arisen in the form of a systematic examination of the tax arrangements that govern highly skilled migrants.

The primary stimulus for analytical developments in this direction was provided by my proposal to levy a supplementary tax on professional migrants

[3] J Bhagwati & K Hamada, 'The Brain Drain, International Integration of Markets for Professionals and Unemployment', in Bhagwati (ed), 1976, *op cit*.

from developing countries, to be levied and assessed on their incomes in the developed countries of immigration. The specific ethical rationale at the time involved the view that highly skilled migrants coming from poor countries ought to make an institutionalised tax contribution from their earnings to their countries of origin, and possibly for development financing to poor countries *en bloc*. It is somewhat hypocritical for developing countries to ask rich countries to tax their citizens in order to finance foreign development aid, while not undertaking any direct tax burden themselves.

A great deal of economic, legal and sociological thinking on the questions that this proposal stimulated, indeed often provoked, as also deliberations on it at international conferences and an intergovernmental expert group meeting in March 1978, suggests that the surest way to defuse emotional reactions and prevent them from overtaking one's ability to look dispassionately at these new ideas is to note that international migration of the highly skilled, often varying in duration and constituting a to and fro movement across countries, is an important aspect of the interdependence that characterises the modern world. It is, therefore, necessary to examine the equity and efficiency aspects of the existing and potential arrangements for taxing highly skilled migrants, much as it has been done by economists, political scientists and tax lawyers for multinational corporations and international capital movements.

It also helps to distinguish between two quite different ideas, namely taxation of the migrants themselves, and tax sharing by the countries of immigration with the countries of origin. The rationales for these alternative proposals, as also their legal, administrative, economic and political implications, are naturally different.

Taxing Migrants

The case for taxing highly skilled migrants on their incomes in the countries of immigration can be developed on alternative rationales. Two major ideas in the literature may be briefly noted here before I move on to a more sustained statement of a third, more compelling, rationale.

An obvious rationale lies in the fact that these migrants typically make substantial earnings when they manage to emigrate (except probably when they are expelled as in Uganda, in which case the decision to migrate is involuntary), whereas there is the distinct possibility that their emigration causes losses to the countries of emigration. It would then be appropriate to ask that some taxation should be levied on those who are allowed to migrate in pursuit of a humanistic world order for the compensatory benefit of those who are unwilling, or more often unable, to migrate.

A very different rationale, but one that is built partly on the identical premise that the migrants derive major gains in income, follows from the oldest argument for taxation in economic science: the taxation of economic rents. The stiff immigration restrictions in the rich countries, and the enormous differentials in economic rewards between rich and poor countries, imply that the professionals migrating from the poor countries into rich ones enjoy windfall gains in the nature of economic rent. These rents, like all economic rents (for example, the monopoly profits enjoyed by those who manage to get the scarce import licences in exchange-control regimes that confer scarcity premia on imports), can be taxed to social advantage without entailing any harmful effects through distortion of resource allocational incentives.[4] Thus, migrants from the poor countries or the South may be taxed to raise resources for development spending in the poor countries, much as profits from the sale of IMF gold stocks at the substantially higher market prices are being used currently to assist needier member countries.

Both the rationales above are likely to apply with much greater force to the migration of the highly skilled from the South to the North than to the intra-North mobility of such people.[5] The windfall gains are much higher for South-North migration; and the disruption and losses are more likely to arise for countries of emigration in the South.

The most compelling rationale, however, emerges if we reflect on the nature of modern migration of the highly skilled. We are, in a sense, back to the nomadic culture. We are born in one country, get educated there and elsewhere, work over a lifetime in several countries and may retire perhaps in a country different from the one we were born in. However, the most characteristic tendency of the modern, highly skilled migrants in this complex world is that they typically tend to retain their nationality as also their ethnic ties. The world has collapsed into a manageable geographical unit, with cheap transportation, conferences and foundation financed short term visits for virtually all those who fall in the highly skilled categories. Few change nationalities any longer, even when they have changed residence permanently. The professional and especially the academic world is truly international and the pressures of assimilation that led to the 'melting pot', and the need to affirm loyalty to one's host nation by changing nationality, are no longer operative in anything like the same degree.

The result is that the professional migrants retain their national status and associated rights, including often the right to vote, but carry no corresponding tax obligation, even of a minimal nature. The situation is one of 'representation without taxation'. The anomaly is particularly compounded because typically these highly skilled migrants are among the more prosperous and successful even prior to their migration, and their ability to work abroad additionally renders them the most taxable, but almost totally untaxed, citizens of their countries. When one considers that in Albert Hirschman's apt conceptualisation

[4]While these rents will generally imply that there are no resource allocational effects from their presence or their being taxed away, recent analysis of 'rent seeking' models has shown that rents, in fact, lead to the wastage of resources because they inevitably lead to 'rent seeking' activities: e.g. firms using people to obtain larger shares of the import licences. Thus, again, a great wastage of resources may be caused in the countries of emigration from 'rent seeking' activities directed at getting the scarce entry permits to jump over the restrictive barriers imposed by immigration authorities. This qualification, however, means that a tax that reduces the net rents accruing to the migrants will only reduce this 'rent seeking' loss of the less developed countries.

[5]The reference here is to first country of origin i.e. an Indian doctor coming to the US from England is still considered a South-North movement.

these migrants have not chosen to 'exit' but have retained 'voice' and 'loyalty', it appears legitimate to regard their escaping the tax system as altogether incongruous.[6]

Curious Anomaly

Curiously, this anomaly of 'representation without taxation' at the emigration end has been matched by the anomaly of 'taxation without representation' at the immigration end. The immigrants have been typically excluded from all voting rights, even in the US which has often been the champion of civil rights and whose Supreme Court has progressively struck down discrimination against resident aliens. However, there have been exceptions to this practice. For example, in the state of Victoria in Australia, aliens owning property within the municipality have been allowed local voting rights; in New Zealand, aliens 'ordinarily resident' for at least a year have the vote even in the general election; and in Ireland all foreigners have the right to vote and even to be ėlected in local elections.[7] The question has further been vigorously debated in recent years in West Germany, France, Switzerland and Luxembourg, whereas Sweden actually allowed non-Swedes to vote in the elections of September 1976 for the first time.[8]

By contrast, the symmetric move towards elimination of 'representation without taxation' has surfaced only recently to the level of intellectual and policy discussions. Such reform, which would bring the highly skilled (and others) working abroad into the tax net, is in fact precisely what is done under the existing 'global tax' system, under which all nationals working and living abroad are taxable, as opposed to the 'schedular tax' system where they are taxed on the basis of residence rather than nationality. Countries such as the US, Mexico and the Philippines practise the global tax system to their advantage, and the poor countries, which generally do not, have forgone their right to tax nationals abroad, when they can least afford it.

Such a global tax system is fully acceptable under existing international tax law, is consistent with human rights conventions at the UN and elsewhere – no one has accused the US yet of violating human rights because of its tax laws – and reflects notions of equity that characterise nearly all western societies

[6]The relevance of Hirschman's concepts to the problems discussed in this paper was suggested by Kindleberger's review article in *Minerva* (1978) of the two volumes by myself, *op cit*, and H Grubel and A Scott's *The Brain Drain: determinants, measurement and welfare effects*, Ontario: Wilfred Laurier University Press. 1977. However, whereas Kindleberger uses Hirschman, to argue against the taxation of migrants, on the false assumption that they have 'exited' in the Hirschman sense, I use it to argue the exact opposite, on the assumption that they have not, but in fact retain 'loyalty' and 'voice'.

[7]Sica, 'Involvement of the Migrant Worker in Local Political Life in the Host Country', *International Migration*, 15 (2/3) 1977.

[8]Hammar, 'The First Immigrant Election,' *International Migration*, 15(2/3), 1977. The election, although described as the 'general election' by Hammar, appears to have been only to local bodies. Interestingly, the Swedish authorities not merely offered the vote to foreign workers, but in fact spent a great deal of time and money to educate them about the Swedish political system.

today.[9] Moreover, it fits in very nicely with the emerging stress in intellectual circles in less developed countries that increased 'self reliance' is necessary. There is also the increased perception that the bargaining power of the less developed countries is not as great as was believed in the early euphoric days of the success of the OPEC cartel. For what could be better for developing countries than taxing their prosperous nationals working and living abroad in order to raise resources, especially when the developed countries are not really critical of this effort, as the tax can be levied and collected unilaterally without bringing them into the picture in any essential way?[10] This is not to deny, of course, that in several cases the collection would be more efficient if, under bilateral or multilateral tax treaties, the developed countries were to agree to supplying minimal tax information on foreign nationals residing in their territories.[11]

Harmonising Transition

While, furthermore, the global tax system can be adopted unilaterally by single countries, an advantage of several countries exercising such an option, more or less simultaneously, would be that they could then harmonise tax rates on nationals abroad, thereby making the transition to the global tax system appear legitimate, fair and hence defensible against special interest lobbying. At the same time, such simultaneous action would make it easier to seek tax treaties that would make the collection easier.

It is interesting to note therefore that in the concerted position of the Group of 77 reached at the UNCTAD Inter-Governmental Group of Experts meeting on highly skilled migration in early 1978, the possible adoption of the global tax system by less developed countries was incorporated in the draft recommendations and, by implication, in the agreed Report, signed, among others, by the developed countries.[12]

While, therefore, my original proposal to tax brain drain visualised a format where developing countries would levy the supplementary income tax with the developed countries of immigration agreeing to its collection and enforcement

[9] From the viewpoint of *efficiency* also, recent work on the theory of public finance underlines how the escape of one set of taxpayers from the tax net, just because they live and work abroad, is harmful to the country of origin. See recent work of Bhagwati, Hamada and John Wilson's thesis at MIT, 1979.

[10] Both the US and the Philippines collect their taxes on nationals abroad without the aid of the countries where their nationals reside and work. In the case of the Philippines, the collection is reportedly geared to passport renewal and the associated requirement that the documentation to be produced for such renewal must include a copy of the tax information that is issued by the tax authorities of the country of residence.

[11] Bilateral renewable tax treaties may be the only way to proceed realistically. It is difficult, for example, to think of the Swedish government agreeing to a multilateral treaty which requires it to yield information on Chilean and Ugandan nationals in Sweden to their governments.

[12] The UNCTAD Expert Group met from 27 February to 7 March, 1978. The Group of 77 in its Draft Recommendations, urged the developed countries to 'render assistance, either on a bilateral or multilateral basis, to developing countries which exercise or wish to exercise their internationally recognised jurisdiction to tax their citizens abroad under a "global" tax system; such assistance could take the form either of "tax collection assistance" and/or of access to information.'[TD/B/C6/AC4/LI/Rev 1, 1978, Committee on Transfer of Technology, p 3, Section A(2)(d).]

under a UN treaty, and the revenues to be disbursed for development spending via some UN agency, the optimal format now seems to be essentially for the developing countries to exercise their global tax jurisdiction abroad and not to involve the developed countries of immigration into the process except through seeking bilateral or multilateral, mutually acceptable, treaties aimed merely at 'normal' exchange of tax information. In this version, the proposal to tax the brain drain turns into an action of 'self reliance' by the developing countries, rather than appearing as something that the developed countries would do for the developing countries. The onus thus shifts to the developing countries as far as policy action is concerned.

The extension of the global tax system to nationals working abroad can be undertaken without, in most cases, involving 'double taxation'. The principle of double taxation, of course, is by no means sacrosanct and its economic basis is derived from the assumption of perfect international mobility of factors, a postulate which is certainly invalid because of severe immigration restrictions. Nonetheless, if this principle were still considered desirable, it would create few difficulties, since tax rates in developing countries applicable to incomes in the developed countries would generally exceed corresponding tax rates in the developed countries, largely because the unadjusted incomes abroad would take these nationals into very high tax income brackets at home.[13] If therefore developing country tax schedules were to be applied to incomes earned by nationals living abroad, it would be natural to make adjustments for the higher cost of living abroad, much as the US does with Section 911 of the Internal Revenue Code. An alternative, simpler procedure would be to follow the Philippines example, and to levy a flat rate of 1 to 3 per cent on the incomes of nationals working abroad, regardless of their residence status. The 'small' tax rate avoids the incidence of double taxation, while sparing the taxpayer and the Filipino authorities the costs of filling out and checking complicated schedules.

Again, it is true that the adoption of a global tax system would encourage some to change their nationality. I doubt, however, if US and Filipino nationals living and working abroad have changed nationality in significant numbers because of the incidence of domestic taxation. But even if nationalities were to be changed, why should that harm the countries of emigration? The revenues earned from global taxation would cease for such ex-nationals; but would that really matter?

Also, the fear that such taxation would cut into remittances appears to be groundless. Not merely casual empiricism, but also such statistics as are available, suggest strongly that remittances go mainly from unskilled and semi-skilled workers rather than from the highly skilled. Typically, the highly skilled migrants tend to come from successful families and hardly need to support needy members left behind. A global tax system which is suitably progressive and taxes skilled higher paid workers rather than the unskilled, lower paid workers, should not cut into remittances in any significant way.

[13]Table 1 in K Hamada, 'Taxing the Brain Drain: a global analysis', in J Bhagwati (ed), *The New International Economic Order: The North-South Debate*. MIT Press. 1977.

Substantial Gains

As for the tax revenues raised, there is little reason to feel that the adoption of the global tax system would not be worthwhile. The Philippines' experience with its extremely small tax rate (1 per cent in the main) and its revenue collection of roughly Filipino $23 million in total during the four year period 1973-6[14] suggests a tax base which is by no means negligible, especially since it is in foreign exchange. The US has been raising substantial revenues, estimated at $150 million in 1975, for example, through its taxation of US citizens residing abroad. Substantially greater revenues are also suggested by tax revenue estimates that I made on the basis of a higher tax rate of 10 per cent on net-of-developed-countries-tax earnings of less developed countries' immigrants (belonging to the professional, technical and kindred category, PTK, in US law) into developed countries, taking the stock of these over a ten year period. The resulting estimate was close to $500 million annually. It seems unlikely, however, that a tax rate of 10 per cent on net-of-developed-countries-tax incomes could be levied and enforced without the active cooperation of developed countries. But if, say, 5 per cent were considered reasonable, it would amount to $250 million and 3 per cent to $150 million at 1976 prices.

While, therefore, the adoption of the global tax system seems on current evidence and reasoning to be equitable, efficient, consistent with existing international tax-legal and human rights practices and conventions, and capable of raising revenues for the less developed countries on a self-reliant basis, its adoption should not necessarily be considered probable. Ultimately, the politicians and the policymakers in the less developed countries, as indeed everywhere, are likely to consider it expedient to avoid taxing their own nationals and to concentrate instead on seeking revenues from foreign governments in one form or another.

The major opposition to the idea from the intellectuals of the developed countries is likely to come from a philosophical direction. The late Harry Johnson, in private conversation, once expressed his distaste for the proposal on the ground that it would help extend the arm of the less developed countries' governments to people who had essentially left the country, and that this was particularly reprehensible since many less developed countries were now dictatorships. This viewpoint could be compelling, given the empirical premises, if the less developed countries' taxes were enforced by the countries of immigration and, besides, applied even after a change of citizenship, if any. The original format of my tax proposal did indeed have these features. However, the format suggested above, in the shape of the adoption of a global tax system, is entirely free from these sources of discord.

Sharing Tax Revenues

The idea of taxing the incomes of the migrants themselves must be distinguished

[14]G F M Sicat, *A Survey of Problems and Policies in the Philippines*, Transfer of Technology Division, UNCTAD, Geneva, TD/B/C6/AC4/5, 1977, p 19.

from the idea of getting the developed countries of immigration to share income tax revenues (raised from the migrants through the routine taxation apparatus) with the less developed countries of origin. The rationale for such migration-related taxation on developed countries can be provided in two alternative wasy: either that the developed countries ought to compensate the less developed countries for the losses that the brain drain imposes on them, or that the developed countries gain from such migration and therefore, regardless of whether there is any loss to the less developed countries, they ought to share these gains (based on the inflow of less developed country nationals) with the less developed countries that need development resources.

The latter moral argument reflects a Nozick type of ethical criterion: the human resources 'belong' to the less developed countries and the division of the gains from their working in the developed countries ought therefore rightfully to be shared with the former. This form of argument, which is evidently not utilitarian in nature, therefore does not fall if it is contended that these human resources would have been utilised less profitably or not at all in the less developed countries themselves.

Of these two notions, the former (suggesting compensation for the less developed countries) would appear to be the main motivating force behind recent pronouncements from spokesmen of the less developed countries calling for a brain drain related transfer of resources/revenues by the less developed countries. Consider, for instance:

> . . . I would also like to propose the establishment of an International Labour Compensatory Facility (ILCF). It could be elaborated along the lines of the Trust Fund for Compensatory Facilities of the IMF. The proposed Facility would draw its resources principally from labour importing countries, but in a spirit of solidarity and goodwill, other ILO members may contribute to it. The accumulated resources will be diverted to developing labour exporting countries in proportions relative to *the estimated cost incurred due to the loss of labour.*[15]

> The Commission on Development recommends that, in order to *compensate* for the reverse transfer of technology, resulting from such exodus, amounting to several billions of dollars for the last decade, special arrangements including the possibility of establishing special funds, should be made to provide the necessary resources for strengthening the technological capabilities of the developing countries.[16]

However, given the controversy that surrounds the question as to the magnitude, if not the existence, of losses to less developed countries in a meaningful and measurable sense, it would appear to be pertinent to rest the case for a migration-related transfer of funds from developed countries to less developed countries so alon the former moral rationale: namely, the gains by developed countries from the influx of highly skilled migrants. That such a gain exists is generally conceded, national immigration policies on levels and composition

[15]Address by Crown Prince Hassan bin Talal of Jordan to the 63rd meeting of the ILO, Geneva, 10 June 1977. Note the emphasis on 'compensation' and the notion of losses suffered by loss of manpower.

[16]*Report* of the Contact Group on Industrialisation and Transfer of Technology, CIEC, Paris, 14 May, 1977.

having generally been dictated by national interest (except in the case of political refugees).[17]

Thus, by bilateral or multilateral tax treaties, individual developed countries could agree, for example, to share tax revenues that they earn from the nationals of less developed countries on the basis of some formula. Thus, for example, if the formula involved the developed countries paying to less developed countries 10 per cent of adjusted gross domestic incomes (and hence definitely less than half of the tax revenues from PTK immigrants from less developed countries), it would appear that the less developed countries would earn under such an assessment formula more than half a billion US dollars annually.

There is legal precedent for such tax sharing, of course. Thus, for example, the revenues from taxing the French workers in the canton of Geneva are shared with the French principalities from which the workers come into Geneva. And again the proposal to have the developed countries share their tax revenues with the less developed countries of nationality/origin fits in well with the notion that the less developed countries are self-reliant. These revenues are, after all, paid by their own talented and skilled manpower which constitutes their 'natural resources' and this legitimises revenue sharing arrangements which enable the less developed countries to share in the taxes generated from the incomes of their nationals.

Other Proposals

Finally, two other tax and quasi-tax proposals have been recently made and are worthy of consideration as supplements to the two major tax ideas developed here.

First, it may be suggested that the US practice of tax exempting contributions to approved charities be extended so as to enable a generous and easier inclusion of many less developed country charities as eligible for such benefits and that this then be extended to other developed countries as well.[18]

Secondly, following the recent US practice of taxpayers being allowed to earmark part of their taxes to finance presidential elections, one might suggest that less developed country immigrants in developed countries be allowed, in the same way, to earmark (up to, say 10 per cent) of their taxes for routing to a

[17]The presumption that the developed countries gain from PTK immigration has recently been challenged by Dan Usher in the *Journal of Political Economy* (85) 1977, on the ground that the immigrants receive more from their share in public expenditures than they give up by way of taxes. However, his calculations are hardly persuasive, being mainly 'quick' estimates, often based on dubious procedures. The general presumption in this regard, which is hardly disproved by Usher's arithmetic, is that PTK immigrants, belonging generally to the developed country groups that are subject to progressive taxation in developed countries are likely to be making a net contribution to, rather than a net claim on, the developed countries through the tax system; hence the presumption of gain by the developed countries from PTK immigration can only be reinforced on this account.

[18]This suggestion is contained in the paper by O Oldman & R Pomp in Bhagwati and Partington (ed), 1976 *op cit* and is also in the Group of 77 Draft Recommendations at the Meeting of Experts, UNCTAD, March 1978. Also see Pomp and Oldman, *Legal and Administrative Aspects of Compensation, Taxation and Related Policy Measures: suggestions for an optimal policy mix*. UNCTAD Geneva, TD/B/C6/AC4/7, 1977. The eligibility need not be confined to less-developed-country-origin taxpayers in developed countries.

designated UN agency for development spending.[19]

Evidently, therefore, economists, lawyers, policymakers in less developed countries and international agencies are beginning to examine the migration of highly skilled labour from the fresh perspectives which are called for in the light of the nature of modern migration in a highly interdependent world. The result is likely to be the development of a whole set of new tax arrangements which, consistent with human rights conventions, replace the existing legal structure, which is a legacy of the past.

[19] J Bhagwati, *The Reverse Transfer of Technology (Brain Drain): international resource flow accounting, compensation, taxation and related policy proposals.* UNCTAD. Geneva. TD/B/C6/AC4/2, 1977.

Errata

Page 28, line 4: “wasy” should read “ways”.

Page 28, line 3 from bottom: “so alon” should read “along”.

II
INTERNATIONAL LABOR MOBILITY: CONSEQUENCES AND POLICIES

Journal of Development Economics 2 (1975) 195–221. © North-Holland Publishing Company

WELFARE–THEORETICAL ANALYSES OF THE BRAIN DRAIN*

Jagdish BHAGWATI

M.I.T., Cambridge, MA 02139, U.S.A.

Carlos RODRIGUEZ

Columbia University, New York, NY 10027, U.S.A.

Received February 1975, revised version received May 1975

The paper reviews and synthesises the theoretical analyses of the brain drain in the earlier literature and in the present symposium in the Journal on the subject. Static analysis and dynamic analysis are distinguished, critical issues are raised relating to how welfare changes should be discussed in the context of migration, and possibilities of fruitful future research are outlined.

1. Introduction

This paper reviews the literature on the theoretical analysis of the welfare effects of the brain drain. The different theoretical analyses, with their occasionally divergent conclusions, can be illuminatingly classified according to whether: (i) they deal with comparative-static or dynamic formulations; (ii) they assume a perfectly competitive model or one with endogenous market or policy-imposed distortions; and (iii) they address themselves to the welfare of the country of emigration or of immigration, or take a world-welfare viewpoint.

In the following review, we begin (section 2) briefly with a discussion of the last set of issues distinguished above, namely, whose welfare should be considered and how welfare should be defined. We next turn, in section 3, to the early, theoretical literature which has focussed on comparative-static analyses in perfectly competitive models. In section 4, we turn to analyses which allow for distortions: policy-imposed (e.g., educational subsidies) and endogenous (e.g.,

*Earl Grinols and Asim Dasgupta have provided excellent research assistance in the course of writing this paper. The first author took primary responsibility for preparing the preliminary drafts of the sections on static analysis and the second author for the section on dynamic analysis; the final outcome is however jointly authored in the full sense of the term. Thanks are due to Harry Johnson and Al Berry for helpful comments.

rigid or sticky real wages). Finally, in section 5, we review the dynamic analyses of the effects of the brain drain.[1]

In reviewing the literature, we naturally synthesise and marginally extend it. Also, we provide an analytical taxonomy into which the theoretical contributions in this volume can be, and are, appropriately fitted, and hence their relationship to the foregoing contributions and to one another is more readily assessed by the reader.

2. Welfare: Whose and how defined

2.1.

A central problem in the analysis of migration relates to the question: whose welfare is being assessed? Even if we assume away intergenerational welfare problems (such as those raised by Rawls (1971) recently), the modern migration of skilled personnel raises in an acute form the question as to whether the welfare of these migrants is to be considered part of the welfare of the LDC (or, for that matter, as in a recent UNCTAD study (1974), part of the welfare of the DC).

If migration were permanent, so that the immigrant could be taken to have left the LDC and arrived in the DC on a for-ever basis, then it would make some sense to consider the question as to what has happened to 'LDC welfare' as identical to the question as to what has happened to the 'welfare of those left behind in the LDC'. However, skilled (PTK in U.S. immigration terminology: professional, technical and kindred) migrants today – including those who take permanent-residence visas in the DC of immigration and are immigrants in the juridical sense as well as in popular parlance – typically move to and fro between the LDC of origin and the DC of destination (and indeed, en route, to other DCs and LDCs at times). Hence, PTK immigrants are not really permanent migrants in many cases.

However, even in the case of permanent, for-ever migrants, it is not entirely clear that they should be excluded altogether from the definition of 'LDC welfare'. Skilled immigrants today enjoy low transport costs which permit frequent returns to the LDCs of origin and hence retention of LDC loyalties and affiliations. Their job opportunities also now tend to cut across different DCs, increasing their capacity to resist the assimilative pressures of the DC in which they reside – a passionate immigrant into the UK, who will not adapt to British phlegm, may be able to migrate to the back-slapping friendliness of the U.S. or to a convex combination of the two cultures in Canada. The identification with the DC of

[1] We should enter the caveat explicitly that our review is by no means exhaustive but touches rather on what appear to us to be interesting contributions from the viewpoint of our focus in this paper. Furthermore, we confine ourselves to explicitly theoretical analyses, using formal models in one way or another: hence we do not review early writings of interest such as Johnson's (1965) article on the Canadian brain drain.

destination is not quite so inevitable in consequence. Furthermore, the melting pot now has itself melted in the U.S., the principal DC of immigration: ethnic diversity is encouraged and Dr. Kissinger finds his Realpolitik hamstrung by ethnic groups whose political and emotional affiliation to countries of emigration is considered a thoroughly acceptable part of the domestic political process.

Thus, several factors have combined to make a continuing link to LDCs of origin and failure to fuse into DCs of destination important aspects of modern, PTK migration from LDCs to DCs. This observation, plus the fact of extensive 'to-and-fro' migration, make it somewhat implausible to assert that, if one is interested in LDC welfare, one must exclude the welfare of the migrants from the analysis. Identically, any procedure which defines 'DC welfare' as inclusive of the PTK immigrants' welfare runs into the same difficulties plus the additional fact that, despite the selective regulation of immigration in the national interest by the legislative and executive branches of DC governments, the average citizen of a DC is more likely to regard the immigrant's welfare as a 'favour' to the immigrant at the DC-citizens' 'expense' than as an augmentation of DC welfare!

It is best therefore to analyse the welfare issues separately for three groups: (i) LDC nonemigrants; (ii) migrants; and (iii) DC non-immigrants. Then, depending on what is appropriate for the analysis of any specific situation, one can add together any of the three components to arrive at what is considered to be 'LDC welfare' or 'DC welfare': clearly, no general rules will apply to all situations.

Among the other implications of to-and-fro migration by migrants, we might also note one consequence of some analytical interest. While the *theoretical* models to be reviewed presently allow for migration from the LDC to the DC in the context of a variety of models of the LDC, none of them allow for the 'return of the native'. Once the return migration is allowed for, one can open up interesting possibilities for theoretical analysis: the modelling of the DC, implying possible learning effects for the (temporary) migrant, for example, could become relevant so that the two-way migration relates to the same (physical) migrant but implies unequal flows in the two directions from the viewpoint of welfare analysis. A 2-period analysis of the welfare impact of such to-and-fro migration would then be called for and would involve the effect of changing locations on the efficiency and wealth of the migrant in an essential way.

2.2.

Next, we ought to distinguish explicitly between the conventional economist's objective function, which admits only goods and services, and augmented objective functions, which allow 'noneconomic' arguments in the objective function as in the analysis of optimal policy intervention to achieve noneconomic objectives in Bhagwati and Srinivasan (1969).

The explicitly theoretical literature to be presently reviewed is exclusively focussed on the conventional objective function. However, the fact that societies may value the presence of technical personnel per se in the interest of modernisation or the possibly associated increase in the size of the 'modern', industrial sector's activity level is manifestly an important aspect of societal concerns, and the economist evaluating the welfare effects of the brain drain must come to terms with these traditionally political, sociological, 'noneconomic' objectives. This is indeed what McCulloch and Yellen (1975) do when they discuss the possible 'demodernisation' effect of an emigration tax in their model of the brain drain at the Bellagio conference.

2.3.

At a different level, the economic analyst may not be able to continue using a well-ordered social utility function because there are no fiscal policy instruments by which incomes can be redistributed in the desired manner. In this event, explicit attention to the (actual) income distributions before and after migration is required for welfare analysis. Thus, in Hamada's (1975) Bellagio contribution, incomes *can* be redistributed but, in the absence of lump-sum taxation as a feasible alternative, only via the income tax: hence income distribution and per capita income levels are *both* to be analysed for examining the welfare consequences of emigration.

2.4.

Similarly, if we depart from the assumption of full employment of factors of production, then the effect of emigration on the unemployment levels (or rates) could well be an additional, 'economic' argument in the objective function: as is done in the Bhagwati–Hamada (1974) paper.

2.5.

Finally, we may note that dynamic welfare analyses would necessarily take the theorist into intertemporal optimisation: and, in this case (as is evident from our detailed analysis in section 5), the welfare presumptions established from static, welfare analysis do not necessarily carry over.

3. Static, welfare theorising without distortions

The focus of most theoretical analyses has been on LDC nonemigrants' welfare, using comparative statics and models without distortions, and assuming permanent migration. These contributions can be reviewed in ascending order of complexity.

3.1. Model 1: One-product, one-factor-emigration model

The simplest neoclassical model which has been used for analysing the impact of migration on the welfare of the LDC nonemigrants is the one-product model with just one factor (labour) migrating at the margin in a closed economy.

In this model, used by Grubel and Scott (1966), it was argued correctly that, for infinitesimal changes, the emigrant will neither harm nor help the nonemigrants: the emigrant will have been contributing his marginal product to national income and earning it as well, so that his presence or absence is irrelevant to the nonemigrants' welfare. To put it graphically, the emigrant will be merely sailing away with his own marginal product.

However, for *finite* changes, as was noted by Berry and Soligo (1969) and later independently by Tobin (1974), there is the familiar 'surplus' that the nonemigrants lose. This is seen readily in fig. 1, where the marginal product of labour (MPL) curve is drawn, falling as a consequence of the usual concave production

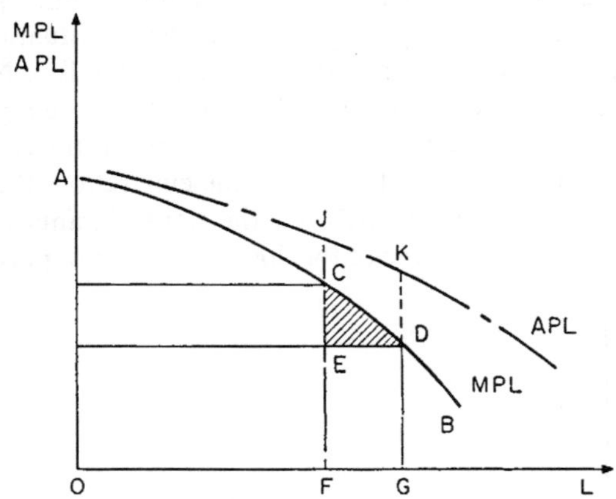

Fig. 1.

function. The finite emigration of *FG* amount of labour then results in a loss of surplus of the shaded area *CDE*.

Note one more point that is sometimes the source of critical confusion. If we draw in an average product of labour (APL) schedule, it is clear that, for both infinitesimal and finite changes, the *per capita income* of the *economy* will rise (from *KG* to *JF* in fig. 1) with emigration as a simple consequence of the assumed diminishing returns. How does this reconcile with the conclusion that the infinitesimal migration does not affect the welfare of those left behind? The paradox is only apparent: the emigrant earns not the per capita income in the premigration situation, but rather the marginal product. The per capita income comparison, to be a correct welfare index of the impact on those left behind, would have to presume that the migrant earned average, rather than marginal, product: in this case, since the average exceeds the marginal product, the migrant was contributing less to national income than earning and making demand on it, so that his migration helps those left behind.[2]

3.2. Model 2: Two-product, two-factor, one-factor-emigration model

The extension of the preceding analysis of one-factor-emigration to the standard trade-theoretic model of two products and two primary factors has been carried out by Kenen (1971) in the Kindleberger Festschrift. Its substance can be readily derived as follows.

For a closed economy, start with given equilibrium. When labour migrates infinitesimally, the Rybczynski theorem implies that, at constant commodity prices, the output of the labour-intensive commodity will fall and that of the capital-intensive commodity will rise. Since domestic income and expenditure fall, however, the assumption of noninferiority in consumption, combined with stability, will yield in the post-emigration, full-equilibrium situation a reduced (relative) commodity price for the capital-intensive commodity. Next, turn to fig. 2a, which sketches the production possibility set of the nonemigrants as *AB*. In the before-migration situation, the commodity price-ratio is *PQ* and the welfare of the nonmigrant group is at U_b. With the emigration, the commodity price-ratio shifts, as just argued, to *SR* and the nonemigrants get worse off ($U_b > U_a$). It is easy to see the source of this loss: the 'trade opportunity' of the

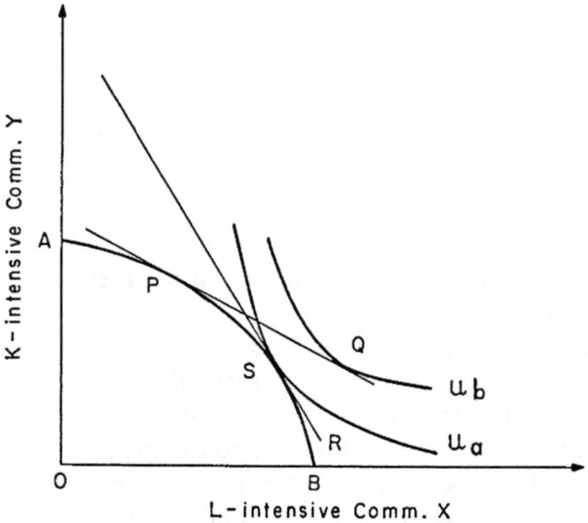

Fig. 2a.

[2]For those familiar with peasant-family-farming models in the Lewis-type literature on dualism, where average product rewards to family members are assumed, the per capita income of the farming *sector* would become the relevant welfare index. It does not seem relevant, however, to the problem of international migration.

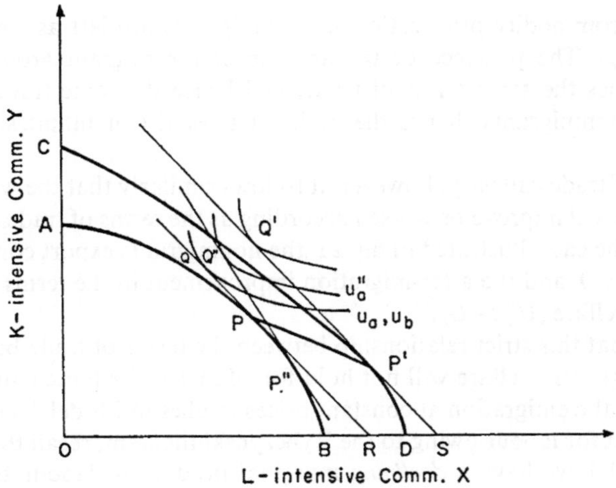

Fig. 2b.

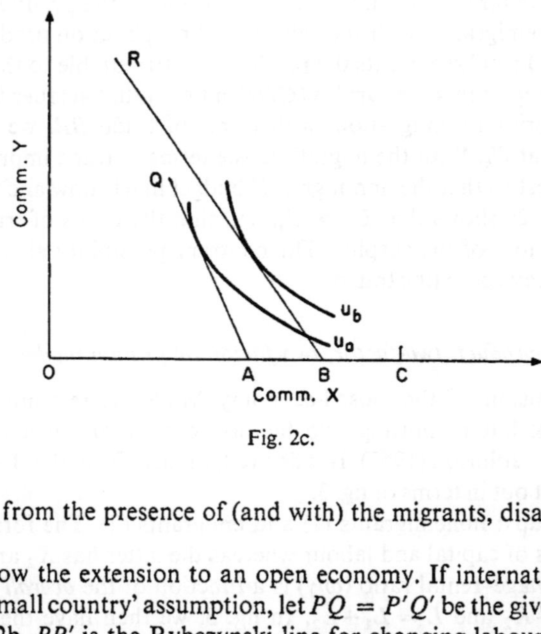

Fig. 2c.

nonmigrants, from the presence of (and with) the migrants, disappears with the emigration.

Consider now the extension to an open economy. If international prices are fixed by the 'small country' assumption, let $PQ = P'Q'$ be the given international prices in fig. 2b. PP' is the Rybczynski-line for changing labour supply. Before the migration, the *total* population has the production set CD, the nonmigrants have the production set AB, the nonmigrants' welfare is at U_b and potential emigrants earn income RS in terms of commodity X. When migration occurs, the migrants essentially disappear with their constant marginal product and, at the unchanged commodity price-ratio, the nonmigrants are left as well off as before ($U_b = U_a$). The presence or the absence of the migrant group in the population implies the same terms of trade, and hence the same trade opportunity, for the nonmigrants: hence the no-impact result (for infinitesimal *and* finite migration).

If the terms of trade can vary, however, it follows similarly that the welfare of the nonmigrants will improve or worsen according as the terms of trade improve or worsen.[3] In the case illustrated in fig. 2a, the nonmigrants export commodity X for commodity Y and the after-migration improvement in the terms of trade improves their welfare ($U_a'' > U_b$).

Note finally that this strict relationship between the terms of trade behaviour and the nonemigrants' welfare will not hold for Model 1, for finite emigration, because whereas the emigration at constant prices implies in Model 2 a constant marginal product for labour owing to the Rybczynski theorem, recall that in the one-good Model 1 we have a *declining* marginal product to labour schedule. Hence, for Model 1, we have to set off the loss of the surplus (CDE in fig. 1) against the terms of trade gain, if any, to arrive at the net impact of the migration on nonemigrants' welfare. Thus, in fig. 2c, OA represents the production possibility set of the nonemigrants, with specialisation throughout on producing X as required by Model 1; AC represents the production attributable to the potential migrants; and AB represents the surplus (CDE in fig. 1) that accrues to the nonemigrants. Thus, prior to emigration, with terms of trade BR, we have nonemigrants' welfare at U_b. With the migration, the terms of trade improve to AQ but the surplus is lost so that the nonmigrants' budget line is now anchored on A rather than B. Fig. 2c shows that $U_b > U_a$, i.e., that the terms of trade gain is outweighed by the loss of the surplus. The contrary possibility also exists and could equally well have been illustrated.

3.3. Model 3: One-product, two-factor, two-factor-emigration model

A different extension of the closed-economy Model 1, retaining the one-product framework but permitting two factors to emigrate in a two-factors framework, is due to Johnson (1967). It is derived, in turn, from the Berry–Soligo paper and is best set out in terms of fig. 3.

Assume two groups: nonemigrants (1) and emigrants (2). The former group has K_1 and L_1 units of capital and labour whereas the latter has K_2 and L_2 such units. The overall wage–rental ratio (ω/γ) is a function of the *overall* K/L ratio, k, where $K = K_1 + K_2$ and $L = L_1 + L_2$. In fig. 3, we then have the post-emigration-of-group-2 equilibrium at Q and $(\omega, \gamma)_{k_1}$ is the wage–rental ratio tangent

[3]This conclusion naturally holds only insofar as the trade pattern for the nonmigrant group is not reversed by the migration. This qualification, explicitly noted by Kenen, has its counterpart in our review of the dynamic analyses where the effects of dissimilar *savings* behaviour by migrants and nonmigrants are considered.

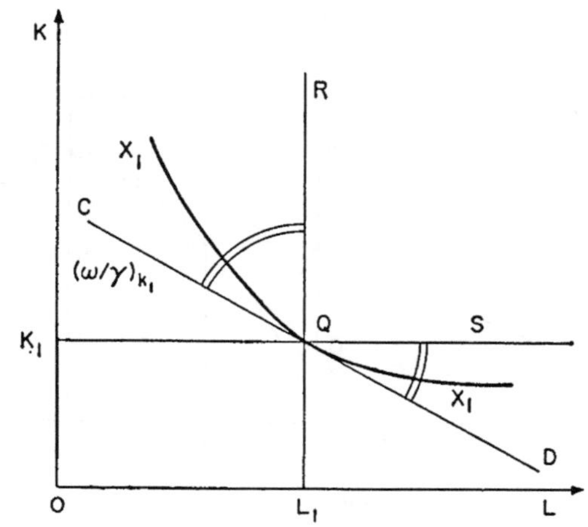

Fig. 3

to the X_1 isoquant. X_1 is therefore the post-migration income of group 1. How does this compare with the pre-migration income level? There are two possibilities to consider but both show a worsening of welfare (except for a singular case of no impact) from the migration. The entire range of feasible (ω/γ) ratios before migration can be divided into (i) the range spanned by QR and QC, which would materialise clearly if $k_2 > k_1$ (where $k_2 = K_2/L_2$ and $k_1 = K_1/L_1$) and thus $k > k_1$; and (ii) the range spanned by QS and QD which would materialise if $k_2 < k_1$. The singular case is where $k_2 = k_1 = k$ and therefore $(\omega/\gamma)_{k_1} = (\omega/\gamma)_k$. It follows immediately that, when $k_2 > k_1$, so that it is the richer group that emigrates, the wage-to-rental ratio will *fall* to $(\omega/\gamma)_{k_1}$; in the other case, where $k_2 < k_1$, it will *rise* to $(\omega/\gamma)_{k_1}$. In *either* case, the 'budget line' for group 1 will shrink in the relevant range and will imply *loss* of income. To read off this loss of income, all that one has to do, in the case where $k_2 > k_1$ for example, is to draw the $(\omega/\gamma)_k$ line through Q and take its tangency with respect to the X_k isoquant; clearly ,$X_k > X_1$ and $(X_k - X_1)$ is the loss of income to group 1 from the migration of group 2.

It follows equally that the nonemigrant group 1 will become *better off* if the wage–rental ratio rises (falls) when $k_2 > k_1 (k_2 < k_1)$. This can happen if, when $k_2 > k_1$ for example, the emigrants leave a sufficient amount of their capital behind to *raise* (instead of lowering) the overall capital–labour ratio, k, with emigration.

The same conclusions can be readily derived in the context of yet another familiar diagrammatic technique.[4] Take fig. 4. It measures the capital–labour

[4]Asim Dasgupta suggested this diagrammatic treatment to us, independently of having seen fig. 5 in section 5, after seeing the preliminary draft of section 3.

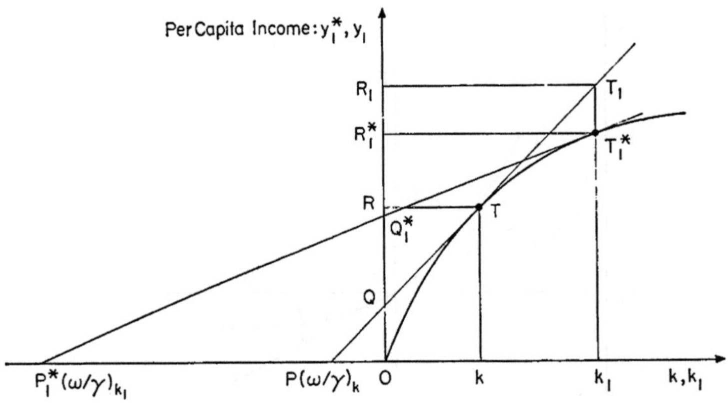

Fig. 4.

ratios along the horizontal axis to the right and per capita incomes y_1^* and y_1 (overall and group 1, respectively) on the vertical axis. Writing the aggregate, constant-returns-to-scale production function in the intensive form as $y = f(k)$, with $f' > 0$ and $f'' < 0$ as usual, we can easily show that the factor rewards, γ and ω, in the premigration situation are

$$\gamma = f'(k) = OQ/PO$$

and

$$\omega = f(k) - kf'(k) = OQ,$$

and therefore

$$\omega/\gamma = PO,$$

so that the wage–rental ratio can be measured as the length of the intercept, on the horizontal axis to the left, of the tangent to the $y = f(k)$ curve OTT_1^* in fig. 4.

Now, $y_1 = \omega(k) + \gamma(k) \cdot k_1$ before migration and $y_1^* = \omega(k_1) + \gamma(k_1) \cdot k_1$ *after* migration. In fig. 4, it is then readily shown that

$$y_1^* = OR_1^*$$

and

$$y_1 = y_1^* + T_1 T_1^*,$$

so that the migration leads to a decline in the per capita income of the non-emigrant group 1 by $T_1 T_1^*$. As with fig. 3, then, we can also think of two possibilities: where $k < k_1$ and $k > k_1$. In the latter case as well, if fig. 4 is so redrawn, there will be a measure $T_1T_1^*$ of per capita income loss for group 1.[5]

Finally, note that it should be possible to derive the results of Model 1 as a special case of Model 3: for Model 1 is where one may think of two factors emigrating, but with one factor (capital) taking zero value. With the emigrant group 2 then being labour-abundant, we have the case where $k < k_1$ and the wage–rental ratio rises after emigration: so we are in the range $(QS-QD)$ in fig. 3 and in the configuration shown in fig. 4 and, in each instance of course, we get the expected loss of income for the nonemigrant group 1.

Consider next the extension to an open economy. For the simplest case (considered by Johnson) of a small country with fixed terms of trade, and staying within the Samuelson range of incomplete specialisation in production, it is immediately obvious that the emigration of group 2, for $k \gtreqless k_1$, will leave group 1 no better or worse off than before the migration.

3.4. *Model 4: One-product, three-factor, two-factor-emigration model*

In his contribution to the Bellagio conference, Grubel (1975) works with a simple model where skilled workers, unskilled workers and capital combine to produce a single output and the skilled workers ('engineers') migrate with the capital embodied in their acquired skills. The main results of his geometrical analysis are readily derived, while relaxing his assumption that skilled and unskilled labourers must be used in fixed proportions, as follows. Thus, consider the system:

$$\theta = \theta(K_0, L_e, L_w), \tag{1}$$

$$\bar{L} = L_e + L_w, \tag{2}$$

$$\bar{K} = K_0 + kL_e, \tag{3}$$

where θ is output, L_e is the number of engineers, L_w the number of workers, $\bar{L}$ the stock of total labour, $\bar{K}$ the capital stock, k the units of capital required (i.e., used up) to train an engineer, and K_0 the capital left over to be employed with L_e and L_w to produce output θ.

Assuming that the system will work efficiently so as to maximise output, we can then easily determine the effect of emigration on per capita income. The implication of the efficiency assumption can be first spelled out simply by using the envelope theorem. Thus substitute the constraints (2) and (3) into $\theta(\cdot)$:

$$\theta = \theta(\bar{K} - kL_e, L_e, \bar{L} - L_e). \tag{4}$$

[5]The above results can also be simply derived by noting that $\mathrm{d}y_1/\mathrm{d}k = (k_1 - k)(\mathrm{d}y/\mathrm{d}k)$. From this it also follows that, for infinitesimal emigration, the cost of the emigration to the nonemigrant group goes to zero *in the limit* and may virtually be treated as zero.

For a maximum, it is necessary that

$$[\theta_1(-k)+\theta_2+\theta_3(-1)] = 0, \tag{5}$$

where θ_i is the ith partial derivative and 1, 2, 3 refer to the first (K_0), second (L_e) and third (L_w) arguments in the function $\theta(\cdot)$.

3.4.1. First consider the emigration of unskilled labour. Now:

$$\begin{aligned}\frac{d\theta}{d\bar{L}} &= \theta_1(-k)\frac{dL_e}{d\bar{L}}+\theta_2\frac{dL_e}{d\bar{L}}+\theta_3(-1)\frac{dL_e}{d\bar{L}}+\theta_3 \\ &= [\theta_1(-k)+\theta_2+\theta_3(-1)]\frac{dL_e}{d\bar{L}}+\theta_3 \\ &= \theta_3 \qquad \text{(using (5)).}\end{aligned} \tag{6}$$

Hence, if unskilled labour emigrates, the loss of national income will be equal to the marginal product of the labour; thus an infinitesimal move will not harm these left behind. Next, we may examine the impact of the emigration on per capita incomes:

$$\frac{d(\theta/\bar{L})}{d\bar{L}} = \frac{\bar{L}(d\theta/d\bar{L})-\theta}{\bar{L}^2} = \frac{\theta_3}{\bar{L}}-\frac{\theta}{\bar{L}^2} = \frac{1}{\bar{L}}\left(\theta_3-\frac{\theta}{\bar{L}}\right). \tag{7}$$

As one would intuitively expect, therefore, the per capita product will rise or fall according as the marginal product to labour (θ_3) falls below or exceeds the average product of labour ($\theta/\bar{L}$).

3.4.2. Next, consider the emigration of an engineer, implying the 'loss' of the k units of capital *along with* a unit of labour.

Therefore,

$$\begin{aligned}\frac{d\theta}{d\bar{L}} &= \theta_1\left(k-k\frac{dL_e}{d\bar{L}}\right)+\theta_2\frac{dL_e}{d\bar{L}}+\theta_3(1-dL_e/d\bar{L}) \\ &= \theta_1 k+\theta_3 \qquad \text{(again using (5)).}\end{aligned} \tag{8}$$

And then

$$\frac{d(\theta/\bar{L})}{d\bar{L}} = \{\theta_3+\theta_1 k\}-\frac{\theta}{\bar{L}}, \tag{9}$$

where, now, the bracketed term includes the marginal product of labour plus the 'lost' marginal product of the capital emigrating via the engineer. Again, we have the intuitive results on the impact of infinitesimal emigration of skilled labour on the national income (and hence zero-impact on those left behind) and on the per capita income of the society.

It is futile to talk of 'presumptions' of loss or gain from emigration. But the weight of the arguments above is that, except for the no-impact outcome for infinitesimal emigration, the different models seem to lead to a prima facie presumption of a loss to those left behind even under conditions of perfect competition. The *magnitude* of this loss is of course conditional on the production functions assumed for the analysis; and as every undergraduate student of economics now must know, 'high' or 'low' costs can emerge depending on whether the elasticity of substitution in production is assumed to be low or high, in turn.[6]

4. Static, welfare theorising with distortions

The theoretical literature embodying distortions, whether policy-imposed or endogenous (in Bhagwati's (1971) terminology), is rather sparse, although the awareness that such distortions can affect the welfare analysis of the brain drain is fairly widespread.

The first paper to consider distortions in a systematic, general-equilibrium framework was by Bhagwati and Hamada (1974). It considers two distortions: an educational subsidy (which is a policy-imposed distortion) and a sticky wage (which is an endogenous distortion). The model, in view of the sticky wage, permits unemployment in the Harris–Todaro (1970) fashion. At the same time, the model enables the authors to analyse the consequences of what is aptly called the 'emulation' effect: the possibility that migration of educated labour can raise the sticky wage as the LDC Joneses emulate and try to keep up with the DC Joneses.

An interesting variation on this model is provided by McCulloch and Yellen (1975) in their Bellagio paper. They modify the Harris–Todaro approach so as to enable the sticky wage to respond *partially* to the degree of unemployment; at the same time, as in one of the Bhagwati–Hamada (1974) variants, they assume that all educational costs are privately borne (i.e., that there is no policy-imposed distortion via an educational subsidy).[7]

[6]This must be kept in mind by any unsophisticated reader of Johnson's (1967, app. III) illustrative, 'small', cost calculations for the Cobb–Douglas case, even though one is only belabouring the obvious here. It is perfectly clear that, by assuming a different production function (e.g., the fixed-coefficients Leontief variety), one can generate 'large' losses. One important implication, again hardly unobvious, is that the cost of the brain drain could very well vary with the kind of professionals one is discussing.

[7]There are other points of difference between the Bhagwati–Hamada and the McCulloch–Yellen models which the readers can note for themselves: they are not pertinent to the discussion in the text.

Both papers lead to more complex welfare analysis than the models without distortions in section 2. They enable one to consider, for example, unemployment as an argument in the objective function. Moreover, there is no longer any necessary equality between the income lost to a country by migration and the wage that the (infinitesimal) migrant earns: the Grubel–Scott proposition is predictably invalid.

Finally, two important results from this type of analysis may be noted. First, it is often argued that if only the emigrant paid for the educational subsidy he had received, that would suffice to leave no adverse welfare impact on those left behind; the Bhagwati–Hamada analysis – of the cases where the educational cost is internalised, and where it is not but the country of immigration compensates the LDC for the educational cost of the immigrant – shows that this is not a valid conclusion.

Second, there is a school of thought which argues that the emigration of PTK manpower from LDCs, when there is unemployment, will not harm the LDCs: that, in fact, we have here an 'overflow' or 'safety-valve', rather than a 'drain', phenomenon. Graphically, as Walter Adams put it to the first author of this paper, 'I saw doctors driving taxicabs in Manila; why should we worry about their migrating abroad?' It is clear from the Bhagwati–Hamada analysis that the emigration, by raising the *expected* return to doctors, can cause further expansion of education and hence lead to loss of income; and that the emulation effect can make even *actual* returns to doctors higher than they might have been, thus reinforcing the loss in income.

Further, as the Hamada–Bhagwati (1975) analysis at Bellagio models the point at issue, it is not really meaningful to think of that doctor as driving taxicabs in Manila forever. He is almost certainly 'waiting' to clear his ECFMG to migrate to the U.S. If the possibility of migration to the U.S. were not available, he would at some stage stop wasting his skills and being a cabdriver and, since returns to being a doctor in Manila are clearly low, he would migrate internally: to the smaller cities where he could practice medicine. The external brain drain (from Manila to New York) therefore inhibits the (desirable) internal diffusion (out of Manila into the hinterland).[8] And, even if one pretends that doctors earn the value of their marginal product (in and out of Manila, in the Philippines), the above argument shows that the social marginal product of the doctor who is 'unemployed' qua doctor is *not* zero, contrary to the argument of Adams.

In short, the assumption that PTK personnel who are unemployed at any one point of time can therefore emigrate at no loss of marginal product to their

[8]The diffusion of doctors from Manila into the hinterland is the slow, capitalist equivalent of the Maoist policy of 'sending' doctors to the countryside. In India, there is growing evidence that doctors in major cities are now opening offices in the adjacent towns, visiting there for periods such as one day a week, thus effectively 'migrating' partially to the hinterland: flirting is easier than marriage!

society is based on the faulty reasoning which assumes that they will forever so remain and omits taking into account the 'search process' aspect of the labour market. And, it ignores additional welfare implications which could follow from phenomena such as the Bhagwati–Hamada emulation effect.[9]

5. Dynamic analyses of international migration

The dynamic treatment of the consequences of migration, whether unskilled or skilled, is more recent; besides, the number of contributions in this framework is yet relatively small.

The dynamic models naturally divide into those which concentrate on steady-state analysis, such as Berry and Soligo (1969), McCulloch and Yellen (1974) and Rodriguez (1975a), and those which additionally or exclusively describe the transition of the economy outside the steady state, as in Mishan and Needleman (1968) and Rodriguez (1975b).

At the same time, their common dynamic feature is the explicit introduction of capital as a factor of production and the ability of the economy to change the level of its capital stock by means of savings: domestic or foreign. Furthermore, the papers addressed to the brain drain, as distinct from what might be called Ricardian labour migration of the purely unskilled variety, incorporate a second produced factor of production: education as human capital. Moreover, all the papers reviewed focus *not* on world-welfare effects, but on the welfare implications of the migration on the nonmigrant populations of the countries of immigration or emigration. Finally, in regard to the measures of welfare changes, the most widely used are the per capita income of native residents together with the relative factor rewards as indicators of the income distribution, although Berry–Soligo and Rodriguez (1975a) follow a utilitarian approach and proceed to evaluate the full changes in the levels of utility enjoyed, the former by means of consumer surplus analysis and the latter by the first-order change in the stationary level of utility enjoyed by each individual in the context of a life-cycle model of saving.[10]

Finally, we must note that, in contrast to the static analyses reviewed in earlier sections, labour mobility in a dynamic context can be analysed (i) as a once-and-for-all labor movement, or instead (ii) as a rate of migration per unit of time which may, in turn, be either constant or varying over time according to the changing domestic or foreign conditions.

[9]The precise implications of building these interpretations of unemployment into the model used for analysing the effects of brain drain will depend, of course, on how the rest of the model is put together. This should be obvious to the reader from contrasting the analyses in, say, Bhagwati–Hamada (1974), McCulloch–Yellen (1975) and Hamada–Bhagwati (1975).

[10]In none of the dynamic models either, therefore, is the issue of to-and-fro migration addressed: emigrants leave for good and the welfare of those left behind is what is considered.

B

In case (i), it is clear that a once-and-for-all labor movement will not affect any of the steady-state values of the relevant per capita variables, provided we assume that migrants have the same preferences as those of the indigenous population. Under those circumstances, the labor movement can be considered as a change in one of the initial conditions (i.e., initial population) such that the steady state of the economy (if it exists) will be unaffected by it. If, however, a steady state does not exist (as in one of the cases discussed by Mishan–Needleman because of their inclusion of Hicks-neutral technological progress in a Solow-type growth model), even a once-and-for-all inflow of labor with the same preferences as the indigenous population will have permanent effects on the long-run paths of the per capita variables. When migrants have different preferences from those of the rest, however, even a once-and-for-all migration will change the preference structure of the population and will thus have both short- and long-run effects on the economy (provided, of course, that those preferences are transmitted to their children). With the exception of McCulloch–Yellen (1974) and Mishan–Needleman, all the other articles reviewed here introduce differences in preferences in one way or another.

In case (ii), where migration is a continuous process through time, we again have to distinguish between two different problems: (a) a constant or variable migration rate will change the rate of population growth and thus the steady-state requirements of per capita savings, and (b) the preferences of the migrants may differ from those of the rest. In either case it is clear that a continuous migration process will affect both the transition and the steady-state behaviour of the economy.

5.1. The dynamic models of Ricardian labour migration

This subsection concentrates on the models that treat labour as a homogeneous input (contrary to those, discussed in the next subsection, which additionally consider skilled labour).

5.1.1. Of the analyses treating international migration in a dynamic context, the Mishan–Needleman paper is probably the one which provides the clearest link between the static and dynamic models. Their production structure is the same as that of the Solow-type growth model: one-sector, neoclassical technology with two inputs: capital and labor. Savings (equated to investment) are a constant fraction of income and population reproduces at a constant exponential rate. Immigrants have the same preferences (i.e., savings ratio) as the natives and are assumed to enter the country of immigration in a constant number per year. After the immigrant group of a given year enters the country, it starts reproducing itself at the same exponential rate as the natives. Since one of the main objectives of the analysis is to investigate the effects of immigration on the welfare of the indigenous population, they incorporate those born to the immigrants (i.e., their descendants) into the stock of the immigrant population.[11]

These simple assumptions provide an ideal framework to test in a dynamic model the static propositions that a discrete labor inflow (outflow) will decrease (increase) aggregate per capita income but raise (reduce) the per capita income of those who were previously in the country (left behind). In this case, of course, the focus of analysis is on the *time-paths* of the different measures of per capita income.

Mishan and Needleman do not solve explicitly their model in order to find out the qualitative properties of the growth path but rather they postulate a CES production function and, using various sets of parameters values presumably appropriate to the UK, they proceed to simulate the paths of the relevant variables for a thirty-year horizon. Some of their results seem to confirm those of the static analysis: for all of the 30 years aggregate income per capita falls short of that under no immigration, while the wage–rental ratio is consistently lower under the immigration regime. However, their results for the effects on the per capita income of the indigenous population do, in some cases (notably, when the production function is Cobb–Douglas), differ from what would be expected: in the Cobb–Douglas case the per capita income of the indigenous population falls short (instead of being in excess) of that under no immigration for the first 21 years. This seems an unusual conclusion in light of the neoclassical nature of the assumptions. We think, however, that a possible explanation for that lies in their treatment of overhead capital. They assume that a constant fraction of total savings is required for the formation of overhead capital, which is not directly productive; although in the text they assume that such savings are provided by the immigrants, the equations that they simulate do not show it but rather imply that the immigrants' savings for overhead capital are provided by the indigenous population at the expense of their own accumulation of physical capital, which of course tends to reduce their own per capita income [Mishan and Needleman (1968, eqs. 13 and 18)]. Furthermore, the moment the immigrant settles in the country there is an additional requirement for overhead capital, which is assumed to be provided by the indigenous population.

Abstracting from the formation of overhead capital and their assumption of a positive constant rate of technical progress, the effects of a once-and-for-all immigrant inflow in the Mishan–Needleman model can be described, in a perhaps more illuminating way, as follows.

Let $Q = F(K, L) = Lf(k)$ be the neoclassical production function for the composite good Q which can be either consumed or transformed into physical capital. The total labor force can be divided into that of indigenous origin, L_d,

[11] Again, there is room here for debate. Even where the immigrants are treated as different from the country of immigration, would it not be unrealistic to assume that those born of first-generation immigrants will still be 'second-class' citizens forever (in the unfolding of our dynamic model)?

and that of immigrant origin, L_m. Since both immigrants and indigenous relidents have the same savings ratio, the capital–labor ratio of the economy changes through time according to the standard formula,

$$k = s\cdot f(k)-n\cdot k, \tag{10}$$

where n is the rate of population growth. At time t_0, when the once-and-for-all immigration takes place, there is a jump in the capital–labor ratio from $k_0 = K(t_0)/L_d(t_0)$ to $k_1 = K(t_0)/\{L_d(t_0)+L_m(t_0)\}$, where $L_m(t_0)$ is the size of the immigrant inflow. From t_0 on, immigration ceases but the initial immigrant population starts reproducing itself at the rate n, while at the same time they save the same fraction of their income as the rest of the population. In consequence, the capital–labor ratio of the economy, after the initial jump at t_0, starts changing through time according to (10).

The amount of capital per head *owned* by the immigrant population then changes according to

$$(2)k_m = s\cdot y_m - n\cdot k_m, \tag{11}$$

where y_m is the per capita income of the immigrant population and equals the sum of their wage earnings, $\omega(k)$, plus the earnings from the capital they own, $\gamma(k)k_m$. Notice that given competition and constant returns to scale the wage rate and the rental rate, ω and γ, are functions only of the economy's aggregate capital–labor ratio k. In fig. 5, per capita income and savings are represented on the vertical axis and ratios of capital to population on the horizontal axis. The curve $q = f(k)$ shows the aggregate per capita income as a function of the aggregate capital–labor ratio; the curve nk shows the steady-state investment requirements; and finally, the curve $sf(k)$ shows the aggregate per capita savings.

We assume that, before the immigration, the economy had reached the steady-state level of the capital–labor ratio k_0. After the immigration, the capital–labor ratio falls instantaneously to k_1 and aggregate income per capita consequently falls to k_1B from the higher level k_0D. The reduction in the capital–labor ratio increases the rental rate and reduces the wage rate (which is now given by the distance OA along the vertical axis). Since initially immigrants have no capital, their income is equal to the wage rate OA, clearly lower than the aggregate per capita income which also includes the earnings from the capital stock. Even though the aggregate capital–labor ratio has been reduced, the per capita amount of capital *owned* by the indigenous population remains unchanged at k_0. Thus, the per capita income of the indigenous population immediately after the immigrant inflow is equal to the new wage rate, OA, plus the rental rate (the slope of the line AC times their per capita holdings of capital, or the distance k_0C which exceeds the per capita income they had before the immigration by the

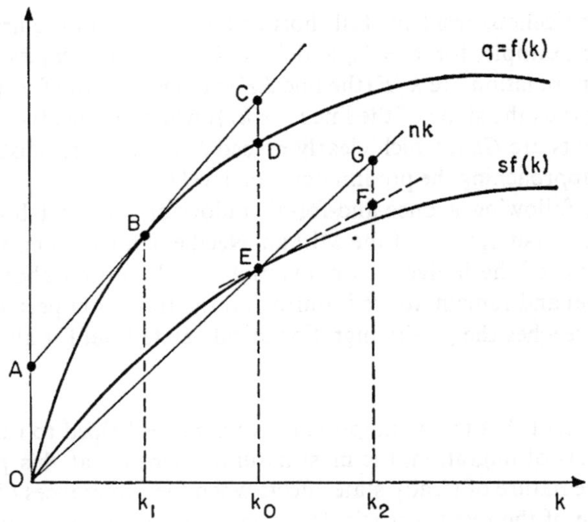

Fig. 5.

amount CD. Thus, the short-run effect of immigration is to raise the per capita income of the indigenous population.[12]

Following the impact effect, it is clear that for the new capital–labor ratio k_1, aggregate savings exceed the amount of investment required to keep it at the same level and thus it will start rising, according to eq. (10), until eventually it will reapproach the pre-immigration steady-state value k_0. There are thus no long-run effects on the aggregate per capita income or capital–labor ratio from a once-and-for-all immigrant inflow. Initially, however, the per capita income of the indigenous population has been increased above the original steady-state level; thus, their per capita savings will exceed the amount required to keep the amount of capital per-head they own constant. In consequence, the ratio of capital per head owned by the indigenous population, k_d, will start rising. It is clear that during the transition process for which $k < k_0$ it will also be $k_d > k_0$, and thus the per capita income of the indigenous residents will exceed its pre-immigration steady-state value. Eventually, however, the aggregate capital–labor ratio will approach k_0 and remain there. At this moment k_d may be also equal to k_0 or still larger. If it is equal, the income per capita of the indigenous population will be the same as the aggregate per capita income, and thus k_d will behave in the same way as k and will remain constant. If k_d still exceeds k_0 while $k = k_0$, then k_d must be falling and finally approaching k_0: for the set of factor rewards implied by $k = k_0$, any k_d larger than k_0 implies that the per capita

[12]The reader may here profitably recall our analysis of fig. 4.

savings of the indigenous residents fall short of the investment required to keep it constant. For example, for $k = k_0$ and $k_d = k_2 > k_0$, per capita savings of the indigenous population are k_2F (the line EF is tangent to the function $sf(k_0)$ at the point k_0; thus the slope of the line is $sy(k_0)$) while the steady-state investment requirements are Gk_2, which clearly exceed k_2F; thus, k_d must be falling and eventually approaching the pre-immigration level k_0.

To conclude, following a once-and-for-all inflow of foreign labor into the country, the basic assumptions of the Mishan–Needleman model imply that the income per capita of the indigenous population will be raised above the pre-immigration level and remain above it during all the transition period until the economy again reaches the pre-immigration steady-state level for all per capita variables.

5.1.2. To the extent that the assumption of equal tastes helped to rule out any steady-state effects of migration, the most natural extension at this point is to inquire about the nature of steady-state effects when the preferences of migrants differ from those of the rest (in particular, when the saving ratios differ). As it happens, this is precisely the question addressed by Berry–Soligo (1969) and Rodriguez (1975a), to whose analyses we now turn.

Both papers differ from Mishan–Needleman in at least two basic respects:

(1) Savings behavior is derived from the individual's maximisation of life-time utility. This, in general, implies that the saving ratios are not constant but rather depend on factor rewards. Individuals do not all have the same utility function.

(2) Both papers are concerned with the effects of emigration on the welfare of those left behind rather than the effects of immigration on the welfare of the indigenous population of the receiving country; it is obvious, however, that both questions are different sides of the same coin.

Basically, their behavioral assumption is that of a life-cycle model of savings where individuals work when they are young and save for their retirement. In this context, the interest rate not only plays the role of being the return to the factor of production 'capital' but also determines the trade-off between present (working period) and future (retirement period) consumption. As proved elsewhere [Samuelson (1958), Diamond (1965)], a competitive market will in general fail to attain the optimal 'golden rule' level of the capital–labor ratio (for which the interest rate equals the rate of population growth) at which society's consumption potential is maximised and the optimal distribution of consumption among generations is attained. To the extent therefore that emigration or immigration changes the aggregate savings ratio of the population, and thus the steady-state level of the capital–labor ratio, there can be aggregate social gains or losses depending on whether the move is towards or away from the golden rule level of the capital–labor ratio.

For the members of each individual group (characterised by a set of preferences) these aggregate gains or losses must be modified to the extent that the individual differs from the average: the change in the steady-state capital–labor ratio brings about changes in relative factor rewards which in turn redistribute income in favor of the group which is relatively better endowed with the factor whose reward has increased in relative terms. For example, if there are only two groups of individuals, high savers and low savers, emigration of some members of the high-savers group will in general reduce the new steady-state capital–labor ratio (through the reduction in the aggregate savings ratio of the population). If the capital–labor ratio was initially below its golden rule level (i.e., the interest rate was larger than the rate of population growth), this move must decrease welfare in the aggregate. The lower capital intensity, in turn, decreases the wage–rental ratio and thus redistributes income towards those remaining members of the high-savers group (those with a higher preference for the ownership of capital) and away from the low savers. It follows that, on both counts, the members of the low-savings group tend to be worse off while the remaining members of the high-savings group may be either worse off or better off. When low savers emigrate, the capital–labor ratio will be increased and, if the movement is towards the golden rule ratio, there is a gain in the aggregate and a redistribution of income towards the remaining low savers (the wage–rental ratio rises). Thus, on both counts, the remaining low savers are better off while the effect on high savers is ambiguous.

It follows from the above analysis that if the capital–labor ratio is below its golden rule level, in the long run emigration of high savers (which decreases the capital–labor ratio even further) will make at least one group worse off, while emigration of low savers will make at least one group better off. If, however, the capital–labor ratio was above the golden rule level, those conclusions should be reversed since in this case reductions in the capital–labor ratio are beneficial in the aggregate.

5.1.3. To summarise, in this section we have concentrated on the description of dynamic models of labor migration where migrants may or may not differ from the rest of the population in regard to their preferences for the accumulation of physical capital. If everyone's preferences are identical and migration is a once-and-for-all phenomenon, there are in general no steady-state effects of migration; the gains of the population of the receiving country (or losses to those remaining in the country of origin) which appear in the static models also appear in this case, except that these gains (or losses) occur in the transitional period during which the economy approaches the original steady state. These transitional gains or losses are shown to depend critically on the per capita ownership of capital by the economic agents and the transitional change in the economy's factor proportions (and factor rewards) brought about by the migration.

When migrants differ from the rest of the population in their savings habits, we have not merely the transitional gains or losses referred to above, but also the permanent changes in the steady state of the economy due to the now different aggregate savings behavior. These effects can be divided into two parts: (i) effects of movements in the steady-state capital–labor ratio towards or away from the golden rule ratio; and (ii) effects of changes in the steady-state distribution of income due to the new prevailing set of factor rewards and the different preferences of members of the population for the ownership of factors of production.

5.2. The dynamic models of the brain drain

We turn next to the brain drain models whose basic feature is that human capital, in addition to unskilled labor and physical capital, appears as a distinctive factor of production. Human capital is assumed to be accumulated through an educational process which uses up some of society's scarce resources.

To the extent that competition prevails everywhere, including the educational market, it is clear that allowing for the international mobility of educated people amounts to little more than an extension of the issues discussed in the previous section to the context of a three-factor model. Neither of the two papers in this area [McCulloch–Yellen (1974) and Rodriguez (1975b)], however, could be described as a straightforward three-factor extension of the models analysed so far. The main differences are:

(1) The educational market is not assumed to be perfect, either because education is not competitively supplied or because, thanks to the existence of capital market imperfections or information costs, the rates of return to physical and human capital are not equalised.

(2) Rather than considering an exogenous population movement or migration rate, the two papers consider as exogenous the foreign rewards of the internationally mobile factors and the migration preferences of those factors in response to the rates of return from international emigration. Since these rates of return depend not only on the foreign rewards but also on the domestic rewards and the costs of the move, it follows that the actual migration rates will be endogenously determined within the system.

(3) The Rodriguez (1975b) analysis also includes the case of labor market distortions of the type analysed in Harris–Todaro (1970), which were also discussed in a static framework in Bhagwati–Hamada (1974) and Hamada–Bhagwati (1975).

The paper which most closely approximates the other dynamic models previously discussed is McCulloch–Yellen (1974), which concentrates on the study of the steady-state effects on the distribution of income of migration of educated (skilled) people within the context of the following basic assumptions:

(1) Only one good is produced, with a constant-returns-to-scale technology and three factors: physical capital, skilled (educated) labor and unskilled labor.

(2) Education (the acquisition of skills) is carried on until the point where the skilled–unskilled wage differential equals the cost of acquiring the education which, in turn, increases with the fraction of the newly-born population getting educated. The educational cost may be either the marginal or average cost depending on the kind of market structure which prevails in this sector. For the purposes of making the comparison, they convert the once-and-for-all education cost into a constant flow per time unit, using an exogenously given discount rate.

(3) Migration is carried on until the foreign–domestic wage differential for skilled labor equals the flow-equivalent migration cost. Unskilled labor does not migrate.

(4) The domestic rate of return on physical capital is equalised with the foreign rate of return by assuming perfect international mobility of foreign capital at constant rental.

Given these assumptions and a constant rate of population growth, the result is, in general, a nonzero migration rate for skilled labor. This is so because there is no reason why the steady-state output of the educational sector will be consistent with the maintenance of that particular stock of skilled labor relative to the other factors which precisely generates a domestic skilled wage such that emigration or immigration is not attractive. There is, however, a band equal to the foreign skilled wage plus or minus the migration cost such that if the steady-state domestic skilled wage falls within it, no migration will occur.

The steady-state factor rewards for skilled and unskilled labor, migration rate and education rate will then depend on certain exogenous parameters, among them the foreign wage for skilled labor, the foreign rental on capital, the migration cost and the interest rate used for discounting investments in human capital or migration. In fact, reduced to its barest essentials, the basic assumptions of this model imply the following steady-state relationships. Assuming that the steady state is consistent with net emigration of skilled labor (a similar analysis follows easily in the case of immigration), the domestic skilled wage is pegged at the world level minus the migration cost (converted into a constant-flow equivalent). The thus-determined skilled wage *plus* constant rental on capital (equal to the world rental) suffice to determine all the steady-state factor proportions in production (the ratios of capital to skilled and unskilled labor) and therefore, by implication, the unskilled wage and also the skilled–unskilled wage differential. The wage differential, in turn, determines the fraction of the newly-born population acquiring education via assumption (2) above. Since for a steady state the growth rate of the skilled labor force must equal that of the total labor force (such that factor proportions remain constant), the equilibrium migration rate is then obtained as the difference between the growth rate in the stock of skilled people, implied by the already-determined equilibrium factor proportions and the fraction of those newly-born getting educated, and the rate of population growth.[13]

From these relatively simple relationships it is then easy to derive the steady-state responses of several endogenous variables to changes in the exogenous parameters. For example, an increase in the cost of emigration (or equivalently, an emigration tax or a fall in the foreign skilled wage) reduces the domestic skilled wage by the same amount. Given the constant rental on capital and the constant-returns-to-scale technology, reductions in the skilled wage are associated with increases in the unskilled wage; thus the skilled–unskilled wage differential must unambiguously fall. The fall in the skilled–unskilled wage ratio makes skilled labor more attractive for use in production than unskilled labor and thus the ratio of skilled to unskilled labor is increased. Similarly, the lower wage differential makes education less attractive and thus the fraction of the newly-born getting educated falls. The lower output of the educational sector plus the higher steady-state requirement of skilled labor relative to the unskilled unambiguously implies a reduction in the rate of emigration.

The only other dynamic analysis of skilled migration is by Rodriguez (1975b). It concentrates on the *differential attitudes* of individuals regarding the decisions of capital accumulation, education and migration. Rather than postulating that education is carried on by everyone up to the point where the wage differential equals the (flow-equivalent) education cost, he assumes that all those born to educated (skilled) parents will get educated *irrespective of* costs and returns (at least within the relevant range), while only a fraction of those born to uneducated parents will seek education (this fraction depending on the pecuniary rate of return to education). Similarly, migration does not necessarily close the gap between foreign and domestic wages (allowing for the migration cost) but rather the fraction of the skilled population which chooses to migrate is assumed to be a function of the rate of return to such a move. It is further assumed that investment in physical capital is a constant fraction of profits earned. On the technology side, Rodriguez assumes two sectors whose outputs are traded at a fixed international relative price, as in Bhagwati–Hamada (1974) and McCulloch–Yellen (1975), but, and in contrast to both, physical capital is used in both sectors while only one type of labor (skilled or unskilled) is used in each sector. The mobility of capital between the sectors and the fixed terms of trade imply a

[13]Denote by S, U and $P = S+U$ the skilled, unskilled and total population, respectively; by g and e the gross rate of population growth and the fraction of those just born getting education; and by m the ratio of skilled migrants to total population. Then, the growth rates in the stocks of skilled labor and total population are

$$(1/S)(\mathrm{d}S/\mathrm{d}t) = (eg-m)(P/S),$$
$$(1/P)(\mathrm{d}P/\mathrm{d}t) = g-m.$$

Since both growth rates must be equal in the steady state, the equilibrium migration rate will be given by

$$m = -g(1-e)(S/U)+ge.$$

technologically-determined *positive* relationship between the returns to both kinds of labor. This makes the income distribution predictions of this model essentially different from those of McCulloch–Yellen (1974), where the assumptions about technology and international mobility of capital implied a *negative* relationship between the skilled and unskilled wage rates. Education is assumed to be supplied by a third sector at a constant cost and capital goods are assumed to be imported from abroad or produced in one of the two domestic sectors.

The paper analyses the stability of the model, the nature of the steady-state solution and comparative statics, proceeding then a la Bhagwati–Hamada to analyse the long-run effects of sticky real wages in the context of a Harris–Todaro (1970) labor market, while also exploring the short- and long-run effects of the implementation of a migration tax on factor rewards and unemployment.

When wages are flexible, the most distinctive result of the model is the complete independence of all steady-state factor rewards from the costs of migration or the foreign wage and thus also from a migration tax. The reason for this result can be easily shown as follows. Denote by x the fraction of those born to unskilled parents who get educated, n the growth rate of population, U and K the stocks of unskilled labor and capital, and s and r the savings ratio out of profits and the interest rate, respectively. Then, the growth rate in the stock of the unskilled population equals

$$(1/U)(\mathrm{d}U/\mathrm{d}t) = n(1-x), \tag{12}$$

and the growth rate in the stock of capital is

$$(1/K)(\mathrm{d}K/\mathrm{d}t) = s\cdot r. \tag{13}$$

In the steady state, both these growth rates must be equalised and thus, in the steady state, we must have

$$s\cdot r = n(1-x) \tag{14}$$

Since x depends only on the constant education cost and the skilled–unskilled wage differential which, in turn, depends only on the interest rate r, it follows that the above condition by itself determines the steady-state interest rate and, by implication, all other factor rewards as functions only of the educational costs s and n. Since none of these three variables depends in any way on the foreign wage or the migration cost, it follows that steady-state factor rewards are independent of these two variables. Notice, however, that if workers were also to save, the rate of growth of the capital stock would *also* depend on their savings ratio and the shares of the different factors in national income. Since these shares will depend on the ratios of the different factor endowments (which are endogenous variables in the steady state), the above steady-state condition would not suffice to determine all factor rewards which will now depend also on the other parameters of the system, including the foreign wage and the migration cost.

As for the short run, Rodriguez returns to the original assumptions, showing that the steady-state independence of factor rewards from a migration tax does *not* prevail in the short run and that, following the imposition of such a tax, the returns to *both* types of labor will fall during the transitional period while the return to capital is increased.

In conclusion, Rodriguez notes for the sticky-wage variant of his model that, with this amendment, it is rather the long-run rate of unemployment that is independent from the foreign wage or the migration cost. However, in the transitional period, following an increase in the migration cost, the unemployment rate is increased; note, however, that since Rodriguez shows that the model is always unstable when there is a minimum wage for skilled labor, this result strictly applies only to unskilled wages and unskilled unemployment.

6. Concluding remarks

Clearly, the preceding review suggests that the theoretical analysis of the brain drain, once dormant after the Grubel–Scott–Berry–Soligo–Johnson phase, has received a fresh lease on life with the analysis of distortions (beginning with Bhagwati–Hamada) and of explicitly dynamic formulations (in Rodriguez). The explicit examination of policy options, in general-equilibrium formulation, is also recent: especially the Bhagwati-type surtax on migrants has been examined, for its welfare impact, in several of the recent papers.

Where can we suggest fruitful avenues for future theoretical work? The following would seem to be rewarding areas for general-equilibrium analysis:

(1) The welfare of the nonemigrants may be examined for to-and-fro migration (as noted earlier) be permitting the migrant to acquire skills, wealth, etc., during the migration to the DCs.

(2) The case of the migration accentuating distortions (e.g., through the emulation effect in Bhagwati–Hamada) may be extended to the case where migration *reduces* distortions (e.g., if a state monopsony is under-remunerating the emigrants' skills, the migration could reduce the monopsonistic power).

(3) The possibility that the migration could affect the foreign trade possibilities (i.e., the foreign offer curve) via its effect on the LDCs overall national income, and hence on its bargaining power in a world of unequal partners or via the efforts exerted by the migrants in their DCs of destination on behalf of their LDCs of origin (e.g., Greek PTK emigrants influencing the U.S. Congress in favour of Greece in matters of importance to Greece), may also be formalised.

References

Berry, R. and R. Soligo, 1969, Some welfare aspects of international migration, Journal of Political Economy, 77.

Bhagwati, J., 1971, The generalized theory of distortions and welfare, in: J. Bhagwati, R. Jones, R. Mundell and J. Vanek, eds., Trade, balance of payments and growth (North-Holland, Amsterdam).

Bhagwati, J. and T.N. Srinivasan, 1969, Optimal intervention to achieve non-economic objectives, Review of Economic Studies, 27–38.

Bhagwati, J. and W. Dellalfar, 1973, The brain drain and income taxation, World Development 1, no. 1.

Bhagwati, J. and K. Hamada, 1974, The brain drain, international integration of markets for professionals and unemployment: A theoretical analysis, Journal of Development Economics 1, no. 1.

Diamond, P.A., 1965, National debt in a neoclassical growth model, American Economic Review 55, December.

Grubel, H., 1975, Evaluating the welfare effects of the brain drain from developing countries, paper presented at the Bellagio Conference on Brain Drain and Income Taxation, Bellagio, Italy.

Grubel, H. and A. Scott, 1966, The international flow of human capital, American Economic Review, May.

*Hamada, K., 1975, Efficiency, equality, income taxation and the brain drain: A second-best argument, paper presented at the Bellagio Conference on Brain Drain and Income Taxation, Bellagio, Italy.

*Hamada, K. and J. Bhagwati, 1975, Domestic distortions, imperfect information and the brain drain, paper presented at the Bellagio Conference on Brain Drain and Income Taxation, Bellagio, Italy.

Harris, J. and M. Todaro, 1970, Migration, unemployment and development: A two-sector analysis, American Economic Review, March.

Johnson, H.G., 1965, The economics of the 'brain drain': The Canadian case, Minerva.

Johnson, H.G., 1967, Some economic aspects of brain drain, Pakistan Development Review 3.

Kenen, P., 1971, Migration, the terms of trade and economic welfare in the source country, in: J. Bhagwati, R. Jones, R. Mundell and J. Vanek, eds. Trade, balance of payments and growth (North-Holland, Amsterdam).

McCulloch, R. and J. Yellen, 1974, Factor mobility and the steady state distribution of income, Discussion paper no. 369 (Harvard Institute of Economic Research, Cambridge, MA).

*McCulloch, R. and J. Yellen, 1975, Consequences of a tax on the brain drain for unemployment and income inequality in LDCs, paper presented at the Bellagio Conference on Brain Drain and Income Taxation, Bellagio, Italy.

Mishan, E.J. and L. Needleman, 1968, Immigration: Some long-term economic consequences, Part A and part B, Economia Internazionale 21, nos. 2 and 3.

Rawls, J., 1971, A theory of justice (Harvard University Press, Cambridge, MA).

Rodriguez, C., 1975a, On the welfare aspects of international migration, Journal of Political Economy, forthcoming.

*Rodriguez, C., 1975b, Brain drain and economic growth: A dynamic model, paper presented at the Bellagio Conference on Brain Drain and Income Taxation, Bellagio, Italy.

Samuelson, P.A., 1958, An exact consumption-loan model of interest with or without the social contrivance of money, Journal of Political Economy, December.

Sjaastad, L., 1962, The costs and returns of human migration, Journal of Political Economy, October (supplement).

Tobin, J., 1974, Notes on the economic theory of expulsion and expropriation, Journal of Development Economics 1, no. 1.

UNCTAD, 1974, The reverse transfer of technology: Economic effects of the outflow of trained personnel from developing countries (brain drain), Trade and Development Board, Intergovernmental group on transfer of technology, Third session, Geneva, July 15.

*Paper appears in this symposium.

Errata

Page 202, last line: "$(\omega,\gamma)_{\lambda_1}$" should read "$(\omega/\gamma)_{\lambda_1}$".

Page 212, line 2 from bottom: "(the slope" should read "(the slope)".

Journal of Development Economics 1 (1974) 19–42. © North-Holland Publishing Company

THE BRAIN DRAIN, INTERNATIONAL INTEGRATION OF MARKETS FOR PROFESSIONALS AND UNEMPLOYMENT

A theoretical analysis*

Jagdish BHAGWATI and Koichi HAMADA

Massachusetts Institute of Technology, Cambridge, Mass., U.S.A.

Received April 1973, revised version Received August 1973

1. Introduction

Nearly the entire *theoretical* literature on the effects of the 'brain drain' from the less developed countries on their welfare has been undertaken in the framework of neoclassical models of the Hicks–Samuelson value-theoretic variety.[1]

While the analysts in this genre have greatly clarified certain issues such as the nature of the objective function to be specified, their analysis and prescriptions have been constrained by the theoretical model which they work with. The central result of their analysis, attributable to Grubel and Scott (1966), that brain drain prima facie should not be a cause for worry as the drained person will only take away the value of his marginal product which he himself earns anyway, can be rather obviously shown to be subject to the limitations that (i) for finite, rather than infinitestimal, shifts of labour, there would still be a loss to those left behind;[2] (ii) if the social marginal product exceeds the private marginal product, thanks to strong externalities, as would seem to be the case with doctors and exceptionally gifted academics about whose emigration typically the underdeveloped countries seem to worry, then again there *is* a loss to those left behind;[3]

*Thanks are due to the National Science Foundation for financial support of the research underlying this paper. The paper was written while K. Hamada (University of Tokyo, Bunkyo-ku, Tokyo) was visiting M.I.T. on a Fellowship from the American Council of Learned Societies. Helpful comments on the paper were received from T.N. Srinivasan, Robert Solow, Herbert Grubel and an anonymous referee. Bhagwati is Visiting Ford Research Professor at University of California, Berkeley, for 1973–1974.

[1]See, in particular, Grubel and Scott (1966) and Johnson (1972).

[2]On the other hand, depending on the size of the emigration and the nature of the production function, this loss may still be very small.

[3]On the other hand, one could stretch things a great deal and argue that, for some emigrants, their contribution to social product still continues to accrue to the home country: e.g. an Indian scientist's achievements abroad 'inspire' his countrymen at home; and that this happens *without* their earning their private product from the home-country's GNP and also that their social product may even *increase* if their achievements improve in a more efficient and productive environment than the one found in their home country.

and (iii) if the State has financed the education which is embodied in the skilled worker who migrates, *and* if it is assumed that the State would have taxed this skilled worker – a realistic assumption when there is progressive taxation – partially or wholly to 'recover' the return on this investment, then his emigration does deprive those left behind of this return and thus worsens their welfare.

These are useful insights into the problem of the 'brain drain'. However, admittedly, the analysis is overly simple and could be extended in many directions. An obvious growth-theoretic extension would be to bring in savings behaviour and maximization of welfare over time for those left behind. Or, within the confines of the Hicks–Samuelson model, the analysis could be enriched to allow for remittances from the emigrated people: an argument which qualifies the conclusions in favour of permitting the brain drain. The neoclassical model could further be extended *fully* in the direction of trade-theoretic models with factor movements: the effect of the labour migration on the commodity terms of trade of the labour–losing country could be readily analysed along the lines of the recent Jones (1967) and Kemp (1966) contributions to the welfare theory of international capital movements.[4]

But few of these extensions of the Hicks–Samuelson value-theoretic model are anything but analytic modifications which admit into the model the kinds of complexities which the model itself, rather than reality, suggests. It is necessary therefore to see whether an alternative value-theoretic model can be devised which comes closer to reality as observed in certain underdeveloped countries.

In particular, certain important aspects of the educated-manpower problem in underdeveloped countries have been noted by the non-theorists:

(1) The presence of international income-inequality implies that, for the educated elite which is better informed about the developed world, and more integrated therewith regarding notions of a 'good life' and related values, the salary levels demanded *and* fixed by the elite groups themselves tend to reflect the salary levels of comparable groups in the more developed countries. René Dumont (1969) has argued for French Africa:

> 'During the last phase of colonialism, the policy was to equalize salaries of Africans and Europeans in similar jobs, a defensible position only in the framework of 'assimilation'. The native civil servant, in addition to his regular salary, received a colonial supplement. This has been reduced in some cases, but not abolished. At independence, this pseudoequality has led to flagrant disparity with the rest of the population, whose standard of living is often a fifteenth of the French.

[4] Johnson (1967) has extended the analysis of the problem in a yet different direction, by assuming that skilled-labour migration reduces *both* the labour and the capital stock of the emigrating country. However, his analysis is limited by his assumption that human capital and physical capital are perfect substitutes – an assumption that would naturally provide a downward bias to the damaging effects of brain drain.

Massive departure of the French resulted in a high rate of promotion of subordinate African civil servants, who thus earn even more now than before, for the same qualifications. The student returning from France is appointed director if he is the only African technician or graduate in his field.' (p. 80)

Indeed, this phenomenon has been noted by Osvaldo Sunkel (1971) for Latin America and by Dudley Seers and Richard Jolly (1972) for a wider group of countries. Thus, we can postulate a socio-economic situation in which the real wage levels of the educated elites are set by fiat, legislation, unionisation, etc., at levels which reflect the degree of response to the international-elite-integration effect just outlined.

(2) This phenomenon of educated-elite wages, 'way out of line with the average per capita income of the underdeveloped countries', is next regarded as often leading to a 'leap-frogging' process under which the lowest wages tend to get pulled up by the highest: hence the phenomenon of such institutionally defined wages tends to run through the entire labour-market.

(3) With these institutionally defined wages, it is inevitable that the labour-market must work so as to have open unemployment of labour (except in singular cases); and this too is an observed phenomenon: educated and also uneducated people are often unemployed in the developed countries.

(4) At the same time, the phenomenon of high wages, accruing to the (employed) educated elite, creates a political demand for education. René Dumont (1969) has again described the French African situation vividly:

Present education obstructs progress

'This statement may appear paradoxical to many readers, particularly coming from the pen of a professor, since education was the essential foundation of development in Europe, America, Japan, the Soviet Union and China. In Africa it has a certain utility, but this is greatly curtailed by the social *milieu* on to which the educational system was grafted. For most African children, in town and country alike, school represents above all a means of entering the *elite* class. Even in the most backward areas of the bush everyone has grasped the fact that the official with clean hands earns more and works much less.

Pushed by his parents, a peasant child realizes that he can never go very far in agriculture; the only way to get ahead is to get out. He goes to school and works very hard, to this end, sometimes at the price of incredible sacrifices. I have heard of a child in Chad who walks twice a day the twenty kilometres separating his house from school.

... Before long, these young people end up in the shanty-towns of the capitals and become social parasites. Their days are spent writing requests for jobs, requests that pile up in all the administrations. Some of them, in Douala for example, join the underground.' (pp. 88–89)

But this is a situation which is to be found in a large number of underdeveloped countries, indeed.

(5) And the demand for education is translated into educational expenditures by the State, in these underdeveloped countries, with visible alacrity. In India, for example, the number of colleges expands, with little time lag, to accommodate the students who qualify with 'passing marks' from the high schools: and the standards in the latter have, in turn, fallen to accommodate the larger flows of students seeking educational qualifications.

A value-theoretic model which accounts for these phenomena is clearly more relevant for analysis of the questions pertaining to the labour market, such as the welfare effect of the brain drain, in several underdeveloped countries than the neoclassical model (which assumes fully flexible wages, for example).

We proceed therefore to the construction of precisely such a model in sect. 2 and then analyse the phenomena of brain drain and increasing international integration of elite groups in its framework in sect. 3. In sect. 4, we discuss a number of variants of this basic model. In sect. 5, we draw together the welfare implications of emigration in the framework of our model and its variants, also examining the effects of taxing emigrants – a policy that has sometimes been advocated in the literature.[5] In particular, since our model allows for the existence of unemployment for both educated and uneducated labour, our discussion of welfare will involve examination not merely of the (conventional) impact on the domestic availability of goods and services for final use but also of the effect of each policy measure on the level and the degree of unemployment, if any, of each class of labour.[6]

2. The basic model

The simplest general equilibrium model, incorporating the features described above, which can be constructed for our analysis is set out below.

Assume two commodities m_1 and m_2. Let their outputs M_1 and M_2 be related to the inputs by the following production functions which possess the standard properties including twice differentiability and linear homogeneity,

$$M_1 = F_1(L_1), \tag{1}$$

$$M_2 = F_2(L_2), \tag{2}$$

where L_1 is the quantity of skilled/educated labour employed in producing m_1,

[5]See, for example, Bhagwati and Dellalfar (1973).

[6]We might as well note explicitly that the kind of model we build and analyse in this paper is not universally valid, even on casual empiricism. Thus, for example, in Japan, the (relative) wage level of intellectuals in Japan has managed to remain virtually unaffected by the significantly higher level of remuneration for their counterparts in the West. This may be one of the many respects in which Japan has apparently differed from the other 'latecomers' in the process of industrialization and integration of the world economy and polity, exhibiting a remarkable ability to adhere to an 'inner-directed' posture in her political and cultural methods.

and L_2 is the quantity of unskilled/uneducated labour employed in producing m_2. Note that educated labour enters only m_1-production and uneducated labour enters only m_2-production. Diminishing returns to L_1 and L_2 are postulated, implying implicit, specific 'non-labour' factors. We further assume that the country is a 'small' country, in Samuelson's sense, so that the commodity price ratio $p_1/p_2 = \pi$ is exogenously fixed and commodity m_2 is the numeraire.

We next assume that the real wage of educated labour is fixed, by international emulation and associated union-fixation or wage legislation, at level $\bar{w}_1$ in m_2-units. Note that this automatically defines $(\partial F_1/\partial L_1)\pi$ and hence L_1 and M_1. Similarly, assume that the 'leap-frogging' process fixed the minimum wages of unskilled labour L_2 at $\bar{w}_2$ $(= \partial F_2/\partial L_2)$, and hence also L_2 and M_2. Thus we can write the following two factor market equations:

$$\partial F_1/\partial L_1 = \bar{w}_1/\pi, \quad \text{or } L_1 = g_1(\bar{w}_1/\pi), \tag{3}$$

$$\partial F_2/\partial L_2 = \bar{w}_2, \quad \text{or } L_2 = g_2(\bar{w}_2). \tag{4}$$

Then with U_1 and U_2 denoting the unemployed, educated and uneducated labour respectively, N_1 and N_2 denoting educated and uneducated labour supply respectively, and $\bar{N}$ representing the total fixed labour supply, we have three balance equations:[7]

$$L_1 + U_1 = N_1, \tag{5}$$

$$L_2 + U_2 = N_2, \tag{6}$$

$$N_1 + N_2 = \bar{N}. \tag{7}$$

But we next need to know how the available labour supply will divide between N_1 and N_2. To do this, we need to introduce equations to determine the supply of educated labour N_1. We shall assume that there will be a positive inducement to get educated as long as the expected wage for educated labour exceeds the expected wage for uneducated labour.

Let the expected wage for educated labour Ew_1 then be the *average* wage for it, namely,

$$Ew_1 = \bar{w}_1(L_1/N_1), \tag{8}$$

and the expected wage for uneducated labour Ew_2 be the *average* wage for it:

$$Ew_2 = \bar{w}_2(L_2/N_2), \tag{9}$$

[7]Bhagwati and Srinivasan (1972) have analysed an alternative adjustment mechanism for the labour market, where the unemployment of skilled labour is not permitted as long as there are enough jobs in the unskilled labour market. Under this theory, the available supply of skilled labour first gets absorbed in the skilled labour market, and the spillover then takes the available jobs in the unskilled labour market (where the two kinds of labour are equally productive but the employers sociologically prefer giving jobs to skilled over unskilled applicants). The Bhagwati–Srinivasan model is designed to study the phenomenon of 'overqualification', whereby the educated seem to get into the uneducated-level jobs over time: a phenomenon which has sometimes also been called the 'upgrading' of jobs.

and the equilibrium condition then is:

$$Ew_1 = Ew_2. \tag{10}$$

Note that this equilibrium condition makes sense insofar as we are assuming that the State undertake the cost of education, and not labour itself. It is assumed therefore that as long as $Ew_1 > Ew_2$, there will be a politically effective excess demand for State-financed educational facilities to be opened up, for N_2 to be turned into N_1 until $Ew_1 = Ew_2$. However, to analyze the effect of this assumption on the level of national income, we may simply subtract the cost of this education from national production of m_1 and m_2 to arrive at the national income available for consumption:

$$Y = (\pi M_1 + M_2) - kN_1, \tag{11}$$

where k is the fixed educational cost, in m_2-units, per person; this cost being subtracted from total output of M_1 and M_2 to arrive at the net output available for consumption Y.[8] It follows that increasing Y is tantamount to increasing the value of a conventional social welfare function defined in terms of goods and services available for domestic consumption.

This basic model thus has eleven equations and eleven unknowns: M_1, M_2, L_1, L_2, U_1, U_2, N_1, N_2, Ew_1, Ew_2, and Y. It is also a model in terms of which we can analyze meaningfully a number of questions relating to the brain drain problem and the phenomenon of international integration of the educated-labour markets.

3. Brain drain and international integration of market for professionals

This basic model can be easily contrasted with the case where both wages are flexible and labour pays for the cost of education. Note first that we have here *three* sources of economic inefficiency: the two sticky wages plus the free education. In the absence of these three inefficiencies, the economy would have reached the standard Pareto-optimal equilibrium with the following first-order conditions:

$$w_1 - k = (\partial F_1/\partial L_1) - k = (\partial F_2/\partial L_2) = w_2, \tag{12}$$

with full employment of labour. In analysing the model with the three inefficiencies which we have noted, we now proceed through successive possibilities, analysing the effects on unemployment and national income in four alternative cases:

Case I. Our-Joneses-keeping-up-with-their-Joneses: This is the case where the country's educated/skilled labour, on integrating with the outside-world's

[8]To ensure proper dimensionality in the analysis that follows, this educational cost must be regarded as the 'annual' flow-equivalent of the educational cost incurred to train a man. Also, to simplify the analysis, we do not introduce private educational expenditure until sect. 4.

educated/skilled labour, demands and achieves an increment in its salary level: this is therefore the case where there is primary increase in w_1.

Case II. Keeping-up-with-our-Joneses: This is the case where we have the well-observed 'leap-frogging' process, so that the rise in w_1 (the wage of skilled labour) leads to a sympathetic rise in w_2 (the wage of unskilled labour).

Case III. Emigration-of-our-Joneses: This is the case where the emigration of skilled labour to higher-wage areas abroad leads to higher expected wage to skilled labour: *either* via mere reduction in unemployment of skilled labour at home and consequent increased assurance of the domestic wage ($\bar{w}_1$) *or* via pushing up the expected wage because the wage-rate abroad is higher than the domestic wage.

Case IV. The general case of emigration and rise of wages: This is the general case where the emigration of skilled labour is also accompanied by a sympathetic rise in the domestic wage ($\bar{w}_1$): a case that is plausible because more emigration could imply more integration of the professional markets for skilled labour internationally. This general case therefore considers the totality of effects from Case II and Case III: the emigration effect of Case III being combined with the dual wage-increase effect of Case II.

We now analyse these cases, in turn. The following analysis is carried out on the assumption that a marginal change in wages or emigration still leaves some unemployment in each sector; otherwise, neoclassical competitive analysis would become applicable.

Case I. Our-Joneses-keeping-up-with-their-Joneses

This is the case where the educated labour force is getting culturally integrated internationally, and the effect is to exercise an upward pull on its domestic salary level. This phenomenon of 'our-Joneses-keeping-up-with-their-Joneses' can be analysed simply then by analysing the effect of a shift in w_1.

We can see the effect of the increase in $\bar{w}_1$ on employment by differentiating (3) and (4):

$$\mathrm{d}L_1/\mathrm{d}\bar{w}_1 = (1/\pi)g_1'(\bar{w}_1/\pi) < 0, \text{ because } g_1'(\bar{w}_1/\pi) = (\partial^2 F_1/\partial L_1^2)^{-1} < 0, \tag{13}$$

$$\mathrm{d}L_2/\mathrm{d}\bar{w}_1 = 0. \tag{14}$$

The employment in m_1-sector will decrease in response to the rise in wages in its own sector and the employment in m_2-sector remains the same.

However, unemployment in both sectors depends on how labour divides into the two types of labour. We can readily see the effect of the wage increase in m_1-sector on the division of labour supply into the two types, by deriving:

$$\mathrm{d}N_1/\mathrm{d}\bar{w}_1 = (1-\eta_1)N_2L_1/(\bar{w}_1L_1+\bar{w}_2L_2), \tag{15}$$

where $\eta_1 \equiv (\bar{w}_1/L_1)(\mathrm{d}L_1/\mathrm{d}\bar{w}_1)$ is the elasticity of the demand for labour in m_1-industry. Further, (15) simplifies to:

$$\mathrm{d}N_1/\mathrm{d}\bar{w}_1 = (1-\eta_1)N_1N_2/(\bar{N}\bar{w}_1), \tag{16}$$

or, in elasticity terms,

$$(\bar{w}_1/N_1)(\mathrm{d}N_1/\mathrm{d}\bar{w}_1) = (1-\eta_1)N_2/\bar{N}. \tag{17}$$

Thus the supply of educated labour increases or decreases depending on whether the elasticity of demand for labour in m_1-industry, is less or more than unity. This result is easy to understand, of course, because the outcome regarding the supply of educated labour depends on the impact effect of the wage change in m_1 on the expected wage (Ew_1) in that sector: and the expected wage will rise insofar as the actual wage rises but fall insofar as (educated) labour is laid off by profit-maximising entrepreneurs in m_1 in consequence. The net outcome is determined by whether the elasticity of demand for labour in m_1 is higher or lower than unity: in the former case, the net effect is to lower the expected wage Ew_1; in the latter case, the net effect is to increase it.[9]

We can now analyze the effect on absolute and relative unemployment of each sector.

(a) *Absolute level of unemployment of educated labour*

$$(\mathrm{d}/\mathrm{d}\bar{w}_1)(N_1-L_1) = (1-\eta_1)N_1N_2/(\bar{w}_1N)+\eta_1L_1/\bar{w}_1. \tag{18}$$

Thus if the elasticity of demand for educated labour is less than unity, the absolute level of unemployment increases because the supply of educated labour increases while the demand decreases. However, even if the elasticity of demand for educated labour is greater than unity, so that the supply of educated labour is reduced (owing to reduced expected wage Ew_1), the absolute unemployment of educated labour would increase if the demand for such labour reduces even more; this would be the case if:[10]

$$L_1/N_1 \geqq N_2/\bar{N}, \tag{19}$$

or

$$L_1/N_1 < N_2/\bar{N}, \quad \text{but} \quad \eta_1 < [1-(L_1/N_1)/(N_2/\bar{N})]^{-1}. \tag{20}$$

[9]At the same time, it is easy to see that the elasticity of demand for labour, η_1, is the ratio of the elasticity of substitution of the production function, σ_1, and the capital share, α_1:

$$\eta_1 = -\frac{\bar{w}_1}{L_1}\frac{\mathrm{d}L_1}{\mathrm{d}\bar{w}_1} = -\frac{F_L{}^1}{L_1F_{LL}{}^1} = \frac{F_L{}^1}{\bar{K}_1F_{LL}{}^1} = \frac{F_L{}^1F_K{}^1}{F^1\cdot F_{KL}{}^1}\cdot\frac{F^1}{F_K{}^1\bar{K}_1} = \frac{\sigma_1}{\alpha_1}.$$

We may therefore restate the above proposition: the supply of educated labour increases or decreases depending on whether the elasticity of substitution in m_1-industry is smaller or larger than the capital share in m_1-industry.

[10]This can be seen by rewriting eq. (18) as:

$$(\mathrm{d}/\mathrm{d}w_1)(N_1-L_1) = \{1-\eta_1+\eta_1(L_1\bar{N}/N_1N_2)\}N_1N_2/(\bar{w}_1\bar{N}).$$

In developing countries the elasticity of substitution in industrial sectors seems to be low, so that it is likely that the elasticity of demand for labour in m_1-sector is less than unity. Moreover, (22) is quite likely to be satisfied unless the unemployment rate in m_1-industry is extremely high. Therefore, we can conclude that the absolute unemployment in educated labour will most probably increase if the wage of educated labour increases.

(b) *Relative unemployment of educated labour*

Similarly, from (14) and (17), we can derive:

$$\frac{N_1}{L_1}\frac{\mathrm{d}}{\mathrm{d}\bar{w}_1}\left(\frac{L_1}{N_1}\right) = -\frac{N_2}{\bar{N}}\frac{1}{\bar{w}_1}\left\{\left(\frac{\bar{N}}{N_2}-1\right)\eta_1+1\right\} < 0. \tag{21}$$

Thus the relative unemployment of educated labour will always increase when the wage in m_1-industry increases.

(c) *Unemployment of uneducated labour*

Since the employment of uneducated labour depends on its unchanged wage, it will clearly not change. However, the *unemployment* of uneducated labour will increase or decrease, depending on whether the supply of uneducated labour increases or decreases. Thus if $\eta_1 < 1$, so that the resulting improvement in Ew_1 has led to increase in educated labour, the stock of uneducated labour (N_2) will have been reduced and hence also the unemployment of uneducated labour. Similarly, if $\eta_1 > 1$, the unemployment of uneducated labour will have increased.

(d) *National income*

Next, it is easy to see that:

$$\mathrm{d}Y/\mathrm{d}\bar{w}_1 = -L_1\eta_1 - k(1-\eta_1)(N_1N_2/\bar{N}\bar{w}_1). \tag{22}$$

National income will therefore change, when $\bar{w}_1$ rises, because of two effects: (i) the decline in employment of (educated) labour will diminish output of m_1 without any offset from increment in output in m_2 where the employment has not changed; and (ii) the cost of educating labour will change, depending on whether the supply of educated labour increases or decreases. Clearly, therefore, when $\eta_1 < 1$, the increase in the supply of educated labour will work to accentuate the reduction in income from the first effect: thus the result must be unambiguously to reduce national income, as is evident from (22). Moreover, even if we take the other case where $\eta_1 > 1$, provided that condition (19) or (20) is satisfied *and* $k < \bar{w}_1$, the *net* effect will be to reduce national income, again as is evident from (22). The only case when income will increase is where k is large, η_1 is extremely large and the initial unemployment rate of educated labour is large and violates eq. (19). The results in this case are summarized under the column (Effect I) in table 1.

Table 1

Effects of rise in wages.

Impact on:	Symbol	*Effect I* Our-Joneses-keeping-up-with-their-Joneses	*Effect II* Keeping-up-with-our-Joneses $\theta \equiv \mathrm{d}w_2/\mathrm{d}w_1$
Educated labour	$\frac{\mathrm{d}N_1}{\mathrm{d}\bar{w}_1}\left(= -\frac{\mathrm{d}N_2}{\mathrm{d}\bar{w}_1}\right)$	$(1-\eta_1)N_1N_2/(\bar{w}_1\bar{N})$	$-\theta(1-\eta_2)N_1N_2/(\bar{w}_2\bar{N})$
Unemployment of educated labour	$\frac{\mathrm{d}}{\mathrm{d}\bar{w}_1}(N_1-L_1)$	$(1-\eta_1)N_1N_2/(\bar{w}_1\bar{N})+\eta_1L_1/\bar{w}_1$	$-\theta(1-\eta_2)N_1N_2/(\bar{w}_2\bar{N})$
Rate of employment of educated labour	$\frac{N_1}{L_1}\frac{\mathrm{d}}{\mathrm{d}\bar{w}_1}\left(\frac{L_1}{N_1}\right)$	$-\eta_1/\bar{w}_1-(1-\eta_1)N_2/(\bar{w}_1\bar{N})$	$\theta(1-\eta_2)N_2/(\bar{w}_1\bar{N})$
Unemployment of uneducated labour	$\frac{\mathrm{d}}{\mathrm{d}\bar{w}_1}(N_2-L_2)$	$-(1-\eta_1)N_1N_2/(\bar{w}_1\bar{N})$	$\theta\{(1-\eta_2)N_1N_2/\bar{w}_2\bar{N}+\eta_2L\bar{w}_2/_2\}$
Rate of employment of uneducated labour	$\frac{N_2}{L_2}\frac{\mathrm{d}}{\mathrm{d}\bar{w}_1}\left(\frac{L_2}{N_2}\right)$	$(1-\eta_1)N_1/(\bar{w}_1\bar{N})$	$\theta\{-\eta_2/\bar{w}_2-(1-\eta_2)N_1/(\bar{w}_2\bar{N})\}$
National income	$\frac{\mathrm{d}Y}{\mathrm{d}\bar{w}_1}$	$-\eta_1L_1-k(1-\eta_1)N_1N_2/(\bar{w}_1\bar{N})$	$\theta\{-\eta_2L_2+k(1-\eta_2)N_1N_2/(\bar{w}_2\bar{N})\}$

Case II. Keeping-up-with-our-Joneses

The next question we ask is what happens if the rise in $\bar{w}_1$ leads, in turn, to a sympathetic rise in $\bar{w}_2$ *via* the well-observed 'leap-frogging' process: this may be called the 'keeping-up-with-our-own-Joneses' phenomenon. We can indeed explore all the questions considered for Case I, for the case where *both* $\bar{w}_1$ and $\bar{w}_2$ rise.

The effect on employment in m_1-sector naturally remains the same as above; but there is now an additional negative effect on employment in m_2-sector, thanks to the induced rise in w_2. Instead of (14) we have

$$\mathrm{d}L_2/\mathrm{d}\bar{w}_1 = g_2'(\bar{w}_2)(\mathrm{d}\bar{w}_2/\mathrm{d}\bar{w}_1) < 0. \tag{23}$$

Thus, defining $\mathrm{d}\bar{w}_2/\mathrm{d}\bar{w}_1 \equiv \theta(\theta > 0)$ and $\eta_2 \equiv -(\bar{w}_2/L_2)(\mathrm{d}L_2/\mathrm{d}\bar{w}_2)$, we get the results tabulated in table 1.

In addition to the effect through the rise in w_1 (Effect I), the effect through the rise in w_2 (Effect II) is superimposed.

Note that, in contrast to Case I, the directions of the impacts are ambiguous because the induced rise in $\bar{w}_2$ can offset the effects of the primary increase in $\bar{w}_1$. Take, for example, the impact of the increase in $\bar{w}_1$ on the level of the educated labour force (N_1). For Effect I, the level of N_1 will rise if $\eta_1 < 1$; however, for Effect II, the induced rise in $\bar{w}_2$, implying $\theta > 0$, will work to reduce N_1 if $\eta_2 < 1$, thus making the direction of the combined effect indeterminate. An interesting implication of the impact on national income in the last row of table 1 is that it is more difficult to exclude the possibility of increased income from the process of wage-increases. For example, take the extreme case where $\eta_1 = \eta_2 = 0$, and $\mathrm{d}\bar{w}_1 = \mathrm{d}\bar{w}_2$, i.e. $\theta = 1$. Then

$$\mathrm{d}Y/\mathrm{d}\bar{w}_1 = k(\bar{w}_1 - \bar{w}_2)N_1N_2/(\bar{w}_1\bar{w}_2\bar{N}) > 0.$$

In this special case where the elasticities are zero, and where the factor intensities are consequently fixed, the simultaneous wage rise will increase national income because less people will get educated, thus reducing the cost of education, while employment in each sector is kept constant.

Case III. Emigration-of-our-Joneses

We can now turn to the issue of actual emigration of educated labour. We can set up the problem by assuming an exogenous emigration of educated labour, Z, which does not *in itself* lead to a simultaneous rise in the (actual) wage $\bar{w}_1$ for educated labour; only in Case IV will we consider the fully general case where the emigration causes rise in $\bar{w}_1$ as also an induced rise in $\bar{w}_2$ as per Case II.

Eq. (5) must then be rewritten as:

$$L_1 + U_1 + Z = N_1, \tag{24}$$

so that the total educated labour is now the sum of domestically employed and unemployed plus emigrated labour.[11]

There are alternative ways in which we can explore now the impact of such emigration on the system, but all of them must operate through the primary impact on expected wage in the educated-labour market. Let us take three possibilities.

(I): We may assume that the migration of a few educated members of the working force does not have any impact on the expected wage, as the migration is not wage-induced and does not lead to similar expectations. Then, in this singular case, *as long as* the migration of labour still leaves *some* unemployment of educated labour, the division of labour into the two types of labour is unaffected, so that the only effect is a reduction in the unemployment of educated labour. Clearly, moreover, production and national income are unchanged. However, since per-capita income and the relative employment rate of educated labour are increased, social welfare should be increased by the 'brain drain' for any reasonable social welfare function. If, therefore, the migration is welfare-improving for the migrants – an assumption that seems reasonable if they are pursuing self-interest – the emigration is a 'good' event, causing welfare improvement for both the migrants and those left behind.

(II): But this 'well-behaved' result will no longer carry through if we assume that the expected wage to educated labour will improve with the migration. This may happen in at least two plausible ways. *Either* the emigration may be treated as reducing the unemployment in the market for educated labour, so that the emigration is treated as raising the wage merely by increasing the number employed, without taking into consideration the incremental wage accruing to those employed abroad as distinct from those employed at home: this may be called the *incremental-employment-effect* variant of the model. *Alternatively*, we may assume that the fact that the emigrants earn a differentially higher wage also affects the expected wage: this may be called the *incremental-employment-and-differential-wage* variant. We examine the former variant first.

For the *incremental-employment* variant, the effect of the emigration is to change the equation for the expected wage in m_1 as

$$Ew_1 = \bar{w}_1(L_1 + Z)/N_1. \tag{25}$$

[11] We should note here the delicate problem of the timing of education and emigration. There would be little difficulty of interpretation, however, if we regard this analysis as the comparison of two stationary states with and without migration, or more precisely one with some migration and the other with marginal increase in migration.

Thus the division of total labour between the two groups (educated and uneducated) is determined now by:

$$\bar{w}_1(L_1+Z)/N_1 = \bar{w}_2 L_2/N_2. \tag{26}$$

Noting that the employment of labour in neither sector is affected by dZ, we can next show that

$$\mathrm{d}N_1/\mathrm{d}Z = N_1 N_2/\{(L_1+Z)\bar{N}\}. \tag{27}$$

We thus see, from (27), that the increase of educated labour supply will be less than the amount of migration of educated labour if $(L_1+Z)/N_1 > N_2/\bar{N}$ [which is a relation very similar to (19) earlier]. Thus, under the above inequality, the unemployment of educated labour increases, and the unemployment of uneducated labour decreases, due to the effect of an increase in N_1.[12]

The effect on *national income* is quite simply:

$$\mathrm{d}Y/\mathrm{d}Z = -k(\mathrm{d}N_1/\mathrm{d}Z). \tag{28}$$

National income is seen, from (28), to diminish unambiguously because of the cost of educating the increment in educated labour.

But we may well ask what happens to *per-capita income*, as the total amount of labour in the system is diminished too. Now, clearly:

$$\frac{\mathrm{d}}{\mathrm{d}Z}\left(\frac{Y}{\bar{N}-Z}\right) = \frac{kN_2}{(\bar{N}-Z)^2}\left(-\frac{(\bar{N}-Z)}{\bar{N}}\frac{N_1}{L_1+Z}+\frac{Y}{kN_2}\right).$$

Hence, if $kN_2/Y < (L_1+Z)N_1$, for example, the average income will increase with the emigration. That is, if the ratio of the hypothetical educational cost of training all uneducated labour to national income is smaller than the employment rate of educated labour, the national income per labour will increase. Another way of looking at it is to see that $\mathrm{d}(Y/(\bar{N}-Z))/\mathrm{d}Z > 0$ if $k(\mathrm{d}N_1/\mathrm{d}Z) < Y/(\bar{N}-Z)$, i.e. the per-capita income would increase if the increase in the education cost is less than the per-capita income.

(III): We may finally explore the *incremental-employment-and-differential-wage* variant. We thus assume now that the labour force will indeed take into

[12]If the unemployment is defined as $U_1/N_1 = 1-(L_1+Z)/N_1$, we can show that

$$\frac{\mathrm{d}}{\mathrm{d}Z}\left(\frac{U_1}{N_1}\right) < 0, \text{ because: } \frac{\mathrm{d}}{\mathrm{d}Z}\left(\frac{L_1+Z}{N_1}\right) = \frac{1}{N_1}\left(1-\frac{(L_1+Z)}{N_1}\frac{N_1N_2}{(L_1+Z)\bar{N}}\right)$$

$$= \frac{1}{N_1}\left(1-\frac{N_2}{\bar{N}}\right) > 0.$$

account the foreign wage level at which the emigrants get hired. If we then denote the foreign wage as $\bar{w}_f$, we can write the expected wage in m_1 as:

$$Ew_1 = (\bar{w}_1 L_1 + \bar{w}_f Z)/N_1 . \tag{29}$$

In this case, we now can derive the following modified results:

$$\mathrm{d}N_1/\mathrm{d}Z = \bar{w}_f N_2/(\bar{w}_1 L_1 + \bar{w}_2 L_2 + w_f Z) = \bar{w}_f N_1 N_2/\{N(\bar{w}_1 L_1 + \bar{w}_f Z)\}, \tag{30}$$

$$\mathrm{d}Y/\mathrm{d}Z = -k(\mathrm{d}N_1/\mathrm{d}Z) = -k\bar{w}_f N_1 N_2/\{N(\bar{w}_1 L_1 + \bar{w}_f Z)\}. \tag{31}$$

It is then easy to see that the change in the level of the educated labour force (N_1) in the new equilibrium will readily exceed the emigration if $\bar{w}_f$ is large enough relative to $\bar{w}_1$. Therefore in the case when the high wage rate in foreign countries is taken account of in assessing the expected wage rate, it is quite probable that unemployment in educated sector increases in both absolute and relative sense.

In addition, as is evident from (31), national income will go down; and it is easy to see that the possibility of decreasing per-capita income as well is more likely than before.[13] Therefore in the society whose welfare function depends on per-capita income and unemployment rates, national welfare will quite possibly go down unless the evaluation of reducing unemployment rate in the m_2-sector more than offsets the loss due to decreasing per-capita income and increasing unemployment in the m_1-sector.

Case IV. The general case of emigration and rise of wages

If the wage of educated labour is rigidly fixed because it reflects the salary levels of comparable groups in the more developed countries, it is quite conceivable that $\bar{w}_1$ itself is affected by the amount of migration of educated labour. The more migration there is, the more then could be the upward pull from the internationalization of this educated elite to domestic wage fixation. This rise in $\bar{w}_1$ may in turn trigger additional wage rise in $\bar{w}_2$, as analyzed in Case II.

Thus the effects of migration on employment, supply of educated labour and national income in this fully general case can now be decomposed as the sum of

[13]This is seen readily as follows. For a unit of emigration, population decreases by $1/(N-Z)$ per cent. On the other hand, national income decreases by $k\bar{w}_f N_1 N_2/\{N(\bar{w}_1 L_1 + \bar{w}_f Z)Y\}$. The fact that the latter may exceed the former can then be readily seen as follows. Let us take the special case of the impact of initiating emigration, that is, $Z = 0$. If the following, quite possible, relationship holds:

$$\bar{w}_f/\bar{w}_1 > (L_1/N_1)(Y/kN_2),$$

then the relative rate of decrease in national income is larger than that of decrease in population, thus leading to the reduction of per-capita income.

Table 2

Total effects of migration.

Impact on:	Symbol	Direct effects of migration	Indirect effects through: Effect I — Rise in $\bar{w}_1$	Effect II — Rise in $\bar{w}_2$
Educated labour	$\frac{dN_1}{dZ}\left(=-\frac{dN_2}{dZ}\right)$	$\frac{\bar{w}_f}{\bar{w}_1}\frac{N_1N_2}{\bar{N}L_1}$	$\frac{(1-\eta_1)N_1N_2}{\bar{w}_1\bar{N}}\frac{d\bar{w}_1}{dZ}$	$-\frac{(1-\eta_2)N_1N_2}{\bar{w}_2\bar{N}}\theta\frac{d\bar{w}_1}{dZ}$
Employment of educated labour	$\frac{dL_1}{dZ}$	0	$-\eta_1\frac{L_1}{\bar{w}_1}\frac{d\bar{w}_1}{dZ}$	0
Unemployment of educated labour	$\frac{d}{dZ}(N_1-L_1)$	$\frac{\bar{w}_f}{\bar{w}_1}\frac{N_1N_2}{\bar{N}L_1}$	$\frac{(1-\eta_1)N_1N_2}{\bar{w}_1\bar{N}}+\eta_1\frac{L_1}{\bar{w}_1}\frac{d\bar{w}_1}{dZ}$	$-\frac{(1-\eta_2)N_1N_2}{\bar{w}_2\bar{N}}\theta\frac{d\bar{w}_1}{dZ}$
Employment of uneducated labour	$\frac{dL_2}{dZ}$	0	0	$-\eta_2\frac{L_2}{\bar{w}_2}\theta\frac{d\bar{w}_1}{dZ}$
Unemployment of uneducated labour	$\frac{d}{dZ}(N_2-L_2)$	$-\frac{\bar{w}_f}{\bar{w}_1}\frac{N_1N_2}{\bar{N}L_1}$	$-\frac{(1-\eta_1)N_1N_2}{\bar{w}_1\bar{N}}\frac{d\bar{w}_1}{dZ}$	$\left\{\frac{(1-\eta_2)N_1N_2}{\bar{w}_2\bar{N}}+\eta_2\frac{L_2}{\bar{w}_2}\right\}\theta\frac{d\bar{w}_1}{dZ}$
National income	$\frac{dY}{dZ}$	$-k\frac{\bar{w}_f}{\bar{w}_1}\frac{N_1N_2}{\bar{N}L_1}$	$-\left\{\eta_1L_1+\frac{k(1-\eta_1)N_1N_2}{\bar{w}_1\bar{N}}\right\}\frac{d\bar{w}_1}{dZ}$	$\left\{-\eta_2L_2+\frac{k(1-\eta_2)N_1N_2}{\bar{w}_2\bar{N}}\right\}\theta\frac{d\bar{w}_1}{dZ}$

(1) the *direct* effect of migration keeping wage levels constant and (2) the *indirect* effect of the resulting wage increases. The latter component is in turn decomposed into (1) the effect of the wage increase in the m_1-sector and (2) the effect of a wage increase in the m_2-sector that it induces. Thus taking the *incremental-employment-and-differential-wage* variant, and evaluating for simplicity the expression for the initial impact, namely, at the point where $Z = 0$, we may summarize the expressions for the total effect of emigration as in table 2.

The following observations, based on these results, are in order concerning the effects of emigration of educated labour in our model.

(1) Note that the *direct* effect of emigration on employment in either sector is nil. However, if the foreign wage level is taken into account in calculating the expected wage (Ew_1), this increases the supply of educated labour (N_1) and will reduce national income by the incremental educational cost. If the foreign wage level ($\bar{w}_f$) is high enough, we could also have increased unemployment of educated labour and reduced per-capita income.

(2) The induced wage-increase of educated labour, if any, will work to reduce the employment of educated labour. If the elasticity of demand for educated labour (η_1) is below unity, the supply of educated labour will increase, thus increasing unemployment of the educated, both absolutely and relatively; further, national income will also be likely to reduce.

(3) Finally, if we have the leap-frogging process, such that $\bar{w}_2$ also rises in response to the rise in $\bar{w}_1$, the effect thereof will be towards reducing the employment of uneducated labour. This effect would thus work to increase the expected wage (Ew_2) in this sector (if $\eta_2 < 1$) and thus to mitigate the increase in the supply of educated labour (when $\eta_1 < 1$): the net result could even be to reduce, in the new equilibrium, the supply of educated labour. The loss of national income would also be reduced insofar as the supply of educated labour is reduced; however, unless the effect of reducing the cost of education is large, it is unlikely that it will offset the loss in national income caused through the contraction of output of m_1 and m_2 resulting from the rise in $\bar{w}_1$ and $\bar{w}_2$ respectively.

Thus, in our model, even without invoking the presence of 'externalities' (leading to differences between the private and social marginal product of the emigrants), we see that the emigration of educated labour can easily lead to unfavourable effects on national income, per-capita income and on the unemployment (absolute and relative) of educated and uneducated labour through the effect of the migration on expected-wage formation in the market for educated labour, the upward pull on the (actual) wage of educated labour, and the leap-frogging upward pull on the (actual) wage of uneducated labour. And, as we proceed now to discuss in more detail in sect. 4, the internalization of the cost of education will not necessarily reduce the income–cost of the migration. Nor will the payment by the foreign country of the cost of education of the immigrants eliminate the adverse effect of the migration.

4. Alternative assumptions

Before we proceed to an explicit welfare analysis of the effects of brain drain in sect. 5, we now sketch briefly the effects of varying some of the assumptions in the model of sects. 2 and 3.[14]

4.1. Internalizing the cost of education

The reader may well ask what happens if we let people pay for their own education, so that the educational cost is 'internalized'. In this case, instead of (10), we will have:

$$Ew_1 - k^* = Ew_2, \tag{10'}$$

where k^* is the amount of educational cost that is internalized ($k^* \leqq k$).

Since employment depends on the *actual* wage, however, the employment effects in the model are unchanged whereas the allocation of the labour force between the two groups (educated and uneducated) will be directly affected. In consequence, we now have:

$$dN_1/d\bar{w}_1 = (1-\eta_1)N_2L_1/[\bar{w}_1L_1 + \bar{w}_2L_2 - k^*(N_1 - N_2)]. \tag{15'}$$

Since it is easy to show that the denominator is positive,[15] the behaviour of N_1 continues, as in the earlier case of free education, to depend on the elasticity of demand for labour.

The resulting impact on the other comparative-statics results established for the case of free education can be readily worked out by the reader. It may be noted, however, that, contrary to general intuition, the internalization of the educational cost does not necessarily reduce the undesirable impact effect of the brain drain in our model: the welfare impact of an increment in $\bar{w}_1$ under free education ($k^* = 0$) is given by (22) for Case I, and under internalized cost by:

$$dY/d\bar{w}_1 = -L_1\eta_1 - k(1-\eta_2)N_2L_1/[\bar{w}_1L_1 + \bar{w}_2L_2 - k(N_1 - N_2)], \tag{22'}$$

and, in general, when a welfare cost is involved (as when $\eta_1 < 1$), the two costs cannot be uniquely ranked.

[14]Incidentally, none of our quantitative conclusions depend on the assumption of allowing only two sectors. In fact, even in the presence of many sectors, we still obtain:

$$(\bar{w}_1/N_1)(dN_1/d\bar{w}_1) = [(\bar{N}-N_1)/\bar{N}](1-\eta_1)$$

and

$$(w_1/N_j)(dN_j/d\bar{w}_1) = -(N_1/\bar{N})(1-\eta_1),$$

where

$$\bar{N} \equiv \sum_{j=1}^{n} N_j, \quad \text{for } n \geqq 2.$$

[15]By (10′), we have: $\bar{w}_1L_1 + \bar{w}_2L_2 - k^*(N_1 - N_2) = \bar{w}_2(L_2/N_2)\bar{N} + k^*N_2$.

Similarly, for Case III, we may note again that the adverse effect of emigration on employment and income is not necessarily reduced if the cost of education is internalized as in (10′). Thus, for example, (27) is modified in the case of internalized educational cost ($k^* = k$) to:

$$\mathrm{d}N_1/\mathrm{d}Z = \bar{w}_f N_2/\{\bar{w}_1 L_1 + \bar{w}_2 L_2 + \bar{w}_f Z - k(N_1 - N_2)\}, \tag{27'}$$

and it is clear that the new, additional term $-k(N_1 - N_2)$ could, in principle, work in either direction. Also, eq. (31) for impact on national income would modify to:

$$\mathrm{d}Y/\mathrm{d}Z = -k\bar{w}_f N_2/\{\bar{w}_1 L_1 + \bar{w}_2 L_2 + \bar{w}_f Z - k(N_1 - N_2)\}. \tag{31'}$$

And this means that the effect of internalizing the cost of education could well be to *increase*, rather than diminish, the cost in national income from the emigration in our model: this being yet another instance of second-best theory.

All this, of course, is not to deny that, for any *given* levels of $\bar{w}_1$, $\bar{w}_2$ and Z, the *progressive* internalization of the cost of education will be employment-and-income-*improving*. We can show that the increased internalization of the cost of education will, while leaving unchanged the employment in each sector, reduce the supply of educated labour (N_1) and hence its (total) cost (kN_1):

$$\mathrm{d}N_1/\mathrm{d}k^* = -N_1 N_2/\{w_2(L_2/N_2)N + K^* N_2\} < 0. \tag{32}$$

Therefore, as long as unemployment in educated labour exists, increasing the education cost borne by labour itself will save the education cost by $-k\mathrm{d}N_1$. Note further that, even if the cost paid by labour (i.e., k^*) approaches the 'true value' of k, the unemployment of educated labour may still exist.[16] In such a case, the imposition of higher cost ($k^* > k$) for education may turn out to be optimal in this second-best problem with wage rigidities![17]

4.2. Irreversibility of education

We may next address ourselves to the question of what happens in the 'short run' when the educated labour force cannot be reduced. The effect of this clearly is to accentuate – by eliminating the possibility of reducing the educated-labour supply, N_1, and thus saving on its cost, kN_1 – the loss possibilities in the model. There is thus no relief for the 'let-us-not-worry-about-brain-drain' economists from shifting to the short run!

[16] Suppose $\bar{w}_1$ and $\bar{w}_2$ are fixed higher than the equilibrium full employment wage rate indicated by (12). Then the phenomenon discussed in the text could readily occur.

[17] Note again that the saving in educational costs, which we have been discussing, applies only in the 'long run', for comparison of two stationary states in our model.

4.3. The case where the labour market in m_2-sector is competitive

Next, what happens if the 'uneducated-labour' sector is 'competitive', so that the sticky-wage assumption applies only to educated labour? In this case, instead of (10) we will now have:

$$(L_1/N_1)\cdot\bar{w}_1 = w_2, \tag{10''}$$

and

$$N_2 = L_2.$$

Further, since w_2 is no longer fixed, it will now be determined by:

$$w_2 = g(L_2), \qquad g' < 0.$$

Finally, we will have the total labour supply constraint as:

$$N_1 + N_2 = \bar{N}.$$

Solving these four equations, we would then get now:

$$\mathrm{d}N_1/\mathrm{d}\bar{w}_1 = L_1(1-\eta_1)/(w_2 - N_1 g'), \tag{33}$$

and it is easy to see that (33) has the same qualitative property as (16) in our basic model in sects. 2 and 3.[18]

4.4. Cost of education paid by country of immigration

It is sometimes asserted that if the host country pays the cost of education, brain drain would cease to be harmful. In our model, this is easily allowed for, of course, by assuming that the country of emigration recovers ($k\mathrm{d}Z$) worth of transfer income from the country of immigration. It is again easy to see, as already noted in sect. 3, that all this does is to modify the last row of table 2 by the addition of the term ($k\mathrm{d}Z$) and that the net effect on income, and the effects on unemployment, can still be adverse.

5. Welfare effects of brain drain and integration of markets for professionals

We may now draw together the main analytical results of sect. 3 to derive welfare conclusions. To do this, however, we need to specify the social welfare function explicitly.

It is our contention that the traditional trade-theoretic analysis of the Grubel–Scott–Johnson variety yields conclusions more favourable to the phenomenon of brain drain and integration of markets for professionals, not merely because

[18] It may be interesting to note, however, that the change in $\bar{w}_1$ will now endogenously change w_2. And, in the case where $\eta_1 < 1$, $\mathrm{d}w_2/\mathrm{d}\bar{w}_1 = -g'(\mathrm{d}N_1/\mathrm{d}w_1) > 0$, since $\mathrm{d}N_2 = -\mathrm{d}N_1$, so that a rise in $\bar{w}_1$ leads to a rise in w_2. This is, of course, not the same as the 'leap-frogging' in our Case II, a phenomenon that is ruled out by the 'competitive' assumption for section m_2.

the model used for analysis is simplistic. It is also because the social welfare function used for analysis is really limited in confining itself to arguments which rule out many relevant variables.

In fact, we think that it could make much sense to define a social welfare function which has at least the following arguments:

(1) *National income*: The sense of security, bargaining power in trade and economic negotiations, the need for defense, and a number of political and economic variables of importance could depend, not just on per-capita income, but on national income as an aggregate.

(2) *Level of emigration*: Those who have lived in the less developed countries know that the emigration of skilled manpower in certain occupations, such as scientific research in particular, creates a sense of inadequacy, which may stiffle creative endeavour in domestic environment.

(3) *Level of educated/professional manpower*: The technological ability of the population may matter much to the independence and creativity of the population; hence a fall in the (short-run and long-run) level of the educated labour force due to the phenomena being discussed by us could cause an adverse effect on social welfare.

(4) *Unemployment*: Unemployment, whether absolute or its rate, is also of importance to social welfare. More directly, it affects political stability and social cohesion, if nothing else, and is of immediate concern to the developing countries. In this regard, the unemployment among the educated may be even more explosive than among the uneducated, as is evident from the fact that the leadership of the revolutionary movements in Calcutta, for example, has derived from the unemployed, educated students.

(5) *Income distribution*: In the absence of fiscal ability to redistribute incomes, the direct income distributional impact of the phenomena under discussion will also often be the final effect. And it should clearly enter the social welfare function. In the context of our model, we could thus include in the arguments of the social welfare function, for example, the relative share of wage income in total national income: $(\bar{w}_1 L_1 + \bar{w}_2 L_2)/Y$.[19]

Thus, a realistic social welfare function should probably read as follows:

$$U = U\{Y,\ Y/N, Z, N_1, L_1/N_1, L_2/N_2, (\bar{w}_1 L_1 + \bar{w}_2 L_2)/Y\}. \tag{34}$$

We forego a taxonomic exercise, exploring the outcomes on welfare and possible tradeoffs among alternative arguments in this welfare function, for different parametric combinations of the elasticities η_1, η_2 and other parameters such as θ and k appearing in the expressions in table 2. The reader can readily

[19] Alternatively, we could use as an argument the weighted sum of per-capita utilities: e.g. where $U(w_i)$ is the per-capita utility in labour class i with $U' > 0$ and $U'' < 0$, the social welfare function could have the argument: $\sum_i U_i(w_i)L_i$.

do this for himself; and we have already discussed briefly in sect. 3 some of the possible outcomes with regard to national income, per capita income, supply of educated labour and the level and rates of unemployment in both classes of labour.[20]

Emigration tax

Rather, we may sketch here the answer to the question as to what would happen if the country of emigration were to impose a tax on emigration. To analyse this policy, assume that a recurring poll tax (that would be paid annually by the migrant) is levied on each emigrant.[21] Restricting our analysis to the effect on the income of those left behind (for reasons of space), we should expect a twofold effect: (i) the direct effect of the tax on revenue, which may then be treated as income redistributed to those left behind; and (ii) the indirect effect on unemployment levels, income, etc., which would operate through the effects on expected and actual wage levels.

(i) If we take T as the (recurring) poll tax paid by the emigrants (Z), the tax revenue will be TZ. As T is changed, this revenue will change by:

$$Z(1-\eta_f^T), \tag{35}$$

where η_f^T is the elasticity of emigration with respect to the poll tax (i.e., $-T/Z \cdot dZ/dT$). Clearly, this *revenue effect* will be positive or negative, depending on the elasticity of emigration with respect to taxation.

(ii) As for the 'indirect' effect, this can be indicated *via* the simplified Case III assumption of the *incremental-employment-and-differential-wage* variant: i.e., by assuming that (only) the expected wage is modified downwards by the tax. Thus, we must rewrite (29) as follows:

$$Ew_1 = [\bar{w}_1 L_1 + (\bar{w}_f - T)Z]/N_1. \tag{29'}$$

[20]The only effects, which we have not worked out in sect. 3, relate to income distribution. This, however, can be readily worked out. Thus, for the general Case IV, we can write:

$$\frac{Y}{\bar{w}_1 L_1 + \bar{w}_2 L_2} \frac{d\{(\bar{w}_1 L_1 + \bar{w}_2 L_2)/Y\}}{dZ} = \frac{1}{\bar{w}_1 L_1 + \bar{w}_2 L_2}\left(L_1(1-\eta_1) + L_2(1-\eta_2)\theta \frac{d\bar{w}_1}{dZ}\right)$$
$$+ \frac{k\bar{w}_f N_1 N_2}{Y\bar{N}\bar{w}_1 L_1} + \frac{1}{Y}\left\{\eta_1 L_1 + \frac{k(1-\eta_1)N_1 N_2}{\bar{w}_1 \bar{N}}\right\}\frac{d\bar{w}_1}{dZ}$$
$$+ \frac{\theta}{Y}\left[\eta_2 L_2 - \frac{k(1-\eta_1)N_1 N_2}{\bar{w}_1 \bar{N}}\right]\frac{d\bar{w}_1}{dZ}.$$

[21]The effect of the usual poll tax would be of a once-for-all nature. However, in order to conform to our analysis in terms of flows, it would be useful to conceive of a recurring poll tax along the lines of the Bhagwati–Dellalfar (1973) proposal (which relates to an income tax related to the income of the emigrant, a difference of unimportance if we assume a unique $\bar{w}_f$).

Substituting (29′) into (10) and differentiating with respect to T, we obtain

$$\frac{\mathrm{d}N_1}{\mathrm{d}T} = -\frac{N_2Z - N_2(\overline{w}_f - T)(\mathrm{d}Z/\mathrm{d}T)}{\overline{w}_1L_1 + \overline{w}_2L_2 + (\overline{w}_f - T)Z},$$

which can be written as

$$\frac{\mathrm{d}N_1}{\mathrm{d}T} = -\frac{N_2Z(1+\varepsilon_f)}{\overline{w}_1L_1 + \overline{w}_2L_2 + (\overline{w}_f - T)Z} < 0, \tag{36}$$

where ε_f is the elasticity of emigration with respect to effective foreign wages $(w_f - T)$.[22] Thus an increase in T will always decrease the supply of educated labour in the long run, and this effect is strengthened if the emigrant is responsive to the recurring poll tax. As before, the income change is then:

$$\frac{\mathrm{d}Y}{\mathrm{d}T} = -k\,\frac{\mathrm{d}N_1}{\mathrm{d}T} = \frac{kN_2Z(1+\varepsilon_f)}{\overline{w}_1L_1 + \overline{w}_2L_2 + (\overline{w}_f - T)Z} > 0. \tag{37}$$

Thus, the net impact on the income of those left behind will be given by the sum of these two, direct and indirect, effects (36) and (37):

$$Z(1-\eta_f^T) + \frac{kN_2Z(1+\varepsilon_f)}{\overline{w}_1L_1 + \overline{w}_2L_2 + (\overline{w}_f - T)Z}. \tag{38}$$

A sufficient (but not necessary) condition for the per capita income of those left behind to improve thanks to the emigration tax, therefore, would be that $\eta_f^T < 1$.[23]

The reader could readily extend the analysis of the poll tax on emigration to examine the impact on the other arguments in the social welfare function; space considerations prevent us from undertaking this task ourselves.

6. Concluding remarks

It is clear, of course, that our results are in contrast with those of the traditional, fully neoclassical model because of the assumptions of 'rigid' wages and resulting unemployment. Under the conventional assumptions of flexible wages and absence of unemployment, the results of emigration are both simpler and easily stated: (i) for internalized cost of education ($k^* = k$), the emigration will reduce national income but, in increasing the average product of labour, will also raise per-capita income under the 'normal' assumption of diminishing

[22] Note that $(\overline{w}_f - T/T)\eta_f^T = \varepsilon_f$.

[23] Note that the 'indirect' effect works only in the long run. Furthermore, we have ruled out the more general case where the emigration may affect the *actual* wage as well. If this were allowed, then the emigration tax might well reduce the *actual* wage in the m_1, and possibly m_2, sectors and hence moderate the income loss on that account.

marginal productivity of labour;[24] and (ii) for free education ($k^* = 0$), the other polar case, and no compensation for educational costs by the country of immigration, it is possible (though not inevitable) that the average product of labour, and hence per-capita income, falls as a result of emigration of educated labour.

Our results are both more complex and less comforting than these. They are also more realistic. They should suffice to raise doubts about the complacency concerning the brain drain phenomenon resulting from the analysis in the existing literature.[25]

[24]The *apparent* contradiction between this statement and the earlier Grubel–Scott argument that emigration leaves unchanged the welfare of those left behind is easily resolved. The Grubel–Scott result is based on the fact that the emigre was earning w (the wage) and thus everyone other than him was getting $(Y-w)$, whereas his departure reduces Y itself by w: hence the result for those left behind is the sum of the reduction in income due to emigration ($\mathrm{d}Y/\mathrm{d}L = -w$) and the increment in available income as the emigrant loses his claim on income defined by his wage ($+w$), which means no-impact. On the other hand, $\mathrm{d}(Y/L)/\mathrm{d}L = (1/L)[w-(Y/L)] > 0$ as the wage, which equals the marginal product, will be below the average product: hence emigration will *raise* per-capita income, i.e. *improve* the welfare of those left behind. This contradiction is easily resolved, however, once it is seen that the Grubel–Scott argument assumes that the income accruing to the emigre prior to emigration is w, the wage, whereas the per-capita-income argument in effect assumes it to be $Y/L(> w)$: the former assumption thus yields no impact whereas the latter yields improvement, for those left behind. In this paper, we have examined the impact on *both* income and per-capita income; results under the Grubel–Scott assumption can however be readily derived by taking the impact on income and adding to it the consumption of the emigrant, defined as his wage rate ($\bar{w}_1$), on the assumption that the emigrant was employed prior to emigration, or possibly a lower sum if we assume that he was unemployed and was subsisting on someone else's income.

[25]We have not modelled here, as an anonymous referee has pointed out, some of the real-world complexities which arise on a different dimension from those (e.g. sticky wages and unemployment) considered in this paper: for example, the effects of the quality and content of higher education and professional training in the advanced countries on the phenomenon of brain drain. Thus, it is well known that the brain drain occurs in part *via* the settling down abroad of LDC students who have been receiving higher education abroad. To some extent, this phenomenon results from the fact that the type of training received abroad makes these students somewhat ill-suited at times to any useful work at home and, if they do return, makes them conduits of disequilibrating disturbances in the domestic economy. We would need however a different model to study these kinds of relationships and effects: to admit everything into one model would be to make it too complex.

References

Bhagwati, J. and T.N. Srinivasan, 1972, Overqualification, education and welfare: A theoretical analysis, mimeo. (M.I.T., Cambridge, Mass.).

Bhagwati, J. and W. Dellalfar, 1973, The brain drain and income taxation: A proposal, World Development 1, no. 1.

Dumont, R., 1969, False start in Africa (Praeger, New York).

Grubel, H. and A. Scott, 1966, The international flow of human capital, American Economic Review, May.

Johnson, H.G., 1967, Some economic aspects of brain drain, Pakistan Development Review 3.

Johnson, H.G., 1972, Labour mobility and the brain drain, in: G. Ranis, ed., The gap between rich and poor nations, Proceedings of the 1970 IEA Conference at Bled, Yugoslavia (Macmillan, New York).

Jolly, R. and D. Seers, 1972, The brain drain and the development process, in: G. Ranis, ed., The gap between rich and poor nations, Proceedings of the 1970 IEA Conference at Bled, Yugoslavia (Macmillan, New York).

Jones, R., 1967, International capital movements and the theory of tariffs and trade, Quarterly Journal of Economics, Feb.

Kemp, M., 1966, Gains from international trade and investment, American Economic Review, Sept.

Sunkel, O., 1971, Latin American underdevelopment in the year 2000, in: J. Bhagwati, ed., Economics and world order: From the 1970's to the 1990's (Macmillan, New York).

DOMESTIC DISTORTIONS, IMPERFECT INFORMATION AND THE BRAIN DRAIN*

Koichi HAMADA
Tokyo University, Tokyo, Japan

Jagdish BHAGWATI
M.I.T., Cambridge, MA 02139, U.S.A.

An earlier paper by Bhagwati and Hamada (1974) presented a theoretical analysis of the brain drain in the context of wage rigidity and unemployment. This paper extends the analysis by modifying the model to incorporate the phenomena of overqualification, internal diffusion of labor from urban to rural areas and imperfect information about the quality of labor. The welfare effect of the brain drain in the presence of these phenomena is analyzed.

1. Introduction

The traditional, theoretic analysis of the welfare effects of the brain drain, initiated by Grubel and Scott (1966) and developed by Berry and Soligo (1969), Johnson (1967) and Kenen (1971) among others, has been based on the assumption of perfect competition, including perfect information and full wage flexibility.

A departure from these assumptions was made in an earlier paper of ours – Bhagwati–Hamada (1974) – by permitting the presence of wage rigidity and unemployment. In the context of this model, the basic Grubel–Scott contention that (infinitesimal) emigration would not affect the welfare (conventionally defined) of those left behind was clearly not valid and a welfare loss could well be imposed on the nonmigrant group. In addition, the Bhagwati–Hamada analysis introduced the possibility of the 'emulation effect' whereby the migration could raise the wage levels of the class of migrants by virtue (or rather, vice) of the implied, consequent integration internationally of this class of labor: such a 'distortion-augmenting' emulation effect could accentuate then the welfare loss imposed on those left behind.

*Thanks are due to the National Science Foundation for partial financial support of the research underlying this paper. The paper was prepared for the Bellagio Conference on The Brain Drain and Income Taxation, 15–19 February 1975. It is best read as a companion piece to the Bhagwati–Hamada (1974) paper, whose analysis it extends.

In this paper, we utilize the same basic model, but extend it in three directions which bring it closer to alternative facets of reality in the LDCs.

First, we consider the phenomenon of 'overqualification', i.e., where jobs have been upgraded and the educated are working in jobs that, objectively speaking, do not 'require' the education.[1] The extension of our analysis to the situation where overqualification is present shows that, in the absence of the emulation effect, brain drain from the class of skills characterized by overqualification can help, rather than hurt, those left behind.

Secondly, we extend our analysis to the phenomenon that has sometimes been described as the 'internal brain drain' but is more aptly called the 'internal diffusion' of professionals. Thus it is well known that doctors tend to congregate in the urban areas and rural areas tend not to attract doctors. However, there is also a process of internal diffusion going on, with doctors, as the congestion in the cities increases and cuts into average incomes, increasingly moving to the countryside partially or fully.[2] This internal diffusion process is likely to be inhibited as the possibility of external brain drain from the LDC (cities) is opened up. We will model this phenomenon and demonstrate formally the welfare-reducing impact of migration in such a context.

Thirdly, we introduce an element of imperfect information into the analysis of the brain drain. Arrow (1973) and Spence (1974) have developed a 'screening' theory of education.[3] In its simplified form, the theory states that education is important not so much because it increases the productivity of workers as because it plays the role of filtering efficient labor from labor in general. We utilize this notion and consider the case where the brain drain serves to identify, and thus screen, the more efficient from the less efficient. It turns out that if the domestic labor market cannot discriminate as effectively as the international market for professionals, then the economy tends to lose, essentially because emigrants are picked up from the category of the more efficient.

This analysis of market distortions and imperfect information will demonstrate that the welfare effects of the brain drain, and accordingly the nature of the policy intervention necessary, differ significantly depending on the nature of distortion or imperfection that the LDC economy is facing; in fact, within each LDC, different classes of professional emigrants (e.g., doctors, engineers, etc.) may correspond to different models. While this analysis takes the domestic distortions as given exogenously, we raise in our concluding section the signifi-

[1]For a statement of this basic model, see Bhagwati (1972) and the systematic, general-equilibrium analysis of education in this framework in Bhagwati and Srinivasan (1975). The latter paper rechristens the overqualification model as the 'job ladder' model.

[2]The partial movement frequently occurs through opening up clinics or offices in the neighboring towns, with the city doctor spending part of the month there.

[3]A concise statement of four alternative theories of education (the Schultz-Becker 'human capital' theory, the radical 'socialization' theory, the Arrow–Spence screening theory and the Bhagwati–Srinivasan 'job ladder' and fairness-in-hiring theory) is provided in Bhagwati and Srinivasan (1975).

cant possibility that migration itself could influence these distortions, accentuating or moderating them.

2. The basic framework and the welfare criterion

We initially state the basic Bhagwati–Hamada (1974) model, with its special features such as the presence of wage rigidity and unemployment.[4] Consider an economy satisfying the small country assumption such that the relative commodity price-ratio between two tradeable commodities is fixed internationally. Let there be two kinds of labor: uneducated and educated. Uneducated labor can be transformed into educated labor at constant costs. Corresponding to the two goods, there are two sectors in the economy: the traditional sector that normally employs uneducated labor, and the developed sector that normally employs educated labor.[5] Wages are assumed to be exogenously given by the international emulation process and possibly by the 'leap-frogging' process discussed in the Bhagwati–Hamada (1974) paper.[6] It is also assumed that unemployment exists in both of the sectors.

The production function of the traditional sector is given by

$$F_0(L_0) \qquad [\text{with } F_0' > 0,\, F_0'' < 0],$$

where L_0 is the employment of labor in the traditional sector. The production function of the developed sector is given by

$$F_e(L_e) \qquad [\text{with } F_e' > 0,\, F_e'' < 0],$$

where L_e is the employment of labor in the developed sector. We shall assume that $F_e'(L_e) > F_0'(L_0)$ for an identical amount of labor $L_e = L_0$.

The total labor force N is divided into two categories: uneducated labor N_0 and educated labor N_e, in such a way that

$$N_0 + N_e = N. \qquad (1)$$

Under the 'normal' assumption that excludes the over-qualification of labor, $(N_0 - L_0)$ and $(N_e - L_e)$ indicate, respectively, the unemployment in the traditional sector and that in the developed sector, in the absence of brain drain. Let us suppose now that brain drain occurs only from educated labor. In the presence

[4]Only the barest details are provided here; the reader can consult the original Bhagwati–Hamada paper for a more leisurely statement of the model.

[5]The use of the qualifying adverb 'normally' is pertinent to our analysis in the next section.

[6]Bhagwati and Hamada (1974). Most of the results below remain valid so long as the wage of educated labor is determined exogenously. The wage of uneducated labor may be determined by marginal or average productivity.

of brain drain equal to Z, $(N_e - Z - L_e)$ then indicates the unemployment in the developed sector.

Wages are fixed as $\bar{w}_0$ and $\bar{w}_e$, and labor is employed to the point of equality with its marginal product, i.e.,

$$F_0'(L_0) = \bar{w}_0, \tag{2}$$

$$F_e'(L_e) = \bar{w}_e, \tag{3}$$

assuming the international price ratio to be normalized to unity. When $\bar{w}_0$ and $\bar{w}_e$ are given, L_0 and L_e will clearly be determined from eqs. (2) and (3).

People decide whether to educate themselves by comparing the expected wage rate for uneducated labor and that for educated labor. That is, in the absence of any constraints on the expansion of education facilities, and if educational cost is provided by the government, the equality

$$\frac{L_0}{N_0}\bar{w}_0 = \frac{L_e}{N_e - Z}\bar{w}_e \tag{4}$$

will determine the amount of educated people. In certain institutional settings discussed below, there will then be permanent excess demand to get educated: in this case, the number of educated people will have to be limited exogenously by governmental fiat.

Let us now turn to the welfare criterion to judge the welfare effect of the brain drain in this economy. We will take the average income of those left behind as the welfare criterion. The resulting formula for welfare change is then readily derived as follows.

The GNP, Y, of the country of emigration can be expressed as

$$Y = F_0(L_0) + F_e(L_e) - kN_e = G(N - Z), \tag{5}$$

where k is the constant cost of education, noting again that the international commodity price-ratio is normalized at unity, and GNP is a function of the available labor force. As soon as we shift, however, to the GNP accruing to those left behind, i.e., Y_d, their income *after* migration becomes

$$Y_d = G(N - Z),$$

and, before migration, it is

$$Y_d = G(N) - vZ,$$

where v is the average income that emigrants are receiving prior to the emigration. It follows immediately then, denoting per capita income of those left behind by y_d, that

$$\frac{dy_d}{dZ} = \frac{1}{N-Z}\left\{v + \frac{dG}{dZ}\right\}, \tag{6}$$

and, evaluated at $Z = 0$, we have[7]

$$\left.\frac{dy_d}{dZ}\right|_{Z=0} = \frac{1}{N}\left\{v + \frac{dG}{dZ}\right\}. \tag{6'}$$

Therefore we must look at the value of $[v+(dG/dZ)]$ in order to assess the welfare effect of the brain drain. All that this formula says is that if the marginal loss due to the reduction of labor is larger than the payment that was received by the marginal emigrant, then those left behind will lose; otherwise they will gain.

We shall not repeat the comparative static analysis of the system of eqs. (1)–(4) that was developed in our earlier paper.[8] It is necessary to note, however, that if the brain drain results (only) in a rise in the wage of educated labor (thanks to the emulation effect), then the effect on GNP will now become

$$\frac{dG}{dZ} = -k\frac{L_0\bar{w}_0}{L_e\bar{w}_e + L_0\bar{w}_0} - \left\{\eta_e L_e + \frac{k(1-\eta_e)N_e N_0}{\bar{w}_e N}\right\}\frac{d\bar{w}_e}{dZ},$$

where η_e is the wage elasticity of the demand for educated labor.[9] Having noted this, we now turn to the extension of the analysis to the phenomena of overqualification, internal diffusion and imperfect information.

3. The overqualification phenomenon

The labor market may function, in response to excess supply, not by cutting the wage as in the usual neoclassical analysis, but rather in the context of a 'job ladder' model, with sticky wages, where the excess supply then spills over from the 'best' to the 'next-best' job. Thus educated labor, on finding no more employment in the educated-labor category of jobs, can be postulated as moving down

[7]This welfare criterion, as Berry and Soligo (1969) noted, is of course different from that which would result if we were comparing, before and after migration, the per capita incomes (as distinct from the per capita incomes of those left behind). For the former case, the criterion would modify to

$$\frac{dY/(N-Z)}{dZ} = \frac{1}{N-Z}\left\{\frac{dG}{dZ} + \frac{Y}{N-Z}\right\}.$$

[8]Bhagwati and Hamada (1974, p. 33, table 2). Note merely that there is a minor difference between eq. (25) there and eq. (4) in this paper concerning the treatment of Z. But this is for the purpose of simpler exposition and does not affect the substance of our analysis.

[9]See Bhagwati and Hamada (1974, p. 33); the difference in the first term in the RHS comes from our new eq. (4), which replaces the earlier eq. (25).

the job ladder and taking the jobs which do not require the education. Bhagwati and Srinivasan (1975) further argue that, in this case, a 'fairness-in-hiring' principle may also be sociologically invoked whereby employers, faced by excess demand for the no-educational-requirement jobs from both educated and uneducated labor, prefer to hire the educated because they think it is 'fair' to reward those who have put in extra effort, as it were. Thus, although both kinds of labor are equally productive in the no-education-requirement jobs, the educated applicants are hired in preference over the uneducated ones.

In the analysis that follows, we then modify our basic model to incorporate this job ladder phenomenon with overqualification (or upgrading of jobs in terms of hiring practice) characterizing the hiring in the sector where educated and uneducated labor have identical productivity. Thus, assume now (as before) that the educated labor may be in excess supply in its market, in the *developed* sector; however, when the expected wage in this sector is equalized with the wage in the *traditional* sector, the educated labor spills over into employment in the traditional sector. And, given the number of jobs in the traditional sector at the exogenously-fixed wage therein, we assume that the incidence of unemployment then falls on uneducated labor. Formally, the model then modifies as follows.

Let L_{ee}, L_{e0} and L_{00} denote respectively the educated labor *employed* in the developed sector, educated labor *employed* in the traditional sector, and uneducated labor *employed* in the traditional sector. Then, by definition, we have

$$L_{ee} = L_e,$$

and

$$L_{e0}+L_{00} = L_0,$$

for labor employment in the two sectors. Now, the assumption that everyone will get educated as long as the expected wage to educated labor exceeds that to uneducated labor (since the educational cost is borne by the government and its indirect tax cost not taken into account by atomistic labor), implies that in this modified model there would be an endless incentive to get educated: the expected return to educated labor would always exceed the expected return to uneducated labor. Hence, we must impose an *exogenous* constraint on how many get educated: i.e., $N_e = \bar{N}_e$ by policy decision.

It is immediately obvious then that, thanks to the constancy of $\bar{w}_e$ (and hence of L_e) and $\bar{N}_e$, the effect of the migration is to create an *identical* reduction in the unemployment of uneducated labor:

$$\mathrm{d}L_{e0} = -\mathrm{d}Z \qquad \text{and} \qquad \mathrm{d}L_{00} = \mathrm{d}Z,$$

so that we have

$$\mathrm{d}G/\mathrm{d}Z = 0. \tag{7}$$

The loss of educated labor is fully offset, at the margin, by unemployed uneducated labor getting employed in their place in the traditional sector, without loss of productivity (as postulated), so that both L_e and L_0, the employment levels in both sectors, and hence the output levels in both sectors are unaffected.[10] It follows therefore that

$$\left\{v+\frac{\mathrm{d}G}{\mathrm{d}Z}\right\} > 0, \tag{8}$$

unless we introduce other complexities into the analysis.

Such a complication, for example, is when the wage $\bar{w}_e$ in the developed sector rises due to the emulation effect, in the presence of migration, and the accompanying move towards integration of the labor market for the migrant class of labor. The number being educated will remain constant (at $\bar{N}_e$) again by assumption; however, GNP will now be reduced by the induced fall in L_e (as $\bar{w}_e$ rises) in the developed sector:

$$\frac{\mathrm{d}G}{\mathrm{d}Z} = -L_e\eta_e\frac{\mathrm{d}\bar{w}_e}{\mathrm{d}Z}. \tag{9}$$

Yet another complication could be introduced if we were to postulate that the governmental educational policy is aimed at providing a constant educational labor force *net* of emigration. In this event, the emigration of educated labor would lead to an identical, offsetting expansion of the educated labor force, so that we must modify eq. (7) as follows:

$$\mathrm{d}G/\mathrm{d}Z = -k, \tag{10}$$

because, while output in the two sectors remains constant, the cost of education increases as more get educated to offset the emigrated educated labor. In this case, again, the welfare criterion $[v+(\mathrm{d}G/\mathrm{d}Z)]$ will become ambiguous unless we postulate (as seems reasonable) that $v > k$.

In conclusion, it would appear that, under the conditions postulated, the overqualification phenomenon tends to mitigate the welfare loss, if any, of the brain drain. In fact, if the brain drain is not accompanied by an induced rise in the wage-level in the developed sector or by an offsetting expansion of domestic educational facilities, the brain drain will increase (rather than decrease) the per capita income of those left behind in the country of emigration.

[10]This argument presupposes, of course, that the magnitude of emigration does not exceed the spillover of educated labor into the traditional sector in the pre-emigration situation.

4. The internal diffusion process

The diffusion of the emigrant class of professionals (e.g., doctors) from the urban to the rural areas, from areas of 'low' to areas of 'high' social marginal product, is a phenomenon that again can be modelled as an extension of our basic framework, leading to the conclusion that the brain drain in the presence of such a diffusion process could harm those left behind.

Suppose now that there are two subsectors in the developed sector, and hence two opportunities for the educated labor therein: urban and rural employment. In the urban occupation, wage $\bar{w}_{eu}$ is paid and is higher than the wage $\bar{w}_{er}$ in the rural occupation; the latter, in turn, is still higher than the wage in the traditional sector $\bar{w}_0$. Educated labor thus chooses between rural and urban occupations such that

$$\bar{w}_{er} = \frac{L_{eu}}{N_e - L_{er} - Z}\,\bar{w}_{eu}, \tag{11}$$

where L_{er} and L_{eu} indicate employment in rural and in urban occupations, respectively. Again, since $\bar{w}_{er} > \bar{w}_0$ and educational costs to individuals are nil, we must contend with excess demand for getting educated. Hence we will assume, as in the preceding section, that the size of the educated labor force N_e is exogenously fixed by the government, consistent with eq. (11).

We further postulate that, in the rural occupation, there is a shortage of educated labor. Formally, the social marginal product in the rural occupation is higher than the wage,

$$F'_{er}(L_{er}) > \bar{w}_{er},$$

while, in the urban occupation, the wage is equal to its marginal product:

$$F'_{eu}(L_{eu}) = \bar{w}_{eu}.$$

If emigration occurs now, without any additional emulation-induced effects on the wages in both occupations, then the constancy of N_e implies that

$$\mathrm{d}L_{er} = -\mathrm{d}Z,$$

and

$$\frac{\mathrm{d}G}{\mathrm{d}Z} = -F'_{er}(L_{er}).$$

Essentially, this means that the educated labor employed in the *rural* occupation decreases by the amount of the emigration: the emigration raises the expected wage in the urban occupation, pulling the educated labor out of the rural occupation. The welfare criterion then is

$$v+\frac{\mathrm{d}G}{\mathrm{d}Z}=v-F'_{er} \tag{12}$$

which has a positive sign if F'_{er} is smaller than v, but can be negative if the social marginal product in the rural occupation is substantially higher than the wage in the rural occupation and further exceeds the wage that was paid to the emigrant.

Introduce now the emulation effect, so that the brain drain induces a rise in $\bar{w}_{eu}$. In this case, clearly the production loss is aggravated. For, in the urban occupation, L_{eu} is reduced by $(\eta_{eu}L_{eu}/\bar{w}_{eu})\mathrm{d}\bar{w}_{eu}$, where η_{eu} is the elasticity of demand for labor in the urban occupation. On the other hand, the labor shortage is increased in the rural occupation because L_{er} is reduced as follows:

$$\mathrm{d}L_{er}=-\mathrm{d}Z-\frac{L_{eu}(1-\eta_{eu})}{\bar{w}_{er}}\mathrm{d}\bar{w}_{eu}.$$

Therefore, the shortage of educated labor in the rural occupation increases by more than the size of emigration if $\eta_{eu}<1$. The total production loss is then

$$\frac{\mathrm{d}G}{\mathrm{d}Z}=-F'_{er}\left\{1+\frac{L_{eu}(1-\eta_{eu})}{\bar{w}_{er}}\frac{\mathrm{d}\bar{w}_{eu}}{\mathrm{d}Z}\right\}-L_{eu}\eta_{eu}\frac{\mathrm{d}\bar{w}_{eu}}{\mathrm{d}Z}. \tag{13}$$

Thus, in spite of the fact that the employment of the urban occupation reduces, the shortage in the rural occupation increases.

If our analysis accurately reflects the reality in some LDCs, then we must consider to be somewhat optimistic the following view of Myint (1968) on the effects of the brain drain of doctors from large cities in the LDCs:

> The pressure of excess demand from the advanced countries is most likely to affect the doctors in private practice in the bigger towns in the underdeveloped countries. In so far as this is true, the welfare effects are less catastrophic than if the doctors were being taken away from the rural areas and the development effect is probably negligible.

The analysis of this section shows that the effect of the brain drain could be significantly harmful even though the direct source of the emigrants was the urban population.

5. Brain drain and the screening process

Consider now the question as to who is likely to emigrate. Several 'high-level' emigrants are individuals who possess some special skills such as language ability, study and experience in the developed countries. They are therefore likely to be specialists who have some special ability 'needed' in the recipient country.[11] Suppose now that these kinds of characteristics or ability are also productive at home. In this case, we have the possibility that the brain drain functions as a screening device of more efficient from less efficient labor.

If these individuals receive their full marginal productivity at home, there is no problem. Or if the fact that a person has a foreign offer for job and emigration results in his getting a correspondingly higher wage, there is no problem either. But does the employer know who possesses differentially higher ability? Or, if he knows this, does he or can he offer higher wages to such people? In other words, if a category of educated labor contains both 'emigrable' and 'non-emigrable' labor, and if the former is more efficient, does the price mechanism duly take account of the difference?[12] This section therefore deals with the possible imperfection of information in the market of educated labor and the consequences it has for the welfare effects of the brain drain.

The basic Arrow (1973)–Spence (1974) framework for analyzing education as a screening (or, as Arrow calls it, filtering) device eliminates any productivity effects of, say, the human-capital variety. In our framework, however, we admit the productivity effect, but at the same time allow for the possibility that the (domestic) market cannot discriminate between the highly-gifted (and consequently 'emigrable') labor and the commonly-educated (and consequently 'non-emigrable') labor.

Now let us return to our basic model. Assume again that educated labor works only in the developed sector, but that educated labor consists of two categories: 'commonly-educated' labor L_c and 'highly-gifted' labor L_h. L_h is λ times more productive than L_c, the difference being of the labor-augmenting type. However, let us assume that employers cannot discriminate between L_c and L_h, so that all the educated labor receives the *average* marginal productivity. Therefore,

$$\bar{w}_e = \{(1-p)+p\lambda\}F_e'(L_e), \qquad \lambda > \tag{3'}$$

where p is the ratio of the highly-gifted labor to all the educated labor: $p = L_h/L_e = L_h/(L_c+L_h)$. In other words, p may be regarded as the probability of educated labor turning out to be highly gifted.

Then, in the system of the basic model (1)–(4), with the only modification that (3) is replaced by (3′), we obtain the same qualitative properties for given values of $\bar{w}_0$ and $\bar{w}_e$ as the basic model. The rise in $\bar{w}_e$ also creates the same qualitative impact as in the basic model.

[11]The labor certification process which is necessary for 'normal' professional immigration in many countries would tend to produce this outcome, of course.

[12]In Japan, for example, all college graduates in a company receive almost the same salary until several years after the graduation. If somebody is offered a higher-paid position in a foreign country, it does not follow that the company pays him a higher wage.

Suppose now that the individuals who emigrate are picked up only from the highly-gifted category. Then, with a given number of educated labor, the *marginal* loss to the economy is

$$\lambda F_e'(L_e),$$

while the emigrant before emigration was receiving the weighted *average*,

$$v = \bar{w}_e = \{(1-p)+\lambda p\}F_e'(L_e).$$

Therefore the direct loss to those who remain behind is given from our welfare criterion as follows:

$$v + \frac{\mathrm{d}G}{\mathrm{d}Z} = -\lambda F_e'(L_e) + \bar{w}_e$$

$$= (1-\lambda)(1-p)F_e'(L_e) < 0, \qquad (14)$$

assuming that the number of the educated labor is held constant.

Naturally eq. (14) indicates only the direct impact. When the marginal outflow of highly-gifted labor occurs, however, the vacancy will be filled with new labor with the expected value of productivity equalling $\bar{w}_e$. Moreover, from (1) and (4), the number of educated labor will then increase by

$$\mathrm{d}N_e = \frac{L_0\bar{w}_0}{L_0\bar{w}_0 + L_e\bar{w}_e}\,\mathrm{d}Z,$$

thus imposing on the economy the education cost $k\mathrm{d}N_e$. Therefore, the *total* effect (ruling out other effects such as emulation-induced wage increases) is given by

$$v + \frac{\mathrm{d}G}{\mathrm{d}Z} = -\lambda F_e'(L_e) + 2\bar{w}_e - k\frac{L_0\bar{w}_0}{L_0\bar{w}_0 + L_e\bar{w}_e}$$

$$= \{1-(\lambda-1)(1-2p)\}F_e' - k\frac{L_0\bar{w}_0}{L_0\bar{w}_0 + L_e\bar{w}_e}. \qquad (15)$$

Eq. (15) has no definite sign but it is easy to see that it can quite easily be negative.

It is worth noting that the direct-impact effect in eq. (14) is valid even if we work with a model with flexible wages in both the educated and the uneducated labor markets. Moreover, in an economy equipped with competitive labor market and the amount of education optimally given by the government, eq. (14) will indicate the *total* effect of emigration in such an economy. For, if N_e is determined optimally,

$$\frac{\mathrm{d}G}{\mathrm{d}Z}=\left.\frac{\partial G}{\partial Z}\right|_{N_e:\text{const}}+\frac{\partial G}{\partial N_e}\frac{\mathrm{d}N_e}{\mathrm{d}Z}$$

$$=\left.\frac{\partial G}{\partial Z}\right|_{N_e:\text{const}}=(1-\lambda)(1-p)F_e'<0,$$

by the envelope relationship.

So far we have worked with the assumption that the emigrating labor is necessarily from the highly-gifted category. Suppose now instead that the probability of an emigrant being highly-gifted is q. Then the expected value of the direct impact on the economy is

$$v+\frac{\mathrm{d}G}{\mathrm{d}Z}=\bar{w}_e-\{(1-q)+\lambda q\}F_e'$$

$$=(q-p)(1-\lambda)F_e', \tag{16}$$

which is negative as long as $q > p$. As long as the screening power of brain drain has *some* informational value, i.e., $q > p$, the impact effect is clearly negative.

We have also assumed thus far that the ratio or the probability of highly-gifted labor is independent of the brain drain. Suppose, however, that the probability of an individual turning out to be highly-gifted is related positively to some trait such as the high school grade. Then, the probability of turning out highly-gifted for the *marginal* student who comes into the educational system because of the emigration will be lower than the *average* probability for the educated. In this case, p is a decreasing function of Z, and this factor gives rise to yet further welfare-reducing effects.

In conclusion, we may note the possible dynamic externality aspects involved in the emigration of the highly-gifted. It is possible that such emigration affects, *via* adverse impact on domestic availability of the highly-gifted (who are not inspired and taught into full maturity of their talent in the absence of the senior highly-gifted people), the welfare of those left behind by affecting the ratio p adversely. Thus, suppose that it takes one period to educate the younger generation for skilled labor. Suppose also that $p(t)$ depends on the density of the preceding generation $p(t-1)$ such that

$$p(t)=\alpha+\beta p(t-1) \qquad [\alpha>0,\ 0<\beta<1].$$

Then it is easy to show that if brain drain is occurring every period, affecting

$p(t)$ by δ, the stationary value of p will be reduced by $\beta\delta/(1-\beta)$.[13] Even a once-and-for-all emigration of highly-gifted labor will have a decaying but enduring effect on the future path of $p(t)$.

6. Brain drain and institutional change

It should be clear by now that the welfare effects of the brain drain differ significantly depending on the institutional setting from which labor is emigrating. If the phenomenon of overqualification exists, then the brain drain may work to improve the welfare, provided that we exclude the emulation effect on the wage level of the emigrant class of labor. On the other hand, if the domestic market for the labor is characterized by the internal diffusion process, the brain drain will harm those remaining behind, regardless of whether or not the emulation effect leads to a rise in the wage level. Finally, if emigrants are chosen from the highly-gifted category and are not so identified in the domestic market, then the brain drain could cause a welfare loss even with flexible wage rates.

The institutional setting concerning wage levels and changes therein and informational structure differs from country to country. Even within a country, it must surely differ from occupation to occupation. Risking oversimplification, we might argue that overqualification is likely to occur most with social scientists and (for certain countries, chiefly India) with engineers; the internal diffusion process is most serious for doctors and nurses, and imperfect information is pertinent to scholars and researchers. Therefore, depending on which LDC is being discussed, and which occupation is the object of attention, the analysis of the welfare effects of the brain drain is likely to vary; and a generalized analysis could well be misleading. Our analysis should be taken as an attempt to underline the importance of setting out the nature of institutional rigidities or imperfect information in the labor prior to analyzing the welfare effects of such emigration.

Note finally that our analysis in this paper has proceeded almost exclusively on the assumption that the institutional distortions in the domestic economy of the LDC of emigration are exogenous to the emigration process. The only exception made was for the Bhagwati–Hamada emulation effect: emigration from a class of skilled labor would raise the (sticky) wage of that labor, thus accentuating the sticky-wage distortion in the labor market.

But we can, and indeed must, ask the question whether the emigration process can be expected to influence, and if so in what direction, each of the market imperfections that we have analyzed in this paper. The analysis of the emulation effect in Bhagwati–Hamada (1974), and in the present paper, demonstrates the significance of modelling this kind of linkage into one's theoretical framework. But this can also be seen from at least two other areas of inter-

[13] Even without considering the above-mentioned mechanism of reducing p, p will be immediately reduced by the emigration of highly-gifted because it takes time to replenish highly-gifted labor in the situation considered here.

national economic analysis. Thus, in tariff theory, it is well known that while a domestic monopoly is distortionary, it does not compromise the case for free trade since the introduction of free trade itself can be regarded as destroying the monopoly: the free trade policy is distortion-destroying and hence continues to be optimal. To take the other example, the welfare effect of foreign investment by MNCs (multinational corporations) may be considered in light of its effects on an 'imperfect' domestic entrepreneurship: it may inhibit and stunt its growth or it may encourage it to be competitive and efficient.[14]

In the present context, we must eventually ask questions such as the following, distinguishing in each case between the 'malign impact' and the 'benign impact' hypotheses:

(1) Will the brain drain accentuate a domestic distortion such as a sticky wage (that exceeds the shadow wage as in Bhagwati–Hamada or falls below it as with monopsonistic pricing of a skill such as medicine under a nationalized health service) or will it promote increased flexibility in wage-setting in the country of emigration (as implied by Johnson (1972))?

(2) Will the brain drain, in the presence of unemployment, reduce the possible subsidy to education or will it lead to greater demands for increasing it?

(3) Will the screening function exercised in the brain drain process induce the domestic labor market to do better screening in the future or will it demoralize it into indiscriminate escalation of the entire wage level regardless of differential productivity?

These are all yet additional instances of the unsettled debate among development economists whether international integration into the world economy leads to development in the LDCs or to their domestic disintegration.[15] The issues raised here are not purely economic; they necessarily encompass sociological, political, ethnic and historical facets. Complex as they therefore are, and almost intractable to conventional economic analysis, they are equally necessary to address and resolve if the analysis of the brain drain is to be complete.

[14] For a discussion of these possibilities of 'malign impact' and 'benign impact' models in analyzing MNCs, see Bhagwati (1975).

[15] This phrasing is from Sunkel; see, for example, his long essay (1973) on import substitution.

References

Arrow, K.J., 1973, Higher education as a filter, Journal of Public Economics 2, no. 3.

Berry, R. and R. Soligo, 1969, Some welfare aspects of international migration, Journal of Political Economy, September–October.

Bhagwati, J., 1972, Overqualification, education and welfare: A theoretical analysis, mimeo (M.I.T., Cambridge, MA).

Bhagwati, J., 1975, What we need to know, contributed at the Princeton Conference on International Trade and Finance, March 1973, forthcoming in: Peter Kenen, ed., Volume of papers and proceedings (Cambridge University Press, Cambridge).

Bhagwati, J. and K. Hamada, 1974, The brain drain, international integration of markets for professionals and unemployment: A theoretical analysis, Journal of Developmental Economics 1, no. 1.

Bhagwati, J. and T.N. Srinivasan, 1975, Education in a job-ladder model and the fairness-in-hiring rule, mimeo (M.I.T., Cambridge, MA).

Grubel. H. and A. Scott. 1966. The international flow of human capital, American Economic Review, May.

Johnson, H.G., 1967, Some economic aspects of brain drain, Pakistan Development Review 3.

Johnson, H.G., 1972, Labor mobility and the brain drain, in: G. Ranis, ed., The gap between rich and poor nations (Macmillan, London).

Kenen, P.B., 1971, Migration, the terms of trade and economic welfare in the source country, in: J. Bhagwati et al., eds., Trade, balance of payments and growth (North-Holland, Amsterdam).

Myint, H., 1968, The underdeveloped countries: A less alarmist view, in: W. Adams, ed., The brain drain (Macmillan, New York).

Spence, A.M., 1974, Market signalling: Informational transfer in hiring and related screening processes (Harvard University Press, Cambridge, MA).

Sunkel, O., 1972, Latin American underdevelopment in the year 2000, in: J. Bhagwati, ed., Economics and world order (Macmillan, New York).

Journal of Public Economics 7 (1977) 1–22. © North-Holland Publishing Company

EDUCATION IN A 'JOB LADDER' MODEL AND THE FAIRNESS-IN-HIRING RULE

Jagdish N. BHAGWATI*

Massachusetts Institute of Technology, Cambridge, MA 02139, U.S.A.

T. N. SRINIVASAN*

Indian Statistical Institute, New Delhi 110029, India

Received December 1975, revised version received June 1976

The paper constructs a general equilibrium model of education which is distinguished by a 'job ladder' or sticky wages, combined with the assumption that educated labor is preferred over uneducated labor, i.e. per a 'fairness-in-hiring' rule, when there is excess demand for jobs at given wages. This theory of education, considered to be relevant to liberal arts education in underdeveloped countries, is contrasted with the human capital doctrine and the Arrow–Spence screening theories. The analysis is mainly focused on examining the social inefficiency properties of the educational process captured in the model constructed.

1. Introduction

Education turns a person into a different 'kind' of labor. Any economic analysis of education therefore must be based on a theory as to what this difference consists in; it must *also* presuppose a theory as to how the market for this kind of labor functions. In consequence, any theory of education may be distinguished from others on either of these two dimensions.

In this paper, we propose, and analyze in general equilibrium, a theory of education that in fact differs from the usual theories on both dimensions. To appreciate this, it is useful to distinguish among the different hypotheses about what education does and about how the market for educated labor functions, including in our taxonomy the ideas that we formalize in this paper.

1.1. *What education does*

(1) The most familiar, and indeed the most obvious as also traditional, theory of what education does is that education confers skills which are tanta-

*The research underlying this paper has been supported by National Science Foundation Grant No. SOC74-13210. We have profited from the comments by Marcello Selowsky and other participants in seminars at the World Bank and at Minnesota, and by George Psacharopoulos, Koichi Hamada, Gary Fields and two referees.

mount to 'human capital' formation. This approach has naturally been developed most extensively by the Chicago School.

(2) The radical economists of present U.S. vintage, on the other hand, have advanced the interesting view that the role of education is to 'socialize' the educated, breaking them into productive workers in the capitalist economy. This view leads to no special wrinkles as far as the divergence between social and private returns to education is concerned and, on that dimension, is indistinguishable from the human capital theory.

(3) An alternative view of education has been advanced by Spence (1973) and Arrow (1973). In this view, education imparts neither training nor socialization. Rather, it acts as a filter, screening and grading the educated. Education, in itself, is therefore *not* productive in the sense of imparting skills or socialization to the educated but it does manage to convey the *information* about ability to prospective employers. By acquiring it, therefore, the ones with ability are able to secure better wages; and hence education offers a private return. But clearly a divergence between private and social returns can follow.

(4) An altogether different view of education however can be that it is an instrument for job competition. Imagine a job specification with a certain number of jobs at a wage. If the wage is sticky, an excess supply of labor at that wage cannot be cleared by lowering the wage. Then, the access to these jobs, in a competitive system, could imply a resort to *either* a randomized choice from among the available labor force *or* another method of choice from that labor force which otherwise preserves a sense of *fairness*. Education can then be perceived as an attribute which, when acquired, gives a member of this labor force precisely the attribute which the employer can utilize to prefer him to other (uneducated or lesser-educated) members of the labor force seeking the jobs.[1] The sociological principle of job selection then is to prefer those who are more educated to those who are less: that seems 'fair' as the educated have 'put in more' to get the job, even though the job does not 'require' any education at all for satisfactory performance.[2] The 'fairness' principle of preferring the

[1]An apt example of our fairness-in-hiring rule is provided by the recent hiring of an Accounts Assistant at the Indian Statistical Institute. Although the required educational qualification was stated as high school diploma, the fact of a large number of applicants led the selection commitee to consider only those applicants who had a Bachelor's or Master's Degree. Additional references to such 'casual empiricism' are listed by Fields (1974). In the U.S. context, also see the interesting piece by Thurow (1972).

[2](*i*) The obverse of 'fairness,' of course, is prejudice. Thus, when jobs are rationed or scarce in relation to applicants, one may not hire those whom one is prejudiced against, e.g., blacks may be ruled out from the jobs by white employers. This is discrimination in hiring rather than discrimination in wages.

(*ii*) The fairness-in-hiring notion, developed in this paper, extends also to other phenomena. Thus, men may be hired in preference to women because 'men have to support families' and therefore it is 'fair' to prefer them. This theme has been developed and its similarity to our fairness-in-hiring rule is noted by Desai (1975).

(*iii*) The 'fairness-in-hiring' rule may, in fact, be 'unfair' if those who manage to get educated have better access to educational facilities owing to status or other privilege-creating mechanism.

educated in hiring thus turns education into an instrument of competition for jobs, yielding therefore a divergence between private and social returns to education.[3]

1.2. How the market for educated labor functions

(1) The functioning of the market for educated labor, in the *traditional* neoclassical writings, takes the form of a flexible wage: excess supply of educated labor leads to a reduction in the wage until the market is cleared.

(2) Alternatively, one can postulate that the wage is sticky and that the educated laborer, when in excess supply, spills over into open unemployment (as in standard Keynesian, short-run analysis). The counterpart to this in trade-theoretic literature is the analysis of a generalized sticky wage in general equilibrium, as in Brecher (1974) and Lefeber (1971). Such a clearance of the labor market for educated labor, however, is unsatisfactory, in general equilibrium analysis, as the educated labor force could always seek employment in the uneducated labor market: an idea which we turn to later.

(3) Yet another version of the spillover under the sticky wage is that introduced by Harris and Todaro (1970) where they equate the employment-rate-weighted, 'expected' wage in the sector with unemployment to the 'actual' wage in the sector with full employment in a homogeneous-labor market model for analyzing intersectoral migration. This approach would imply that the excess supply of educated labor would spill over into unemployment, with the 'expected' wage in educated employment then becoming the sticky wage weighted by the jobs as a proportion of the educated labor force. This is a sensible assumption if we think of every member of the educated labor force as having equal, randomized access to the available jobs, i.e. that, in the steady state, everyone is earning the expected wage and is therefore 'underemployed' rather than 'unemployed.' Note that this assumption implies that the *average wage*

[3](i) It may be argued that, in some cases, the 'fairness-in-hiring' rule may only be an indirect proxy for screening for better ability. This is however not necessarily so; and the nonequivalence in reality of the two alternative hypotheses is evident to us from the fact that employers advertise for jobs, specifying lower educational requirements than they 'settle for,' as also from the fact that most educational qualifications have been 'objectively speaking' reduced in terms of their intellectual input anyway, degenerating often into sheer lapse of time, energy and financial resources by the candidate (as with law degrees in India, which are acquired typically *via* diets of capsuled questions and answers).

(ii) Next, we may note that labor market imperfection could also account, in some cases, for the preference for a once-and-for-all upgrading of educational requirements. Thus, if jobs 1 to *n* objectively require increasing qualification but the access to the more-skilled jobs is partly or wholly biased in favor of those who already hold the less-skilled jobs (because of unionized rules giving preference to those already within the organization), then it could well pay the employer to 'overbuild' the skills at the lower end of the job ladder. This argument however explains why the employer may advertise for candidates with greater qualifications than (currently) necessary for a job; it does not really explain why he would advertise for the job with specification of lesser qualifications and then hire those who have more.

to educated labor has indeed been cut but that, unlike with the flexible wage assumption, the cost of hiring to the employer is *not*. We therefore have here a source of inefficiency in the economic system: the method of cutting the wage is inefficient.

(4) Finally, we can stick to the sticky wage assumption and instead assume that if the educated labor force exceeds the jobs for which it is qualified, then the excess supply filters down to the 'next-best' job in the 'job ladder.' Thus the *average* wage of educated labor is again cut in effect: for, it is a weighted average of the 'best' and the 'next-best' wages.

In the model of education that we analyze in this paper, we take the last assumption on how the labor market works (i.e. we take a job ladder model) and we analyze its implications for issues such as: in what way is the system suboptimal *vis-a-vis* a flexible-wage model, would education be overexpanded in such a regime, and how precisely would the private and social marginal product to education diverge?

The job ladder model is reduced to its essential framework by assuming only two noneducational sectors: sector 1 which employs only educated labor and sector 3 which employs, at identical wage, both educated and uneducated labor. Sector 2 employs educated labor as teachers at an exogenously specified student–teacher ratio. The 'job ladder' phenomenon is then introduced by assuming that wage in sectors 1 and 2 is fixed–sticky and that the supply of educated labor in excess of its employment in sectors 1 and 2 then 'spills over' into sector 3.

Now, in section 2, we compare this model with the flexible wage model and with the socially optimum solution, in order to examine its economic implications. This analysis is thus predicated on the assumption that the top rung in the job ladder, sector 1, uses only educated labor because it 'needs' educated labor. Thus, the job ladder model in this section presupposes the use of educated labor, in 'its' sector 1, as 'productive' along the lines of the training models; and our theory of education therefore departs from them essentially in regard to the 'job ladder' assumption: an assumption which leads us to characterize the model equivalently as the 'minimum wage' model.

In section 3, however, we proceed to interpret the job ladder model rather as one where sector 1 employs only educated labor because employers 'prefer' educated to noneducated labor in hiring on the fairness principle: the fourth assumption delineated above under subsection 1.1. Thus both educated and uneducated labor could, in principle, be employed with equal productivity in sector 1 but the educated enjoy preference in hiring. Hence, as long as the educated labor force available for employment in sector 1 exceeds the jobs in sector 1 at the fixed wage, sector 1 will hire only educated labor. Thus, the 'job ladder'–minimum-wage model in section 2 applies equally to the case where the 'fairness' principle in hiring is in force. What does change however is the *comparison* with the flexible wage model and the social optimum. For, in the flexible wage model with the 'fairness' principle, we would now have to allow for the hiring of uneducated labor in sector 1 as well: and, with both kinds of labor equally productive within each of sectors 1 and 3, educated labor supply will fall to zero even if there is no direct or opportunity cost to getting educated.

Note next that we will compare the 'job ladder' (or 'minimum wage') model with the flexible wage model and with the social optimum solution, in each of sections 2 and 3 as already explained, using two alternative devices for handling the education sector: (*i*) that there is a domestic education sector which uses educated labor to produce educated labor; and alternatively, in the Appendix, (*ii*) that education is undertaken with foreign teachers.

Finally, we should note that the 'job ladder *plus* fairness-in-hiring' education theory presented here was described in an earlier draft [cf. Bhagwati (1972)] as the 'overqualification' theory of education – since jobs get upgraded in regard to educational requirements under the process captured by the theory. As it happens, the same theory, in its essence, has been developed independently in an elegant contribution by Fields (1974), who describes the model as a 'bumping' model where the educated displace the uneducated through the preferential hiring phenomenon. The Fields model, which corresponds closely to that earlier developed by us [cf. Bhagwati (1972)], is based on his (1972) thesis and differs from our present analysis in the following respects: (*i*) Fields works with a prespecified number of jobs in alternative markets whereas we formally specify a general equilibrium model where the number of jobs is determined by the specification of the sticky wage; (*ii*) the Fields analysis is in partial equilibrium whereas our model is specified in general equilibrium terms, with commodity prices, the market for production of educated labour, etc., explicitly set out, so that our model is amenable to analysis of familiar issues such as the welfare effects of subsidising or taxing education; and (*iii*) whereas Fields considers the effects of his model for the demand for education in LDCs, our analysis is focused on the precise nature of the breakdown in economic efficiency that such an educational process implies in an economy (though consequences for the size of the educated labour force etc. are also spelled out in the analysis).

2. The 'pure' job ladder model and analysis

We now set out the job ladder model in its different dimensions, describing the production functions, the education sector, the determination of the wage structure, etc. We also describe, in the process, how the model modifies if we instead assume a flexible wage. Recall that we will be interpreting the job ladder in its 'pure' version in section 2 (where sector 1 employs only educated labor because it 'needs' educated labor) and in its 'augmented' version in section 3 (where sector 1 can employ both educated and uneducated labor equally at identical wage but the 'fairness' principle in hiring leads to hiring of only educated labor in sector 1 as long as the supply of educated labor for such employment is not below the jobs available in sector 1).

2.1. The production functions and relative output prices

We set up the following simple two-sector model which enables us to capture the essence of the job ladder phenomenon without bringing in any inessential complications. In sector 1 output is a function $f(L_1^E)$ only of L_1^E, the number of educated laborers employed, the production function being strictly concave with marginal product $f'(L_1^E)$, being positive for all $L_1^E > 0$ and infinite (zero) for $L_1^E = 0$ (∞). (One could, if one wishes, postulate a two-factor production function with the factor other than labor being kept constant). In sector 3, output is a linear function wL of labor employed.[4] (Again, one could, if one wishes, postulate that sector 3 relates to agriculture in a land-abundant economy.) Let as assume that our economy is 'small' and open in the sense that the relative price of output of sector 1 to that of sector 3 is exogenous to it. Without loss of generality we can assume this relative price to be unity.

2.2. The education sector

It is assumed that the only direct costs of education are teaching costs per unit of time per person in school. We consider two alternative ways in which the education sector is organized. In the first version, the education sector is domestic and the teachers are drawn from the pool of the educated labor force, with the teacher–student ratio exogenously specified. The direct cost per student year will then equal the teacher–student ratio times the teacher's wage. In the second version (in the Appendix), the direct cost of education is assumed to be payment for foreign teachers and hence a charge on national income.

2.3. The determination of the wage structure

The wage of an uneducated laborer is set equal to his marginal value product w (in terms of the numeraire, the output of sector 1, given the exogenously-specified relative output price of unity) in the only sector employing him, namely sector 3. In the minimum wage version of the model, the wage of an educated laborer employed in sector 1 is set at $\lambda_1 w (\lambda_1 > 1)$ and that of a teacher in the domestic education sector at $\lambda_2 w (\lambda_1 > \lambda_2 > 1)$. In the flexible wage version of the model, however, the wage of an educated laborer as a worker in sector 1 or as a teacher in the domestic education sector equals his marginal value product in sector 1.

[4]The assumption that educated and uneducated labor in sector 3 have the same productivity is, of course, the essence of our model. Remember that, as with all theory, we are building a 'stylized' model that focuses on one central idea. In reality, it may well be that, in certain sectors, the employment of educated labor, in the long run, may wind up causing unanticipated productivity gains or that the employment of such labor in upgraded jobs may even cause *loss* of productivity due to inaptitude—could a Nobel Laureate in Economics sweep the streets well?—or discontent at the desk.

2.4. The determination of the size of the educated labor force

The size of the educated labor force is determined such that, for an educated worker, the present value of his income stream net of any educational costs charged to him during his period of education equals the present value of his income stream had he not educated himself but was employed in sector 3 throughout his working life. More precisely, let the working life of a worker be T periods, of which the first t periods are spent in school if he chooses to educate himself. Let the nonnegative rate of discount be r. Let c be the educational costs charged to the worker per each period in school. Let $\bar{w}$ be the wage per period of an educated worker. Then,

$$-c\int_0^t e^{-r\tau}\,d\tau+\bar{w}\int_t^T e^{-r\tau}\,d\tau = w\int_0^T e^{-r\tau}\,d\tau. \tag{1}$$

Denoting by γ the ratio of $\int_t^T e^{-r\tau}\,d\tau$ to $\int_0^T e^{-r\tau}\,d\tau$, we have

$$\gamma\bar{w} = w+(1-\gamma)c. \tag{1'}$$

In the flexible wage model, entrepreneurs in sector 1 will then equate the marginal product of labor in that sector to $\bar{w}$. In the minimum wage model, $\bar{w}$ will further equal the weighted average of the wages in sectors 1, 2 and 3, with the weights equalling the proportion of the educated labor force employed in each of these sectors respectively. However, in determining c, we will allow for situations in which c differs from the direct costs of education as, for instance, in the case where the state subsidizes in full or partially the costs of education.

2.5. The steady state

Except for some brief remarks later, we shall be concerned mainly with comparison of steady states and not with the dynamic approach to the steady state. In the steady state it will be assumed that the total labor force is set at unity by choice of units and a portion L^E of the labor force is educated. Given that the working life of a person is T periods, of which t periods are spent in school in the case of an educated worker, it is clear that the number of persons in school in a steady state is $(t/(T-t))L^E$. Let us denote the fraction $(t/(T-t))$ by δ. Hence the number of students in a steady state is δL^E. Denoting by ε the teacher–student ratio in the domestic education sector, it follows that the number of teachers in a steady state is $\varepsilon\delta L^E$. Since the employment of educated workers in sector 1 is L_1^E, the number of workers employed in sector 3 will therefore equal $[1-L_1^E-(1+\varepsilon)\delta L^E]$ in the case of the domestic education sector (and $[1-L_1^E-\delta L^E]$ in the case where teachers are foreign).

2.6. Equilibrium

We discuss at length only the case in which there is a domestic education sector. As noted already, the case in which the teachers are foreign is briefly discussed in the Appendix.

Note that the size of the total labor force is given and normalized at unity and that the employment in the domestic education sector is determined once the size of the educated labor force is determined because of our assumptions of a fixed student–teacher ratio and a steady state. Hence, the equilibrium values of only two variables, namely the size L^{E} of the educated labor force and the part of it, L_1^{E}, that is employed in sector 1, are to be determined. We have also two equations: one that equates the marginal value product of labor in sector 1 to the relevant wage rate thus determining the level of employment in that sector, and eq. (1′) determining the size of the educated labor force.

Finally, the job ladder or equivalently the minimum wage model (with superscript M) will be distinguished from the flexible wage model (with superscript F) in the determination of wage rate in sector 1. We therefore proceed now to discuss these two alternative models in detail.

2.6.1. The job ladder or minimum wage model

Here the employment L_1^{EM} in sector 1 is determined, given the wage $\lambda_1 w$ and the production function f, through the following marginal productivity equation:

$$f'(L_1^{\mathrm{EM}}) = \lambda_1 w \quad \text{or} \quad L_1^{\mathrm{EM}} = g(\lambda_1 w), \tag{2}$$

where $g(\cdot)$ is the inverse function f'. Given our assumptions on f, $g(\cdot)$ is a decreasing function of its argument with $g(0) = \infty$ and $g(\infty) = 0$.

A part of the educated labor force, $\varepsilon\delta L^{\mathrm{EM}}$, is employed as teachers at a wage rate $\lambda_2 w$ in sector 2 in the steady state. This means that the expected wage rate $\bar{w}$ of an educated worker is a weighted average of the wage rates $\lambda_1 w$, $\lambda_2 w$ and w in the sectors 1, 2 and 3 respectively, with weights $L_1^{\mathrm{EM}}/L^{\mathrm{EM}}$, $\varepsilon\delta$ and $[1-\varepsilon\delta-(L_1^{\mathrm{EM}}/L^{\mathrm{EM}})]$. Hence, in this case, (1′) becomes

$$\gamma w\left(\frac{\lambda_1 L_1^{\mathrm{EM}} + \lambda_2 \varepsilon\delta L^{\mathrm{EM}} + (1-\varepsilon\delta)L^{\mathrm{EM}} - L_1^{\mathrm{EM}}}{L^{\mathrm{EM}}}\right) = w + (1-\gamma)c\,. \tag{3}$$

This yields

$$L^{\mathrm{EM}} = \frac{\gamma(\lambda_1 - 1)wL_1^{\mathrm{EM}}}{(1-\gamma)(w+c) - \gamma w(\lambda_2 - 1)\varepsilon\delta}\,. \tag{3'}$$

This equilibrium solution is meaningful provided $(1-\varepsilon\delta)L^{\mathrm{EM}} \geqq L_1^{\mathrm{EM}}$, i.e. the size of the educated labor force net of teachers is at least as large as the employment in sector 1, and $(1+\delta)L^{EM} \leqq 1$, i.e. the educated labor force and the student body does not exhaust the total labor force. The first condition will be satisfied provided:

$$(1-\gamma)(w+c)-\gamma w(\lambda_2-1)\varepsilon\delta \geqq 0 \tag{4}$$

or

$$w+(1-\gamma)c \geqq \gamma w[\lambda_2\varepsilon\delta+(1-\varepsilon\delta)], \tag{4'}$$

and

$$\gamma w(\lambda_1-1)(1-\varepsilon\delta) \geqq (1-\gamma)(w+c)-\gamma w(\lambda_2-1)\varepsilon\delta \tag{5}$$

or

$$\gamma w[\lambda_1(1-\varepsilon\delta)+\lambda_2\varepsilon\delta] \geqq w+(1-\gamma)c. \tag{5'}$$

Now, the LHS of (4′) which is the same as the RHS of (5′), $[w+(1-\gamma)c]$, is the opportunity cost (but for a multiplicative factor of $\int_0^T e^{-r\tau}\,d\tau$) of education including the discounted sum of income foregone and tuition charges. The RHS of (4′) is the discounted sum (but for the same factor) of the expected income of an educated worker when no educated worker is employed in the highest-paying sector 1. Inequality (4′) thus ensures that it is not worthwhile to educate oneself if the job opportunity outside sector 3 consists of a teaching job! On the other hand, the LHS of (5′) is the discounted sum of the expected income of an educated worker when no educated worker is employed in the lowest-paying sector 3. Thus (5′) ensures that this sum is not below the opportunity cost of education. Thus (4′) and (5′) together ensure that the opportunity cost of education lies between the minimum expected income of an educated worker (when none of them is employed in sector 1) and the maximum expected income (when none of them is employed in sector 3).

Finally, the welfare measure W for comparing the outcomes of different models will be the value of output of sectors 1 and 3 (except in the Appendix when teachers are foreign, in which case the payments to them have to be subtracted). Essentially, therefore, we are placing no value on education as a consumption good. Thus:

$$W^M = f(L_1^{EM})+w[1-L_1^{EM}-(1+\varepsilon)\delta L^{EM}]. \tag{6}$$

2.6.2. The flexible wage model

Turning now to the flexible wage model, we note that there can no longer be any difference in the wages of an educated worker by sector of employment.

Nor can there be any spillover of educated workers into employment in sector 3. Thus, in this model:

$$L_1^{EF} = (1-\varepsilon\delta)L^{EF}, \tag{7}$$

$$L_2^{EF} = \varepsilon\delta L^{EF}, \tag{8}$$

$$L_3^{EF} = 0. \tag{9}$$

The size of the educated labor force L^{EF} is determined by (1′), with $\bar{w}$ satisfying

$$f'(L_1^{EF}) = \bar{w}. \tag{10}$$

Substituting (10) in (1′), we get

$$rf'(L_1^{EF}) = w+(1-\gamma)c, \tag{11}$$

or

$$L_1^{EF} = g\left(\frac{w+(1-\gamma)c}{\gamma}\right). \tag{11′}$$

This solution is clearly meaningful provided

$$1 \geqq \left(\frac{1+\delta}{1-\varepsilon\delta}\right) L_1^{EF} \geqq 0\,,$$

i.e. the educated labor force together with the student body does not exceed the total labor force.

The welfare level attained in this model is given by

$$W^F = f(L_1^{EF})+w[1-(1+\delta)L^{EF}]. \tag{12}$$

2.6.3. The social optimum model

In this model, the size of the educated force L^{ES} is so chosen as to maximize welfare, i.e. such that L^{ES} maximizes $f\{(1-\varepsilon\delta)L\}+w\{1-(1+\delta)L\}$ with respect to L.

In defining this maximand, we have implicitly taken into account the fact that all educated workers are used either as teachers or as production workers in sector 1 and that, given L educated workers, $\varepsilon\delta L$ have to be employed as teachers (since there will be δL students in school). Thus the employment in sector 1 is $(1-\varepsilon\delta)L$ and, in sector 3, it is $\{1-(1+\delta)L\}$.

Maximization of the above function leads to the first-order condition:

$$f'\{(1-\varepsilon\delta)L^{ES}\} = \frac{w(1+\delta)}{1-\varepsilon\delta}, \tag{13}$$

or

$$L^{ES} = \frac{g\left(\dfrac{w(1+\delta)}{1-\varepsilon\delta}\right)}{1-\varepsilon\delta}. \tag{13'}$$

It is easy to interpret (13). The LHS represents the marginal social product of an educated worker. The RHS represents the marginal social cost (in terms of output foregone in sector (3) of adding one more person to employment in sector 1: this is so because maintaining one more educated person employed in sector 1 involves, in the steady state, withdrawing this person from sector 3 *and* in addition $[\delta+\delta(\varepsilon\delta)+\delta(\varepsilon\delta)^2\ldots] = \delta/(1-\varepsilon\delta)$ students as well as $[\varepsilon\delta+(\varepsilon\delta)^2+\ldots] = \varepsilon\delta/(1-\varepsilon\delta)$ teachers. These persons,

$$1+\frac{\delta}{1-\varepsilon\delta}+\frac{\varepsilon\delta}{1-\varepsilon\delta} = \frac{1+\delta}{1-\varepsilon\delta},$$

would have produced $w(1+\delta)/(1-\varepsilon\delta)$ in sector 3.

Finally, it is clear that the welfare level attained in this model is

$$W^S = f\{(1-\varepsilon\delta)L^{ES}\}+w\{1-(1+\delta)L^{ES}\}. \tag{14}$$

2.7. The comparison of steady states

We will now compare the steady state outcomes of the job ladder model with those of the flexible wage model on the one hand, and the latter with those of the social optimum model on the other. The variables whose values will be compared are: employment in sector 1, the size of the educated labor force, private and social marginal products of education, welfare levels, and the share of the educated labor force in total wage income.

2.7.1. The employment in sector 1

(A) Minimum vs. flexible wages. Comparing the minimum wage and flexible wage models, it is easy to see from (2) and (11′) that $L_1^{EM} \leqq L_1^{EF}$. This is because $g(\cdot)$ is a decreasing function and $\lambda_1 w \geqq w[\lambda_1(1-\varepsilon\delta)+\lambda_2\varepsilon\delta] \geqq (w+(1-\gamma)c)/\gamma$ in view of $\lambda_1 \geqq \lambda_2$ and (5′). Thus the flexible wage model leads to equal or higher employment level in sector 1 than the minimum wage model.

(*B*) *Flexible wage vs. social optimum.* Furthermore, comparing the flexible wage with the social optimum models, we see from (11′) and (13) that

$$L_1^{\mathrm{EF}} \gtreqqless L_1^{\mathrm{ES}} = (1-\varepsilon\delta)L^{\mathrm{ES}},$$

according as

$$\frac{w+(1-\gamma)c}{\gamma} \lesseqqgtr \frac{w(1+\delta)}{1-\varepsilon\delta}. \tag{15}$$

Rewriting (15) slightly differently, we get:

$$L_1^{\mathrm{EF}} \gtreqqless L_1^{\mathrm{ES}}$$

according as

$$\frac{w}{\gamma}+c\left(\frac{1-\gamma}{\gamma}\right) \lesseqqgtr w(1+\delta)+\varepsilon\left(\frac{w(1+\delta)}{1-\varepsilon\delta}\right)\delta. \tag{15′}$$

Now, it can be easily shown that for nonnegative discount rates r, $1/\gamma \geqq (1+\delta)$ and $(1-\gamma)/\gamma \geqq \delta$ with equality holding only for a zero discount rate. Note also that $\varepsilon[w(1+\delta)/(1-\varepsilon\delta)]$ is the social cost of schooling per student year, being the product of the teacher–student ratio ε and the social wage of the teacher, $w(1+\delta)/(1-\varepsilon\delta)$.

It is evident, therefore, that as long as a student is charged at least as much as it costs socially to educate him,[5] employment in sector 1 under a flexible wage model will not exceed the socially optimal level. This conclusion will hold even if the charge is below social cost, *provided* the private discount rate is sufficiently high. Of course, the two employment levels will be the same if either (*i*) the students are charged the social cost of education *and* the private discount rate is zero (as is the implicit social discount rate) or (ii) students are charged less than the social cost of education but the private discount rate is suitably high. The flexible wage model will lead to overemployment in sector 1 (i.e. to greater employment than is socially desirable) only if students are charged less than the social cost of education and the private discount rate is sufficiently low.

A perhaps more illuminating way of illustrating the effect of private discount rate and the fee charged to students is to note that if the education sector itself is privately organized with no subsidies or taxes from the state, the students will have to pay the direct cost of their education, namely, the product of the teacher–student ratio ε and the wage of a teacher. In the flexible wage model the

[5]It would seem that the most prevalent situation is one where students are charged substantially less than the social cost of the education they receive.

latter equals the wage of an educated worker in sector 1, which in turn equals the marginal value product of labor in that sector. Hence we have

$$\gamma f'(L_1^{EF}) = w + (1-\gamma)\varepsilon f'(L_1^{EF}),$$

or

$$L_1^{EF} = g\left(\frac{w}{\gamma - (1-\gamma)\varepsilon}\right).$$

Comparing this value of L_1^{EF} with L_1^{ES}, we note the two will be equal when $\gamma = 1/(1+\delta)$. And γ will equal $1/(1+\delta)$ when the private discount rate is zero, and will be less than $1/(1+\delta)$ when the private discount rate is positive, resulting in L_1^{EF} being less than L_1^{ES}. Thus, the fact that individuals have a positive time preference, while our implicit social rate of time preference is zero, leads to an underexpansion of the education sector in the flexible wage model even if the students pay the full market cost of education. A subsidy towards educational costs will be needed to reach the social optimum in such a situation.

(*C*) *Minimum wage vs. social optimum.* Our third and final comparison of the minimum wage and the social optimum models in respect to employment in sector 1, on the other hand, is straightforward. As long as the minimum wage in sector 1, namely $\lambda_1 w$, is greater (less) than the social product of labor $w(1+\delta)/(1-\varepsilon\delta)$, then L_1^{EM} will be less (greater) than L_1^{ES}.

2.7.2. *The size of the total educated labor force*

(*A*) *Minimum vs. flexible wages.* Again, we begin by comparing the minimum wage and flexible wage models. We first note that, from (3′) and (7),

$$L^{EM} = \theta L_1^{EM},$$

where

$$\theta = \frac{\gamma(\lambda_1 - 1)w}{(1-\gamma)(w+c) - \gamma w(\lambda_2 - 1)\varepsilon\delta},$$

and

$$L^{EF} = \frac{1}{1-\varepsilon\delta} L_1^{EF}.$$

Now, it will be apparent from our earlier analysis that if we set $\lambda_1 w = (w + (1-\gamma)c)/\gamma$, then $L_1^{EM} = L_1^{EF}$, i.e. if the minimum wage in sector 1 is set just equal to what it would have been under a flexible wage model, the employment in sector 1 would have been the same in the two cases. However, as is to be expected, for this to be feasible in the minimum wage model, the teachers also have to be paid the same wage, i.e. $\lambda_2 = \lambda_1$. (For, if $\lambda_2 < \lambda_1$, then

B

(5′) will be violated.) Then, given $\lambda_1 w = \lambda_2 w = (w+(1-\gamma)c)/\gamma$, it follows that $\theta = 1/(1-\varepsilon\delta)$ as well. Hence $L^{EM} = L^{EF}$.

Suppose next that λ_2 is now left unchanged while λ_1 is increased. It is clear then that, as λ_1 is increased, employment L_1^{EM} in sector 1 decreases. However, θ increases with λ_1. Hence, θ will exceed $1/(1-\varepsilon\delta)$ and it is therefore possible that L^{EM} could exceed L^{EF} because of this factor. We can, however, say more than this. Thus, writing $L^{EM} = \theta g(\lambda_1 w)$, we get

$$\frac{\mathrm{d}L^{EM}}{\mathrm{d}\lambda_1} = \frac{L^{EM}}{\lambda_1 - 1}\left(1+\frac{\lambda_1-1}{\lambda_1}(\lambda_1 w)\frac{g'}{g}\right)$$

$$= \frac{L^{EM}}{\lambda_1 - 1}\left(1+\frac{\lambda_1-1}{\lambda_1}\eta\right),$$

where η is the elasticity of employment with respect to the wage rate in sector 1. If this (negative) elasticity is less (greater) in absolute value than $\lambda_1/(\lambda_1-1)$, then L^{EM} will increase (decrease) as λ_1 increases. Thus we conclude that if the demand for labor in sector 1 is not very elastic with respect to the wage rate, the minimum wage model will lead to a *larger* educated labor force than the flexible wage model in the case where the specified minimum wage in sector 1 exceeds that under the flexible wage.

So far, in our comparison of the two models, we have kept the wages of teachers fixed at the value they take in the flexible wage model. Now, continue keeping $\lambda_1 w$ (the minimum wage in sector 1) fixed at some value higher than its level in the flexible wage model, but increase λ_2. Since λ_2 does not affect L_1^{EM}, and an increase of λ_2 increases θ, L^{EM} will increase. Thus, in the case where the demand for labor in sector 1 is not very elastic with respect to the wage rate, increasing λ_1 and λ_2 works in the *same* direction and results in increasing L^{EM} *above* L^{EF}. However, if the demand for labor in sector 1 is sufficiently elastic, we will have two opposing effects: while the increase in λ_1 will push L^{EM} below L^{EF}, a simultaneous increase in λ_2 will raise L^{EM}. The net result could then clearly go either way.

(B) Flexible wage vs. social optimum. Next, since $L_1^{EF} = (1-\varepsilon\delta)L^{EF}$ and $L_1^{ES} = (1-\varepsilon\delta)L^{ES}$, our earlier comparison of L_1^{EF} and L_1^{ES} is equivalent to comparing L^{EF} and L^{ES}, and therefore we do not repeat our analysis.

(C) Minimum wage vs. social optimum. The comparison of L^{ES} with $L^{EM}(=\theta L_1^{EM})$ is similar to the comparison of L^{EF} and L^{EM}, as we now show.

Suppose that the social wage $w(1+\delta)/(1-\varepsilon\delta)$ is less than $(w+(1-\gamma)c)/\gamma$. In this case, clearly (3) cannot be satisfied if $\lambda_2 w \leqq \lambda_1 w \leqq w(1+\delta)/(1-\varepsilon\delta)$ – as such, a minimum wage equilibrium cannot exist. If we now raise λ_1, so that

$\lambda_1 w$ exceeds $w(1+\delta)/(1-\varepsilon\delta)$, such that a minimum wage equilibrium does exist, L_1^{EM} will fall below L_1^{ES} while θ will exceed $1/(1-\varepsilon\delta)$. Again, the elasticity of demand for labor in sector 1 will then determine what happens to L^{EM}.

Suppose instead that the social wage $w(1+\delta)/(1-\varepsilon\delta)$ equals $(w+(1-\gamma)c)/\gamma$. If we now set $\lambda_1 w = \lambda_2 w = w(1+\delta)/(1-\varepsilon\delta)$, the minimum wage equilibrium is naturally identical to the social optimum one. Again, elasticity considerations will determine whether L^{EM} will exceed or fall short of L^{ES} as λ_1, and λ_2, are increased from this common value.

The interested readers can readily work out the results for the third case where $w(1+\delta)/(1-\varepsilon\delta)$ exceeds $(w+(1-\gamma)c)/\gamma$.

2.7.3. *The marginal product of education*

In our model, there is no possibility of varying 'education' at the margin, since the activity of education consists in spending a fixed 't' periods of one's lifetime in school. There are, however, a number of ways in which one can evaluate the contribution of education to an individual as well as to society. The first approach, a flow approach, is to attribute to education the difference in the wage of the educated laborer and that of an uneducated laborer, in the alternative models (flexible wage, minimum wage and social optimum). The second approach, a stock approach, is to attribute to education the difference in the sum of discounted earnings of an educated laborer and that of an uneducated laborer over their lifetime or (what is the same thing) over the period of lifetime after schooling. Since the lifetime as well as the schooling periods are the same in all models and since we are comparing steady states, the flow and stock approaches will lead to *identical* results with respect to the difference between private and social returns to education, *provided* the same rate of discount is applied in all cases. This is so because the stock return is a multiple of the flow return, the multiplication factor depending only on the discount rate, the length of schooling and the span of life. However, as we will see below, if we apply the private discount rate (presumed positive) in models other than the social optimum, and the implicit social discount rate of zero to the social optimum model, the stock and flow approaches could lead to different results.

Under the *flow* approach, the *private* marginal product of education is the difference between the wage $\bar{w}$ that an educated laborer expects to earn and the wage of an uneducated laborer. In both the minimum wage and the flexible wage models this is the same and equals

$$\frac{w+(1-\gamma)c}{\gamma} - w = \left(\frac{1-\gamma}{\gamma}\right)(w+c).$$

The *social* marginal product of education, on the other hand, is the difference between the wage of an educated laborer and an uneducated one in the social optimum. This equals $w(1+\delta)/(1-\varepsilon\delta)-w$.

The difference between the private and social marginal product of education thus equals

$$\left(\frac{w+(1-\gamma)c}{\gamma}-\frac{w(1+\delta)}{1-\varepsilon\delta}\right).$$

The factors influencing this difference have already been discussed in section 2.7.1.

It is also possible to compute a 'second-best' social marginal product to education in the following way. Suppose one more person is educated: what would be his net addition to output? In the minimum wage model, this will be zero as long as there are educated workers employed in sector 3, whereas in the flexible wage model it will equal the private marginal product to education.

Turning now to the *stock* approach, the difference in the discounted sum of lifetime earnings of an educated worker and that of an uneducated worker equals

$$\bar{w}\textstyle\int_t^T e^{-r\tau}d\tau - w\int_t^T e^{-r\tau}d\tau = (\bar{w}-w)\int_t^T e^{-r\tau}d\tau - w\int_0^t e^{-r\tau}d\tau.$$

Now, $\bar{w}$ equals $(w+(1-\gamma)c)/\gamma$ in the flexible (or minimum) wage model and $w(1+\delta)/(1-\varepsilon\delta)$ in the social optimum model. It is seen from the above that if we apply the same discount rate r, the comparison of returns to education in the flexible (or minimum) wage model to that in the social optimum model reduces to a comparison of $\bar{w}$ with w, as in the flow approach. Suppose, instead, we were to apply the positive private discount rate r to the flexible and minimum wage models and the implicit social discount rate of zero in the social optimum model. It can then be verified that the private (stock) return to education in the flexible and minimum wage models is $c\int_0^t e^{-r\tau}d\tau$, as it should be, since in equilibrium the discounted excess earnings of an educated worker equal the discounted private cost of education. The corresponding figure in the social optimum model is $\bar{w}(T-t)-wT$, where $\bar{w}=w(1+\delta)/(1-\varepsilon\delta)$, or $[w(1+\delta)/(1-\varepsilon\delta)]t$, this being the direct cost of education (the teacher–student ratio (ε) multiplied into the wage of a teacher $w(1+\delta)/(1-\varepsilon\delta)$ and the period of schooling, t). For any $r>0$, t exceeds $\int_0^t e^{-r\tau}d\tau$. Hence if the charge levied, c, is not larger than the social cost $w\varepsilon(1+\delta)/(1-\varepsilon\delta)$ per student year, the stock return to education will be necessarily higher in the social optimum than in the flexible and the minimum wage models.

2.7.4. The welfare levels

It is obvious that the welfare level W^S attained in the case of the social optimum model is the maximum attainable, and as such exceeds W^F and W^M, the welfare levels attained in the case of flexible and minimum wage models.[6] It only remains to compare W^{F} and W^{M}.

Now

$$(W^{\mathrm{F}}-W^{\mathrm{M}}) = f(L_1^{\mathrm{EF}})+w\left(1-\frac{1+\delta}{1-\varepsilon\delta}L_1^{\mathrm{EF}}\right)-f(L_1^{\mathrm{EM}})$$

$$-w(1-\delta(1+\varepsilon)\theta L_1^{\mathrm{EM}}-L_1^{\mathrm{EM}}),$$

where θ (as defined earlier) equals $\gamma(\lambda_1-1)w/[(1-\gamma)(w+c)-\gamma(\lambda_2-1)w]$. And, using the concavity of f, we get

$$(W^{\mathrm{F}}-W^{\mathrm{M}}) \geqq f'(L_1^{\mathrm{EF}})(L_1^{\mathrm{EF}}-L_1^{\mathrm{EM}})$$

$$-w\left(\frac{1+\delta}{1-\varepsilon\delta}L_1^{\mathrm{EF}}-\delta(1+\varepsilon)\theta L_1^{\mathrm{EM}}-L_1^{\mathrm{EM}}\right)$$

$$\geqq \left(f'(L_1^{\mathrm{EF}})-\frac{w(1+\delta)}{(1-\varepsilon\delta)}\right)(L_1^{\mathrm{EF}}-L_1^{\mathrm{EM}})$$

$$+\left(\theta-\frac{1}{1-\varepsilon\delta}\right)\delta(1+\varepsilon)L_1^{\mathrm{EM}}. \tag{16}$$

Now, we have already shown that $L_1^{\mathrm{EF}} \geqq L_1^{\mathrm{EM}}$ and $\theta > 1/(1-\varepsilon\delta)$. Now $f'(L_1^{\mathrm{EF}}) = (w+(1-\gamma)c)/\gamma$ and, as discussed earlier, will exceed the social wage rate $w(1+\delta)/(1-\varepsilon\delta)$ as long as the students are charged at least what it costs society to educate them and the private discount rates are positive.[7] Hence, in these cases, $W^{\mathrm{F}} > W^{\mathrm{M}}$: the flexible wage model leads to higher welfare than the minimum wage model.

[6]The difference between W^{S} and W^{F} arises only because of the difference in private and social cost of education. This difference is due to two factors, as we have seen earlier: (*i*) the difference between c, the cost borne by the student, and the direct cost of teaching him; and (*ii*) the fact that private discount rate is positive while the implicit social discount rate is zero. Hence, if the student pays his cost of education and the private discount rate is also zero, W^{S} and W^{F} will be equal. However, if the private discount rate is positive, then c has to be sufficiently less than the cost of education to bring about an equality between W^{S} and W^{F}.

Incidentally, it may be worth noting that if we treat c, the tuition fee per student, as a policy parameter, increasing it will improve welfare in the minimum wage model by reducing the incentive to get educated even though some educated workers are employed in sector 3. In the flexible wage model, increasing c will improve welfare only if the education sector is overexpanded relative to the social optimum.

[7]In fact, as we argued, even if the students are charged less, this result holds provided discount rates are sufficiently high.

2.7.5. The share of educated labor in wage income[8]

We finally turn to the income distributional implications of our educational model. The share α^i of educated labor in total wage income can be written as

$$\alpha^i = \frac{\bar{w}^i L^{Ei}}{\bar{w}^i L^{Ei} + w[1-(1+\delta)L^{Ei}]}, \qquad i = \mathrm{M, F, S},$$

where $\bar{w}^i$ is the expected wage of an educated worker. In the flexible wage and social optimum models $\bar{w}^i$ equals the actual wage of an educated worker (in sector 1 or sector 2), while in the minimum wage model it equals the weighted average of the wage rate $\lambda_1 w$ in sector 1, $\lambda_2 w$ in sector 2, and w in sector 3. However, the private optimization decision regarding education ensures that this expected wage is the same in the minimum and flexible wage models.

(*A*) *Minimum vs. flexible wages.* Hence, we can conclude that $\alpha^F \gtreqless \alpha^M$ according as $L^{EF} \gtreqless L^{EM}$, i.e. according to whether the size of the educated labor force under a flexible wage model exceeds, equals, or falls short of that under the minimum wage model: conditions determining the latter having been already discussed earlier under section 2.7.2.

(*B*) *Flexible wage vs. social optimum.* As for the comparison of α^F and α^S, however, it is clear that $\alpha^F \gtreqless \alpha^S$ according as $\bar{w}^F L^{EF} \gtreqless \bar{w}^S L^{ES}$. Since $L^{EF} = [1/(1-\varepsilon\delta)]L_1^{EF}$ and $L^{ES} = [1/(1-\varepsilon\delta)]L_1^{ES}$, it follows that $\alpha^F \gtreqless \alpha^S$ according to whether the labor income in sector 1 under a flexible wage model exceeds, equals, or falls short of that under the social optimum model. Clearly the answer depends in an obvious way on the elasticity of demand for labor with respect to the wage rate in sector 1.

(*C*) *Minimum wage vs. social optimum.* Finally, the comparison of α^M and α^S leads to the similar conclusion that $\alpha^M \gtreqless \alpha^S$ according as $\bar{w}^M L^{EM} \gtreqless \bar{w}^S L^{ES}$. In this case, however, we have $L^{EM} = \theta L_1^{EM}$, $L^{ES} = [1/(1-\varepsilon\delta)]L_1^{ES}$ and $\theta \geqq 1/(1-\varepsilon\delta)$. Thus, in addition to the elasticity discussed above (for the α^F–α^S comparison), the factor θ has to be taken into account in determining the behavior of the shares. For instance, if the expected wage $\bar{w}^M$ exceeds $\bar{w}^S$ and the demand for labor in sector 1 is inelastic with respect to wage rate, then we will find that $\alpha^M > \alpha^S$, i.e. the share of educated labor in the minimum wage model will exceed that in the social optimum model.

[8]Income distributional questions have not been formally investigated in all theories of education, although the different views regarding education have led to fragmentary remarks and empirical work, as in Bhagwati (1973b). However, for a systematic treatment, using the human-capital approach, see Dasgupta (1975), and for an analysis in the screening framework, see Stiglitz (1975).

2.8. The approach to steady states

We now briefly discuss the approach to steady states. If one postulates the simple and natural adjustment mechanism that the rate of change of the size of the educated labor force is proportional to the difference between the expected lifetime discounted income (net of costs of education) of an educated worker and that of an uneducated worker, then it is easy to see that the steady states postulated in the earlier sections are reached asymptotically if the economy is not initially in the steady state, *provided* a steady state exists. The crucial equations to examine in this connection are (3) under the minimum wage situation and (11) under the flexible wage situation.

It is then immediately obvious that, with our assumptions on the production functions, a unique solution for L^{EF} exists in the *flexible* wage model. Provided this unique solution does not exceed the available total labor force net of teachers and students, it is also the unique steady state solution that is approached asymptotically. However, under the *minimum* wage situation, if $\gamma = 1$ (i.e. education requires no time) *and* $c = 0$ (i.e. students are charged nothing for their education), the LHS of (3) will always exceed the corresponding RHS as long as there is at least one educated worker.[9] Thus the process of education goes on until *all* workers are educated. Thus *either* $\gamma < 1$ (i.e. education requires time or equivalently the opportunity cost in terms of income foregone is positive) *or* $c > 0$ (i.e. some of the direct cost of education is passed on to the students) is a *necessary* condition for the existence of a steady state. Of course, these (γ or c or a combination thereof) have to be sufficiently high if we are to preclude the situation in which the education process ends up with everyone educated.

3. Education as a competitive instrument: 'Fairness-in-hiring' in the job ladder model

If we now interpret the sole employment of educated labor in sector 1 as attributable to the 'fairness-in-hiring' principle, the analysis of the job ladder (i.e. minimum wage) equilibrium is not altered. However, we can no longer analyze the equilibrium in the flexible wage and social optimum models as in section 2.

Now that educated and uneducated labor are perfect substitutes for each other in sector 1 *as well as* sector 3, but education has resource costs, the size of the educated labor force will fall to zero in both the flexible wage and social optimum models, and thus together with it the employment opportunities for teachers! This means that in *both* these situations, the allocation of the labor

[9] To be exact, we assume that, if initially the size of the total educated labor force is less than L_1^{EM} (this latter being the level of employment in sector 1 when the marginal product equals the minimum wage), then each educated worker receives a wage which exceeds $\lambda_1 w$.

force between sectors 1 and 2 will be such as to equate the marginal value productivity of labor in the two sectors. Thus $L_1^S = L_1^F$ and $f'(L_1^S) = w$. The rest of the labor force, namely $(1-L^S)$, will be employed in sector 3.

The welfare level in this case is $W^S = f(L_1)+w[1-L_1]$. It is trivially obvious that this exceeds W^M, the welfare under the minimum wage model, for

$$W^S - W^M = f(L_1^S)+w[1-L_1^S]-f(L_1^M)-w[1-L_1^M-(1+\varepsilon)\delta\theta L_1^M \quad (17)$$

$$\geqq f'(L_1^S)[L_1^S-L_1^M]-w[L_1^S-L_1^M(1+\varepsilon)\delta\theta L_1^M] \quad (17')$$

$$\geqq w(1+\varepsilon)\delta\theta L_1^M \geqq 0, \quad (\text{since } f'(L_1^S) = w). \quad (17'')$$

Thus, as is to be expected, when education has no productivity, the minimum wage model with the fairness-in-hiring rule necessarily leads to a wasteful creation of an educated labor force.

4. Concluding remarks

In the foregone analysis, we have provided a general equilibrium analysis of a model of education in a job ladder model, with and without the fairness-in-hiring rule.[10] The analysis has embraced positive aspects, as also efficiency and income-distributional implications.

The job ladder model *with* the fairness-in-hiring rule, as depicted in section 3, represents the 'pure' version of our theory, emasculating education of *all* productivity connotation of the human-capital or socialization variety. Hence it is the 'ideal' version to be compared with the alternative theories of education in their idealized versions. In particular, the contrast with the Arrow–Spence screening theory, which also departs from the productivity principle, should be noted.

Next, note that the analysis can be readily extended to cover the effects of alternative policy interventions in our job ladder model of the economy. In particular, we should remark in conclusion that the policy instrument to counter the fairness-in-hiring rule (whose inefficiency has been precisely modelled in section 3) is to ensure selection processes which eliminate the use of (excess) educational attainment as a hiring criterion. One way in which this can be done is to ensure randomized access by all qualified *and* overqualified applicants through the use of a lottery system.[11] Note however that this would be a second-best policy, since it would nullify the fairness-in-hiring rule while continuing the job ladder economy;[12] the first-best policy would clearly be to eliminate the

[10]Note that the presence of the fairness-in-hiring rule requires a job ladder but the reverse is not true.

[11]This has been proposed in Bhagwati (1973a).

[12]The counterpart of this, in the Arrow–Spence screening theory, would be the question: is there a cheaper way of screening than using the educational system? This question has been discussed in Taubman and Wales (1973).

job ladder (and *hence* also the fairness-in-hiring practice) and to restore full flexibility of wages.

Finally, we should note that no simple theory of education – ours (job ladder and fairness-in-hiring) or the Schultz–Becker (human-capital) or the radical (socialization) or the Arrow–Spence (screening) – is likely to fit the entire educational system in any country. If we had to generalize at the peril of oversimplification, we would guess that the fairness-in-hiring theory is likely to apply most to liberal arts education in the less developed countries with developed educational systems inherited from progressive colonial governments (e.g. in Asia),[13] the screening theory most to liberal arts education in the developed countries, and the human-capital doctrine to technical and scientific education in both LDCs and DCs.

Appendix: The foreign teachers model

We discuss briefly the implications of assuming that the education sector is operated exclusively by hiring foreign teachers. Let us assume that the payment to foreigners per student is k in terms of the numeraire. Naturally the payment to foreigners, $k\delta L^{Ei}[i = \mathrm{M, F \text{ or } S}]$, has to be subtracted now from the sum of the values of output of sectors 1 and 3 to arrive at welfare levels.

Now, since only c, the fees charged per student, enters the private cost calculations of the flexible and minimum wage models, the parameter k is irrelevant for this purpose. However, recall that the teacher–student ratio ε plays a role in the determination of equilibrium when domestic teachers are assumed. So, now we must set $\varepsilon = 0$ to obtain the equilibrium values of the size of the educated labor force in the minimum and flexible wage models from eqs. (3′) and (7). However, the welfare levels will now be

$$W^{\mathrm{M}} = f(L_1^{\mathrm{M}}) + w[1 - L_1^{\mathrm{M}} - \delta L^{\mathrm{M}}] - k\delta L^{\mathrm{M}},$$

$$W^{\mathrm{F}} = f(L_1^{\mathrm{F}}) + w[1 - (1+\delta)L_1^{\mathrm{F}}] - k\delta L_1^{\mathrm{F}}.$$

The fact that payment to foreign teachers has to be subtracted also affects the maximand in the social optimum model. Thus we maximize $f(L) + w[1 - (1+\delta)L] - k\delta L$ with respect to L. This leads to

$$f'(L^{\mathrm{S}}) = w(1+\delta) + k\delta.$$

This is the analogue of (13) and has a similar interpretation. The LHS is the social product of an educated laborer while the RHS is the social cost in terms

[13] For an application of our theory of education to the welfare analysis of the brain drain problem of less developed countries (LDCs), see Hamada and Bhagwati (1975).

of output foregone in sector 3 (from the withdrawal of $(1+\delta)$ persons, one person being added to the educated labor force and δ persons to the student body) plus the direct cost of education equaling k per person in the educated labor force.

Comparisons of the sort made in sections 2.7.1–2.7.5, in the context of the present models with foreign teachers, lead to similar results as in those sections, provided it is understood that the direct social cost of education is k per student.

References

Arrow, K.J., 1973, Higher education as a filter, Journal of Public Economics 2, 193–216.

Bhagwati, J., 1972, Overqualification, education and welfare: A theoretical analysis, M.I.T., mimeo.

Bhagwati, J., 1973a, India in the international economy, Lal Bahadur Shastri Lectures (Osmania University Press, Hyderabad).

Bhagwati, J., 1973b, Education, class structure and income equality, World Development 1, 21–36.

Brecher, R., 1974, Optimal commercial policy for a minimum-wage economy, Journal of International Economics 4, 139–150.

Dasgupta, A., 1975, Two essays on the distribution of Income, Ph.D. dissertation, M.I.T.

Desai, Padma, 1975, Participation of women in the economies of developing and developed countries, ways of recognizing their contribution to national income, and strategies for ensuring their economic independence in developing countries, Prepared for the International Women's Year Conference, United Nations, Mexico.

Fields, G., 1972, A theory of education and labor markets in less developed countries, Unpublished Ph.D. dissertation, University of Michigan, Ann Arbor.

Fields, G., 1974, The private demand for education in relation to labour market conditions in less-developed countries, Economic Journal 84, 906–925.

Hamada, K. and J. Bhagwati, 1975, Domestic distortions, imperfect information and the brain drain, Journal of Development Economics 2, 265–279.

Harris, J. and M. Todaro, 1970, Migration, unemployment and development: A two-sector analysis, American Economic Review 60, 126–142.

Lefeber, L., 1971, Trade and minimum wage rates, in: J. Bhagwati, et al., eds., Trade, balance of payments and growth (North-Holland, Amsterdam) 91–114.

Spence, M., 1973, Job market signalling, Quarterly Journal of Economics 87, 355–374.

Stiglitz, J., 1975, The theory of 'screening,' education, and the distribution of income, American Economic Review 65, 283–300.

Taubman, P.J. and T. Wales, 1973, Higher education, mental ability, and screening, Journal of Political Economy 81, 28–55.

Thurow, L., 1972, Education and economic equality, Public Interest 28, 66–81.

Erratum

Page 10, equation (11): "r" should read "γ".

Editor's Note

Also see Jagdish N. Bhagwati, "Education, Class Structure and Income Equality," *World Development* 1(5) (May 1973):21–36. The "job-ladder" model and the fairness-in-hiring rule type of theory is discussed therein. It also explores at length, with evidence, the relation of class structure to the educational process and its income distributional consequences.

Journal of Public Economics 18 (1982) 285–289. North-Holland Publishing Company

INTRODUCTION

Jagdish N. BHAGWATI*

Columbia University, New York, NY 10027, USA

Received January 1982

If citizens can work or reside abroad, i.e. if there is international mobility of people, how should the income tax jurisdiction of a country be exercised over the subset that is so mobile? That is, should the income tax be extended to citizens abroad, on a citizenship nexus, or should it be levied on the basis of residence, thereby effectively exempting from its scope those citizens who are abroad? The Symposium in this issue addresses this novel and interesting question in public finance theory for open economies.[1]

This question has come to theoretical scrutiny by the rather indirect route of a proposal to 'tax the brain drain', i.e. to extend income taxation to skilled migrants from the developing to the developed countries. This proposal had several different moral–philosophical and economic rationales: among these being the raising of revenue from successful, internationally mobile citizens to assist development in the countries of their origin or citizenship.[2] It seemed therefore that if the developing countries could exercise their income tax jurisdiction over their citizens abroad, contrary to the current practice, they would have an added source of revenue and would also bring into the tax net a generally high-income set of citizens who were hitherto exempt simply on grounds of their locale. In short, to put the matter quite generally, one should reject 'representation without taxation', i.e. citizenship without the obligation to pay the income tax.[3]

*Arthur Lehman Professor of Economics, Columbia University. Thanks are due to the Ford Foundation, the German Marshall Fund, the Guggenheim Foundation and the National Science Foundation Grant no. SCS-80-25401 for support of the research underlying this Symposium. John Wilson made helpful comments.

[1]The papers in this Symposium, among others, were presented at a Conference on The Exercise of Income Tax Jurisdiction Over Citizens Abroad, held in New Delhi during January 1981, with financial support from the Ford Foundation and the National Institute of Public Finance and Policy, New Delhi.

[2]Cf. Bhagwati (1977, 1979, 1980), Bhagwati and Partington (1976), and Oldman and Pomp (1975, 1977, 1979), among several discussions of the proposal from economic, legal, human-rights, administrative, sociological and moral–philosophical viewpoints.

[3]This phraseology, while colorful and apt, may be a trifle misleading if 'representation' is taken to mean not citizenship generally but the specific right to vote. The voting right is occasionally abridged for citizens abroad owing to administrative and procedural restrictions and considerable diversity obtains in regard to this situation.

The problem that emerges then for public finance theory is evident: we need an extension of the usual income tax theory to an open economy (where openness implies international mobility). Many problems then immediately spring to attention. For example, what is the optimal income tax rate for citizens abroad relative to the optimal tax rate for citizens at home [Bhagwati and Hamada (1982), Mirrlees (1982), Wilson (1982a)], and what is the nature of the distortions that follow and what are the second-best solutions and policy instruments if the tax rate on citizens abroad is arbitrarily set at zero, as in many countries today [Bhagwati and Hamada (1982), Wilson (1982b)]? The papers in this Symposium address many of these issues.

But many more issues need further modelling. For example, the possibility of tax evasion, a critical one insofar as taxing non-residents is a serious problem[4] (though, taxing even residents is for many developing countries possibly an equally, if not more, difficult administrative problem), needs to be incorporated into the theoretical analysis.

Yet another significant issue arises because of the harmonization question implied by the co-existence of different income tax systems. In the United States (and the Philippines)[5] the 'global' income tax system that extends the income tax to citizens abroad is practised; other countries are on the 'schedular' income tax system that does not.[6] For the United States, this has meant a twofold problem, with consequent opposition to its global system from political lobbies preferring the schedular system.

(1) Private US citizens abroad, who are taxed on the basis of the global system, allege that they are unfairly taxed because nationals of other countries abroad (e.g. Frenchmen in Bangkok, alongside Americans) are not so taxed by their own governments and because nationals of the countries where they reside (e.g. the Thais in Bangkok) are subject only to domestic taxes (e.g. the Thai income tax) which are equally borne by the US citizens on top of such US income tax as becomes applicable. Hence, the *intra-*

[4]This problem is addressed in an informed analysis of the administrative and legal aspects of the experience of the Philippines with taxing citizens abroad, by Pomp (1982) in his paper at the New Delhi Conference.

[5]It is interesting that the US practice has spread to its former colony, whereas the European practice has spread to their former colonies. Since the Americans have not been colonizers on the scale and gusto of the Europeans during Europe's outward expansion, it is inevitable therefore that the global system is currently being practised in near isolation by the Philippines and the United States. Incidentally, Mexico also theoretically taxes citizens everywhere; in practice, in a sad commentary on the state of tax administration in many developing countries, the income tax is not enforced in the case of residents abroad.

[6]These contrasts are not wholly pure. Thus, for example, the United States does extend several exemptions (other than double-tax avoidance) to citizens abroad; and there are certainly restrictions in European systems on the definition of foreign residence which justifies exclusion from tax liability. The central thrust, and principles, of the two tax systems are very clear and different, however, in both cases.

national (*horizontal*) *equity* of the global system runs afoul of the *international* (*horizontal*) *equity* claims.

(2) Also, once trade in goods is considered, the harmonization issue becomes one of efficiency, rather than only equity. If US firms have to pay US income tax on US citizens they employ abroad, whereas French firms employing Frenchmen abroad do not have to pay the French income tax, distortion of comparative advantage could easily follow. That is to say, French firms, having to pay certain net-of-tax salaries for, say, Saudi construction contracts, would then have a smaller real cost, ceteris paribus, than US firms competing for the same contracts. Of course, this assumes that the incidence of the global tax system, unlike in the models of personal income taxation in this Symposium in the tradition of the classic papers of Mirrlees (1971) and Atkinson (1973), does not fall on the taxed individuals. It also assumes, in the stark version outlined above, that the French firms must hire Frenchmen and the US firms must hire Americans: if the two were total substitutes, as they almost certainly are not for different reasons, the harmonization issue would disappear. This problem needs formal analysis but has certainly played a major role in the political economy of American income taxation. People such as Senator Proxmire, who accept the equity underlying the global system and argue that the café-crawling Americans in Paris ought to pay their share of American taxes instead of leaving the burden to be borne by the workers in Detroit, have been traditionally pitted against pressure groups such as the corporations handling construction works abroad.[7]

Quite remarkably, the countries that are on the schedular system have hardly ever debated the merits of the alternative, global tax system. Thus, to cite just a single instance, the Meade Commission on direct taxation failed even to raise the matter in its otherwise comprehensive report, implicitly taking for granted the existing schedular system in consequence. Indeed, an interesting question in the historical evolution of the two rival systems of taxation, the global in the United States and the schedular in the European countries, is why these contrasts exist.

The United States, from the very beginning, appears to have defined tax equity on a citizenship basis, the judicial determination of the issue going so far as even to maintain that payment of the income tax was a privilege, if not a duty, of citizenship. By contrast, in the British case, the levy of the income tax has always been on a residence principle, from the time of its imposition by Pitt to pay for the Napoleonic War. The failure however to extend the tax, no matter what its original design, to citizens resident abroad may have been due to any or all of the following factors. (i) A colonial power such as Great Britain, unlike a newly-established immigrants' country such as the

[7]For a historical review of this tussle, see Bhagwati (1981).

United States, had several citizens abroad during the period of European outward expansion. It was likely that the many such British abroad had powerful connections with the Parliament, and were unlikely to be taxed by their friends. (ii) A more agreeable reason might simply be that, if many abroad were civil servants running the Empire, then the incidence of the global tax might fall on the Treasury itself: if so, only transaction costs would be incurred by taxing these citizens overseas. (iii) Again, the idea that all citizens should bear an appropriate burden of taxation is an egalitarian notion that is more consistent with the early American notions of democracy and political ideals than those of the more stratified, hierarchical European societies of the nineteenth and early twentieth centuries.[8]

[8]These questions are raised, and addressed with a skeletal historical analysis for the United States and for Great Britain, in Bhagwati and Wooton (1982). They await more sustained and penetrating historical research.

References

Atkinson, Antony B., 1973, How progressive should income tax be?, in: Parkin, M., ed., Essays in modern economics (Longman, London).

Bhagwati, Jagdish N., 1977, The brain drain: International resource flow accounting, compensation, taxation and related proposals, Paper for the Intergovernmental Group of Experts Meeting, UNCTAD, Geneva.

Bhagwati, Jagdish N., 1979, International migration of the highly skilled: Economics, ethics and taxes, Third World Quarterly, July.

Bhagwati, Jagdish N., 1980, North–south dialogue: An interview, Third World Quarterly, April.

Bhagwati, Jagdish N., 1981, Taxation and international migration: Recent policy issues, in: Chiswick, Barry, ed., U.S. immigration: Issues and policies. Proceedings of a Conference held at University of Illinois, Chicago Circle, 10–11 April 1980 (American Enterprise Institute, Washington D.C.).

Bhagwati, Jagdish N. and Koichi Hamada, 1982, Tax policy in the presence of emigration, Journal of Public Economics 18, this issue.

Bhagwati, Jagdish N. and Martin Partington, 1976, Taxing the brain drain: A proposal, vol. I (North-Holland, Amsterdam).

Bhagwati, Jagdish N. and Ian Wooton, 1982, The political economy of the global and the schedular income tax systems: A historical analysis of the United States and Great Britain, mimeographed, July.

Mirrlees, James A., 1971, An exploration in the theory of optimum income taxation, Review of Economic Studies 38, 175–208.

Mirrlees, James A., 1982, A theory of taxation and migration, Journal of Public Economics 18, this issue.

Oldman, Oliver and Richard Pomp, 1975, The brain drain: A tax analysis of the Bhagwati proposal, World Development 3.

Oldman, Oliver and Richard Pomp, 1977, Consideration of policy issues at the international level, legal and administrative aspects of compensation, taxation and related policy measures: Suggestions for an optimal policy mix, Paper for the Intergovernmental Group of Experts Meeting at UNCTAD, Geneva, UN Doc. TD/B/C.6/AC.4/6, Geneva.

Oldman, Oliver and Richard Pomp, 1979, Tax measures in response to the brain drain, Harvard International Law Journal 20, Winter.

Pomp, Richard, 1982, The exercise of tax jurisdiction over citizens abroad: The Philippines experience, Harvard International Law Journal, forthcoming; paper presented to the New Delhi Conference in January 1981 on The Exercise of Income Tax Jurisdiction over Citizens Abroad.

Wilson, John D., 1982a, Optimal linear income taxation in the presence of emigration, Journal of Public Economics 18, this issue.
Wilson, John D., 1982b, Optimal income taxation and migration: A world welfare point of view, Journal of Public Economics 18, this issue.

Erratum

Page 4, line 1: "several" should read "many".

Editor's Note

Related to the questions discussed in this paper are Jagdish N. Bhagwati and Martin Partington, eds., *Taxing The Brain Drain: A Proposal*, Amsterdam: North-Holland, 1976, chapters 1 and 2 by Bhagwati; and Jagdish N. Bhagwati, ed., *The Brain Drain and Taxation: Theory and Empirical Analysis*, Amsterdam: North-Holland, Amsterdam, 1976, chapter 1 by Bhagwati.

Journal of Public Economics 18 (1982) 291–317. North-Holland Publishing Company

TAX POLICY IN THE PRESENCE OF EMIGRATION*

Jagdish N. BHAGWATI
Columbia University, New York, NY 10027, USA

Koichi HAMADA
Tokyo University, Tokyo 113, Japan

Received June 1981, revised version received January 1982

1. Introduction

Recent policy and theoretical discussions of the effects of highly skilled migration from the underdeveloped countries, the so-called 'brain drain', have focused on a proposal [Bhagwati (1972)] to levy a (supplementary) income tax on those who migrate, the proceeds of such a tax to be transmitted to the developing country of origin or to developing countries *en bloc* for developmental spending.[1]

The welfare implications of such a tax were analyzed in an earlier paper of ours [Bhagwati and Hamada (1974)] in the context of a model of the country of emigration, characterized by sticky wages and Harris–Todaro (1971) type of unemployment. In subsequent papers, the tax has been analyzed also in the context of modified models, still incorporating the unemployment phenomena, by Rodriguez (1975) and McCulloch–Yellen (1975).[2] Essentially, these models analyze the impact of the income tax on emigrants' incomes as arising primarily through the reduced differential

*This paper is a significantly revised and augmented version of an earlier, unpublished paper [Bhagwati and Hamada (1976)]. Thanks are due to NSF Grant no. SCS-80-25401, to the Ford Foundation and to the German Marshall Fund for financial support of the research underlying this paper. The stimulating atmosphere at the SSRC Workshop on Public Economics at Warwick, England, 1978, also must be gratefully acknowledged by Koichi Hamada. We are also indebted to Peter Diamond, William Baumol, Assar Lindbeck, John Wilson and other participants at the New Delhi Conference in January 1981 for their helpful suggestions. The excellent comments of two referees have led to substantial improvements in this paper.

[1]This tax proposal has been explored from the viewpoint of its economic rationale, its revenue implications, and its legal (constitutional, tax and human rights) implications in Bhagwati and Partington (1976). The present paper can be seen as developing a yet further rationale for such a tax (in the version where the tax proceeds accrue to the country of emigration).

[2]For a review of these and other brain drain models in recent theoretical writings, see Bhagwati and Rodriguez (1975).

between foreign (net-of-tax) and domestic salaries for the emigrant class of labor: this reduction in differential, in turn, reduces the expected and possibly the actual salaries in the home countries and thus generates consequences for education, unemployment, income and income distribution (among the educated, uneducated, employed and unemployed).

The present paper takes an altogether different, public-finance-theoretic approach to the analysis of the income tax on emigrants. We employ rather the framework of income taxation originated by Mirrlees (1971), and particularly in the form developed by Atkinson (1973). There, the choice for individuals is the length of education, which affects their productivities after graduation so that education increases the earnings of individuals while simultaneously postponing the realization of these earnings. Atkinson studies, in the context of this model, the conflict between efficiency and equity: the income tax would redistribute income but also distort the educational choice and hence reduce efficiency.[3]

In this paper we utilize this basic model to analyze the welfare impact of the possibility of emigration to earn incomes abroad and to assess the role of taxing migrants' incomes under alternative assumptions within the model.

Section 2 lays out the model, with the required modification to consider foreign earnings by migrants. It also outlines three policy instruments — the income tax (on domestically earned incomes), an educational subsidy, and the income tax on migrants' foreign earnings — which are appropriate to analyze in the model, for reasons spelled out herein. Section 3 considers the use of only one policy instrument, the tax on non-migrants' incomes, which we will refer to simply as the 'income tax' throughout the paper.[4] Section 4, on the other hand, considers the case where the home country can use both the income tax *and* an income tax on migrants' incomes, simply called hereafter an 'income tax on migrants'.[5] Section 5 considers the case where *all three* instruments are available to the home country. Section 6 offers concluding observations, including the possible extension of our results for tax policy in relation to migrants.

[3]Note that lump-sum taxation to redistribute income is not being permitted; if it were, the conflict between efficiency and equity naturally would disappear! The conflict between efficiency and equity in the presence of factor mobility has also been mentioned by Cooper (1973, p. 54).

[4]Our model does not allow for non-migrants to earn foreign income or for migrants to earn domestic income, for simplicity. Therefore, an income tax on non-migrants' income is the same as an income tax on domestically earned income.

[5]The United States, Philippines and (in theory) Mexico tax citizens who work abroad, regardless of length of residence or legal migration status. Therefore, the 'income tax on migrants', discussed in this paper is a well-established, international tax-legal policy instrument as long as migrants do not change their nationality. Under *current* international practices, therefore, if migrants change their nationality, the 'income tax on migrants' would become an infeasible instrument. For a lucid tax-legal discussion of these issues, see the valuable papers by Oldman and Pomp (1975, 1977, 1979).

2. The model and policy instruments

2.1. The model

Following Atkinson's model of optimal income taxation, we assume that differences exist in the innate ability of the individuals of the home country. Let n be the index of innate ability and S be the length of education that an individual undertakes. The innate ability in the initial population, before immigration possibility opens, is assumed to be distributed by the density function $p(n)$, such that

$$\int_{n_1}^{\infty} p(n)\,\mathrm{d}n = 1,$$

where n_1 indicates the lower bound of the index of innate ability. Let the domestic earning of an individual be a function of his ability and his length of education such that $f(n, S)$ indicates the resulting earnings.[6] Let $f^*(n, S)$ be the earnings if the individual migrates and therefore has foreign earnings instead, even though we assume that he has received his education at home. These earnings are defined *gross* of income tax levied by the foreign country. Moreover, these earning functions are assumed to be increasing functions of n and S, while the marginal productivity of S is assumed to be non-increasing. That is to say,

$$f_n, f_n^* > 0, \qquad f_S, f_S^* > 0,$$

$$f_{SS}, f_{SS}^* \leqq 0,$$

with subscripts denoting the partial derivatives with respect to the subscripted variables. We further assume, for simplicity, that the length of working period after education is identical at home and abroad and designate it as R.

The decision whether or not to migrate is then assumed to depend on the comparison between the discounted earnings stream at home and that in the country of immigration. We assume that if the former exceeds the latter, individuals will remain at home; if the former is less than the latter, they will decide to migrate and work abroad instead.[7] Further assumptions on the migration decision will be spelled out in section 3.

[6]George Psacharopoulos has pointed out to us that, while it is plausible to write earnings as a function of innate ability, the econometric attempts at isolating this relationship have not been particularly successful so far.

[7]We could have assumed instead that only a fraction of those who could earn more abroad would choose to migrate, with this fraction an increasing function of the difference between income earned by migrating and domestic income. However, our assumption simplifies the analysis while sacrificing nothing that is critical.

2.2. The policy instruments

With this basic framework set up, we now list the three policy instruments that we will consider in the paper.

(1) *Linear income tax.* Following Atkinson (1973), a linear income tax implies that the after-tax (non-migrants') income will be written in the form $[\alpha+\beta f]$, where $\alpha>0$, $1>\beta\geqq 0$, $(1-\beta)$ is the marginal rate of taxation and α constitutes the uniform lump-sum payment to each individual.

(2) *Subsidy to education.* Following Hamada (1974), who demonstrated that the use of an appropriate educational subsidy could virtually resolve the Atkinson conflict between equity and efficiency, an educational subsidy will be considered as implying that the subsidy (G) is given directly to individuals enrolled in the educational system.

(3) *Linear income tax on migrants.* Following Bhagwati, we will consider a linear income tax on migrants so that their after-home-country-tax income can be written in the form $[\alpha^*+\beta^* f^*]$, with the asterisk indicating migrants. If we assume that the country of immigration levies its own income tax on the migrants' income such that $y^*=\gamma+\delta f^*$, where y^* is then the net-of-immigration-country-tax income of the migrant, and that the home country's income tax on migrants is levied on y^* so as to leave the migrant finally with net income equal to $[t+\tau y^*]$, then we must have $\alpha^*+\beta f^*=t+\tau(\gamma+\delta f^*)$ so that we obtain the following relationship between the tax parameters:[8]

$$\alpha^*=t+\tau\gamma; \qquad \beta^*=\tau\delta.$$

(4) *The welfare criteria.* Next, we note that three alternative welfare criteria might be deployed to analyze the outcomes under these alternative policy combinations. (a) We will generally deploy the criterion of the welfare impact of the migration on those left behind (TLBs), examining in turn their average income or utility and alternatively the minimum income among them à la Rawls (1971). (b) Alternatively, we could have examined the welfare impact on TLBs plus the migrants:[9] as discussed briefly in the concluding section.[10] (c) Finally, we could have taken a global or 'internationalist' criterion embracing the non-migrant nationals of the country of immigration as well in a two-country framework.

[8]Note that the linearity of the income tax on migrants is assumed here, parallel to Atkinson's income tax, but is not a necessary feature of the proposal in Bhagwati (1972).

[9]This criterion would seem more consistent with the view that many migrants do not change their nationalities today and hence are, from a legal *and* sociological viewpoint, members of the home country. Cf. Bhagwati (1979).

[10]Wilson considers, in his illuminating paper (1978) based on the leisure-work choice model of Mirrlees (1971), the effect of migration on the optimal linear tax rate, assuming that the only policy instrument is the income tax (on domestic residents).

3. Income tax in the presence of migration

We now consider the case, applicable to countries which neither subsidize education nor exercise their income tax jurisdiction over citizens working abroad, where the home country has only an income tax (on domestic incomes) at its command. Precisely, we will analyze the welfare impact on TLBs when, in the presence of the possibility of migration to work abroad, the income tax is levied at an optimal rate.[11] Our reference point will be the standard Atkinson solution where the possibility of migration is *not* allowed, so that we will then be able to deduce what the introduction of the possibility of migration implies for the welfare of the TLBs and the associated optimal parameters/rates of income taxation.

3.1. Two fundamental individual decisions

We begin by first indicating how the possibility of migration to earn foreign income will influence the two fundamental choices facing an individual in this modified Atkinson economy: (1) the choice of the length of education; and (2) the decision to migrate or work at home. Note immediately, however, that in the Atkinson model without migration, efficiency is sacrificed for equity, the loss of efficiency taking the form of a reduced length of education since individuals are taxed on their (education-augmented) earnings. In our modified version with migration, on the other hand, the sacrifice of efficiency will occur on two dimensions: a distorted length of education by migrants and non-migrants, *and* overmigration since migrants escape (whereas non-migrants must pay) the income tax because the home country fails to exercise its tax jurisdiction over citizens working abroad.

3.1.1. Choice of length of education

Assuming throughout that education is always undertaken at home, we can see that an individual will maximize his lifetime income from domestic earnings, I_d, with respect to S (the length of education). Now,

$$I_d = \int_S^{S+R} (\alpha + \beta f(n,S))e^{-it}\,dt$$

$$= A(\alpha + \beta f)e^{-iS}, \tag{1}$$

where i is the rate of discount, R is the length of working period, and $A \equiv$

[11]The optimality will reflect the precise choice of the objective function, of course.

$(1-e^{-iR})/i$. Since we assume that R is constant,[12] A can also be regarded as a constant. Maximizing I_d with respect to S, we then obtain the first-order condition for a privately optimal decision:

$$A\{-i(\alpha+\beta f)+\beta f_S\}=0. \tag{2}$$

The second-order condition is satisfied because of the assumption that $f_{SS} \leqq 0$.

Similarly, if the individual concentrates on foreign earnings as a migrant, he will maximize

$$I_f = \int_S^{S+R} (\alpha^* + \beta^* f^*(n, S))\, e^{-it} dt - Ce^{-iS}$$

$$= A(\alpha^* + \beta^* f^*)e^{-iS} - Ce^{-iS}, \tag{1a}$$

where C is the lump-sum cost of migration (e.g. transportation, etc.) that is incurred at the time of departure, $f^*(n,S)$ is the foreign income to be earned before tax by an individual with index n, and $(\alpha^*+\beta^* f^*)$ is the foreign income of the migrant net of all income taxation. Recall from our earlier discussion of policy instruments that when the home country does not tax citizens abroad, α^* and β^* will equal the parameters of the income tax schedule of the *foreign* country, i.e. $\alpha^*=\gamma$ and $\beta^*=\delta$.

The corresponding first-order condition for the migrants' privately optimal decision then is yielded by maximizing I_f with respect to S, and is

$$A\{-i(\alpha^*+\beta^* f^*)+\beta^* f^*_S\}+iC=0. \tag{2a}$$

3.1.2. *Decision to migrate and work abroad*

Next, consider the problem of the choice between staying at home and working abroad. As stated above, potential migrants are assumed to decide whether or not to migrate by comparing the discounted value of income streams to be obtained from home and abroad. They decide to migrate therefore if the following expression is positive, and not to migrate if it is non-positive:

$$\Gamma(n)=\{A(\alpha^*+\beta^* f^*(n,S^*))\, e^{-iS^*} - Ce^{-iS^*}\} - A(\alpha+\beta f(n,S))\, e^{-iS}. \tag{3}$$

[12]Alternatively, we may assume that the total length $(S+R)$ of life, instead of R, is constant. However, this does not change our main results, as indicated by Hamada (1974). In fact, it even simplifies some expressions. For example, the optimal subsidy formula becomes $G=\alpha$ instead of $G=Ai\alpha$.

Here S and S^* indicate, respectively, the length of education given the opportunity to work at home or abroad.

To facilitate our analysis, we additionally assume now that, corresponding to the parameters of the income tax schedules of the home country and the foreign country, there is a *unique* value n^* of ability above which everyone will migrate.[13] Hence:

$$\begin{aligned} &\Gamma(n)>0, \quad \text{if } n>n^*, \\ &\Gamma(n)\leqq 0, \quad \text{if } n\leqq n^*. \end{aligned} \tag{4}$$

Evidently, the value of n^* depends on the tax parameters, α and β, through their effect on realized discounted incomes. Moreover, since β's effect on this income equals α's effect multiplied by $f(n,\hat{S})$, we can show that:[14]

$$\frac{\partial n^*}{\partial \alpha}>0; \qquad \frac{\partial n^*}{\partial \beta}=f(n^*,\hat{S})\frac{\partial n^*}{\partial \alpha}>0. \tag{5}$$

Next, reflecting the reality that (thanks to the nature of immigration restrictions which are biased in favor of professional, skilled immigrants) migration is feasible often for the skilled alone, we will assume that this

[13]The analysis of the more general possibility where migration is feasible over the entire interval of ability endowment is considerably more complex. Cf. Wilson (1978).

[14]With given values α^* and β^*, n^* is determined by

$$I_d(\alpha,\beta,n^*)-I_f(\alpha^*,\beta^*,n^*)=0.$$

Therefore

$$\frac{\partial I_d}{\partial \alpha}\cdot d\alpha+\frac{\partial I_d}{\partial \beta}\cdot d\beta+\frac{\partial I_d}{\partial n^*}\cdot dn^*-\frac{\partial I_f}{\partial n^*}\cdot dn^*=0.$$

Thus

$$\left.\frac{\partial n^*}{\partial \alpha}\right|_{\beta=\text{const.}}=\frac{\partial I_d}{\partial \alpha}\Bigg/\left\{\frac{\partial I_f}{\partial n^*}-\frac{\partial I_d}{\partial n^*}\right\}$$

$$\left.\frac{\partial n^*}{\partial \beta}\right|_{\alpha=\text{const.}}=\frac{\partial I_d}{\partial \beta}\Bigg/\left\{\frac{\partial I_f}{\partial n^*}-\frac{\partial I_d}{\partial n^*}\right\}.$$

Now, from the expressions of I_d and I_f, we have:

$$\frac{\partial I_d}{\partial \beta}\Bigg/\frac{\partial I_d}{\partial \alpha}=f(n,S).$$

Moreover, since the assumption underlying relation (4) presupposes that $[(\partial I_f/\partial n)-(\partial I_d/\partial n)]$ is positive in the neighborhood of n^*, it follows that both $\partial n^*/\partial \alpha$ and $\partial n^*/\partial \beta$ are positive.

critical value n^* is larger than the mean value $\bar{n}$ of the ability index, i.e.

$$n^* > \bar{n}. \tag{6}$$

Finally, the reader may find it illuminating to consider the critical value n^* in fig. 1, where I_d and I_f are drawn as functions of the ability index n and the given tax parameters. Our assumption underlying (4) implies that the I_f curve intersects the I_d curve from below only once, with the value of n at the intersection being n^*. I_d shifts upward with an increase in either α or β. However, the increase in the latter case is proportionally $f(n, S)$ times greater than in the former case. It follows that the value of n^* will increase with either α or β, as in (5).

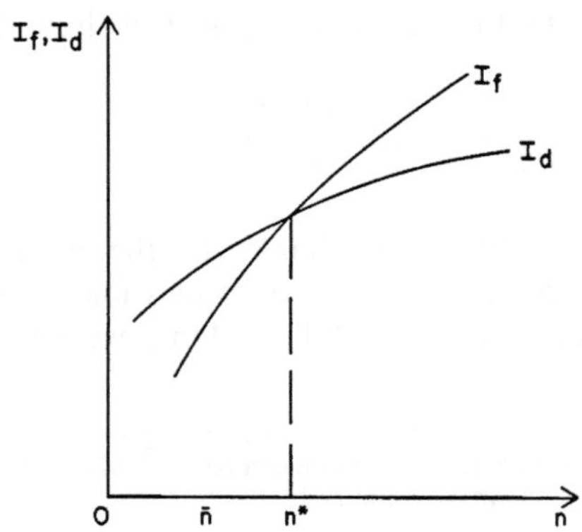

Fig. 1

3.2. *Defining TLBs*

Next, before we undertake our analysis of the nature of the optimal income tax schedule in the presence of migration, we must carefully consider the implication of the welfare criterion we plan to adopt, i.e. the impact on TLBs. For, one final complexity needs to be cleared up in discussing the TLBs in our modified Atkinson economy. The TLBs turn out, in general, to be a variable number of individuals because the critical value n^* that serves to divide the population in the home country into migrants and non-migrants is a function of the tax parameters, α and β. Thus, if we were to compare (say) the average welfare of TLBs under one set of (α, β) with the average welfare of TLBs under another set of (α, β), we would in fact be comparing different subsets of original population.[15] To avoid this difficulty, we resort to the following stratagem. We take a value N such that $N \leq n^*$ for

[15]And we would have an ill-defined problem! Cf. Hamada (1975).

all n^*'s associated with the range of tax parameters,[16] α and β, that emerge in our analysis. We then redefine TLBs to include only those whose ability index lies in the interval $[n_1, N]$. This procedure clearly avoids the ambiguity concerning the size of the TLB population by making it invariant to changes in n^*.

3.3. The formal optimization problem

We are now in a position to analyze the optimal choice of the tax parameters, α and β, in this modified, 'open' Atkinson economy. Consider first the utilitarian criterion for judging welfare impact on TLBs. We then have the formal problem of maximizing[17]

$$\int_{n_1}^{N} U(I_d(n,\alpha,\beta))\, p(n)\, \mathrm{d}n \tag{7}$$

subject to the budget constraint

$$\alpha \int_{n_1}^{n^*} p(n)\, \mathrm{d}n = (1-\beta) \int_{n_1}^{n^*} f(n,S)\, p(n)\, \mathrm{d}n. \tag{8}$$

The general solution to this problem being difficult to secure, we assume the particular forms of earning function, distribution-of-ability function and the utility function that were assumed by Atkinson (1973) in the original analysis without migration. Thus, our earning function will be

$$f(n,S) = nS \tag{9}$$

and we will use the Pareto distribution whose density function is written as:

$$\begin{aligned} p(n) &= \mu n^{-\mu-1}, \quad &&\text{for } n \geqq 1 \\ &= 0, &&\text{for } n < 1, \end{aligned} \tag{10}$$

where μ is parametrically assumed to exceed 2 and n_1 is assumed to equal unity.[18] It follows also from eq. (6) that

$$n^* > \mu/(\mu-1) = \bar{n}. \tag{6'}$$

[16]This requirement is in fact stronger than needed. If we solve the problem following the procedure discussed below for an arbitrary N, and if the resulting optimal tax parameters α and β do not give rise to n^* smaller than N, then our our analysis is completely legitimate.

[17]Recall that $I_d(n,\alpha,\beta)$ is the discounted value of income stream for individuals with ability n and with disposable income $\{\alpha + \beta f(n,S)\}$.

[18]So long as the Pareto distribution is assumed, the restriction on n_1 does not change the value of the optimal tax rate in a closed economy. We owe this observation to Tony Atkinson. [Cf. Atkinson (1973)].

3.4. The optimal choice of tax parameters

Our analysis then proceeds by first discussing the implications of individual optimizing behaviour in this model, second deriving the feasibility locus between the tax parameters that this behavior implies in the presence of the restriction that the government's budget be balanced, and finally utilizing this tax feasibility locus to derive the optimal choice of the tax parameters, given the welfare criterion adopted.

3.4.1. Individual optimization

The individual optimization implies that the non-migrant will choose the length of education so as to maximize

$$I_d = A(\alpha + \beta nS)e^{-iS}$$

which, under the assumption that everybody spends some time in educating himself, will result in:

$$\hat{S} = \frac{1}{i} - \frac{\alpha}{\beta n}, \tag{11}$$

$$nS = \frac{n}{i} - \frac{\alpha}{\beta}, \tag{12}$$

and

$$I_d = A\frac{\beta n}{i}\exp\left(\frac{\alpha i}{\beta n} - 1\right) = A\frac{\beta n}{ie}\exp\left(\frac{n_0}{n}\right), \tag{13}$$

where $n_0 = \alpha i/\beta$.

3.4.2. Tax feasibility loci

Next, given this individual-optimizing behavior, we can derive the *tax feasibility locus*, reflecting additionally the government's budget constraint. Following Atkinson, we derive this for β and $n_0 = i\alpha/\beta$ (rather than α and β), where n_0 corresponds to the value of the ability index where an individual stops educating himself. In a closed economy, n_0 is smaller than unity if $\mu > 2$. This justifies the above assumption that everybody spends some time in educating himself.[19] Thus, we shall follow this assumption throughout the

[19] See Atkinson (1973, p. 100, footnote 2). Since the optimal n_0 in an open model is smaller then the optimal n_0 in the corresponding closed model [cf. fig. 2, and proposition 3(2)], we can justify this assumption in an open model as well.

paper. Thus, we note that the budget constraint (8) can be expressed as:

$$\alpha \int_1^{n^*} p(n)\,\mathrm{d}n = (1-\beta)\int_1^{n^*}\left(\frac{n}{i}-\frac{\alpha}{\beta}\right)p(n)\,\mathrm{d}n, \tag{8'}$$

where n^* itself is a function of α and β. Moreover, by substituting the Pareto distribution, we get:

$$\alpha(1-n^{*-\mu}) = (1-\beta)\left\{\frac{\bar{n}}{i}(1-n^{*-\mu+1})-\frac{\alpha}{\beta}(1-n^{*-\mu})\right\}.$$

Following Atkinson's procedures, we can then deduce the following, critical relationship:

$$\beta = 1-\frac{n_0}{\bar{n}}\cdot\frac{1-n^{*-\mu}}{1-n^{*-\mu+1}} = 1-\frac{n_0}{\bar{n}}h(n^*), \tag{14}$$

where $h(n^*) \equiv (1-n^{*-\mu})/(1-n^{*-\mu+1})$.

Now, it is readily seen that if we were to 'close' this economy and eliminate migration, $n^* \to \infty$ and $h(n^*)$ reduces to unity. The tax feasibility loci for the 'closed' (i.e. without-migration) economy and for the 'open' (i.e. with-migration) economy, depicting the relationship between β and n_0 from (14), are drawn in fig. 2 with a straight line AC for the former case and with a curve AB for the latter.

Before proceeding to the last step of choosing the optimal tax parameters from this feasible set, however, we must investigate the properties of these loci. First, we must note that the closed-economy locus will be straight line.

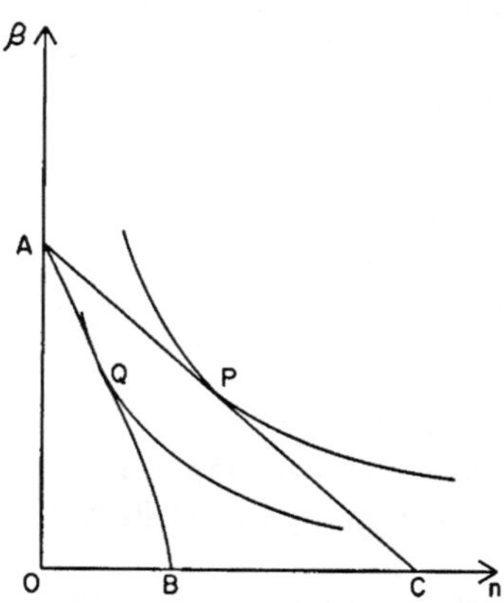

Fig. 2

Moreover, since (as shown in the appendix, remark 1) $h(n^*)>1$ for the relevant values of $n^*>2$ and $\mu>2$, the tax feasibility locus for the open economy must lie below that for the closed economy (except when $n_0=0$).

Second, the slope of the tangent line for the tax feasibility locus for the open economy can be shown everywhere to be steeper than the (unique) slope of the focus for the closed economy. That is to say (as per the appendix, remark 3), we can show that

$$-\frac{d\beta}{dn_0}>\frac{1}{\bar{n}}. \tag{15}$$

3.4.3. The logarithmic utility function

Now we can turn to the optimal choice of the tax parameters, given these tax feasibility loci. With Atkinson, we will begin with the utilitarian welfare criterion, i.e. we will maximize the average utility of TLBs.[20] Following Atkinson again, we will initially assume a specific utility function, i.e. the logarithmic utility function. In this case the utilitarian objective is written as:

$$\int_1^N \log\left\{\frac{\beta n}{ie}\exp\left(\frac{n_0}{n}\right)\right\} p(n)\,dn$$

$$=\text{const.}+\log\beta\int_1^N p(n)\,dn+n_0\int_1^N n^{-1}p(n)\,dn. \tag{16}$$

The social indifference map for the population with ability between 1 and N can then be obtained by equating the above expression to a constant, and the indifference curves can then be drawn convex, as in fig. 2. Moreover, the slopes of the tangent lines to the indifference curves are identical for a given value of β or, in other words, the tangent lines are parallel along any hozizontal line, because the slope

$$-\frac{d\beta}{dn_0}=\beta\frac{\int_1^N n^{-1}p(n)\,dn}{\int_1^N p(n)\,dn} \tag{17}$$

does not depend on the value of n_0.

We then arrive immediately at two important conclusions, noticing that the optimal tax parameters chosen by the TLBs will reflect the tangency of a

[20] In Atkinson's analysis the economy is closed of course. Our analysis of the open economy, on the other hand, applies the utilitarian criterion to TLBs alone.

social indifference curve with the tax feasibility locus, i.e. eq. (15) with (17). First, the welfare level attained by the TLBs is strictly inferior to that in a closed economy, because the feasibility locus of an open economy is inside that for a closed economy.[21] Second, we see that the home country, pursuing the utilitarian objective on behalf of TLBs, will choose a *lower* marginal tax rate $(1-\beta)$ if the economy is open rather than closed: the emigration possibility, in this sense, forces a less egalitarian policy on the home country. To see this, consider fig. 2 again. If the economy is closed, point P will be chosen; if it is open, point Q will be chosen. Because the tangency slope of the indifference curves along the horizontal line through P is constant, and because the tangency slope of the opportunity curve for an open economy is steeper than that of the dotted line as indicated by (15), the vertical coordinate of Q must be larger than that of P. Since the marginal rate of taxation equals $(1-\beta)$, this amounts to choosing a lower marginal tax rate if the economy is open.

3.4.4. The iso-elastic utility function

We turn next to the more general case of an iso-elastic utility function:

$$U=\frac{I_{\mathrm{d}}^{1-\rho}}{1-\rho}, \qquad \rho\geqq 0, \qquad \rho\neq 1, \tag{18}$$

where ρ indicates the degree of inequality-aversion of society and, as is well known, this utility function converges to a logarithmic function when ρ approaches unity. The welfare of TLBs can then be expressed as:

$$W=\frac{A'}{1-\rho}\int_1^N \beta^{1-\rho}n^{1-\rho}\exp\left(\frac{(1-\rho)n_0}{n}\right)p(n)\,\mathrm{d}n, \tag{19}$$

where $A'=$const. The marginal rate of substitution between β and n_0 can then be written as:

$$-\frac{\mathrm{d}\beta}{\mathrm{d}n_0}$$

$$=\beta\int_1^N n^{-\rho}\exp\left(\frac{(1-\rho)n_0}{n}\right)p(n)\,\mathrm{d}n\Big/\left[\int_1^N n^{1-\rho}\exp\left(\frac{(1-\rho)n_0}{n}\right)p(n)\,\mathrm{d}n\right]. \tag{20}$$

Along a horizontal line, such that β is constant, this absolute slope of the indifference curve can be shown to be an increasing function of n_0 if $\rho<1$,

[21]This was shown also in Hamada (1975).

and a decreasing function of n_0 if $\rho > 1$ (cf. the appendix, remark 4). This has immediate consequences for the optimal choice of the tax parameters in our open economy vis-à-vis the closed economy.

Thus, if $\rho < 1$, exactly the same argument as for the case of the logarithmic utility function applies and the open economy will be characterized by the choice of a lower marginal tax rate. (Note that when $\rho = 0$, we have the linear utilitarian criterion and we are maximizing average *income*.)

On the other hand, if $\rho > 1$, i.e. the inequality-aversion exceeds that in the logarithmic case, the tangency slopes to the indifference curves become steeper as one moves horizontally to the left of P. Hence, we cannot assert now that the marginal rate of income taxation is necessarily less for the open economy.[22]

This paradoxical possibility when $\rho > 1$, however, can be shown to be ruled out in the extreme, Rawlsian case where, as is well known, we are dealing with the limiting case of the utilitarian welfare criterion when $\rho \to \infty$. In this extreme case of inequality-aversion, where we are maximizing the discounted income of the individual with the lowest ability, we can write this discounted income, since $n_1 = 1$, as:

$$I_d = A \frac{\beta}{ie} e^{n_0},$$

so that we have the indifference curve:

$$\beta e^{n_0} = \text{const.}, \tag{21}$$

with a marginal rate of substitution, $-\mathrm{d}\beta/\mathrm{d}n_0 = \beta$, which is independent of n_0. Hence, the argument can proceed exactly as with the logarithmic utilitarian case (i.e. $\rho = 1$), and therefore the open economy would be characterized by a *lower* marginal tax rate.

3.5. Three major propositions

We can therefore summarize our results thus:

Proposition 1. The welfare level of the TLBs is definitely inferior in an open, vis-à-vis the closed, economy.

Proposition 2. If the individual utility function is iso-elastic with $\rho \leqq 1$ — the logarithmic function, with $\rho = 1$, and the linear function, with $\rho = 0$, being two

[22]The deviation from $1/n$ of the slope of the tax feasibility locus is independent of the deviation of the tangency slope of indifference curves from the slope at P. Therefore, one may get the paradoxical situation in the text if $h(n^*)$ is very close to unity, i.e. the possibility of emigration is very small.

special cases — then the criterion of maximizing the welfare of TLBs will lead to choice of a reduced marginal tax rate for an open economy.

Proposition 3. (1) *If, however, $\rho > 1$, one cannot preclude the possibility that the open economy is characterized by an increased marginal tax rate.* (2) *For the extreme Rawlsian case, where $\rho \to \infty$, the open economy, however, will be characterized by a lower marginal tax rate.*

3.6. Efficiency implications

Our analysis has focused thus far on the effect on the choice of the tax parameters, and the associated welfare impact on TLBs, when the economy is open. In doing this we demonstrated the deterioration in the tax feasibility locus that the migration possibility entails. Now, however, we shift our focus to a related, but distinct, question: How precisely does efficiency get compromised in our open Atkinson economy?[23]

We must distinguish between *domestic* (i.e. home-country) and *global* efficiency. By the former, we will mean the equalization of the relevant marginal rates of substitution (MRS) within the home country. By the latter, we will mean the equalization of the MRS within the home country and between the home and foreign countries.

But we will define global efficiency in a *restricted* fashion: the foreign country will be assumed to be behaving optimally vis-à-vis its own population, setting its own tax parameters correspondingly. Global efficiency will then be defined purely in the sense that the *home country* migrants' decision to migrate must reflect the comparison of their gross, unadjusted productivities/returns.

Moreover, we must note that domestic efficiency is not tantamount to maximization of domestic income since the latter would also reflect the distribution of world income among the two countries.

3.6.1. Domestic efficiency

Now, domestic efficiency requires the individual non-migrant to choose the *socially* optimal amount of education. The corresponding first-order condition, necessary for a maximum, is yielded by maximizing:[24]

$$\int_{S}^{S+R} f(n,S)\,e^{-it}\,dt = Afe^{-iS},$$

[23]This question is pertinent to our analysis in section 5.

[24]In order that the individual productivity maximization over time coincides with the socially optimal choice, we need to use the correct discount rate. As discussed in Hamada (1972), the correct discount rate should be the biological rate of interest, i.e. the growth rate of the population (plus the posiitive rate of labor-augmenting technical progress).

which yields:

$$A\{-if+f_S\}=0. \tag{22}$$

This condition is evidently not met in our Atkinson economy where, it will be recalled, individuals optimize so as to satisfy

$$A\{-i(\alpha+\beta f)+\beta f_S\}=0. \tag{2}$$

The equality of (22) and (2) would require that $\alpha=0$ and $\beta=1$, i.e. the absence of income taxation!

If we consider next the migrants' income as part of domestic income, there is a similar failure of equality between the migrants' choice of the individually optimal length of education and the *socially* optimal choice thereof. The former will imply

$$A\{-i(\alpha^*+\beta^* f^*)+\beta^* f^*_S\}+iC=0, \tag{2a}$$

whereas the latter will require

$$A\{-if^*+f^*_S\}+iC=0, \tag{22a}$$

and (22a) and (2a) will not be equal unless $\alpha^*=0$ and $\beta^*=1$.

3.6.2. Global efficiency

In addition to satisfying the preceding two first-order conditions, (22) and (22a), for a globally optimal choice (in the restricted sense as defined above) of the educational length, global efficiency further requires that the decision to migrate depend on whether the following expression is positive or not:

$$\begin{aligned}\hat{\Gamma}(n) &= \int_{\hat{S}^*}^{\hat{S}^*+R} f^*(n,\hat{S}^*)\,\mathrm{e}^{-it}\,\mathrm{d}t - C\mathrm{e}^{-i\hat{S}^*} - \int_{\hat{S}}^{\hat{S}+R} f(n,\hat{S})\,\mathrm{e}^{-it}\,\mathrm{d}t \\ &= \{Af^*(n,\hat{S}^*)-C\}\,\mathrm{e}^{-i\hat{S}^*} - Af(n,S)\,\mathrm{e}^{-i\hat{S}},\end{aligned} \tag{23}$$

where $\hat{S}$ and $\hat{S}^*$ are the values of S and S^* satisfying (22) and (22a). However, the actual decision to migrate is made depending instead on whether (3) is positive or non-positive. Unless, therefore, coincidentally $\beta=\beta^*=1$ and $\alpha=\alpha^*$, the two conditions will be different. With only domestic income tax available as a policy instrument, the home country cannot affect the values of α^* and β^*, which are solely determined by the foreign government. Thus, this third and final requirement for (restricted) global efficiency will not be met either.

4. Income tax and income tax on migrants in the presence of migration

Consider now a modification to the Atkinson, open economy. In addition to the (domestic) income tax, let us now utilize also an income tax on migrants. The effect of this is essentially to close the economy from the viewpoint of the budget constraint. This, however, will not restore, in general, the tax feasibility locus of the closed economy without migration *even if* the income tax is uniformly applied to non-migrants' domestic incomes and migrants' net-of-foreign-tax foreign incomes.

For, as long as (some) migrants' net-of-foreign-tax incomes exceed what they could earn domestically, corresponding to any educational level, this is tantamount to keeping the economy closed to migration but increasing the productivity of these 'migrants'. Hence, evidently, the tax feasibility locus of the open economy with such utilization of the added policy instrument constituted by the income tax on migrants will dominate that for the closed economy confined only to the use of the (domestic) income tax, the latter in turn dominating of course the tax feasibility locus for the open economy confined to the (domestic) income tax.

In fig. 3 this is illustrated by the numbered tax feasibility loci in terms of α and β referring to the open economies and the locus C referring to the closed economy. Locus *II* is the locus for the open economy with income tax on migrants' net-of-foreign-tax incomes at the same rates as the tax on non-migrants' domestic incomes (assuming that these incomes exceed what the migrants would have earned (gross) domestically), i.e. when

$$t=\alpha \quad \text{and} \quad \tau=\beta$$

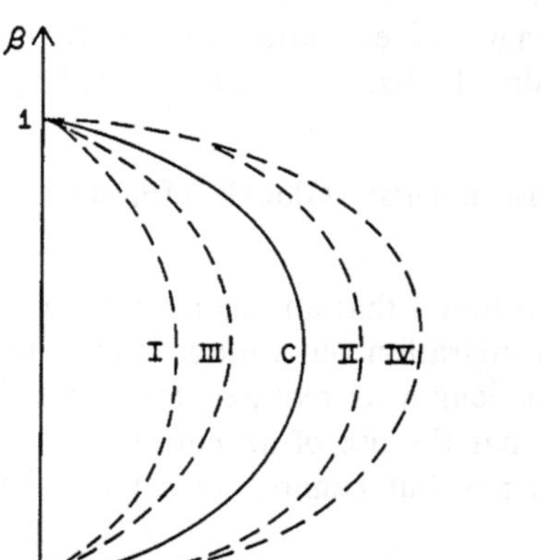

Fig. 3

in terms of eq. (5). Locus I, on the other hand, is the tax feasibility locus when the open economy cannot use the income tax on migrants. In fig. 3, locus $II \supset$ locus $C \supset$ locus I.

If the home country were to use 'prohibitive' tax rates on migrants, t and τ, so that it pays migrants to stay home, we revert of course to the closed economy locus C. On the other hand, the home country could set these tax rates, t and τ, 'monopolistically' so as to extract the entire rent, if any, from the migrants' working abroad rather than at home, in which case the corresponding tax feasibility locus IV will be the 'best' one; but it is likely to run afoul of explicit human-rights conventions!

On the other hand, choosing the tax parameters t and τ at values that substantially reduce the migrants' tax liability to the home country will result in a shrinking-in of the tax feasibility locus. In the limiting case of zero income tax on migrants, it will revert to locus I, but will otherwise dominate it. However, it may be dominated in turn by the closed economy locus, as when it is locus I in fig. 3, where locus $I \subset$ locus $III \subset$ locus C.

While all this is perfectly clear, it is not possible, without added restrictions, to say anything more than that the availability of the income tax on migrants generally permits the tax feasibility locus to be improved over that in the open economy without this added policy instrument. Hence, whether one maximizes TLB welfare more generally or takes the extreme Rawlsian case, it would be possible to improve welfare with the use of the income tax on migrants.[25]

At the same time, it is important to note that the income tax on migrants can be utilized so as to correct the choice on migration so as to fulfill the global-efficiency requirement that the migrants choose to migrate when their gross, unadjusted incomes abroad exceed the gross, unadjusted incomes at home. However, it cannot obviously be used to correct the inefficiency of the choice regarding the length of education (which requires the use of the educational subsidy, as already discussed in the preceding section).

5. All three policy instruments: Global efficiency and TLB welfare maximization

Now, we know from section 4 that an income tax on migrants can be used to correct the choice on migration but cannot correct for the inefficiency in the choice of educational length as required for domestic efficiency. At the same time, it is evident that the use of an educational subsidy can assist in achieving domestic efficiency but cannot correct for the socially inefficient

[25] We have therefore not elevated this simple, but important, conclusion into a proposition in the text. Note also that we *could* say something more if we were to attempt a solution to the very difficult analytical problem of choosing α, β, t and τ so as to secure the best tax feasibility locus in the 'monopolistic' case discussed in the text.

(from the global viewpoint in the restricted sense discussed above) choice on migration. It should be evident, therefore, that the use of *both* the educational subsidy *and* the income tax on migrants ought to enable us to achieve domestic *and* global efficiency.

An interesting problem for us to analyze, therefore, is the characterization of the optimal levels of these policy instruments. Moreover, it would be important to ask whether, if the educational subsidy and the income tax on migrants were set in this way so as to achieve domestic and global efficiency, the tax feasibility locus for this open Atkinson economy would lie outside the tax feasibility locus for the open Atkinson economy which cannot use these policy instruments at all. In fact, it will. Therefore, we can argue that the use of the income tax, the income tax on migrants and the educational subsidy at appropriate values can both achieve domestic and global efficiency *and* improve the welfare of TLBs, vis-à-vis an economy that uses only the income tax and experiences migration. Indeed, we can go further and show that this global efficiency solution will also be characterized by virtual, full equity *and* will, in fact, be the first-best solution for TLB welfare.

5.1. Achieving global efficiency

Thus, consider first the achievement of (restricted) global efficiency by a suitable use of the three policy instruments, by examining the three choices in our model: the choice of the educational lengths for non-migrants and migrants respectively, and the decision to migrate.

5.1.1. Choice of the lengths of education

As for the educational choice of the *non-migrant*, it is easy to see that the first-order condition for a private maximum will be given by

$$A\{-i(\alpha+\beta f)+\beta f_S\}+G=0, \tag{24}$$

as shown in Hamada (1974) for a closed economy, and where G is the educational subsidy. On the other hand, we get from (22) the first-order condition for a social maximum as: $A\{-if+f_S\}=0$. Hence, equality between (22) and (24) implies an educational subsidy such that

$$G=Ai\alpha=\alpha(1-e^{-iR}). \tag{25}$$

By a similar reasoning, we can deduce the educational subsidy for the migrants. Thus, the private-maximum first-order condition for potential migrants is readily shown to be

$$A\{-i(\alpha^*+\beta^*f^*)+\beta^*f_S^*\}+iC+G=0, \tag{24a}$$

and for a social maximum it is

$$A\{-if^*+f_S^*\}+iC=0, \tag{22a}$$

so that reconciling (24a) and (22a) yields the educational subsidy for the potential migrants as

$$G=\alpha^*(1-e^{-iR})-(1-\beta^*)iC. \tag{25a}$$

However, the educational subsidy must evidently be given uniformly to all individuals. Therefore (25) and (25a) should be equated so that we must have

$$\alpha^*=\alpha+\frac{i}{1-e^{-iR}}(1-\beta^*)C=\alpha+\frac{(1-\beta^*)}{A(R)}C, \tag{26}$$

i.e. if the migration cost C is negligible, the same intercept must be chosen for the (domestic) income tax, and the income tax on migrants' schedules.

5.1.2. Decision to migrate

There remains now the problem of the choice between staying at home and going abroad. One therefore has to choose the tax scheme in such a way as to ensure the socially efficient choice in this regard. In fact, we shall prove that the linear income tax on foreign income combined with educational subsidy and the domestic income tax, satisfies this requirement provided that β^* is set equal to β.

Now, the condition for the globally efficient choice for deciding to emigrate is

$$\hat{\Gamma}=\left[\int_{\hat{S}^*}^{\hat{S}^*+R} f^* e^{-it}\,dt-Ce^{-i\hat{S}^*}\right]-\int_{\hat{S}}^{\hat{S}+R} fe^{-it}\,dt>0, \tag{26'}$$

where both $\hat{S}$ and $\hat{S}^*$ are chosen to satisfy the marginal condition for securing the efficiency of the length of education. On the other hand, individuals will migrate according to the (private) condition:

$$\Gamma=\int_{\hat{S}^*}^{\hat{S}^*+R}(\alpha^*+\beta^*f^*)e^{-it}\,dt-Ce^{-i\hat{S}^*}+G\int_0^{\hat{S}^*}e^{-it}\,dt$$

$$-\left[\int_{\hat{S}}^{\hat{S}+R}(\alpha+\beta f)e^{-it}\,dt+G\int_0^{\hat{S}}e^{-it}\,dt\right]>0$$

which, in view of (26), equals:

$$\alpha\left[\int_{\hat{S}^*}^{\hat{S}^*+R} e^{-it}\,dt-\int_{\hat{S}}^{\hat{S}+R} e^{-it}\,dt\right]$$

$$+\left[\int_{\hat{S}}^{\hat{S}^*+R}\frac{(1-\beta^*)}{A}Ce^{-it}\,dt-(1-\beta^*)Ce^{-i\hat{S}^*}\right]$$

$$+G\left[\int_{0}^{\hat{S}^*} e^{-it}\,dt-\int_{0}^{\hat{S}} e^{-it}\,dt\right]$$

$$+\beta^*\left[\int_{\hat{S}^*}^{\hat{S}^*+R} f^*e^{-it}\,dt-Ce^{-i\hat{S}^*}\right]-\beta\int_{\hat{S}}^{\hat{S}+R} fe^{-it}\,dt>0.$$

It is easy to see, however, that the second bracket vanishes. Moreover, if we substitute here $G=\alpha(1-e^{-iR})$, it can be seen that:

$$\alpha\left[\int_{\hat{S}^*}^{\hat{S}^*+R} e^{-it}\,dt-\int_{\hat{S}}^{\hat{S}+R} e^{-it}\,dt\right]+G\left[\int_{0}^{\hat{S}^*} e^{-it}\,dt-\int_{0}^{\hat{S}} e^{-it}\,dt\right]=0.$$

Therefore, the criterion for the private decision on migration reduces to:

$$\Gamma=\beta^*\left[\int_{\hat{S}^*}^{\hat{S}^*+R} f^*e^{-it}\,dt-Ce^{-i\hat{S}^*}\right]-\beta\int_{\hat{S}}^{\hat{S}+R} fe^{-it}\,dt>0. \qquad (27)$$

Therefore, if and only if β^* is set equal to β, permitting the fulfillment of (26) and (27) simultaneously, will the criterion for the optimal decision for emigration be satisfied.

The equalization of (26) and (27) therefore yields the condition for securing the globally efficient choice on the decision to migrate:

$$\beta=\beta^*. \qquad (28)$$

5.2. Properties of the globally efficient solution

Therefore, setting the three policy instruments at appropriate values, i.e. those that satisfy (26) and (28), will ensure global efficiency in our open Atkinson economy.

At the same time, it is immediately obvious that setting $\beta=\beta^*$ virtually close to zero would again ensure, as argued in Hamada (1974), that full equity would be achieved alongside domestic (*and*, now restricted global) efficiency. Therefore we have a generalization of the closed-economy Hamada (1974) result to an open economy, thanks to the availability of one more instrument (i.e. the income tax on migrants) when the economy is opened. Thus, we can conclude:

Proposition 4. By a combined, appropriate use of the (domestic) income tax, the income tax on migrants and the educational subsidy, (restricted) global efficiency can be achieved while the home country achieves both domestic efficiency and 'almost' full equity. This requires that the marginal rate of taxation for the two income taxes be identical and virtually equal to unity, whereas the intercept for the income tax on migrants' schedule will differ from that for the (domestic) income tax schedule by virtue of the migration cost.

Now it is obvious that the tax feasibility locus for this globally efficient open economy will lie outside that for the inefficient open economy which cannot use the educational subsidy and the income tax on migrants, so that TLBs ought to *improve* their welfare. But, we can go beyond the obvious and show something much stronger: namely, that our generalized solution of efficiency *plus* virtually full equity constitutes also the first-best, i.e. the welfare-*maximizing*, solution for TLBs. For global efficiency implies that world output, produced by both TLBs and migrants, is maximized provided that there is no distortion abroad. At the same time, $\beta^*\rightarrow 0$ implies that maximal revenue is being collected by the home country (α^* cannot be reduced below α without *both* disrupting the efficiency condition *and* eliminating migration altogether and therefore resulting in a closed economy, given $\beta=\beta^*\rightarrow 0$). Therefore, TLB welfare ought to be at a maximum in this solution. Thus we can conclude:

Proposition 5. The solution in proposition 4 is, at the same time, the welfare-maximizing first-best solution for TLBs.

Note finally that β^* is the marginal slope of the disposable income of the migrants *net* of both foreign-country and the home-country income taxes. How then are β and β^* to be equated by the home country given the fact that the foreign-country tax schedule is to be considered as exogenously determined? This equality can be achieved simply in the following way. First, let the home country extend its (domestic) income tax schedule to migrants. Second, as per double-taxation-avoidance arrangements, let the tax payments to the foreign country be made deductible as tax credits from tax liability to the home country. Third, to allow for the migration cost (C) complication already noted, let amount $(1-\beta^*)iC$ be credited also against the tax liability of the migrants to the home country. The satisfaction of the first two conditions will then ensure that $\beta = \beta^*$ and, of the third, will ensure that the required relationship between α and α^* [in eq. (26)] will also be satisfied, *provided* the marginal income tax rate for the foreign country is less than that of the home country.[26,27]

6. Concluding observations

The main objective of the present paper has been to initiate a formal public-finance-theoretic analysis of an important policy issue that has come to attract attention from policymakers: namely, the exercise of home-country income tax jurisdiction over nationals working abroad.

Our main results have been developed by assuming that the home country maximized the welfare of the TLBs ('those left behind'). This social objective may appear reasonable to policymakers even though nationals who work abroad are part of the national population, especially if the TLBs are at the lower end of unadjusted income distribution and the migrants at the upper end. Our welfare criterion can be regarded as an extension of the Rawls criterion, not applied to the individual with minimum income but to a predetermined band of individuals who are in lower income brackets. On the other hand, one may well want to ask what happens to the migrants' welfare in our exercises in this paper since policies that improve the welfare of the TLBs may well be worsening that of the migrants, resulting in a trade-off that may need to be addressed in policymaking.[28] To adapt our analysis to this newly defined objective function, which extends over the augmented and full set of nationals, we do not need to amend the derivation of the tax feasibility loci in the analysis but rather to amend the (indirect) social indifference curves defined on the tax parameters. We hope to return to this task in another paper.

Appendix

This appendix is designed to prove some properties of the $h(n)$ function, the tax feasibility locus, and the social welfare function. These properties are

[26] As Hamada (1978) has noted, this proviso is generally satisfied for migration from the developing to the developed countries. The extension of domestic tax schedules to migrants, with double-taxation relief, was proposed there as a device to restore global efficiency in a two-country world.

[27] Of course, one cannot actually *recommend* this first-best solution without reservations. In the real world, the threshold of perception or incentives may be quite high. Moreover, the administrative cost of redistribution may not be negligible. Our analysis in this section only shows that there is a *structure* implied in the model of income taxation deployed such that the conflict between equity and efficiency can be undone by a combination of proper instruments.

[28] The delicate issue of comparing the welfare of different groups of people, in an environment where equity and efficiency considerations interact, is beautifully analyzed in the companion paper by Baumol (1982) in this Symposium.

utilized in the text, as noted at appropriate places. We define, as in the text,

$$h(n^*) \equiv (1-n^{*-\mu})/(1-n^{*-\mu+1}).$$

Remark 1. **If $n^*>1$, and $\mu>1$, then $h(n^*)>1$.**

Proof.

$$h(n^*)-1=\frac{n^{*-\mu+1}-n^{*-\mu}}{1-n^{*-\mu+1}}>0, \quad \text{for } n^*>1.$$

Remark 2. If $n^*>\mu/(\mu-1)$, then $h'(n^*)<0$.

Proof.

$$h'(n^*)=\frac{-(\mu-1)n^{*-\mu-1}\left\{n^*-\dfrac{\mu}{\mu-1}\right\}-n^{*-2\mu}}{(1-n^{*-\mu+1})^2}<0.$$

Remark 3. The slope of tangent line to the opportunity locus expressed by eq. (14) in the text is steeper than $1/\bar{n}$ as long as the opportunity locus is downward-sloping.

Proof. Totally differentiating (14), taking account of the fact that n^* depends on β and n_0, one obtains:

$$\mathrm{d}\beta=-\frac{\mathrm{d}n_0}{\bar{n}}h(n^*)-\frac{n_0}{\bar{n}}h'(n^*)\left(\frac{\partial n^*}{\partial\beta}\mathrm{d}\beta+\frac{\partial n^*}{\partial n_0}\mathrm{d}n_0\right).$$

Therefore

$$\frac{\mathrm{d}\beta}{\mathrm{d}n_0}=-\frac{1}{\bar{n}}\left\{h(n^*)+n_0h'(n^*)\frac{\partial n^*}{\partial n_0}\right\}\Bigg/\left\{1+\frac{n_0}{\bar{n}}h'(n^*)\frac{\partial n^*}{\partial\beta}\right\}. \tag{A1}$$

When the opportunity locus is downward-sloping, the denominator in the brace is positive. (If the denominator changes its sign from positive to negative, then the opportunity locus becomes tangent to a vertical line at some value of β and tilts into an upward-sloping locus. However, this upward-sloping locus does not interest us because the point on this portion of locus can never be efficient.)

On the other hand, from (11), (13) and the definition of n_0, one obtains:

$$I_{\mathrm{d}}=\frac{An}{ie}\beta\exp\left(\frac{n_0}{n}\right).$$

It is easy to notice that a marginal change in n_0 shifts the I_{d} schedule just β/n^* times as the change of β shifts it. Therefore, by applying the same reasoning as used to derive (5) (cf. fig. 1), one obtains:

$$\frac{\partial n^*}{\partial n_0}=\frac{\beta}{n^*}\frac{\partial n^*}{\partial \beta}. \tag{A2}$$

Therefore,

$$\left\{h(n^*)+n_0 h'(n^*)\frac{\partial n}{\partial n_0}\right\}\Big/\left\{1+\frac{n_0}{\bar{n}}h'(n^*)\frac{\partial n^*}{\partial \beta}\right\}$$

$$=h(n^*)\left\{1+\frac{\beta}{n^*h(n^*)}\left(n_0 h'(n^*)\frac{\partial n^*}{\partial \beta}\right)\right\}\Big/\left\{1+\frac{1}{\bar{n}}\left(n_0 h'(n^*)\frac{\partial n^*}{\partial \beta}\right)\right\}. \tag{A3}$$

Because $h(n^*)>1$, $\beta<1$ and $n^*>\bar{n}$, we get:

$$\frac{\beta}{n^*h(n^*)}<\frac{1}{\bar{n}}. \tag{A4}$$

Since $n_0 h'(n^*)(\partial n^*/\partial\beta)$ is negative, and since the denominator is assumed to be positive, one can conclude from (A4) that the r.h.s. of eq. (A3) is larger than $h(n^*)$, because the brace in the numerator is larger than the brace in the denominator, which itself is positive. Therefore, we can conclude from (A1) and (A3) that:

$$\frac{\mathrm{d}\beta}{\mathrm{d}n_0}<-\frac{1}{\bar{n}},$$

which is in fact (15).

Remark 4. The absolute slope of the indifference curve is an increasing function of n_0 along a horizontal line if $\rho<1$, and a decreasing function of n_0 if $\rho>1$.

Proof. The Schwarz Inequality says [e.g. Royden (1968, p. 210)]: Let g_1 and g_2 be integrable functions with respect to $\mathrm{d}F$. Then

$$|\int g_1\,\mathrm{d}F|\cdot|\int g_2\,\mathrm{d}F| \geqq [\int g_1 g_2\,\mathrm{d}F]^2.$$

Let us write, for economy of space:

$$\int_1^N n^{-\rho}\exp[(1-\rho)n_0/n]\,p(n)\,\mathrm{d}n \equiv \int n^{-\rho},$$

$$\int_1^N n^{1-\rho}\exp[(1-\rho)n_0/n]\,p(n)\,\mathrm{d}n \equiv \int n^{1-\rho},$$

and so forth.

Then

$$\frac{\partial}{\partial n_0}\left[-\frac{\mathrm{d}\beta}{\mathrm{d}n_0}\right] = \beta\frac{\partial}{\partial n_0}[\int n^{-\rho}/\int n^{1-\rho}]$$

$$= \beta(1-\rho)\frac{[\int n^{-1-\rho}][\int n^{1-\rho}]-[\int n^{-\rho}]^2}{[\int n^{1-\rho}]^2}$$

$$\begin{cases} >0, & \text{if } \rho<1, \\ <0, & \text{if } \rho>1. \end{cases}$$

For, by the Schwarz inequality applied to $\mathrm{d}F = \exp[(1-\rho)n_0/n]\,p(n)\,\mathrm{d}n$

$$[\int n^{-1-\rho}][\int n^{1-\rho}] \geqq [\int n^{-\rho}]^2$$

and the equality does not hold because the integrands are not proportional to each other.

References

Atkinson, A.B., 1973, How progressive should income tax be?, in: M. Parkin, ed., Essays in modern economics (Longman, London).

Baumol, W.B., 1982, The income distribution frontier and taxation of migrants, Journal of Public Economics 18, this issue.

Bhagwati, J., 1972, The United States in the Nixon era: The end of innocence, Daedalus.

Bhagwati, J. 1976, ed., The brain drain and taxation: Theory and empirical analysis (North-Holland, Amsterdam).

Bhagwati, J., 1979, International migration of the highly skilled: Economics, ethics and taxes, Third World Quarterly 1, 17–30.

Bhagwati, J. and W. Dellalfar, 1973, The brain drain and income taxation, World Development 1, 94–101.
Bhagwati, J. and K. Hamada, 1974, The brain drain, international integration of markets for professionals and unemployment: A theoretical analysis, Journal of Development Economics 1; reprinted in revised version in Bhagwati (1976).
Bhagwati, J. and M. Partington, eds., 1976, Taxing the brain drain: A proposal (North-Holland, Amsterdam).
Bhagwati, J. and C. Rodriguez, 1975, Welfare-theoretical analyses of the brain drain, Journal of Development Economics 2; reprinted in Bhagwati (1976).
Cooper, P.N., 1973, Economic mobility and national economic policy (Almquist and Wicksell International, Stockholm).
Hamada, K., 1966, Strategic aspects of taxation on foreign investment income, Quarterly Journal of Economics 80, 351–375.
Hamada, K., 1972, Lifetime equity and dynamic efficiency on the balanced growth path, Journal of Public Economics 1, 379–396.
Hamada, K., 1974, Income taxation and educational subsidy, Journal of Public Economics 3, 145–158.
Hamada, K., 1975, Efficiency, equity, income taxation and the brain drain: A second best argument, Journal of Development Economics 2, 281–287.
Hamada, K., 1978, Taxing the brain drain: A global point of view, in: J. Bhagwati, ed., The new international economic order: The north–south debate (MIT Press) ch. 5.
Harris, J. and M. Todaro, 1970, Migration, unemployment and development: A two-sector analysis, American Economics Review 60, 126–142.
McCulloch, R. and J. Yellen, 1975, Consequences of a tax on the brain drain for unemployment and income inequality in the LDCs, Journal of Developments Economics 2; reprinted in Bhagwati (1976).
Mirrlees, J.A., 1971, An exploration in the theory of optimum income taxation, Review of Economic Studies 38, 175–208.
Oldman, Oliver and Richard Pomp, 1975, The brain drain: A tax analysis of the Bhagwati proposal, World Development 3; reprinted in Bhagwati (1976).
Oldman, Oliver and Richard Pomp, 1977, Consideration of policy issues at the international level, legal and administrative aspects of compensation, taxation and related policy measures: Suggestions for an optimal policy mix, Paper for the Intergovernmental Group of Experts Meeting at UNCTAD, Geneva, UN Doc. TD/B/C.6/AC.4/7, Geneva.
Oldman, Oliver and Richard Pomp, 1979, Tax measures in response to the brain drain, Harvard International Law Journal 20, Winter.
Rawls, John, 1971, A theory of justice (Harvard University Press).
Rodriguez, D., 1975, Brain drain and economic growth: A dynamic model, Journal of Development Economics 2.
Royden, H.L., 1968, Real analysis, 2nd edn. (Macmillan, New York).
Wilson, John D., 1978, The effect of potential emigration on the optimal linear income tax, Journal of Public Economics 14, 339–353.

III
TRADE AND WELFARE IN THE PRESENCE OF FOREIGN FACTORS OF PRODUCTION

Journal of Development Economics 7 (1980) 71–83. © North-Holland Publishing Company

TARIFF CHANGE, FOREIGN CAPITAL AND IMMISERIZATION

A Theoretical Analysis*

Jagdish N. BHAGWATI
M.I.T., Cambridge, MA 02139, USA

Ernesto TIRONI
CIEPLAN, Santiago, Chile

Received January 1979, final version received April 1979

This paper analyzes the possibility that tariff reductions in the presence of foreign capital may be immiserizing. Other impacts of tariff revisions in a Latin America-like context are also discussed.

1. Introduction

It is now fully appreciated that foreign capital inflow may be immiserizing in the presence of a distortionary tariff, as noted by Bhagwati (1973), Uzawa (1969), Hamada (1974), Minabe (1974) and most elegantly and definitively by Brecher and Alejandro (1977).

The concerns of Latin American policymakers with the implications of trade liberalization in the presence of private foreign investment suggest the obverse and novel analytical possibility: that tariff reduction, in the presence of foreign capital, may be immiserizing.

This paper is addressed to analyzing this immiserization possibility, as also more generally the welfare impact of tariff change, in the context of the traditional 2×2 model of trade theory. Section 2 develops briefly one case of immiserization in such a model, sufficing to prove the possibility of such immiserization. Section 3 then systematically traces the effects of continuously varying tariffs and trade subsidies, from autarky to complete specialization, on overall welfare change, gross and net of the 'redistribution

*The credit for noting the fact that foreign capital raises difficulties for trade liberalization belongs fully to Ernesto Tironi whose MIT dissertation (1976a) discussed this in relation to the Andean Common Market, using partial-equilibrium analytical tools. Also see Tironi (1976b, 1977). Thanks are due to the National Science Foundation, Grant No. SOC77-07188 and the Program of Research on the International Economic Order of the Ford Foundation for support of the research underlying this paper. We are grateful to Richard Brecher and T.N. Srinivasan for many helpful comments.

effect', under specified assumptions concerning the domestic and foreign ownership of primary factors of production, the distribution of tariff proceeds and the incidence of taxes to pay the trade subsidy (if the tariff is a subsidy), and the factor-intensity of traded goods. Section 4 extends the analysis briefly to tariff changes in the context of customs unions.

2. Immiserization: An example

Take two primary factors, K (capital) and L (labour) in fixed supply, and two traded goods, X and Y. Let all capital be foreign-owned. Assume the country is small in the Samuelson sense, i.e., the terms of trade are fixed. Let Y be the importable good and assume it to be L-intensive while good X is K-intensive. To avoid tariff-revenue problems, we will compare free trade with autarky.

Then starting from autarky, the move to free trade should unambiguously improve welfare if all factors were domestic. However, the decline in the relative price of the importable good Y, which is L-intensive, will lead (as per the well-known Stolper–Samuelson argument) to a decline in the real wage of labour and a rise in the real rental of capital. Since labour is in fixed supply, it is clear that it is unambiguously hurt and, since all capital is foreign-owned, this is tantamount to net welfare for the country having declined.

3. Welfare effects of continuous tariff variation in the presence of foreign capital

The preceding analysis is sufficient to establish how trade liberalization in the presence of foreign capital may yield immiseration. However, a complete categorization of the effect of continuous tariff variation on net welfare of a country with foreign capital can be made, as in the rest of this paper.

We will simplify our analysis in two critical respects, throughout this paper. First, we will assume that the country has no monopoly power in trade, i.e., its external terms of trade are fixed. Second, all labour is domestic and all capital is foreign. The latter assumption enables us to carry over here, without serious modification, the existing theoretical analysis of the impact of tariff change on the domestic rewards of different factors of production, as initiated by the celebrated Stolper-Samuelson analysis.

Note initially that the variation of the tariff from the prohibitive to the zero level, in the 2×2 model, will raise now the problem of deciding on the allocation of the tariff revenue between domestic and foreign factors of production. Equally, if we permit the tariff variation to negative values and thus to include trade subsidies, we will need to decide on the allocation of the tax burden to pay these subsidies. Since the welfare implications depend critically on the assumptions made in these two respects, as also on whether the importable good is capital-intensive or labour-intensive, a taxonomic mapping of the welfare implications must be undertaken.

We need to distinguish between two primary possibilities determined by whether the importable is capital-intensive (Case I) or labour-intensive (Case II). In regard to tariff revenues, it makes little economic sense to consider the case where they are distributed to foreign capital. Therefore, all cases will assume that tariff revenue accrues to domestic factors through lump-sum redistribution à la Meade's analysis (1950). However, since we extend the analysis to trade subsidies, and taxes to pay the trade subsidies can well fall on foreign capital, we will explicitly consider this possibility as also the possibility that the incidence of such taxation is wholly on domestic labour. Moreover, we will assume that there is no repatriation of earnings of foreign capital, all such earnings being spent in the host country itself.

3.1. Welfare change as tariff varies, with no foreign capital

First, let us recall the welfare impact of continuous tariff variation in this small country on the assumption that all factors are domestically owned. We will then be able to contrast these results with the implications of the presence of foreign capital that we derive in the rest of this paper.

Denote overall, 'gross' welfare, *as if* all capital were domestic, by the ordinal index U^G and the national welfare (i.e., welfare of the domestic factors *alone*), by U^N, the standard assumptions being made in each case to make the implied social utility function valid.[1]

Then, for a small country, in fig. 1, with production possibility curve QS and world prices fixed at EF, autarky production and consumption are at A and free trade production and consumption are at F and E respectively. The corresponding utility levels show that $U^G(A) < U^G(F)$, since free trade is superior to autarky.[2]

Now, it is known that,[3] ruling out inferior goods (which we do, throughout here), continuous tariff variation leading from F to A in fig. 1 will yield a monotonically decreasing U^G. Any further shift beyond A towards Q however is impossible with only a tariff since any further increase in the prohibitive tariff at A would only be redundant.[4] On the other hand,

[1]The distinction between U^G and U^N in utility terms corresponds to the distinction between *GDP* and *GNP* in terms of income.

[2]Strictly speaking, $U^G(A) \leqq U^G(F)$ since A may coincide with F; and $U^G(F)$ is also the maximal utility obtainable under the assumptions made.

[3]Cf. Bhagwati (1968) and Kemp (1968). For the large-country tariff ranking by welfare impact, see Bhagwati and Kemp (1969).

[4]However, as Richard Brecher has pointed out to us, the *simultaneous* use beyond A of an *export* subsidy for good Y would make a move to Q feasible. This possibility is ignored below.

it is possible with a trade subsidy to move from F to S and the continuous increase in the trade subsidy until it leads to complete specialization at S will yield a monotonically declining social utility. The total plot of U^G, as the

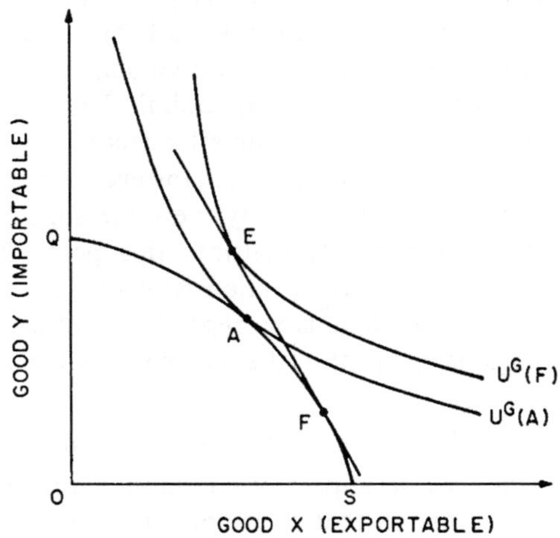

Fig. 1

tariff is therefore varied from the prohibitive level at A to the negative value that brings specialization at S, is then in fig. 2. Since $U^G(S)\gtreqless U^G(A)$, the left-hand side subsidy quadrant shows these three alternative possibilities;[5] on the other hand, $U^G(F)>U^G(A)$ and $U^G(F)>U^G(S)$.[6]

3.2. Case I: Importable capital-intensive, tariff revenue accruing only to domestic factors, capital wholly foreign

Consider now the effect on national welfare (U^N), accruing only to domestic factors, for the same range of tariff variation, when (homogeneous) capital is wholly foreign-owned and tariff revenue goes only to domestic factors. We consider here the case where the importable is capital-intensive.

Consider first the variation in the tariff from A to F, from autarky to free trade. As the domestic relative price of the importable falls, so does the real rental of capital a la Stolper–Samuelson. With no tariff revenue assumed to be going to foreign capital, foreign capital therefore unambiguously and

[5] $U^G(S^1)=U^G(A)$, $U^G(S^2)>U^G(A)$, and $U^G(S^3)<U^G(A)$.

[6] Again, strictly speaking, $U^G(F)\geqq U^G(A)$ as A and F may coincide, and $U^G(F)>U^G(S)$ as F and S may coincide, although figs. 1 and 2 are drawn to exclude the equality signs and our arguments in the text consistently exclude them.

continuously loses. On the other hand, the fact that U^G would unambiguously increase as the tariff is reduced for this small country means also that, with all tariff revenue being redistributed to domestic factors

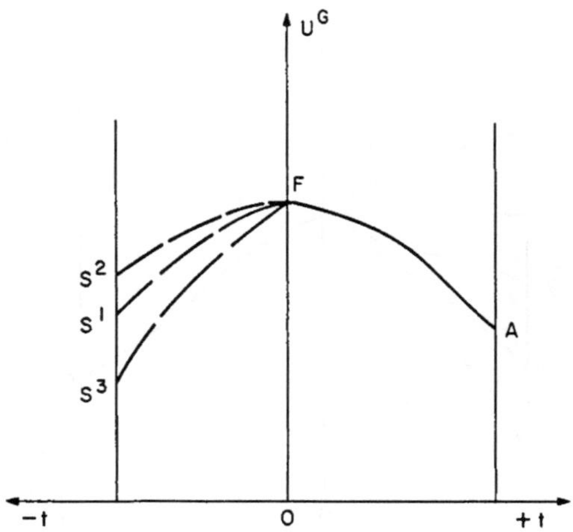

Fig. 2

(labour) by assumption, the real income of labour in terms of either good must increase with successive tariff reductions.[7] It follows of course that national welfare would correspondingly improve since it must reflect labour's welfare in our model. The plot of the changes in U^N, as the tariff is varied from the autarkic level to zero, is therefore monotonically welfare-improving for U^N (as it was for U^G), as seen in the right-hand side quadrant of fig. 3.

As the tariff goes from zero to negative values with a trade subsidy, the 'redistribution effect' à la Stolper–Samuelson real wage argument continues to operate against capital. However, the tariff revenue is now replaced by the trade subsidy which must be paid for by lump-sum taxation on the factors. If the incidence of the taxation is on domestic factors as well, then the fact that U^G is declining from F to S (instead of rising, as from A to F) will imply that the improved real wage of domestic labour may well be accompnied by a decline in its real income (i.e., wage net of taxes) and hence by reduced U^N.

Thus, in principle, trade subsidy variation in the presence of foreign capital may result in specialization with a range of welfare outcomes regarding the

[7]For a similar argument in the context of the Stolper–Samuelson theorem, see Bhagwati (1959). This paper introduced for the first time the distinction, relevant here, between real wage and real income, the latter defined as real wage plus redistributed tariff revenue. For a brilliant subsequent analysis of the extension of the Stolper–Samuelson theorem on real wages to real incomes, see Rao (1971).

free trade and the autarkic levels of national welfare: $U^N(S) \gtreqless U^N(F)$ and $U^N(S) \gtreqless U^N(A)$, as illustrated in fig. 3.[8] Moreover, unlike the the right-hand side quadrant, there will be lack of monotonicity in the left-hand side quadrant in fig. 3.

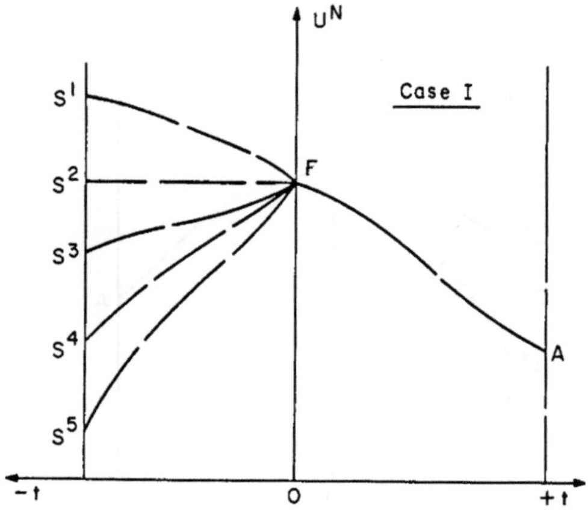

Fig. 3

3.3. *Case II: Importable labour-intensive, tariff revenue accruing only to domestic factors, capital wholly foreign*

For the alternative case where the importable good is labour-intensive, the redistribution of earned income is now in favour of capital.

As the economy moves from autarky to free trade, the falling price of the importable will then imply a falling real wage of labour and a rising real rental of capital. We have already noted, in section 1, that $U^N(A) > U^N(F)$ because the real wage of labour, which alone constitutes domestic factors, is lower under free trade than under autarky. However, for tariff rates in the interval of A and F, tariff revenue arises and will be redistributed to domestic factors, i.e., to labour. Therefore, there *could* be welfare-improving tariff-reduction, between A and F and the decline of U^N from $U^N(A)$ to $U^N(F)$ need not be monotonic: as indicated by the two alternative schedules drawn in the right-hand side quadrants of fig. 4.

If we extend the argument now to trade subsidies, increasing trade subsidy from free trade (F) to complete specialization (S) will keep increasing the real rental of capital and lowering the real wage of labour. However, if part of all of the incidence of taxation to pay the subsidy falls on labour, its real income

[8]In fig. 3, $U^N(S^4) = U^N(A)$, $U^N(S^2) = U^N(F)$, $U^N(S^1) > U^N(F)$, $U^N(S^5) < U^N(A)$ and $U^N(S^3) > U^N(A)$. $U^N(F) > U^N(A)$, always.

will collapse even more. Therefore, assuming that the subsidy payments rise monotonically with the rate of trade subsidy, $U^N(F)$ will decline monotonically to $U^N(S)$ with increasing trade subsidy rate, as illustrated in the left-hand side quadrant of fig. 4. It follows moreover that $U^N(A) > U^N(F) > U^N(S)$, as drawn in fig. 4.

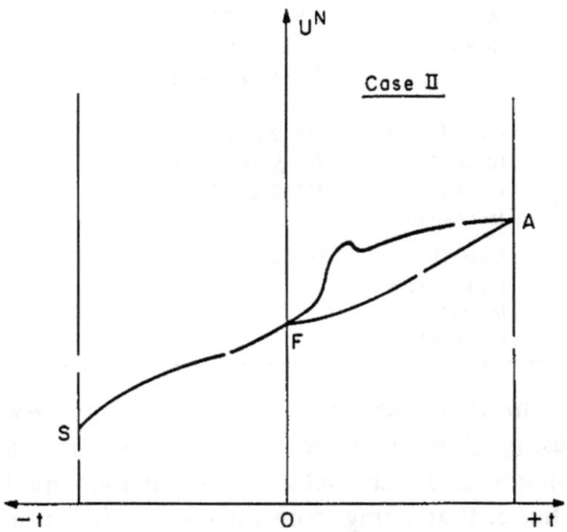

Fig. 4

3.4. *Summary of welfare rankings of zero tariff, prohibitive tariff and trade subsidy (just) producing complete specialization*

The results of welfare rankings, by U^G and U^N, for the tariff rate producing autarky, for free trade with zero tariff, and for the trade subsidy just producing complete specialization on the exportable good, can then be summarized, as in table 1. Evidently, the presence of foreign capital affects the welfare impact of tariff variation critically.

3.5. *Illustrating with the Johnson technique*

The results derived above can be readily illustrated with the aid of the general-equilibrium diagrammatic technique introduced by Johnson (1959, 1960) to deal with income distribution in the 2×2 model. This technique, as adapted from Tironi (1976b), brings out well the role of the Stolper–Samuelson theorem in determining the behaviour of real wages, while also permitting the reader to see clearly the role that tariff revenue (or subsidy payment) plays in determining the impact on real income (i.e., earned wages *plus* redistributed tariff revenue or *minus* lump-sum taxation to pay the trade

Table 1

Welfare rankings of autarky (using tariff), free trade and complete specialization (using trade subsidy), by U^G and U^N.

Utility index	Case	Comparisons of autarky (A), free trade (F) and complete specialization (S)
U^G (on assumption of no foreign capital)	All cases	$U^G(A)<U^G(F)$ $U^G(S)<U^G(F)$ $U^G(S)\gtreqless U^G(A)$
U^N (national welfare on assumption of wholly foreign capital and wholly domestic labour)	Case I (importable capital-intensive)	$U^N(A)<U^N(F)$ $U^N(S)\gtreqless U^N(F)$ $U^N(S)\gtreqless U^N(A)$
	Case II (importable labour-intensive)	$U^N(A)>U^N(F)>U^N(S)$

subsidy) and hence on national welfare. To economise on space, we illustrate only the following, using Case II where the importable is labour-intensive, capital is wholly foreign and the welfare comparison involves no tariff revenue effect: (i) in fig. 5, that going from autarky to free trade will *worsen* U^N, i.e., $U^N(F)<U^N(A)$, and (ii) in fig. 6, that a tariff reduction from autarky to a non-zero *non-prohibitive* level could however *raise* U^N because the tariff revenue in the new situation, when redistributed to domestic labour, could more than offset the effect of the reduced real wage.

Thus, in fig. 5, QS is the production possibility curve, with good X capital-intensive and good Y, the importable, labour-intensive. As the price-ratio faced by producers shifts in favour of the exportable good, i.e., from Q through A, F and S, the Stolper–Samuelson argument implies that the real wage of labour keeps going down. Q_LS_L is then the well-known 'income distribution' locus for labour, as derived by Johnson (1959): for each point on it, draw the ray from the origin to QS, and the ratio of labour's factor income to total income then is the ratio of the ray's length to Q_LS_L to its entire length to QS. Thus, for end-points Q and S, the labour share in income is OQ_L/OQ and OS_L/OS respectively. The decline in the absolute and relative share of labour in total income implies that $OQ_L/OQ>OM/OA>ON/OF>OS_L/OS$.

The budget line for labour is correspondingly given, for each equilibrium production point on QS, by drawing a line parallel to the price-line tangent to that production point and at the same time going through the intersection of the ray from the intersection of the ray from the origin to that production point with the Q_LS_L locus. Thus, for example, corresponding to autarkic production at A, labour's budget line is $A'MA''$, for production at F, it is

$F'NF''$, and for production at S, it is $S'S_L$. Moreover, given the real wage behaviour a la Stolper–Samuelson, it is clear that $A'MA''$ lies uniformly outside $F'NF''$ and the latter in turn uniformly outside $S'S_L$.

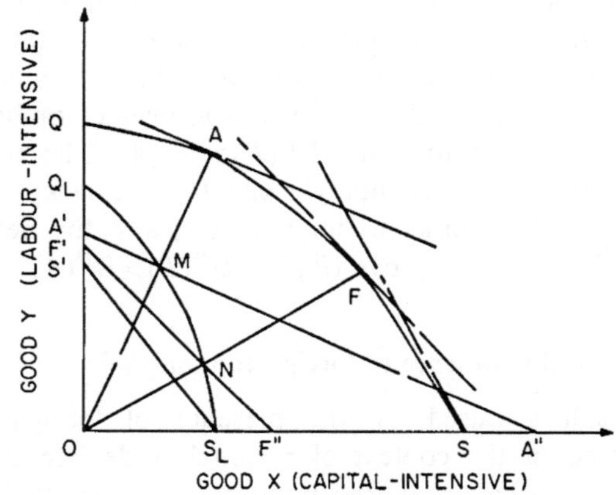

Fig. 5

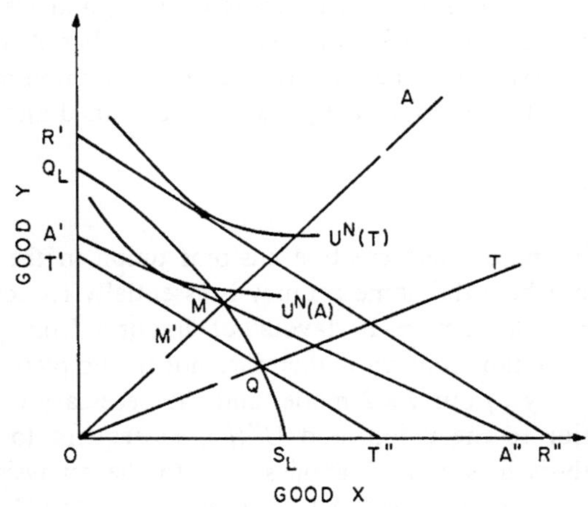

Fig. 6

It is then evident that, when the economy shifts from autarky at A to free trade at F, the relevant budget line for labour shifts from $A'MA''$ to $F'NF''$. With all capital foreign-owned, it follows therefore that the shift to free trade will result in immiserization: $U^N(F)$, tangent to $F'NF''$, will be less than $U^N(A)$, tangent to $A'MA''$.

Consider next fig. 6 where we have shifted to comparison of the autarkic equilibrium with a non-prohibitive tariff which must be characterised by tariff revenue. We eliminate QS from fig. 6, while indicating production equilibria at A and T for autarky and non-prohibitive tariff and concentrate on $Q_L S_L$. For the autarkic equilibrium, labour's budget line – relevant for U^N – will remain $A'MA''$, as in fig. 5. But, for the non-prohibitive tariff equilibrium, the real-*wage*-determined budget line $T'M'T''$ (at *tariff-inclusive* price-ratio) must be augmented by redistributed tariff revenue which could take it, if tariff revenue were $T''R''$, to the real-*income*-determined budget line $R'R''$. The result would be to make $U^N(T) > U^N(A)$. The real-wage effect works to worsen U^N as the economy shifts from autarky but the tariff-revenue-distribution effect works to improve U^N, and the net effect in the case illustrated in fig. 6 is to improve U^N, i.e., $U^N(T) > U^N(A)$.

4. Customs unions in the presence of foreign capital

Since the difficulties raised by the presence of foreign capital were originally considered in the context of regional trade liberalization in the format of common markets and free trade areas, it would be relevant to show that our analysis can be readily applied to tariff change in the context of customs union. Thus, consider Viner's trade creating and trade diverting customs unions, in turn. We will consider only the 'basic' Viner–Lipsey models where offer curves from the partner and the non-union countries are perfectly elastic and only two goods are produced, consumed and traded.

4.1. Trade creating union

If we consider the 'pure' trade creating customs union in the well-known Lipsey (1957) model where the home country is essentially reducing its fully-protected importable production in favour of imports from the partner country, and the non-union country is therefore not in the picture at all, the model reduces basically to our 2×2 model and the necessary comparison is between $U^N(A)$, prior to the union, and $U^N(F)$, subsequent to the union.[9] Therefore, our analysis in section 3 applies *fully* to the analysis of a trade creating union: table 1 comparisons of $U^N(F)$ and $U^N(A)$ for Cases I and II are fully applicable. Evidently therefore, in Case II, a trade creating customs union *can* be immerserizing in the presence of foreign capital.

4.2. Trade diverting union

Where, however, the customs union diverts imports from the non-union to the partner country – Viner's trade diverting union – we may consider two

[9]The free trade position, however, is with the partner country, *not* with the world at large. Overall free trade, F^*, would lead to $U^N(F^*)$, which is not relevant here.

sub-cases: (i) where, as in Lipsey's (1957) classic paper on how the consumption gain can offset the terms of trade loss to make such a trade diverting union beneficial, we assume domestic production to be always specialized on the exportable; and (ii) where we allow home production to change with the union.

(i) In the former case, there is clearly no redistributive effect in production from the union as the importable price domestically falls within the union. However, the tariff revenue is lost as imports are switched from the non-union country before the union to the partner country after the union. If the tariff revenue was entirely redistributed to domestic labour, and capital is wholly foreign, we then can get a redistributive effect *against* domestic factors. Thus, even a 'large' consumption gain and 'small' terms of trade loss may be compatible with welfare loss (i.e., lower U^N) if this 'redistributive' effect from the tariff revenue is large enough in a pure trade diverting union. And, if we were to assume that some or all revenue goes to foreign factors – an unrealistic assumption, not made in section 3 – then clearly a trade diverting union, with no substitution in consumption and hence no consumption gain, may still result in improved U^N because of the 'redistributive' effect related to the tariff revenue.

Fig. 7 illustrates the case where such improvement in U^N takes place in a pure trade diverting union with zero consumption gain. Assume there that consumption takes place in the fixed proportion along the ray $OC_1C_2C_3$. Let

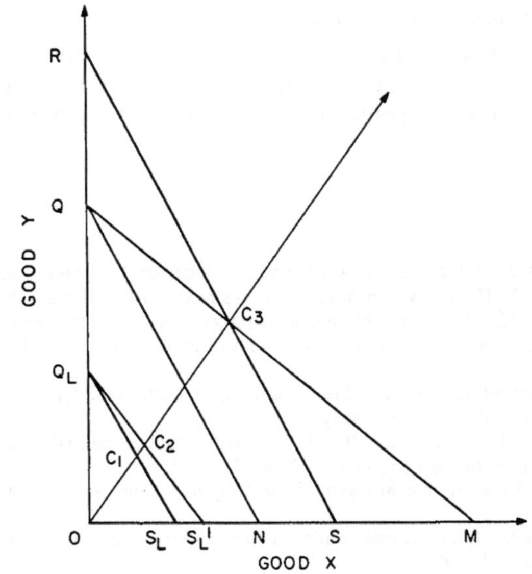

Fig. 7

Q be the endowment of Y-goods, with these being divided between foreign capital and domestic labour in the ratio QQ_L/Q_LO. Prior to the customs union, trade takes place from Q to C_3 at non-union country foreign price-ratio QM and domestic price-ratio is RS. The tariff revenue generated is NS and is redistributed to foreign capital. The tariff-revenue-inclusive income of foreign capital is therefore Q_LR(QQ_L of earnings plus QR of revenue) whereas the income of labour is Q_LO. With consumption of each factor group lying along the same ray $OC_1C_2C_3$, the pre-union consumption point for labour is C_1 on its budget line Q_LS_L whereas the difference between C_3 and C_1 constitutes the bundle consumed by foreign capital. The union then eliminates trade with the outside country and diverts it to the partner country at its price-line $Q_LS_L^1$. Since $Q_LS_L^1$ is steeper than QM, the country's terms of trade have deteriorated. However, the loss and more is absorbed by foreign capital; and domestic labour improves its welfare because its new budget line is $Q_LS_L^1$ and therefore, the shift from C_1 to C_2 implies a corresponding *improvement* in U^N, i.e., national welfare. The trade diverting union has clearly been beneficial, therefore, even though there is no consumption gain (nor production gain, i.e., decline in domestic production of protected importable in favour of imports from the partner country, or Viner's 'trade creation' in production): an outcome attributable solely to the assumption made regarding the distribution of tariff revenue to foreign capital alone.

(ii) In the case where production will also vary, the trade diverting union will also involve changes in income distribution à la Stolper–Samuelson with the production change and the net welfare impact of the union will be correspondingly complicated, exactly as in section 3. The details of this Case can be left for the interested reader to work out, in the manner set out in section 3.

References

Bhagwati, Jagdish N., 1959, Protection, real wages and real incomes, Economic Journal, Dec.

Bhagwati, Jagdish N., 1968, The gains from trade once again, Oxford Economic Papers, July.

Bhagwati, Jagdish N., 1973, The theory of immiserizing growth: Further applications, in: M. Connolly and A. Swoboda, eds., International trade and money (Allen and Unwin, London) 45–54.

Bhagwati, Jagdish N. and Murray Kemp, 1969, Ranking of tariffs under monopoly power in trade, Quarterly Journal of Economics, May.

Brecher, Richard and Carlos Diaz-Alejandro, 1977, Tariffs, foreign capital and immiserizing growth, Journal of International Economics 7, Nov., 317–322.

Hamada, Koichi, 1974, An economic analysis of the duty-free zone, Journal of International Economics 4. 225–241.

Johnson, Harry G., 1959, International trade, income distribution and the offer curve, Manchester School 27, 241–260.

Johnson, Harry G., 1960, Income distribution, the offer curve and the effects of tariffs, Manchester School 28, 215–242.

Kemp, Murray C., 1968, Some issues in the analysis of trade gains, Oxford Economic Papers 20, July.
Lipsey, Robert E., 1957, The theory of customs unions: Trade diversion and welfare, Economica, Feb.
Meade, James E., 1950, A geometry of international trade (Allen and Unwin, London).
Minabe. Noburo, 1974, Capital and technology movements and economic welfare, American Economic Review 64, 1088–1100.
Rao, V.S., 1971, Tariffs and welfare of factor owners: A normative extension of the Stolper–Samuelson theorem, Journal of International Economics 1, 401–416.
Tironi, Ernesto, 1976a, Foreign direct investment and economic integration policies: The Andean case, Unpublished doctoral dissertation (Massachusetts Institute of Technology, Cambridge, MA).
Tironi, Ernesto. 1976b, The theory of the costs and benefits from foreign investment and economics integration, Discussion Paper Series no. 20, Nov. (Center for Latin American Development Studies, Boston University, Boston, MA).
Tironi, Ernesto, 1976c, Customs unions theory and foreign direct investment, Discussion Paper Series no. 21 (Center for Latin American Development Studies, Boston University, Boston, MA).
Tironi, Ernesto, 1977, Customs union theory in the presence of foreign firms, Paper presented at the University of Wisconsin–Ford Foundation Conference on Trade and Development Research Projects on the International Economic Order, Madison, WI, Nov.
Uzawa, Hirofumi, 1969, Shihon jiyuka to kokumin keizai, Economisuto 23, 106–122 (in Japanese).

Errata

Page 74, footnote 6: "$U^{G^i}(F) > U^{G^i}(S)$" should read "$U^{G^i}(F) \geqq U^{G^i}(S)$".

Page 75, line 4: "either good" should read "the importable or actual consumption bundle".

Page 76, figure 3: the slope of AFS^i, for $i=1,2,\ldots,5$, should be negative at the point F in all cases, since the slope of aggregate welfare (U^{G^i} in figure 2) is zero at F while the welfare of foreign capital is rising for increases in t: national welfare is the difference between aggregate welfare and that of foreign capital. The intercepts S^i in figure 3, $i=1,2,\ldots5$, are not affected by this change.

Journal of International Economics 10 (1980) 103–115. © North-Holland Publishing Company

NATIONAL WELFARE IN AN OPEN ECONOMY IN THE PRESENCE OF FOREIGN-OWNED FACTORS OF PRODUCTION*

Jagdish N. BHAGWATI

MIT, Cambridge, MA 02139, USA

Richard A. BRECHER

Carleton University, Ottawa, Ontario K1S 5B6, Canada

Received October 1979

In the presence of foreign-owned factors of production in the economy, the effect of trade policy changes on national welfare needs to take into account the possible redistributive effect between foreign-owned and domestic factors. Therefore, an otherwise welfare-improving trade liberalization may paradoxically worsen national welfare. This paper analyzes this important, new area of trade theory and establishes the condition under which this paradox of immiserizing trade liberalization arises. The analysis is also applicable to analyzing the effects of external tariff variation in customs unions, with full internal factor mobility, on member countries' welfare.

1. Introduction

In the presence of foreign-owned factors of production in an economy, the traditional conclusions regarding the effects of exogenous parametric changes or policy changes on national welfare need to be modified. Thus, in an open economy, the absence of the usual foreign and domestic distortions *à la* Bhagwati (1971) and Johnson (1965) will not ensure that an exogenous term-of-trade improvement or a policy shift from autarky[1] to free trade will improve national welfare.

For example, take the traditional 2×2 model of trade theory and assume that the importable good is labour-intensive, labour is wholly national, and capital is wholly foreign. A shift from autarky to free trade will then, by lowering the relative domestic price of the importable good, lower the real wage of labour *à la* Stolper–Samuelson (1941) and thereby result in national

*Thanks are due to the National Science Foundation Grants Nos. SOC77-07188 and SOC79-07541 for financial support of the research underlying this paper. The comments of John Black, Alan Deardorff, Murray Kemp and Alasdair Smith have led to improvements.

[1]The term 'autarky' in the present context is taken to mean the absence of trade across national *borders*, in conformity with conventional terminology of economic policy discussions. More elaboration of this point is provided in section 4 below.

immiserization from the shift to free trade. Free trade therefore worsens rather than improves welfare, given the presence of foreign capital in this example.

Bhagwati and Tironi (1978) formulated the original problem as relevant to analyzing the widespread concerns of Latin American policymakers, who feared that regional trade liberalization would benefit foreign investors and could harm the Latin American nations themselves in consequence. In addressing this particular problem recently for the 2×2 model, the Bhagwati–Tironi analysis allows the tariff to vary by policy, but assumes that each of the two factors of production is wholly foreign or wholly national. This latter assumption permits them to adapt readily to their problem the well-known results on income distribution by factor class, originating from Stolper–Samuelson (1941) and developed in Bhagwati (1959), Johnson (1959, 1960) and Rao (1971).

Unfortunately, the real world does not permit us to divide all factors exclusively into the national or the foreign category. Capital flows to countries that cannot be assumed to have no capital of their own, and labour moves into countries that surely have native populations. Thus, it is necessary for this reason alone to examine the problem at hand by permitting the factors of production to be both national and foreign, as we do presently.

More importantly, while it is clear that a redistributive effect resulting from changing goods price-ratio could lead to paradoxical outcomes for national welfare, we are able to demonstrate a stronger proposition in this paper. Namely, the paradox of national immiserization following improvement in the country's external terms of trade will arise *if and only if* the redistributive effect against nationals goes so far as to result in the *differential-trade-pattern* phenomenon, as defined below.

Our geometric analysis, moreover, has the added advantage of using familiar trade-geometric techniques to simplify and resolve what appears to be a potentially complex problem. Furthermore, although the explicit focus of this paper is the national-foreign distinction, the two-group analysis presented here applies equally well to a broad spectrum of alternative domestic distinctions, e.g. those based on race, ethnicity or sex.[2] Moreover, the analysis is just as readily applicable, as we demonstrate later, to the theory of customs unions.

In section 2 we trace the effects of variation in the goods price-ratio on the income accruing to national factors, thus defining their 'income line' at alternative price-ratios. In section 3, we relate this perfectly general analysis first to exogenously-induced changes in external terms of trade, assuming free

[2]Thus, our general-equilibrium analysis can throw light on the conditions under which parametric changes at the national level may lead to conflicting outcomes for differently-endowed racial, ethnic, sexual and other differentiated groups within the nation.

trade, and therewith discuss the effects on national welfare that would follow from such changes. We also relate the analysis next to effects of tariff variation on national welfare. Section 4 offers some concluding observations.

2. National income variations as goods price-ratio is varied

The first problem that we analyze relates to the behavior of the national 'income line' as the prevailing price-ratio for goods is varied.

The model has two factors of production, K (for capital) and L (for labour). The overall factor endowment is $\bar{K}$ and $\bar{L}$, while the national (i.e. domestically-owned) factor endowment is $\bar{K}_n$ and $\bar{L}_n$. The two traded goods are X and Y.

With the usual restrictions on the linear homogeneous production functions for the two goods, and assuming the absence of factor-intensity reversals for the rest of our analysis, we can define an aggregate production possibility curve, $T_x'T_y'$ in fig. 1 for the aggregate factor endowments ($\bar{K}$, $\bar{L}$).

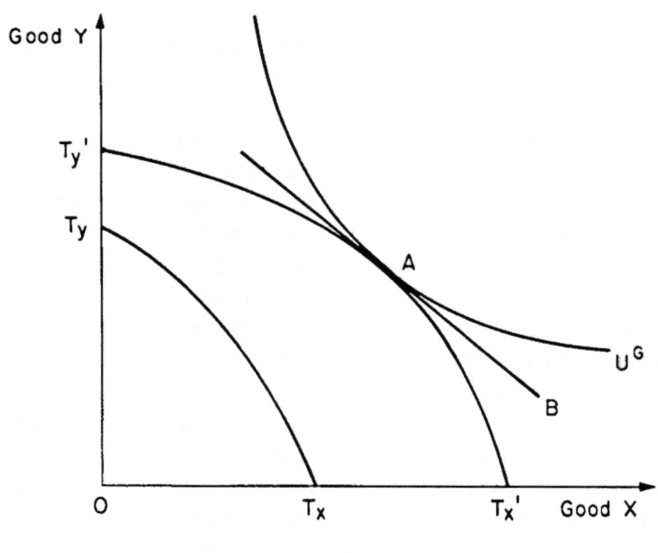

Fig. 1.

For the usual trade-theoretic analysis, with well-behaved social utility curves, a goods price-ratio AB will be defined for autarky and the utility index U^G would rise monotonically as P_x/P_y (the relative price of X in terms of Y) was varied up from A to T_x' or down from A to T_y' (with reversed pattern of trade). (For simplicity of exposition, we assume that all income earned by factors from abroad is consumed locally, to avoid having to show repatriation of such income in fig. 1.) This relationship between P_y/P_x and U^G, as illustrated in fig. 2, follows from deriving *first* the implication of the goods price-ratio variation for the aggregate budget line and *then* deducing the welfare level (U^G) achieved in fig. 1.

For *national* welfare, however, we need to define these two steps for domestically-owned factors *alone*. First, as in this section, we must derive the national budget line, as defined by the domestic goods price-ratio. Next, as in the following section, we must deduce the national welfare level (U^N) reached in consequence.

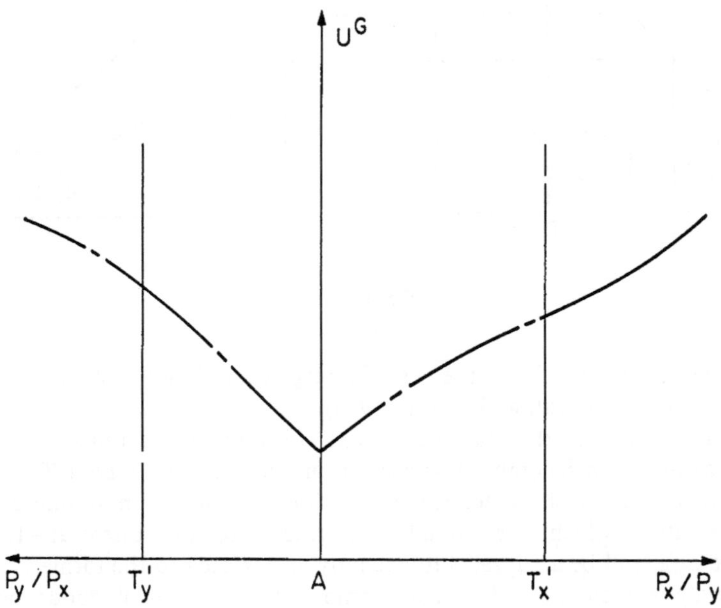

Fig. 2.

The natural way to proceed with the analysis then would appear to be to draw onto fig. 1 the national production possibility curve, T_xT_y, defined by the domestically-owned endowments $\bar{K}_n$ and $\bar{L}_n$. One may then be tempted to draw the goods price-ratio tangent to it, as to $T'_xT'_y$, and to treat the resulting income line as the *national* budget line.

But, except for a range of possible cases, this cannot be done. To see why, and to state the correct and complete analysis of the problem, let us turn to the familiar Samuelson diagram in fig. 3 – which relates the goods price-ratio (P_y/P_x), the factor-price (rental-wage) ratio P_K/P_L, and the sectoral capital–labour ratios K_x/L_x (for good X) and K_y/L_y (for good Y). Assume, without loss of generality, that $\bar{K}_n/\bar{L}_n<\bar{K}/\bar{L}$, i.e. the foreign-owned endowment is

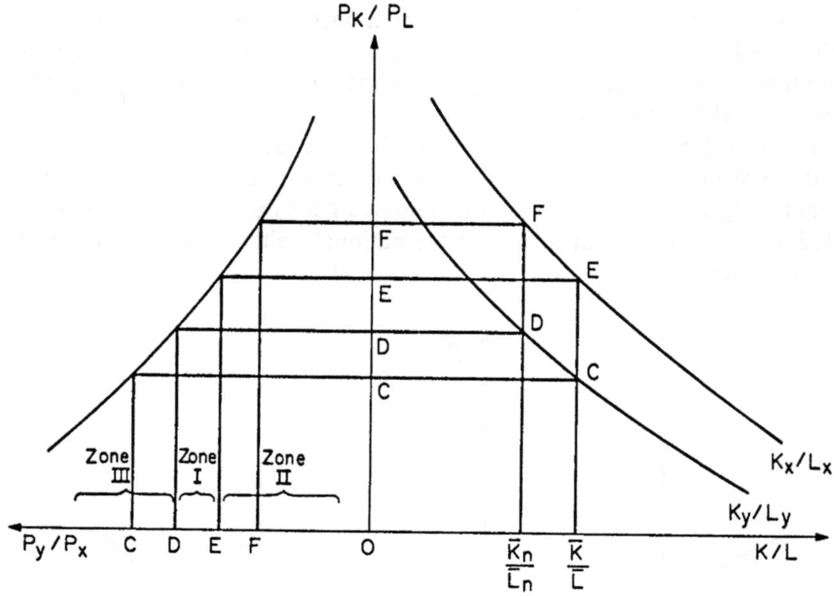

Fig. 3.

capital intensive (as would be the case if foreign capital alone had come into the country *à la* Bhagwati and Tironi (1978)).

There are two cases that can arise then: *either* there is a range of factor price-ratios at which incomplete specialization will obtain on *both* T_xT_y and $T'_xT'_y$ *or* there is no such range. Fig. 3 illustrates the former, more interesting case; the latter, which corresponds incidentally to the Bhagwati–Tironi restrictive case, will be analyzed subsequently and related to the former.

The analysis then must distinguish among three zones of goods price-ratios: *Zone I*, where they lead to incomplete specialization in production for both the production possibility curves T_xT_y and $T'_xT'_y$; *Zone II*, where complete specialization on the capital-intensive good X occurs on $T'_xT'_y$ before it does on the national curve T_xT_y; and *Zone III*, where complete specialization on the labour-intensive good Y occurs on T_xT_y before it occurs on the aggregate curve $T'_xT'_y$. Take each, in turn.

Zone I. For the aggregate endowment ratio, $\bar{K}/\bar{L}$, the range of factor price-ratios for incomplete specialization is clearly CE (i.e. OC to OE) on the vertical axis of fig. 3. For the national endowment ratio, $\bar{K}_n/\bar{L}_n$, the range for incomplete specialization is DF. Therefore, DE represents along the vertical axis the range of factor prices over which *both* T_xT_y and $T'_xT'_y$ will show incomplete specialization. Consequently, for any goods price-ratio in the range DE (i.e. OD to OE) along the left-hand horizontal axis, it is evident that the choice of capital–labour ratios in X and Y will be *identical* for T_xT_y and for $T'_xT'_y$, and hence there will be a unique set of real factor prices (P_K/P_i and P_L/P_i, $i=x,y$) along both of these production possibility curves.[3] Given this uniqueness, the value of national income ($\bar{L}_nP_L/P_i+\bar{K}_nP_K/P_i$, $i=x,y$) can be represented by the goods price-ratio tangent to T_xT_y, for the same reason that the value of aggregate income ($\bar{L}P_L/P_i+\bar{K}P_K/P_i$, $i=x,y$) is representable by the goods price-ratio tangent to $T'_xT'_y$. Thus, even though T_xT_y is only a hypothetical construct and national factors combine with foreign factors to produce at common techniques throughout the economy along $T'_xT'_y$, we can see immediately that the foregoing procedure for deriving the national budget line (by putting the goods price-ratio tangent to T_xT_y) will be valid as long as P_y/P_x is in the range DE.

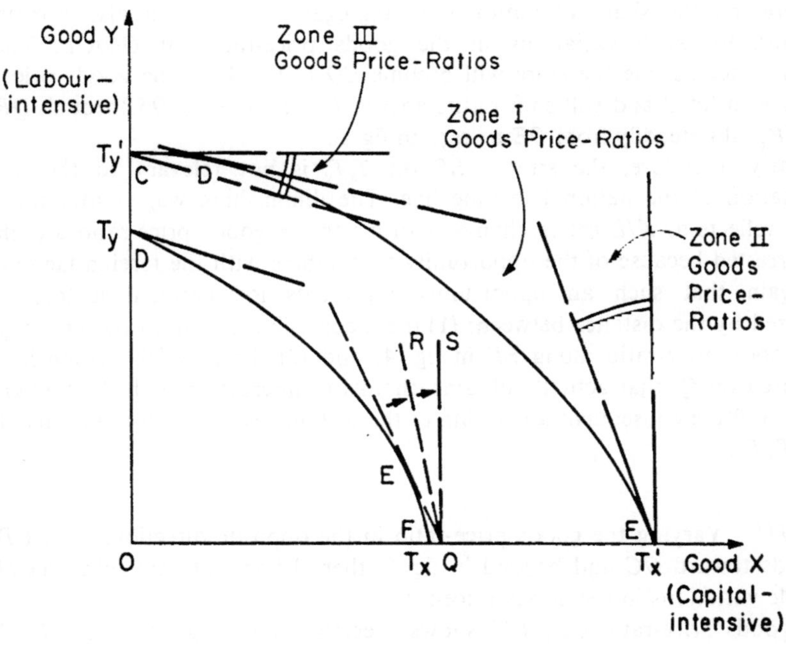

Fig. 4.

[3]For ease of identification, fig. 3 is marked, both for P_K/P_L and for P_y/P_x, with identical lettering: C, D, E, and F. Thus, the factor price-ratio range DE corresponds to the goods price-ratio range DE. Similarly, the positioning of the letters C, D, E and F on the K_x/L_x and K_y/L_y schedules indicates, as noted in the text, corresponding points of specialization in production on T_xT_y and $T'_xT'_y$. Again, the lettering on T_xT_y and $T'_xT'_y$ in fig. 4 will correspond to the lettering in fig. 3, to facilitate grasp of the relationship between the two illustrations.

Therefore, for this overlapping range (DE) of incomplete specialization, we can indeed proceed in fig. 4 to place the goods price-ratio tangent to $T_x T_y$ to derive the national income line. Besides, a movement from E to D along $T_x T_y$ and $T'_x T'_y$ will imply – given the resulting rise in the wage-rental ratio and the condition $\bar{K}_n/\bar{L}_n < \bar{K}/\bar{L}$ – a rise in the share of aggregate income going to domestically-owned factors.

Zone II. But vary now the goods price-ratio P_y/P_x down from OE in fig. 3. It is evident that there will be complete specialization on good X on $T'_x T'_y$ while, on $T_x T_y$, we would get incomplete specialization in production until the goods price-ratio becomes OF (fig. 3). Since the returns to domestically-owned factors must reflect what happens on $T'_x T'_y$, however, it follows that the relative rewards of K and L will remain fixed at $P_K/P_L = OE$ in fig. 3 for all changes in the goods price-ratio from OE to OF *and* further.

Therefore, the share of national in aggregate income will also remain constant, for such variations in the goods price-ratio, at OQ/OE. The national income line therefore will become EQ in fig. 4 for the goods price-ratio OE in fig. 3 and will shift on its anchor Q thereafter to QS through QR as P_y/P_x falls steadily from OE to zero in fig. 3.

Clearly, therefore, the stretch EF on $T_x T_y$ is not relevant to the determination of the national income line. The diminishing wage-rental ratio that it reflects as K/L ratios change with a varying goods price-ratio are, in fact, arrested because of the opportunity to combine with the foreign factors. The gain that such an opportunity represents for national factors is measured by the distance between: (1) the income line produced by tangency of a goods price-ratio along EF in fig. 4; and (2) the parallel income line (anchored on Q) that actually obtains, thanks to interaction with the foreign factors and the consequent anchoring of the techniques and factor rewards at E on $T'_x T'_y$.

Zone III. Varying the goods price-ratio in the opposite direction, from OD upwards toward OC and beyond in fig. 3, then defines the remaining set of possible variations in the goods price-ratio.

At goods price-ratio OD, $T_x T_y$ shows specialization on good Y and $T'_x T'_y$ shows incomplete specialization, in fig. 4. If factor prices were constant as P_y/P_x rises, $T_x T_y$ would have led to continuous improvement in the national budget line, each successive budget line being anchored on D and rotating upwards. However, P_K/P_L is *not* fixed, but will continue to fall as the aggregate economy moves along $T'_x T'_y$ from D to C. Therefore, given the associated increase in the wage-rental ratio and the condition $\bar{K}_n/\bar{L}_n < \bar{K}/\bar{L}$, the share of national in aggregate income will rise with the move from D

towards C on $T'_xT'_y$. However, the move to C from D is also accompanied by a declining intercept of the aggregate income line with the vertical axis. Therefore, while the former effect works to raise the national income line, the latter effect works to lower it.

It is possible to establish, however, that the combination of these two effects yields an unambiguously upward shift in the national income line, according to the following reasoning. The real value of national income in terms of good Y is given by $Q_y = \bar{L}_n P_L/P_y + \bar{K}_n P_K/P_y$. By differentiation of this equation, $dQ_y/d(P_L/P_y) = [\bar{L}_n/\bar{K}_n + d(P_K/P_y)/d(P_L/P_y)]\bar{K}_n$. Since the first-order conditions for profit maximization can be manipulated easily to show that $d(P_K/P_y)/d(P_L/P_y) = -L_y/K_y$, then $dQ_y/d(P_L/P_y) = (\bar{L}_n/\bar{K}_n - L_y/K_y)\bar{K}_n$. Thus, $dQ_y/d(P_L/P_y) \geqq 0$ because $\bar{L}_n/\bar{K}_n \geqq L_y/K_y$ within zone III, with the strict equality holding only for the borderline case of goods price-ratio OD. Consequently, as P_L/P_y increases continuously with P_y/P_x (*à la* Stolper–Samuelson) within zone III, Q_y rises correspondingly, and hence the national income line shifts upwards while becoming flatter.[4] Once the goods price-ratio reaches OC in fig. 4, however, and specialization on good Y ensues at T'_y for the aggregate economy, successive increases in P_y/P_x will not change the share of national in aggregate income and the national income line will rotate upwards (along with P_y/P_x) from a fixed anchor on the vertical axis in fig. 4.

What happens in the goods price-ratio range from OD to OC is that the presence of foreign factors introduces diminishing wage-rental ratios, which would have been avoided if national factors had operated in isolation (at D in fig. 4). At the same time, *à la* Stolper–Samuelson, an 'income-redistribution' phenomenon works to labour's and hence to national advantage. Apparently, however, the net impact on the national income line is unambiguously favourable in the general case for the subrange of goods-price ratios $OD \leqq P_y/P_x \leqq OC$. For price-ratios in the subrange $P_y/P_x > OC$, there is, of course, only a favourable rotation of the national income line as P_y/P_x improves and the economy is specialized on good Y. These two subranges together define all the possibilities in zone III.

In concluding this section, note that the T_xT_y curve clearly would be of little use if $\bar{K}_n/\bar{L}_n$ were so much below $\bar{K}/\bar{L}$ that zone I did not exist.[5] In this case, we can see immediately that the situation can be described fully by the

[4] Of course, $dQ_x/d(P_L/P_x) \geqq 0$ also because $\bar{L}_n/\bar{K}_n \geqq L_x/K_x$. Except for the borderline case of goods price-ratio OD, it is evident that $\bar{L}_n/\bar{K}_n$ exceeds both L_x/K_x and L_y/K_y as P_y/P_x varies from D to C and therefore *both* Q_y and Q_x will improve unambiguously with increase of P_y/P_x.

[5] If, as in the Bhagwati–Tironi analysis, there is only labour in the national endowment, and capital is essential for production, T_xT_y would shrink to the origin! Otherwise, in their model, it would have a Ricardian shape if capital is dispensable.

foregoing analysis of zones II and III. Of course, it is clear that this case, where there is no zone I, is implied by the Bhagwati–Tironi analysis where capital is wholly foreign and labour is wholly domestic. For, in this case, where the Stolper–Samuelson–Bhagwati–Johnson–Rao analysis can be applied directly, the overall factor endowment ratio is $\bar{K}/\bar{L}_n$ and the national endowment ratio is $\bar{K}_n/\bar{L}_n=0$. Indeed, in this case, it is evident that the national income in units of $Y\,(Q_y)$ *and* of $X\ (Q_x)$ will unambiguously rise as the real wage of labour rises in terms of *both* Y and X with the rise of P_y/P_x, *à la* Stolper–Samuelson.

3. Welfare implications in an open economy

The preceding analysis can be readily grafted onto two familiar problems of the theory of trade and welfare: (1) the welfare effects of exogenously-induced changes in the external terms of trade (as a result of some type of parametric shift abroad) under free trade, and (2) the welfare comparison of free trade and autarky. The critical role of the *differential-trade-pattern* phenomenon emerges from our analysis. The discussion holds equally well for both the large-country and small-country cases, even though the magnitude of adjustment in the equilibrium value of international prices could depend upon the economy's degree of monopoly power in world trade.

3.1. Exogenously-induced changes in the terms of trade

As noted above, in the context of fig. 2, the conventional result, with a standard social utility function, is that improvements in the terms of trade monothonically improve welfare under free trade, given the pattern of trade. This result, however, does not hold necessarily in the presence of foreign factors of production. To see this, consider terms of trade variations *within* the three zones distinguished in section 2 for the general case where zone I also obtains. The analysis can be readily extended by the reader to terms of trade changes *between* the Zones.

3.1.1. Changes within zone I. Within zone I, the domestic price-ratio (which is identical to the external terms of trade under free trade) can be put tangent to T_xT_y to derive the national income line, as shown above in section 2. It follows therefore that terms-of-trade improvement within zone I ought to increase national welfare.

It should be observed, however, that a given change in P_y/P_x may mean both an improvement in the terms of trade for the economy as an aggregate and a simultaneous terms-of-trade deterioration from the national point of view. This apparent paradox is easily seen and quickly resolved, by noting simply that the equilibrium value of P_y/P_x may differ between aggregate autarky (along the actual production possibility curve $T'_xT'_y$) and national autarky (along the hypothetical curve T_xT_y), so that the aggregate (actual) pattern of trade may differ from the national (hypothetical) pattern of trade. For this reason, although national welfare improves monotonically with the national terms of trade, aggregate terms-of-trade improvement will not imply an increase in national welfare unless the aggregate and national patterns of trade happen to be the same.

This is illustrated in fig. 5, where the $T'_xT'_y$ curve has been omitted, to avoid cluttering the diagram. The aggregate-autarky price-ratio (determined along the omitted curve $T'_xT'_y$) is drawn tangent to T_xT_y at A'. The national-autarky price-ratio is tangent to T_xT_y at A. (To have ray OA' steeper than ray OA as drawn, a sufficient but not necessary condition is a unique set of homothetic indifference curves corresponding to both U^G and U^N, in view of

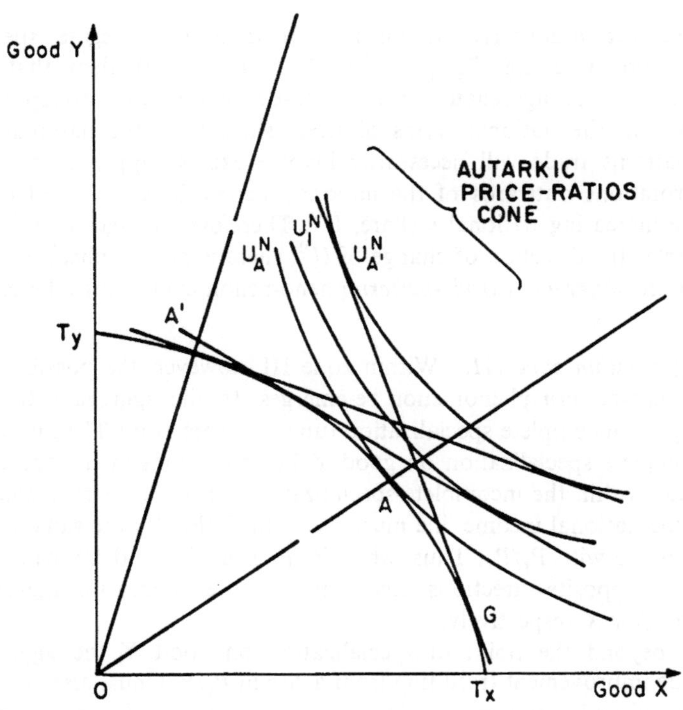

Fig. 5.

the well-known Rybczynski Theorem) For any reductions in P_y/P_x from A', U^G would have improved. However, for all such changes between A' and A, within the autarkic price-ratios cone AOA', U^N obviously declines because for national factors the aggregate terms-of-trade improvement is a terms-of-trade deterioration. Therefore, U^N declines steadily from $U^N_{A'}$ through U^N_1 to U^N_A. However, further declines in P_y/P_x will start improving U^N and fig. 5 shows the P_y/P_x at G which raises U^N back to the level A' consistent with the aggregate-autarky price-ratio. Obviously, then, still further decline in P_y/P_x would have raised U^N above the level at A'.

It follows that the net result of terms-of-trade improvements for the aggregate economy may be to raise, lower or leave national welfare unchanged. This general result still would hold if ray OA' were flatter than ray OA. Only if the two rays coincided would aggregate terms-of-trade improvement necessarily imply an increase in national welfare. We have thus shown that, in zone I, the paradox of conflicting movements in aggregate and national welfare will arise when there is a difference between the national and aggregate patterns-of-trade. *This differential-trade-pattern* phenomenon will now be discussed in the context of the other two zones.

3.1.2. Changes within zone II. Within zone II, there is (aggregate) specialization on good X along $T'_xT'_y$ in fig. 4. It is evident then that any improvements in the aggregate terms of trade will imply corresponding improvements in the national terms of trade since both the national and aggregate patterns trade will necessarily involve excess supply of good X. Successive rotations outwards of the national income line, anchored on Q, will produce increasing national welfare, U^N. Therefore, changes in U^G may be used to infer the direction of change of U^N; there is no complication as in zone I, since the *differential-trade-pattern* phenomenon cannot arise here.

3.1.3. Changes within zone III. Within zone III, however, the possibility of *differential-trade-pattern* phenomenon re-emerges. In the aggregate, there is first the range of incomplete specialization (up to C from D on $T'_xT'_y$ in fig. 4) and then complete specialization on good Y. For variations in the aggregate terms of trade within the incomplete-specialization range, our earlier analysis shows that the national income line must rise with P_y/P_x. By the same token, U^N must also rise with P_y/P_x. Thus, when P_y/P_x rises, U^N and U^G will move together or in opposite directions according as the economy (in aggregate) exports good Y or X respectively.

However, beyond the point of specialization on good Y, the aggregate terms-of-trade improvement (resulting from a rise in P_y/P_x) must also increase national income and therefore U^N. The net effect of terms-of-trade improvements in zone III therefore may be to *lower* or increase national welfare when there is incomplete specialization along $T'_x T'_y$, but must be to raise national welfare when aggregate specialization is complete on good Y.

Note, moreover, that the contrary behaviour of U^N and U^G, possible in the case of incomplete specialization, does require that the aggregate pattern of trade be different from the national pattern of trade: for, such a possibility will arise if and only if the aggregate trade pattern involves the export of good X[6] and the national trade pattern (owing to complete specialization on good Y, necessarily in zone III) involves the export of good Y instead.

It is evident therefore that directional changes in national welfare generally cannot be inferred from the direction of changes in the terms of trade in the aggregate, if the economy is in zones I and III. Interestingly, for both these zones, the paradoxical behaviour of national welfare arises simply because the aggregate pattern of trade masks a contrary pattern of trade for the domestically-owned, national factors of production. If only we could draw aside the veil imposed by the presence of foreign factors, and see directly the national (hypothetical) equilibrium production and consumption, the paradox would have disappeared.[7] Therefore, we may describe the paradox of zones I and III as arising from the *differential-trade-pattern* phenomenon. The redistribution of income *à la* Stolper–Samuelson does indeed take place in both zones I and III; but it might not be sufficiently strong to create the paradox of deterioration (improvement) in national welfare when the economy's terms of trade improve (deteriorate). Sufficient strength, moreover, is here synonymous with a difference between the national and aggregate patterns of trade.

3.2. *Autarky versus free trade*

Since neither free trade nor autarky creates tariff revenue, the analysis of this paper can be readily used also to rank these two trade policies in the presence of foreign-owned factors of production.

It is seen immediately that, in zones I and III, the *differential-trade-pattern* phenomenon may arise and thus lead to autarky (in the aggregate) being better for national welfare than free trade. (Zone II can be ignored at this stage in the discussion, since aggregate autarky cannot occur when only

[6]This is, in fact, the paradoxical case considered in Bhagwati and Tironi (1978, section II), but without the underlying explanation and argumentation *à la* the national production possibility curve, as set out in this paper.

[7]Of course, this does not mean that the paradox cannot arise if national and foreign tastes are homothetic. For, it is the difference in the trade pattern, as determined by the production and consumption choices at the specified goods price-ratio, that is the critical variable in creating the paradox in both zones. Nor should the reader forget that the hypothetical national equilibrium production will reflect, in zone III (as also zone II, for that matter), the interaction with foreign factors: the national income line cannot simply be drawn by reference to $T_x T_y$ alone by tangency of the goods price-ratio with it. In zone I, however, the presence of foreign factors does nothing to affect the correctness of such a procedure.

good X is produced along $T'_xT'_y$, assuming that aggregate consumption is always positive for each good.) Thus, the conventional welfare ranking (of free trade being superior to autarky) may be reversed, in the presence of foreign-owned factors of production within an economy.

4. Concluding remarks

In conclusion, a few words should be said about the meaning of the term 'autarky,' as used by us in this paper. By general convention in practical parlance, autarky refers to the absence of trade across national borders. At the same time, evidently 'autarky' does not exclude domestic 'trade' between resident citizens of different countries. The national and foreign factors in our analysis are indeed engaged in domestic trade[8], even in the absence of international (i.e. trans-border) trade. The analytical problem is therefore identical to that which would arise in the case of customs unions. For, once a customs union is formed with common external tariff and free internal trade *and* factor mobility, changes in individual member countries' welfare as external conditions change for the union as a whole are evidently analyzable in precisely the same fashion as changes in national welfare in the presence of foreign factors of production!

[8]This intra-national trade might be *either* goods for goods (in zone I where trade in factor services is not necessary to equalize marginal products) *or* goods for factor services (in zones II and III where marginal products would otherwise remain unequal).

References

Bhagwati, Jagdish N., 1959, Protection, real wages and real incomes, Economic Journal, December.

Bhagwati, Jagdish N., 1971, The generalized theory of distortions and welfare, in: Jagdish Bhagwati et al., eds., Trade, balance of payments and growth: Essays in honor of Charles P. Kindleberger (North-Holland, Amsterdam).

Bhagwati, Jagdish N. and Ernesto Tironi, 1978, Tariff change, foreign capital and immiserization: A theoretical analysis, MIT mimeo, forthcoming in: Journal of Development Economics.

Johnson, Harry G., 1959, International trade, income distribution and the offer curve, Manchester School 27, 241–260.

Johnson, Harry G., 1960, Income distribution, the offer curve and the effects of tariffs, Manchester School 28, 215–242.

Johnson, Harry G., 1965, Optimal trade intervention in the presence of domestic distortions, in: Robert E. Baldwin et al., eds., Trade, growth and the balance of payments: Essays in honor of Gottfried Haberler (Rand McNally, Chicago).

Rao, V.S., 1971, Tariffs and welfare of factor owners: A normative extension of the Stolper–Samuelson theorem, Journal of International Economics 1, 401–416.

Stolper, Wolfgang and Paul Samuelson, 1941, Protection and real wages, Review of Economic Studies 9, November.

Errata

Page 109, paragraph 3, line 2: After "at *OQ/OE*" add "in fig. 4".

Page 111, paragraph 3, line 3: "monothonically" should read "monotonically".

Page 113, paragraph 3, line 5: "patterns trade" should read "patterns of trade".

Page 113, paragraph 3, line 5: After "good *X*" add "where position *Q* in fig. 4 is treated as the national production point".

Foreign Ownership and the Theory of Trade and Welfare

Richard A. Brecher

Carleton University

Jagdish N. Bhagwati

Columbia University

Some standard topics in the theory of international trade are reconsidered in this paper by distinguishing between national and aggregate income when fixed supplies of foreign inputs are present within the home country. Under conditions that would ensure a national welfare gain if foreign ownership were absent, international transfer, economic growth, or tariff policy might cause a national welfare loss in the presence of foreign ownership. The techniques developed could be applied to other domestic distinctions (such as those based on race, sex, age, or ethnicity) and to the theory of customs unions in a three-country world.

I. Introduction

This paper reconsiders a number of standard topics in the theory of international trade by taking explicit account of the distinction between national and aggregate income when fixed supplies of foreign-owned inputs are present within the domestic economy. Extending the work of Bhagwati and Brecher (1980),[1] the following

Thanks are due to the National Science Foundation grant no. SOC79-07541 for partial financial support of the research underlying this paper. The comments and suggestions of Alan Deardorff, Jacob Frenkel, Alasdair Smith, and anonymous referees are gratefully acknowledged.

[1] Their work, in turn, extends the analysis of Bhagwati and Tironi (1980), who concentrate on a special case mentioned in n. 3 below.

[*Journal of Political Economy*, 1981, vol. 89, no. 3]

analysis takes a new look at welfare-theoretic aspects of international transfer, economic expansion, and tariff policy, while it emphasizes significant departures from conventional wisdom that arise in the presence of foreign ownership. As these selected departures suggest, many standard results are open to serious question when part of the domestic product accrues to factor inputs from abroad.

Originally, the motivation for the present two-group analysis (based on the national-foreign distinction) came from a recent concern in Latin America, where policymakers have been worried about the impact of trade liberalization on national welfare, given the domestic presence of foreign-owned multinational corporations. After further reflection, however, it is clear that the treatment below has much greater applicability to a broad range of analytically similar cases. For example, it is possible to treat in much the same way a wide variety of alternative domestic distinctions, including those based on race, sex, age, or ethnicity. The following techniques and results, moreover, are directly relevant for the fully analogous two-group issue relating to the distribution of gains (or losses) between trading partners in a customs union (such as the European Economic Community) with factor mobility. While these other policy problems are of considerable importance and interest as well, only the national-foreign distinction is pursued explicitly here for the sake of brevity.

Section II reviews the basic model of an open economy, in which foreign-owned and national supplies of two homogeneous factors are combined to produce two commodities. As Section III then shows, a transfer-receiving country might suffer a loss in national welfare, even under the usual conditions which would ensure a welfare gain if foreign ownership were absent. As established next by Section IV, a country experiencing economic expansion (due to factor-endowment growth or technological advance) might encounter a deterioration in national welfare, even under well-known conditions which would preclude this possibility of "immiserizing growth" in the absence of foreign ownership. Afterward, Section V explains why free trade might be inferior to *both* no trade and subsidized trade, as far as national welfare is concerned.[2] Section VI summarizes the paper's main results, based on the possibility of aggregate and national welfare moving in opposite directions.

Needless to say, this possibility would not arise if foreign-owned factors were taxed to the nationally optimal extent. Indeed, with these factors in perfectly inelastic supply, the optimal tax on each foreign

[2] This result is obtained also by Bhagwati and Tironi (1980), for a special case identified in n. 3 below. In addition, since Bhagwati and Brecher (1980) compare free-trade equilibrium with autarky, the present paper will emphasize instead the comparison of free versus subsidized trade.

input clearly would be 100 percent, thereby removing the after-tax distinction between aggregate and national welfare. Assuming that this type of optimal taxation of factors is politically infeasible, however, the present analysis cautions nationally oriented policymakers against the usual, automatic adoption of the standard welfare conclusions which reflect an aggregate point of view. More specifically, this paper shows precisely how the traditional (aggregate) propositions must be modified for a truly national perspective, when political constraints eliminate optimal taxation of inputs from abroad.

II. The Basic Model

Following the analysis of Bhagwati and Brecher (1980), the present section summarizes the basic two-commodity, two-factor model of an open economy (large or small), which plays host to given quantities of inputs from abroad. The aggregate factor endowments of the country are fixed at $\bar{K}^a$ units of capital and $\bar{L}^a$ units of labor, while the given amounts $\bar{K}^n$ and $\bar{L}^n$ are the national endowments of capital and labor, respectively. (Thus, the fixed supplies of foreign-owned capital and labor within the home country are $\bar{K}^a - \bar{K}^n$ and $\bar{L}^a - \bar{L}^n$, respectively.) It is assumed that $\bar{K}^a > \bar{K}^n > 0$ and $\bar{L}^a > \bar{L}^n > 0$, excluding the possibility that either factor within the home economy is owned wholly by nationals or completely by foreigners.[3] Commodity two is always labor intensive relative to capital-intensive commodity one, and the well-behaved technology exhibits constant returns to scale.

In figure 1, the home country is depicted in free-trade equilibrium. Aggregate production is at point Q^a on production-possibility frontier $T_2^aT_1^a$ (corresponding to $\bar{K}^a$ and $\bar{L}^a$), aggregate income is represented by budget line Q^aD^a, and aggregate consumption occurs at point D^a on indifference curve $I_2^aI_1^a$. (For simplicity of exposition, it is assumed that all income earned by factors from abroad is consumed locally, to avoid having to show repatriation of such income within the diagram.) By the reasoning of Bhagwati and Brecher (1980), national consumption takes place at point D^n on indifference curve $I_2^nI_1^n$, with national income given by budget line Q^nD^n (parallel to Q^aD^a), *as if* nationals produced separately at point Q^n on production-possibility frontier $T_2^nT_1^n$ (drawn for $\bar{K}^n$ and $\bar{L}^n$).[4] To emphasize that the main results of this paper qualitatively do *not* require any differences in consumer preferences between nationals and foreigners within the home country, assume throughout the text that the same set of indifference

[3] For the special case in which $\bar{K}^a > \bar{K}^n = 0$ and $\bar{L}^a = \bar{L}^n > 0$, see Bhagwati and Tironi (1980).

[4] The discussion could be extended readily to allow for the possibility of complete specialization, following the analysis of Bhagwati and Brecher (1980).

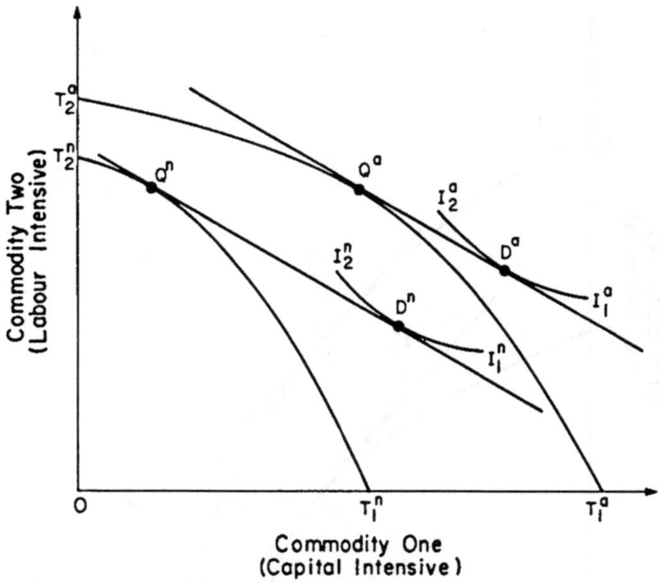

FIG. 1.—Differential trade-volume phenomenon

curves with unitary income elasticities of demand represents both national and aggregate tastes in consumption, although this simplification of the exposition could be dropped (as in footnotes to this paper) without detracting from the essence of the analysis.[5]

The model may be summarized conveniently as follows:

$$X^j_i = F^j_i(p), i = 1, 2, j = a, n; \tag{1}$$

$$Y^j = X^j_1 + pX^j_2,\ j = a, n; \tag{2}$$

$$W^j = U^j(C^j_1, C^j_2), j = a, n; \tag{3}$$

$$C^j_1 + pC^j_2 = Y^j, j = a, n; \tag{4}$$

where p denotes the relative price of the second commodity in terms of the first; X^j_i denotes output of commodity i on frontier $T^j_2T^j_1$; each F^j_i is a conventional function of p, given $\bar{K}^j$, $\bar{L}^j$ and the (uniform) technology for commodity i; Y^a and Y^n denote the real value of aggregate and national income, respectively, in terms of the first commodity; C^a_i and C^n_i denote aggregate and national consumption, respectively, of commodity i ($i = 1, 2$); W^a and W^n denote aggregate and national welfare,

[5] Nn. 6–8, 10, and 15 below extend the discussion to let tastes differ between nationals and foreigners within the home country. These extensions bring out the essentially "three-country" flavor of the analysis, in which nationals, domestically located foreigners, and the rest of the world can be treated as three distinct components of the international economy.

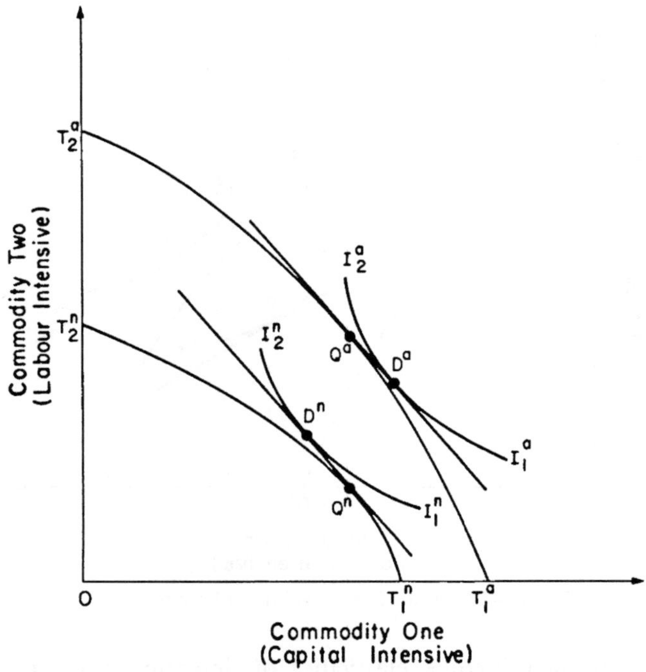

FIG. 2.—Differential trade-pattern phenomenon

respectively; and each U^j is a concave function of C_1^j and C_2^j, with positive partial derivatives denoted by $U^j_i \equiv \partial U^j/\partial C^j_i$ $(i = 1, 2)$.

Later in the paper when a change in relative prices is induced by various parametric shifts, either of the following phenomena might lead to a fall in national despite a rise in aggregate welfare, depending on the strength of other induced effects. The differential trade-volume phenomenon is shown in figure 1, where the aggregate (actual) volume of trade (defined by line segment Q^aD^a) is less than the national (hypothetical) volume of trade (defined by line segment Q^nD^n), implying (ceteris paribus) that a terms-of-trade deterioration worsens national by more than aggregate welfare. Figure 2 (labeled similarly) illustrates the Bhagwati and Brecher (1980) differential trade-pattern phenomenon, which arises when the aggregate and national patterns of trade differ (in direction), so that an aggregate terms-of-trade improvement (tending to raise W^a) means a national terms-of-trade deterioration (tending to lower W^n). The national relative to the aggregate endowment of factors is labor abundant in figure 1 (with $\bar{K}^a/\bar{L}^a > \bar{K}^n/\bar{L}^n$) but capital abundant in figure 2 (with $\bar{K}^a/\bar{L}^a < \bar{K}^n/\bar{L}^n$), as suggested by the relative shapes of frontiers $T_2^aT_1^a$ and $T_2^nT_1^n$, in accordance with the reasoning of Rybczynski (1955).

To understand the possibility of a fall in national welfare despite a rise in aggregate welfare, it might be tempting to go no further than the following simple observation. Whenever the national and aggregate endowments exhibit different capital/labor ratios, the domestic distribution of income might deteriorate for nationals, as a change in relative commodity prices alters the wage/rental ratio for reasons expounded by Stolper and Samuelson (1941). It is important to recognize, however, that generally this income-redistribution effect will not be strong enough to produce the differential responses in national and aggregate welfare if the relative factor-endowment discrepancy is too small to create either the differential trade-volume or the differential trade-pattern phenomenon. Even when either of these phenomena arises, moreover, a fall in national welfare despite a rise in aggregate welfare can occur if and only if certain specific conditions (derived below) are satisfied.

III. International Transfer

According to a standard result in the literature (see Mundell 1960), a transfer-receiving country cannot suffer a loss in aggregate welfare despite any possible deterioration in the aggregate terms of trade, as long as international commodity-market equilibrium is stable. In other words, the transfer-induced change in W^a cannot be negative, assuming that an excess demand for or supply of the second good in world markets can be cleared by a rise or fall in p, respectively. As the following argument demonstrates, however, a (large) transfer-receiving country might suffer a deterioration in national welfare, even under the assumption (maintained throughout the present paper) that commodity markets are stable. This demonstration of a transfer-induced fall in W^n, moreover, does not even require a rise in the relative price of home importables.

If it is assumed that the transfer is given only to nationals, equations (2) are modified as follows:

$$Y^j = X_1^j + pX_2^j + \tau, j = a, n, \tag{5}$$

where τ is the real value of the transfer in terms of the first commodity. If any part of the transfer were given to foreigners within the home country, the chances for a decline in W^n would simply be enhanced, thereby strengthening the argument below.

To examine the welfare implications of the transfer, differentiate equations (1), (3), (4), and (5) totally with respect to τ—assuming (without loss of generality) that initially $U_1^j = 1$, while noting that $U_2^j/U_1^j = p = -(dF_1^j/dp)/(dF_2^j/dp)$ from the first-order conditions for maximizing utility and profit. In this way, it is a straightforward exercise to derive

$$dW^j/d\tau = 1 + (E^j dp/d\tau), j = a, n, \tag{6}$$

where $E^j = X_2^j - C_2^j$. Consistent with figures 1 and 2, which depict the home country exporting the second good, $E^a > 0$ by assumption throughout the present paper. As illustrated above, however, E^n can be either positive (in fig. 1) or negative (in fig. 2).

As equations (6) confirm, $dW^a/d\tau$ is the familiar sum of the following two components: the primary gain (= 1) from the transfer-induced increase in aggregate income, at the initial (pretransfer) set of relative prices; plus the secondary effect ($= E^a dp/d\tau$) from the possible increase or decrease in the real exchange value of the initial volume of home exports, in the event of a transfer-induced change (if any) in relative prices. The expression for $dW^n/d\tau$ is analogous. If foreign inputs were entirely absent from the home country, the distinction between national and aggregate variables would disappear, thereby implying that $E^n = E^a$ and (hence) that $dW^n/d\tau = dW^a/d\tau$. Given the actual presence of factor inputs from abroad, however, $dW^n/d\tau$ generally differs from $dW^a/d\tau$, except in the special case where either $E^n = E^a$ (despite the foreign presence) or $dp/d\tau = 0$.

To determine precise conditions for the direction of change in welfare, consider the standard transfer-induced terms-of-trade response, analyzed previously by Samuelson (1952, 1954) and subsequently by Mundell (1960). Thus, by well-known reasoning,

$$dp/d\tau = (1 - m - m^*)/(e + e^* - 1)E^a, \tag{7}$$

where e (> 0) and m denote the relative-price elasticity of import demand and the marginal propensity to consume the importable, respectively, for the home country; e^* (> 0) and m^* denote the corresponding variables for the rest of the world; and $\tau = 0$ in the initial (pretransfer) equilibrium.[6] Given the assumption above that world commodity-market equilibrium is stable, $e + e^* > 1$ throughout the present paper.

If equation (7) is substituted into equations (6), simple manipulation confirms that

$$dW^a/d\tau = (\epsilon + \epsilon^*)/(e + e^* - 1) > 0, \tag{8}$$

[6] If preferences in consumption were allowed to differ between nationals and foreigners within the home country, it would be necessary to rewrite eq. (7) as follows, to reflect the present assumption that the entire transfer goes exclusively to nationals:

$$dp/d\tau = (1 - m^n - m^*)/(e + e^* - 1)E^a, \tag{7'}$$

where m^n denotes the national marginal propensity to consume the home importable.

but shows that

$$dW^n/d\tau \gtreqless 0 \text{ as } (e + e^* - 1)E^a \gtreqless (m + m^* - 1)E^n, \qquad (9)$$

where ϵ (> 0) and ϵ^* (> 0) denote the compensated (constant-utility) relative-price elasticity of import demand for the home country and the rest of the world, respectively, while $e = \epsilon + m$ and $e^* = \epsilon^* + m^*$, according to a standard decomposition.[7] Although $dW^a/d\tau > 0$ unambiguously, it is evidently possible to have $dW^n/d\tau < 0$ nevertheless.[8]

To highlight the important role of the differential trade-pattern and differential trade-volume phenomena, it is helpful to revert to equations (6), which imply that a fall in national despite the rise in aggregate welfare can occur only if $(E^n - E^a)dp/d\tau < 0$. This necessary condition for a fall in W^n holds if either $dp/d\tau < 0$ in presence of the differential trade-volume phenomenon of figure 1 (where $E^n > E^a > 0$) or $dp/d\tau > 0$ in conjunction with the differential trade-pattern phenomenon of figure 2 (where $E^n < 0 < E^a$).[9] Correspondingly, if home exportables were relatively intensive in their use of capital (rather than labor), a transfer-induced deterioration in national

[7] Alternatively, if eq. (7′) from n. 6 above were substituted into eqq. (6), simple manipulation could show that

$$dW^a/d\tau = [(\epsilon + \epsilon^*) + (1 - \gamma)(m^f - m^n)]/(e + e^* - 1) \qquad (8')$$

and

$$dW^n/d\tau = [(\epsilon + \epsilon^*) + (1 - \gamma)(m^f + m^* - 1)]/(e + e^* - 1), \qquad (9')$$

where m^f denotes the marginal propensity to consume the home importable for foreigners within the home country; $\gamma \equiv (C_1^n - X_1^n)/(C_1^a - X_1^a) = E^n/E^a$; and use is made of the fact that $m = \gamma m^n + (1 - \gamma)m^f$. Eq. (8′) indicates that $dW^a/d\tau$ can be decomposed into two comparative-static components. As could be shown readily, the first component $[(\epsilon + \epsilon^*)/(e + e^* - 1)]$ is the transfer-induced change in W^a that would occur initially if the transfer were given temporarily to nationals and domestically located foreigners in the respective amounts $\gamma\tau$ and $(1 - \gamma)\tau$, whereas the second component $[(1 - \gamma)(m^f - m^n)/(e + e^* - 1)]$ is the subsequent change in W^a that would occur as the portion $(1 - \gamma)\tau$ was passed from domestically located foreigners to nationals (the ultimate recipients of the entire transfer). Eq. (9′) could be interpreted analogously, since $-dW^n/d\tau$ equals the worldwide sum of transfer-induced changes in welfare for everyone excluding home-country nationals, as could be shown readily.

[8] Under the present assumption that $m^f = m^n = m$, eq. (8′) of n. 7 above is equivalent to eq. (8), while eq. (9′) leads directly to condition (9). Alternatively, if it were the case that $m^f \neq m^n$, there would arise the new possibility of having $dW^a/d\tau < 0$ in eq. (8′). Also if it were supposed that $m^f = 1 - m^*$, it would be the case that $dW^n/d\tau > 0$ unambiguously in eq. (9′). This last result can be understood intuitively as follows: If foreign tastes are uniform throughout the world, the reasoning behind eq. (8) shows equally well that the transfer must lower worldwide foreign welfare; that is, $-dW^n/d\tau < 0$, recalling n. 7 above. Incidentally, in view of the fact that worldwide foreign welfare otherwise can rise (when $dW^n/d\tau < 0$) if $m^f \neq m^*$, international aid might be especially attractive for a donor country with investments in the aid-receiving economy.

[9] Although $(E^n - E^a)dp/d\tau < 0$ also if $0 < E^n < E^a$ when $dp/d\tau > 0$, $dW^n/d\tau > 0$ in this case, as implied by eqq. (6). The reader may also see alternatively that, from condition (9), $dW^n/d\tau < 0$ if and only if $(\epsilon + \epsilon^*)E^n + (E^a - E^n)(e + e^* - 1) < 0$. Therefore, national welfare *may* decline despite the increase in aggregate welfare if $E^n < 0 < E^a$ (i.e., the differential trade-pattern phenomenon holds) or if $E^n > E^a > 0$ (i.e., the differential trade-volume phenomenon holds).

(though not in aggregate) welfare would still be possible, provided that either the aggregate terms of trade improve in the case of labor-abundant nationals or an aggregate terms-of-trade decline occurs in the presence of capital-abundant nationals.

Consequently, the basic results of this section can be summarized generally in the following terms. When the home exportable uses intensively the factor that is relatively abundant in the national (as compared with the aggregate) endowment, the national and aggregate patterns of trade are the same, in which case a fall in national welfare might occur through a differential trade-volume phenomenon if the (national and aggregate) terms of trade worsen unambiguously. Alternatively, when the home exportable uses intensively the factor that is relatively scarce in the national (as compared with the aggregate) endowment, the aggregate and national patterns of trade could differ, in which case the differential trade-pattern phenomenon might give rise to a deterioration in national welfare if the national terms of trade worsen through an aggregate terms-of-trade improvement. These general results, moreover, hold equally well for changes in p induced by economic expansion and tariff policy, as will be clear from the analysis below.

IV. Economic Expansion

As Bhagwati (1958*a*) has demonstrated, a once-for-all increase in a factor endowment or in a technological level might deteriorate the aggregate terms of trade enough to worsen aggregate welfare of the home country, but this immiserizing growth can occur only if either the rest of the world has an inelastic offer curve or growth would decrease the production of home importables at the initial product-price ratio. In other words, if the offer-curve elasticity for the rest of the world is not less than unitary and economic expansion is not "ultrabiased" against the production of home importables, the growth-induced change in W^a cannot be negative. Even under these circumstances (assumed throughout the present section) which preclude a fall in aggregate welfare, however, the following analysis demonstrates that a (large) country might suffer a loss in national welfare. This demonstration of a growth-induced decline in W^n, moreover, does not even require a rise in the relative price of home importables.

To allow for factor-endowment expansion or technological advance, equations (1) may be rewritten as follows:

$$X^j_i = F^j_i(p, \theta), i = 1, 2, j = a, n, \tag{10}$$

where θ is a general shift parameter, a rise in which indicates either a factor-endowment increase (for $\bar{K}^j$ or $\bar{L}^j$) or a disembodied technological improvement for an industry (one or two). It is assumed that any addition to the aggregate supply of capital or labor is owned fully by nationals. If any part of such addition were foreign owned, the likelihood of a decline in W^n would simply be enhanced, thereby strengthening the argument below. However, the ability of domestically located producers to take advantage of disembodied technological progress should be independent of the source of ownership of the inputs used, as assumed here.

Differentiating equations (2), (3), (4), and (10) totally with respect to θ, while recalling that $U_1^j = 1$ initially and that $U_2^j/U_1^j = p = -(\partial F_1^j/\partial p)/(\partial F_2^j/\partial p)$, we readily obtain the following result:

$$dW^j/d\theta = Y_\theta^j + (E^j dp/d\theta), j = a, n, \tag{11}$$

where $Y_\theta^j \equiv \partial Y^j/\partial\theta > 0$. Thus, each $dW^j/d\theta$ is the sum of a primary growth effect (Y_θ^j) plus a secondary relative-price effect ($E^j dp/d\theta$), which are analogous to the welfare-related effects of the transfer mentioned above in Section III. Although national and aggregate welfare again would remain equal if foreign inputs were entirely absent from the home country, the actual presence of foreign ownership gives rise to the possibility of having $dW^n/d\theta < 0$ when $dW^a/d\theta > 0$, except in the special case where $dp/d\theta = 0$.

Turning to the standard growth-induced terms-of-trade response, analyzed previously by Bhagwati (1958*b*) and subsequently by Kemp (1969, p. 110), we see that it is a well-known fact that

$$dp/d\theta = (\beta - m)Y_\theta^a/(e + e^* - 1)E^a, \tag{12}$$

where $\beta \equiv (\partial X_1^a/\partial\theta)/Y_\theta^a$. When this result is substituted into equations (11), straightforward manipulation confirms that

$$dW^a/d\theta = (\epsilon + \beta + e^* - 1)Y_\theta^a/(e + e^* - 1) > 0 \tag{13}$$

but shows that

$$dW^n/d\theta \gtreqless 0 \text{ as } E^a(e + e^* - 1)Y_\theta^n \gtreqless E^n(m - \beta)Y_\theta^a, \tag{14}$$

where $\beta \geqq 0$, which recalls the assumption that growth would not reduce production of home importables at the initial commodity-price ratio; and $e^* \geqq 1$, which recalls the assumption that the rest of the world's offer curve is not inelastic. Thus, despite the fact that $dW^a/d\theta > 0$ unambiguously under these circumstances, it is still possible to have $dW^n/d\theta < 0$ nevertheless.[10]

[10] Along lines suggested by nn. 6–8 for the case of international transfer, the analysis of economic expansion could be extended readily to distinguish between m^n and m^f. It is worth noting, however, that it would still be possible to have $dW^n/d\theta < 0$ even if it were the case that $m^f = 1 - m^*$.

Equations (11) imply that a fall in national despite the rise in aggregate welfare can occur only if $(E^n - E^a)dp/d\theta < Y_\theta^a - Y_\theta^n$. As could be shown readily, this necessary condition for a fall in W^n can result from each of the following alternative events, for example: an increase in either the national endowment of capital or the technological level of industry one, with $dp/d\theta > 0$ in the presence of the differential trade-pattern phenomenon (fig. 2); and an increase in either the national endowment of both factors or the technological level of both industries, if $dp/d\theta < 0$ with the differential trade-volume phenomenon (fig. 1).[11] Correspondingly, if home exportables were relatively capital intensive, it would be possible to have an expansion-induced deterioration in national (though not in aggregate) welfare under a variety of circumstances, including the following: an increase either in the national stock of labor or in the level of technology for the production of importables, when the national endowment is labor abundant; or an increase either in the national endowment of both factors or in the level of technology for both sectors, when nationals are capital abundant.

V. Tariff Policy

According to a standard result in the literature (see Bhagwati 1968), free trade is ranked superior to both no trade and subsidized trade (assuming that both offer curves are well behaved),[12] from the viewpoint of aggregate welfare. In other words, the home country cannot increase W^a above the free-trade level either by using an import (or export) tax to eliminate trade or by imposing an export (or import) subsidy to encourage trade. From the national-welfare point of view, however, the ranking above may be reversed. Since Bhagwati and Brecher (1980) already demonstrated the possibility of such a reversal for free trade versus autarky, the following analysis concentrates on free versus subsidized trade.

To allow for tariff policy, equations (2) may be modified as follows:

$$Y^j = X_1^j + pX_2^j + [(C_1^a - X_1^a)\,\alpha/(1-\alpha)], j = a, n; \tag{15}$$

where α denotes the *ad valorem* tariff, which is an import tax (if $\alpha > 0$) or an import subsidy (if $\alpha < 0$); the domestic relative price of the

[11] Although $Y_\theta^a = Y_\theta^n$ with a national factor-endowment increase, it is possible that $Y_\theta^a > Y_\theta^n$ for a technological advance. Thus, with the latter (but not the former) type of economic expansion, a fall in national welfare despite the rise in aggregate welfare might occur even without the differential trade-volume and differential trade-pattern phenomena—if both industries experience the technological advance and $dp/d\theta < 0$.

[12] I.e., the offer curve is assumed to represent imports as a monotonic decreasing function of their relative price in world markets. For the significance of this assumption in tariff analysis, see Bhagwati and Kemp (1969).

second good is still denoted by p, so that the relative price of this good in world markets is now equal to $p(1 + \alpha)$; and $(C_1^a - X_1^a)\alpha/(1 + \alpha)$ equals the real value (in terms of the first good) of tax revenues or subsidy payments, evaluated at domestic prices.[13] In writing equations (15), it is assumed (for the sake of simplicity) that all tax revenues or subsidy payments, respectively, are returned to or collected from *national* consumers in lump-sum fashion. If foreigners within the home country were to receive or finance any part of these revenues or payments, respectively, comparison of the free-trade and autarkic equilibria (which generate no tax revenues) clearly would be unaffected, while the chances of having free trade inferior to subsidized trade simply would be enhanced (thereby strengthening the analysis below).

To show that free trade might be inferior to subsidized trade from the national point of view, it is sufficient to establish the possibility of having $dW^n/d\alpha < 0$ in free-trade equilibrium. Consequently, throughout the following discussion, let $\alpha = 0$ in the initial (pretariff) equilibrium.

Differentiating equations (1), (3), (4), and (15) totally with respect to α and again recalling that $U_1^j = 1$ initially and that $U_2^j/U_1^j = p = -(dF_1^j/dp)/(dF_2^j/dp)$, we may verify readily that

$$dW^j/d\alpha = pE^a + (E^j dp/d\alpha), j = a, n; \qquad (16)$$

note that $pE^a = C_1^a - X_1^a$ when (balanced) trade is initially free (with $\alpha = 0$). By well-known reasoning (see Kemp 1969, p. 96),

$$dp/d\alpha = p(1 - m - e^*)/(e + e^* - 1); \qquad (17)$$

note that $1 - m$ equals the home country's marginal propensity to consume the exportable and recall that $\alpha = 0$ initially. When this result is substituted into equations (16), simple manipulation confirms that[14]

$$dW^a/d\alpha = \epsilon pE^a/(e + e^* - 1) \geqq 0 \qquad (18)$$

but shows that

$$dW^n/d\alpha \gtreqqless 0 \text{ as } (e + e^* - 1)E^a \gtreqqless (m + e^* - 1)E^n. \qquad (19)$$

Thus, despite the fact that $dW^a/d\alpha \geqq 0$, it is evidently possible to have $dW^n/d\alpha < 0$ nevertheless.[15]

[13] Although the corresponding value at *world* prices would be $(C_1^a - X_1^a)\alpha$, consumers respond directly to *domestic* (tariff-inclusive) prices instead.

[14] Note that $dW^a/d\alpha = 0$ only in the small-country case where $e^* = \infty$, and even then the change in W^a does not equal zero for any discrete change in α, by well-known reasoning.

[15] Along lines suggested by nn. 6–8, the analysis of tariff policy could be extended readily to let $m^f \neq m^n$, without eliminating the possibility of having $dW^n/d\alpha < 0$ even if $m^f = 1 - m^*$.

As implied by the equations (16), it is possible to have $dW^n/d\alpha < 0$ (even though $dW^a/d\alpha$ cannot be negative) if either a differential trade-volume phenomenon arises (fig. 1) when $dp/d\alpha < 0$ (the "normal" price response) or a differential trade-pattern phenomenon occurs (fig. 2) when $dp/d\alpha > 0$. (The "perverse" price response [$dp/d\alpha > 0$] can occur only in the large-country case, under conditions discussed by Metzler [1949].) Correspondingly, if home exportables were relatively capital intensive, it would be possible to have $dW^n/d\alpha < 0$ (even though $dW^a/d\alpha$ cannot be negative) if either nationals are labor abundant when $dp/d\alpha > 0$ or nationals are capital abundant when $dp/d\alpha < 0$.

Thus a trade subsidy might raise national (but not aggregate) welfare above the free-trade level. This analysis of a small subsidy (tax) on trade, moreover, complements the discussion of Bhagwati and Brecher (1980), who concentrate on prohibitive taxes on trade and thus are able to avoid the issue of tariff revenues.

The analysis of this section has an important implication for the traditional method of estimating the cost (benefit) of tariff protection or trade liberalization. Since the conventional method (as outlined by Johnson [1960]) ignores the source of ownership of domestically located inputs, the concept measured (in present notation) is clearly $dW^a/d\alpha$ rather than $dW^n/d\alpha$. Thus, the traditional estimate of the impact of protection or liberalization is an aggregate measure, which overstates or understates the national cost (benefit) if $(E^n - E^a)dp/d\alpha \lesseqgtr 0$, respectively, as suggested by equations (16). This misstatement arises because the conventional estimate simply sums the three standard components (namely, the external terms-of-trade effect and the costs of distortion in both production and consumption), while it fails to exclude the foreign-factor portion of the tariff-induced change in aggregate welfare.[16]

VI. Summary

As demonstrated by this paper, welfare aspects of international trade theory need to be reconsidered, when national and aggregate income

[16] The foreign-factor portion of the change in aggregate welfare is represented by the expression $(E^a - E^n)dp/d\alpha$, which must be excluded from $dW^a/d\alpha$ to give $dW^n/d\alpha$, as suggested by eqq. (16). Also by repeating the procedure of Bhagwati, Ramaswami, and Srinivasan (1969), it is possible to write (in present notation) that $dW^a/d\alpha = (E^a dp^*/d\alpha) + [(p^* - p)dX_2^a/d\alpha] + [(p - p^*)dC_2^a/d\alpha]$, where the relative price of the second good in world markets is denoted p^*, which equals $p(1 + \alpha)$. The components $E^a dp^*/d\alpha$, $(p^* - p)dX_2^a/d\alpha$, and $(p - p^*)dC_2^a/d\alpha$ are the effects due to the terms-of-trade change, the production distortion, and the consumption distortion, respectively. When evaluated in free-trade equilibrium (where $\alpha = 0$ and $p = p^*$), the latter two (distortion-related) components disappear, leaving only the first (terms-of-trade) component. This remaining (first) component, moreover, is equivalent to the right-hand side of eqq. (16) for $j = a$, since (in free-trade equilibrium) $dp/d\alpha = (dp^*/d\alpha) - p$.

differ in the presence of foreign ownership. Examples of this need are provided by the analysis of international transfer, economic expansion, and tariff policy. For a country receiving a transfer from abroad, national (but not aggregate) welfare might deteriorate even when international commodity-market equilibrium is stable, regardless of the direction of change in the world product-price ratio. In the case of economic expansion from factor-supply growth or technological advance, national (but not aggregate) welfare might worsen even when the rest of the world does not have an inelastic offer curve and domestic expansion is not ultrabiased against production of home importables, no matter what the direction of change in the world commodity-price ratio. As for tariff policy, free trade might be ranked inferior to both no trade and subsidized trade (in either direction), from the viewpoint of national (but not aggregate) welfare. Moreover, the conventional empirical estimates of the cost of protection à la Johnson's (1960) methodology are generally seen to be in need of correction if the economy has foreign-owned factors of production. In fact, many economies typically do have substantial labor inflows under *gastarbeiter* or other programs defined by immigration-quota policies, and, of course, equally there are substantial flows of capital among nation states.[17]

References

Bhagwati, Jagdish N. "Immiserizing Growth: A Geometrical Note." *Rev. Econ. Studies* 25 (June 1958): 201–5. (*a*)

———. "International Trade and Economic Expansion." *A.E.R.* 48 (December 1958): 941–53. (*b*)

———. "The Gains from Trade Once Again." *Oxford Econ. Papers* 20 (July 1968): 137–48.

———. "Shifting Comparative Advantage, Protectionist Demands, and Policy Response Options." Paper presented at a Ford-NBER conference on Import Competition and Adjustment: Theory and Policy, Cambridge, Mass., May 1980.

Bhagwati, Jagdish N., and Brecher, Richard A. "National Welfare in an Open Economy in the Presence of Foreign-owned Factors of Production." *J. Internat. Econ.* 10 (February 1980): 103–15.

Bhagwati, Jagdish N., and Kemp, Murray C. "Ranking of Tariffs under Monopoly Power in Trade." *Q.J.E.* 83 (May 1969): 330–35.

Bhagwati, Jagdish N.; Ramaswami, V. K.; and Srinivasan, T. N. "Domestic Distortions, Tariffs, and the Theory of Optimum Subsidy: Some Further Results." *J.P.E.* 77 (November/December 1969): 1005–10.

[17] Variations in protection may, in turn, lead to variations in the presence of foreign factors in the economy. Thus, for instance, Bhagwati (1980) has considered linkages between reduction in protection and reduction in the restrictiveness of immigration quotas. However, the analysis in the text has taken the endowment of *both* national and foreign-owned factors to be invariant to policy changes.

Bhagwati, Jagdish N., and Tironi, Ernesto. "Tariff Change, Foreign Capital and Immiserization: A Theoretical Analysis." *J. Development Econ.* 7 (March 1980): 71–83.

Johnson, Harry G. "The Cost of Protection and the Scientific Tariff." *J.P.E.* 68 (August 1960): 327–45.

Kemp, Murray C. *The Pure Theory of International Trade and Investment.* Englewood Cliffs, N.J.: Prentice-Hall, 1969.

Metzler, Lloyd A. "Tariffs, the Terms of Trade, and the Distribution of National Income." *J.P.E.* 57 (February 1949): 1–29.

Mundell, Robert A. "The Pure Theory of International Trade." *A.E.R.* 50 (March 1960): 67–110.

Rybczynski, T. M. "Factor Endowment and Relative Commodity Prices." *Economica* 22 (November 1955): 336–41.

Samuelson, Paul A. "The Transfer Problem and Transport Costs: The Terms of Trade When Impediments Are Absent." *Econ. J.* 62 (June 1952): 278–304.

———. "The Transfer Problem and Transport Costs, II: Analysis of Effects of Trade Impediments." *Econ. J.* 64 (June 1954): 264–89.

Stolper, Wolfgang F., and Samuelson, Paul A. "Protection and Real Wages." *Rev. Econ. Studies* 9 (November 1941): 58–73.

Editor's Note

The analysis of international transfers in section III of this essay is complemented by the treatment of transfers in the presence of distortions, as in essay 68 in this volume (coauthored by R. A. Brecher). The case of transfers under foreign ownership—or, more generally, bilateral transfers in a multilateral world—and the case of transfers under distortions—exogenous or endogenous—are unified by a "Generalized Theory of Transfers and Welfare," the title of two recent papers (unpublished) coauthored by Jagdish N. Bhagwati, Richard A. Brecher, and Tatsuo Hatta, 1982.

IV
FOREIGN INVESTMENT, IMPORT COMPETITION, AND OLIGOPOLY

Journal of International Economics 2 (1972) 455–462. © North-Holland Publishing Company

BOOK REVIEWS

Raymond Vernon, Sovereignty at Bay: The Multinational Spread of U.S. Enterprises. (Basic Books, New York, 1971; pp. 336; $8.50.)

The multinational corporation (MNC), as an institution that interacts significantly with the pattern of world trade and factor movements and at the same time poses obvious questions relating to the exercise of national sovereignty, has been the subject of intensive research in recent years. Raymond Vernon's volume represents in many ways the overall synthesis of the principal results of his Harvard Multinational Enterprise Project. As such, and in its wide-ranging review of the numerous economic and political issues raised by MNC's, this volume is a useful contribution and should be recommended to all students of the subject.

However, the book is irritating and inadequate at several levels. MNC's raise ideologically-loaded issues and even the most fair-mined, "old-fashioned, down-to-earth" economist is unlikely to be immune to this fact. Vernon's work claims to a neutrality and objectivity which often conceals only ineffectively his sub-conscious bias in favour of MNC's. Thus, typically he starts with strong leftwing positions on MNC's, proceeds to argue that "unfortunately" the facts as usual are "muddled", cites evidence against these positions, and then in a gesture of fairness gives a few examples that go the other way. A leftwing economist could well go in the reverse direction and leave the reader with the impression that the pro-MNC positions are somewhat ridiculous.

But the subconscious pro–MNC bias in this work goes deeper; it also affects the quality of the arguments deployed plus the judgment which is reached on the evidence cited in support of pro-MNC positions. Two examples should suffice.

In discussing the impact of the MNC's on LDC's, he argues:

> But these foreign-owned subsidiaries were much more than conduits for foreign capital; they were mobilizers of local resources... For less-developed economies, where local institutions for the mobilization of resources were generally not very strong, this function had a significance all its own. The degree of mobilization of resources by U.S.-owned subsidiaries is suggested by the fact that for every dollar of capital transferred from the United States to these subsidiaries in the less-developed countries, about $4 more of capital were collected by the subsidiaries from other sources, including sources internal to the less-developed areas (p. 171).

This argument must be rejected on two counts. First, several thoughtful people in the LDC's have been worried precisely by the fact that the foreign capital inflow which materialises from private firms is much too small a part of the total resource cost of the investments being undertaken, and that for small sums of money, these firms get control of large investments which are actually being financed by domestic capital. Indeed, in some instances, the bulk of the capital comes from foreign aid which would have been available anyway for domestic use. This was notoriously so in the case of the Bokaro steel plant in India where the U.S. Steel Corporation was planning to invest only $33 million and take control over an aid-financed steel mill requiring a total investment of at least $1 billion: a situation described by the then U.S. Ambassador to India as "a real bargain" for the U.S. Steel Corporation.* The use of the phrase

* See Padma Desai, The Bokaro Steel Plant: A Study of Soviet Assistance to India. (North-Holland Publ. Co., 1972.)

"mobilization" for such phenomena would be reminiscent of the use of sanitised words such as "pacification" in Asia. Second, it is amply clear that even in the poor countries Vernon cannot legitimately regard the use of domestic capital and foreign aid by MNC's as necessarily implying the net "mobilization" of resources by MNC's; and the uncritical use of "muddled" figures as the 1 : 4 ratio of own-to-other-resources is, at best, misleading and wrong.

Yet another example of ready resort to dubious evidence and argument in support of MNC's is to be found in Vernon's citation of Katz's study on Argentina where Katz argues that there is a positive correlation between the estimated rates of technical progress in industries and the participation of foreign investment therein. But the methodology of this study is suspect. The econometric technique by which technical progress is estimated requires one to assume that, at each point of time, all firms have identical production functions. But this contradicts the hypothesis that foreign firms, as against domestic firms, have greater technical progressivity or that they have superior productivity which diffuses gradually to the less efficient domestic firms. The assumption of perfect competition in making the estimates also contradicts the hypothesis that domestic firms coexist with more efficient foreign firms. On these grounds alone, as also on well-known objections to estimating production functions in highly *aggregated* industries, I would regard this study as unpersuasive unless one wants to be persuaded.

Examples such as these could be multiplied. The careful reader will therefore do well to examine each argument and consult each original source of evidence before he accepts the frequent claim that the weight of evidence, on balance, shows that MNC's promote the economic welfare of the LDC's.

The disappointing analytical quality of this work shows up even in chapter 3 on the pattern of U.S. MNC manufacturing investments abroad. Vernon restates succinctly here his "product cycle" thesis, which seems to have two components to it. (1) U.S. firms develop new products which come to dominate the U.S. export pattern. This is nothing but the familiar "availability" thesis of Irving Kravis: emerging availability of new products, combined with the demonstration effect on foreign demands, leads to inevitable exports by U.S. innovators. (2) "...When their export position is threatened they establish overseas subsidiaries to exploit what remains of their advantage; they retain their oligopolistic advantage for a period of time, then lose it as the basis for the original lead is completely eroded" (p. 66).

The latter part of the "product cycle" thesis, as quoted above, is its apparently novel feature; but it is also extremely unsatisfactory to the professional economist. (1) Examination of the studies cited in support, as also Vernon's own account, show that nearly everything that has always been argued as influencing overseas investment is thrown into the catchall phrase "threatened export position": host-country tariffs and quotas, the growth of domestic production in the host-country, the entry of *other* MNC's there, and so on. The multitude of these factors, with no quantitative analysis of their relative importance in explaining the alledgedly product cycle variety of overseas investments by the U.S. MNC's, contrasts unhappily with the fact that the "export threat" interpretation of some of these phenomena is not the only possible one. Thus, for example, it is conceivable *and* probable that even a pure monopoly, once external sales in an overseas market reach sufficient scale, would be able to find overseas production profitable relative to exports if tariffs and transports costs are reasonably high and local factor and input costs are advantageous. Since such cost-reducing elements for undertaking production abroad in preference to exports are *always* present in some degree or the other in all cases, and *could* presumably be considered often the decisive factors when overseas production is undertaken, how does one discard this kind of hypothesis in favour of Vernon's "export-threat" thesis? Vernon and his associates not only do not settle such issues; they do not even raise them. (2) Nor does Vernon consider the other critical question for his thesis: why do some firms in an industry respond to export-threats and not others? After all, not all firms in an industry go abroad; and some are content to continue exporting. (3) And then there is one more unasked question: why do the MNC's investing in external production, while choosing that option in preference to exports, not prefer to sell the knowhow for undertaking such production? Since there *is* a large market for sale of technology, and many R&D intensive firms occasionally enter it, this is indeed a pertinent question and a theory of external investment cannot be logically complete unless it is answered.

But, despite these difficulties with the product-cycle thesis, the fact that MNC's substitute foreign production for exports is admittedly an important part of the MNC activities. But it is surely only a part. Leaving out the extractive ventures, on which Vernon has a very useful chapter 2, the MNC's indulge in one or both of the following additional varieties of external investments: (i) they produce, even before exports are undertaken, in some markets; and (ii) they assemble *components* in some countries and ship them out to home base or to third markets where the final production facilities are located.

There is also at least one more dramatic form of international investment which neither Vernon nor other researchers in the MNC field has noted but which may well be the pattern to emerge as a dominant form. In contrast to the case where the MNC's, having developed new products *via* R&D, export them and then transit to producing them abroad, there is an alternative "model" where MNC's in different countries have R&D-induced advantages in producing different types of sub-products (e.g. one MNC in Japan is excellent with small cars and one MNC in U.S. has an edge on large cars; or tire firms in different countries have acquired edge in producing and competing effectively in different types of tires). In competing in each other's home countries or in third markets in both types of sub-products, it is natural that each MNC would find it difficult to compete effectively with the other in sub-products where it does not have the edge. I would expect that, in this situation, there is likelihood of these MNC's deciding that mutual equity inter-penetration, with productionwise accommodation in sub-product specialization according to the advantage possessed, is profitable. Thus, the MNC in U.S. (say, GM) that finds it difficult to compete in the small-car field with the MNC in Japan (say, Toyota) that finds it difficult to compete with the MNC in U.S. in the large-car field, would each decide that the best strategy if you cannot compete with comfort is to follow the policy: "if you cannot beat them, buy them". Thus GM would want to buy equity in Toyota for the small-car production and Toyota in GM for the large-car production; and GM in U.S. would go off spending resources in producing and improving its own small cars while Toyota in Japan would similarly hold back on its own large-car efforts. One thus gets mutually interpenetrating MNC's within industries, with accompanying division of labour and a novel form of "cartelisation" which goes by sub-products. Linder has made us familiar with trade in commodities between similar countries as consisting of sub-product exchanges; and Hymer and Rowthorn have noted that MNC's from different countries penetrate into each other's countries. My "model" essentially combines these two and predicts that MNC's with R&D-induced specialization in different types of sub-products *within* an industry in *different* countries will interpenetrate.

This model is almost ideally illustrated by the following example which Martin Zimmerman has unearthed for me. *Forbe's* of November 15, 1970, (p. 22) notes the following "international marriage":

> Long the friendliest of competitors, Dunlop and Pirelli neatly complement each other. Dunlop is primarily a manufacturer of conventional cross-ply tires. Pirelli concentrates on radials. In Europe, Dunlop has perhaps 18% of the market, Pirelli 12%, as against 12% for Michelin, the next largest competitor. In Europe, Pirelli crosses Dunlop's path only in West Germany: Elsewhere, where Dunlop is active, Pirelli stays out; where Pirelli is active, Dunlop stays out. Outside of Europe, Pirelli is active mostly in Latin America, Dunlop in the Commonwealth and North America.
>
> The two companies have even diversified into different areas – Dunlop into sporting

> goods and precision engineering products, Pirelli into paper, electronics and cables.
>
> Eventually, of course, both marketing organizations will work as one, with Dunlop pushing Pirelli products where Dunlop is strong, and Pirelli pushing Dunlop products elsewhere. " The greatest benefits should come from a pooling of R&D, however, " explains J. Campbell Fraser, a Dunlop director: "In the 'seventies and 'eighties, competition will be more and more in terms of innovations. In the U.K. we have a home base of about 55 million people – that isn't big enough for the kind of R&D we'll need. Pirelli has an even smaller home base, about 45 million. By merging, we'll have a home base of 100 million, enough for the kind of R&D we'll need around the world... There will not even be any exchange of public shares. Instead each will acquire an interest in the other's operating subsidiaries. The British and Italian companies will operate on their own.'

The report goes on to note (p. 23) that there will be four companies: Dunlop Home (U.K. and Europe) with Dunlop owning 51% and Pirelli 49%; Dunlop International (rest of the world) with Dunlop holding 60% and Pirelli, Milan and Switzerland, 20% each; Pirelli Milan (Common Market) with Pirelli Milan holding 51% and 49%; and Pirelli Switzerland (all other Pirelli operations) with Dunlop holding 40%, Pirelli Milan 20% and Pirelli Switzerland 40%.

But interpenetration among MNC's with competing R&D-induced specializations in different sub-products may not be the only important new form of international MNC investments to emerge. Alternative possibilities are one-way penetrations by MNC's. Thus, it is entirely possible for GM to expect to buy its way into profitable Japanese small-car production, for example, by merely offering its distributive outlets, access to funds and/or R&D facilities, and perhaps the political offer of not clamouring for quota protection. Indeed, the recent political pressures on MITI in Japan to open up Japan to U.S. investment in several areas has been so considerable that it seems entirely probable that the model of one-way penetration is about as relevant as the model of interpenetration.

These emerging new patterns of MNC investment are not merely interesting in marking new departures from traditional patterns of MNC investments. They also have differential impact on several questions of a political-economy nature. Consider, for example, the impact of MNC's on the pressure groups for free trade *versus* protectionist policies. An own-export-substituting type of MNC investment, along Vernon's lines, would normally imply that the MNC would transit from being interested in free trade to relative apathy on the issue (except insofar as export of components to the overseas subsidiary is involved or later expansion abroad leads to third market or reverse-flow sales). On the other hand, the penetration-model MNC is going to shift to a free trade position from having protectionist impulses prior to the penetration.

The political economy of MNC's clearly therefore varies with the *type* of MNC investment abroad. The focus on only the so-called product-cycle model prevents Vernon from considering such questions, thereby limiting also the utility of his chapters on the social and political factors which interact with MNC's. In fact, Vernon misses the main point about MNC's and political economy today: as his own detailed statistics show, MNC's are different from 19th century private investments abroad, *not* in being more significant in relation to the recipient-country economies but rather in having become tremendously important in the countries of their *origin*, especially in the United States. The nature of the political influence that they can, and almost certainly seek to, exercise in matters concerning international economic policy positions, mainly on trade and aid matters, as also in regard to the pressures brought to bear on the recipient countries' government and politics, is therefore of the utmost concern and merits serious analysis. The relative complacency on such issues in this volume contrasts dramatically with the recent disclosures of I.T.T.'s politicking on President Allènde's election in Chile and the recurring evidence of considerable corporate lobying in Washinton as the normal way in which at least this Anglo-Saxon democracy works. The issues here are admittedly complex; and, as I have argued, the implication for all these issues will vary with the *type* of MNC investments. Unfortunately, the reader is unlikely to get a proper sense of the importance of these issues, or even a useful and sharp definition thereof in this volume.

Nonetheless, the volume will repay careful and critical reading; and it must be considered indispensable for anyone who wants to know quickly the major sources and familiarise himself with many of the principal concerns which currently dominate research in the area of MNC's.

Journal of Development Economics 4 (1977) 387–400. © North-Holland Publishing Company

A REVIEW SYMPOSIUM

Stephen H. Hymer, *The International Operations of National Firms: A Study of Direct Foreign Investment* (M.I.T. Press, Cambridge, MA, 1976) pp. xxii+253, $12.50.

This slim volume is a real dividend. Its crisp style, the clarity of its thesis and the revolutionary shift of focus on a traditional question are manifest even at a cursory glance. Inevitably, therefore, for those of us who are familiar with the tortuous history of Hymer and his work as also for those who must discover it from Charles P. Kindleberger's simply splendid introduction, the all-too-familiar question poses itself: why was Hymer faced with the hostility of international economists to the extreme point where the doyen of international trade theorists (all but recognizable from Kindleberger's account) would find the substance of Hymer's theory unacceptable and would in fact be a party to holding up (on grounds of academic conviction, of course) its publication in professional journals of repute? And, perhaps equally paradoxically, when Hymer's work would have eventually found its way into the orthodox literature on direct investment, why should there be manifest a tendency to deny

Hymer credit for the fundamental impact of his work and to divert it instead to the very same traditional economists whom Hymer often castigated for rejecting his theory and who were later to take it over with few additional insights to those already contained in Hymer's early work (e.g. witness Kindleberger's gentle but firm criticism of Horst for ascription of Hymer's main thesis to another such economist, in the *Journal of International Economics*, November 1974, p. 397)?

Hymer's thesis was absurdly simple. Until his Ph.D. dissertation, it was customary to treat direct, equity investment abroad on a par with 'capital flows' in general; the distinction between portfolio and equity investment, for example, was not important to this way of analytical thinking. Admittedly, this deficiency was one that afflicted orthodox economic thinking of the day: thus, international trade theory focused on interest rate differentials as explanatory of 'capital flows'. It certainly could not be attributed to Marxist thinking which characteristically focused on the nature of monopoly capitalism for its insights into the capitalist drive to foreign lands (though, the Hobson 'underconsumptionist' theory would appear to be closer to the orthodox economic theory). Hymer's breakthrough, coming interestingly from the recognition of stylised facts such as the presence of cross-investments and the concentration of foreign equity investments in a few oligopolistic industries which did not rest happily with the interest-rate-differentials theory, was to focus on the notion that the primary insights into foreign direct investments could come only from recognising the oligopolistic industrial structure of the firms making such investments: a viewpoint dominating and defining the recent review of writings on direct foreign investments by Richard Caves ('International Corporations: the Industrial Economics of Foreign Investment,' *Economica*, February 1971).

Hymer evidently came to his original thesis, therefore, not from Marxist sources but from thoroughly neoclassical industrial–organizational Bain-inspired reflection on a few facts about foreign direct investment. On the other hand, the natural affinity of his thesis with Marxist perceptions, combined with the neoclassical hostility to his ideas from trade-theoretic circles, must have surely propelled him into the embrace of Marxism towards the end of his short life.

Moreover, while Hymer's basic notion was that the international direct investments had to be seen in the context of the search for control by oligopolistic enterprises, he had an admirably lucid statement of the so-called 'advantages' theory of direct, horizontal investments by multinationals. Thus, Hymer distinctly discussed how the firm would go abroad rather than license or sell its technology, if the special advantages that it possessed (and whose value outweighed the special advantages that local firms would enjoy in their own markets) required own control. Thus, Hymer was the first to pose sharply the atlernatives of licensing technology and of direct investment and to argue the different reasons why special advantages may not be cashed for the same returns through licensing arrangements and may thus require direct investments abroad (see pp. 41–54, in particular); and interestingly, he also described these as 'horizontal' investments!

But if Hymer is to be so completely credited with the modern industrial–organizational theory of foreign direct investment, two natural questions arise at this later date: how does his original dissertation compare with later developments, and how did his own thinking evolve?

The major developments in the 'advantage' theory of Hymer's (this in turn, being only a principal strand in his more general proposition that the study of foreign direct investments belongs in the field of industrial organization, reflecting oligopolistic considerations), would appear to be twofold: first, Harry Johnson's elegant explorations of the efficiency and welfare implications of Hymer's theory (cf. his paper in C.P. Kindleberger, ed., *The International Corporation*, M.I.T. Press, 1970); and second, Raymond Vernon's highly innovative and influential notion of the 'product-cycle' which provided an insightful analysis of the reasons why technological breakthroughs would lead to exports and then to horizontal investments by the firms making these innovations (with their associated Schumpeterian type monopolistic advantages).

It is worth noting that Vernon's product-cycle is possibly the most telling and analytically developed example of Hymer's notion that 'the fiirm's advantage may be that . . . it may have knowledge or control of a more efficient production function . . . or a differentiated product' (pp. 41–42). And it builds on the role of technological innovation in modern corporations and indeed in the dynamic process of capitalism that Marxists focus on but which is missing from the basic Debreu version of neoclassical general equilibrium theory. But it is still a theory that focuses on horizontal foreign direct investment as an act of going abroad to manufacture 'one's own' R and D- produced, differentiated product.

On the other hand, a careful reading of the volume under review shows unmistakeably that Hymer would have regarded, and indeed quite correctly, *any* oligopolistic act of equity investment abroad in the same industry as an example of horizontal direct (as against portfolio) investment. [Thus for example, Hymer argues: 'Trade brings the enterprises of one country into contact with the enterprises of another country; this contact often causes conflict, and international operations are one means of resolving the conflict' (p. 81). Also, his eclectic approach to possible outcomes from the oligopolistic process involved is evident throughout the volume; for example: 'the association of oligopoly elements with international operations . . . introduces a certain degree of indeterminacy into the extent of international operations' (p. 88).] And, if one does this, it is possible to construct yet another (sub-)theory of horizontal direct investment which, in contrast to the Vernon product-cycle (sub-)theory, involves *mutual* foreign equity investments in *each other's* (rather than one's own) differentiated advantages.

Thus, if corporation *X* in one country has differentiated advantages in large cars and corporation *Y* in another in small cars, these two oligopolistic corporations may well decide that, rather than compete on both kinds of cars, they stand to gain most by specializing on their own advantages and each investing in the *other's* advantage. In short, the response to international competition in *differentiated* products in the same industry (e.g. cars, in the above example) could be to prompt foreign equity investment in one's erstwhile competitor's firm: sharing, therefore, *not* markets but product-specialization. Thus, one gets (firmwise) *mutual* cross-investments in the same industry. This theory, christened the MPI theory of mutually penetrating investments by this reviewer elsewhere, is clearly in the Hymer tradition, crossing his notions with those of Linder (who related product differentiation from technological innovation etc. to *trade* flows and argued that countries at similar income levels would have a higher share of mutual manufacturing trade to GNP than those with dissimilar incomes). The conditions under which the oligopolistic response to trade-in-products competition would lead to own-advantage (product-cycle or defensive variety) or to MPI (merger or alternatives form of quasi-merger) equity investments abroad by multinationals is an interesting question that might be addressed theoretically. Such an analysis would enable one to understand the conditions determining when, starting from exportation of an innovation-generated differentiated product, a corporation would choose to invest directly abroad in its manufacture or to go the MPI route directly or as a sequel to the own-product-manufacture-abroad stage.

Hymer's own interests, however, were not to develop in these narrowly professional directions. The fields of sociology, history and political science were to attract him intellectually for the light that they would throw on the larger issues that MNCs (multinational corporations) raised and in which he was to get increasingly involved. For, the 'neutral' Hymer of the 1960 dissertation, focusing purely on the oligopolistic nature of the MNCs with a view to explaining why direct investment took place, was to grow into a policy 'advisor' (in Canada, *via* the Watkins Report, prepared for the Privy Council) and, more important, into a self-declared Marxist.

By a strange irony of fate, therefore, just as Hymer's work was working its way indelibly into the thinking of orthodox economists, these changes in Hymer's lifestyle and worldview were to alienate him again from their preoccupations and deny him their wholehearted approbation. For, professional economics does not take kindly to 'big' issues such as the interaction of MNCs with nation states, their role in international capitalism and the social value of their technological know-how: these are relegated to the softer social sciences. Hymer's Marxism, in turn, reinforced the resulting alienation. For, dismal science as it is called, orthodox economic thinking is basically steeped in optimism: at Chicago, we believe that this is the best of all possible worlds and, at M.I.T., we diagnose the malfunctioning of the invisible hand but typically tend to think that, given the optimal policy interventions that we figure out, a 'quick-fix' can follow. By contrast, Marxist thought is characteristically pessimistic: except in the utopia that comes in the post-revolution but undated steady state, the capitalist system we inhabit must be characterised by unavoidable crises. Hymer's thinking on MNCs was, in this fundamental philosophical sense, therefore to become somewhat uncomfortable to several orthodox exonomists.

But this was surely their own loss, as during the 1960s when the Hymer ideas would face hostility and rejection. For those (such as Kindleberger) who cared to listen, but not necessarily accept, there were still new insights that Hymer could come up with.

A single example, drawn from personal experience and constituting on this occasion a legitimate lapse from the impersonal professional style demanded by book review editors, may illustrate. As we strolled through the exquisite garden of the International House of Japan in Tokyo several years ago, refreshed by saké and stimulated by the discussions of world order organized by Saul Mendlovitz, Hymer developed an argument about MNCs as a vehicle for the transmission of ideology. Imagine the structure of the MNC. The man who heads the branch at the 'periphery' in New Delhi is only a lower-level executive in the overall organization; and, as per the organization-man thesis, he is keen to absorb the ideology of his bosses who are back at the 'center' (and therefore capitalist-minded): But, in India, he is the top dog, with his air-conditioned Cadillac and resources, so that *he* is the one whose ideology will be emulated locally. Therefore, the ideology would pass from the center to the periphery *via* the MNC structure. I recall an animated exchange with Hymer: for, fascinating as this argument was, I maintained that the local MNC bureaucrats were not necessarily the value-setting elite, that in India for instance there were other elites and that the man who ran Coca Cola, for example, was treated with the faint contempt that was lavished on most businessmen. But the argument was brilliant, a kind of Marxist Lemma, suggesting the kind of flash and sudden illumination that had characterised his dissertation.

Editor's Note

The MPI (mutually penetrating investments) theory of direct foreign investments discussed on page 394 is developed in essay 55 and elaborated on in essay 57, both in this volume.

Shifting Comparative Advantage, Protectionist Demands, and Policy Response

Jagdish N. Bhagwati

6.1 Introduction

Although the threat of "new protectionism" has arisen with reference to a whole range of industrial activities in the Western countries and although there is a tendency to consider all such threats as part of a general political-economic phenomenon to be attributed to factors such as generalized unemployment, increased demands for job security from the state, etc., it is useful to distinguish between two extreme, idealized situations.

On the one hand, the pressure of import competition, no matter how significant, can be seen as being addressed to industries undergoing a basic shift in comparative advantage, not because of technological advances arising in different parts of the world which are not being shared by competing nations, but rather because of shifts in labor costs or because "learning by doing" by latecomers is altering the traditional competitive edge of industries in the West. These are the "senescent," "declining" industries such as textiles, and shoes and footwear which are labor-intensive and mostly unintensive in skills and R & D, where the newly industrializing countries of the South are increasingly demonstrating comparative advantage. Since these industries are characterized by low technical progress—which is perfectly compatible with increasing

Jagdish N. Bhagwati is the Arthur Lehman Professor of Economics at Columbia University. He has written on trade theory, developmental theory and policy, internal and international migration, and education models. He is editor of the *Journal of International Economics* and author (with T. N. Srinivasan) of *Lectures on the Theory of International Trade*, to be published by MIT Press.

Thanks are due to NSF Grant no. SOC 79-07541 for financial support, to Robert Feenstra for helpful conversations, and to Robert Baldwin, T. Bayard, Charles Kindleberger, Gene Grossman, Jean Waelbroeck, and John Williamson for valuable comments.

capital intensity, of course—Schumpeterian responses in the nature of induced technical progress à la Weiszacre-Kennedy-Samuelson are not in evidence. Hence the responses of the enterpreneurs, labor, and communities or townships in which these industries are located, as well as the nature of the governmental policy options and responses, are likely to be quite different from those occurring when the industries are of the type considered immediately below.

This second class of industries is at the other end of the technological scale, being largely characterized by changing comparative advantage because R & D leads to technical change that gives the competitive edge to new countries. These industries are at the front end of the dynamic, Schumpeterian capitalist process. The resulting shifts in comparative advantage yield a very different set of responses by the industries losing comparative advantage, and the policy options available to the countries where they are located are also correspondingly different.

In considering these two idealized models, it will be critical to note that the response to shifting comparative advantage will involve differential interaction with international "factor" mobility. In the former case, a possible and indeed empirically important response (hitherto neglected altogether in the literature) is lobbying for a greater inflow of foreign *labor.* In the latter case, however, among the important responses are a variety of patterns of direct foreign *investment*: for example, the use of threats of protection to induce a reverse flow of foreign investment into the country or mutually penetrating investments in differential but similar products where the different countries have differential advantages.

Moreover, it will be useful to distinguish the following "actors" among the lobbies seeking governmental response to the shift in comparative advantage: (i) the entrepreneurs, who may be interested in sales à la Burnham and Galbraith but are generally identified in the formal arguments below with the owners of equity capital in the industry; (ii) labor, distinguished in practice by nationality, skills, and age but again treated in the formal analysis below as a homogeneous entity; and (iii) the community-cum-township where the affected industry may play a dominant role. The analysis will try to identify which policy responses will be sought by one or more of these actors and therefore what political forces the government is likely to confront by choosing one policy response option in preference to another.

6.2 Technically Unprogressive, "Traditional" Industries

Since technical change is not important in these industries, the *shift* in their comparative advantage largely reflects changing factor endowments and/or learning in the newly industrializing countries. They are thus also primarily labor-intensive, low-skills industries—in competition with the less developed countries (LDCs). How are these industries in the developed countries likely to react to the adversely shifting comparative advantage?

6.2.1 The Relaxation of Immigration Quotas as a Policy Response Option

As comparative advantage shifts against these unprogressive industries, pressuring them toward a (relative or absolute) contraction of their output, it might appear that all the potential lobbies that were distinguished above—entrepreneurs, labor, and the community—would be seeking relief via only one type of governmental response, namely, some sort of protection. However, this is plainly not the case. For these unprogressive industries are often at a comparative disadvantage precisely because cost conditions have moved against them, and in labor-intensive industries this is often because labor abroad has become relatively cheaper. Now, introduce into this picture the fact that international mobility of labor is severely regulated by immigration quotas and that the real wages of labor are substantially higher in the West than in many developing countries. It follows immediately that one additional policy response in which entrepreneurs could be interested is for the government to increase the availability of imported labor.

Note that the entrepreneurs' response will typically not include in this case their leaving for the foreign countries where the comparative advantage has shifted. This is due to the fact that these are unprogressive industries where, with no Hymer-like firm-specific know-how to take advantage of, the migration of domestic entrepreneurship is likely to mean merely that the migrant entrepreneurs will have to operate in unfamiliar, relatively riskier foreign situations, without any offsetting technological advantage, and hence at a competitive disadvantage with local producers.[1]

On the other hand, domestic labor should find its own interests better served by a policy of protection rather than by the alternative policy of relaxed immigration quotas. Therefore, while a governmental response in the form of allowing the increased importation of foreign labor will satisfy entrepreneurs, it will not generally satisfy domestic labor. To consider these issues rigorously, turn now to the formal analysis below.

6.2.2 Some Formal Models

Heckscher-Ohlin-Samuelson Model

Take first the $2 \times 2 \times 2$ model of trade theory to develop the main implications of our policy-choice problem rigorously. Assume two goods X and Y, and two factors K and L, and let Y be L-intensive and the importable good, in conformity with the empirical reality of the problem at hand. I would like to distinguish between the two types of shift in comparative advantage that may affect the L-intensive importable industry Y: (1) that which arises *externally*—either from a shift in the foreign offer curve facing our country or from a tariff cut by our country as in the across-the-board tariff cuts of the Kennedy Round; and (2) that which results *internally*, e.g., from capital accumulation or productivity change. In each case, it will also be relevant whether the comparisons between the two policies involve a tariff-free or a tariff-ridden economy when the policy chosen is to import more labor. Throughout, I assume a small country and negligible lobbying costs.

Case I: External shift in comparative advantage, zero initial tariff. Figure 6.1 shows the economy moving from external price ratio P_1 to P_2, adversely affecting production of good Y.

The tariff policy will then restore production of Y to the initial level Y^0 at Q_1 but, as seen in figure 6.2, will yield welfare U_t. The alternative policy of restoring Y production to Y^0 by importing labor, on the other hand, will lead to welfare level U_{Lm} as follows. As labor is imported, holding the goods price ratio unaltered at its new free-trade position P_2, we can trace the Rybczynski line Q_2R which, at Q_3, yields Y production equal to Y^0. Importation of the corresponding amount of labor (Lm) would then restore domestic importable output to the initial, preshift level. But the *national* welfare level, defined *exclusive* of imported labor's welfare, would be U_{Lm}, with the national budget line Q_2C_{Lm}, since imported labor earns the value of its marginal product, which, in turn, equals the increment in output along the Rybczynski line.

A comparison of the two policies, both achieving identical production in the importable industry and thus satisfying entrepreneurs equally in that respect,[2] then shows that the policy of reduced restrictions on the importation of labor dominates that of increasing trade protection insofar as economic welfare conventionally defined is concerned ($U_{Lm} > U_t$), and hence should be the preferred option of an economic-welfare-oriented government.[3] At the same time, from the viewpoint of international relations, it should again be a preferred option, since relaxing immigration restrictions gives the government good marks whereas increasing trade protection gives it bad marks. On the other hand, at Q_3 and Q_2 under the policy of reduced immigration restrictions, the real wages of labor are less than at Q_1 under the tariff policy, à la the Stolper-Samuelson argument.[4]

The choice between the policy option of reducing immigration restrictions and increasing trade protection in response to an adverse shift in comparative advantage therefore primarily involves the conflicting interests of the *government* (or, more precisely, that part of the government [e.g., in the United States, the executive rather than the legislative] which

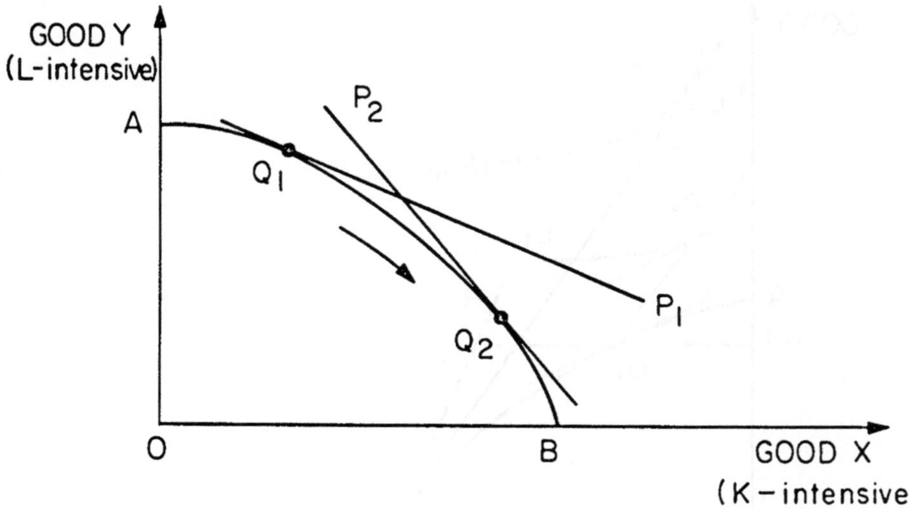

Fig. 6.1

is presumably interested in welfare as defined by conventional economics) and *consumers*, who face lower prices for importables, on the one hand, and *domestic labor*, on the other hand, while leaving the entrepreneurs somewhat indifferent between the two policy options insofar as industry output is concerned but in favor of the policy of importing more foreign labor since this implies greater reward to capital. I shall later amplify other aspects of the conflicting interests involved in the choice between these policies, especially those involved at the community-cum-township level, which cannot be accommodated in the present model. For the present, however, let me go on to show that this basic pattern of conflicts between the different sectors resurrects itself when the external shift is in the presence of a trade restriction, though there are important differences to note, as argued immediately below.

Case II: External shift in comparative advantage, positive initial tariff. The presence of an initial tariff makes a significant difference to the analysis of the effects of different policy responses to an external shift in comparative advantage. This is because the policy of increasing the importation of labor is itself to be judged in the context of a tariff-ridden economy. For the choice now, when the external price ratio shifts from P_1 to P_2, is between increasing the tariff to restore production of Y to Y^0 at Q_1 and, instead, increasing the importation of labor to achieve Y^0 while maintaining the tariff at the initial level.

While in case I, with zero initial tariff, the importation of labor left the national welfare unchanged at the free-trade level (since imported labor earned the value of its marginal product at domestic prices as well as at

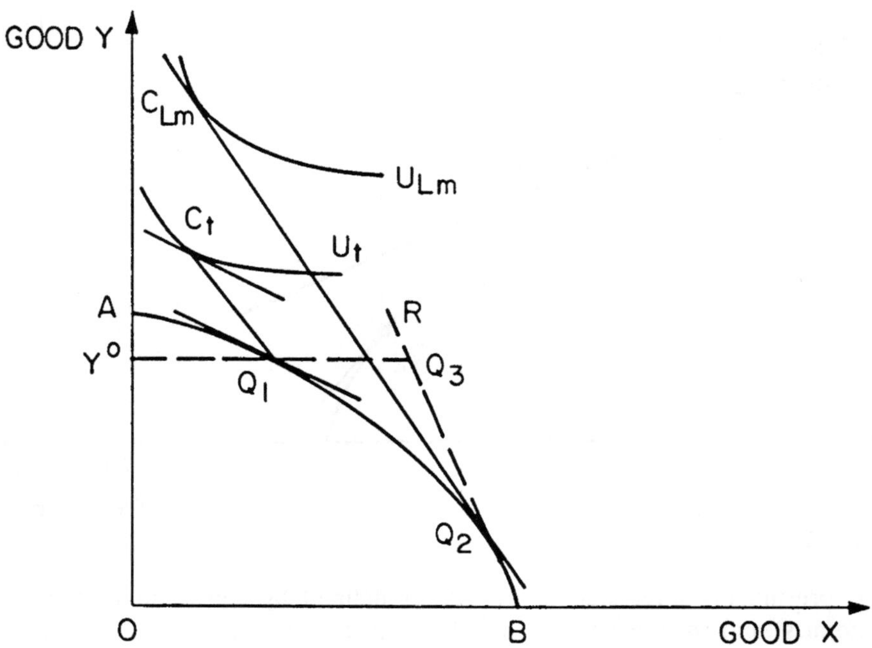

Fig. 6.2

international prices thanks to free trade), the importation of labor when the labor-intensive importable industry is protected by a tariff is necessarily immiserizing! This result, derived by Uzawa (1969) and Brecher and Alejandro (1977) independently of one another, is seen in figure 6.3. There, after the shift of the external price ratio to P_2, the continuing initial tariff makes P_2^D the new tariff-inclusive domestic price ratio. With labor imported, the corresponding Rybczynski line is then Q_2R. Now, if no labor were imported, the equilibrium consumption would be at C_2, which lies on P_2 and on the income-consumption line IC (P_2^D) which is drawn with reference to price ratio P_2^D. If, however, labor is imported and is paid the value of its marginal product at domestic tariff-inclusive prices, the *national* income at domestic prices will be identical to P_2^D through Q_2. Thus, if labor importation takes production on the Rybczynski line to Q_3, and (for simplicity) we assume that foreign labor consumes entirely in the country of residence, the *national* (net-of-foreign-labor-consumption) bundle of production will be along the stretch EF on the national income line P_2^D through Q_2. And, by putting the new international price line P_2 through E and F, and cutting IC (P_2^D), we see that the resulting national consumption will lie in the range of $C'_{Lm}C''_{Lm}$. Evidently therefore importing labor will necessarily be immiserizing.

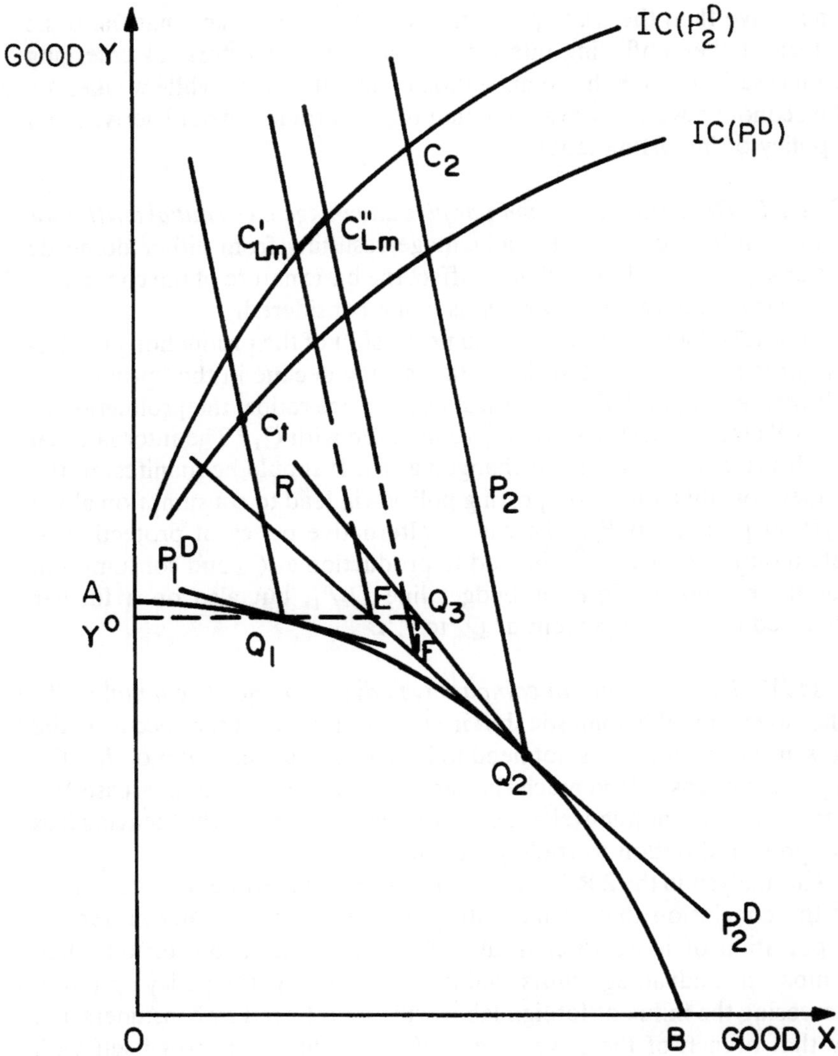

Fig. 6.3

However, it is equally evident that the alternative policy of resorting to trade protection to restore Y production to Y^0 by shifting back to Q_1, with the new international price ratio P_2, yields consumption at C_t on the income-consumption curve IC (P_1^D) which is drawn with reference to P_1^D (tangent to AB at Q_1). Evidently this is *inferior* to any equilibrium consumption, on C'_{Lm} C''_{Lm}, reached under the labor importation policy.

Note therefore that the welfare loss from importing labor is constrained so as to make the labor-importing policy nonetheless a better alternative than the trade protection policy.[5] This means that the basic nature of the conflicting interests of the different actors, as emerging from case I, survives the complication of an initial tariff while weakening the economic-welfare advantage that the government would derive from a policy of importing labor.

Case III: Domestic shift in comparative advantage, zero initial tariff. Nor does a shift in comparative advantage resulting from either domestic factor supply or technical change affect the basic nature of the conflicting interests on the two policy options being considered.

Thus take figure 6.4, where a domestic shift of the production possibility curve from AB to $A'B'$ leads to a strong decline in the "production advantage" of good Y: at identical goods price ratios, the production of good Y actually declines, as at Q_2 compared with Q_1.[6] The international goods price ratio remains unchanged at P_1. It should be manifest to the reader now that a labor-importing policy will lead to consumption along Q_2P_1 at price ratio P_1, whereas an alternative policy of protection to retain output of Y at Y^0 will lead to production at Q_4 and consumption not merely on the inferior budget line Q_4P_1, but also on a further distorted price-ratio tangent at Q_4 to $A'B'$.

Case IV: Domestic shift in comparative advantage, positive initial tariff. The case where the domestic shift in comparative advantage occurs in the presence of a tariff does not need to be spelled out, since it modifies the argument of case III in much the same way as case II modifies case I: it weakens the economic-welfare case for importing labor while leaving it as the preferred option to trade protection.

The analysis in the $2 \times 2 \times 2$ model therefore underlines the robustness of the conclusion that, while entrepreneurs will marginally prefer the importation of more foreign labor to an increase in protection when comparative advantage shifts against their industry, the policy option of increasing the influx of foreign labor will be preferred by consumers and by that branch of the government (if any) which concerns itself with economic welfare conventionally defined, while being considered detrimental to its interests by domestic labor.

However, I might add that cases III and IV, where the shift is domestically induced, suggests an important difference from cases I and II, where the shift is externally induced. In the former case, if the shift results from capital accumulation leading to a decline in the output of the labor-intensive importable activity (à la Rybczynski), the real wages of labor will be *maintained*; it is just that the "drawing power" of the importable activity for domestic labor has been reduced as a result of the change in the accumulation. In this case, it is not likely that domestic labor will oppose the import of foreign labor; the labor import will be seen rather as

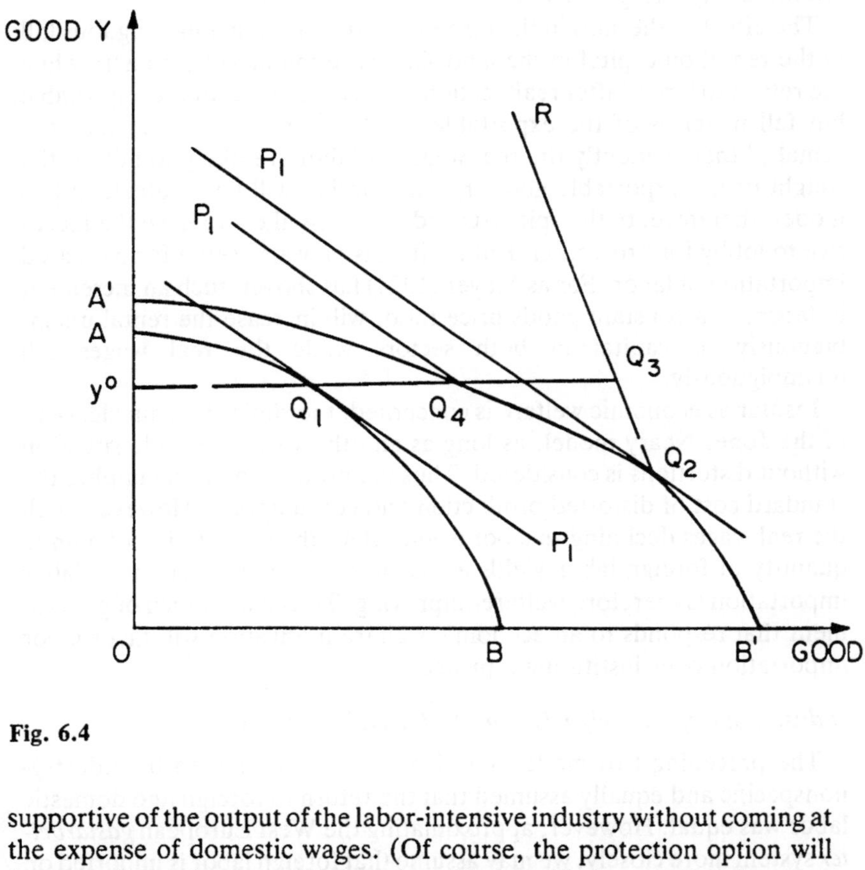

Fig. 6.4

supportive of the output of the labor-intensive industry without coming at the expense of domestic wages. (Of course, the protection option will *increase* the real wages of labor; but this is unlikely to make the same impression on labor as actually *losing* ground through reduced real wages). In cases where the shift in comparative advantage is external, however, the loss of real wages in the present model is necessarily actual, not just in an opportunity-cost sense, when the shift occurs; and therefore the importation of labor as a policy option is likely to be opposed passionately.

Jones-Neary Model

Consider instead the model of Jones (1971) and Neary (1978) in which capital is specific but labor is mobile between the two sectors. This may be considered to be the "short-run" version of the standard 2 × 2 model, if labor is assumed to be mobile in the short-run but capital is not, an interpretation given by Neary (1978), Mussa (1974), and Mayer (1974).[7] What happens to the choice between labor importation and protection in this model when the terms of trade shift adversely against the labor-intensive importable activity?[8]

The effect of the shift in the terms of trade is now an unambiguous fall in the rental on capital in the labor-intensive importable industry while the return to labor (after reallocation) will rise in terms of the importable but fall in terms of the exportable good. (If the importable sector is "small," then evidently the real wages of labor are likely to fall, as the weight of the exportable good in consumption will be greater). In this model, therefore, both capitalists and labor are likely to have the incentive to lobby for protection. But capitalists may also settle for increased importation of labor. For as Mayer (1974) has shown, such an increment in labor, at a constant goods price ratio, will increase the rental unambiguously to capital in both sectors while the real wages fall unambiguously.[9]

Insofar as economic welfare is concerned, the choice is again clear-cut in the Jones-Neary model, as long as an otherwise free-trade situation without distortions is considered. Thus the protection option implies the standard cost of distorted production and consumption. However, with the real wages declining as labor is imported, the importation of a finite quantity of foreign labor yields a "surplus" to the host country: labor importation is therefore welfare-improving. Thus that branch of government that responds to an economic-welfare motivation will favor labor importation over instituting a protective tariff.

Industry-specific Foreign Labor Paid a Differential Wage

The preceding two models considered foreign labor to be industry-nonspecific and equally assumed that the return to foreign and domestic labor was equal. However, approximating the West European *gastarbeiter* system more closely, we may assume that foreign labor is imported on an industry-specific contractual basis and can be effectively paid lower wages than domestic labor.

Take this model then and assume a Haberler-Brecher model with Haberler (1950)–type sector-specific factors and Brecher (1974*a*, *b*)–type sticky real wages for labor. Let Q_1 be the initial production vector, AQ_1B being the production possibility curve, given the immobility of factors. When the terms of trade shift from P_1 to P_2, turning against the importable, labor-intensive good Y, labor in Y production insists on maintaining its real wages in terms of good X. This leads to workers being laid off in industry Y until the marginal physical product of labor in Y rises sufficiently at Q_2 to restore Y labor's real wages in terms of good X.

In this situation, if the Y capitalists are allowed to import foreign labor to restore their output to Q_1, and foreign labor allows itself to be hired at lower real wages than what local labor insists on, then part of the incremental output of good Y (this increment being Q_2Q_1) will accrue to

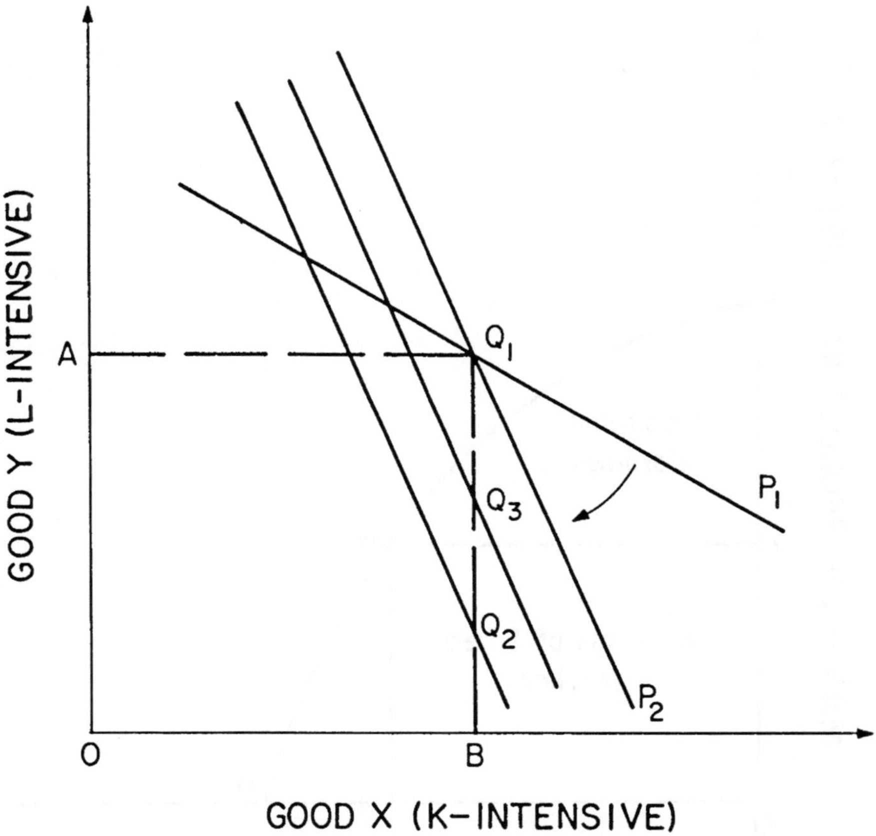

Fig. 6.5

the capitalists, as demonstrated in figure 6.6. There, *OS* represents the real wages of domestic labor in terms of *Y* at Q_2 in figure 6.5; *OZ* is the lower, fixed real wages at which foreign labor can be imported in numbers permitted by the immigration quota; *OJ* is the immigration quota; *SHR* is the marginal product curve for imported labor in industry *Y*, given the employment of domestic capital and labor at Q_2 in figure 6.5. The total increment in *Y* output that results is then *SHJO*, which is assumed to correspond to Q_2Q_1 in figure 6.5. But of this increment, only *OZHJ* accrues as earnings of foreign workers, and the rest, *SHZ*, accrues to the domestic capitalists; this division corresponds to Q_3Q_1 for foreign workers and Q_2Q_3 for domestic capital in figure 6.5. Thus, reverting to figure 6.5, national welfare is now defined, in the labor-importation option, by the availability line P_2 passing through Q_3.

By contrast, the protection option will maintain domestic labor's real wages while restoring labor employment as well; it will also increase

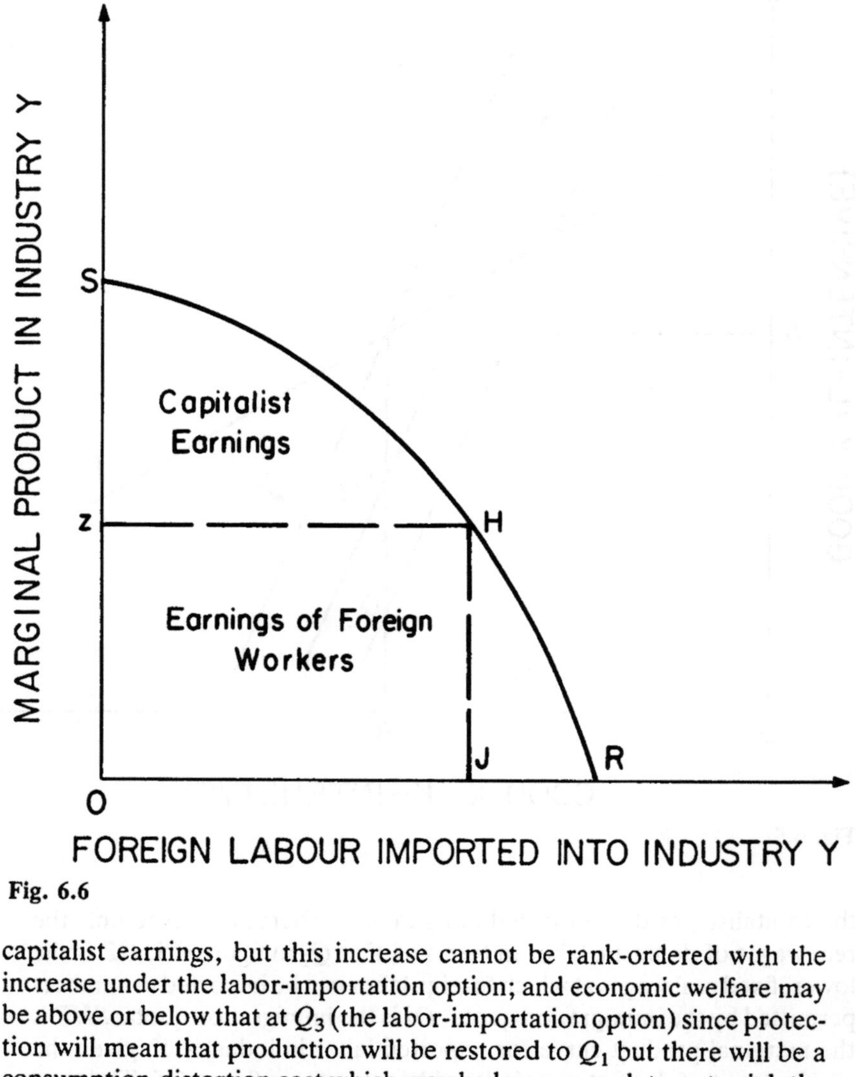

Fig. 6.6

capitalist earnings, but this increase cannot be rank-ordered with the increase under the labor-importation option; and economic welfare may be above or below that at Q_3 (the labor-importation option) since protection will mean that production will be restored to Q_1 but there will be a consumption-distortion cost which may be large enough to outweigh the production gain vis-à-vis the labor-importation option.[10]

6.2.3 Likely Lobbying Outcomes

What type of lobbying may then be expected in the labor-intensive industries, once we recognize the possibility of using immigration quotas as a policy instrument? Evidently the answer depends critically on the production-cum-trade model that applies to a specific situation; it is also clearly dependent on the precise immigration control system that the country operates. Thus, if we contrast the results of the three models, it is interesting that, in the Heckscher-Ohlin-Samuelson (HOS) model, capitalists would find protection harmful and labor importation of no effect on their earnings whereas in the other two models *both* options are helpful. Again, labor is actually hurt by labor importation in the Jones-Neary model but is neither hurt nor helped in the other models, whereas protection helps it in all three models. The precise conflicts of interests, reflecting the implications of the two policy options of protection and labor importation, will therefore depend on the specifics of the situation concerning factor-market and immigration-system behavior. No general conclusions are possible, as indicated by table 6.1, which categorizes the outcomes.

On the other hand, the models uniformly suggest that entrepreneurs have an interest in getting governments to agree to relax immigration quotas, that governments themselves have a potential interest in the relaxation of immigration quotas since economic welfare is such an important objective, and that labor, in contrast, has a relatively greater interest in the adoption of protection measures instead. I would therefore expect governments to expedite the inflow of foreign labor whenever (*a*) domestic labor's opposition to this policy option is weak and its lobbying for protection is correspondingly weak (as when labor is not effectively organized due to geographical dispersion of the industry, for example), (*b*) the government's ability to grant protection is weak (because, for example, of fear of retaliation or respect for GATT Article XIX), and (*c*) the government's ability to augment immigration is not constrained greatly by the social consequences of increased immigration. More specifically, the following types of hypotheses may well be worth exploring.

1. When the shift in comparative advantage is domestically induced (as in cases III and IV of the HOS model above), the opposition of domestic labor to the importation of labor will be the less, for reasons spelled out earlier. By contrast, when the shift comes from external changes (as in cases I and II), the opposition of domestic labor to the importation of labor will be the greater. Therefore I would expect that the policy response to a shift in comparative advantage would be, *ceteris paribus*, greater for imported labor when the shift is domestic rather than external.

2. Moreover, where the external shift in comparative advantage is combined with the presence of a native labor force which has low-mobility characteristics (e.g., higher age, residency traditionally in towns or communities in which the roots and ties are strong, which raises the nonpecuniary costs of mobility), the likelihood of protection emerging as the outcome of the lobbying response will be all the greater. For in this case, the option of importing foreign labor will appear particularly unattractive to the low-mobility labor, whose real wages will otherwise face a significant decline. The role of the community or township as a lobbying

Table 6.1 **Effects of Output-restoring Labor-Importation and Protectionist Responses to Import Competition in Labor-intensive Industries**

Model	Policy Response	Capitalists*	Labor	"Economic Welfare"
Heckscher-Ohlin-Samuelson	Labor Importation	Earnings unchanged	Earnings unchanged	Welfare Unchanged (cases I & III)
	Protection	Earnings reduced	Earnings increased (back to preshift level)	Reduces welfare
Jones-Neary	Labor Importation	Earnings increased	Earnings lowered	Increases welfare
	Protection	Earnings increased	Earnings increased	Reduces welfare
Haberler-Brecher	Labor Importation	Earnings increased	Earnings unchanged	Increases welfare
	Protection	Earnings increased	Earnings increased (via increased employment)	May increase or lower welfare (while increasing domestic employment)

Note: The comparison is with the situation where import competition (i.e., shift in comparative advantage) occurs and there is no policy response. The comparison is *not* therefore with the situation *before* import competition

*The entries here relate, in the Jones-Neary and Haberler-Brecher models, to capitalist earnings in the importable industry.

force in cases where labor has strong historical ties to an area, as in traditional "textile towns," may also be very important quite independently of the labor force itself. For where such geographical specificity is involved, other jobs are likely to be seen as being dependent not merely on the size of the industry's output but also on traditional spending patterns, and imported labor, with its usual high savings and remittance rates, is unlikely to be quite an adequate replacement in that regard! Moreover, the social cohesion of the community itself may militate against introducing a sizable foreign labor component into such communities.[11]

What type of evidence would indicate that such hypotheses make empirical sense? The foregoing arguments suggest that one may be able to examine episodes such as the response to across-the-board tariff cuts in the Kennedy Round and hypothesize a set of testable propositions.

I would expect, for example, that when across-the-board tariff cuts are made, as after the Kennedy Round, the tariff-cut exemptions (adjusted insofar as they were offset by domestic subsidies—as they were often, and in varying degree, in West Germany according to Riedel 1977) would be generally greater in those traditional industries where the labor force is largely domestic, is geographically concentrated in close-knit communities, or is relatively immobile. In contrast, when quota restrictions are relaxed, I would expect there to be a relatively greater growth of the foreign labor component in those industries in which the labor force already has a significant foreign element, is geographically dispersed, or has a domestic component that is relatively skilled and mobile.

Furthermore, if cross-sectional regressions were run, I would not be surprised if (the subsidy-adjusted) tariff-cut exemptions were inversely related to the initial proportion of foreign labor in the total labor force and to the skill level of the labor force, and positively related to the average age of the labor force, as seems to be indicated to some degree in Cheh's (1974) analysis of the United States and Riedel's (1977) analysis of West Germany. And this is the important *new* possibility: that the growth rate of foreign labor (absolute or relative to domestic labor) in these industries, reflecting the relaxation of immigration quota restrictions, may be positively related to the initial proportion of foreign labor in the total labor force and to the skill level of the labor force, and inversely related to the average age of the labor force. And thus, also, there may then exist an inverse correlation between the tariff-cut exemptions an industry receives and the growth rate of its foreign labor force, in cross-sectional analysis.

6.2.4 Labor Lobbying and the Efficient Tariff: An Aside

Where the labor interest in protection is deep-seated, the foregoing arguments suggest that the governmental response will be to yield to protectionist pressures from the labor lobby; the relaxation of immigration quota restrictions will not be the preferred option.

In these cases, the "bargaining" between the government and labor may be visualized as being over the degree of protection to be granted to the industry when the comparative advantage has shifted, with labor's primary interest consisting in fully restoring its preshift economic position and the government's in minimizing the cost of such restoration of labor's economic position.

Viewing the conflict this way, we can develop the notion of an "efficient tariff" (as is done rigorously by Feenstra and Bhagwati in chapter 9), once we recognize that the levy of a tariff will generally raise revenue. Thus, consider for simplicity the $2 \times 2 \times 2$ model where labor's real wage declines with the relative price of the importable good. A shift in comparative advantage improving the terms of trade will hurt labor, triggering the lobbying for a tariff. If then the tariff is used for restoring the real wages of labor, there will be an associated loss of welfare to society. However, since the tariff raises revenue, we may consider the following alternative. Suppose that this tariff revenue itself is used to compensate labor through a direct subsidy such that labor's real income (defined as the *sum* of its real wages in employment and this subsidy, as in Bhagwati 1959) is equivalent to its preshift real wages. Then the resulting welfare cost to society would generally be lower. Thus a tariff which restores the real *wages* of labor to their original level would generally be inferior to the efficient tariff which is chosen so as to minimize the welfare cost of a tariff which restores labor's real *income* to the original (real wage) level by additionally utilizing the tariff revenue proceeds to subsidize labor's income.[12] This notion of the efficient tariff makes a good deal of sense insofar as the revenue used for redistribution is being generated as a side effect of the protection itself and is *not* being raised *ab initio* for the redistribution![13]

What this notion of the efficient tariff does therefore is to provide a rationale for a direct subsidy to lobbying labor, as long as it is kept within the bounds of the tariff revenue raised from the partial protection granted, when the labor lobby seeking protection is strong and the government feels that there is no political alternative to maintaining the labor lobby's economic position in face of a shift in comparative advantage.

6.2.5 Protectionist Response to Import Competition and the Welfare of the Exporting Country: Some Paradoxes

While the foregoing analysis was addressed to lobbies, policy options, and likely outcomes, focusing exclusively on the country facing import competition, the novel element of foreign labor additionally introduces an interesting, and surely important, element of paradox into the situation regarding protectionist responses to import competition as far as the welfare of the *other* trading countries is concerned.

For it is no longer possible to identify the levying of protective tariffs on one's exports by another country as necessarily welfare-worsening—short of standard paradoxes in trade theory—for the simple reason that the protection also redounds to the welfare of foreign labor, and this labor may very well be one's own emigrant labor. Thus, if the United States levies protective tariffs on Mexican textile exports, this will worsen the welfare of the Mexican nonemigrant population but, since some Mexican labor is employed in textiles production in the United States, it will also improve the welfare of the Mexican emigrant population. So, depending on what distributional welfare weights are assigned, one could easily argue that United States protection *improves* the welfare of the Mexicans (emigrants *plus* nonemigrants)![14] Interestingly, this paradox is the mirror image of the paradox (analyzed in Bhagwati and Tironi 1980, Bhagwati and Brecher 1980 and Brecher and Bhagwati 1981) in which the reduction of a tariff in the presence of foreign-owned factors of production may be accompanied by a decline in national welfare even though the country is small and no other domestic distortions are present.[15]

Another interesting paradox that arises in the presence of foreign labor from LDCs and the DCs (developed countries) is that the country from which foreign labor is coming and the country producing the imports may not coincide. Thus textiles in the United States may be using Mexican labor while they face competition from South Korea. Hence there may be inter–LDC conflicts inherent in the decision of the DCs to use or not to use protection in the face of a shift in comparative advantage. For instance, West Germany uses a great deal of Turkish, Yugoslav, and Greek labor in industries that face competition from the less developed newly industrializing countries such as Brazil, Taiwan, South Korea, Hong Kong, and Singapore.

6.3 Technically Progressive, Schumpeterian Industries

The scenarios concerning lobbying and policy response options discussed in the preceding section change dramatically as attention is shifted to technologically progressive industries. These industries might be described as Schumpeterian since they represent the essence of the dynamic capitalist system that Schumpeter described so beautifully. Technological change, resulting from R & D (whether private or public), is critical to the shifts in comparative advantage in these industries, and this essential fact fundamentally transforms the nature of the lobbying responses and policy options that open up in the face of the ongoing shifts in comparative advantage.

6.3.1 Two Alternative Models of Direct Foreign Investment in Progressive Industries

It will be appropriate to distinguish in the analysis that follows between two models in the direct investment literature, both an offshoot of Hymer's (1960) ground-breaking work on direct foreign investment: the "product cycle" (PC) model of Vernon (1966) and the "mutual penetration of investment" (MPI) model set forth in my review of Vernon's *Sovereignty at Bay* (Bhagwati 1972) and then amplified in Bhagwati (1978, 1979).

The "Product Cycle" Model

In the PC model, firms develop R & D–based new products in one country, with a corresponding conferral of comparative advantage of manufacture in that country. As long as the product and its associated processes need to be "debugged" and simplified, the location of production at home, close to the R & D facilities, is important. With the passing of this stage, the production of the products is freed from this locational requirement and production facilities will shift to wherever wages are cheapest. Thus this model is premised on a shift in comparative advantage in the location of production that reflects a process where R & D–created comparative advantage self-destructs and the process is essentially a result of domestic R & D rather than a result of external changes induced by R & D.

The "Mutual Penetration of Investment" Model

In contrast, the MPI model is based on the observation that competition occurs among differentiated but similar products and that increased competition can typically occur in the progressive industries through R & D–induced intensification of the advantages enjoyed by the competitors for their differentiated products. For example, European and Japanese small cars compete with American large cars; and this competition intensifies with time as the Japanese get better at the game (e.g., Toyota started production only after World War II) of R & D in production, marketing, and sales and the Americans get steadily better at producing the "gas guzzlers." The MPI thesis then is that the response to such intensified competition could be a mutual investment by the competing firms in one another's R & D–induced advantages. Contrasting the resulting MPI pattern of direct investment and Vernon's PC model, I wrote the following in 1972:

> There is also at least one more dramatic form of international investment which neither Vernon nor other researchers in the MNC field has noted but which may well be the pattern to emerge as a dominant form. In contrast to the case where the MNC's, having developed new

products via R&D, export them and then transit to producing them abroad, there is an alternative "model" where MNC's in different countries have R&D–induced advantages in producing different types of sub-products (e.g. one MNC in Japan is excellent with small cars and one MNC in U.S. has an edge on large cars; or tire firms in different types of tires). In competing in each other's home countries or in third markets in both types of sub-products, it is natural that each MNC would find it difficult to compete effectively with the other in sub-products where it does not have the edge. I would expect that, in this situation, there is likelihood of these MNC's deciding that mutual equity inter-penetration, with productionwise accommodation in sub-product specialization according to the advantage possessed, is profitable. Thus, the MNC in U.S. (say, GM) that finds it difficult to compete in the small-car field with the MNC in Japan (say, Toyota) that finds it difficult to compete with the MNC in U.S. in the large-car field, would each decide that the best strategy if you cannot compete with comfort is to follow the policy: "if you cannot beat them, buy them." Thus GM would want to buy equity in Toyota for the small car production and Toyota in GM for the large-car production: and GM in U.S. would go off spending resources in producing and improving its own small cars while Toyota in Japan would similarly hold back on its own large-car efforts. One thus gets mutually interpenetrating MNC's within industries, with accompanying division of labour and a novel form of "cartelisation" which goes by sub-products. Linder has made us familiar with trade in commodities between similar countries as consisting of sub-product exchanges: and Hymer and Rowthorn have noted that MNC's from different countries penetrate into each other's countries. My "model" essentially combines these two and predicts that MNC's with R&D–induced specialization in different types of sub-products within an industry in different countries will interpenetrate.

I then noted that the MPI model was perfectly illustrated by an account in *Forbe's* magazine of 15 November 1970 (p. 22) of the following "international marriage":

> Long the friendliest of competitors. Dunlop and Pirelli neatly complement each other. Dunlop is primarily a manufacturer of conventional cross-ply tires. Pirelli concentrates on radials. In Europe, Dunlop has perhaps 18% of the market, Pirelli 12%, as against 12% for Michelin, the next largest competitor. In Europe, Pirelli crosses Dunlop's path only in West Germany: Elsewhere, where Dunlop is active, Pirelli stays out; where Pirelli is active, Dunlop stays out. Outside of Europe, Pirelli is active mostly in Latin America. Dunlop in the Commonwealth and North America.

> The two companies have even diversified into different areas—Dunlop into sporting goods and precision engineering products, Pirelli into paper, electronics and cables.
>
> Eventually, of course, both marketing organizations will work as one, with Dunlop pushing Pirelli products where Dunlop is strong, and Pirelli pushing Dunlop products elsewhere. "The greatest benefits should come from a pooling of R&D, however," explains J. Campbell Fraser, a Dunlop director: "In the 'seventies and 'eighties, competition will be more and more in terms of innovations. In the U.K. we have a home base of about 55 million people—that isn't big enough for the kind of R&D we'll need. Pirelli has an even smaller home base, about 45 million. By merging, we'll have a home base of 100 million, enough for the kind of R&D we'll need around the world. . . . There will not even be any exchange of public shares. Instead each will acquire an interest in the other's operating subsidiaries. The British and Italian companies will operate on their own.

The report went on to note (p. 23) that there will be four companies: Dunlop Home (the United Kingdom and Europe) with Dunlop owning 51 percent and Pirelli 49 percent; Dunlop International (the rest of the world) with Dunlop holding 60 percent and Pirelli Milan and Pirelli Switzerland 20 percent each; Pirelli Milan (the Common Market) with Pirelli Milan holding 51 percent and 49 percent; and Pirelli Switzerland (all other Pirelli operations) with Dunlop holding 40 percent, Pirelli Milan 20 percent, and Pirelli Switzerland 40 percent.

6.3.2 Shifting Comparative Advantage, Lobbying, and Policy Response Options: Three Patterns

The preceding review of major models of direct foreign investment evidently bears directly on the questions being addressed in the present paper: namely, what kind of lobbying responses can one expect, and what options are open for governmental response, when a shift in comparative advantage occurs in technically progressive industries? For one can now think of three idealized patterns: (i) the *"product cycle" scenario*, where the shift in comparative advantage occurs from the emergence of cheaper factor costs abroad overtaking the relative cheapness of domestic production due to the proximity to R & D facilities once the new product processes are simplified and debugged; (ii) the *"mutual penetration of investment" scenario*, where international competition is among similar products and technical change intensifies competition among them without conferring a dominant advantage to one class of products (and hence firms and nations) as against another; and (iii) the *"growing dominance of external products" scenario*, where, as in the MPI case, there is international competition among similar products but the technical change (or even a shift in demand, as in the case of the shift in demand away from "gas guzzlers" toward small cars and hence in favor of non-American car makers, who have traditionally specialized in small cars) favors the external producers and represents a growing, adverse shift in comparative advantage.

The first two patterns evidently include, as possible responses to the shift in comparative advantage, the corresponding patterns of direct foreign investment, i.e., the outward migration of entrepreneurs and firms. The last pattern, on the other hand, opens up a more complex set of responses.

The "Product Cycle" Scenario

In this case, the shift in comparative advantage toward producing abroad and the subsequent transfer of production abroad essentially reflect entrepreneurial decision making. Besides, the direct foreign investment response is consistent with governmental interest insofar as it represents an economic-welfare-improving move (unless there are domestic or foreign distortions present).

The lobbying response is therefore to be expected from domestic labor insofar as labor feels that it is "losing jobs" as a result of this response by the entrepreneurs.[16] Again, therefore, the actors likely to be involved in the lobbying process, in response to the shift of production abroad as comparative advantage shifts abroad, are likely to be labor lobbies.

However, the policy instruments that the labor lobby can turn to are not identical to those in the case of the "traditional" industries. Thus, if the market for the product shifts mainly overseas before the production shift overseas takes place, as in some of the PC folklore, then protecting domestic production evidently does not help! Rather, labor would have to ask for a subsidy on production or trade, neither of which is likely to appeal very much to the government because of its budgetary implications and because it opens up the possibility of countervailing action under GATT rules. An obvious alternative instrument which labor is likely to seek therefore is the imposition of restrictions on foreign investment—which is indeed what labor unions in the United States have occasionally done. Together with this route, one can also expect the unions and labor lobbies to attempt to make such direct foreign investment less attractive by complaining that the practices resulting in cheaper costs abroad are in violation of GATT and other standards, and thus require the imposition of countervailing duties, a procedure which again can help only insofar as the domestic (as against the overseas) market is still of some importance for the product. Again, this option is also occasionally exercised, as in the frequent complaints about the exploitation of child labor abroad in violation of International Labour Organization (ILO) standards, about regional subsidies that aid competing firms abroad, about special concessionary treatment of profits made by foreign firms, etc.

Given, therefore, the nature of the shift in comparative advantage to produce abroad, the lobbying game reduces in the present instance essentially to one between the government and the entrepreneurs, on one hand, and labor lobbies, on the other. But instead of the lobbying essentially focusing on trade protection, it is likely to focus primarily on the need for controls on investment abroad except in cases where the domestic market still accounts for a major fraction of total sales. Such a situation therefore contrasts with the case of "traditional" industries, where the tariff is a more effective instrument for protecting labor's economic interests. Here, the question of controlling foreign investment by the domestic entrepreneurs is a meaningless option; entrepreneurs in these industries do not seek to respond by out-migration since they do not have Hymer-type know-how that would make it economical to do so, as already noted in section 6.2.

But it *is* pertinent to ask whether the importation of foreign labor is not an option that entrepreneurs would seek as an alternative to investing abroad when the product is standardized and debugged and cheap foreign labor becomes correspondingly decisive. It must be admitted that the failure to consider this option altogether is a major weakness of the PC doctrine, which has focused wholly on the choice between producing at home with local factors and producing abroad with foreign factors. This omission does make sense when immigration quotas are taken as exogenously specified, but it does not when firms can seek to have the quotas liberalized in response to a shift in comparative advantage. Eschewing formal analysis of a firm's choice between going abroad and seeking more importation of foreign labor, I think it would be fair to assert that, since the wage costs of imported labor are likely to be substantially higher than the wage costs of similar labor abroad, the labor importation option will be outweighed by the out-migration of production option unless the industry and the countries involved are such as to make the potential risks and costs of direct foreign investment unduly high. It would appear from casual observation that United States entrepreneurs have followed the direct investment route à la Vernon's PC model fairly automatically whereas West European entrepreneurs in technically progressive industries have followed a mixed strategy, investing in cheap-labor countries abroad but also relying on increasing numbers of *gastarbeiters* much as in the "traditional," labor-intensive industries of section 6.2. It may well be that the greater willingness of West European governments to increase importation of *gastarbeiters* in the 1960s and much of the 1970s and the relative stringency of United States immigration policy in regard to unskilled labor account for this differential. Whether domestic labor unions would have permitted a shift in United States policy in this regard, leading to a shift from the Vernon-style direct investment abroad to importation of cheap labor to the United States in the technically progressive industries for their standardized, debugged, labor-intensive operations, is a question that I cannot answer but one that would be interesting to explore. In fact, it is not at all clear that domestic labor would be worse off under a policy where entrepreneurs out-migrate à la the PC scenario than it would be under a policy where entrepreneurs are allowed to import cheaper foreign labor!

The "Mutual Penetration of Investment" Scenario

In contrast to the case of PC–type shifts in comparative advantage, I have earlier distinguished shifts in comparative advantage that occur from increased competition from similar products, a state of affairs often brought about by R & D–induced changes in know-how. I have also distinguished between two polar cases: the case in which the intensification of competition does not confer an advantage to one product (and nation) as against another, and that in which the competitive advantage of one product (and nation) increases at the definite expense of the other. Before I proceed to analyze these two cases, however, it is necessary to discuss how trade in similar products comes about.

Alternative theories of trade in similar products. Recent analytical work in trade theory by Lancaster (1980), Dixit and Norman (1980), and Krugman (1979) has undertaken formalization of the original notion, inherent in Linder's (1961) pioneering work and in subsequent writings by Balassa (1967) and Grubel and Lloyd (1975), that much of the trade in manufactures among developed countries occurs in what might be called "similar" products. This formalization has proceeded on the basis of models that assume *identical* know-how among different countries and that specialization in different "similar" products ensues primarily as a result of scale economies, with basic indeterminacy as to which country produces which of the similar products and with Linder-like conclusions concerning the *volume* of trade in place of the Heckscher-Ohlin emphasis on predicting the *pattern* of trade. Therefore these theories share the Heckscher-Ohlin assumption of identical know-how but emerge with a contrasting set of outcomes concerning whether the volume or the pattern of trade can be explained.

On the other hand, I find it difficult to accept this type of formalization of trade in similar products among nation-states, neat as it is, and prefer an alternative "theory," which I will sketch below with a broad brush. Essentially, it seems to me that if we want to introduce the notion of "similar" products, with different nations trading such products to one another, we really have to give up the Heckscher-Ohlin assumption that all firms, and nations, share identical know-how *ex ante.* I would thus start with the notion that, just as in biological theorizing the "environment" interacts with "genetic factors" to produce a phenotype, we can think of an economic process whereby a specific choice of a product type emerges within a nation-society.[17] Thus, think of the income level and the level of R & D in manufacturing as defining the capacity of the society to come up technologically with a given set of characteristic product combinations, e.g., small, medium, and large cars.

The United States and Japan share this "genetic" set of traits; Zaire and Gabon do not. But which phenotype is selected in the market depends on the interaction of this common set of genetic traits with the specific "environment" of Japan and the United States. Thus the land-man ratios, the size and structure of the family, etc., may lead to the evolution of "gas guzzlers" in the United States and of smaller, fuel-economy cars in Japan, as, in fact, has been the case. At the next stage of the argument, then, the successful development of small cars in Japan and of gas guzzlers in the United States gets reinforced by localized technical change in precisely these types of cars with the result that one is now dealing with a situation of *ex ante* differentials in the know-how of producing and selling different types of cars. Next, since "cars" represent a generic product, representing a certain manner of transportation, the taste for small cars diffuses to the United States and for gas guzzlers to Japan as part of the Schumpeterian process of dynamic capitalism, aided by advertising in search of new markets. Thus trade in similar products arises. Scale economies with identical *ex ante* production functions do not play any role in this "theory," of course, and I believe that this scenario may have a greater claim to truth than the recent formal theorizations regarding trade in similar products. A formal characterization of this theory building on his recent theoretical work is presented in the appendix by Feenstra.

The MPI scenario. Whether the trade in similar products arises owing to scale economies in the presence of *ex ante* identical production functions or because of an "ecobiological process" theory like the one I have delineated above, what happens when the competition among similar products intensifies? When it results in a standoff, with the products of neither country's firms gaining dominance through R & D breakthroughs or taste shifts (whether exogenous or advertising-induced), the response of the entrepreneurs is likely to be of the MPI variety if the competition gets tough.[18]

Because no jobs are threatened, this then is an outcome to which unions ought to be indifferent. The entrepreneurs reduce the threat to their profits from import competition by *de facto* product-wise cartelization, and the government may not be unduly disturbed about the outcome (unless the result is the total elimination of competition in the industry *and* the government has an antitrust policy which it seeks to implement to this instance.)[19] The results are therefore far more sanguine in the MPI scenario than in the PC scenario!

The "Growing Dominance of External Products" Scenario

However, as soon as the comparative advantage has shifted dramatically in favor of the foreign products so that the domestic and foreign products do not both have a comfortable niche in the market, the picture changes drastically.

In this case, the entrepreneurs will want protection but may settle for greater access to cheaper foreign labor to offset the loss of comparative advantage if they can get the government to oblige them. While entrepreneurs may be indifferent between protection and greater access to foreign labor, the labor lobby will generally prefer protection to labor importation for reasons which need not be spelled out again. However, labor may be indifferent between a policy of actual protection and one in which they can merely use the *threat* of protection to get the foreign firms to invest where labor is, for the policies will equally secure their jobs. On the other hand, the entrepreneurs will prefer actual protection to the policy that merely uses protectionist threats to draw in foreign firms. For, while the United Auto Workers, for example, does not care whether its members are employed by Datsun or Ford, Ford does!

Thus we have the intriguing response possibility of domestic labor trying to import foreign entrepreneurs (with superior know-how), whereas in the "traditional" industries (of section 6.2) we had the spectacle of domestic entrepreneurs trying to import foreign labor (which will imply lower wages)!

As it happens, the protectionist threat resulting from the deteriorating competitive position of the United States car industry is a splendid example of the scenarios spelled out above. The American car industry, thanks largely to the steady erosion of the market for gas guzzlers in recent years, has been turning increasingly to producing small cars for survival, and this has shifted the problem of competition from one where the makers of American and foreign cars each had their own special niche in the market, with MPI (and variants thereof in the form of mutually supportive and profitable arrangements for marketing, joint production, etc.) as the relevant model, to one where the competition is more fierce and over a product type (the small car) where the makers of foreign cars have always had the edge. The result has been indeed for labor unions to go abroad and threaten the makers of foreign cars to produce in the United States or face protection. The following *New York Times* reports are revealing:

Douglas A. Fraser, head of the United Automobile Workers union, warned Japanese car makers today that they must invest in auto assembly plants in the United States or face the threat of immediate legislation to restrict rising imports of their small fuel-efficient cars.

He told Prime Minister Masayoshi Ohira and Foreign Minister Saburo Okita at separate meetings today that 220,000 auto workers were unemployed in the United States and that there was a 10.3 percent unemployment rate in Michigan, his home state and the center of American auto industry. Japanese auto makers should open operations in the United States to reduce unemployment there, even if only by small amounts, Mr. Fraser said. "You ought to have a sense of urgency," Mr. Fraser said he had told the Japanese leaders. He is making a short trip to Japan at the suggestion of Mike Mansfield, the United States Ambassador.

American vehicle imports totaled 2.2 million units in 1979, including about 1.7 million cars, and shipments in 1980 may increase as Americans turn to light, front-wheel-drive Japanese cars. By contrast, Japan imported fewer than 20,000 American cars last year.

The tall, heavily built U.A.W. chief said that Nissan Motor, a leading auto maker here that markets Datsun cars, offered yesterday to build a truck assembly plant in the United States, to avoid a pending 25 percent import tariff.

"That won't be sufficient," Mr. Fraser said. (*New York Times*. 1980*a*)

A stiff Congressional warning went out to Japan today to cut back voluntarily on automobile exports to the United States or face protectionist quota legislation that would damage the trading interests of both countries.

The chairman of a House trade sub-committee, Charles A. Vanik, Democrat of Ohio, called on the Japanese to roll back their American exports to 1977 levels over a two-year period to avoid what he called the "last resort" of legislated quotas.

In addition, he said, underscoring recent demands by Douglas A. Fraser, president of the United Automobile Workers, the Japanese must be convinced of the necessity to build important quantities of cars in the United States to avoid protectionist reaction here.

Declining international values for the yen, which make it more profitable to export from Japan, and the current emphasis on producing competing small cars by the American industry are behind the resistance of the two biggest Japanese producers—Toyoto and Nissan—to construct assembly plants in the country. But Honda, a smaller company, has announced plans to manufacture relatively modest numbers of cars in an assembly plant in Ohio.

Mr. Vanik's call for voluntary restraint, made at committee hearings crowded today with Japanese reporters, came shortly after two bills were introduced by Michigan legislators to impose quota restraints.

> But Congressional analysts believe that sentiment is not yet ready to jell, though it well might if automotive unemployment continues to rise. More than 200,000 auto workers have already been laid off.
>
> At 1977 levels, Japanese sales here would be some 25 percent below the current rate of 2 million cars a year, which represents well over 20 percent of all cars sold in the United States.
>
> No other country permits such penetration, Fred G. Secrest, executive vice president of the Ford Motor Company, told the panel.
>
> He reported that, by agreement between British and Japanese producer associations, Japanese imports into Britain were held to about 11 percent of the market. France, he said, applies an informal but very effective share limit of 3 percent to Japanese cars. By bilateral agreement, Italy limits Japanese imports to 2,000 cars and trucks, while Spain limits imports of automobiles to a value of $500,000 from any exporting country.
>
> Thomas J. Downey, Democrat of Suffolk County, said that American consumers were welcoming Japanese products "with open arms" and that even during the committee proceedings news photographs were being made by Nikon cameras and voice recordings by Panasonic.
>
> He warned that failure to cut back the flow of Japanese cars would mean "a wave of protectionism that will sweep across the country and do irreparable harm to the Japanese economy and ultimately to us." (*New York Times*, 1980c)

The reaction to this protectionist lobbying by Japanese car makers is likely to be a response which combines some voluntary export restraints (VERs) and some accommodation to the demands for direct investment in the United States either à la Honda in Ohio or in some joint ventures in the United States with United States car makers like the proposed deal in Italy between Alfa Romeo, the state-owned car maker, and Nissan, which produces the Datsun, to produce a new medium-sized car at Alfa's plant in Alfasud in Pamigliano, Naples, with Alfa engines and Nissan bodies.[20]

6.4 Concluding Remarks

The primary emphasis of this paper has been to examine the strong relationship that exists between the response to intensifying import competition in goods and the nature of international labor and entrepreneurial mobility. In doing this, the paper has sought to provide a framework to systematize alternative patterns of responses to shifts in comparative advantage, without undertaking a rigorous, theoretical formulation of many of the ideas set forth.

Perhaps the major analytical limitation of the paper is the lack of consideration of what political scientists would call the issue of how a nation is governed. Whether, for example, the importation of foreign labor is legal, as in Western Europe, or illegal, as in the United States, and whether the unions are successful in their bid for protection instead of permitting a market-oriented adjustment to shifting comparative advantage are issues that require an analysis of how the corporate state works, i.e., how representative democracy interacts with industry and labor. Such a "political" and public-choice-theoretic analysis would nicely complement the analysis I have set forth here, essentially by explaining cross-country contrasts in the choices of policy response that have actually occurred as comparative advantage has shifted in recent years.

Notes

1. The only important exception to this hypothesis (i.e., that in the declining, senescent, unprogressive, labor-intensive industries the typical response would not be for entrepreneurs to move) would appear to come from Japanese experience. However, the shift of some Japanese textiles, for example, to South Korea and other countries in the Far East appears to have been partly a question of "investment shunting" prompted by GSP. It may also be useful to examine whether the shift has occurred from the technologically more progressive firms among these industries. Again, the few United States apparel producers who have gone abroad to take advantage of United States tariff provisions under GSP or 806.30-807 (the offshore assembly provision) seem to be the smaller firms with special designing or marketing skills. For a discussion of how Japanese direct investment differs in this respect (i.e., insofar as it occurs also in the "traditional" labor-intensive industries) from Western direct investment, see Kojima (1978).

2. In fact, the reward to capital is higher at Q_2 and Q_3 under the labor-importation policy and thus should please entrepreneurs more.

3. Note that, even if a production subsidy were used for protection, the corresponding welfare (U_{ps}) would, while avoiding the consumption cost of the tariff, still be inferior to that under the policy of relaxing the immigration restrictions on labor.

4. Note that the real rewards at Q_2 and Q_3 are identical, since the goods price ratio does not change along a Rybczynski line.

5. This strong ranking would not have followed if the policy comparison had not required identical Y^0 production. Thus it is easy to see in figure 6.3 that further shifts up along the Rybczynski line and hence IC (P_2^D) could lead eventually to welfare levels below that at C_r. Note also that the strong ranking might not hold if we were to use a sticky-wage model of either the Brecher (1974*a*, *b*) or the Harris and Todaro (1970) variety since that would introduce a domestic distortion in the sense of Bhagwati and Ramaswami (1963), Johnson (1965), and Bhagwati (1971).

6. Types of factor accumulation or technological progress which can lead to an increase in the production of the exportable good X and a fall in the production of Y are as follows: an increase in the stock of capital (used intensively in the export industry), and neutral or labor-using technological progress in the export industry (see Findlay and Grubert 1959).

7. It is a moot point whether labor is, in fact, always more mobile than capital is malleable!

8. The analysis of this model and the next could be extended to cases where the shift in comparative advantage is domestically induced, as in cases III and IV above. This can be done readily by the interested reader.

9. Note that the output of the importable industry expands under a policy of protection or labor importation.

10. The production is, of course, identical under both options; i.e., both policies are assumed to take the economy back to Q_1. However, under the labor-importation option, the net-of-remuneration-for-foreign-workers "production" point is Q_3 ($<Q_1$).

11. The project at Sussex University's Center for European Studies under the direction of Professor Ronald Dore ought to shed more light on these questions.

12. In chapter 9 of this volume, the analysis considers the lobbying costs of the labor lobby as well.

13. If we could raise any amount of revenue in a lump-sum fashion, it would of course be trivially true that we could bribe the labor lobby out of any protectionist pressure! The notion of the efficient tariff, on the other hand, is a second-best one, and the beauty of it is that the revenue being used for the bribe to labor is generated by the tariff itself. For further discussion, see chapter 9.

14. In the standard $2 \times 2 \times 2$ model, it is possible to work out the conditions under which the paradox of welfare-worsening tariff imposition will arise. See Bhagwati and Rivera-Batiz (1980). This paradox was first noted in Bhagwati (1979).

15. Needless to say, varying the tax on foreign capital to its optimal level would eliminate the paradox. This is, however, as removed from reality as differential taxation of foreign labor in the argument in the text and in Bhagwati and Rivera-Batiz (1980).

16. Of course, it is easy enough to construct analytical cases where the shift outward of technology-cum-capital, by profit-maximizing entrepreneurs, neither increases domestic unemployment in a Brecher-type model nor lowers the real wages of labor with full employment in the $2 \times 2 \times 2$ model.

17. Thus a typical popularized statement of the modern genetic theory is the following: "The phenotype is the result of a particular heredity acting on a particular environmental background. Any variation we observe among the members of a related group of organisms living under natural conditions must be phenotypic variation, because it will be the result of different environmental pressures and different genetic histories. Phenotypic variation in a population is the sum of genotypic variation inherent in the combined heredity of the group plus that part of the environmental variation which affects the phenotype" (Alland, Jr., 1972, p. 9).

18. Impure forms of the MPI phenomenon may involve a one-way equity purchase in exchange for marketing facilities.

19. Governments, of course, manage to get worried about direct foreign investments for all sorts of reasons; so perhaps I ought not to be overly optimistic about their benign neglect in this case!

20. However, the foreign investment response, as already indicated, may not meet with the approval of the entrepreneurs in the Honda type of investment or with that of the entrepreneurs other than the one going into joint venture in the Alfa-Nissan type of investment. In fact, as the *New York Times* (1980*b*) reported on the Alfa-Nissan proposal: "Fiat, not surprisingly, reacted strongly against the proposal, charging that the Nissan deal could become the opening wedge for a Japanese invasion of the Italian automobile market. Fiat, auto industry experts say, is particularly vulnerable to fresh competition because it has been losing some of its market share to other European car makers. . . .

"Fiat is also beset by sabotage and work stoppages by its workers. The company says that the violence and wildcat strikes caused a 12 percent decline in production last year and pushed its operating costs up sharply.

"To head off the Nissan-Alfa venture, Fiat made a proposal of its own to Alfa early this month, offering to buy 40,000 to 50,000 Alfa engines—the same number that would be involved in the Nissan deal—and mount them on new flat models over the next several years. There has also been talk about possible construction of a new Fiat body factory near the Alfasud plant."

Trade unions, if organized by firms, may also then have conflicting interests; and differential location of different firms may also pose questions of conflicting interests, e.g., workers in Alfa Romeo versus workers in Fiat.

References

Alland, Jr., A. 1972. *The human imperative.* New York: Columbia University Press.

Balassa, B. 1967. *Trade liberalization among industrial countries.* New York: McGraw-Hill.

Bhagwati, J. 1959. Protection, real wages, and real incomes. *Economic Journal* 69: 733–44.

———. 1971. The generalized theory of distortions and welfare. In J. Bhagwati et al., ed., *Trade, balance of payments, and growth.* Amsterdam: North-Holland.

———. 1972. Review of Vernon, *Sovereignty at bay. Journal of International Economics* 2 no. 4: 455–62.

———. 1977. Review of Hymer. *Journal of Development Economics* 4: 391–95.

———. 1978. *Anatomy and consequences of exchange control regimes.* Cambridge, Mass.: Ballinger.

———. 1979. The economic analysis of international migration. Plenary lecture to Nordisk Migrasjonsforskerseminar, Nordic Council of Ministers, Oslo, Norway, October.

Bhagwati, J., and R. Brecher. 1980. National welfare in an open economy in the presence of foreign-owned factors of production. *Journal of International Economics* 10 (May): 103–16.

Bhagwati, J., and V. K. Ramaswami. 1963. Domestic distortions, tariffs, and the theory of optimum subsidy. *Journal of Political Economy* 71, no. 1 (February): 44–50.

Bhagwati, J., and F. Rivera-Batiz. 1980. Protection in the presence of immigrant workers and sending country's welfare: Some paradoxes. Mimeographed, May.

Bhagwati, J., and E. Tironi. 1980. Tariff change, foreign capital, and immiserization: A theoretical analysis. *Journal of Development Economics*, February, pp. 103–15.

Brecher, R. 1974*a*. Minimum wage rates and the pure theory of international trade. *Quarterly Journal of Economics* 88, no. 1: 98–116.

———. 1974*b*. Optimal commercial policy for a minimum-wage economy. *Journal of International Economics* 4: 139–49.

Brecher, R., and C. D. Alejandro. 1977. Tariff, foreign capital, and immiserizing growth. *Journal of International Economics* 7 (November): 317–22.

Brecher, R., and J. Bhagwati. 1981. Foreign ownership and the theory of trade and welfare. *Journal of Political Economy* 89, no. 3 (June): 497–511.

Cheh, J. 1974. United States concessions in the Kennedy Round and short-run labor adjustment costs. *Journal of International Economics* 4 (November): 323–40.

Dixit, A., and V. Norman, 1980. *The theory of international trade: A text.* Cambridge: Cambridge University Press.

Findlay, R., and H. Grubert. 1959. Factor intensities, technological progress, and the terms of trade. *Oxford Economic Papers*, nos. 111–21. Also in J. N. Bhagwati, ed. 1970. *International trade: Selected readings,* pp. 327–40. Harmondsworth, UK: Penguin

Grubel, H., and P. Lloyd. 1975. *Intra-industry trade.* London: Macmillan.

Haberler, G. 1950. Some problems in the pure theory of international trade. *Economic Journal* 60 (June): 223–40.

Harris, J., and M. Todaro. 1970. Migration, unemployment, and development: A two-sector analysis. *American Economic Review* 60 (March): 126–42.

Hymer, S. 1960. The international operations of national firms: A study of direct foreign investment. Dissertation, MIT. Published with the same title in 1976 by MIT Press, Cambridge, Mass. (See pp. xxii and 253 of the latter.)

Johnson, H. G. 1965. Optimal trade intervention in the presence of domestic distortions: In R. E. Caves, P. B. Kenen, and H. G. Johnson, eds., *Trade, growth, and the balance of payments*, pp. 3–34. Amsterdam: North-Holland.

Jones, R. 1971. A three factor model in theory, trade, and history. In J. Bhagwati et al., eds., *Trade, balance of payments, and growth*, pp. 3–21. Amsterdam: North-Holland.

Kojima, K. 1978. *Direct foreign investment.* London: Croom Helm.

Krugman, P. 1979. Increasing returns, monopolistic competition, and international trade. *Journal of International Economics* 9 (November): 469–80.

Lancaster, K. 1980. Intra-industry trade under perfect monopolistic competition. *Journal of International Economics* 10: 151–76.

Linder, S. 1961. *An essay on trade and transformation.* New York: Wiley.

Mayer, W. 1974. Short-run and long-run equilibrium for a small open economy. *Journal of Political Economy* 82: 955–68.

Mussa, M. 1974. Tariffs and the distribution of income: The importance of factor specificity, substitutability, and intensity in the short and long run. *Journal of Political Economy* 82: 1191–1204.

Neary, J. P. 1978. Short-run capital specificity and the pure theory of international trade. *Economic Journal* 88 (September): 488–510.

New York Times. 1980*a*. Fraser bids Japan build cars in U.S. 14 February, Section D.

———. 1980*b*. Italy debating auto future. 29 February, Section D.

———. 1980*c*. Rep. Vanik warns Japan to curb auto exports. Clyde Farnsworth. 14 February, Section D.

Riedel, J. 1977. Tariff concessions in the Kennedy Round and the structure of protection in West Germany: An econometric assessment. *Journal of International Economics* 7, no. 2 (May): 133–44.

Uzawa, H. 1969. Shihon jiyuka to kokumin keizai. *Ekonomisuto*, 23 December, pp. 106–22.

Vernon, R. 1966. International investment and international trade in the product cycle. *Quarterly Journal of Economics* 80 (May): 190–207.

Appendix *Product Creation and Trade Patterns: A Theoretical Note on the "Biological" Model of Trade in Similar Products*

Robert C. Feenstra

Introduction

In this appendix I shall draw on the recent research of Feenstra (1980) to formalize the "biological" model of trade in similar products outlined by Bhagwati in this chapter.[1] The main features of the model to be presented are as follows: (1) As in models of "learning by doing" (see Arrow 1962) or induced technological innovation (see Kennedy 1964; Samuelson 1965), the technologies available within a country are endogenously determined by tastes, research and development (R & D) costs, and other parameters. (2) The returns to R & D activity are the monopoly profits associated with developing and marketing a new product, and an equilibrium of the R & D process is determined as a Chamberlinian "tangency solution" where profits on the last R & D project are zero. (3) If we allow countries to reach an R & D equilibrium in autarky, then it follows from (1) and (2) that countries with differing tastes, R & D costs, etc., will have different sets of available products and technologies. We shall assume that technological knowledge cannot be transferred abroad. Then opening the countries to international trade, we may observe trade in "similar" products arising from the fact that some countries may

Robert C. Feenstra is assistant professor of economics at Columbia University and was a Post-Doctoral Fellow in International Economics at the University of Chicago. He has published in the *Journal of International Economics* and has written on international trade theory and econometrics.

The author acknowledges helpful discussions with Richard Eckaus, Paul Krugman, and Martin Weitzman and the financial support of National Science Foundation Grant SOC 79-07541.

produce unique varieties of a differentiated product, and therefore export these varieties and import others. This bilateral trade in similar products, or intraindustry trade, is not related to scale economies in the post–R & D technologies (which are assumed to exhibit constant returns to scale), but, rather, depends on differences in the post–R & D technologies across countries and therefore, from (1), on cross-country differences in tastes, R & D costs, and other parameters.

It can be seen from this brief outline that our model is closely related to the ideas sketched by Bhagwati, and offers an alternative explanation for trade in similar products from the models of monopolistic competition and trade given in, among others, Krugman (1979) and Lancaster (1980), and in these authors' contributions to this volume. In the next section we shall present our model in detail and show how the autarky equilibrium is established. The pattern of trade between two countries is analyzed in the third section. In the last section we contrast our results to those from models of monopolistic competition and trade, and give brief conclusions.

Autarky Equilibrium

We shall consider the group of markets for a differentiated product, where the aggregate demand for product (i.e., variety) i is given by

$$\text{(A1)} \qquad q_i = a_i d^i(p, I; S(t)),$$

where p is the vector of prices, I is total consumer income, a_i is a parameter reflecting tastes for different varieties, and $S(t)$ denotes the set of products which are currently available for purchase and which change over time due to R & D. It is assumed that the demand functions d^i correspond to a *symmetric* utility function.[2] It is also assumed that demand is homogeneous of degree one in income and negative one in prices, and that goods are substitutes in the sense that an expansion in the set $S(t)$ of goods available implies a fall (or no change) in the demand for any good previously available.[3]

Note that the aggregate demand functions given in (A1) can be aggregated from individual demand functions under either of the following conditions: (1) all consumers have identical homothetic utility functions, in which case the parameters a_i, reflecting tastes for different varieties, are identical across consumers; (2) the distribution of income across consumers is fixed, and the individual utility functions are homothetic and differ only in the parameters a_i, in which case the *aggregate* parameters a_i reflect *differences* across individuals in their tastes for different varieties.[4]

We shall model an R & D project as spending fixed costs of f to discover the technology to produce good i. It is assumed that the post–R & D unit costs c_i of producing good i are nonstochastic and known even before the R & D takes place: this assumption is made for simplicity, but may not be unrealistic in situations where, prior to R & D, one has an accurate estimate of the inputs needed to produce a good even though the manner in which the inputs will be combined (i.e., the design of the product) is unknown. The post–R & D technologies are assumed to be linearly homogeneous, and the factor prices which determine c_i are held constant throughout the analysis. If the fixed costs $\tilde{f}$ of R & D are stochastic, then f denotes the certainty equivalent of $\tilde{f}$.[5] We shall assume that after the technology for producing any particular good is known, no further R & D on this good takes place; our model is thus one of *product creation* rather than process innovation on the technologies of existing goods.

In general terms, the R & D process we wish to model is one in which R & D proceeds sequentially over different products, where private firms decide which products to develop and when to stop creating new goods. It will be convenient to assume that, at any point in time when R & D is occurring, only *one* product (and corresponding technology) is being developed, and only *one* firm is engaged in this R & D. We shall suppose that the knowledge embodied in any new technology is protected by a one-period patent and that after the patent expires this knowledge is fully appropriable by all firms in the domestic (but not foreign) market. It follows that the returns to creating a new product through R & D are simply the one-period monopoly profits associated with the product:

$$\text{(A2a)} \qquad \Pi_i(S(t)) = (p_i^* - c_i)a_i d^i(p^*, I; S(t) \cup \{i\}) - f,$$

where p_i^* denotes the profit-maximizing price (where marginal revenue equals marginal cost), p^* is the corresponding vector of prices, and the notation $S(t) \cup \{i\}$ denotes the set obtained by adding product i to the set of products $S(t)$ previously available for purchase.

After a patent expires and other firms begin production of that good, it is assumed that the market structure is perfectly competitive, so that the good is sold at its marginal (and average) cost of c_i. Thus the prices p_j in the vector p^* are determined as follows:

$$\text{(A2b)} \qquad p_j = \begin{cases} c_j & \text{for } j \in S(t) \\ p_i^* = c_i \left[\dfrac{e_i}{e_i - 1}\right] & \text{for } j = i \\ +\infty & \text{for } j \notin S(t) \text{ and } j \neq i, \end{cases}$$

where e_i denotes the elasticity of demand for product i, $e_i > 1$, and we adopt the convention of setting prices equal to $+\infty$ for products which are not available for purchase. The monopolistic equilibrium given in (A2a, b) is assumed to exist.

To complete our model, we must specify how R & D proceeds over time, that is, how the set of products $S(t)$ available for purchase at the competitive price changes. Loosely speaking, we shall assume that starting from any set of initial products S_0, R & D occurs on the product of highest profitability and then proceeds sequentially (i.e., one good at a time) to the products next highest in the rank order of profitability, stopping when the remaining profits are nonpositive. This description is not precise, since it is possible for the rank order of products by profitability to depend on the set of goods $S(t)$, and therefore the rank ordering can change over time.

More formally, given any set of products $S(t)$ available for purchase at the competitive price, we shall assume that the next product selected for development is i^*, which satisfies

(A3) $$\Pi_{i^*}(S(t)) = \max_{i \notin S(t)} \Pi_i(S(t)).$$

If more than one product i^* satisfies (A3), any one can be selected. Let $\Delta(t)$ denote the length of time between the introduction (availability) of the last, and next, product sold at its competitive price. We shall assume that $\Delta(t)$ is inversely related to the current profitability of R & D:

(A4a) $$\Delta(t) = 1/\psi(\Pi_{i^*}(S(t))),$$

where

(A4b) $$\psi(x) = 0 \qquad \text{for } x \leq 0,$$

$$\psi'(x) > 0 \qquad \text{for } x > 0.$$

Finally, note that the set of products $S(t)$ available for purchase at the competitive price changes in the following manner:

(A5) $$S(t + \Delta(t)) = S(t) \cup \{i^*\}, \qquad t \geq 0$$

$$S(t) = S_0, \qquad 0 \leq t < \Delta(0),$$

where the set S_0 of initial products is given and nonempty. Equations (A2)–(A5) are a complete description of our R & D process.[6]

From (A4) we see that as the profitability of the most attractive remaining R & D project falls, the length of time $\Delta(t)$ between the introduction of new products increases, and when $\Pi_{i^*} \leq 0$, then $\Delta(t) = +\infty$ in which case no further R & D takes place and we shall say that the set $S(t)$ of available products has converged.[7] We shall refer to the set $\bar{S}$ of available products and the associated competitive prices as an *autarky equilibrium* of the R & D process.

What products do we expect to be produced in the autarky equilibrium (i.e., included in the set $\bar{S}$)? Clearly, those products which are most profitable—which have a high a_i or low c_i—will be produced. Thus, suppose that $c_i = c$ for all i so that products differ only in the demand parameter a_i. We can rank-order products from the highest to lowest a_i, and this clearly corresponds to the rank ordering by profitability and is invariant to the set $S(t)$ of goods produced. Then R & D will begin at the product with highest a_i and proceed down the rank ordering, stopping when the profits from R & D become nonpositive. Similarly, if $a_i = a$ for all i and products differ only in their unit costs c_i, then the rank ordering of products from lowest to highest c_i corresponds to the rank ordering by profitability and is invariant to the set of goods produced, and R & D will begin at the product with lowest c_i and proceed along the rank ordering until the profits from R & D are nonpositive.

For given demand parameters a_i and unit costs c_i, the number of goods produced in the autarky equilibrium is determined by total consumer income I and the fixed R & D costs f. From our assumption that goods are substitutes, an increase in the number of products (i.e., an expansion of $S(t)$) lowers the returns to R & D on any remaining product. A rise in consumer income or fall in fixed costs of R & D increases the profits from R & D, and therefore expands the number of goods produced in the autarky equilibrium.[8]

To make explicit the relationship between our formalization and the "biological" model of trade in similar products outlined by Bhagwati, note that we can identify the total consumer income I spent on all varieties of the differentiated product, and the fixed costs of R & D, as "genetic" traits defining the capacity of an economy to create products through R & D. Given countries with similar "genetic" traits, the actual set of product varieties developed (i.e., phenotype selected) depends on the interaction between this common set of genetic traits and the specific "environment" of a country, where we identify the demand parameters a_i and post–R & D unit costs c_i as determined by the environment (e.g., factor endowments; transportation and communication infrastructure, including advertising; social habits) of a country. We have seen that slight differences in the environmental parameters may lead to marked differences in the set of product varieties developed in autarky, and thus a situation of technological differentials across countries in the production of different varieties.[9] These cross-country differences in the sets of products developed in autarky will lead to trade in similar products, as we shall analyze in the following section.

Trade Equilibrium

We shall consider trade between two countries A and B, where it is assumed that the functions d^i in (A1) are identical in the two countries so that tastes differ only in the demand parameters a_i. The countries may also differ in consumer income I, unit costs c_i, or fixed R & D costs f, which are measured in terms of a common numeraire in the two countries and are denoted with a superscript A or B. Note that given any set $S(t)$ of products available in both countries, the *world* demand for product i is

$$\text{(A6)} \qquad a_i^A d^i(p,I^A;S(t)) + a_i^B d^i(p,I^B;S(t)) = (a_i^A I^A + a_i^B I^B) d^i(p,1;S(t)),$$

since the demand functions d^i are homogeneous of degree one in income. The sets $S^A(t)$ and $S^B(t)$ denote those products which have been *developed* in countries A and B, respectively, and the set $S(t)$ of goods *available* in both countries with trade is given by $S(t) = S^A(t) \cup S^B(t)$.

Because of the dynamic nature of our R & D process, in order to determine the set of products available in a trade equilibrium we must specify the *timing* of trade liberalization. Accordingly, we shall assume that each of the two countries A and B reaches an autarky equilibrium $\bar{S}^A$ and $\bar{S}^B$, respectively, and that trade is opened only *after* the autarky equilibria have been established. This assumption corresponds to the empirical observation that firms usually develop new products for the home market before considering export possibilities, and can be justified on the basis of various forms of uncertainty when marketing products abroad. We shall also assume that technologies cannot be transferred internationally, so that if firms in any country wish to produce a good which is not yet produced at home (but may be available through trade), they must first develop the technology through R & D.[10]

Within our model, the trade equilibrium is determined in the following manner. After the opening of trade, the profits from R & D activity are evaluated using world rather than domestic demand so that, from (A2a) and (A6), the returns to R & D on product i are given by

$$\text{(A2a')} \qquad \Pi_i^k(S(t)) = (p_i^* - c_i^k)(a_i^A I^A + a_i^B I^B) d^i(p^*,1;S(t) \cup \{i\}) - f^k, k = A,B,$$

where at the time T when trade is opened the set $S(t)$ of products available in both countries is $S(t) = \bar{S}^A \cup \bar{S}^B$.

Note that in general R & D in one country may occur in goods which are already produced abroad, where this *product imitation* may be profitable if one country has a sufficient cost advantage in production over the other country. However, if countries have similar post–R & D unit costs (measured in terms of a common numeraire), then product imitation is unlikely to occur, and we shall assume that this is the case. It follows that in (A2a') product i is not included in the set of products already available for purchase ($i \notin S(t) = S^A(t) \cup S^B(t)$) and that the vector of prices p^* is given by

$$\text{(A2b')} \qquad p_j^* = \begin{cases} \min\{c_j^A, c_j^B\} & \text{for } j \in S^A(t) \cap S^B(t) \\ c_j^A & \text{for } j \in S^A(t), j \notin S^B(t) \\ c_j^B & \text{for } j \in S^B(t), j \notin S^A(t) \\ c_i^k \left[\dfrac{e_i}{e_i - 1}\right] & \text{for } j = i \text{ and when evaluating } \Pi_i^k, k = A,B \\ +\infty & \text{for } j \notin S(t) \text{ and } j \neq i. \end{cases}$$

In this specification of p^* it is recognized that for products which have been developed in both countries ($j \in S^A(t) \cap S^B(t)$), production and export will take place in the country of minimum unit cost and competitive price.

Turning to the dynamics of R & D, we shall assume in general that, after the opening of trade, R & D will occur in a country if and only if the monopoly profits from R & D as given in (A2′) are positive for some product. When the maximum profits over all remaining products are nonpositive in both countries, then the sets $S^A(t)$, $S^B(t)$, and $S(t)$, of the R & D process will have converged to some sets $\bar{\bar{S}}^A$, $\bar{\bar{S}}^B$, and $\bar{\bar{S}} = \bar{\bar{S}}^A \cup \bar{\bar{S}}^B$, respectively, and we shall refer to these sets of products developed and available, and the associated competitive prices, as a *trade equilibrium* of the R & D process.[11]

While it is difficult to specify a general set of equations governing the R & D process with trade, one can easily describe certain special cases. For example, suppose that the countries "take turns" in R & D in the sense that the first country—say, country A—engages in R & D in a manner analogous to the autarky process until the profits (as given in [A2′]) from remaining R & D activity are nonpositive, after which country B develops products sequentially until profitable R & D opportunities have been exhausted. From our assumption that goods are substitutes, this process will converge after the two "turns" we have indicated, since the introduction of new products by country B will lower the profits from R & D activity in country A.

As another example, suppose that the time intervals $\Delta^A(t)$ and $\Delta^B(t)$ between the introduction of the last, and next, product sold at its competitive price are equal and constant in both countries whenever profits from R & D are positive; that is,

$$\text{(A4')} \qquad \Delta^k(t) = \begin{cases} \bar{\Delta} & \text{if } \Pi_{i_k^*}^k > 0, \\ +\infty & \text{if } \Pi_{i_k^*}^k \leq 0, \end{cases} \qquad k = A,B,$$

where i_k^* satisfies

$$\text{(A3')} \qquad \Pi_{i_k^*}^k(S(t)) = \max_{i \notin S(t)} \Pi_i^k(S(t)), \qquad k = A,B.$$

Then the change in the set of products $S(t)$ available for purchase at the competitive price is determined by

(A5′)
$$S(t) = S^A(t) \cup S^B(t),$$
$$S^k(t+\bar{\Delta}) = \begin{cases} S^k(t) \cup \{i_k^*\} & \text{if } \Pi^k_{i_k^*} > 0 \\ S^k(t) & \text{if } \Pi^k_{i_k^*} \leq 0, \end{cases} \qquad t \geq T,$$
$$S^k(t) = \bar{S}^k \quad \text{for} \quad T \leq t < T + \bar{\Delta}, k = A,B.$$

In this case the R & D process with trade is completely described by (A2′)–(A5′), and is assumed to converge to a trade equilibrium.

What trade patterns do we expect to observe in a trade equilibrium? First, let us consider the pattern of trade which emerges in the *temporary* competitive equilibrium immediately following the opening of trade, but before any additional R & D has occurred. Suppose that the sets $\bar{S}^A$ and $\bar{S}^B$ of products developed in countries A and B, respectively, have no products in common, where the difference between these sets may be attributed to differing demand parameters a_i^k and post–R & D unit costs c_i^k in the two countries, $k = A,B$, which leads to different products being developed in autarky (e.g., small and big cars, different varieties of furniture, etc.). In this equilibrium, all products in the set $\bar{S}^A$ will clearly be exported from country A to country B, and conversely for products in the set $\bar{S}^B$. The volume of exports from one country to the other is determined by the number of goods the exporting country produces (i.e., in $\bar{S}^k$), where for given tastes and post–R & D unit costs, the number of goods produced in the autarky equilibrium is directly related to total consumer income I^k and inversely related to the fixed costs of R & D f^k, $k = A,B$.

More generally, suppose that the sets $\bar{S}^A$ and $\bar{S}^B$ of products developed have some goods in common. For these goods, production and export in the temporary equilibrium will take place in the country of minimum unit cost and competitive price, while for goods developed in only one country, the trade pattern is determined as before. In this case the volume of trade depends on the relative unit costs of production between the countries, since the country with a cost advantage in the larger number of products will tend in aggregate to be a net exporter of those products both countries have developed.

Do we expect to observe additional R & D after trade is opened to move the economies away from the temporary equilibrium we have just described? Such R & D will occur if and only if the evaluation of profits from R & D is changed from nonpositive to positive as a result of using world rather than domestic demand (i.e., shifting from [A2] to [A2′]). This shift in demand has two effects on profits: (1) profits are increased due to the expansion of market income, that is, evaluating profits using $I^A + I^B$ rather than I^A or I^B; (2) profits are decreased due to the greater variety of products available, that is, evaluating profits using

$S(T) = \bar{S}^A \cup \bar{S}^B$ rather than $\bar{S}^A$ or $\bar{S}^B$. It is quite possible for effect (2) to dominate effect (1) so that there is *no* additional R & D after trade is opened, and the *temporary* equilibrium which we have just analyzed is identical to the *trade* equilibrium.

In fact, the following result can be established.[12] Suppose that demand and unit costs of production are identical across products and countries, $a_i^A = a_i^B = a$ and $c_i^A = c_i^B = c$ for all i, that as more products are introduced goods become stronger substitutes, that the sets of goods $\bar{S}^A$ and $\bar{S}^B$ produced in each country in the autarky equilibrium have no products in common, and that the number of goods produced in each country in the autarky equilibrium is large. Then after trade is opened there is *no* additional R & D activity. By continuity, we can allow slight differences in the demand parameters a_i^k and c_i^k across commodities and countries, $k = A,B$, and under the remaining hypotheses still find that the amount of R & D activity after trade (if any) is small. The difference between the sets $\bar{S}^A$ and $\bar{S}^B$ of products developed in autarky is now determined by cross-country differences in tastes and post–R & D unit costs (as well as differences in total consumer income and fixed costs of R & D), and the implications for trade patterns are as previously described: products in $\bar{S}^A$ will be exported to country B, and conversely. We have thus arrived at the model of trade in "similar" products outlined in the introduction to this appendix and a formalization of the ideas sketched by Bhagwati.

Last, we must consider the case where additional R & D activity *does* occur after the opening of trade. The products which firms in each country select to develop need not be identical across countries, though identical rank orderings by profitability will obtain if the post–R & D unit costs of production are equal in the two countries. In general we expect the rate of product creation in each country to depend on the profits from R & D, which may differ across countries due to different unit costs of production or fixed costs of R & D, and some exogenously specified "rate of product creation" function (or parameter) such as ψ in (A4) (or $\bar{\Delta}$ in [A4′]). Countries with a quicker rate of product creation will tend in aggregate to be a net exporter of those products which are developed after trade is opened.

Conclusions

A general conclusion from models of monopolistic competition and trade, such as Krugman (1979) and Lancaster (1980), is that the *volume* of trade between countries is determined in the trade equilibrium, but the geographical origin of any particular product is indeterminate; the latter result follows since countries are assumed to have identical technologies. The above model of product creation differs in several respects. First, the geographical origin of production is determinate for any good which is developed in one country but not the other, where this situation is likely to occur whenever one country has a demand bias or cost advantage in certain product varieties while the other country has a demand bias or cost advantage in other varieties. In particular, countries will tend to export those products which are developed in autarky.[13] The resulting intraindustry trade is not related to scale economies in the post–R & D technologies, but, rather, is determined by scale economies (due to the spreading of fixed costs) of R & D and cross-country differences in tastes, post–R & D unit costs, etc. Note that for goods which are developed in *both* countries, the location of production is indeterminate if the post–R & D unit costs are identical.

The volume of trade in any particular product is determined by the number of goods produced, and, as in models of monopolistic competition, this number is established in a Chamberlinian "tangency solution" and is directly related to total consumer income and inversely related to the fixed costs of production or R & D.[14] For the case where additional R & D activity occurs after the opening of trade, the aggregate volume of trade in equilibrium is determined by the rates of product creation in the two countries, whereas this effect does not enter the models of monopolistic competition and trade (which are primarily of a static nature).

In conclusion, we should indicate that the model of product creation we have presented can be fruitfully extended in a wide variety of directions (see Feenstra 1980), e.g., modeling "product imitation" by one country to lead to a model of the "product cycle", or an examination of the Linder (1961) hypotheses concerning the importance of domestic demand in determining potential and actual trade.

Notes

1. This formalization demonstrates how the "biological model" of trade in similar products can be cast in theoretical terms, but is incomplete in that certain aspects of the proposed model are not fully investigated.

2. In order to correspond to a symmetric utility function, the demand functions d^i must satisfy the following condition: if the vector $\tilde{p}$ is equal to p except that the components p_i and p_j have been interchanged, then

$$d^i(p,I;S(t)) = d^j(\tilde{p},I;S(t)).$$

An example of a utility function leading to demand equations as in (A1) is

$$U = \sum_{i=1}^{N} a_i v(q_i/a_i), \qquad v'>0, v''<0.$$

The corresponding demand functions are

$$q_i = a_i \phi(\lambda p_i),$$

where ϕ is the inverse function of v' and λ is the marginal utility of income.

3. That is, for $i \varepsilon S$ and $S \subseteq S'$, we have

$$d^i(p,I;S') \leq d^i(p,I;S).$$

4. Lancaster (1980) assumes that each consumer has a most preferred product variety, that demand for neighboring varieties decreases in a uniform manner, and that the distribution of consumers' preferred varieties is also uniform across products, in which case *aggregate* demand is identical across product varieties.

5. If firms evaluate profits using the utility function U, an approximate certainty equivalent to $\tilde{f}$ is given by

$$f = \bar{f} + \frac{1}{2}\sigma_f^2 R_A,$$

where $\bar{f} = E(\tilde{f})$, $\sigma_f^2 = E(\tilde{f} - \bar{f})^2$, and $R_A = -U''/U'$ is the index of absolute risk aversion.

6. I have permitted myself one sleight of hand in specifying the equations for the R & D process. Specifically, given equation (A4), it would be natural to let $\Delta(t)$ denote the length of time between the introduction of the last, and next, product sold at its *monopolistic* (rather than competitive) price. However, this definition would complicate the specification of p^* in (A2b) since, depending on the length of time needed to complete the R & D for one product, at any point in time a variable number of products are sold at their monopolistic price. Because of this complication, we have adopted the simpler, but less natural, definition of $\Delta\ (t)$.

7. We shall assume that convergence is obtained; that is, the R & D eventually stops. This seems to be a reasonable assumption of a market where total demand is stationary (i.e., consumer income I is fixed) and the introduction of new goods does not affect the demand or cost parameters a_i, c_i, and f_i.

8. But note that, starting from an autarky equilibrium, a *fall* in I or *rise* in f has *no* effect on the set $\bar{S}$ of available products: these parameter changes decrease the profits from remaining R & D projects and also decrease the *hypothetical* profits from duplicating the R & D activity on any existing product (and hypothetically selling the product at its monopoly price for one period), but neither of these outcomes has any effect on the set of products available. This illustrates a basic difference between our model and models of monopolistic competition: in the model being presented the set of products available can expand but never contract, since the fixed costs of R & D are borne in only one period, whereas in models of monopolistic competition where fixed costs are paid every period, the number of products available can expand or contract as a result of parameter changes. However, if we compare two *different* economies which are identical except that the first has lower consumer income or higher fixed costs of R & D than the second and these parameters have not changed over time, then in their autarky equilibria the first economy will have a smaller number of products available than the second.

9. Note that even if the demand parameters a_i and unit costs c_i are *identical* across commodities, in which case *any* undeveloped product satisfies (A3) and may be selected for development, we may still obtain cross-country differences in the sets of products developed in autarky due to random differences in the products selected for R & D. If the number of potential product varieties is large relative to the number actually developed, this random selection procedure will probably lead to little overlap across countries in the sets of products developed in autarky, and therefore to a considerable amount of trade in these similar products (as analyzed in the next section).

10. That is, in the model being presented we shall assume that the fixed costs of R & D in any country do not depend on whether the product has previously been developed abroad. In some cases it may be more realistic to assume that the additional fixed costs of adapting a foreign technology for production at home are considerably less than if the technology had not been developed abroad, and our model can be extended in this direction (see Feenstra 1980).

11. Note that our analysis is partial equilibrium, and we do not require that trade is balanced in the trade equilibrium.

12. A similar result, using a CES utility function, is established in Feenstra (1980).

13. Note that in the models of Krugman and Lancaster it is assumed that aggregate demand and production costs are identical across goods. If we adopted this assumption within our model, then we would not be able to predict which goods would be developed in autarky (as discussed in note 9), though it would still be the case that countries would tend to export the autarky set of products. On the other hand, if we weakened the "symmetry" assumption of identical aggregate demand and production costs within Lancaster's model, but retained the assumption that countries have identical technologies and factor prices, then we would still find that the geographical origin of production is indeterminate (in contrast to the model of product creation). The "symmetry" assumption cannot be weakened within Krugman's model, since this would lead to the nonexistence of a long-run equilibrium with zero profits for every firm in the industry; this existence problem may be recognized as a weakness of the Chamberlinian approach to monopolistic competition theory, as also discussed by Chipman in his comment to chapter 7.

14. A difference in the determination of the number of goods produced between our model and that of monopolistic competition is discussed in note 8.

References

Arrow, K. J. 1962. The economic implications of learning by doing. *Review of Economic Studies* 29, (June): 155–73.

Feenstra, R. C. 1980. Product creation and trade patterns. Mimeographed, November.

Kennedy, C. 1964. Induced bias in innovation and the theory of distribution. *Economic Journal* 74 (September): 541–47.

Krugman, P. 1979. Increasing returns, monopolistic competition, and international trade. *Journal of International Economics* 9: 469–79.

Lancaster, K. J. 1980. Intra-industry trade under perfect monopolistic competition. *Journal of International Economics* 10, no. 2 (May): 151–75.

Linder, S. B. 1961. *An essay on trade and transformation.* New York: Wiley.

Samuelson, P. A. 1965. A theory of induced innovation along Kennedy-Weizsacker lines. *Review of Economics and Statistics* 47 (November): 343–56.

Erratum

Page 154, line 2: "Weiszacre" should read "Weizsacker".

Editor's Note

The reference to "Feenstra and Bhagwati in chapter 9" on page 168 applies to essay 27 in volume 1 of this two-volume collection of essays.

OLIGOPOLY THEORY, ENTRY-PREVENTION, AND GROWTH*

Jagdish N. Bhagwati†

1. The focus of the theory of oligopoly has been shifted towards entry-prevention models since the recent work of Sylos Labini and Bain, especially after its brilliant formalization by Franco Modigliani.[1] This paper examines the entry-prevention approach critically, while relating it to the traditional approaches to the analysis of oligopoly behavior. The analysis is also extended to incorporate the phenomenon of "growth of firms."

2.1. Traditional oligopoly theory was founded on two basic assumptions: (1) each firm maximizes its profits; and (2) each firm concerns itself with the repercussions of its action on the behavior of other firms *already* in the industry, firms which could be described as actual rivals. The former assumption was universal and extended to all market structures. The latter assumption, of interdependence among firms, was supposed to be the hallmark distinguishing oligopoly theory (the "small group" case) from the traditional competitive theory (the "large group" case).[2]

2.2. Under the perfectly competitive structure, the firm is assumed to act as if an infinitesimal "cut" in its price will enable it to sell as much as it likes and an infinitesimal "raise" will lose it its entire sales. This follows from the

*From *Oxford Economic Papers*, N. S., Vol. XXII, No. 3 (November, 1970), pp. 297–310. Reprinted by permission of the Clarendon Press, Oxford, and the author.

†Jagdish N. Bhagwati, Professor of Economics, Massachusetts Institute of Technology. The author is grateful to G. C. Archibald, W. M. Gorman, Ian Little, Harry Johnson, Walter Eltis, and N. Kaldor for helpful comments on earlier drafts of this paper.

[1]Franco Modigliani, "New Developments in the Oligopoly Front," *Journal of Political Economy*, Vol. LXVI, No. 2 (June, 1958), pp. 215–32; Sylos Labini, *Oligopolio e progresso tecnico* (Milan: Guiffre, 1957); and J. S. Bain, *Barriers to New Competition* (Cambridge, Mass.: Harvard University Press, 1956). Two earlier commentators on Modigliani's paper are: F. Fisher, "New Developments on the Oligopoly Front: Cournot and the Bain-Sylos Analysis," *Journal of Political Economy*, Vol. LXVII, No. 4 (August, 1959), pp. 410–13, and D. E. Farrar and C. F. Phillips, Jr., "New Developments on the Oligopoly Front: A Comment," *Journal of Political Economy*, Vol. LXVII, No. 4 (August, 1959), pp. 414–17.

[2]It should thus be emphasized that the distinction between the small and the large group cases is a matter, *not* of numbers, but of the pattern of behavior that characterizes the firm.

fact that it is assumed to be atomistic in relation to the industry and hence, the effects of its action will be "spread over many sellers" and hence, provoke no attempt on their part to alter their prices in response to this firm's action. Oligopoly theory departs from competitive theory basically in so far as each oligopolistic firm is *conscious* of the impact of its decisions on the economic behavior of its rivals. Under this view, the solution to the oligopolistic system would be quite different from the competitive solution unless each firm, in reaching its policy decision, assumed that the rival firms would keep their prices unchanged (so that the demand curve for each firm becomes infinitely elastic, as in the competitive case, at least in the relevant range).[3] Traditional theory thus proceeded by assuming some rule under which each firm played the game of maximizing its profits: the firm assumes the rivals' outputs to be maintained in the face of a change made by the firm (Cournot); the rivals' price is assumed to be constant (Bertrand; this is the competitive solution); and so on with Fellner and Stackelberg.[4]

3. It is often wrongly thought that the "kinked demand" analysis, developed independently by Hall and Hitch in England and by Sweezy in the U.S.A. in 1939, represented an innovation in oligopoly theory.[5] Actually, it is no more than a variation upon the traditional formulation, designed to explain rigidity in prices. It assumes that, *given* a market price, the firm will argue that a price increase by it will not be followed by its rivals but that a cut will be; hence, the kink. With the demand curve so derived, the firm is assumed to maximize its profits.[6]

4.1. The really fundamental innovation in oligopoly theory came with the realization that oligopoly theory must deal with "potential" competition as

---

[3]This obviously is the well-known Bertrand solution to the oligopoly problem. It is difficult, however, to consider this solution plausible because the firms are going to learn soon that prices will *not* be maintained by their rivals in the face of price cuts!

[4]For an extensive discussion of these various solutions, see Chamberlin, *The Theory of Monopolistic Competition* (4th ed.; Cambridge, Mass.: Harvard University Press, 1942), Chapter III; and W. Fellner, *Competition Among the Few* (New York: A. Knopf, 1949). Edgeworth and Chamberlin were both skeptical about the possibility of a determinate solution of the problem in the general case; cf. Chamberlin, *op. cit.*, Chapter III.

[5]Hall and Hitch, "Price Theory and Business Behaviour," *Oxford Economic Papers*, No. 2 (May, 1939), pp. 12–45; and Sweezy, "Demand Under Conditions of Oligopoly," *Journal of Political Economy*, Vol. XLVII, No. 4 (August, 1939), pp. 568–73; the latter is also reprinted in *Readings in Price Theory*, American Economic Association Series (London: Allen and Unwin Ltd., 1953).

[6]There is thus no radical departure involved in this model and the only advantage of the model consists in providing testable hypotheses relating the variability of prices to the several factors affecting the extent of the kink and hence the magnitude of the discontinuity in the marginal revenue curve. On some elementary tests, see Stigler, "The Kinky Oligopoly Demand Curve and Rigid Prices," *Journal of Political Economy*, Vol. LV, No. 5 (October, 1947), pp. 432–49.

distinct from "actual" competition (with *existing* rivals).[7] In perfect competition (and, indeed, in any "large group" case regardless of product differentiation), the firm does not worry about the reactions of existing rivals; the question of "potential" rivals is hence irrelevant. The distinction between the "short" period and the "long" period, in Marshall, concerns only the question of excess profits in an industry but has nothing to do with each individual firm's economic behavior (which continues to be the same under both periods). This is not so, however, with oligopolistic firms which *do* worry about rivals' reactions. The distinction between the short and long periods becomes of great relevance because the rivals multiply in the long period. More important, except when the firm wants to leave the industry, the firm's decision must *always* be affected by *both* actual competition and the possibility of potential competition.

4.2. This shift of focus makes it necessary to examine afresh the second assumption of traditional oligopoly theory as well. Profit maximization must now be reinterpreted. Firms already in an industry at any point of time will often have the following choice: *either* to maximize profits in the short period (defined, *á la* Marshall, as the period when entry cannot take place)—this being the framework of the traditional oligopoly solutions; or to maximize the value of profits (duly discounted) over the long period, *taking into account the repercussions on entry, and hence on future profitability, of any price policy pursued in the short period*—this being the hallmark of the new approach to oligopoly theory.

4.3. The recent thinking on oligopoly theory, therefore, departs from tradition in two important and related ways: (1) it focuses on the problem of "potential" competition; and (2) it correspondingly distinguishes between short-period and long-period profit maximization and takes the latter to be the objective of firms that maximize profits (excepting, of course, those that are planning to move out of the industry).[8]

---

[7]This is described as a "fundamental innovation" because it represents a radical departure in the theoretical formulation of the problem. Whether this stands up better against the test of empirical verification than the traditional approach is, of course, a separate issue.

[8]Firms may not want to maximize profits. They may desire a stable stream of profits even if the present discounted value thereof may be less than that of an alternative stream that is variable. Alternatively, they may pursue the objective of increasing their share of the market in preference to profit maximization, as W. Baumol has argued in *Business Behavior, Value and Growth* (New York: Macmillan Co., 1959). In either case, however, the impact of the current price-policy on potential competition and thus on the long-period stream of profits and share of the market must still be considered by existing firms.

5. This shift of focus may be primarily associated with the work of P. W. S. Andrews, who has developed this theme in numerous writings on the subject.[9] Several Oxford economists have followed with discussion of the ways in which potential competition affects a firm's price-policy.[10] Much of the analysis, principally of Harrod, Andrews, and Edwards, has assumed that firms, faced with potential competition, will pursue a price-policy designed to prevent the entry of potential competitors—with strong overtones that this is equivalent to long-run profit maximization.[11] However, there is disagreement on the level of the entry-prevention price which reflects, in turn, differences in the postulates made concerning the existing firms' expectations, and hence strategy, with respect to the entrant's evaluation of the possibility of successful entry.

6.1. *The Harrod strategy.* Harrod, explicitly citing Andrews' analysis, has advanced an entry-preventing strategy which is based squarely on the assumption that the potential entrant can be put off if, and only if, the existing firms are making merely normal profits. Hence, the existing firms will equate average cost, inclusive of normal profits, to average revenue instead of maximizing profits in relation to the demand curve derived on the basis of

[9]The following are of particular interest: P. W. S. Andrews, *Manufacturing Business* (London: Macmillan and Co., 1949); and P. W. S. Andrews, "Theory of Individual Business," *Oxford Economic Papers*, N.S., Vol. I, No. 1 (January, 1949), pp. 54–89. Mr. Kaldor has drawn my attention to the following paragraph on pp. 69–70 of his paper on "Market Imperfection and Excess Capacity," *Economica* (February, 1935), reprinted in his *Essays on Value and Distribution* (London: Duckworth, 1960):

> Thus a producer, if far-sighted, will take the effect of his own actions not merely on his existing competitors into consideration but also on his *potential competitors.* He will act on the basis of an "imagined demand curve" which shows the amount he can sell at different prices *in the long-run,* under the assumption that his competitors' products, prices and the number of his competitors are all adjusted to his price. If a producer knows that if he charges a high price today a competitor will appear tomorrow whose mere existence will put him in a *permanently worse position,* he will charge a price which will afford him only a low profit, if only he hopes to secure his profit permanently; i.e., he will act in a manner *as if* his own demand curve were very much more elastic than it is.

Indeed, references to the importance of potential competition abound in the literature even prior to Kaldor's paper (including, in the United States, the writings of J. M. Clark). However, nothing like a complete theoretical system appears to have been based on the idea of potential competition until Andrews placed it squarely at the center of his analysis of oligopoly prices and behavior.

[10]The major contributions may be listed here. R. F. Harrod, "Theory of Imperfect Competition Revised," in *Economic Essays* (London: Macmillan and Co., 1952), Chapter VIII; J. R. Hicks, "The Process of Imperfect Competition," *Oxford Economic Papers*, Vol. VI, No. 1 (February, 1954), pp. 41–54; and H. R. Edwards, "Price Formation in Manufacturing Industry and Excess Capacity," *Oxford Economic Papers*, Vol. VII, No. 1 (February, 1955), pp. 94–118.

[11]This equivalence, however, does not necessarily obtain in the case of any of the different strategies discussed in this paper. Hicks, *op. cit.*, however, is explicit on this question.

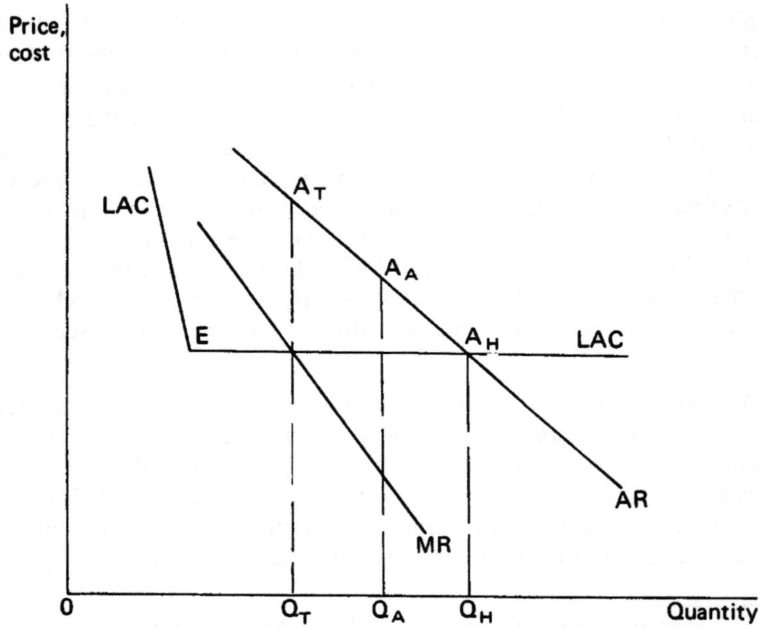

Figure 21-1

competition with existing rivals.[12] Thus, assume that, in view of existing competition, the demand curve facing the (typical) firm is AR in Figure 21-1.

[12]Harrod wishes to make this behavior applicable to firms in the "large group" case. This, however, is not persuasive. If firms are unconcerned about the reactions of existing rivals (the definition of the large group), it is impossible to see why they should bother about potential rivals! Harrod's strategy is plausible only in the case of oligopoly. This leads up to a problem which has been treated only cursorily, at best, in the literature on potential competition. How are existing rivals to *agree* on the entry-preventing price? How is such mutual agreement to be obtained? Curiously enough, some of the contributors almost wholly neglect this problem of actual competition in their concern with potential competition: the pendulum has swung to the other end! Hicks, *op. cit.*, skilfully frames his analysis in terms of a single firm which has no current rivals. Harrod does not analyze actual competition either. Edwards, *op. cit.*, in developing Andrews' theory, does have much to offer, however, in this direction. The most efficient firm in the industry, as currently constituted, will usually set the price at the entry-preventing level and other firms will have to follow it as best they can. If they cannot, the efficient firm(s) will expand at their expense and still keep the price at the entry-preventing level. Actual competition, therefore, adjusts itself to the demands of potential competition. Modigliani, *op. cit.*, does not pose the problem in the way it has been formulated here. While concentrating on potential competition, however, he offers several comments, based on Sylos's work, concerning "industrial structure," which closely parallel the arguments of Edwards concerning actual competition. Alternative solutions to the problem raised here would be *either* to have actual collusion *or* to argue, as Schelling has recently done with persuasiveness in *The Strategy of Conflict* (Cambridge, Mass.: Harvard University Press, 1960), that firms will often arrive at similar policies without actual collusion if attractive mutual gains follow from this event.

LAC, the long-run average cost curve of the firm, shows constant costs beyond *E*. Under traditional doctrine, the equilibrium output is Q_T and price A_T. Under Harrod's strategy, however, the output is Q_H and price A_H.[13]

6.2. However, even if this strategy were successful in preventing entry, one must ask why firms should wish to eliminate entry at the cost of all excess profits currently. Why make normal profits throughout (as per Harrod's strategy) instead of making excess profits immediately (ignoring the resulting entry) and normal profits later? Such a curious scale of preference on the part of Harrod's firms may be explained, of course, in terms of the firms seeking, for instance, a "stable" stream of profits or a larger share of the market, at the expense of extra profits. However, a rationale may be found for the Harrod-type behavior even within the framework of profit maximization. The optimum plant may be *different* for the pre-entry and post-entry situations. If the firm decides to invite competition by maximizing profits currently with a plant optimal to this objective, the profits following on entry will become subnormal *until* the plant is adjusted to the post-entry, optimum level. If the time-lag by which an existing plant can be adapted (at worst, through amortization and new purchase) to the post-entry optimal size is greater than the time-lag required for entry (as, one may suspect, may be the case for many plants), then subnormal profits are inevitable initially when entry occurs. If so, Harrod's strategy acquires cogency, from the viewpoint of profit maximization, if the initial losses on entry, duly discounted, exceed the gains that would have accrued from short-period profit maximization.

7.1. *The Andrews strategy*. Much of Andrews' writing suggests, however, that some *premium* in the form of a profit margin in excess of normal profits (as with output Q_A and price A_A) can be secured where entry is not "easy."[14] Entry can be difficult if it is hard to get a "foothold in the market" (i.e., the demand that accrues to the entrant may be insubstantial). A large market may further be needed to reach the "scale of efficient production" (i.e., the minimum size of plant, with least average cost, with which the entrant can come in, may be large).[15] The premium that can be enjoyed by the existing firms will thus reflect both the entrant's requirement of demand (determined by the scale of his plant) and his possibility of securing that demand.

[13]Harrod does allow a firm with advantages "peculiar to itself" to make abnormal profits. But the premium considered here is that which does not rest on such advantages but merely on the fact of being *already* inside the industry. Advantages such as Harrod has in mind are discussed by Bain, *op. cit.*, and are referred to in this paper in paragraph 10.

[14]Thus, Edwards, *op. cit.*, who offers an excellent account and extension of Andrews' theory, shows a premium being charged by an Andrews firm in Figure 2 on p. 110. Edward's analysis seems to be the best formal statement of Andrews' theory, and I shall draw upon it frequently. It is only fair to warn the reader that Andrews does not himself regard this as the correct interpretation of his theory; hence, it is probably best to regard the theory in the text as an "Andrews type" rather than as an Andrews theory.

[15]Edwards, *op. cit.*, pp. 96, 97, 99, among others. Numerous references to Andrews' own statement of the theory can be found in his book, *op. cit.*; for instance, pp. 151–4.

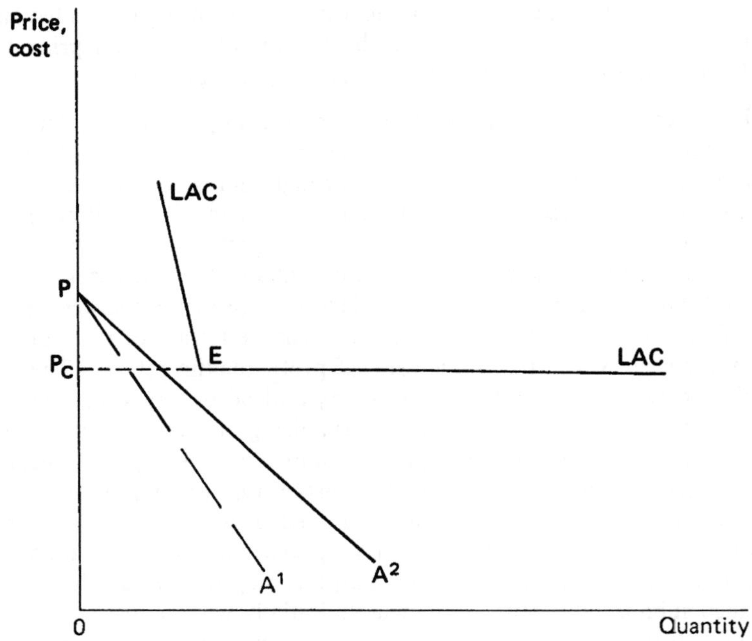

Figure 21-2

7.2. It is assumed that the entrant and the existing firms will expect (1) the existing firms to follow the entrant's price-cuts;[16] and (2) the customers of the existing firms not to switch to the entrant except in pursuit of a price-advantage.[17] Under these assumptions, the demand for the entrant's output is restricted to a share in the *marginal* increment in aggregate (industry) demand when the price falls below the pre-entry level. This increment may be equally divided among the existing firms and the entrant. However, if part of the increment ensues from the buyers attached to the existing sellers, the entrant's share is likely to be lower than that of (at least some of) its rivals. The demand curve so derived for the entrant is PA^1 in Figure 21-2. However, Andrews admits an important qualification to the assumption that buyers do not switch to the entrant except when there is a price-advantage. Buyers *will* be expected to transfer custom (in chagrin) to the entrant if the post-entry

[16]Cf. Edwards, *op. cit.*, pp. 107–9.

[17]With a single exception to be considered shortly, this is one of the central assumptions of Andrews' theory. It is held to be particularly true when the buyers themselves are manufacturing firms. Thus, consider: "The buyers of the product—themselves manufacturers at a higher stage of production—will tend to look first to their customary suppliers because of the confidence gained by previous custom, and it is from these firms that they will normally buy." Edwards, *op. cit.*, pp. 95–6. It should be noticed that this argument contradicts the premise of *random* pairing of buyers and sellers. In the absence of this assumption, the premium that could be charged, consistent with entry-prevention, would be *reduced*.

price reveals the pre-entry price to have been unduly high in relation to cost and hence exploitative.[18] Thus, the demand curve for the entrant will be more elastic — PA^2 in Figure 21-2. If the entrant's demand curve so derived for any given price, say PA^2 for price P in Figure 21-2, is below the average cost of production for the range of outputs at which the minimum average cost obtains,[19] entry will be expected to be unprofitable and hence is barred. The existing firms will then choose the maximum price — P_0 in Figure 21-3 — which is consistent with the prevention of entry.[20]

7.3. The premium charged under Andrews' strategy is then *approximately* given by the formula:

$$P_0 = P_C\left[1 + \frac{\bar{x}}{X_C\{\zeta/(N+1)+\varepsilon\}}\right],$$

where P_0 is the entry-preventing price, P_C the competitive price (equal to the minimum average cost of the potential entrant), $\bar{x}$ the minimum scale of plant (of the entrant) at which the minimum average cost is achieved, X_C the industry demand at price P_C, N the number of existing firms, ζ the price-elasticity of industry demand at price P_C, and ε the elasticity, with respect to change in price, of the current buyers' transfer of custom to the entrant.[21] It follows that the premium obtainable in an industry will vary directly with (1) the minimum size of the scale of most efficient production and (2) the number of existing firms; and inversely with (1) the size of the total market, (2) the price-elasticity of industry demand and (3) the extent to which existing buyers will transfer custom to the entrant consequent upon entry.[22]

[18] "In the event that the price has been maintained high, gratuitously, by otherwise efficient producers, it will very soon be reduced to match the price of the new entrant. But the resentment of the buyer-firms at the high price now revealed to have been not warranted by costs, provides a reservoir of ill-will which, properly exploited, will ensure the new entrant access to the market." (Edwards, *op. cit.*, p. 97.)

[19] Andrews rules out the possibility of a stable equilibrium at levels of production which involve operating at falling costs to the level of the minimum average cost point, the argument being that in this situation firms will feel that they must expand production and drive out existing rivals until at least the efficient scale is achieved. Analogously, the entrant will not enter if he cannot cover his costs at a level of output characterized by *minimum* average costs.

[20] Assuming, of course, that prices and profits are positively correlated. This assumption is shared by Modigliani, *op. cit.*

[21] The sign of ζ is negative and of ε (since custom is lost to the entrant and hence *reduced* when price *falls* with entry) positive. Some of the symbols have been borrowed from Modigliani, *op. cit.* For simplicity, it has been assumed that the increase in demand, as price falls with entry, is shared equally by all firms.

[22] Three observations are in order here. (1) The "Andrews strategy" presented here abstracts, for the purpose of analyzing the problem of price-formation, certain key postulates from, and hence is only a segment of, a full-blooded and rich account of the industrial process contained in Andrews, *op. cit.* (2) On the other hand, the testable hypotheses listed here as deductions from this strategy represent an extension of Andrews' analysis in so far as they are not all to be found (at any rate in the form given here) explicitly in Edwards and Andrews, *op. cit.* (3) It should further be noted that Andrews considers that, with the possibility of entry by multi-product firms into adjacent markets, the relevant minimum size of the entrant's plant will often be sufficiently small to make the premium chargeable negligible.

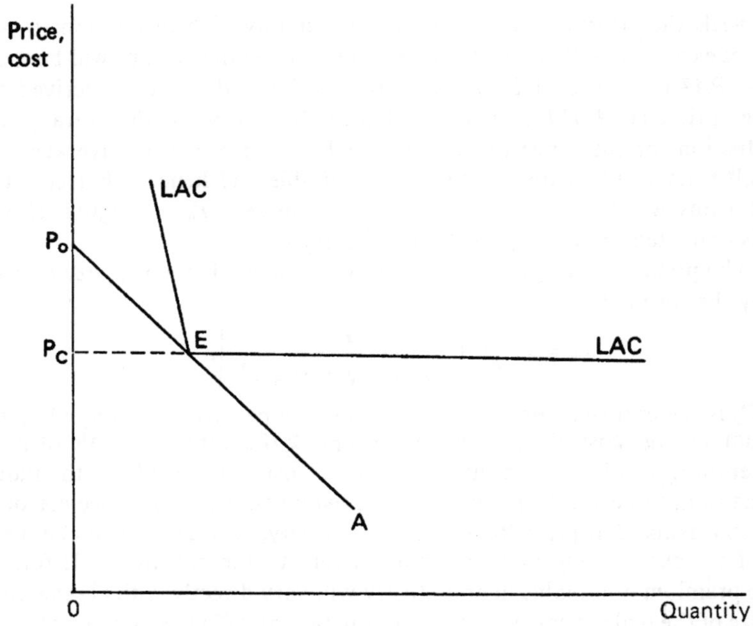

Figure 21-3

8.1. *The attractiveness of entry.* Andrews often appears to argue as though, in addition to making entry easier for the potential entrant, a higher premium also makes entry more "attractive"; however, no cogent discussion of such attractiveness is to be found in his work. It would appear, however, that *the mere enjoyment of lucrative premium by existing firms (no matter how amply justified in terms of difficulty of entry as defined previously) will attract firms into the industry who may want to undergo initial losses with a view to driving some existent firms out, in the hope of surviving and earning the lucrative premiums that are being made in the industry.* If, therefore, it is possible that if the premium charged appears lucrative enough, the entrant will risk coming into the industry in the hope of securing a foothold at the expense of some existing firm(s), the premium that will be charged will be *lower* than otherwise available.

8.2. This argument is illustrated in Figure 21-4. *OE* represents the profits, discounted back to the current period, that will be earned by the existing firms in the industry, *in the absence of entry*, at different premiums.[23] *LP* represents the expected losses and profits, duly discounted again, of an Andrews

[23]It is assumed that the greater the premium charged, the greater the profits made. The schedule could be easily adjusted to incorporate any alternative assumption.

entrant, corresponding to the premiums being charged currently by the existing firms. For premiums up to P_0, the entrant is supposed to take losses; with premiums exceeding P_0, the entrant will expect to make profits.[24] O then represents Harrod's entry-prevention price; and P_0 that of Andrews. If the attractiveness-of-entry argument is considered, however, the entrant will now have a new schedule of profits expected in case of *survival*, corresponding to the range of (lucrative) premiums form O' to P_0. These profits will be expected with uncertainty and are likely to accrue after an initial period of losses; hence, the schedule ought to be left of OE. However, the profits must be computed from the level of losses estimated in deriving LP_0, to permit lateral aggregation with the latter; hence, the schedule *may* be to the right of OE (for some premiums). The resulting schedule is $O'R$ in Figure 21-4. By aggregating LP_0 and $O'R$ for each premium charged, we arrive at the truly relevant curve LR. This curve intersects the Y-axis at P_0^1 which is the entry-prevention price.

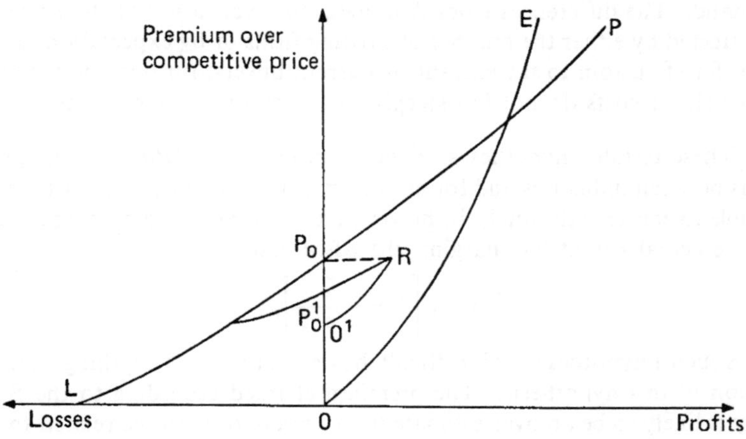

Figure 21-4

9.1. *The SBM strategy.* The Sylos-Bain model, as presented by Modigliani, and referred to hereafter as the SBM model, is startlingly similar to, though not identical with, Andrews' analysis.[25] The SBM firms agree on sharing the following expectations: (1) the potential entrant will not enter if the post-entry price does not cover its average cost of production; and (2)

[24]The expected losses could be estimated presumably at the minimum level of output at which minimum average cost is obtained; and the expected profits in a similar way.

[25]Modigliani, *op. cit.*, in a brief footnote on p. 216, refers to Edwards, *op. cit.*, as having anticipated "many of the conclusions of Sylos and Bain." However, he misses the differences between the two strategies.

the existing firms, assumed to be producing at minimum average cost, maintain their output unchanged when entry occurs. Under these rules, the entrant's demand curve starts from the price-axis at the pre-entry price and is drawn so that the entire increment in aggregate industry demand with each price-reduction accrues to the entrant. In other words, this demand schedule is the industry demand schedule minus the unchanging output of the existing firms. Assuming then that costs fall steeply to the minimum average cost level,[26] the following approximate formula holds for the maximum entry-preventing price (using the notation of paragraph 7.3):

$$P_0 = P_C\left[1 + \frac{\bar{x}}{X_C\,\zeta}\right].$$

9.2. In common with Andrews' results, the following testable hypotheses are obtained: the premium that can be charged, consistent with the prevention of entry, varies directly with the minimum scale of the entrant's plant and inversely with both the size of the total market and the price-elasticity of industry demand. The differences from Andrews, however, are that the premium is not affected by either the number of existing firms or by expectations about the transfer of custom to the entrant by current buyers; further, the premium will now rise if costs do not fall steeply to the minimum average cost level.

9.3. These testable hypotheses relate, however, to *variations* in the profit margins between industries and for an industry at different points of time. It is possible to construe the analysis, however, as also stating something testable about the actual size of the margin: the SBM result,

$$P_0 = P_C\left[1 + \frac{\bar{x}}{X_C\,\zeta}\right],$$

provides such a hypothesis. It is difficult, however, to expect anything except a refutation of this hypothesis. The premium charged according to the SBM strategy is likely to be an over-estimate for a variety of reasons, related to the attractiveness-of-entry factor considered in paragraph 8.1. If lucrative premiums are charged in an attempt to capitalize on the difficulty of entry, the attractiveness of entry becomes great and firms will enter the industry in the hope of survival. The reasons for this type of behavior by the entrant are quite plausible:

(1) When the entrant enters the industry, *every* firm makes losses; it should thus be a matter of chance as to which firm goes out. If the premium is lucrative enough, it could pay the firm to take the chance that it (rather than some existing firm) will survive.

(2) Indeed, if the SBM strategy is pursued, the entrant will be making *smaller* losses than the existing firms, except in a limiting case, under the assumptions made concerning costs; and hence, its chances of survival will be *greater* than those of existing firms,

[26]The SBM model, in contrast to Andrews' model, admits the possibility of equilibrium at ranges of output where the average cost is in excess of the minimum. The formula in the text, however, ignores this complication.

so that the argument about survival is considerably strengthened. In Figure 21-5, designed to illustrate the SBM strategy, AR^1 is the demand curve for an existing firm (symmetry of demand for each firm is assumed for the sake of simplicity; nothing substantive in the following argument hinges on this); P^1 is the entry-preventing price; P^2 is the price *after* entry; OW is the output of the existing firm before entry, which is now maintained, *à la* the Sylos Labini strategy, in the face of entry; OK is the (minimum) plant with which the entrant has entered the industry; and AR^2 is the demand curve for each *existing* firm *after* entry. The pre-entry profits, in excess of normal, are P^1RMN; the post-entry loss for each pre-entry firm is $NMQP^2$; and the post-entry loss for the entrant itself is only $NEHP^2$ ($< NMQP^2$). In the limiting case, when each existing firm produces, prior to entry, at E, each firm (inclusive of the entrant) must make identical losses after entry.

(3) Further, if the question is one of survival, to earn lucrative premiums, it is quite possible that the entrant may have greater financial reserves than some existing firm(s) —an assumption clearly compatible with the assumption of homogeneity of cost curves—and hence, also a greater capacity to survive. Since the entrants are often, and will almost always be assumed to be, multi-product firms, this argument acquires special cogency.

(4) The entrant may quite possibly be willing to take initial losses and to consider them as inevitable "investment in a market," particularly if a market that is already substantially being exploited is being entered.

(5) Finally, multiple-product firms can always set off losses on a new venture against profits from existing activities and hence let the Treasury share the losses, so that the

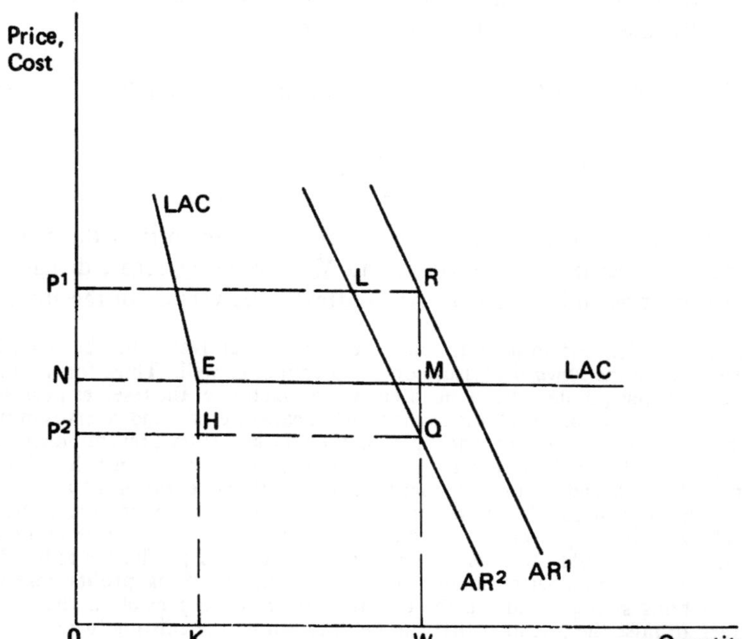

Figure 21-5

prospect of initial losses again is relatively less inhibiting than might otherwise be supposed. For these various reasons, therefore, the premium that will be charged by oligopolistic firms is likely to be overstated by the SBM formulation and is unlikely to be successfully verified empirically.[27]

10. All this is *not* to deny that sometimes existing firms may have absolute cost advantages over entrants, which may persist for long periods. For instance, patents provide an example. Where such advantages obtain and are likely to persist for long periods, the premium charged will be *higher* than that indicated by Andrews', as also Sylos Labini's analysis. Bain provides a careful and valuable analysis of these advantages, and several testable hypotheses about variations in the size of the available premium follow directly from his analysis.[28]

11. Many of the paces through which the entry models are taken involve the assumption of a *given* demand curve for the industry. Sylos Labini and Modigliani argue, for instance, that the implications of a growing demand will be (1) to put a downward pressure on the premium that can be charged (because the aggregate demand is now larger) and hence (2) to cause the existing firms to ration out scarce supplies instead of raising prices if capacity creation has lagged behind the expansion of demand.[29] It is possible, however, to incorporate the effects of growing demand formally into the entry analyses of the variety discussed here; and the results are interesting.

12.1. The formula for the equilibrium price, under the Andrews strategy, should now read:

$$P_0 = P_C\left[1 + \frac{\bar{x} - k\lambda}{X_C\{\zeta/(N+1) + \varepsilon\}}\right]$$

where λ is the growth of aggregate demand subsequent to entry, k the proportion thereof that accrues to the entrant, and X_C now the aggregate demand at the competitive price *after* growth. An Andrews-type version of the share of

[27]Of course, under certain assumptions, the issue of survival could be plausibly shown to exercise some *upward* pressure on the premium as well. Thus, for instance, as Mr. Archibald has pointed out to me, if entry is a function of the reserves possessed by existing firms and usable in a "war to the ruin" in case of entry, and reserves in turn depend on the level of profits in the short period, then the best entry-prevention strategy would appear to be to maximize current profits. However, it seems to me that this argument must be balanced against the fact that the worth-whileness of a "war to the ruin" to the entrant is itself a function of the presence of lucrative premiums in the industry. The Archibald-type argument thus merely makes the *O'R* curve in Figure 21-4 steeper than it would otherwise be, because the expected profits are reduced at higher premiums if the higher premiums improve the existing firms' profits, reserves, and hence fighting strength and thereby dim the entrant's prospect of survival. The result is then to raise the premium that can be obtained by the existing firms.

[28]Modigliani, *op. cit.*

[29]Modigliani draws attention to the fact that these conclusions are found in Edwards, *op. cit.*

the increasing demand accruing to the entrant would probably be: $k\lambda = qm\lambda/(N+1)$, where $(1-m)$ is the proportion of increased demand that accrues through current buyers attached to existing sellers, and $(1-q)$ the fractional scalar by which the entrant's share in the increased demand must be reduced because the existing sellers' "goodwill" gives them a more than equal share of the demand accruing through new buyers. The prospect of increasing demand will thus reduce the premium available; and the reduction will vary directly with q, m, and λ and inversely with the number of current sellers.

12.2 However, there is a further implication which is positively startling. It is no longer possible to argue that entry, even though "free," can be closed by the "very effective and legitimate weapon of a competitive price based on the costs of efficient production."[30] Thus, where $\bar{x} < k\lambda$, the entry-prevention price is lower than P_c. However, the price cannot be set (permanently) below P_c, so that the use of price-policy to prevent entry becomes an ineffective device. From this, there follow two significant conclusions. (1) The entry-prevention approach can now be turned around to provide testable hypotheses concerning the *incidence of entry* itself. Thus, the testable hypothesis provided here is that entry occurs when $\bar{x} < qm\lambda/(N+1)$.[31] Moreover, viewed from the angle of the existing firms, this also becomes a hypothesis about the growth of firms; the share of a firm in increased aggregate demand will fall below its average share of the market when $\bar{x} < qm\lambda/(N+1)$.[32] (2) It is also now evident that the only efficient entry-preventing strategy that the existing firms can pursue, in a situation of increasing demand, is to ensure, in so far as this is feasible, *the maximum appropriation to themselves, rather than to any potential entrant, of the segment of growing demand.* The theoretical problem thus shifts from devising an entry-preventing *price* to a formal analysis of the *non-price* factors which determine the share of the existing firms in the growing market and the ways in which these are within the range of influence of these firms.

---

[30]Edwards, *op. cit.*, p. 96.

[31]Similar hypotheses would be that the incidence of entry would vary directly, for instance, with the rate at which industry demand is growing and inversely with the share thereof that accrues through current buyers.

[32]An SBM-type argument, however, would make the growth of existing firms an independent variable (which determines both entry and price). The SBM formula would now read somewhat like: $P_0 = P_c[1 + \{\bar{x} - (\lambda - \alpha)\}/X_c\,\zeta]$ where α is the creation of new capacity by existing firms in anticipation of growing demand. It in only when this falls short, for reasons such as incorrect anticipation or difficulties of expansion peculiar to some existing firms(s), of the growth in demand that the entry-prevention price could be reduced to the extreme level when entry would become inevitable.

V
SURVEYS AND CONTROVERSIES IN INTERNATIONAL TRADE AND COMPARATIVE ADVANTAGE

The Pure Theory of International Trade: A Survey[1]

This Survey[2] covers that branch of international trade theory which, following Marshall, is generally described as 'pure'. This epithet separates it from 'monetary' theory. It is *not* to be taken to imply exceptional esotericism and abstraction from the problems of the real world. Indeed, I propose to give prominence to that part of the growing, new literature in pure theory which attempts explicitly to bring the theory on to the ground – through empirical verification of testable propositions, through measurement of the gains and losses from changes in trade policy and through the formulation of analytical and operational models to assist the developmental planning that is becoming a characteristic of the developing nations.

The pure theory of international trade represents essentially the application of the theories of value and welfare to questions of international economics.[3] Although the distinction between them has not always been clear in many writings, it is none the less true that two different species of problems have been the subject of analysis in pure theory. There are questions of 'positive' or 'objective' analysis: for instance, what determines the composition of trade; how will tariffs affect factor prices; what is the effect of trade on the terms of trade?

[1] This is the fourth of the series of Surveys supported by the Rockefeller Foundation.

[2] This Survey was partly written when I was with the Indian Statistical Institute. For correspondence and/or discussions, I am thankful to Professors H. G. Johnson, R. W. Jones, C. P. Kindleberger, B. S. Minhas, P. A. Samuelson and T. N. Srinivasan. V. Balasubramanian and R. Tagat have assisted with the computational work.

[3] The pure theory of trade thus differs structurally from general theory in the kinds of questions asked, rather than in the kinds of assumptions made. This vexed question has been considered at length by Haberler [4, Chapter 1].

On the other hand, there are questions in 'welfare' or 'normative' economics: among them, does free trade maximize world real income; are tariffs superior to free trade from the viewpoint of national advantage; how do tariffs compare with subsidies as forms of State intervention?[1]

The range of questions that have been asked is impressive. The recent literature which is addressed to them runs into several dozen books and over two hundred papers. This makes a brief survey exceptionally difficult, even if confined to the developments in the last two or three decades.[2] This difficulty is compounded by the fact that the subject has already been extensively, frequently and recently surveyed. We currently have a cogent and lucid survey in a brief monograph by Haberler [4], revised only in 1961; a nearly exhaustive, full-length account in a 1960 volume by Caves [3]; an excellent, theoretical survey of some of the central analytical propositions of pure theory by Mundell [11] in 1960; and, most embarrassingly, a survey of some of the more impressive recent developments in pure theory by myself [1] as recently as 1961.[3]

To collapse the immense literature into a concise survey, to exercise the inevitable selectivity (with respect to both authors and problems of analysis) to maximum advantage, it is necessary to have a precise, logical frame. The structure of this paper is built squarely on the

[1] The distinction between 'positive' and 'welfare' questions is recent in trade theory and appears to have been stated explicitly and emphatically only as late as 1933 by Ohlin [34]. Ohlin, who distinguished between these two aspects, criticized the classical economists for muddling them. As Haberler [4, p. 3], however, has charmingly pointed out: 'That his demand for not just a clear distinction between political evaluation and theoretical explanation, but for actual separation of these two areas by putting them into separate books or chapters, is easier postulated than accomplished is demonstrated by Ohlin himself. Thus, in an early passage of his celebrated treatise, in the midst of "objective theory", he proves in typical classical manner that interregional trade and division of labour results in an increased social product without making it clear that this statement implies a value judgment on his part and is not merely "objective analysis".'

[2] Thus Lipsey's [7] concise and brilliant review of the theory of customs unions (part of the theory of discriminatory tariff changes) in this *Journal* runs into several pages. And it deals with a comparatively recent field which forms only a small segment of the literature on pure theory.

[3] To these may be added Meade's celebrated works [8, 9, 10], which cover the entire field and the writings of Johnson [5, 6], which have done much to synthesize the literature on many aspects of trade theory. Mention may also be made of two papers: Lipsey's [7] 1960 survey of customs-union theory and the review in 1960 by myself and Johnson]2] of certain historical controversies in pure theory, reprinted as chapter 2.

clear distinction between 'positive' and 'normative' pure theory.

Under positive theory, in turn, a distinction has been drawn between: (1) the propositions of 'statics', which describe the properties of an equilibrium situation at *any given point* of time; (2) the propositions of 'comparative statics', which concern the *differences* in the equilibrium values of variables between situations at *two different points of* (conceptual) time; and (3) the propositions of 'dynamics', which involve time in an essential way.

The static propositions which have attracted the greatest analytical interest concern: (1) the pattern of trade: the determination of commodities as exports and imports; and (2) the configuration of factor prices. The analysis of the former question has further been enriched greatly by a recent, noticeable trend towards empirical verification. The propositions of comparative statics (which continue to be almost exclusively deductive) fall again into two classes: (1) those that concern the effect, on equilibrium prices and quantities, *under a pre-defined trade policy*, of an autonomous change in one of the following data: production functions, demand and factor supply; and (2) those that relate to the effect, on equilibrium prices and quantities, of a change in trade policy itself, while other data are constant. The development of pure theory has witnessed a synthesis and simplification of these propositions in comparative statics which eludes the few, though diverse, attempts at dynamic analysis. This synthesis has also been accomplished in terms of an analytical framework characterized by primary factors of production and integrated processes of production. This constitutes a central limitation of the theory in a theoretical world where this conceptualization has been replaced generally by the more general approach of process analysis and in a real world where a large portion of the world trade consists of intermediates and capital goods and an increasing number of developing nations' imports are coming to consist almost exclusively of these commodities.

The parts of this paper dealing with positive theory have therefore been divided into the following five groups:

1 Section 1: *Theorems in Statics: The Pattern of Trade.*
2 Section 2: *Theorems in Statics: Factor Price-Equalization.*
3 Section 3: *Theorems in Comparative Statics.*
4 Section 4: *Theorems in Dynamics.*
5 Section 5: *Central Limitations of Pure Theory: Intermediates and Capital Goods.*

In the theory of welfare and trade the classification has been easier. There is, on the one hand, the 'traditional' theory which is addressed to *qualitative* propositions that rank different trade policies (*e.g.*, free trade is superior to no trade) and can be classified according to whether they satisfy Samuelson's superior-for-all-income-distributions criterion. On the other hand, there is a growing, important segment of the literature which aims at *quantitative* measures of costs and benefits – prompted by the objective of making economic analysis policy-oriented. At the same time the growth of centralized planning in many developing countries has raised the interesting questions of the *operational* use of trade theory's welfare insights and results as part of the complement of planning techniques; and some useful experience has been obtained.

The survey of welfare propositions in trade theory, therefore, has been divided into three major groups:

1 Section 6: *Welfare Propositions: Gains from Trade.*
2 Section 7: *Measurement of Welfare.*
3 Section 8: *Trade Theory and Development Planning.*[1]

1. Theorems in Statics: The Pattern of Trade

The theory of comparative advantage (or cost), which concerns the determination of the pattern of trade, constitutes perhaps the oldest set of analytical propositions in pure theory. It belongs to the realm of 'statics' because traditionally it has been formulated as a theorem concerning the determination of (traded) commodities into exports and imports in a static, analytical framework. This is certainly true of the two major theories, Ricardian and Heckscher–Ohlin [1], that have dominated this field.

There are, no doubt, different possible ways in which an 'international economy' may be simulated by a theorist. Each such 'model' could be used to deduce analytical propositions. Indeed, the literature on pure theory contains a large number of such idealizations, among the most celebrated being those of Yntema, Mosak and Graham [3].[2]

[1] Although the paper falls neatly into these eight sections, there are inevitably some overlaps. None the less, I would maintain that the proposed classification is the most advantageous from the viewpoint of assessing the current state, limitations and trends of the pure theory of trade.

[2] For a summary statement of these and other models, Caves [3] is an excellent reference. A cataloguing of such models, however, is of limited interest as any number of models can be put down as one wishes. Only those models are of

From the viewpoint of propositions concerning the pattern of trade, the two models of significance are those of Ricardo and Heckscher–Ohlin [19, 34]. Not merely have these models been used to derive 'logically true' theorems concerning the trade pattern.[1] These theorems have also now been adapted to formulate testable hypotheses (based on factors stressed in the respective models). And these hypotheses have been subjected to empirical verification in a series of excellent papers. In consequence, new theories have now been devised, which provide *alternative* explanations of the pattern of trade. Prominent among these are the analyses of Kravis [22] and Linder [27]. These four theories concerning the pattern of international specialization are discussed here, distinguishing clearly between the formulations as deductive, analytical propositions (which are logically true under a specified set of sufficient conditions) and formulations as testable hypotheses.

The Ricardian Theory

The Ricardian Theory can be construed in either of two ways: (1) as a highly simplified model which was intended to be, and served as, an eminently successful instrument for demonstrating the welfare proposition that trade is beneficial; or (2) as a serious attempt at isolating the crucial variables which can be used to 'explain' the pattern of trade. There is little doubt that the former view is plausible. A careful study of the original texts yields supporting evidence; the most persuasive element is the fact that when both Ricardo and Mill discussed the 'positive' (as opposed to 'normative') proposition relating to the effects of cheap corn *imports* from the colonies on profits, wages and rents, and thence on the approach of the stationary state, they were using the full-fledged classical model characterized by three factors and diminishing returns [1]. And yet the impact of the Ricardian 'constant cost' model in recent literature has been predominantly as an idealization which affords a significant clue to the structure of foreign trade.[2]

significance which have been used to yield theorems; and then it is only in considering those theorems that they are best discussed.

[1] The phrase 'logically true' is used there in the strict mathematical sense: a statement that is true in every logically possible case is said to be *logically true*.

[2] This has been the result of two factors: (i) traditionally the question whether the Ricardian theory should be construed as positive or normative has rarely been raised; it has always seemed 'natural' to construe Ricardo as though he were

On the latter interpretation the Ricardian theory can be deduced directly from the celebrated England–Portugal example in Ricardo's *Principles.* If it is assumed that there are two commodities, a single factor (labour) and constant returns to scale (in each activity),[1] the pre-trade commodity price ratio will be a function exclusively of the (scale-free) output-factor ratios contained in the production functions. The combination of a single factor with constant returns to scale ensures that neither demand nor the level of factor supply makes any difference to the equilibrium commodity price ratio in a closed economy.[2] Since Ricardo assumes a similar model for each country, it follows that the pre-trade commodity price ratio, and hence the composition of trade, is exclusively determined by international differences in relative output-factor ratios. If a_1 and a_2 are the output-factor ratios for country I and b_1 and b_2 for country II in activities 1 and 2 respectively, country I will export commodity 1 and import commodity 2 if $a_1/a_2 > b_1/b_2$ (as this will imply that commodity 1 will be cheaper, and commodity 2 dearer, in country I than in country II *prior to trade*). The algebraic condition is frequently written as $a_1/b_1 > a_2/b_2$, which states the condition in terms of 'comparative factor productivities'. If, however, the number of commodities is increased beyond two, while maintaining the two-country assumption, it is no longer possible to derive the 'strong' Ricardian theorem that the trade pattern is determined exclusively by international differences in production functions (*i.e.*, by comparative factor productivities). The model now implies a weaker proposition: there will be a chain in which all commodities are ranked in terms of their comparative factor-productivity ratios such that *it will always be true that each of a country's exports will have a higher factor-productivity ratio than each of its imports.* The precise composition of exports and imports (*i.e.*, where the chain will be cut, dividing the exports and

---

genuinely attempting to explain the pattern of trade with his simple model; and (ii) the Ricardian 'demonstration' of the benefits of trade, long since challenged as inadequate by Barrett Whale, has now been superseded by the elegant and more rigorous formulations of the new welfare economics and Samuelson's classic proof of 1939 – so that it is no longer easy to see that the Ricardian preoccupation was predominantly with normative aspects.

[1] The last assumption listed here need not be implicit in the preceding one, since fixed factors like land may well be subsumed in the shape of the production function.

[2] The reason is that the resulting production possibility curve is non-strictly convex and characterized by a constant rate of transformation.

the imports) can be determined only by bringing demand into the model [20]. This proposition will continue to hold also in the more general framework of many countries and commodities, which represents a generalization of Ricardo's two-country model by Graham. In an elegant generalization of Ricardo's theory, drawing upon McKenzie's earlier work [78], Jones [69] has shown that, taking each pair of countries, only comparing the labour cost ratios of the commodities they are producing in specialization, the Ricardian bilateral cost comparisons are necessarily satisfied. (These propositions relate, more generally, to the location of production in a free-trade world: their implications for the trade pattern are in conformity with the Ricardian theory.)

When international trade economists have attempted to formulate hypotheses, based on the Ricardian theory, and test whether observable trade conforms to the postulated pattern, the real difficulty has been that of trying to adapt the one-factor, Ricardian approach to the multi-factor real world. Two ways in which this adaptation may be made can be distinguished.

One way would be to focus on the fact that the Ricardian model emphasizes the crucial role of comparative differences in *production functions* so that the testable proposition should be developed in these terms. For instance, if the technology in activity i could be characterized by $Q_i = \lambda_i^{\mathrm{I}} Q_i(K_i; L_i)$ for country I and by $Q_i = \lambda_i^{\mathrm{II}} Q_i(K_i; L_i)$ for country II so that the *only* difference between the two countries' production functions for an identical activity is a multiplicative scalar ($\lambda_i^{\mathrm{II}}/\lambda_i^{\mathrm{I}}$ in this case), then the Ricardian testable hypothesis could be construed to mean that

$$\frac{\lambda_i^{\mathrm{II}}}{\lambda_i^{\mathrm{I}}} > \frac{\lambda_j^{\mathrm{II}}}{\lambda_j^{\mathrm{I}}}$$

$$i = 1, 2, \ldots m \quad j = m + 1, \ldots n$$

where commodities $i = 1, 2, \ldots m$ are country II's exports and commodities $j = m + 1, \ldots n$ are its imports. This would be a Ricardian hypothesis – as much as any other.[1] The possibility of testing such a

[1] The conditions under which this proposition is logically true could be established by an extension of the theoretical work on the Heckscher–Ohlin theory and on the effects of neutral technical progress [5, Chapters I and III]. For instance, if all the assumptions which are shown to be sufficient for the logical validity of the Heckscher–Ohlin theorem are made with the *only* difference that the production functions are not identical, but differ between countries in the manner postulated in the text, it follows that the (Ricardian-type) hypothesis in the text concerning the pattern of trade will be logically true (provided, of course, that international differences in relative factor endowments are ruled out).

hypothesis is not, by any means, remote. Minhas [33, p. 154] states, in a brilliant paper on the Heckscher–Ohlin theory, that 'the isoquants in different countries, except for a pure scale change, look alike; and the marginal rates of substitution are unchanged at given capital: labour ratios' when homohypallagic production functions are fitted to the data for certain comparable industries in Japan and the United States. This empirical evidence seems to provide the means to test the kind of Ricardian hypothesis formulated here.[1]

The most frequent interpretation for the purpose of formulating a testable proposition, however, has been in terms of the factor productivities themselves. The comparative factor productivities, defined in terms of an arbitrarily chosen factor (almost always labour),[2] have been taken as providing the necessary clue to the trade pattern.

The intuitive and ultimate rationale behind this interpretation is easily stated (and, as will be evident later, has an important bearing on the procedure of testing). Since exports will take place only when domestic (pre-trade) prices are lower than abroad, it follows that

$$\frac{P_i^{\mathrm{I}}}{P_i^{\mathrm{II}}} \nless 1$$

$$i = 1, 2, \ldots m$$

where $\frac{P_i^{\mathrm{I}}}{P_i^{\mathrm{II}}}$ refers to the price-ratio of commodity i, exported by country I, *prior to trade*.[3] Similarly,

[1] Minhas comes close to doing this, but does not see the problem in this way because he is focusing on the implications of such 'neutral' differences in production functions for the Heckscher–Ohlin theorem. Credit must be given to him, however, for having seen the possibility of construing the Ricardian approach in the broader way (of differences in production functions) suggested here, as against the narrower approach of labour productivity ratios that is to be found in the literature.

[2] There is nothing in the basic *structure* of the Ricardian model which requires that this single factor be labour. It could be anything else. However, it has mostly been taken to be labour. The reasons for this exclusive preference may be that: (i) the historical context of the labour theory of value, in terms of which Ricardo's comparative cost doctrine has usually been understood, makes it inevitable that the formal identity between labour and any other factor, as noted here, should have been missed, and (ii) there has been, until recently, also a widespread tendency, in economic literature generally, to take labour productivity as the index of 'productivity' rather than, say, capital productivity.

[3] Where transport costs are present, lower pre-trade prices are only a *necessary* condition for exports; where transport costs (and similar cost-raising factors) are ignored, lower pre-trade prices also become a *sufficient* condition.

$$\frac{P_j^{\mathrm{I}}}{P_j^{\mathrm{II}}} > 1$$
$$= m + 1, \ldots n$$

where the commodity j is exported by country II. Hence.

$$\frac{P_i^{\mathrm{I}}}{P_i^{\mathrm{II}}} < \frac{P_j^{\mathrm{I}}}{P_j^{\mathrm{II}}}$$
$$i = 1, \ldots m \quad j = m + 1, \ldots n$$

Now it is possible to write these prices (defined as equal to costs) in terms of three component factors:

$$P_i = a_i \,.\, \frac{W_i}{L_i} \cdot \frac{TC_i}{W_i}$$

where a_i is the labour: output ratio, W_i is the wage bill (so that $\frac{W_i}{L_i} = w_i$ is the wage-rate) and TC_i the total cost (inclusive of profits, by definition) in activity i. If we now argue that it is, in practice, enough to focus attention on a_i and to ignore the other two factors (on the ground that either they are insignificant *or* they are identical between countries individually or as a product), then we could substitute a_i for p_i in the above price-comparison. We could also alternatively assume that the inter-industrial pattern of wage rates (w_i) and the total-cost/wages ratio $\left(\frac{TC_i}{W_i}\right)$ is identical internationally. We would then get the condition

$$\frac{a_i^{\mathrm{I}}}{a_i^{\mathrm{II}}} < \frac{a_j^{\mathrm{I}}}{a_j^{\mathrm{II}}} \quad . \quad . \quad . \quad . \quad (1)$$
$$i = 1, 2, \ldots m \quad j = m + 1, \ldots n$$

This is, in fact, the condition stated frequently as the Ricardian hypothesis.

This chain of reasoning also leads to a further formulation. It is possible to advance a variation of the hypothesis, which brings into the picture the structure of the wage-rates as well. This can be done by rewriting the previous hypothesis thus:

$$\frac{a_i^{\mathrm{I}}}{a_i^{\mathrm{II}}} \cdot \frac{w_i^{\mathrm{I}}}{w_i^{\mathrm{II}}} < \frac{a_j^{\mathrm{I}}}{a_j^{\mathrm{II}}} \cdot \frac{w_j^{\mathrm{I}}}{w_j^{\mathrm{II}}} \quad . \quad . \quad . \quad (2)$$
$$i = 1, 2, \ldots m \quad j = m + 1, \ldots n$$

This is, in fact, a statement of the Ricardian hypothesis which is in terms of comparative *unit labour costs* and not *labour productivity*. It is the hypothesis which is to be found in much of the empirical literature [1].

Although it appears relatively simple to go on from these formulations to their tests, there are some points of interest that need to be spelled out.

(1) To begin with, 'indirect' tests of these hypotheses readily suggest themselves but can be treacherous. For instance, it has been customary to argue through an attempted demonstration of the international 'similarity' of the inter-industrial wage-rate structure and the pattern of the total-cost/wages ratio. Caves [3, p. 272] has cited Kravis' [21, pp. 145–6] empirical results, which show that the ranking of industries by hourly earnings of workers is almost identical between Japan and the United States, to argue that these data lend force to the Ricardian hypothesis in terms of comparative labour productivity differences (as the determinants of relative price differences).[1] However, such a deduction leaves out of reckoning the possibility that the structure of the costs–wages ratio may be largely dissimilar between trading countries and makes implicitly an unverified assumption of 'similarity' of this structure. This procedure, in any case, is unsound, since, although each of the two structures (costs–wages and wage-rates) may be internationally 'dissimilar', their product may be similar as a result of these dissimilarities being offsetting. A method which proceeds in terms of investigating the similarities of individual structures will leave out this possibility and thereby constitute an unduly restrictive and false test for the empirical verification of the Ricardian hypothesis in question.

(2) But then, if a direct test of the Ricardian hypotheses were adopted, examining whether the labour productivity or unit wage–cost ratios for the exports and imports for two countries (taken bilaterally) conform to the postulated relationships, would that be enough? I do not think so. Let me cast my argument in terms of hypothesis (1), which relates to labour productivity ratios – it is equally valid for hypothesis (2) relating to unit wage–cost ratios.

It will be recalled that hypothesis (1) is derived in two steps. (*a*) First, it is argued that the (pre-trade) prices are such that the relative price (defined as the domestic over the foreign price) of an exported good

[1] Similar data, showing similarity of industrial wage structures, have been produced for the United States, United Kingdom, Canada and (only a little less successfully) Sweden by Lebergott [23]. None of this, however, adds up to anything impressive, since the coverage in terms of both activities and nations is severely limited.

must be lower than the relative price of an imported good. This is a natural assumption to make; it merely reflects the assumption that the profit motive will direct the pattern of trade.[1] This, however, relates to the *pre-trade* prices. But the observed prices are inevitably *post-trade* prices. This should have posed an impossible difficulty in testing any proposition concerning the pattern of trade and prices. However, it is easy to get around the problem when one reckons with the fact of transport (and other) costs that lead to a difference in the post-trade f.o.b. and c.i.f. (landed) prices. This difference in f.o.b. and c.i.f. prices means that the price–trade proposition that the relative price of an exported good must be lower than that of an imported good will continue necessarily to hold (with the domestic price of a good defined f.o.b. and the foreign prices c.i.f. for exported goods). The proposition is necessarily valid empirically in a world which is characterized by natural and artificial cost-raising factors. It therefore calls for no conscious attempt at verification. This is indeed a great gain. It is, however, an advantage not shared by the other postulate that must be made before the Ricardian hypothesis can be derived. (*b*) This other assumption consists in arguing that prices can be approximated by labour productivities. This proposition takes generally the strong form that the linear regression equation fitted to observed labour productivity ratios (for each activity in both countries) and corresponding price ratios would yield a 45 degree line from the origin.[2] This strong assumption, which is equivalent to arguing that the inter-industry structure of the total cost per unit labour is identical between the trading countries, is only a sufficient condition for yielding, along with the price–trade assumption, the required Ricardian hypothesis. It is also the condition that is most frequently found in the literature on Ricardian theories [3, Chapter X]. A weaker, but still sufficient, assumption would be to make labour productivity ratios a monotonically increasing function of price ratios. But the

[1] Theoretically, of course, one can think of cases where the pattern of trade does not conform to this rule. For instance, the contrary possibility can arise if there are domestic distortions (i.e. divergence of the domestic rate of transformation in production from the commodity price-ratios) [112]. In anticipation, I may point out that this qualification does not apply to the *post-trade*, relative price comparison for exportables and importables, to which I proceed immediately in the text.

[2] The labour productivity ratio here must be defined as the foreign labour productivity divided by the domestic; and the price ratio is defined as the domestic price divided by the foreign.

weaker this assumption gets, the more difficult it becomes to interpret it in meaningful, economic terms.[1]

Since one does want to know why it is that the trade pattern is characterized, if at all, by the comparative labour productivity ranking postulated by Ricardian hypothesis (1), I would argue that it is also necessary to supplement such a direct verification by a further verification of whether labour productivity ratios exhibit the (underlying) hypothesized relationship with price ratios.[1] Unfortunately, neither the direct verification of the rankings of exports and imports (for a pair of trading countries) in terms of their comparative labour productivities or unit wage–cost ratios nor the necessary, supplementary test of the implied relationship between price ratios and labour productivity or unit wage–cost ratios has yet been attempted.

The empirical literature that exists, in some abundance, concerns itself with really different kinds of testable propositions concerning trade. These hypotheses do have some overlap with the Ricardian hypothesis (1) and (2), with the unfortunate consequence that the surprisingly good results that attempts at verifying them have turned up have been construed frequently as validating the Ricardian approach [3, Chapter X]. The pioneering study in this field is by MacDougall [28, 29], with follow-up by Balassa [13], Stern [40] and MacDougall [30] himself.

Taking American and British exports of similar commodities to third markets, MacDougall [28, 29] has conducted analysis which is

[1] In the tests of this assumption which I later attempt in this paper even the weaker hypothesis does not get through: the linear regressions yield very poor fits.

[2] Concerning the derivation of the Ricardian hypothesis (1) in this two-step fashion, however, there is just a little more that may be said. It may be contended that labour productivities approximate the *pre-trade* prices but that trade leads to boosted profits in the export industries with no imputation to wages and no impact on labour productivities. If so, one *could* find evidence for the trade pattern exhibiting the Ricardian ranking in terms of comparative labour productivities and/or unit wage–cost ratios, but *not* necessarily for the productivity or unit wage–cost ratios being related in any way to the price ratios. While, of course, this is theoretically possible (and such a theory would have its own further implications which should then be tested), I do not find it plausible. Why should labour productivity ratios, for instance, be a good approximation to relative prices before trade but cease to be so after trade? This asymmetry seems to have no rationale. In any case, the particular chain of reasoning used in the text, aside from being more plausible, is also the one generally subscribed to; and hence its implications have been fully spelled out.

tantamount to investigating three hypotheses: $\frac{a_i^{\text{II}}}{a_i^{\text{I}}}$ is positively correlated with

$$\frac{E_i^{\text{I}}}{E_i^{\text{II}}}, \quad (i = 1, \ldots k); \quad . \quad . \quad . \quad . \quad (3)$$

if

$$\frac{a_i^{\text{II}}}{a_i^{\text{I}}} \cdot \frac{w_i^{\text{II}}}{w_i^{\text{I}}} > 1,$$

then

$$\frac{E_i^{\text{I}}}{E_i^{\text{II}}} > 1, \quad (i = 1, \ldots k): \quad . \quad (4)$$

and $\frac{a_i^{\text{II}}}{a_i^{\text{I}}} \cdot \frac{w_i^{\text{II}}}{w_i^{\text{I}}}$ is positively correlated with

$$\frac{E_i^{\text{I}}}{E_i^{\text{II}}}, \quad (i = 1, \ldots k) \quad . \quad . \quad . \quad . \quad (5)$$

where $E_i^{\text{I}}/E^{\text{II}}_i$ is the ratio of exports of commodity i by countries I and II respectively to third markets.[1] Stern has recently followed MacDougall's hypotheses and procedures closely, but introduced more recent data on productivity. MacDougall [30] has done the same. Balassa has tested hypothesis (3), using again the same new data on productivity, but does not consider hypothesis (4) and approaches hypothesis (5) differently, through multiple-correlatoin analysis.

Now, each of these three hypotheses has two main elements: (*a*) the adequacy of labour productivity (or unit labour-cost) ratios as an approximation to price ratios; and (*b*) the relation of price ratios (between prices of similar commodities exported to third markets by the United States and the United Kingdom) to quantity-ratios (of United States and United Kingdom exports of similar commodities).

It is easy to recognize the former as a proposition borrowed from the Ricardian analysis. The latter proposition, however, represents a departure from the Ricardian price–trade assumption. The assumption that the relative prices of exported goods will be lower than those of imported goods is now replaced by the postulation of some relationship between (United States–United Kingdom) price ratios of third-market exports and (United States–United Kingdom) shares in third markets. In hypotheses (3) and (5), for instance, the relationship takes the form of a negative correlation between the relative export prices

[1] Hypothesis (3) is clearly inspired by Ricardian hypothesis (1) and hypotheses (4) and (5) by Ricardian hypothesis (2). It should be made clear here that MacDougall's papers contain much *other* analysis of considerable interest and that the papers neither are confined to testing the hypotheses listed here nor approach those questions in the same formal manner as set out here.

and shares; in hypothesis (4) the form is shifted: a country's exports are postulated to be greater when its price is relatively cheaper than its rival's, but nothing is stated about the effects of different degrees of relative price advantage on export shares.

Neither of the hypothesized price–trade relationships, however, seems to be plausible. It is difficult to see, for instance, the theoretical reason why the ratio of two rivals' third-market exports should, in a cross-section analysis, turn out to increase as the corresponding price ratio falls. The argument that relative prices of similar commodities and their relative sales can be correlated in *cross-section analysis* cannot be justified on the presumption that, for *any given industry*, a reduction in the relative price of a competitor will increase its relative sales. It is difficult to imagine that this presumption can be extended to cross-section data where different commodities will have varying 'elasticities of substitution', depending on different degrees of product differentiation, quality differences, etc., as between different sources of origin (the United States and the United Kingdom in the present example).[1]

Despite these difficulties with the hypotheses (3), (4) and (5), the empirical verification is remarkably successful.[2] And yet, as already

[1] This is perhaps what Caves [3, p. 269] also is hinting at in his critique of the MacDougall papers.

[2] If one examines the evidence MacDougall [28, pp. 715–17] has produced one is astonished at the empirical support which is turned up for this hypothesis. For United States: United Kingdom export shares and price ratios, MacDougall produces supporting evidence, with twenty-three regressions and correlations, from 1913 to 1948; the lowest two correlation coefficients are −0·73. Fairly high correlation coefficients, with nicely negative regression slopes, are turned up, moreover, for United States : United Kingdom, United States : Japan, United States : Germany, United States : France, United Kingdom : France, France : Japan, France : Germany, United Kingdom : Japan and United Kingdom : Germany. As for the evidence on hypotheses (3), (4) and (5) themselves, the results can be systematized as follows:

I. *Hypothesis (3)*. The results of MacDougall, Stern and Balassa can be stated briefly (*see table on opposite page*).

[a] x and y refer to the logarithms of the United States : United Kingdom export ratio and United States : United Kingdom labour productivity ratio respectively. x^* and y^* in the last regression refer to the ratios themselves. MacDougall does not state his 1937 regression equation.

[b] The productivity data refer to 1950 and the source is the same as that used by MacDougall and Stern. However, the export data refer to values instead of quantities and are for 1951 instead of 1950. For the latter, the reason is that 1950 was an 'abnormal' year. For the former, the reason is that it is very tricky to

Author		Sample	Year	Regression equation[a]	Correlation coefficient
MacDougall	(1)	25 industries	1937	Regression slope = − 4	−0·70
	(2)	39 "	1950	$x = -2{\cdot}19 + 1{\cdot}89y$	0·61
Stern	(3)	24 (= MacDougall 1937 sample)	1950	$x = 0{\cdot}98 + 1{\cdot}65y$ (0·57)	0·52
	(4)	39 industries	1950	$x = -0{\cdot}68 + 1{\cdot}27y$ (0·43)	0·44
	(5)	25 "	1950	$x = 0{\cdot}91 + 1{\cdot}49y$ (0·59)	0·46
Balassa[b]	(6)	28 "	1950 and	$x = -1{\cdot}761 + 1{\cdot}594y$ (0·181)	0·86
	(7)	28 "	1951	$x^{*} = -53{\cdot}32 + 0{\cdot}721y^{*}$ (0·103)	0·80

separate export prices and quantities. Balassa prefers to work with values and justifies this choice on the ground that, with the estimates of elasticity of substitution being high in general, a positive correlation between productivity and export quantities will exist, so that the tests proposed are not vitiated. This argument, however, rests on the estimates of high elasticities of substitution – which, in turn, are based upon the very same separation of prices and quantities which Balassa is shying away from.

The results, on the whole, seem clearly to support the stated hypothesis mildly.

II. *Hypothesis (4)*. Here only MacDougall and Stern have produced evidence. Two different approaches can be distinguished. (1) One is to examine the industries directly and see how many conform to the pattern laid down by the hypothesis. (*a*) Using only the *average* wage levels for the United States and the United Kingdom (instead of individual industry wages), MacDougall found for 1937 that 'where American output for worker was more than twice the British, the United States had in general the bulk of the export market, while for products where it was less than twice as high the bulk of the market was held by Britain' [28, p. 698], while the average American wage was twice as high as the British wage. Thus, out of 25 industries investigated, 20 conformed and 2 more would have if the measure of productivity were suitably adjusted. (*b*) Stern, with the average American wage 3·4 times the British wage in 1950, found that from 24 industries (comparable to MacDougall's 25), 20 conformed to the expected pattern. (*c*) For the larger sample of 39 industries, the exceptions were only 5. These three strikingly favourable results were obtained when the *average* American and British wages were taken. Both MacDougall and Stern, however, attempted to analyse the effect of taking individual wages for different products as well. (*d*) Owing to data limitations, MacDougall could attempt this only for 13 industries. His results showed a slight improvement: cigarettes became an exception, whereas pig-iron, glass containers and hosiery held the line. (*e*) Stern, using the same sample, found a slight deterioration, although the expected pattern still continued.

(2) The other approach to examining hypothesis (4) is through statistical estimation procedures. Both MacDougall and Stern have estimated regression

equations for logarithms of labour productivity ratios and export ratios, already listed earlier here. These are used to estimate the validity of hypothesis (4). (*a*) For instance, MacDougall found that his regression line, fitted to the 1937 data plotted on a double logarithmic scale, passed through the horizontal dividing line of 2 (i.e. American output per worker twice the British) at a point considerably to the left of a vertical dividing line at unity, marking the point of equality in the two countries' exports. This implied that America tended to export only about *two-fifths* as much as Britain in 1937, when the American advantage in output per worker was exactly offset by the inferiority in advantage in average wage. (*b*) For the same sample of industries, Stern found in 1950 that America tended to export only about four-fifths as much as Britain when American output per worker and average wage-rates were 3·4 times higher. This clearly came closer to hypothesis (4). (*c*) For 39 industries, Stern's regression line passed almost exactly through the 3·4 point, appearing to verify hypothesis (4) totally. All these estimates are for data using *average* wage-rates. While this approach, on the whole and especially for 1950, appears to support hypothesis (4), it must be admitted that it represents an inadequate test from the viewpoint of hypothesis (4) itself: even though all observations conform to the postulated pattern, the estimated regression may register a deviation (from the point of intersection of the dividing lines); whereas the regression line may pass exactly through the point of intersection while the observed points deviate from the postulated pattern.

III. *Hypothesis* (5). This hypothesis, relating unit labour cost ratios and export shares, has been tested directly only by Stern and, with a different formulation, by Balassa. (*a*) For *average* wage data, of course, the regression and correlation coefficients for the estimated regression equations in the labour productivity hypothesis (3) should hold again, because all that happens is that the productivity ratios get each multiplied by a scalar (equal to the wage ratio). The results derived earlier, therefore, hold. (*b*) Stern, however, has produced the regression equation

$$x = 0{\cdot}01 - \underset{(0\cdot 38)}{1{\cdot}40}y, \; r = -0{\cdot}43$$

(where y is the logarithm of unit costs ratio), which lends some, though not very strong, support to the hypothesis being tested. (*c*) Balassa approaches the problem in terms of the question whether the introduction of the wage ratios as an *additional* explanatory variable (in a multiple correlation analysis) improves the explanation of export shares. Balassa's regression equation is

$$x^* = -181{\cdot}2 + \underset{(0\cdot 167)}{0{\cdot}691}y^* + \underset{(0\cdot 102)}{0{\cdot}140}z^*$$

where x^* is the export ratio, y^* the productivity ratio and z^* the wage ratio. The multiple correlation coefficient is 0·81 (as against 0·80 in the simple correlation). The partial coefficients are 0·77 (for x^* and y^*) and 0·24 (for x^* and z^*); the latter is not significant at the 5% level. For logarithms, Balassa's regression equation is:

$$x = -5{\cdot}164 + \underset{(0\cdot 328)}{1{\cdot}457}y + \underset{(0\cdot 566)}{1{\cdot}250}z$$

The multiple correlation coefficient is 0·88 (as against the simple coefficient of 0·86). The partials are 0·84 (x and y) and 0·11 (x and z); the latter is not significant at the 5% level. The explanation which comparative labour productivities argued, this has little to do with the empirical verification of the Ricardian hypotheses (1) and (2). While this is true, the authors of these empirical exercises have turned up a great deal of data on export prices and on labour productivities and unit wage-costs. These data can be used to examine the proposition that relative prices can be approximated by comparative labour productivities and/or unit wage–cost ratios. This can only result in the verification (or refutation, as it turns out) of the prop on which the Ricardian hypotheses (1) and (2) are generally rested. A full-blooded test of these hypotheses, directly examining the ranking of (bilateral) exports and imports by comparative labour productivities and/or unit wage–cost ratios, is

TABLE 1 *Labour Productivity Ratios and Export Price Ratios (United States/United Kingdom) for 1937 and 1950*

Industry	1937		1950	
	Output per worker, US/UK	Price of exports, US/UK	Output per worker, US/UK	Price of exports, US/UK
1 Tin cans	5·25	0·68	—	—
2 Pig iron	3·60	0·84	4·10	1·33
3 Wireless sets	3·50	0·64	4·00	0·95
4 Motor cars	3·10	0·91	2·40	2·63
5 Glass containers	2·40	0·69	—	—
6 Paper	2·20	0·72	3·40	0·90
7 Beer	2·00	1·30	3·00	1·00
8 Linoleum and oil cloth	1·90	1·04	2·60	1·11
9 Coke	1·90	1·08	1·90	1·36
10 Hosiery	1·80	1·24	—	—
11 Cigarettes	1·70	1·08	2·50	1·08
12 Rayon weaving and making	1·50	1·19	—	—
13 Cotton spinning and weaving	1·50	1·03	—	—
14 Leather footwear	1·40	1·31	1·70	1·28
15 Woollen and worsted	1·35	1·42	1·80	1·44
16 Margarine	1·20	1·34	1·80	1·46
17 Cement	1·10	2·12	1·20	1·33
18 Electric lamps	5·40	0·51	3·60	0·92
19 Biscuits	3·10	1·01	2·40	1·24
20 Matches	3·10	0·86	—	—
21 Rubber tyres	2·70	1·12	2·40	1·42
22 Soap	2·70	1·24	2·50	1·10

Source: Stern [40, p. 278].

provide is not improved by adding wage ratios as an additional explanatory variable. (It follows, therefore, that wage-structure differences between ratios do not have any systematic relationship with price differences.)

impossible to carry out with this information and must await further research.

For the limited test outlined here, I have used two sets of data. For the MacDougall sample of 25 industries (reduced to 24 in Stern's calculations for 1950), the necessary data are available for 22 industries for 1937 and for 16 of these for 1950 (Table 1). There is a slightly larger and different sample of 25 industries, used by Stern for 1950 (Table 2). There are certainly many limitations to these data. The most serious ones, from the viewpoint of the current analysis, are three: (i) the f.o.b. price reflects gross value, whereas the labour

TABLE 2 *Labour Productivity Ratios, Export Price Ratios, Unit Labour Cost Ratios and Wage Ratios (United States/United Kingdom) for 1950*

	Export prices, US/UK	Output per worker, US/UK	Unit labour costs, US/UK	Wage-rates US/UK
1 Cement	1·33	1·16	2·33	2·70
2 Sugar factories and refineries	1·32	1·48	1·89	2·79
3 Tanneries	1·01	1·68	1·92	3·23
4 Footwear (except rubber)	1·28	1·71	1·68	2·88
5 Woollen and worsted	1·33	1·85	1·96	3·63
6 Metal-working machinery	2·64	2·21	1·79	3·96
7 Rayon, nylon and silk	1·15	2·26	1·51	3·42
8 Generators, motors and transformers	2·63	2·39	1·49	3·56
9 Tyres and tubes	1·23	2·41	1·50	3·62
10 Wirework	1·28	2·44	1·52	3·72
11 Soap, candles and glycerine	1·18	2·49	1·58	3·93
12 Rubber products (excluding tyres and footwear)	1·31	2·50	1·45	3·62
13 Tobacco manufactures	1·08	2·51	1·02	2·56
14 Linoleum and leather cloth	1·11	2·56	1·27	3·25
15 Bolts, nuts, rivets and screws	2·06	2·56	1·71	4·31
14 Breweries and manufacturing of malt	1·00	3·00	1·33	3·99
17 Pulp, paper and board	0·90	3·38	1·08	3·65
18 Electronic tubes	0·68	3·55	1·10	3·91
19 Electric-light bulbs	0·92	3·56	1·10	3·92
20 Paint and varnish	0·09	3·63	0·96	3·50
21 Basic industrial chemicals	0·95	3·72	0·91	3·38
22 Radio	0·95	4·00	0·85	3·39
23 Blast furnaces	1·33	4·08	0·72	2·96
24 Electrical household equipment	1·70	4·12	0·96	3·95
25 Containers, paper and card	1·12	4·28	0·96	4·09

Source: Stern [408]., p. 28

productivity refers to the final, value-adding industry; the results would surely be more in conformity with the spirit of the Ricardian approach if the *indirect* labour productivities were also computed; (ii) the f.o.b. prices also include transport and other costs which add to the ex-factory price, whereas the labour productivity figures are not adjusted for this when necessary; and (iii) in most exporting industries a differential is observable between the average domestic price and the average foreign price [3, p. 281], so that the approximation of labour productivity ratios to relative (export) prices may have to be adjusted analytically for this phenomenon. Notwithstanding these limitations, however, I have carried out the analysis in consonance with the tradition of economists to catalogue the difficulties and thereafter to ignore them. The results, as already hinted at, are seriously prejudicial to the usefulness of the Ricardian approach: though, it should be emphasized, the verdict cannot be final in the absence of better and fuller tests.[1]

The linear regressions of export price ratios on labour productivity ratios are almost entirely hopeless, whether we take logarithms or not. The six regressions, listed in Table 3, uniformly fail to be significant except for the unlogged, MacDougall sample for 1937. The failures clearly overwhelm the success in verification.

Testing the relationship between comparative unit labour-costs and export price ratios, we find the results to be equally disappointing.

TABLE 3 *Relationship between Labour Productivity Ratios and Export Price Ratios*

Data	Regression equation*	Coefficients
1937 (Table 1)	$Y = 1{\cdot}72 \quad - 0{\cdot}211X$ $(0{\cdot}2291) \quad (0{\cdot}0450)$	$r^2 = 0{\cdot}525$ $r = -0{\cdot}724$
1937 (Table 1)	$\log Y = 0{\cdot}252 \quad - 0{\cdot}525 \log X$ $(0{\cdot}1925) \quad (0{\cdot}432)$	$r^2 = 0{\cdot}0686$ $r = -0{\cdot}262$
1950 (Table 1)	$Y = 1{\cdot}58 \quad - 0{\cdot}169\ X$ $(0{\cdot}32605) \quad (0{\cdot}1204)$	$r^2 = 0{\cdot}129$ $r = -0{\cdot}359$
1950 (Table 1)	$\log Y = 0{\cdot}264 \quad - 0{\cdot}611 \log X$ $(0{\cdot}3769) \quad (0{\cdot}5155)$	$r^2 = 0{\cdot}0912$ $r = -0{\cdot}302$
1950 (Table 2)	$Y = 1{\cdot}7044 \quad - 0{\cdot}1470X$ $(0{\cdot}3291) \quad (0{\cdot}1095)$	$r^2 = 0{\cdot}0728$ $r = -0{\cdot}2698$
1950 (Table 2)	$\log Y = 0{\cdot}2056 \quad - 0{\cdot}2773 \log X$ $(0{\cdot}0816) \quad (0{\cdot}1831)$	$r^2 = 0{\cdot}0906$ $r = -0{\cdot}301$

* Y = Export price ratio, and X = Labour productivity ratio.

[1] I am indebted to B. S. Minhas for assistance with the statistical analysis in this paper. The responsibility for any errors, however, is entirely mine.

Table 4 lists the two linear regression equations for the 1950 data (Table 2). Both relationships are insignificant (though they register a negligible improvement over the regressions for export price-ratios and labour productivity ratios alone).

TABLE 4 *Relationship between Unit Labour Cost Ratios and Export Price Ratios*

Data	Regression Equations*	Coefficients
1950 (Table 2)	$Y = 0{\cdot}7227 + 0{\cdot}4141X$ $(0{\cdot}33194) \quad (0{\cdot}23021)$	$r^2 = 0{\cdot}1233$ $r = 0{\cdot}3512$
1950 (Table 2)	$\log Y = 0{\cdot}03785 + 0{\cdot}42113 \log X$ $(0{\cdot}0335) \quad (0{\cdot}1997)$	$r^2 = 0{\cdot}162$ $= 0{\cdot}40248$

* Y = export price ratio, and X = unit labour cost ratio.

Handling the influence of relative inter-country wage-rates alternatively through the introduction of wage ratios as an additional explanatory variable in a multiple correlation analysis, further, we find that the results for the available data are again poor (Table 5). The correlations continue to be insignificant (though they register a slight improvement over the simple correlation, for the same data, between export price ratios and labour productivity ratios alone).

TABLE 5 *Multiple Regressions between Export Price Ratios, Labour Productivity Ratios and Wage Ratios*

Data	Multiple regression equation*	Coefficients
1950 (Table 2)	$Y = 0{\cdot}5572 - 0{\cdot}2286\, X_1 + 0{\cdot}3905\, X_2$ $(7{\cdot}8) \quad (0{\cdot}1140) \quad (0{\cdot}2182)$	$r^2 = 0{\cdot}191$ $r = 0{\cdot}437$ Partial: $X_1 = -0{\cdot}3931$ $X_2 = 0{\cdot}3564$
1950 (Table 2)	$\log Y = 0{\cdot}1646 - 0{\cdot}4304 \log X_1 + 0{\cdot}8011 \log X_2$ $(0{\cdot}0599) \quad (0{\cdot}2015) \quad (0{\cdot}5018)$	$r^2 = 0{\cdot}1850$ $r = 0{\cdot}4301$ Partial: $X_1 = -0{\cdot}4143$ $X_2 = 0{\cdot}3220$

* Y = export price ratio; X_1 = labour productivity ratio, and X_2 = wage-rate ratio.

These results, limited as they are, cast sufficient doubt on the usefulness of the Ricardian approach (as generally understood). Contrary, therefore, to the general impression (based on the MacDougall, Balassa and Stern results), there is as yet no evidence in favour of the Ricardian hypotheses. This is perhaps not as unfortunate as it seems. For ultimately the practical utility of the Ricardian hypotheses is somewhat limited. Labour productivity, after all, is not a datum in the sense that production functions are. The reliance of the prediction on labour productivity unaccompanied by any explanation of why the labour productivity is what it is, and how therefore it may be expected to change, restricts the utility of the prediction. Moreover, even if we could forecast changes in labour productivity, we could not tell exclusively therefrom that the pattern of imports and exports would change in a specified manner; all we could say is that, if the pattern of exports and imports changes in any way, the new pattern will also be characterized by the postulated Ricardian ranking in terms of comparative labour productivities and/or unit wage ratios.[1]

The Heckscher–Ohlin Theory

An alternative approach to explaining the pattern of trade is attributed to the works of Heckscher [19] and Ohlin [34], but owes much to the work of Samuelson [38, 91]. Indeed, in its current form it has discarded so many of the variables which Ohlin explicitly listed as significant that it is almost certainly liable to be rejected by Ohlin as an adequate version of his original analysis!

This approach breaks away from the Ricardian model and works in terms of an analytical framework which is in striking contrast to its predecessor. As we saw, the Ricardian model assumes one factor, and therewith (through the supporting assumption of constant returns to scale) makes the factor supply irrelevant in determining the trade pattern;[2] on the other hand, as we shall soon see, the Heckscher–Ohlin model assumes two factors and makes international differences in factor endowments the crucial and sole factor determining comparative advantage.[3] Moreover, whereas the former attributes to

[1] I would not claim that *any* type of prediction concerning change in the pattern of trade is impossible. But even apparently simple predictions are not possible. For instance, if labour productivity increases in an export industry we *cannot* necessarily predict that the industry will continue to export its product (even if all other autonomous change in the trading countries is ruled out).

[2] This is, strictly speaking, not true in a model with more than two commodities. In this case demand must be brought in to 'break the chain' of ranked commodities into exports and imports. But demand itself will be a function of the level of income, which will depend, among other things, on the factor supply.

[3] Viner [44] has attempted to demonstrate that the factor endowment approach is to be found in classical writings. But his contention is not persuasive, based as it is on fragmentary remarks which do not add up to systematic analysis.

international differences in production functions the explanation of comparative advantage, the latter explicitly postulates the international identity of production functions.[1] The Heckscher–Ohlin theory is also different from the Ricardian analysis in having been presented *explicitly* as a contribution to the 'positive' theory, as an attempt at explaining the structure of foreign trade, rather than with a view to establishing the welfare propositions of trade theory.

The Heckscher–Ohlin theorem states that *a country's exports use intensively the country's abundant factor*. This is an eminently 'plausible-looking' proposition. One would expect that a country should be able to produce more cheaply those goods that are intensive in the use of a factor when that factor of production is (physically) abundant in the country relative to its trading partner. Of course one can think of some exceptions immediately. For instance, it is clear that this presumption rests on the similarity of production conditions between trading countries. There could obviously be a contradiction of the Heckscher–Ohlin proposition if *production functions* for individual industries were different between countries. Alternatively, the country may quite well have an offsetting preference for the *consumption* of these commodities – so that the pre-trade (relative) prices of commodities may turn out to be higher (rather than lower) abroad – thus refuting the Heckscher–Ohlin proposition. Some qualifications are less intuitively seen. One of the theoretically interesting qualifications[2] follows from the fact that although, technologically, the production function for an activity may be identical between countries, the operative segments of it may be intensive in the use of a different factor in each country. Where such 'reversals of factor-intensity' can

[1] It should be emphasized that these contrasts, which are based partly on the distinction between production functions and factors of production, raise the well-known question as to the proper definitions of these two concepts. It is interesting, in this connection, to recall that Ohlin appears to have taken it as apparent that production functions would be the same everywhere, because the same causes everywhere (and at any time) produce the same effects. However, as Haberler [4, p. 19] has pointed out, 'if the concept of the production function is to be a useful tool of analysis, it cannot be identified with, or derived from, such unverifiable metaphysical propositions as "the constancy of the laws of nature". By hypothesizing every conceivable circumstance which may affect output as a separate factor, the production function can, no doubt, be endowed with constancy, invariability, homogeneity, and what not, but at the price of emptying the theory of all empirical content and reducing it to a useless tautological system.'

[2] It is also empirically possible, as Minhas' [33] study shows.

occur the effect can be similar to that of differences in production functions and the Heckscher–Ohlin proposition need not hold.

Theorists have established a set of conditions which ensure the 'logical truth' of the Heckscher–Ohlin theorem. These conditions differ, depending on the definition of 'factor abundance'. It is possible to choose between two definitions: the physical and the price definitions. Under the former, country I is abundant in factor x and country II in factor y when $(X/Y)^{I} > (X/Y)^{II}$, where X and Y refer to the quantities of factors x and y respectively and the superscripts to the countries.[1] Under the latter, the countries are similarly described when $(Rx/Ry)^{I} < (Rx/Ry)^{II}$ *prior to trade* where Rx and Ry refer to the rentals on factors x and y respectively.

When the physical definition is used the set of sufficient conditions for the logical truth of the Heckscher–Ohlin proposition is: (1) international identity of production functions; (2) non-reversibility of factor-intensities, such that a given commodity is factor x-intensive in relation to another at *all* relevant factor price-ratios; (3) constant returns to scale and diminishing returns (along isoquants) in each production function; and (4) identity of the consumption pattern between countries at each relevant commodity price ratio.[2] Samuelson [38, 39] has established that, under perfect competition and profit maximization in perfect markets, condition (3) will suffice to generate a strictly convex production possibility curve, characterized by a unique relationship between factor and commodity price ratios (except at positions of complete specialization in production). Using

[1] The physical definition raises serious conceptual difficulties when applied to the factor 'capital'. As is obvious, it is impossible to collapse different varieties of capital equipment into a single index of 'capital' in the same way as we reduce labour to man-hours. Of course, even with labour, the element of 'human capital' raises equally knotty issues.

[2] Identity of tastes, i.e. the aggregate preference map, is not adequate, since two countries may be at different levels of income and hence at different positions on their preference maps. Unless, therefore, the maps have homothetic isoquants the result can be different consumption patterns at identical price ratios. For a disaggregated economy, with many individuals, the conditions which give rise to such aggregate identity of tastes are quite restrictive [66, 67]. It is also necessary, of course, that transport costs for individual commodities are not such as would shatter this chain of comparative advantage when the c.i.f. prices are considered (as they have to be from the viewpoint of the determination of the trade pattern). The trade theorists generally disregard transport costs; the omission of 'distance' as a factor in most trade models represents a serious deficiency which vitiates the utility of many conclusions.

these propositions, it is possible to demonstrate in a two-commodity system that where two countries, with identical production functions for each activity (condition 1) and non-reversible factor intensities (condition 2) have different capital: labour ratios in the aggregate, the capital-abundant country will have a higher ratio of capital-intensive: labour-intensive outputs at *each* commodity price ratio. When condition (4) is added to this result it follows that the pre-trade commodity price ratios will be such that the capital-intensive commodity will be cheaper in the capital-abundant country. Hence the Heckscher–Ohlin theorem will be logically true. This result is valid for a multi-commodity model as well:[1] as Jones [20] has demonstrated, commodities can still be ranked, from technological and factor-supply data, in terms of factor ratios, and are thereby uniquely ranked also in terms of comparative advantage, with demand being introduced (as in the Ricardian system) to 'break the chain' into exports and imports.

When the price definition of factor abundance is chosen we can dispense with the condition of identity of consumption patterns. This is because, when the other assumptions are made, a country which is capital-abundant will, by virtue of the unique Samuelsonian relationship between commodity and factor price ratios, necessarily have cheaper capital-intensive output. The use of the price definition, while it has this advantage over the physical definition, correspondingly leaves less scope for 'explanation'.[2]

Where the theory is deficient is in its not having been extended to a multi-country, multi-commodity framework. The prediction holds when there are many commodities and two countries. However, when there are many countries and commodities it is not clear, in the absence of theoretical analysis, what conditions will suffice to make the Heckscher–Ohlin hypothesis true – in any of the several alternative versions that are possible in a multi-country framework: (1) the comparison of factor endowments may be between country I and the sum of *all* the other countries of the world; or (2) it may be between country I and the *sum* of *all* the countries directly in trade with it; or

[1] The definitions of 'factor abundance' and 'factor-intensity' in a multi-factor model, however, are not so intuitive; but one can always adopt a convention [35, 53]. The results, however, are both more restrictive and less intuitive.

[2] Lancaster has proposed inadvertently a third definition which states that a country is abundant in that factor which is used intensively in the exportable industry [14]. From the viewpoint of the Heckscher-Ohlin theory, this is totally tautologous and leaves *no* scope for 'explanation'.

(3) between country I and the sum of *all* the countries directly or indirectly in trade with it; or (4) between country I and *each* of the countries in direct trade with it, so that the Heckscher–Ohlin hypotheses would hold for *each* pair of countries (*bilaterally*). There is little in the traditional analysis of the Heckscher–Ohlin hypotheses which affords a reliable clue to a meaningful choice among these different ways in which a Heckscher–Ohlin hypothesis can be interpreted in a multi-country framework. Nor need we expect the conditions under which each of these hypotheses will be logically true to be identical either with each other *or* with those that have been spelled out for the restrictive traditional frameworks.[1] This amounts to a deficiency in the literature (especially from the viewpoint of empirical testing, since the real world unfortunately constitutes a multi-country, multi-commodity international economy).

Empirical testing of the Heckscher–Ohlin hypotheses has indeed been attempted in the literature, starting with Leontief's pioneer attempt at ascertaining the factor-intensities of the average exports and competitive imports in the United States [25]. It is typical of his and other contributions that, while factor-intensities are carefully ascertained, the factor-abundance of the country in question is usually left uninvestigated, except tangentially and vaguely. The result has been a failure to face up to the question raised by multi-country, multi-commodity analysis: how is factor-abundance to be interpreted? By *implication*, Leontief [25, pp. 386, 399] seems to favour the

[1] For instance, it is clear that if country I is K-abundant in relation to country II and L-abundant in relation to country III, and the Heckscher–Ohlin hypothesis holds for each pair of countries (say, I and II, II and III), then it is *impossible* that the export and import commodities of country I can be ranked in terms of K : L ratios such that all exports are K-intensive in relation to all imports. The export and import commodities inevitably criss-cross, fouling up the strictly ordered chain on which the traditional Heckscher–Ohlin hypothesis and proof depend. However, if this chain cannot criss-cross under the usual assumptions, as Jones has demonstrated, we have a contradiction *in terms of the traditional model* and apparently the pattern of international specialization in production and in trade will necessarily have to turn out such that the bilateral formulation of the Heckscher–Ohlin hypothesis holds in a multi-country world. Of course, what I have argued here is not intended to be a proof, in the strict sense, of an extension of the Heckscher–Ohlin hypothesis to the bilateral, multi-country formulation within the fold of traditional postulates concerning technology, etc. The point I am making is really that the analysis of the Heckscher–Ohlin variety of hypotheses, in any or all of their possible versions in a multi-country framework, is not yet available and represents a serious lacuna in the literature.

bilateral interpretation: 'A comprehensive, two-sided explanation of our economic relationships with the rest-of-the-world will not, of course, be possible before the internal economic structure of at least one of the most important of our trading partners has been studied as fully as that of our own'. Recent studies by Bharadwaj [16] for India, Tatemoto and Ichimura [42] for Japan and Wahl [45] for Canada have also implicitly adopted the bilateral interpretation by considering, in addition to the factor intensities of the average *aggregate* exports and competitive imports (which necessitates viewing the country's factor-abundance in a non-bilateral way), the factor-intensities of the average exports to and competitive imports from *specific* trading countries or regions.[1]

While Leontief [25], and nearly all of his many followers, have left this crucial aspect unsatisfactory, Leontief's attempted test has been of significance – for the perverse reason that it turned up the startling result that the United States exports are labour-intensive and its competitive imports capital-intensive.[2] Since the United States may be conceded to be capital abundant by any definition, this result did seem to contradict the Heckscher–Ohlin hypothesis – provided the statistical information and procedure could be accepted. There *were* objections on statistical grounds. For instance, the agricultural capital–output ratio was considered unreliable [18], but recomputation under different assumptions did not reverse the findings. Balogh [12] voiced compelling doubts concerning the implications of aggregation in the input–output matrix (used to compute indirect capital–labour ratios). Thus, the labour-intensity of the American export industries might be spurious and attributable to the aggregation of capital-intensive exportable products with 'similar', non-export, labour-intensive activities. No evidence was produced to support this objection [1]: yet, it leaves a degree of doubt.

While Leontief's exercise spurred the majority of the theorists on to a re-examination of the sufficient conditions for the Heckscher–Ohlin hypothesis [20, 36, 37], the plausibility of the Heckscher–Ohlin

[1] In each of these instances, however, there is no discussion either of the alternative ways in which the Heckscher–Ohlin hypothesis can be interpreted or of the theoretical implication of the specific (bilateral) form of the hypothesis that is chosen or suggested.

[2] The tests have uniformly used the two factors, capital and labour. This choice, as also the definition of capital, is necessarily arbitrary. This arbitrariness is inevitable, and its justification lies in the argument that the theory being tested represents an abstraction.

propositions is so powerful that some ingenuity was addressed to the task of rescuing it from the refutation that had emerged from Leontief's exercises (Leontief himself being one of this small group of analysts).[1] This task is not entirely hopeless, since, although Leontief's results may be accepted, it is possible for the economist, *not* to change the form of the hypothesis, but to retain this form while redefining the concepts used. This is a perfectly valid, scientific procedure: the hypothesis, with redefined concepts, can once again be subjected to empirical verification [1]. This is precisely what may be done with the Heckscher–Ohlin hypothesis, in the expectation that Leontief's United States results may be reversed.

There are many ways in which this can be done. For instance, one could argue that the factor-abundance comparison should refer to the quantities of factors employed in the traded-goods sector, since the original formulation of the Heckscher–Ohlin theorem is logically deduced in a framework assuming no non-traded goods [1]. Or it could be argued that, since the traded-goods sector in some countries represents merely a geographical extension of a country's activities, these sectors being really foreign enclaves based on foreign capital

[1] Leontief also produced subsequently another paper [26] which reworked the calculations in the light of criticism addressed to his original work. For instance, instead of the inversion of only a 50-sector matrix earlier, he inverted a 192-sector matrix. Adjustments were carried out concerning agricultral data. None of this, however, reversed the findings concerning the refutation of the (unadjusted) Heckscher–Ohlin hypothesis. Leontief also went into some theoretical issues, such as the examination of a linear, input–output model for international trade. This has unfortunately been responsible for some confusion concerning the limitations of the empirical verification of the Heckscher–Ohlin hypothesis itself. For instance, Valavanis-Vail [3, p. 279] has objected to Leontief's exercise on the ground that 'input–output models (except with rare luck) are logically incompatible with international trade'. Whatever the analytical support for (any interpretation of) this statement, it is really irrelevant to the objective of Leontief's exercise and the methods used by him to achieve it. The input–output table is used by Leontief (along with the labour and capital coefficients matrices) merely to *compute* the indirect capital and labour requirements for unit exports and imports. The assumptions of input–output *analysis* are *not* necessary. Although Leontief loosely talks of 'reducing' exports by a million dollars and seeing what capital and labour are 'released' thereby, this is *not* what is actually required. All that is necessary, and this is really how Leontief's exercise should be construed, is to compute the total capital and labour requirements of the *current* (level and composition of) exports. And this can be done by a purely 'notional reduction' of (a representative bundle of) exports and the corresponding, computed notional 'release' of capital and labour.

and dominated by foreign economic considerations, it is sensible in such cases to merge these enclaves with the foreign country in question for obtaining the data for the Heckscher–Ohlin test [18].[1] The most interesting attempts, however, have centred around the fact that labour embodies (human) capital, and its implications for both factor-abundance and factor-intensity.

The easiest way of handling this has been to argue that the human capital element should be allowed for in the factor-intensity comparisons. For the United States, this seems to provide an important escape from the refutation of the Heckscher–Ohlin hypothesis. As many of the commentators have noted: (i) American export industries employ relatively more non-agricultural labour,[2] and agricultural labour is likely to be less educated and trained than non-agricultural labour [18]; and (ii) American export industries pay an average wage in excess of the national wage (suggesting that they intensively use skilled labour)[3] [21]. Thus, this computation of human capital (from an analysis of the labour inputs in the exporting and import-competing industries) added to the capital employed in measuring factor-intensities may quite possibly reverse the factor-intensity findings for the United States. However, we should also have to adjust correspondingly the measurement of factor endowments, adding the computed human capital to the measure of capital stock: a procedure which highlights the great conceptual difficulties that attend on both measuring capital meaningfully and comparing it between countries.

An alternative way in which the fact of labour efficiency differences between countries has been handled is by adjusting the labour supply

[1] It is not necessarily correct to use such an adaptation of the Heckscher-Ohlin hypothesis. For the latter, what is relevant is the *availability* of factors of production *regardless of their ownership*. It is only in the extreme case where the investment is accompanied by full, complementary migration of other necessary factors to a piece of foreign territory (which itself does not serve as a factor of production) that it would be proper, from the Heckscher–Ohlin viewpoint, to adopt this approach. Not otherwise.

[2] The breakdown of labour (for a million dollars of exports and import replacements) between agricultural and non-agricultural labour was given by Leontief [25] as follows:

	Exports	Import replacements
Agricultural labour, man years	22·436	40·394
Non-agricultural labour, man years	159·872	127·069

[3] An alternative explanation, of course, is that they are the 'dynamic' innovating industries, and hence pay higher wages.

itself by an efficiency factor.[1] Leontief [25, p. 26], in his original paper, argued that 'labour' should be defined in 'standard' units, after adjusting for varying degrees of efficiency. On this basis he asserted that the average American worker is three times as efficient as elsewhere and that 'spread thrice as thinly as the unadjusted figures suggest the American capital supply per 'equivalent worker' turns out to be comparatively smaller, rather than larger, than that of many other countries'.[2] Hence, the Heckscher–Ohlin theory could be rescued from an apparent refutation (on the implicit assumption that this efficiency factor concerning labour is not neutralized by a similar efficiency factor attributable to the other factor of production).

Leontief's procedure, however, is not valid, although his suggestion is valuable. He does not state how the efficiency factor of three was arrived at. Leontief's argument in support of the assumed efficiency factor of three is that if it were not so it would be impossible to 'explain the comparative surplus of labour which our figures unmistakably reveal' [25, p. 28]. This argument is unpersuasive because (as I have already argued elsewhere [1]) 'it already assumes that the Heckscher–Ohlin theorem provides a valid explanation of the American pattern of trade when, in fact, the question being asked is precisely whether it does'; and (2) 'it also assumes that only the hypothesis about threefold efficiency of American labour can reconcile the results with the Heckscher–Ohlin type hypothesis when, in fact, there *are* other ways in which such reconciliation could be attempted'. The most interesting analysis, which has a bearing on this issue, is by Minhas [33]. As noted earlier, Arrow, Chenery, Solow and he continuously found that for individual industries in different countries the only significant difference between the estimated homohypallagic (CES) production functions consisted of an overall efficiency term, which meant that whereas the isoquants continued to remain more or less the same, the scale factor changed. This means, as Minhas concluded [33, p. 159], that Leontief's requirement that the efficiency factor can be attributed

[1] This method adjusts the measurement of the labour input, whereas the earlier method alters the measurement of the capital stock.

[2] In the original paper [25] Leontief argued for this threefold efficiency, but did not make any differential adjustment for the efficiency factor in export- and import-competing industries. This implicit assumption of an identical efficiency factor for labour in both these sectors was removed by Leontief in his later exercise [26] by an explicit weighting of labour in each sector by its average wage.

to one factor *alone* is unsupported by his specific investigations.[1]

While these different ways in which the definitions of capital and labour have been adjusted, to explore the possibility of reconciling the United States pattern of trade with the Heckscher–Ohlin hypothesis, are of interest, perhaps the more significant innovations have emerged from the work of those who proceeded to apply Leontief's methods to the trade patterns of other countries. There have been four Leontief-type studies so far: Bharadwaj [15, 16] on India, Stolper and Roskamp [41] for East Germany, Tatemoto and Ichimura [42] for Japan and Wahl [45] for Canada. These have now given us a larger range of evidence with which to attempt an assessment of the Heckscher–Ohlin hypothesis. For Japan, exports are capital-intensive and imports are labour-intensive – on the surface again, a black mark against the tested hypothesis. For East Germany exports are capital-intensive and imports are labour-intensive – the authors find this consistent with the stated hypothesis, since the East German trade is three-quarters with the Communist block, where she is probably among the most industrialized of these nations. For Canada, exports are capital-intensive and imports are labour-intensive – presumably an unsuccessful verification, as Canadian trade is primarily United States-orientated.

Where many of these studies innovate is in departing from the Leontief method of taking the *aggregate* exports and competitive imports. They begin to explore the possibility of defining the Heckscher–

[1] Diab [18] also has attempted to test Leontief's conjecture, using Colin Clark's data. His results appear to sustain this conjecture. Diab's methods show that the United States has. in terms of 'standard' labour, a lower capital : labour ratio than Canada, Great Britain, Netherlands, France and Norway. The procedure by which this conclusion is reached, however, is arbitrary. Diab assumes that: (1) labour is the factor which has to be reduced to 'standard' units in each country; and (2) the Cobb–Douglas production function, identical for all countries studied, is known for national output, in terms of capital and 'standard' labour. With this production function, national output and capital known, it is then easy to determine the single unknown, 'standard' labour, with the one equation [1]. Diab postulates a hypothetical production function (with 'standard' labour), uses observed values of output and capital to deduce his 'standard' labour and then attributes the discrepancy between the quantities of 'standard' and observed labour to an 'efficiency' factor. This is surely an arbitrary procedure, which can yield no acceptable results. For instance, one could well use the procedure, assuming that capital, and not labour, is the factor which should be reduced to 'standard' units. Out of curiosity, I did this: the United States turned out to be overwhelmingly 'capital'-intensive [1]!

Ohlin hypothesis in the *bilateral* form[1] (*i.e.*, for each pair of countries) rather than in terms of one country and (presumably) the rest of the world. Thus, Bharadwaj [16] goes on from the aggregative analysis to work out the factor-intensities of Indian trade with the United States, Wahl works with Canada–United States and Canada–United Kingdom trade, and the Tatemoto–Ichimura result is interpreted in terms of the geographic composition of Japanese trade. In the Indian case, when the Indo–United States trade is isolated for analysis, the factor-intensities are the *reverse* of those that obtain for total Indian trade. The Indian exports to the United States turn out to be capital-intensive and imports from the United States are labour-intensive, thus appearing to refute the Heckscher–Ohlin hypothesis. For Canada, the results again are identical with the aggregate results and refutation continues. For Japan, however, the result of disaggregation is beneficial. In the Japanese case the aggregative result is supposed to be attributable to the fact that 75% of Japanese exports go to the (presumably labour-abundant) underdeveloped areas and only 25% to the (presumably capital-abundant) advanced countries. It is widely accepted in Japan that the Japanese economy is somewhere in the middle of the advanced and underdeveloped countries and the 'disaggregated' explanation is only a logical consequence. Tatemoto and Ichimura have computed the capital–labour ratios of Japanese exports to the United States and imports from the United States and find the latter higher than the former. Unlike the Indian case, therefore, a disaggregated approach *supports* the Heckscher–Ohlin approach in the Japanese study. The Japanese result thus demonstrates the possibility of profitably adapting the Heckscher–Ohlin hypothesis so as to state it in terms of *each pair of trading countries* (instead of in aggregate terms).

When these diverse bits of evidence and arguments are added up there is little doubt that an attitude of agnosticism is certain to be left in the reader's mind concerning Leontief's original refutation of the Heckscher–Ohlin theorem.[2] Meanwhile, the empirical verification is

[1] This bilateral formulation, it may be recalled, is only one of several formulations of the Heckscher–Ohlin hypothesis that we can have in a multi-country world.

[2] It is of interest to note that the Ricardian hypothesis (in terms of comparative labour productivities) may be verified and yet the result may equally be in conformity with the Heckscher–Ohlin hypothesis. Thus, for instance, a capital-abundant country I may be exporting capital-intensive commodity x to country II in exchange for commodity y. Then, if transport costs are introduced and the

progressing apace and evidence is accumulating on either side. The most interesting recent result has been Minhas' [33] demonstration that, far from being a theoretical curiosum (as Samuelson [38, 39] believed it to be), the reversal of factor-intensity is an empirical possibility of some significance. Since his data relate to the United States and Japan, the results appear to furnish additional ammunition to those who are sceptical of the utility of the Heckscher–Ohlin approach.[1]

The Kravis Theory

While the Ricardian and the Heckscher–Ohlin approaches have dominated the thinking on comparative advantage for many decades, recently some original theories have appeared in the field. Kravis [22], for instance, in the early period of gloom after Leontief's paper [25], argued that the commodity composition of trade is determined primarily by 'availability'. Trade tends to be confined to goods which

---

necessary technological assumptions which underlie the Heckscher–Ohlin theorem are made, the capital–labour ratio in x will be higher in country I than in country II and therefore the output–labour ratio in x will also be higher in I than II. Similarly, the output–labour ratio in y will be lower in I than in II. Therefore, *both* the Ricardian and the Heckscher–Ohlin hypotheses will be valid in this case. A similar example can also be produced for the more sophisticated Ricardian hypothesis stated in the text (involving comparisons of production functions). For instance, assume that the production function is identical for commodity y in both countries and that country I has 'neutral' advantage in producing commodity x such that the same capital and labour produce λ times more of x in I than in II. Assume x to be capital-intensive at all factor price ratios and I to be capital abundant. Then if the Heckscher–Ohlin thesis holds, so does the sophisticated Ricardian hypothesis automatically. Further, it follows that in free trade equilibrium (with zero transport costs), the capital–labour ratios in I will be lower in each activity than in II. Since constant returns to scale are being assumed, the labour productivity in both x and y would be lower in I than in II, except that the efficiency factor λ in the production of x in I would offset the fall in labour productivity due to lower capital–labour ratio. Assuming that this offset leaves the labour productivity in x greater in I than in II, the comparative labour productivity ratio in x will be greater for I than in y. Hence the Ricardian hypothesis will be sustained in its comparative labour productivity form as well.

[1] Minhas' demonstration of the possibility of factor-intensity reversals is quite serious, since it contradicts one of the premises on which the Heckscher–Ohlin hypothesis is traditionally based. In fact, the damage it does is fatal because, if factor-intensities *are* reversed between two trading countries, for exports and imports, it is logically *impossible* for *both* countries' trading patterns to pass the Heckscher–Ohlin test (though, of course, one will).

are 'not available at home' [22, p. 143]. By this phrase, Kravis intended to describe goods which are 'unavailable in the absolute sense (for example, diamonds)', and goods where 'an increase in output can be achieved only at much higher cost (that is, the domestic supply is inelastic)'. The reason for trade to be restricted to items characterized by such unavailability is that tariff policies, transport costs, cartelization, etc., tend to eliminate from trade those commodities which are available through domestic production, although at 'slightly' higher cost. The reasons cited for unavailability, as defined, are: lack of natural resources (relative to demand) or technical change and product differentiation which confer temporary monopoly of production on the innovating country (until the trading partners have learnt to imitate).

The theory appears attractive. However, it is noticeable that Kravis does not get down to stating precise, testable hypotheses. While he fails to do so, one can still derive several from his suggestive ideas. (1) For instance, one could seize on his idea of the 'inelasticity' of domestic supply and state the refutable proposition that *a country's imports will be characterized by domestic inelasticity of supply*. (Such an hypothesis would, naturally have to be backed by an explicit definition of 'inelasticity'.) (2) Another hypothesis, based also on the concept of inelasticity, might be that *a country's imports will be characterized by the excess of foreign over domestic elasticity of supply.*[1] Both these hypotheses, and related formulations, however, neither get down below the surface *qua* explanations nor are capable of being tested without elaborate econometric estimates of supply elasticities. (3) A more interesting way of formulating Kravis-type hypotheses seems to be to go *directly* to the scarcities of natural resources and temporary scarcities through innovations. Kravis himself indicates that *a country's export-industries will show rates of technical progress higher than the national average*. (4) This could be turned into an alternative, plausible proposition, with traces of Ricardo [1]: *a country's export-industries will show higher rates of technical progress than the same industries in the trading partners*. (5) Perhaps the most promising approach would be to utilize Kravis' distinction between 'unavailability' due to scarce natural resources and due to innovation. Thus, to the preceding two propositions, one could add a further clause: *or, will be intensive in the use, or consist, of raw materials which*

[1]Cf. Kravis' remark: 'it is the elasticity of supply abroad and its inelasticity at home that gives rise to [the United States imports].' [22, p. 150].

are relatively abundant in the country.[1] Such Kravis-type hypotheses have, however, neither been clearly formulated and analysed so far nor tested systematically with empirical evidence.

The Linder Theory

Another novel and ingenious approach is attributable to a recent Swedish author, Linder [27]. He begins by attempting to explain the pattern of trade, but ends up by doing something quite different – and it is precisely in this way that Linder makes a contribution of some significance.

Linder starts with the distinction between trade in primary products and in manufactures. The former is natural resource-intensive, and Linder accepts the thesis that such trade must be explained in terms of 'relative natural-resources endowments' [27, p. 92].[2] Trade in manufactures, however, cannot be so explained. Linder explicitly rejects the analogy.

He despairs, however, of being able to predict the *precise* composition of trade in manufactures. This is a function of many factors: 'technological superiority, managerial skills and economies of scale are perhaps the most important . . .' [27, p. 103]. The results cannot be congealed into a precise, predictable pattern.[3] Economists, when confronted with questions that they could not answer, have usually changed the question. Linder likewise virtually gives up the traditional inquiry and argues that, while the precise composition of trade in manufactures cannot be forecast, what one *can* have instead is a theory

[1] This, of course, begs the question of defining relative abundance. Some working definition would have to be devised. In practice, of course, it is relatively easy to identify the industries whose advantage consists in access to raw materials; although, once again, the distinction between abundance in terms of price and physical units is relevant. For an interesting attempt at estimating the 'resource-intensiveness' of activities entering trade in the United States see Vanek [43].

[2] Linder construes this as consistent with the Heckscher–Ohlin theory because he accepts the original Ohlin statement of his theory, which mentioned a whole host of factors of production, *inclusive* of natural resources. Of course, to the extent that other factors of production are also brought in, the theory both becomes less impressive as an abstraction and is less successfully tractable analytically because of the consequences, for the definitions of 'factor-abundance' and 'factor-intensity', of more than two factors of production.

[3] Linder, while he admits this, does not quite reconcile himself to the conclusion. He feels that *something* can still be said about the trade pattern. But his observations (e.g. that Sweden will export paper because of forest resources or that Eskimos are unlikely to export refrigerators) do *not* constitute a theory.

concerning the *volume* of trade (as proportion of national income) between different pairs of trading nations.

Linder's central thesis is that the *volume of trade in manufactures of a country with each of her trading partners, when taken as a proportion of the corresponding national incomes of these countries, will be higher, the greater the similarity in the demand patterns of the pair of trading countries.* The 'similarity of demand patterns' would be associated with the similarity of incomes *per capita* – although income distribution and similarity of taste patterns are additional variables. However, tastes are internationally not very dissimilar according to recent evidence [27, p. 95]. Hence, provided income distribution is ignored, the last clause in the thesis can be rewritten to state: '*the closer the pair of trading countries in their incomes* per capita'.

Although Linder has not rigorously formulated his analytical framework, the chain of reasoning which leads to this hypothesis is available. (1) The pre-condition for a non-primary commodity to emerge as an export is the presence of 'home demand'. This is attributed to several reasons: foreign trade is only an extension of domestic trade; innovation centres on existing industries and gives them export possibility; etc.[1] (2) The existence of industry catering for internal demand implies that the internal demand pattern will determine the range of commodities that constitute potential exports. (Linder tries here to introduce the concept of 'representative demand' – to narrow down the range of potential exports. The intention is to exclude those commodities for which the internal production is presumably not 'large enough'. But Linder really leaves this idea hanging in the air, without chiselling it down into clarity and precision.) (3) Where the overlap in the commodity-composition of the potential-export range of any pair of trading countries is *greater*, the possibility of a *larger* volume of trade will obtain. (4) The potential volume of trade will be larger, the larger the income-level of either trading country [27, p. 111]. (5) Where the potential volume of trade is larger, the actual volume of trade will also be larger (though tariffs, transport costs, political connections which prompt discriminatory trade promotion, etc., may 'distort' the relationship). (6) A similar set of arguments applies to imports. Linder qualifies only to the extent of stating that

[1] One might add: the foreign market is risky (through QRs and the possibility of entry which cannot be 'controlled' with tariffs as in the domestic market) and the home market is not, so that producers generally do not wish to rely on the foreign market alone.

his 'representative demand' concept is no longer necessary: this hardly matters, however, in view of its imprecision. (7) Hence the Linder thesis.

Many questions inevitably come to one's mind. Aside from, and related to, the looseness of concepts such as 'representative demand', there is lack of precision concerning the concept of the potential-export range. Is it to be defined entirely in terms of the number of commodities with domestic production, or is one to assign weights to commodities in terms of their relative size in terms of some relevant index? What are the conditions under which the size of the trading countries can be expected to affect the volume of trade? And so on.[1] But, despite these limitations (which inevitably attend on pioneering analyses), Linder's work remains significant.

Our survey thus demonstrates that the theory of comparative advantage has been greatly advanced recently. New theories have emerged. And it has been the vehicle of the significant, recent trends towards empirical verification. This trend has synchronized with a more general investigation of the empirical validity of traditional theses about the structure of the international economy: among the prominent contributions being Michaely's [31] study of concentration in world trade and Coppock's [17] analysis of the incidence of economic instability among the trading nations.

Meanwhile, analytical theory of the 'traditionalist' persuasion, concerned with the statement of 'logically true' theorems, has proliferated at a great pace. To this, we must now turn.

2. Theorems in Statics: Factor Price Equalization[2]

The problem which has engaged the attention of many of the most distinguished trade theorists concerns the relationship between factor prices in different countries, under free trade in goods but factor

[1] Linder's brief attempt at empirical verification is also not fully satisfactory. The trade figures relate to aggregate imports, instead of imports of manufacture goods. The relationship investigated is with respect to *per capital* income, with no attempt at examining whether the explanation improves with additional variables like regional or fractile equations. Linder's hypothesis, while brilliantly suggestive, awaits both rigorous analytical formulation and empirical verification.

[2] I have had the invaluable opportunity of corresponding with Professor P. A. Samuelson in writing this Section. Although I have drawn freely on this correspondence, especially for the general case of many goods and many factors, the responsibility for any errors is entirely mine.

immobility between countries.[1] The question dates back to the writings of Heckscher [19] and Ohlin [34]. They considered trade to be an equalizing factor with respect to factor returns in trading countries, though they cited several reasons why *full* factor price equalization would not occur in practice. In 1948 Samuelson [38] initiated the rigorous investigation of the conditions under which complete factor price equalization would follow.

Samuelson [38, 39] stated everything that has ever been said subsequently as far as the restrictive case of two goods and two factors is concerned and, subject to certain sufficient assumptions to be noted shortly, managed to prove factor-price equalization by establishing a *unique* relationship between (relative) factor and commodity prices. In 1953 Samuelson [53], preceded by an investigation of Meade [50] into the two-factor, three-product case, offered the first serious analysis of the general case of many goods (n) and many factors (r), thereby extending the analysis to all the $n \geqslant 2 \leqslant r$ cases. In the process it turned out that the more general analysis was limited by the non-existence of the required mathematics, Samuelson having to content himself with the formulation of what were clearly overly-strong sufficiency conditions for uniqueness in the large (for $n = r > 2$). Subsequent to Samuelson's 1953 analysis, progress has been registered in this area in the following respects: (1) Kuhn [47] has added an alternative sufficiency condition for uniqueness when $n = r \geqslant 2$;[2] (2) McKenzie [49] has provided a basic theorem which seems to overlap with Samuelson's 1953 sufficiency theorem, without either

[1] I have referred only tangentially in Section 7 to one other problem, on which there is some, though scant, literature. This is the question of the pattern of international specialization in *production* (as distinct from *trade*). The papers of McKenzie [78] and Jones [69] discuss this problem most elegantly in a Ricardo–Graham model with one primary factor of production and many countries. While I am on the subject of omissions, I should also note that I have not dealt at any length with the question of the stability of trade equilibrium, although I might have included it in Section 4. The interested reader will find useful and adequate discussion of the problem in the papers of Mundell [11] and myself and Johnson [2, Section 4] and in the volumes by Meade [9] and Vanek [93].

[2] Pearce [51], in an excellent paper which brings out the essence of the problem in an extremely simple fashion, has attempted to provide alternative sufficiency conditions. But apparently Professor McKenzie has produced an example which contradicts Pearce's conjecture and the mathematical results of Nikaido and Gale also have had a similar effect. Mention may also be made of Reiter's [52] contribution which demonstrates the intuitive, inverse theorem that identical production functions are implied by 'universally observed factor price equalization'.

implying or being implied by it; (3) Nikaido and Gale are reported to have discovered a basic flaw in Samuelson's mathematical proof of the sufficiency condition for the uniqueness of equilibrium in the large; and (4) Samuelson [54] has extended the analysis to an investigation of the conditions under which free trade would equalize not merely rentals but also interest rates between countries.

In contrast to the difficulties of the general case, the case where $n = r = 2$ is strikingly simple and, since Samuelson's pioneering analysis, has been extensively surveyed [5, Chapter I; 3, Chapter III]. Samuelson used the following assumptions, which proved to be sufficient for the purpose: (1) linear, homogeneous production functions in each good; (2) diminishing returns along isoquants for each good; (3) non-reversible and different factor-intensities of the two goods at all (relevant) factor prices; (4) identity of production functions for each good between countries; (5) perfect competition and valuation of factors according to marginal value productivity; (6) incomplete specialization in production in each country; and (7) absence of transport costs. The last assumption ensures commodity price equalization, under free trade, between countries. The first five assumptions ensure a unique relationship between commodity and factor prices, under incomplete specialization in production, which obtains identically between countries. With assumption (6), ruling out complete specialization, therefore, commodity price equalization necessarily entails factor price equalization.[1]

When the general case, $n \geqslant 2 \leqslant r$, is considered the analysis is the simplest for the case $n = r > 2$. The kernel of the argument can be summarized easily.[2] If x_{ij} is the quantity of the ith factor used in the production of the jth good, ϕ_j the output of the jth good and q_j its selling price, constant returns to scale ensure that

$$\sum_{i=1}^{n} p_i x_{ij} = q_j \phi_i \quad (j = 1, 2, \ldots n)$$

The quantities x_{ij} of factors used are determined by factor prices p_i and commodity prices q_j so that the n equations can be thought of as

[1] Of all these assumptions, the postulate concerning the non-reversal of factor-intensities has aroused the greatest analytical and econometric interest. The principal analyses in this direction were noted earlier, in Section 7, when discussing the Heckscher–Ohlin theorem.

[2] Samuelson's [53] Appendix contains a lucid account of the argument concerning uniqueness. Pearce's [51] paper contains an easily comprehensible account, from which I have borrowed.

equations in $2n$ variables, p_i and q_j. For uniqueness, therefore, it is necessary that there be only one set of p_i corresponding to each set of q_j, and vice versa. It can then be shown that uniqueness follows if $|x_{ij}| \neq 0$, which constitutes a sufficient condition for factor-price equalization in the small. It should be noted that, in the $n = r = 2$ case, $|x_{ij}| \neq 0$ turns into the familiar factor-intensity-difference condition, and uniqueness can be established *both* in the small and in the large because every element of the determinant is essentially one-signed. For the $n = r > 2$ case, however, Samuelson [53] argued that the condition that $|x_{ij}| \neq 0$ was not sufficient and an *additional* sufficiency condition would be that there should be *some* numbering of factors such that the leading principal minors of $|x_{ij}|$ of *every* order should be non-zero. It is this 'strong factor-intensity' condition which has recently been reportedly re-examined by Nikaido and Gale and found to be inadequate. However, a further strengthening of the factor-intensity postulate, such that *every* principal minor is non-zero (for *all* naturally ordered sets, as distinct from only one, corresponding to *all* numbering of factors), appears to constitute a sufficient condition for uniqueness in the large (as per Samuelson's correspondence).

The cases where $n \neq r$ are more difficult and the results of the analysis more devastating to the prospects for factor price equalization. Samuelson's results are most conveniently summarized as follows. Let the observed number of goods actually produced in both countries be $n^* < n$ and the factors actually used in production of these goods, and with positive prices, be r^*. Then, if $n^* \geqslant r^*$, and if for *some* subset of r^* goods of the n^* goods, the strong factor-intensity conditions of Samuelson–Nikaido–Gale (or alternatively Kuhn and McKenzie, not detailed here) are realized, then equalized goods prices imply equalized factor prices. If, however, $r^* > n^*$, factor price equalization is generally not implied (though it may obtain under certain strong and bizarre assumptions).[1]

Although the bulk of the analysis has been centred on the question of the equalization of the *rentals* earned by factors of production in a Walrasian general equilibrium system (with extension to intermediate products), the effect of free trade on *interest rate* equalization has recently been subjected to analysis by Samuelson [54] in a hitherto unpublished paper. The analysis supports the inference that rental

[1] Several illustrative examples could be produced. For instance, if $n = 1$ and $r = 2$, factor price equalization will generally be forbidden.

equalization (except in certain limiting situations) will be accompanied by interest rate equalization.[1] The possibility of introducing intermediate products without invalidating the factor price equalization theorem, while demonstrated by Samuelson generally in his 1953 analysis, has further been recently demonstrated by Vanek [55], whose $n = r = 2$ analysis dovetails neatly into Samuelson's more powerful work.[2] Laing [48] has, on the other hand, opened up the investigation of the effects of increasing returns to scale; his results serve to underline the implication of Samuelson's analysis that constant returns to scale cannot be given up without invalidating the logical truth of the factor price equalization theorem. Although the subject is, therefore, both of historic interest and still continues to attract fresh minds, one cannot help feeling that perhaps too great a proportion of the intellectual energy of trade theorists has been directed towards a question of limited utility. Of greater importance are the propositions in comparative statics which we must now discuss.

3. Theorems in Comparative Statics

The bulk of the analytical literature in pure theory is concerned with the implications of *differences* between two general equilibrium situations – or putting it differently, with the effects of specific *changes* in a given general equilibrium situation.

Two classes of questions can be distinguished. (1) On the one hand, the effects of a change in *trade policy* are considered while assuming as given, for the trading country, the general equilibrium 'data' (*i.e.*, tastes, the distribution of ownership or resources and transfer claims, factor supplies, production functions and general economic policy plus a specific trade policy from the outside world

[1] The inapplicability of the traditional models (used to examine factor prices equalization) for the purpose of analysing the effect of trade on interest rates was suggested originally, by a reading of Harrod's [46] paper, to V. K. Ramaswami and myself at Oxford in 1958. We noticed Harrod's unwarranted transition from rental to interest-rate equalization, while operating within the framework of Samuelson's 1948 and 1953 models. I wrote subsequently to Samuelson concerning this question, and he worked out the required analysis. Ramaswami also wrote independently a paper which is yet unpublished.

[2] Samuelson has drawn my attention to the fact that Vanek [55] has managed to prove the following intuitive theorem: that (where $n = r = 2$ and both goods also serve as intermediates) if the *direct* factor-intensities are in one direction, then the *total* factor-intensities (including indirect factor requirements as well) will always be in the same direction.

such that the precise offers of trade at varying terms of trade which the country has open to it are known and given): for instance, the effect of a change in a country's tariff rate on its terms of trade may be analysed. (2) On the other hand, the effects of a change in these 'data' may be considered, while assuming the trade policy as given: for instance, the effect of capital accumulation on the terms of trade may be investigated.

Naturally it is not true, *strictly speaking*, that trade theorists have always considered the given 'data' (trade policy), in the context of which the stipulated change in trade policy (data) takes place, as independent of the change itself. Thus, for instance, Myint [83] has argued that a change in trade policy from no trade to some trade will change the country's taste pattern itself – though no formal analysis is founded on this observation. An interesting illustration of the change in trade policy when the 'data' shift is furnished by Kindleberger's [73] brilliant study of the trade policy reaction of different European governments to the influx of cheap American corn in the 1870s. The only other, and the most formal, example of such interaction is provided by the analysis of tariff retaliation. A change in trade policy prompts retaliation which alters the trade possibilities open to the country. A full, sequential analysis is usually presented, with the response mechanisms of each country specified, which properly belongs to the next section on dynamic analysis [5, Chapter II]. Aside from these instances, the last of which belongs elsewhere, while the others are not formalized into theorems, it does continue to be true that the interactions between changes in trade policy and in 'data' have not been the object of serious analysis in the comparative statics of pure theory.

The effects of the shifts in trade policy and in data have been studied generally with reference to certain variables which recur with varying frequency in the numerous analyses. The terms of trade, the internal commodity price-ratios, the factor price ratio, output levels, the composition of trade and the levels of individual exports and imports are among those that turn up almost regularly. Yet, even among them, frequently important extensions of theory have bypassed the analysis of the impact on some variables, leaving many gaps in the literature (which merely need patient and much tiresome work to be filled out).

The models in terms of which the effects of the stipulated changes on these variables are studied vary as well. And yet, it is true that, in the last three decades, an astonishing amount of synthesis has been effected and a large number of theorems worked out in terms of the model (already used in Section 7) which, while inspired by the work of Ohlin and Heckscher, is very much the creation of Samuelson, springing directly out of his early work on the factor price equalization theorem [38, 39] and, with Stolper, on the effect of protection on factor rewards [91].

This Heckscher–Ohlin–Samuelson (HOS) model is characterized by two countries and (within each country) two commodities, two factors of production, production functions characterized in each activity by constant returns to scale and diminishing returns along isoquants, perfect competition and full employment of the given supply of the factors of production.[1] The supply of each commodity, in this system, is exclusively a function of the terms of trade between the two commodities. On the other hand, the demand for each commodity is taken to be determined by both the terms of trade and the level of domestic expenditure. A detailed specification of an HOS type model for the international economy (but omitting the specifications concerning the number of factors) has been provided recently by Mundell [11], who has also furnished therewith an excellent summary of many of the principal results (excluding those that depend upon the HOS specification concerning the number of factors) in comparative statics of the pure theory of trade. Meade's [9] work on trade and welfare contains many formal statements and applications of the HOS model.[2] Recently the HOS model has been strikingly extended, with many of its 'restrictive' characteristics removed. Among the more significant of these extensions are: (1) the investigation of the *multiple country* (and multiple-commodity) case by Mundell [11, pp. 101–9] drawing upon Mosak's earlier work; (2) the analysis of demand explicitly in terms of the pattern of income distribution associated with an equilibrium situation, in contrast to the standard HOS practice of assigning to aggregate, community demand the same properties as to individual demand – an extension introduced independently by Meade [9] and Johnson [66, 67]; and (3) the relaxa-

[1] For certain limited purposes, the assumption of international identity of production functions for each activity is sometimes made.

[2] On the other hand, the *geometrical* applications of the HOS model are innumerable. Much ingenuity has also been expended on alternative geometrical depictions. I am afraid this runs into rapidly diminishing returns, and I have deliberately refrained from entering into a survey of these geometrical techniques.

tion of the assumption of fixed factor supply to include the classical case of factors *in elastic supply* with respect to their rentals by several writers: Walsh [95], Vanek [92], Kemp and Jones [72], and myself and Johnson [60].

The theorems derived with the HOS model (and its recent extensions) and others, can be surveyed under the two main heads:[1] (A) *shifts in data* (*other than trade policy*); (B) *shifts in trade policy*. Under the former the analysis subdivides further into shifts in data internal and external to the trading country. Among the internal shifts are: (1) *changes in demand*; (2) *changes in factor supply*; (3) *technological change*; and (4) *changes in* (*non-trade*) *economic policy*. The external shift in data involves some shift in the foreign offers to trade and may be prompted by changes internal to foreign countries or by changes in trade policy abroad. Such external shifts are classified generally as (5) *changes in international demand*. Under shifts in trade policy, I shall consider mainly tariff policy, distinguishing between: (1) *non-discriminatory tariff change*, and (2) *discriminatory tariff change*. The literature on other forms of trade policy is either largely symmetrical with tariff analysis (as in respect of quotas and subsidies) or limited (as with state trading) so that it will be surveyed only tangentially in the course of the analysis of tariffs which dominate the analysis in the pure theory of commercial policy.

A. *Shifts in Data* (*other than Trade Policy*)

(i) *Changes in Demand*

Problems relating to the changes in demand in trade theory have to be carefully defined, since demand is frequently understood by trade theorists as 'international demand', which is different from demand *per se*. By international demand is meant the demand for imports (and supply of exports) at some given terms of trade.[2] This demand for imports represents the excess of domestic consumption over domestic production of *importables* corresponding to the defined terms of trade. A shift in international demand is therefore to be traced to a shift in domestic consumption and/or production (which, in turn,

[1] Since the literature using the HOS model is admirably synthesized, I shall focus largely on this, while noting the main respects in which other types of models, which have been employed, differ in assumptions and/or conclusions. A fuller survey is ruled out by limitations of space.

[2] The locus of these international demands is nothing but the Marshallian 'offer curve'. International demand is also Mill's 'reciprocal demand'.

may be autonomous or induced by policy). International demand therefore reflects, and is to be distinguished from, internal (overall) demand. Internal demand in turn reflects individual tastes and the level and distribution of purchasing power. Shifts in internal demand therefore must be distinguished again from changes in individual tastes and in the level and distribution of (earned and unearned) income.

The propositions of pure theory have very nearly sidestepped the question of the effects of changes in *internal* demand. There is no formal analysis associated with the effects of changes in a country's tastes. The changes in the internal distribution of income have been brought into the fold of economic analysis only in so far as they *result* from changes in trade policy rather than as autonomous changes whose effects are spelled out. The only striking contrast is provided by the analysis of the effects of changes in the *level* of expenditure (and its accompanying effects on demand). This is nothing but the celebrated '*transfer problem*' which concerns the analysis of the effects on the terms of trade of a transfer of expenditure from one country to another. As for changes in 'international' demand, trade theory is well endowed with controversies and literature concerning the effects on the terms of trade when the foreign reciprocal demand shifts while the country's own demand for the foreign product is unchanged. In the following summary I proceed to the transfer problem, leaving shifts in international demand (which relate to changes in the external data given to the country) to be treated in a later sub-section.

The effect of a transfer on the terms of trade has been of interest because a deterioration in these terms, from the viewpoint of the transferor country, would represent a 'secondary burden' supplementary to the principal burden implicit in the transfer itself. Ignoring transport costs and using the HOS model (without the assumptions with respect to the factors of production and competition), the answer is immediately obvious: the terms of trade will deteriorate or improve according as $m_a + m_b \lesseqgtr 1$, where m_a is the marginal propensity to spend on importables in the transferor country A and m_b in the transferee country B [11, 88, 89].[1] Since the propensity to spend on exportables, x_a and x_b, is here merely unity minus the propensity

[1] It need hardly be stressed that the full-blooded HOS model is not necessary for the present analysis. Only the stability conditions have to be assumed, to determine the direction of the terms of trade change purely in terms of the marginal propensities to spend on importables with respect to expenditure change.

to spend on importables, the criterion can be rewritten in any number of alternative forms such as $m_a \lessgtr x_b$. Where tariffs obtain, and it is assumed that the tariff proceeds are redistributed and spent by private consumers as part of their income, the proportion of the transfer eventually turning up as expenditure on imports will be naturally smaller than m_b, since there is a 'leakage' each time the revenue is earned from expenditure directed at imports. The criterion thus changes to whether the sum of the marginal propensities to spend on importables is greater or less than a value which is greater than unity [5, Chapter VII, p. 173]. Where transport costs are incurred, the formula must change again, except in the extreme case when the transport cost is incurred in the form of the exported good itself. Where the transport cost is incurred, at least, partially, in the form of the imported good, it follows that the entire import expenditure does *not* accrue to the foreigner and, therefore, the criterion would again have to be that the sum of the marginal propensities to spend on importables be greater or less than a value greater than unity [89; 5, p. 174].[1] Mundell [11, p. 107] has extended the analysis to the multi-country case where a transfer from country *i* to country *j* will rearrange demand throughout the international economy – for commodities exported from countries other than *i* and *j*. The resulting formula does not admit of any *a priori* generalization.[2]

[1] Economists have a propensity to answer impossible questions, and they have done so in the context of the transfer problem. There has been a great deal of discussion as to whether, in the *real world*, the classical proposition that the terms of trade would turn against the transferor country still remains a '*presumption*'. Fundamentally, this seems to be the wrong question to pose *until* one has *first* investigated the empirical applicability of the analytical model used. The failure to ask this key question seems to me to vitiate the utility of the entire discussion concerning what is 'plausible' as a prediction. I also wonder whether it is useful to discuss what is generally 'likely' when economic analysis and empirical work can enable us, subject to errors of interpretation and estimation, to make a precise prediction whenever necessary.

[2] Johnson [5, p. 176] anticipates this conclusion in a literary analysis. He also proceeds to introduce additional commodities differently – as non-traded goods in the two countries. However, the analysis is again not presented with full algebraic treatment and it is merely stated that: 'The introduction of non-traded goods does alter the criteria, since changes in demand for such goods must be classed either as changes in (virtual) demand for exportables or as changes in (virtual) demand for imports, according to whether they are more substitutable in production and consumption for one or the other. In both these cases, however, the direction of change of the commodity terms of trade is not uniquely determined by whether the transfer is undereffected or overffected at constant prices.'

While these criteria are devised in a full-employment framework Johnson [5, pp. 177–83], drawing upon earlier work by Meade, Harberger, Metzler, and others, has synthesized and extended the analysis for a Keynesian framework where output in each country is in perfectly elastic supply at a fixed domestic-currency price level, so that output, income and employment are determined by the aggregate demand for output. The resulting criterion involves, in the most general formulation, not merely the marginal propensities to spend on imports and exportables but also now the marginal propensities to save out of both pre-transfer and transfer income. As with the full-employment case, the criterion permits the transfer again to be under-effected or over-effected at constant terms of trade.[1]

(ii) *Changes in Factor Supply*

There are three ways in which changes in factor supply enter the analysis in pure theory: (i) The effect of an *autonomous* change in factor supply has been analysed. We know now, for instance, how capital accumulation or population expansion will affect the terms and volume of trade. (ii) The effect of a *shift* in a factor of production from one country to its trading partner, on the terms and volume of trade, has also been investigated. (iii) Finally, changes in factor supply *resulting* from changes in trade policy, when the supply of factors is elastic with respect to their rentals, have also been considered. These, however, are properly treated with the analysis of the effects of changes in trade policy.

(i) *Autonomous Changes in Factor Supply.* In surveying the literature on this problem, two central difficulties arise. Firstly, there is the difficulty of distinguishing models of growth into 'static' and 'dynamic'; only the former belong here. Sometimes a model is presented with factors increasing at a steady rate over time, and the resulting time-paths of several variables are worked out. And yet the analysis does

[2] The transfer will be under-effected or over-effected according as

$$\left(m_a' + m_b' - \frac{m_a}{s_a} . s'_a - \frac{m_b}{s_b} . s'_b - 1\right) \lesseqgtr 0$$

where the transferor is country A and the transferee country B and $m_a' + m_b'$ is the sum of the proportions of the transfer by which expenditure on imports is altered by the financing and disposal of the transfer, m_a and m_b are the (non-transfer-income) marginal propensities to import in A and B respectively, s_a and s_b are the marginal propensities to save (from non-transfer incomes) in A and B and s_a' and s_b' are the proportions of the transfer by which savings are altered [5, p. 179].

not really involve time in any essential way except with respect to the 'disturbance' itself. Basically, what is involved is working out, for each unit of time, the effects of the factor expansion and then repeating the analysis for each other period: time merely defines the nature of the 'disturbance' (*i.e.*, the increase in the factor supply) which is itself independent of the equilibrium parametric values of the preceding periods. Surely it is sensible to treat such models as 'static' in nature. The second difficulty consists in separating out models that refer to increase in factor supply and those that concern technical change. Frequently the same authors, for instance Johnson [5, Chapter III], analyse both questions in the same framework. Sometimes, however, the two are not even distinguished and merely 'productivity increases' defined as increases in output (attributable naturally to either cause) are discussed, as by Mundell [11], or shifts in demand and supply schedules over time are defined without explicit distinction between different causes, as by Black [59]. Where these models are discussed is inevitably arbitrary, and I have brought them in under the present sub-section.

The simplest and yet the most influential analysis of the effects of economic expansion accruing through increased factor supply is that of Johnson [5, Chapter III], who uses the HOS model.[1] There is a great flood of subsequent contributions, among them by Corden [61], which explores the HOS model further on this issue. The analysis of the effect on the terms of trade proceeds simply by noting that the excess demand for imports (dm) at unchanged terms of trade would equal the difference between the change in the demand for importables (dc) and in their supply (dp).[2] If this excess demand for imports is positive, then the terms of trade will shift against the growing country provided the stability condition is satisfied. And the precise change in

[1] Historically, the contributions occurred as a result of the interest in the causes of dollar shortage in the post-war world. The explanation of the shortage, first propounded by Balogh [58], was in terms of the rapidly increasing productivity in the United States. Translated in terms of the HOS model, with the adjustment mechanism defined in terms of the terms of trade, the explanation was inevitably formalized into a theory of the effect of growth (due to capital accumulation and technical change) on the terms of trade. The connecting link between Johnson's important contributions and the less formal writings of Balogh and others is a seminal paper of Hicks [3, p. 154] which reflects all the difficulties of a pioneering contribution.

[2] In the HOS model the excess demand for imports implies an equivalent excess supply of exports, and the analysis can proceed in terms of *either* good.

the terms of trade can be obtained by equating the excess demand for imports due to growth with their excess supply due to adverse terms of trade [11, 111].

Since $dm = dc - dp$, the question of the properties of dc and dp has been raised. The former involves merely a weighted sum of the individual marginal propensities to consume importables. The latter, however, has prompted interesting analytical contributions. A proposition of Rybczynski [87] states that $dp \gtrless 0$ according as importables are factor K-intensive or factor L-intensive as the supply of K increases. Where the two commodities postulated have different factor-intensities, the output of the commodity intensive in the use of a factor will decrease absolutely as the supply of the other factor rises at unchanged terms of trade.[1] A taxonomic exercise, therefore, can be carried out, using such theorems to define the possible properties of dc and dp [5, Chapter III].

In an influential paper, written prior to the analysis discussed hitherto, Johnson [5, Chapter IV] used a model which assumed that each country consumed and exported one commodity and imported, but did not produce, the other.[2] In this model, which amounts to only a special case of the HOS model, $dp = 0$, and it follows that dm must necessarily be positive unless the consumption of importables

[1] This proposition follows immediately as follows. $\frac{K}{L} \equiv \frac{Kx}{Lx} \cdot \frac{Lx}{L} + \frac{Ky}{Ly} \cdot \frac{Ly,}{fL}$ which states that the aggregate factor endowment ratio is a weighted sum of the factor ratios in the two activities, X and Y. If the terms of trade are kept fixed so are the factor proportions in the model used. Therefore, $\frac{Kx}{Lx}$ and $\frac{Ky}{Ly}$ are fixed. So is L. Let K now increase. The resulting increase in $\frac{K}{L}$ can be accommodated then *only* by reducing Ly and increasing Lx if X is the K-intensive activity, such that $\frac{Kx}{Lx} > \frac{Ky}{Ly}$. Thus, the output of Y, the L-intensive activity, falls when K increases at unchanged terms of trade [61]. Since this argument is in terms of the relative factor endowments, it is easy to generalize the argument to the case where both factors increase in supply. Thus, for instance, if both factors increase at the same rate there will be a uniform expansion of the outputs of X and Y. If K increases more rapidly the analysis implies notionally a uniform expansion of X and Y (at the rate of growth of L) plus a *reduction* in the output of Y from this expanded level (resulting from the *excess* growth of K). And so on.

[2] Johnson [5, Chapter IV] formulated his analysis in terms of exchange-rate adjustment. In the model used by him, however, it is obvious that this is tantamount to terms-of-trade adjustment. An extension to the n-country case is also available.

falls as output increases with factor expansion. Although it is tempting to say this is ruled out if there is no inferior good, it should be noted that although the good is not inferior in any *individual's* consumption, it *may* be for the economy in the aggregate owing to changing income distribution (associated with a changed factor supply).[1]

Three other contributions are of interest – by Mundell [11], Ramaswami [86] and Black [59]. Mundell has extended Johnson's analysis to the multi-country case, noted earlier here. The same conclusions hold as in Johnson's [5, Chapter III] analysis, provided gross complementarity among the exports of different countries is ruled out.[2]

More novel is the analysis of Ramaswami [86], who has recently attempted to distinguish between the effects of 'completed' accumulation and accumulation-in-progress on the terms of trade. Characterizing the analyses of Johnson and others as relating to the latter question, Ramaswami deploys altogether four models to explore the former problem. These models reduce to two basic 'types'. (1) One of the two goods in Johnson's model is assumed to play a dual role – as a consumer and also as a capital good, and accumulation is conceived as a demand shift, at constant prices, from consumption to investment goods. The model is simple and can be easily put through the various paces. For instance, any investment increase means increased demand for the dual-role good. If the reduction in consumption exclusively falls on that good there is no reason to expect the terms of trade to shift. If not, adjustment is clearly necessary. (2) The other approach is to assume a *third* industry ('tools') which serves as the capital good. The analysis is a little more complex but still manageable. The relative ranking of the factor ratios in the three industries adds to the scope for interesting taxonomic analysis.

While the analyses of Johnson, Mundell and Ramaswami are in the general equilibrium framework, Black [59] has produced a model which is strictly partial-equilibrium in its approach and correspondingly of lesser significance.[3] Using the partial-equilibrium supply

[1] Mundell [11], in his otherwise excellent survey, does not make this point clear and relies on the 'non-inferiority' of goods to give him necessarily positive terms.

[2] It is necessarily ruled out in the two-good model, for these two goods have to be substitutes. Gross substitutability among goods is shown by Mundell to guarantee the equivalence of the two-country and multi-country (-cum-multi-commodity) case.

[3] Black describes his approach as Marshallian because his model essentially amounts to using the Marshall–Lerner devaluation analysis and introducing

and demand schedules for commodities in a four-commodity (an export and domestic good for each country), two-country model, he introduces trend-shifts in these schedules to derive changes over time in the balance of payments and terms of trade. In contrast to the general equilibrium models, however, this approach leaves untouched the crucial question of how exactly these schedules may be expected to shift in response to accumulation (technical change, etc.).

(ii) *Transfers of Factors between Countries.* Trade theory has also examined the impact of transfers of factors of production between trading countries. The analyses fall into two classes: (1) either the movement of a factor between countries is made contingent upon the presence of an international differential in its rental and the equilibrium condition postulates the elimination of international factor movements when international factor returns are equalized; or (2) an autonomous shift in a factor's location is analysed. The former is clearly more relevant when there is perfect freedom for factor mobility between countries; the latter is more appropriate to modern conditions where this freedom does not exist and the international migration of factors is subject to political decision-making.

Practically the only rigorous analysis in the former class is by Mundell [82], who uses the HOS model. Mundell postulates a tariff imposed on a situation characterized by international equality of factor rentals. The tariff raises the rental of the factor intensively used (in the strict Samuelson sense) and thereby precipitates a movement of that factor from the other into the tariff-imposing country.[1] Ultimately, the factor prices are equalized, factor movement eliminated and commodity prices are also equalized. The tariff is redundant and can be removed without affecting the new equilibrium reached. Mundell has merely turned the factor price-equalization theorem on its head and effectively proved a commodity price-equalization theorem (when factor mobility is perfect but commodity mobility is not, thanks

trend-shifts in the supply and demand schedules. The Marshallian analysis can be interpreted, of course, in a partial sense or as an unhelpful general equilibrium approach (where the elasticities are *total* elasticities). Black is interpreting the Marshallian approach in the former sense.

[1] It is equally possible to argue that the other factor may also more in the contrary direction. In fact, multiple (indeed, an infinite number of) solutions are possible, characterized by different international distributions of factors of production.

to the tariff). The terms of trade and factor prices will be identical in the new equilibrium as prior to the tariff.[1]

Of greater interest than this variation on the factor price-equalization theorem is the analysis by Johnson [5, Chapter III] of the effects of *given* transfers of productive factors between trading countries. It represents essentially an extension of the analysis of the effect of growth on the volume and terms of trade: a transfer of factors can be analysed as a simultaneous (and equal) increase and decrease in the two countries' factor supply. Aside from the inevitable taxonomy, using propositions such as Rybczynski's, Johnson carefully argues that an income transfer may be associated with the factor shift. Thus, for instance, profit remittances may follow upon capital transfer. Or gifts may attend upon labour migration. The 'transfer problem' analysis may thus have to be super-imposed upon the 'growth and trade' analysis to get a *total* picture. Meade [9, Chapter XIX] has presented a more elaborate model, permitting international differences in production functions for each activity.[2] However, his formal analysis excludes the 'transfer problem' aspects of the question.[3]

(iii) *Technological Change*

Although recent writings have underlined the desirability of treating technical change integrally with capital accumulation, trade theory is cast in the neo-classical tradition which separates them out. The formal analyses of changes in technology again divide into those that treat such changes as autonomous and those which concern the transfer of technical knowledge from one trading country to another.

In the former category there are several contributions. Using the HOS model, on the technological side, Johnson [5, Chapter III] has formulated the proposition that 'neutral' change in an activity will decrease the output level in the other activity, at constant commodity prices.[4] This proposition can be used to define the sign of *dp*

[1] This is easy enough to see when the factor-losing country has no monopoly power in trade. When the terms of trade can vary, the result still continues to hold.

[2] This extension is of considerable significance, since the formal HOS model, with the assumption of internationally identical production functions, rules out one of the central reasons why international factor migration may be *desirable*.

[3] Caves [3, Chapter V] includes several Continental and other writings on capital movements in his survey. It is difficult, however, to extract anything formally rigorous from these writings.

[4] Unlike with the Rybczynski proposition, the factor prices will change although the commodity prices are held constant.

and the taxonomic analysis thereon is similar to that for the change in factor supply, considered in the earlier sub-section. Findlay and Grubert [62] have extended the analysis of the effects of technical change, on output-composition at constant commodity prices, to the case of biased change. For two factors, say land and labour, they have shown that for labour-saving technical change in the labour-intensive activity there will be an absolute decrease in the output of the land-intensive activity. And that, for land-saving change in the labour-intensive activity, the fall in the output of the other activity does not necessarily follow. In general terms, there will be a fall in the output of an activity when there is technical progress in the other activity which saves on the factor used intensively in that activity.[1] Intuitively, these results are obvious. For instance, land-saving invention in the land-intensive activity has two effects: (1) the technical change, conceived *neutrally*, decreases the output of the other activity (Johnson proposition); and (2) the 'notional' release of land reduces the output of the other, labour-intensive activity as well (Rybczynski proposition). The two effects thus reinforce the fall in the other activity's output. On the other hand, they oppose each other when the invention saves on the factor in which the activity is *not* intensive.[2]

Seton [90] has produced an alternative model to analyse the effects of technical change on the terms of trade. It has practically all the features of Johnson's [5, Chapter III] model, but Seton formulates his analysis in terms of concepts which underline the significance of the 'weight' of the trading countries in international trade.[3] A distinguishing feature is his defining technical change exclusively as the 'neutral' change discussed earlier, though Seton does not establish any propositions concerning its effect, at constant commodity prices, on the composition of output.

[1] The definitions of 'neutral', 'labour-saving' and 'land-saving' are in terms of technology alone. Neutral change merely amounts to multiplying the numbers on the isoquants by a scalar. Under 'labour-saving' invention, at the *same* factor price-ratio, the land–labour ratio is increased; and for 'land-saving' progress the land–labour ratio is decreased.

[2] Johnson [65] has ingeniously combined the analysis of technical change with a disaggregated-economy assumption to trace the effects of different types of technical change on the sign of *dc*.

[3] Seton's analysis is lucid, but the results are quite cumbersome, largely by virtue of the novel concepts used by him and his use of proportionate rather than absolute changes. I suspect, since his propositions are consistent with those deducible from Johnson's analysis, that Seton's formulae could be reduced to forms made familiar by the other models.

Kemp's [71] is practically the only other contribution of some interest in this field. He departs from the preceding analyses in introducing Keynesian unemployment. This renders the supply curves of exports and domestic goods perfectly elastic in his four-good model (with an export and a domestic good in each of the two trading countries).[1] The results of the analysis are worked out for technological progress in both the domestic and export industries.

(iv) *Changes in Non-trade Policy*

A shift in 'data' can also come from a change in the (non-trade) economic policy pursued by the government. For instance, the government may decide to impose a tax on *importables* (instead of on imports via a tariff) in an open economy engaged in free trade. How will this affect the volume and terms of trade? Such questions have rarely been posed directly in trade theory. They have, no doubt, been raised tangentially – mostly in relation to *welfare* analysis. For instance, Meade [9, Chapters V and VI] has analysed the choice between an import duty and a consumption tax, and between an export duty and a production tax, as a means of raising revenue, the preference function being defined with respect to world advantage. These analyses indirectly involve contributions to pure theory.

Practically the only *direct* analysis of such problems, however, is due to Mundell [11], who has extended his survey of pure theory to include an original contribution on the effect of consumption and production taxes on the terms of trade (at market prices and factor cost). For instance, a consumption tax on the imported good (with the revenue redistributed as income subsidy to consumers) will always improve a country's terms of trade because its net effect is to reduce the demand for imports by the product of the compensated elasticity of demand for importables and the tax change. This proposition is intuitively obvious, since the tax can be expected normally to reduce the world demand for importables. Mundell also notes the interesting fact that tariffs and (trade) subsidies can always be simulated in their 'real' effects by taxes and subsidies on commodities. Thus, for instance, a tariff on Y (or an export duty on X) is equivalent,

[1] In this respect Kemp's analysis comes close to that of Asimakopoulos [56], who has investigated the effects of a third non-traded good in a constant-cost model which is otherwise analogous to the Johnson model. Kemp's analysis, however, is rigorous, whereas that of Asimakopoulos lacks in formal rigour in so far as the formal model is not fully specified.

C

among several other combinations, to a consumption tax on Y plus a production tax on X or a consumption tax on Y plus a production subsidy on Y.

(v) *Changes in International Demand*

Until now, the autonomous shift has been located within the trading country itself. But the problem can also be posed in terms of an *external* shift – *i.e.*, a shift in the *foreign offer curve* (which represents a schedule of trade offers to the trading country at varying terms of trade).[1] There is indeed a considerable literature on the effect of such shifts on a trading country's terms and volume of trade. This literature was sparked off by an apparent contradiction, in the results reached by Marshall and Graham, which has now been traced to different *definitions* of a shift in the offer curve.[2]

Naturally the results will vary with the definitions chosen; and, as Kemp [70] and Oliver [84] have demonstrated by analysing the effects of three different definitions, any number of definitions may be devised as one wishes. From the viewpoint of the usefulness of the economic analysis, however, the two definitions, adopted each by Marshall and Graham, appear to be the most meaningful and have their counterpart in the standard analysis of value. Marshall's analysis defines the change in international demand in terms of a change in the price at which the given quantity (of imports) is demanded; whereas Graham's definition is in terms of a change in the quantity demanded at given terms of trade. Johnson and myself [2] have argued that each of these approaches has utility in the analysis of trade problems, and hence merits retention in the repertoire of trade theorists.[3]

[1] This shift will naturally be *internal* to the foreign country itself and will reflect any or more of the four types of changes discussed earlier and or a trade-policy change. By the same token, the analysis of this sub-section is of limited interest.

[2] In their analysis, however, the shift was in the country's *own* offer curve, the *foreign* country's offer curve remaining unchanged.

[3] I may quote [2, pp. 78–9]: 'Broadly speaking, Graham's approach is likely to be more convenient when . . . the direction of change of international equilibrium can be predicted from the effect of the change on quantity demanded at the initial price. Examples are the transfer problem and the effect of economic expansion on international trade equilibrium. Marshall's approach, on the other hand, is likely to be more convenient when the problem concerns the effects of a change in a country's commercial policy on its equilibrium prices and quantities, since the direction of change of this equilibrium can be predicted from the effect of the tariff on the quantity of imports demanded at the initial internal price, and

B. *Shifts in Trade Policy*

So far I have surveyed much of the central analysis of pure theory which concerns the effects of shifts in 'data' while the trade policy (usually free trade) is assumed unchanged between the two situations being compared. However, many of the principal questions in trade theory have related to the effects of a shift in the trade policy itself. This is quite natural in view of the traditional preoccupation with the choice of commercial policy. Moreover, the trade policy most frequently analysed is tariff policy.

(i) *Non-discriminatory tariff change.* Within tariff theory, further, the analysis of non-discriminatory tariff change has received a disproportionate attention. Indeed, from the viewpoint of *systematic* theoretical analysis in its positive aspects, non-discriminatory tariff change is practically the only type of tariff change to have been analysed. As with all other positive analysis of trade policy, the theory of non-discriminatory tariff changes has sprung directly out of concern with questions of trade and welfare.

The assertion of the vulgar protectionists that tariffs would increase the share of labour in the national income has, in fact, prompted a thorough analysis, in terms of the HOS model,[1] of the entire question of the effects of non-discriminatory tariffs on commodity prices, factor prices, and the absolute and relative shares of either factor in national income. In a classic analysis Stolper and Samuelson [91] revived the controversy concerning the effect of protection on the real incomes of factors and focused on the issue which was baffling most discussants – namely, how anything definitive could be said concerning the question posed *unless* the consumption pattern of the factors was specified. In an ingenious exercise, within the framework of the HOS model, the authors successfully demonstrated that conditions *could* be specified under which the impact of protection on the absolute and relative shares of factors could be definitively predicted without reference to the consumption pattern of the factors. This was accomplished via the analysis of the impact of tariffs on factor prices. Since, in the HOS model, a unique relationship exists between factor

of the corresponding reduction of the external price on the quantity of imports the foreigner would supply. Marshall himself used this technique for the analysis of tariffs and subsidies; . . .'

[1] The assumptions concerning the factors of production are, however, not necessary to the analysis.

and commodity prices, Stolper and Samuelson opened up, in effect, the entire modern analysis of the effects of tariffs on commodity and factor prices and on absolute and relative shares of factors in national income. Metzler [80, 81] has subsequently extended the analysis to the 'paradoxical' câse where a tariff *reduces* the (relative) price of the importable commodity in the tariff-imposing country. The analysis has been further extended with respect to an elastic factor supply by Kemp and Jones [72] and myself and Johnson [60], the interdependence of public and private consumption by Baldwin [57] and myself and Johnson [60], changes in income distribution by Johnson [67, 60] and the multi-country case by Mundell [11].

In the analysis the distinction between a prohibitive (*i.e.*, trade-eliminating) and a non-prohibitive tariff is of crucial importance, for two reasons: (i) with a prohibitive tariff, starting from free trade, the price of importables cannot be lowered by the imposition of the tariff (in the specified HOS model), whereas it can be when the tariff is non-prohibitive; and (ii) a prohibitive tariff generates no revenue, whereas a non-prohibitive tariff does, creating the necessity to make some assumption about the revenue disposal. The assumption about revenue disposal is, in turn, of significance, since the results of the analysis depend upon it. The two common assumptions in tariff theory are that *either* the government spends it directly *or* that the revenue is re-distributed as an income-subsidy to the consumers, who then spend it like earned income. (The results vary unless the government spends the revenue at internal prices in the same way as consumers do and government consumption does not alter private consumption.)

Subject to these further specifications, the HOS model can be readily employed to work out a large number of formulae concerning the impact of tariff change on domestic and international terms of trade (and hence also on the absolute and relative shares in national income of each of the two classes of factors) [11, 60]. It would be tedious to record the numerous results here; besides, a fairly exhaustive survey has been provided by me elsewhere [1]. I would merely note here that the results under the strict HOS model naturally get modified when any of the assumptions is changed. For instance, letting one of the factors vary in response to its rental complicates the analysis considerably [60, p. 245]. Thus, in this case, the proposition that, when the tariff proceeds are spent by the private sector, the terms of trade will *necessarily* improve for the tariff-imposing country (which follows from the fact that, at constant terms of trade, there is an excess supply of importables measured by the product of the compensated elasticity of demand for imports and the tariff change), is no longer valid and the terms of trade can deteriorate, even though this condition is satisfied [60, p. 246].[1] Similarly, for the case of a disaggregated private sector where changes in income distribution are allowed to play a role in determining the pattern of demand, the net result of such disaggregation is to make the aggregate marginal propensity to spend on imports a weighted sum of these propensities for the different individuals constituting the economy [60, pp. 235–8]. The extension to the multi-country case by Mundell [11], however, does not destroy the simple elegance of the traditional conclusions, for instance, with respect to the effects on the external and internal terms of trade. Gross substitutability among the exports of different countries to the tariff-imposing country is sufficient to sustain the two-country result; further restrictions need not be imposed on the pattern of expenditure out of redistributed revenue [68]. Kemp has also re-examined the standard HOS conclusions in the framework of Keynesian unemployment [3, p. 74], establishing the conditions under which Metzler's 'paradoxical' result would continue to hold.[2] Of some interest is also the recent analysis by MacDougall [75, 76], which utilizes the flood of empirical studies on the international price mechanism to investigate the empirical 'likelihood' of Metzler's results and deduce the conclusion that it is relatively small.

(ii) *Discriminatory Tariff Changes.* Discriminatory tariff changes can be distinguished according as the discrimination is between countries or between commodities. Any particular tariff may

[1] Kemp and Jones [72] have examined additionally the question of the levels of importable production and the variable factor's supply.

[2] (1) Under competitive conditions quotas are identical with tariffs (with redistributed revenue) and the analysis in the text is valid for them as well. Each tariff implies an equivalent quota and the other way round. Where, however, the quota system confers a domestic monopoly, the results are different. (2) Subsidies are perfectly symmetrical with the case where tariff proceeds are redistributed to the private sector. However, there is no sensible counterpart to the case where the Government spends the tariff proceeds itself [11]. (3) State trading can be easily analysed as well, for it merely turns tariff analysis on its head. Where tariff theory analyses the effect of specific tariffs (and subsidies) on the volume and terms of trade, the theory of state trading is concerned with the investigation, in effect, of the tariffs (and subsidies) which must be imposed to make a particular volume and terms of trade feasible [9]. (It may be remembered that *trade* taxes and subsidies can be reduced invariably to equivalent *production* and *consumption* taxes and subsidies.)

discriminate in both ways, of course, as when it is levied on a commodity which is imported only from a single foreign source.

In contrast to the analysis of non-discriminatory tariff changes, the theory of discriminatory tariff changes, in its positive aspects, is singularly lacking in formal propositions concerning the determinants of behaviour of equilibrium variables. This is to be accounted for partly by the analytical dominance of the two-good, two-country (HOS) model, which rules out the possibility of discriminatory tariff changes. Partly it is also the result of the preoccupation of discriminatory tariff analysts with welfare analysis. For instance, the formal analysis of preferential tariff reduction, prompted by the post-war interest in customs unions and free-trade areas, has been almost exclusively oriented towards questions like: will a customs union increase world welfare? rather than towards problems like: how will the terms of trade of the non-member countries be affected? No doubt, welfare analysis must be founded on positive analysis. But it happens that the kind of positive analysis that is subsumed in these welfare exercises in tariff discrimination rarely has the formal neatness that is now associated with the theory of non-discriminatory tariff changes.[1]

The formal theory of customs union begins with Viner's [94] examination of the assertion that a customs union, by virtue of its being a move towards free trade, would *improve* welfare. The models employed were not fully stated, but the arguments have none the less proved seminal. Viner considered merely shifts in the given production (of a single commodity), in an essentially three-country model, from one country to another. (Where the union results in the shift of imports from the lower-cost outside country to the higher-cost partner country, he described the shift as trade-diversion. Where the preferential tariff reduction merely eliminates the inefficient, domestic industry and replaces it with imports from the member country, he named the change trade-creation.) Lipsey [121] and Meade [79] have subsequently elaborated upon these basic concepts,

[1] This is itself attributable frequently to the way in which welfare analysis has been pursued. For instance, Lipsey [121], in a brilliant paper on customs union theory, is content with demonstrating a *possibility* (that despite 'trade diversion', both national and international welfare may be improved by a customs union) and does not carry the analysis through to a formal algebraic statement of the conditions under which the possibility will occur. Further again, Meade's [79] analysis is more in the nature of the demonstration of a method than a fully taxonomic and formal exercise.

stating their models more fully and introducing both the possibility of an *increase* in the volume of imports (as distinct from a mere shift in their origin) due to their cheapening domestically, as also the existence of imperfectly elastic supply curves. This has been done in the context of both a simple formalization of Viner's (implicit) model into a two-good, three-country model [121] and a more complex version with more than two goods which admits of complementarity between imports from different sources [7, 79].

Unfortunately, all these analyses are welfare-orientated and, for reasons outlined earlier, fail to contribute, in their extant form, anything systematic and substantive to positive theory. It is only recently that Vanek [93] has directly posed the questions of positive theory in an interesting extension of the standard, Marshallian offer-curve analysis to the case of preferential tariff reductions in a two-commodity, three-country model. However, he halts his analysis short of the derivation of the conditions under which the possibilities stated by him will occur.[1] In a real sense, therefore, the question of discriminatory tariff change invites systematic and fresh analysis – in its positive aspects.[2]

[1] However, see his later work on customs union theory.

[2] Part of the difficulty in systematically analysing the customs-union problems consists in the vast number of possible cases which logically must be catalogued and analysed. For instance, even in the extremely simplified two-good, three-country model we have seven logically different possibilities (as distinct from four mentioned by Vanek [93]), catalogued in the following matrix, *presented in terms of a single commodity* which may be an export (X) or import (M) of, or not traded (O) by, a country and where the three countries are the home country (H) the partner country (P) and the non-member country (N). The categorization is in terms of the pre-customs-union position.

	H	*P*	*N*
(1)	X	M	M
(2)	M	X	X
(3)	M	M	X
(4)	X	X	M
(5)	O	O	O
(6)	M	O	X
(7)	X	M	O

From the viewpoint of economic analysis, cases (1) and (2) are identical in structure; so are cases (3) and (4), so that the number of distinct cases may be considered to reduce to five. For the three-commodity model the possibilities are greater in number, and depend further on relations of substitution and complementarity between different goods.

4. Theorems in Dynamics

In contrast to the general richness and synthesized character of much of pure theory in its comparative statics, dynamic propositions in international trade are comparatively few and bear no trace of any uniform design, each having been developed in virtual isolation. Dynamic trade theory, where it exists, has grown up in an essentially *ad hoc* fashion and has witnessed none of the interaction of analysis which usually accompanies the development of an area of knowledge and produces a common design, a unifying frame.

At the same time there is no dearth of interest in the dynamic aspects of trade theory, and a vast amount of non-rigorous but suggestive literature is available [3, Chapter IX]. This is supplemented by the occasional attempts of growth theorists to include international trade in their models ('for completeness', and more frequently to 'show that it does not affect the validity of the approach and/or conclusions') – as, for instance, by Chakravarty [137]. I have kept away from either kind of literature – from the former because these unverified conjectures provide a fertile source for fresh theoretical analysis but themselves do not constitute it;[1] and from the latter because the trade aspects of the models are frequently the least interesting, for they are also treated as the least important.

Broadly speaking, the scant formal literature on dynamic propositions divides itself into: (1) those analyses where the inquiry concerns the effects of an *initial* change in the *trade policy*, and (2) those where the effects of an *initial* change in other *data* are being considered.[2]

1. *Change in Trade Policy*

Perhaps the neatest dynamic analysis of the effects of a change in trade policy concerns that involving adaptive, mutual and sequential changes in tariffs. Starting with the imposition of an optimum tariff, levied by a country in a two-country world, the Cournot-type adjustment mechanism where each country alternatively imposes an optimum tariff leads eventually to the two possibilities demonstrated

[1] There are a few exceptions that I have made, partly to illustrate the non-rigorous character of these analyses, but mostly because they come close enough to formal analysis to merit brief comment.

[2] The initial change itself may be defined to be a *continuing* one: for instance, a change in the rate of saving may be *permanent*.

by Johnson [5, Chapter II]: (i) an eventual equilibrium where the optimum tariff of each country is the existing tariff; or (ii) each country moves into a 'tariff cycle' such that the two countries oscillate between a pair of own tariffs. While the possibility of generalizing the theory by changing the postulated reaction mechanism has been recognized previously, Panchmukhi [124] has recently formulated the theory of tariff retaliation in explicitly game-theoretic terms. It is highly improbable, however, that tariff retaliation can be studied profitably on the assumption that tariffs are levied, autonomously or in retaliation, to maximize the tariff-imposing country's advantage. Surely, the tariff levels *and* structure are prompted by distributional considerations (operating through pressure groups) rather than by considerations of national advantage.[1]

By contrast, the literature on the effects of changes in trade policy in the absence of retaliation is characterized by less sophistication, though greater relevance. Practically all the analyses relate to the effect of trade on the rate of growth of income – but the mechanisms postulated vary considerably, and so do the clarity and rigour that attend these contributions.

The earliest of these, and analytically impressive for its time, is the classical analysis of the effect of cheap food imports from the colonies on the approach of the Stationary State. Among the clearest exponents of this theory was Mill [32], who attempted to demonstrate how, through the consequential increase in the rate of profit and hence in the accumulation of savings and capital, the approach of the Stationary State would be put off. What is not available, however, is the *precision* that we have now come to expect in theoretical writing; and unfortunately the recent mathematical formulations of the Ricardian systems (by Samuelson and Pasinetti) leave out international trade altogether, although Ricardo traced out the essence of the sequence that Mill elaborated. Other ways in which such a dynamic link between trade and growth has been established are: (i) via the effect of trade on the marginal capital–output ratio by virtue of the proposition that (free) trade increases real income [27, 132]; (ii) via the effect of trade on the distribution of income and hence on the average savings ratio [97, 99, 100]; and (iii) via the effect of trade through factor price rigidity on the level of employment, hence on real income

[1] The question of tariff retaliation is considered at greater length in Section 6, since it has important implications for welfare analysis.

and savings [27].[1] None of these analyses is fully rigorous. For instance, the analysts who argue via the effects on the distribution of income and hence on the average savings ratio never specify a model. And yet the sequence is clear and the models are easy to invent.[2]

2. *Change in Data*

The most interesting (though insufficiently formal) model, designed to analyse the effects of continuous accumulation on the trade pattern, has been presented by Bensusan-Butt [96]. He operates in a two-country, multi-commodity framework, with a simplified production technology such that each commodity has two alternative processes, one with and the other without machinery, which are known in both countries. Starting with a situation where no accumulation has previously taken place, and the cost and price structure is identical between countries, and trade is absent in consequence, Bensusan-Butt unfolds a sequence in which the steady accumulation of capital in one country leads to progressive mechanization, and emergence as exports, of industries in the accumulating country. The resulting improvement in the other country's real income (initially through the rise of trade and subsequently through the postulated improvement in the terms of trade as the accumulation proceeds) is linked with the emergence of savings there, and the effect of this on the pattern of trade is examined.

While Bensusan-Butt's analysis examines the structure of trade, as

[1] Linder [27] considers his model applicable to underdeveloped countries and uses it to turn up immiserating growth paths of output. The model is, in fact, quite symmetrical between movement from free trade to no trade and a reverse movement. For any change will bring about unemployment (due to factor-price rigidity) in the industry which should contract, and hence the contraction of real income and possible reduction in the rate of growth. The model, not being mathematically formulated, does not specify *where* the incremental output is allocated and whether the mechanism of factor allocation envisaged would be compatible with the factor-price rigidity assumption. Also, it would be pertinent to consider whether it is right to ignore the effects of change brought about by increased output: it may well be that the change implicit in trade may *offset* the change involved by growth. The analysis offered by Linder is thus not fully satisfactory.

[2] For example, a model where tractors produce tractors and corn, and corn is exchanged for toys when trade opens, could easily be used to demonstrate how the possibility of trade can reduce the marginal capital–output ratio and raise the rate of growth (with given average savings ratio). For a treatment of several types of causal links between trade and growth in a historical context, Kindleberger [101] is an excellent reference.

it *evolves* sequentially, the rest of the dynamic analyses in the literature are concerned instead with the equilibrium time-paths of variables such as output, real income and terms of trade in a growing economy engaged in a *pre-defined* pattern of trade.

Srinivasan [104] has constructed an interesting two-country, three-commodity model where one country produces two goods (a consumer good and a capital good which produces all goods in the system) and the other country produces the other (consumer) good. Assuming: (1) the Paretian allocation mechanism to allocate the fully employed factors, labour and capital (good); (2) a fixed trade pattern involving the exchange of the former country's capital good with the latter country's consumer good; and (3) international lending predetermined by a linear relationship between exports and import values, Srinivasan introduces growth into the system by letting labour grow exponentially, capital accumulate through savings and neutral technical progress characterize industries in both countries. The equilibrium time-paths of income, terms of trade and comparative factor rewards are analysed.

While in Srinivasan's model the import demand functions are ingeniously implicit in the production and trade patterns specified, Johnson [5, Chapter V] has used the more conventional approach of specifying marginal propensities to import (and spend on imports) and used them in the context of a Harrod–Domar type of flow-analysis extended to the international economy. Johnson explores, in effect, the behaviour of the equilibrium rate of growth of output and income of a country over time under the assumption of international lending and also under the more realistic postulate of exchange-rate adjustment (when the time profile of the terms of trade becomes relevant).[1]

Far more complex, and for the same reason ineffective as theory, is the analysis of Brems [98], who, using a 52-equations system (among whose novelties is trade in producers' goods), solves it to derive two L-order difference equations (where L is the durability, in years, of capital goods). These yield solutions which establish relations, over

[1] Verdoorn [105] has attempted a rigorous analysis, of similar intent, but under the restrictive assumptions of: (1) fixed coefficients of production, and (2) independence of the foreign rate of growth from the rate of growth of the economy under consideration. Johnson [5, Chapter V] eliminates the former type of analysis altogether (because he operates with the concept of the marginal propensity to import), while his analysis is fully general on the latter question.

the time-path, between the equilibrium values of variables such as the growth rates of the two trading countries.

These analyses nearly exhaust the literature on dynamic theory – except for the 'omissions' justified earlier.[1] There is little doubt that, in contrast to the comparative statics of pure theory, dynamic trade theory still calls for further systematic analysis and synthesis.

5. Central Limitations: Intermediates and Capital Goods

Of greater significance is the negligible dent made so far by intermediate and capital goods in the theoretical models employed by analysts of international trade. To state this is *not* to assert that the present stock of knowledge will not survive the required change in the formulation of the models. In fact, we do know, from such little analysis as already obtains in this direction, that the survival rate tends to be quite high! More important, however, is the fact that a vast range of interesting problems, applicable to economies using intermediate and (produced) capital goods, cannot get within the range of analysis until the theorists get away from the traditional picture of primary factors and integrated processes of production (with the inevitable concomitant feature of trade in consumer goods).

The introduction of intermediates and (produced) capital goods can be accomplished in principle in either of the following alternative ways: either these enter only domestic processes but not trade or they enter trade as well. For instance, a sector producing capital goods may exist though capital goods do not enter trade. The existing theoretical analyses in trade theory exhibit the entire range of these possibilities. For example, Samuelson's [54] interest-rate equalization model has produced but untraded capital goods. So has Ramaswami's [86] model, which analyses the effect of trade on growth. On the other hand, Srinivasan's [104] dynamic model has a capital good which is both produced and traded. As for intermediate goods, the models used by McKenzie [78, 108] and Jones [69], which explore the pattern of trade in a Ricardo–Graham framework, distinguish between the cases where intermediate goods are traded and where

[1] Perhaps the only omission that I regret is that of some Japanese analyses that seem extremely interesting, though the sources I have been able to consult in English [102, 103] do not give enough formal account of these theories. I refer to the analysis of the 'Marxist' economists, S. Tsuru and H. Ktamura, which links cyclical fluctuations with the *pattern* of trade [102].

they are not. Vanek [55], on the other hand, uses a two-sector model where the intermediates are identical with the final goods which enter trade.

A large number of propositions continue to be valid despite the introduction of intermediates and/or capital goods in the analytical models. For instance, as Samuelson [125] and Kemp [120] have shown, the proposition that free trade is superior to no trade is valid even when intermediates exist and enter trade. Similarly, Jones [69] has shown that the pattern of efficient specialization in the Ricardo–Graham model will continue to satisfy the bilateral comparative cost rankings postulated by Ricardo, even when intermediates enter trade. The factor price equalization theorem again has been examined, in the light of traded intermediate goods, by Samuelson [53] and Vanek [55] without leading to any qualitative change in the traditional propositions. On the other hand, certain propositions *do* change. For instance, the *exact* pattern of specialization in the Ricardo–Graham model naturally changes with the possibility of trade in intermediate goods [69, 78]. The effect of growth on the terms of trade again is shown by Ramaswami [86] to change qualitatively with the introduction of a (produced) capital-goods sector.

Of far greater significance, however, is the fact that a whole range of interesting and important questions slip through the analyst's hands unless intermediates and (produced) capital goods are introduced into the formal models. For instance, the recent GATT [107] discussions on the exports of 'new manufactures' from the industrializing underdeveloped countries have drawn attention to the disparity between tariffs levied on unprocessed and semi-processed items (on which tariffs are relatively lower) and those on finished manufactures. It is surely interesting to examine the effects, in both positive and welfare terms, of such tariff discrimination. But the analysis just cannot get off the ground with the traditional types of analytical models![1] Let me take another important illustration. The traditional multiplier analysis in trade theory (which has already been discussed

[1] We may note the related point that an apparently non-discriminatory tariff adjustment on all imports (say, 10% reduction in the tariffs on both alumina and aluminium) would be *de facto* discriminatory in its effects when the imports consist of both the raw material and the finished product. The effective reduction in the protective effect would be greater on the raw material. Incidentally, an analysis of the problem discussed in the text would call for some method of demarcating intermediates in a world where circularities in the Leontief flow-matrix may prevent an easy solution.

earlier in relation to the Keynesian treatment of the transfer problem) postulates the impact of exports and/or autonomous investments on the balance of payments and the levels of domestic output and employment. But there is an extension to the concept of the *import multiplier* as well, when one considers the situation frequently experienced by economies importing raw materials, when excess capacity develops due to the shortage of foreign exchange. An extra unit of exchange (say, through foreign aid) will then increase the level of domestic output directly by a multiple which is the ratio of value added to imported inputs (the latter being the only constraint). If, however, this output enters as input into other processes lying idle for want of materials, one can easily work out (through the input–output mechanism) a whole chain of increased outputs which, on summation, yields a multiplier-measure of the increased output attributable to the incremental unit of imports. This idea has been independently formulated in various writings, by Stolper [109, 110], several Japanese economists such as Akamatsu [106] and Kojima [103], and writers on the Indian balance of payments in recent years. It demonstrates forcefully how the exclusion of intermediates from analysis would rule out from examination one of the most significant aspects of the international trade problems besetting many economies. Since imported intermediates may also lead to extra output of domestically produced capital goods which may help break other bottlenecks at a future date, or the incremental exchange may be used to import capital goods which create capacity to break bottlenecks to domestic utilization of capacity in other sectors of use, this whole notion of the import multiplier has a further time dimension to it and equally illustrates the role of produced and traded capital goods in any realistic analysis of the trade phenomena in the real world.

6. Welfare Propositions: Gains from Trade

Welfare propositions are among the oldest in pure theory. Trade theory developed in the effort to demonstrate the fallacy of the protectionist prescriptions of the Mercantilist School. Today the range of analytical questions has increased astonishingly beyond the early preoccupation with the comparison of free trade with protection. To seek design and order in this vast literature is no mean ambition.

It is useful to start with the basic proposition that the aim of policy-orientated welfare economics is to provide a *ranking of policies*. This ranking may relate to *trade* policies (while the general equilibrium parameters and relationships, such as the known technology, are given). For instance, is a zero tariff (*i.e.*, free trade) superior to no trade? Is a 15% (non-discriminatory) tariff superior to a 20% tariff? Would an increase in the tariff rate be beneficial? On the other hand, the ranking may refer to policies relating to the general equilibrium *parameters and relationships*, such as the factor supply level (given the trade policy). For instance, for an open economy engaged in free trade, is migration desirable? Should the increment in capital stock be absorbed as domestic or foreign investment?[1]

The ranking of policies in pure theory further divides into two classes of propositions: (1) those that relate to *national* advantage; and (2) those that concern *international* advantage. Thus, for instance, the proposition that free trade is superior to no trade is sought to be established from both national and international standpoints. On the other hand, the proposition that (for a variable tariff rate) the optimum tariff is superior to free trade concerns only national advantage.

These rankings can further be classified according to the *criterion of welfare* employed. The Samuelsonian superior-for-all-income-distributions criterion has been widely used in the early development of the theory subsequent to the new welfare economics. On the other hand, it has been replaced extensively in recent years by criteria which handle the problem of income-distribution in a non-purist fashion. Among them, two approaches can be distinguished, which divide mainly on the issue of the measurability of utility.

The *ordinalist* method sets up a community welfare function which *assumes* that the State adopts a policy of lump-sum transfers to fix

[1] Although I have not done so in the text, the ranking of policies could also be classified into the ranking of *specific measures* and of *general forms of policy intervention*. Under the former, a characteristic illustration would be the ranking of two rates of tariffs. For instance, would a 5% tariff be inferior to a 3% tariff? Would a marginal reduction in the tariff rate increase welfare? Under the latter, a typical example would be the ranking of a tariff policy (without specifying a specific tariff rate) and free-trade policy. For instance, the proposition that an optimum tariff is superior to free trade is not formulated in terms of a unique tariff-rate comparison, but is rather valid in the sense that, corresponding to any income distribution chosen, there will be an optimum tariff rate which will be superior to free trade so that the utility possibility curve for an optimum tariff situation, with variable tariff rates, will lie outside (though it may touch) that for the free-trade situation.

the income-distribution at some 'desired' level. The properties of this welfare function are then assumed to be parallel to those which are taken normally (with some 'plausibility') to characterize individual welfare functions. It is only recently that Samuelson [126] has established the exact conditions under which 'social indifference curves' will enjoy these properties – so that, in effect, the trade theorist must assume, *ipso facto*, these conditions to obtain if he uses a social-welfare function with those properties.[1] The ranking of trade policies can then be carried out in terms of such a community preference function, corresponding to any 'desired' income distribution.

The other, alternative method of handling the problem of income distribution so as to achieve a unique ranking of policies has been that extensively used by Meade [8, 9]. He explicitly combines equity and efficiency in a single welfare function by assuming *cardinality* and the possibility of *interpersonal comparisons of welfare* (through assigned weights). This method enables the analyst to judge the change in welfare between two situations for the actual market income-distributions achieved and without having to conjure up a state of lump-sum transfers (which itself may be construed to be an advantage, from the ethical and practical viewpoints, over both the Samuelson criterion and the ordinalist method sketched earlier).[2]

[1] Often trade theorists omit mentioning the problem of lump-sum transfers and use community preference functions as if the community were an individual. This procedure is clearly sloppy. It is also not uncommon for some theorists to assume that the economy is composed of individuals with identical tastes and income (kept equal presumably by lump-sum transfers). This, however, is tantamount to assuming a single individual and, only in a limited, formal sense can one concede the 'reduced restrictiveness' of such an assumption! It is also sometimes stated that the state 'ignores the question of income distribution' and then the analyst proceeds to operate with the community indifference curves [129, p. 329]. This, however, is open to objection because: (1) the assumptions under which the community preference function would be characterized by the required properties (*e.g.*, convexity) would still have to be specified; and (2) the position implied by the statement is untenable. In what sense can one be 'indifferent' to income distribution? The only meaning that can possibly be attributed is that the state attaches equal weight to the marginal utility of each individual – in which case the analyst ceases to be an ordinalist!

[2] Caves' [3, pp. 233–4] neat summary of Meade's method is useful. 'Suppose that a change is made somewhere in the economy, such as the elimination of a monopoly position. There will be a primary gain in economic efficiency, because consumers now receive extra units of this particular product which they value above the cost to the suppliers. In addition, because of relations of substitutability and complementarity between this and other products, both in consumption and

Aside from the possible preferences on ethical and practical grounds, however, the shift in favour of these less-restrictive criteria has been prompted essentially by a change in the kinds of questions that economists are willing to accept from policy makers. The traditional analysis concerned itself with the ranking of specific policy measures (themselves distortionary) under otherwise 'first-best' assumptions or, in ranking forms of policy intervention, compared only policies achieving fully optimal situations with those resulting in sub-optimal ones. In the former category, for instance, is the proposition that a higher tariff is inferior to a lower tariff. In the latter class the most prominent proposition has always been that an optimum tariff (which attains the first best solution) is superior to free trade (which leads to a sub-optimal solution when the country can influence its terms of trade). These rankings satisfy the Samuelson welfare criterion. Now, however, the range of policy questions has increased enormously. The policy-makers wish to know the answers to questions which inevitably involve comparing sub-optimal situations. Problems are posed such that 'second-best' assumptions as also sub-optimal comparisons have to be made.[1] For instance, some distortionary

---

production, expenditure patterns will change throughout the economy. Spending on products with no cost-value divergence may rise; spending on other products with very large divergences may fall. Changes of this type represent secondary losses; their opposites would represent secondary gains. The process of summing these changes over the whole economic system is shown by the expression:

$$u = \sum_{i=1}^{n} \sum_{j=1}^{n} \sum_{s=1}^{e} (U_{ij} D_{ijs} - 1) \mu_j R_{js} \lambda_{ijs}$$

where the net change in utility (u) represents a summation, over all sellers, buyers, and commodities, of the unit revenue from each commodity (R) times the change in the quantity of that commodity exchanged (x), times the rate at which the marginal value to the purchaser exceeds the marginal cost to the seller ($D-1$). Subscript s denotes a commodity, i a buyer, j a seller. In addition, distributional weights appear as μ_j, the weight attached to marginal income for the seller, and U_{ij}, which stands for the ratio μ_i/μ_j.'

[1] Second-best assumptions imply that, from the entire set of assumptions that are made to demonstrate the Pareto optimality of the competitive solution, one (or more) does not obtain. Given this definition of second-best assumptions, it is useful to classify these constraints, the departures from first-best assumptions, into two categories: (1) *Behavioural* constraints; and (2) *Environmental* constraints. In the former class we can consider non-utility maximization and non-profit maximization by decision-making units. In the latter category we may further distinguish between (i) *state-imposed* constraints and (ii) *others*. Among the state-imposed constraints, we have the imposition of direct and indirect taxes, subsidies,

tariffs, restrictions of output levels, etc. The other constraints divide broadly into '*market imperfections*' (for instance, the presence of monopoly, a distortionary wage differential between sectors, divergence of the shadow rental to a factor from its actual rental, and national monopoly power in trade), '*technological characteristics*' (for instance, increasing returns to scale, and non-convexity of isoquants) and '*interdependence*' (for instance, externalities in production and in consumption).

Corresponding to the notion of second-best *assumptions* is the concept of second-best *solutions*. The difference between first-best and second-best solutions is, I suggest, best comprehended if it is founded on a distinction between those second-best assumptions that are *meaningfully* looked upon as removable (*in principle*) by intervention and those that are not. For instance, one can look upon a tax as removable and a wage differential as capable of being offset by a tax-cum-subsidy-on-labour-use, etc., so that the *standard first-best solution* (with all the first-best assumptions holding) is restorable. On the other hand, interdependence of utilities of consumers or increasing returns to scale or monopoly power in trade are not second-best assumptions which can be looked upon as capable of 'elimination' so as to restore the *standard* first-best situation. With this distinction in principle, between the different types of second-best assumptions, we can define the respective first-best and second-best solutions.

In the *former* class, where the second-best constraint is removable, the first-best solution is that which would obtain if the constraint *were* removed, *i.e.* it is the standard first-best solution. The functional forms (of the optimizing conditions), as also the values of the solution, will naturally be identical with those obtaining for the standard first-best solution. In the *latter* case, whree the second-best assumption is irremovable, the *first-best solution is that obtained by maximization subject to the second-best assumption.* This solution may have the same functional form (of the optimizing conditions) as for the solution under standard first-best assumptions. In general, the functional forms *will*, however, differ from those of the conditions for the *standard first-best solution.* Thus, for instance, where consumption externality obtains, it would be necessary for a consumer to take into account the impact of his utility on the other consumers. Or there may be production externality, for instance, under which a producer's decision concerning the level of production may be a function of another producer's level of production. Here again, the optimizing condition for producers will differ from that when no such interdependence obtains (yet the utility level reached will be identical under a policy where the state, by policy intervention, assures the fulfilment of this optimizing condition under interdependence, and under the standard first-best solution when no such interdependence obtains). The second-best solution can then be defined in terms of this first-best solution not being available under the postulates made.

We thus have: (1) the *standard first-best solution* (which obtains under universally first-best assumptions); (2) the first-best solution (equivalent to the standard first-best solution) when the second-best assumption is removable in principle; (3) the second-best solution when the second-best assumption, though removable in principle, is not removable and removed in practice; (4) the first-best solution (which may differ from the standard first-best solution in both functional forms of the optimizing conditions and, where comparison is meaningful, in welfare taxes may have to be admitted into the analysis when two tariff rates are being compared. The policy-maker is apt to say: 'I cannot take

---

level reached) when the second-best assumptions are irremovable in principle; and (5) the second-best solution when these second-best assumptions are irremovable in principle and the corresponding first-best solution cannot be obtained.

This analytical classification can be supplemented with a further set of remarks concerning the ways in which the effects of second-best assumptions are (and often, without clarity, have been) analysed.

(1) To begin with, the precise way in which the second-best solution should be delimited has to be clarified. For instance, if a country has monopoly power in trade the first-best solution would involve the imposition of an optimum tariff. Suppose that this is ruled out; then, is the second-best solution to be determined on the assumption that no tariff can be levied or on the assumption that only the optimum tariff cannot be levied? Similarly, if a wage differential cannot be eliminated entirely, are we to seek a second-best solution on the assumption that it cannot be offset in any degree or that it cannot be offset fully? There is no unique answer: it all depends on what restraints the policy-maker wishes to impose on himself. But the need for a clear definition of the problem must be underlined.

(2) Secondly, one has to distinguish between the second-best solution, which may necessitate intervention in a decentralized economy, and the *actual* solution that would prevail (under the second-best assumptions made) in the absence of the intervention that is necessary to bring about the second-best solution. Thus, if a distortionary wage differential between sectors obtains, the actual solution will be different from the second-best solution [112]; the latter will call for intervention.

(3) It also follows that, starting from any actual solution, under second-best assumptions one can ask how any intervention (other than that which produces the second-best solution) will influence the level of welfare. Thus, rather than investigate what is the second-best solution, the theorist may merely interest himself in *changes* in welfare resulting from the variation in the use of one or more policy instruments when second-best assumptions obtain. Or he may even, using this method, engage in 'partial optimization' and attempt to seek the optimal level of a particular policy (*e.g.*, the tariff rate) instead of seeking the optimal, second-best policy from the *entire* range of policy instruments. In trade theory it is *only* the latter two varieties of approach which have been used extensively; the question of the second-best solutions has hardly ever been posed.

This long footnote, highlighting different aspects of second-best theory, has been inserted primarily to gain a clearer grasp of the structure of many contributions to the theory of trade and welfare. I do not claim any special merits for the analytical classification proposed here over those currently available, except that it appears consistent and illuminates the logic of second-best analyses purposively. I am indebted to T. N. Srinivasan for many helpful conversations and for drawing my attention to, as also making available to me, an important unpublished paper by Otto Davis and Andrew Whinston on 'Welfare Economics and the Theory of Second Best' (*Cowles Foundation Discussion Paper*, No. 146).

off certain taxes. Given these taxes, will a reduction in the tariff rate be desirable?' Another familiar illustration is provided by the policy-makers, who argue that they cannot have universal free trade, but that a free-trade area with continuing tariffs on outside countries may be feasible. If so, would a move to a free-trade area be beneficial (to the member countries and/or the world)? Trade theorists have found that, in general, answers to such questions cannot be given, *even for particular cases* (*i.e.*, for instance, the latter question being asked in relation to a *specific* group of countries joining or opting out of a free-trade area rather than being formulated more generally so that the answer must be valid for all possible free-trade areas), unless the income distribution is specified. In general, *both* the particularizing of a question (in the sense just outlined) and the choice of an income distribution are necessary to the ranking of two alternative policies. Since these questions are of interest to policy-makers, the trade theorist has naturally eschewed all Samuelsonian scruples and, in either of the two ways discussed earlier, decided to handle income distribution in a non-purist fashion so as to enable him to get along with the business of ranking the contrasted policies.

This shift towards policy-orientation of a more realistic variety has logically led to the emergence of a new trend towards the *measurement* of losses and gains from changes in policy. Partly this is a result of the shift to the non-purist welfare criteria. Meade's method, for instance, is candidly cardinal, and the sheer process of determining the direction of the welfare change from a shift in policy involves the evaluation of the magnitude of this welfare change. The measurement of losses and gains in welfare, however, has also been given great currency by ordinalists such as Johnson [132, 133], and the principal reason for this has ultimately to be found in the general demand for such measurement by those who debate policies. Policies are maintained or changed largely for non-economic reasons; and the (economic) 'cost' involved is a magnitude that is commonly demanded and bandied about in discussions of public policy. Whether we like it or not, this is what the policy-makers do want; and the trade theorist, in consonance with the best traditions in the profession, has begun to meet this need in an attempt to bring economic analysis closer to fulfilling the objective that provides its ultimate *raison d'être*.[1] The result has been a definite and significant trend, in the welfare analysis of pure theory,

[1] Other interesting and important uses of the measures of gains and losses in welfare will be discussed in Section 7.

towards measurement of welfare change. It is important enough to merit detailed analysis in Section 7.

In the present Section we will survey the qualitative propositions of welfare analysis in pure theory, utilizing the analytical classifications developed so far. A full survey of the entire range of propositions is not necessary; there are endless ways in which the same theoretical principle may be applied so that a full mapping of these applications in the literature would be both tedious and exhausting. The analytical skeleton of the contributions to the analysis of welfare and trade has already been laid bare. All that needs to be done now is to survey the central analyses so that the skeleton acquires flesh.

Ranking of Policies by Samuelson Criterion: National Advantage

Among the simplest rankings by the Samuelson criterion, in relation to national advantage, is the proposition that a *higher tariff rate is inferior to a lower tariff rate.* This is valid under first-best assumptions (inclusive of the absence of national monopoly power in trade) [1]. There are clearly a very large number of such propositions that could be worked out: for instance, that a *lower trade subsidy is superior to a higher trade subsidy* (under first-best assumptions).[1]

The rankings which have traditionally held the stage in the welfare theory of trade are, however, the two celebrated propositions that: (1) *free trade is superior to no trade*; and (2) *an optimum tariff is superior to free trade* (when a country has monopoly power in trade). To these Kemp [120] has recently added the proposition that (3) *restricted trade is superior to no trade*, and Ramaswami and myself [112] have argued that (4) *an optimum subsidy is superior to a tariff policy* (when there are domestic distortions).

The proposition that free trade is superior to no trade was shown by Samuelson [125], in a classic paper, to hold with standard first-best assumptions. However, its validity has subsequently been extended to the case where a country can influence its terms of trade through the exercise of monopoly power [120]. Although there have always been those who erroneously believe, and have sometimes continued to assert despite proofs to the contrary, that the proposition rests on an

[1] These listed propositions hold because, in each case, the superior policy represents a 'weakening' of the sole second-best assumption (*i.e.*, a tariff or a subsidy) in an otherwise first-best situation. Throughout the following analysis the statement that a policy is 'superior' to another is to be taken to include whenever necessary the borderline case where the two produce identical welfare.

assumed mobility of factors of production, the proposition rests on no such postulate. Samuelson's 1939 proof [125] is clear on this issue; and Haberler [117] has subsequently provided a supporting geometrical argument which must make the truth accessible to more numerous economists. It is also necessary to note that the proposition, valid for all income distributions, holds only in the situation sense – such that the utility possibility curve corresponding to the free-trade policy will lie uniformly outside (though it may touch) the utility possibility curve corresponding to the no-trade policy [120].[1]

The proposition that restricted trade is superior to no trade, which is also valid in the situation sense, has been shown by Kemp [120] to hold under the standard first-best assumptions (except that the country may have monopoly power in trade). By restricted trade is meant essentially trade restricted in a manner which merely brings about a divergence between foreign and domestic commodity prices. Thus, the trade may be restricted by tariffs, quotas or exchange control. It is *not* correct to infer from this proposition that *any* manner of restricted trade will be beneficial in relation to no trade: for it is easy to conceive of forms of trade, where the volume and/or value of trade is lower than under free trade and yet the net effect is to lower the country's welfare below the no-trade level. Nor should the proposition be read to mean that any trade is superior to no trade. In fact, it can be shown that (subsidy-) expanded trade may, for some income distribution, be inferior to no trade. The proposition refers exclusively, therefore, to restricted trade (of the form defined here).[2]

The third proposition in this class is the celebrated dictum that an optimum tariff is superior to free trade when a country has monopoly power in trade. This proposition was formulated, though not with modern sophistication, as early as Mill's *Principles* [32]. When a country has the ability to influence its terms of trade the marginal

[1] It is not possible to demonstrate that the actual bundle of goods obtained by adopting free trade can be redistributed so as to make at least one person better off while leaving others as well off as with the *actual bundle* in the preceding no-trade condition. This has always been understood, although some confusion has cropped up in the literature occasionally. Johnson [66, p. 259] has produced a good example, illustrative of the proposition that the redistribution of the *actual* bundle of goods so as to demonstrate the superiority of free trade over no trade may be impossible.

[2] The analysis in the text could be adapted to develop the proposition that welfare increases to a maximum as restriction decreases to free trade, then falls as trade is increasingly subsidized until welfare has fallen below the no-trade level.

terms of trade diverge from the average terms of trade and a discrepancy arises, under free trade, between the domestic rate of transformation in production and the foreign rate of transformation. This divergence can be eliminated and the equality of these with the domestic rate of substitution in consumption achieved, resulting in the first-best optimum solution, when a suitable tariff rate is levied [5, Chapter II; 118]. This optimum tariff rate will naturally depend on the income distribution chosen. Hence, the proposition holds only for *variable* tariff rates, and in the situation sense. For the multi-commodity case an optimum tariff *structure* will exist, which in turn will vary with the income distribution [118].

The proposition concerning the superiority of the optimum tariff has been sought to be extended to the case where the imposition of the tariff results in retaliation. An investigation of this question requires a behavioural assumption concerning the foreigner's response (mechanism) and another with respect to the country's own method of accommodation to such response. The early assertions that, in the event of retaliation (insufficiently defined), a country could not gain from imposing an (initially, pre-retaliation) optimum tariff have subsequently been rejected as a result of the demonstration that, for any given income distribution, with a Cournot-type adjustment mechanism such that each country imposes an optimum tariff while assuming the other's tariff rate as fixed, it is *possible* (though *not* necessary) that, if and when final equilibrium is achieved with no country under incentive to change the tariff rate, the country imposing the initial optimum tariff may still be better off than under free trade.[1] While this proposition is valid, it should be noted that the result of a retaliatory system depends naturally on the response mechanisms assumed. Alternative 'rules of the game' can be readily imagined. For instance, the retaliation may plausibly be a function of the ability of the affected income group to coalesce into an effective pressure group – as Kindleberger's [73] historical study of the political sociology of the European tariff response to the influx of cheap American corn underlines. In this case, an integration of the protection-and-real-wages theory with the tariff-retaliation theory is called for. The easiest

[1] Two other results are of interest: (1) the adjustment process may result in a 'tariff cycle': countries may mill around the same set of tariff rates and not settle down to an equilibrium pair of tariff rates [5, pp. 42–3]; and (2) the equilibrium pair of tariff rates, where existent, will generally differ, depending on which country starts off the process.

way in which one can demonstrate the dependence of the stated proposition on the response-mechanism assumed is to postulate a retaliatory tariff that eliminates trade (for all income distributions). Here the reversion to no trade clearly leaves the country in a position inferior to free trade, *ruling out the possibility* of an improvement over the free-trade situation.

While the preceding propositions rank *trade policies*, the final proposition considered here involves a ranking of one trade policy and another *trade policy in conjunction with a different form of policy intervention*. This proposition is that, when domestic distortions (*i.e.*, a divergence between domestic rates of transformation and domestic price ratios) obtain, an optimum (production) subsidy (with free trade) is superior to any tariff intervention. The former policy equates the foreign rate of transformation (FRT) with the domestic rates of transformation in production (DRT) and of substitution in consumption (DRS), and thus turns out to be superior to a tariff policy which cannot ensure this [112].[1]

Ranking of Policies by Samuelson Criterion: International Advantage

From the viewpoint of international advantage, the proposition that *free trade is superior to any trade policy* is held to be valid [126]. The proposition holds when all the first-best assumptions obtain (though the possession of national monopoly power in trade, as long as not exercised, is permissible). The propositions that *free trade is superior to no trade*, *free trade is superior to expanded trade and free trade is superior to restricted trade* are only special cases of the preceding proposition.[2]

[1] I have deliberately refrained from describing the optimum subsidy policy which equates FRT, DRT and DRS as a policy which produces the first-best solution. This is because, whether it does or not, will depend on *which* second-best assumption causes this domestic distortion. Where an external economy produces such a distortion, the optimum subsidy will produce the standard first-best solution [112]. Where, however, it results from a wage differential, for instance, the optimum subsidy *cannot* produce the standard first-best solution, although it will, of course, be superior to any tariff intervention [112]. Incidentally, this also helps to illustrate the undesirability of trying to develop the theory of the second-best in terms of the violations of optimum conditions rather than in terms of the second-best assumptions themselves as proposed here.

[2] Several diagrammatic proofs of these propositions can be found in the literature. Formal mathematical proofs, however, are not easy to come by, although they could be easily devised.

Ranking by Other Criteria: National Advantage

The bulk of the literature in the theory of trade and welfare, however, concerns the ranking of policies, which yield sub-optimal results under second-best assumptions, with the aid of non-purist criteria of welfare change. These analyses can be conveniently divided into those exercises that seek to evaluate the change in welfare when a trade policy is changed and those that concern the welfare change when (the trade policy remaining unchanged) some given parameter or functional relationship (*e.g.*, factor supply, known technology, etc.) shifts.

A. *Trade Policies*

The most frequent way in which the problem is posed involves a primarily negative orientation. For instance, much of the analysis in this area concerns the demonstration that, even if the income distribution is fixed at an arbitrary level, the proposition that free trade is superior to no trade will *not necessarily* hold if there are, say, domestic distortions in the economy. Meade, using his cardinal method, extends his analysis, on the other hand, to deriving the precise conditions (*e.g.*, elasticity of transformation in domestic production, the degree of distortion, etc.) under which the trade policies being compared will rank one way or the other.[1] The analysis is sometimes extended also beyond the ranking of two trade policies. For instance, instead of merely ranking a 5% tariff and zero tariff, using either the cardinal or the ordinal method, the analyst proceeds to ask what tariff rates (constituting the policy instrument available to the policy-maker) will *maximize* welfare. The optimum level at which the available policy instrument should be used is thus the aim of this analysis, which goes beyond a mere ranking of two arbitrarily chosen levels at which the policy instrument may be used.[2] While such analysis represents a process of social-utility maximization, it should be emphasized that, except in the highly restrictive case where *all* other forms of policy intervention are excluded from the range of available policy instruments, this optimum level of the assigned policy instrument will not

[1] Of course, he is concerned with the effects of *marginal* changes in policies, so that his analysis amounts to ranking, say, a given tariff and a marginally increased tariff.

[2] Since Meade's analysis is usually directed at investigating the effect on welfare of a marginal change in some tariff rate (*i.e.*, du/dt where u is the level of social welfare and t the tariff rate), the optimum tariff level can be discovered readily by putting du/dt equal to zero.

generally represent the optimum, second-best solution under the stated, second-best assumptions (irrespective of what welfare criterion is being employed). This is really a point of some importance, since the bulk of the optimizing welfare analysis in trade is constrained by the fact that it has been directed at finding the optimum level at which a *specific* trade policy instrument (*e.g.*, a tariff) should be used rather than the optimum level at which the optimum policy instrument (or combination of instruments) should be used to maximize social utility, subject to the stated assumptions, in an open economy.

The kinds of problems analysed can be divided broadly into two classes according as the second-best assumptions relate to the: (1) domestic, or the (2) foreign sector. In the former category a wide assortment of second-best assumptions has been considered: external economies; monopolies in commodity markets; infant industry arguments; factor-reward differentials between sectors of use; factor-price rigidity and increasing returns to scale. In the latter class the stage is held by the theory of discriminatory tariff reduction. These arguments are briefly discussed here, to illustrate the prefatory analysis.

(a) *External Economies.* Where the standard first-best assumptions obtain, with the exception of externalities in production, the actual market solution will be characterized by a domestic distortion (*i.e.*, a divergence between the commodity price-ratio and DRT). The classic example of such externality is the dependence of honey production on the level of neighbouring apple output. The time-honoured infant-industry argument also involves externality [8].[1] Recently the theoretical interest in the co-ordination of investment decisions has also given us another impressive example of external economies under a régime of decentralized decision-making [97].

The resulting domestic distortions have been shown to invalidate, for instance, the proposition that free trade is (necessarily) superior to no trade [112, 117]. It is no longer possible to rank these two trade policies uniquely, either for all income distributions or (more im-

[1] Although the infant industry case has been classified here, it must be admitted that, formally, it has dimensions of dynamic analysis which go beyond the traditional range of external economies. Allowing for this fact, however, the case for assistance to infant industries *does* rest on an assumption of externality, as pointed out by Meade [8] and recently by Johnson [133]. For a different formal description and analysis of the infant-industry case, Haberler [117] may be consulted: his analysis, however, does not bring out the externality aspect as forcefully as it needs to be.

portantly) even with any assigned income distribution for all possible cases.[1] Similarly, it can be shown that no tariff rate may exist, in any given empirical case, which will produce greater welfare than free trade [112]. The reason is obvious. Under free trade, domestic distortions imply that FRT(= FP) = DRS(= DP) ≠ DRT (where DP and FP are the domestic and foreign price ratios respectively). On the other hand, a tariff may equate FRT and DRT, but will disrupt the equality of FRT with DRS. Since two sub-optimal positions are being compared, the conclusions already stated follow readily. The optimal solution for domestic distortions is clearly a production subsidy (or tax-cum-subsidy) which will equate FRT, DRT and DRS, and thereby achieve the first-best solution.[2]

(b) *Monopoly in Product Markets.* The monopoly argument is frequently taken to collapse into a simple case of domestic distortion.

[1] As stated earlier, the ranking will depend, among other things, on the degree of divergence, the elasticity of transformation in production and so on. In this connection it is probably necessary to point out that, in the standard analysis of external economies, it is not made clear that the externality may disappear at certain levels of output of either activity. With apple blossoms and bees, where the former are already too large relative to the latter, any increase in blossoms output by diversion of resources from bee production will not be subjected to externality effects. In terms of the standard geometry (ignored throughout the text of this paper), the production possibility curve, for certain ranges of output combinations, may thus be characterized by the quality of DRT and DP (domestic prices). If, then, free trade carries the economy's production within this range, the domestic distortions will be inapplicable and the standard, first-best solution (*i.e.*, free trade is superior to no trade) will become applicable. Thus, strictly speaking, the analysis in the text requires that the domestic distortions should be within the relevant ranges of production. This, in turn, makes very clear the crucial nature of income distribution: for, with one income distribution, an *x*% tariff may bring the economy within the range of domestic distortions, whereas, for another, it may not, thereby influencing the ranking of policies.

[2] In the light of this analysis it is possible to understand the significant qualification introduced by Haberler [4, p. 57] in his discussion of the correct prescription in the infant-industry case: 'It should also be added that it is, *a priori*, probable that in many cases not a customs duty but an export bounty would be in order in as much as external economies may be realizable in the export rather than in import industries. . . . The fact that the infant industry argument is almost exclusively employed to recommend import restrictions and practically never to justify the opposite . . . shows clearly the bias of those who employ it.' Of course, Haberler's case would require, as the optimal solution, an optimum (production) subsidy to the export industry. It cannot be argued, however, that if this is ruled out the trade-subsidy policy (believed guardedly by Haberler to be desirable) will necessarily produce, or will even be 'likely' to produce, better results than any alternative form of trade or other intervention.

Hence, it is regarded as formally equivalent to the external economy argument. It follows, then, that, once again, free trade cannot be shown to be (necessarily) superior to no trade; and also that no tariff may exist, in any given case, which may yield higher welfare than free trade.

Where, however, the monopoly argument differs from the external economy case is in the fact that the degree of monopoly itself may be a function of the rate of tariff [133]. Take, for instance, the extreme case where the introduction of free trade eliminates the monopoly power and turns the domestic monopolist into a perfect competitor. In this case the proposition that free trade is superior to no trade, for instance, will still be valid. The formal identity with the external economy case therefore breaks down.

(c) *Factor-reward Differentials between Sectors.* The presence of a wage differential between sectors (for remunerating the same factor) represents a market imperfection, constituting a departure from first-best assumptions under certain circumstances.[1] Where it is distortionary, there are two immediate consequences. The rate at which this factor and any other factor are being substituted in production in different sectors will no longer be equal. This will result in a reduction in the transformation possibilities. The production possibility curve will 'shrink in'. Further, at each point on the shrunk-in locus the domestic price ratio will diverge from the domestic rate of transformation (*along the shrunk-in locus*), so that we also are in a situation characterized by domestic distortions.

From these two effects, it is easy to see that: (1) free trade is not (necessarily) superior to no trade; (2) an optimum production subsidy (or tax-cum-subsidy) which equates DRS, FRT and DRT (along the shrunk-in transformation locus) is superior to any tariff; and (3) an optimum subsidy on labour-use, which directly offsets the wage differential, produces the standard first-best result.

(d) *Factor-price Rigidity.* Haberler [117] has sharply distinguished between factor immobility and factor-price rigidity, showing that the former leaves the welfare propositions valid under first-best conditions unaffected, whereas the latter manages to invalidate them. By arguing that factor-price rigidity in the face of commodity price-shift will lead

[1] A detailed discussion of the conditions under which a wage differential may be regarded as distortionary is contained in the paper by myself and V. K. Ramaswami [112]. The qualifications to which the present analysis is subject are also considered there. Further comments on the problem are found in Johnson [133]. Credit for pioneering the problem belongs to Hagen [118].

to unemployment, Haberler has demonstrated the possibility that free trade, for any assigned income distribution and given empirical situation, may produce a deterioration in welfare in relation to no trade.[1] Haberler's analysis has recently been refined by Johnson [133], who has investigated alternative ways in which factor-price rigidity may be defined and, in turn, combined with assumptions concerning mobility of the factors of production, to produce a varying range of propositions which confirm Haberler's results.

(e) *Increasing Returns to Scale.* When an activity in the system is subject to increasing returns to scale the locus of transformation possibilities may lose its convexity. Matthews [123] has demonstrated how, in this case, a country may be worse off under free trade than under no trade. Thus, under this technological assumption, it is not possible to maintain that free trade is (necessarily) superior to no trade.[2]

[1] This is illustrated by Haberler [117], for a given income distribution, as follows. Taking factor immobility as well, he shows production and consumption under no trade at S, with SR as the price ratio between exportables and importables. With free trade at foreign price ratio FP, the production in importables

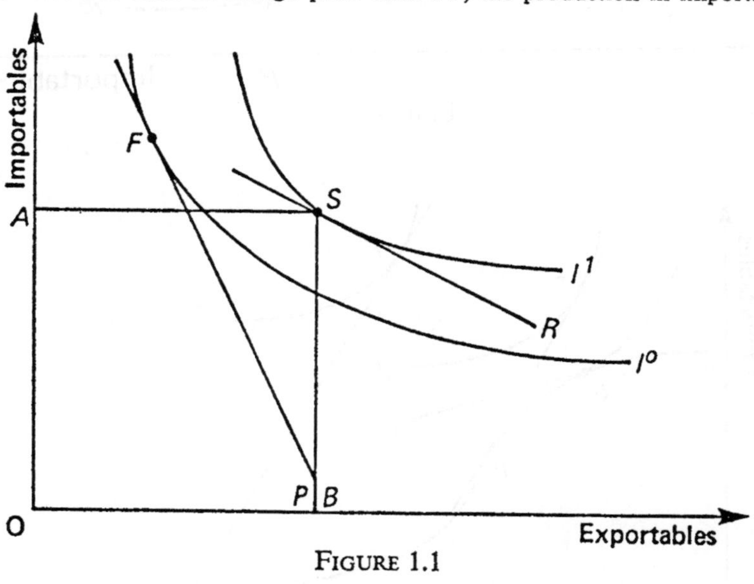

FIGURE 1.1

falls to P and consumption moves to F. The result is a deterioration in welfare. Free trade, for the given income distribution, is inferior to no trade. (It has to be assumed, of course, that the factor-price rigidity is due to institutional rather than voluntary reasons.) I might refer, incidentally, to the analysis of a similar problem [97], where the wage-rate in the agricultural sector is different from the marginal value product (whereas the industrial sector pays according to the marginal productivity principle), the wage-rate being 'rigid' in the agricultural sector.

[2] However, questions of stability of equilibrium arise here which have to be

carefully tackled. Tinbergen [127] has constructed an ingenious example which also illustrates the point in the text. In the accompanying illustration the production associated with free trade happens to be at *P* (which is a stable point) and the result is welfare deterioration in relation to no trade.

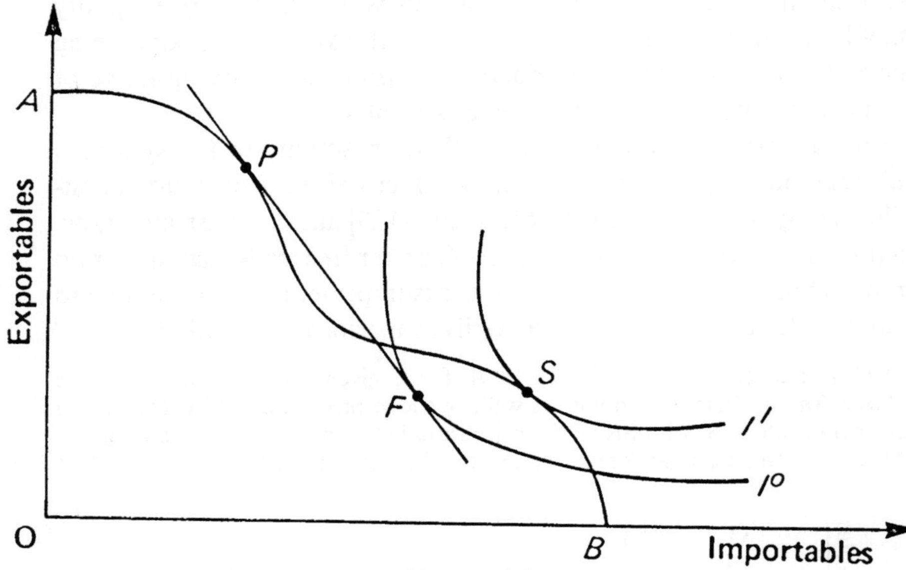

FIGURE 1.2

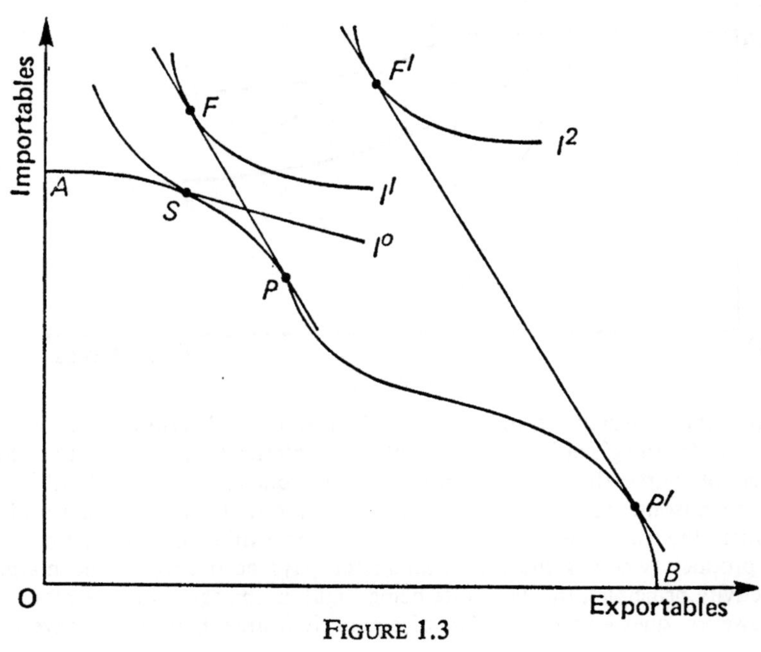

FIGURE 1.3

Concavity also underlines the fact that the optimizing solutions (and corresponding conditions) strictly imply only local maximization. It can be shown that the optimum optimorum may not be reached by free trade when there is concavity over some (though not the entire) range of the transformation locus, although free trade may continue to be superior to no trade.[1]

(f) *Customs Unions*. So far we have been concerned with departures from first-best assumptions on the domestic side. The welfare problem has, however, also been posed in terms of distortions arising from the presence of tariffs, subsidies and other such policies in foreign trade. Thus, for instance, a typical question has been whether, with tariffs continuing on one country, if the tariffs on another are reduced the national welfare will be increased. For any two tariff rates compared in such a situation, the ranking is subject to the income distribution chosen. Even with the income distribution chosen, no unique ranking is generally possible on an *a priori* basis.

Take, for instance, the model where the home country A can import, without having the power to affect the terms at which it can import, a commodity from either of two countries B and C. For the levels of demands relevant to the defined situation, C supplies M cheaper than B, while A is the highest-cost producer. In the initial situation, assume a tariff rate t_0 which permits C to compete successfully and secure A's market. Suppose, however, that A removes the tariff on imports from B but must continue to impose it on C's exports. If this makes B's export of M to A cheaper than C's, A is shifting its source of supply to a higher-cost producer. The former situation was characterized by DRT = DRS $\neq$ FRT; the latter is as well (since the most favourable rate at which A can transform its exports into imports is that determined by C's c.i.f. price in A). The choice between them cannot be made on an *a priori* basis; the choice of income distribution will also influence the ranking [7, 121]. For any given income distribution, using the ordinalist method, the ranking can naturally be worked out for any *given* empirical situation. Meade's cardinalist method would also give a unique ranking for a specific *empirical* situation.

There are many other ways in which a similar problem can be set up. One may take a case where A specializes in X and exchanges it

[1] Thus, in Figure 1.3, S represents the no-trade point, F and P the consumption and production points corresponding to free trade but representing only a local maximum, while F' and P' represent the equilibrium points corresponding to the optimum optimorum position under free trade.

for both Y (from B) and Z (from C). There is a uniform tariff rate on the (perfectly elastic supply of) imports of both Y and Z into A. The actual situation, from the viewpoint of A's welfare, is characterized by

$$\left(\frac{P_y}{P_z}\right)_F = \left(\frac{P_y}{P_z}\right)_D \text{ but } \left(\frac{P_x}{P_y}\right)_F \neq \left(\frac{P_x}{P_y}\right)_D \text{ and } \left(\frac{P_x}{P_z}\right)_F \neq \left(\frac{P_x}{P_F}\right)_D$$

where the suffixes F and D refer to foreign and domestic price-ratios in A. Suppose now that the tariff on Z is abolished *while that on Y is continued*. Then the country moves into a situation where

$$\left(\frac{P_x}{P_z}\right)_F = \left(\frac{P_x}{P_z}\right)_D \text{ but } \left(\frac{P_y}{P_z}\right)_F \neq \left(\frac{P_y}{P_z}\right)_D \text{ and } \left(\frac{P_x}{P_y}\right)_F \neq \left(\frac{P_x}{P_y}\right)_D$$

The comparison is again between two sub-optimal situations in this case. No *a priori*, unique ranking is possible [7]; and the income distribution will in general influence the ranking even when a *specific* situation has been defined (with reference to the functional and parametric aspects).

B. *Non-trade Policies*

So far only different trade policies have been compared. However, there is a considerable literature even on the effects of changes in the general equilibrium parameters and functional relationships on national welfare. Among the prominent contributions in this field are analyses of: (1) the effect of change in factor supply, and (2) the effect of technical change on welfare, when the economy is engaged in trade.

In the former category the analysis by Johnson [5, Chapter III] and myself [111] has shown how the effect of a change in factor supply on the growth of real income can be approximated, making allowance for the effect of the adjustment of the terms of trade *when the country has monopoly power in trade*. The analysis has also been extended to establish the conditions under which the growth of factor supply may actually result in the deterioration of the country's welfare through the loss of real income from worsened terms of trade outweighing the direct gain from expansion – a possibility seen independently by Edgeworth, Johnson [5, Chapter V] and myself and now widely known as the case of 'immiserizing growth'. Basically the same analysis can be adapted to the investigation of the impact of transfers of factors of production from one country to another on each's welfare, since the only substantive difference is that the growth of factors of production is, in one case, net for the two countries, while in the latter case there is no addition to the factor supply of the two countries together but only its redistribution [5].

This analysis has also been turned around to examine the relative advantages of absorption of marginal increment in population or capital stock at home or abroad [119, 122].[1] The analysis has further been reworked in relation to the effects of shifts in technology. The results of Findlay and Grubert [62] have been used to examine the effect of different types of technical progress on national welfare, again under the second-best assumption of national monopoly power in trade [2].

Ranking by Less-restrictive Criteria: International Advantage

So far, the rankings have been concerned with national advantage. Largely owing to the nineteenth-century concern with international advantage, however, much interest still continues to be exhibited in questions of international advantage.

The great bulk of the questions have again related to the ranking of trade policies when some second-best assumption obtains. Meade [8, 9] has worked out numerous problems, investigating the optimum level of a specific trade policy under the stated second-best assumptions. There are other contributions, such as Viner's [9] and Lipsey's [121] analyses of customs unions and Ozga's [85] examination of unilateral tariff reduction by a country in a world with other tariffs. These reinforce the proposition that, in general, no *a priori* ranking of policies is possible and that the choice of income distribution can affect the ranking when second-best assumptions obtain and sub-optimal situations are being ranked.

[1] This problem (unlike the others listed here) is of interest even under first-best assumptions for the economy. For instance, if the rental on capital abroad is higher than at home, and reflects the marginal value product, it would appear to be to private and social advantage to invest abroad. However, this is not correct, as what is socially relevant is the marginal return on the investments abroad. If the country already has invested capital abroad a fall in its rate of return through further investment will reduce the previous return, and the net benefit to the country will be *less* than the average rate of return, as Jasay [119] has noted in a valuable contribution. An important practical point may also be that the rate of return on foreign investment will always be less than the marginal-value product abroad because of corporation taxation [122]. And so on. The possibility of affecting the terms of trade differently according as home or foreign investment is chosen, which arises only under the second-best assumption of national monopoly power in trade, introduces still further theoretical questions of interest.

Meade's exercises, for instance, range over many such comparisons: (1) A imports Y_1 and Y_2 from B; Y_1 and Y_2 are substitutable or complementary in A's consumption. A duty at $t_2\%$ is levied on the import of Y_2 and cannot be removed. Would a tariff on the import of Y_1 be then worthwhile and, if so, what is its optimum level? (2) A imports Y_1, which is complementary or substitutable in A's consumption with X_2, which A exports to B and on whose exports B levies an import duty. Should a tariff be imposed on the import of Y_1 into A, and if so, what is the optimum level? (3) Or there might be second-best assumptions in the domestic economy of a country. For instance, if there is a divergence in the marginal cost and value of a commodity which competes with imports, would a tariff be worthwhile, and if so, what is its optimum level?

Central Limitations of the Propositions

Regardless of the criterion of welfare change employed, the rankings considered hitherto are valid only in a static context. At least two serious limitations of these propositions spring from the admission of dynamic elements.

(1) The ranking of two tariff rates will be a function of how these two rates are reached. Starting from a current tariff rate of $\alpha\%$, moves to a tariff of $x\%$ and $y\%$ will, in general, rank x and y differently (for the same income distribution) than when the move takes place from an initial tariff rate of $\beta\%$. In fact, even the paths of adjustments from a single current position to each of the pairs of rates of tariffs ultimately reached may not be unique, so that, for different paths chosen, the ultimate ranking may be different. These possibilities, however, are ruled out, for instance, by the restrictive assumption of constant terms of trade (for all tariff rates) in Samuelson's 1939 proof [125] of the proposition that free trade is superior to no trade and, in Kemp's extension [120] of the proof to the case when the terms of trade will vary with the volume of trade, by the (implicit) assumption that the foreign countries' trade offers at different terms of trade are not a function of the trade policy of the country. This restrictiveness is serious in a world where policy changes, especially in international trade, are inevitably accompanied by protracted negotiations concerning the reciprocity of 'benefits', and the interdependence of countries' trade policies is an impressive and irrefutable fact [107].

(2) These propositions are further limited in their reliance on one-period, static criteria. There are undoubtedly ways in which one can

demonstrate that free trade is superior to no trade, for instance, in a multi-period, dynamic, welfare framework. Thus, for instance, it can be established that, for the *same* initial conditions, time profile of consumption in each period, time-horizon and the structural composition of the terminal capital stocks (*e.g.*, the ratio in which they are to be held), free trade will lead to a *greater* quantity of terminal capital stocks than no trade [1].[1] While, however, the conclusions of welfare statics can be sustained in welfare dynamics within certain frameworks, they are also refuted within others. For instance, with a *terminal* preference function (*e.g.*, the income level in the terminal period), savings ratio a function of the income distribution, and the income distribution entirely a function of the market-imputed incomes it is possible for free trade to be *inferior* to no trade.[2]

7. Measurement of Gains and Losses

While, in these significant respects, the welfare propositions of pure theory have continued to be limited, the static methods of welfare analysis have been strikingly extended into the field of measurement of losses and gains (as between the welfare levels reached under the ranked policies). Some of the principal factors motivating this shift have already been analysed: the impact of the shift to less purist criteria of welfare and the general demand for such measurement. To these we must add a third, interesting factor: the analytical use of such measurement in determining a 'scientific tariff' [132]. This itself has its origin in the practice of computing the economic cost of given policies.

Frequently policies are pursued for a specific non-economic objective. For instance, a tariff may be imposed to achieve an assigned level of domestic production of an importable commodity. The cost of that tariff then is the cost of achieving this level of domestic production (which constitutes the non-economic objective). This notion can be extended in two profitable ways.

[1] This model, from the seminal work of Dorfman, Solow and Samuelson [113], relies on two main assumptions: (1) perfect foresight; and (2) a centralized authority whose preference function specifies the time-profile of consumption, etc.

[2] I am afraid, therefore, that Caves [3, p. 265] is not correct in arguing that 'static welfare economics is perfectly valid in a dynamic setting for the welfare problems discussed here if the assumption is made that factors of production and commodities are perfectly mobile, that is can be re-allocated with infinite speed and zero cost.'

(1) Suppose that a tariff is the only policy instrument available. However, the non-economic objective, which consists of a *fixed-target* type of assignment (*e.g.*, achievement of a given level of import-competing production or the reduction of imports to a specific value), can be fulfilled in numerous ways. For instance, if the objective is to achieve a given reduction in the value of imports this could be achieved by tariffs on *one* or *more* of the various imported commodities. We have here, then, a problem of choosing that tariff *structure* which *minimizes* the cost of achieving the assigned non-economic objective. This is a familiar problem in economic analysis, with a standard solution.

Johnson [132], in a powerful and ingenious paper, has developed this analysis, christening the minimum-cost tariff structure as 'scientific' [on the (*Oxford English Dictionary*) ground that it is evolved with the aid of expert knowledge]. He uses the notion of the scientific tariff to consider the kinds of tariff structure that would be called for under a wide range of non-economic objectives such as self-sufficiency, promotion of a 'way of life', increased diversification, etc., each such general non-economic objective being reduced to a suitable, operational objective, such as reduction in the value of imports and increase in the value of import-competing production.[1]

(2) But this notion of the tariff structure that minimizes the cost of a fixed-target type of non-economic objective is itself restrictive. For the analysis can be meaningfully extended to the case where the policy-maker is willing to consider a whole range of variables, representing *varying degrees of fulfilment of a non-economic objective.* For instance, a policy-maker interested in reducing the value of

[1] There are two respects, however, in which the analysis, as presented by Johnson, may be misleading. (1) He equates the marginal benefit: marginal cost ratios for tariffs on different imports, as a condition for minimum-cost tariff structure. It should be emphasized that this is only a necessary condition (which would have to be rewritten for cases involving inequalities). (2) Secondly, he frequently talks of 'measuring' a non-economic objective in terms of some observable variable: for instance 'the simplest possible measure of the benefit achieved by such a tariff [to provide national self-sufficiency and independence] in the value of imports excluded by it' [132, p. 342]. This gives the impression that Johnson is setting up an *independent* utility function to *measure* the welfare level reached (with respect to a non-economic objective) by a tariff structure: a procedure which may well be debated. What Johnson really is doing, however, is to translate vague objectives like 'national self-sufficiency' into *precise* and usable objectives such as 'reduction in the value of imports'. And that is both necessary for the analysis to get off the ground and also a valid procedure.

imports may not lay down a specific value of imports as the target, but would like to choose from varying values of imports *after* ascertaining the (*minimum*) costs attached to the tariff structures that lead to these targets. The choice made would then have the usual property (associated with maximizing behaviour): any departure from the selected tariff structure would change the value of imports by an amount which, for the policy-maker, is not worth the change in cost involved. The scientific tariff structure associated with this choice thus exhibits the familiar optimality property from the viewpoint of the policy-maker.[1]

An important limitation of the foregoing analysis is that it specifies a non-economic objective and considers tariffs as the only available instrument variables. While, however, this approach does yield the scientific *tariff* structure, it is possible that the same non-economic objective could have been achieved at a *smaller* cost if the range of policy instruments had been wider. An interesting paper of Corden [128] illustrates this principle tangentially. Working with a two-good model (which eliminates the question of a tariff *structure*) and the fixed-target objective of attaining a *given level* of production of the importable good, Corden has shown that, for unchangeable terms of trade, a (production) subsidy is less expensive than a tariff, whereas, for variable terms of trade, a tariff-and-subsidy measure is superior to either a tariff or a subsidy. Johnson [133], drawing on Young's earlier work, has shown, on the other hand, that, for unchangeable terms of trade, a tariff is more efficient than a subsidy when the non-economic objective is an assigned reduction in the volume of *imports* (in a two-good model). These contributions already begin to pull away in the direction of a scientific *economic* policy, as distinct from a scientific tariff (or even trade) policy.[2]

[1] Johnson [132, p. 341] refers to this question of choice among scientific tariff structures in terms of choosing the tariff 'level' (which is presumably to be obtained, in his formulation, by equating the marginal benefits and costs). This may be a little misleading because, in general, the scientific tariff structure for varying degrees of fulfilment of a non-economic objective may *not* be just scalar multiples of each other.

[2] Although the papers by Johnson [131, 132] and Corden [128] have been singled out in the text for their ingenious and path-breaking approach to the analysis of non-economic objectives, there are two other prior contributions which merit mention here. (1) Johnson's [129] analysis of the relationship between the tariff that would produce maximum revenue (a non-economic objective) and the optimum tariff (that equates FRT with DRT and DRS under variable terms of

While the measurement of gains and losses has been used *theoretically* to derive scientific tariffs, its *empirical* application has been for the more pedestrian but surer task of estimating the cost of changes in tariff policies. Among the most striking of these exercises must be reckoned Johnson's [131] attempt at measuring the gain to the United Kingdom from joining the European Common Market and Wemelsfelder's [135] study of the short-term effect of the lowering of import duties in West Germany.[1] These analyses carry the application of the welfare propositions of pure theory of trade very much further than the early, interesting attempts, most prominently that of Marris [134], at estimating the foreign rate of transformation with a view to deriving directional policy conclusions concerning tariffs.[2]

Although these exercises represent a significant, new trend in the welfare analysis of pure theory, they none the less have limitations which reflect essentially the deficiencies of the conceptual framework underlying the measurements employed.

Two different ways in which measurement has been attempted can be distinguished. They reflect, in turn, the ordinalist and cardinalist methods of (non-Samuelsonian) welfare analysis discussed in the previous section.[3]

The former, ordinalist procedure yields several alternative measures as in other applications of 'surplus' theory. The theorist can choose from a large number of possible measures, some of which have been analysed at length by Johnson and myself [2]. Johnson [132] happens to choose Hicks' compensating variation for his measurement.[4]

---

trade) dates back to 1951–2. (2) Meade [9, Chapters V, VI] had also handled, in 1955, two problems which consist in the choice between a tariff and a domestic tax with a specific non-economic objective (of raising given revenue) from the viewpoint of minimizing the loss in world welfare – thereby anticipating the approach in the contributions of Corden [128] and Johnson [133] towards the formulation of policy questions, not just in terms of trade policy, but in more general terms.

[1] There are other, less-impressive estimates by Verdoorn and Scitovsky [7] of the gains from European integration.

[2] Marris' [134] study, while important as a pioneering empirical exercise in trade and welfare, is unpersuasive in interpretation and analysis of the statistical data.

[3] A partial-equilibrium approach to measurement has also been suggested by Corden and Johnson [130], but is subject to well-known drawbacks that are explicitly recognized by these authors.

[4] Hence, the cost of protection, when a tariff is levied, is measured in terms of the compensation that would leave the country as well off, under the tariff, as previously under free trade.

Meade's method, on the other hand, yields a unique measure of the cost of a change in policy. This measure is tantamount to the Marshallian surplus measures, as is evident from the fact that his method estimates gains (losses) as the increase (decrease) in the volume of transactions in each commodity multiplied by the excess of utility derived by the buyer over the utility of that commodity to the seller, a divergence that is measured, for instance, in the case of a tax, by the rate of tax on the assumption that the price paid equals the marginal utility to the buyer and the price received the utility to the seller. Both Johnson's and Meade's measures are identical except for the differences caused by: (1) Meade's assumption of small and Johnson's of large changes,[1] and (2) Meade's Marshallian measure and Johnson's use of the compensating variation.[2]

The identity, except for the differences noted, obtains despite the different views concerning utility measurement because of the fact that, from the present viewpoint, Johnson's assumption of a well-behaved community preference function (enjoying the properties of a *single* individual's preference function) converges on Meade's *de facto* assumption of equal weights for each buyer and seller. In the two respects in which the measurements diverge, Johnson's analysis clearly is an improvement. And yet, from the *operational* viewpoint, Johnson's ordinalist approach runs into an insuperable difficulty. How is the analyst to estimate the contours (albeit at the relevant points) of the hypothesized social indifference map? Meades' (theoretically less attractive) method runs into no such snags (though *other* difficulties of econometric measurement no doubt persist). Since the aim of these exercises is to measure welfare changes *in practice*, operational methods may well be judged to be superior to analytically more impressive results.

Either method, however, leaves out of reckoning, in consonance with the limitations of the conceptual static approach to welfare on which it is based, the dynamic elements in the absence of which the exercises are reduced in their usefulness. For instance, in relation to

[1] This introduces the fraction $\frac{1}{2}$ into Johnson's formulae, stemming from his having to integrate the area under the triangle for large changes.

[2] This leads Johnson to argue in terms of the 'compensated' (*i.e.*, constant-utility) indifference curve and to use a pure substitution term for changed consumption, whereas Meade does not adjust for changed utility and takes the entire change in consumption in his measure of the gain in utility to buyers. Johnson is equally more cautious in trying to adjust for rent in his measure of the production costs.

the estimates of the gains from European integration, it has frequently been noted that these estimates ignore significant considerations like the effects of competition on efficiency, on innovation, etc. They also omit the implications of improved bargaining power in negotiating tariff and other trade concessions.[1]

The most serious limitation springs from the conceptual difficulty of applying the surplus analysis when the economy is producing and/or absorbing commodities for purposes other than consumption. How, for instance, is the 'consumer's surplus' on the purchase of investment goods to be estimated? To assert that this can be done as with consumer goods is to assume that the price paid for investment goods currently reflects the ultimate utility that will accrue from the production resulting from them. This assumption, however, begs a whole lot of questions which are central to the issues of dynamic welfare economics. For instance, the 'correct' valuation of the investment goods will vary in general with the choice of the time-horizon.[2] These issues cannot be conjured away. They are compelling when welfare comparisons are being made.

While these limitations persist, welfare analysis in pure theory has clearly reached a degree of sophistication and feasibility of useful empirical application which is impressive. These developments have brought within the fold of economic analysis many problems with direct policy relevance.

One of the major 'casualties' of this progress has been the historic intellectual dominance of the 'free trader'. The reorientation in the view concerning the role of the analyst – the acceptance of non-economic objectives, the willingness to consider sub-optimal situations instead of strictly utopian prescriptions – has overwhelmed the profession with a new mood of judging 'each case on its merits' and tailoring policies to specific objectives and situations. The few, surviving 'free traders' have, in consequence, been in disarray. At the turn of the century they readily admitted the solitary, twin examples of 'good' tariffs: the optimum (under national monopoly power) and the infant industry tariffs. They even proudly claimed that it was a 'free trader', John Stuart Mill, who foresaw the formal arguments to

[1] It should be noted, however, that the authors of the estimates are generally aware of most of these limitations.

[2] Moreover, the decentralization of decision-making adds to the difficulties (*e.g.*, inconsistency and myopia in behaviour) created by imperfect foresight and necessitates a revised approach to the notions of 'rational' decision making, and hence of welfare.

support them. With the breath-taking increase in the 'deviations' from the free-trade case, however, this easy 'theoretical' superiority over the pragmatic protectionists has disappeared.[1] With it, the free traders, greatly reduced in number, have now taken to resting their case exclusively on 'empirical', practical bases. Two varieties of arguments are frequent: (1) The unsophisticated argument is that, in practice, it is impossible to estimate the 'distortions' and hence the tariff structure and level which they justify. Hence, faced with this ignorance, the economist should not advocate a move away from the free-trade situation. This contention must be rejected. Not merely does it ignore the growing trend towards estimation. It also attaches an unacceptable special weight to the situation of a zero-tariff. Indeed, even if the fact of ignorance were admitted, the most one could say was that no ranking of trade policies was possible in practice. Why should the free trader be at an advantage here? If it were contended that a departure from a given position would be incapable of positive justification, and hence free trade should be the policy, the free trader is surely worsted in the debate, since the given situation is almost always characterized by the absence of free trade. This entire approach to the validation of the prescription of free trade is thus unpersuasive. (2) A more sophisticated approach admits that distortions exist and welfare-increasing tariffs may be devised by economists. However, in practice, the way tariffs are politically engineered, they are almost always imposed so as to bring about a deterioration in welfare. This argument admits that the zero-tariff position may not be the optimal one. It merely asserts that the admissibility of tariffs will lead in practice to another sub-optimal position which is inferior. Hence the economist ought to support free trade as a political prescription.[2] It is

[1] I use the objective 'pragmatic' with special emphasis. The theological protectionist is as much at fault as the theological free trader. But whereas the former has always been taken lightly, the latter has traditionally had an intellectual respectability which is now a rapidly wasting asset.

[2] This argument has a long, historical tradition. It is worth quoting the famous passage of Edgeworth, arising out of Bickerdike's discussion of the case for optimum tariffs. 'Thus the direct use of the theory is likely to be small. But it is to be feared that its abuse will be considerable. It affords to unscrupulous advocates of vulgar Protection a peculiarly specious pretext for introducing the thin edge of the wedge. Mr. Bickerdike may be compared to a scientist who, by a new analysis, has discovered that strychnine may be administered in small doses with prospect of advantage in one or two more cases than was previously known; the result of this discovery may be to render the drug more easily procurable by those whose intention is not medicinal. . . . Let us admire the skill of the analyst, but label the subject of his investigation POISON' [4, p. 53].

surely difficult to accept this logic. Surely it is not demonstrable that tariffs will always be 'perverse' or are 'likely' to be perverse. It is equally unpersuasive to assume that politicians will readily accept the free-trade prescription when their revealed preference has continuously been for *some* tariffs (though not for no trade), but that they will reject the prescription concerning the 'correct' tariffs and instead settle for perverse tariffs.[1]

8. Trade Theory and Developmental Planning

While any 'orthodox' survey of international economics would undoubtedly have terminated with the preceding Section, it would be singularly unfortunate if I did not address a few closing remarks to the small but important and growing literature on developmental planning (*in practice*) in its trade aspects. Happily, the subject has been brilliantly analysed in a companion Survey paper by Chenery [139] so that I can confine myself to certain ideas which have value in supplementing Chenery's account.

Broadly speaking, the classes of models that have been used to guide the choice of trade (and production) policy divide conveniently into two sets: (1) the highly simplified, decision models which usually anchor on some striking characteristic of the planned economy; and (2) more elaborate, inter-industry models. The latter, in turn, classify into models that deal with mere consistency and those that also attempt partial or fuller optimization.

Among the class of simple, decision models, several can naturally be identified. The two most interesting, however, appear to be those that are associated with the notions of a wage-goods bottleneck and a capital-goods bottleneck. For instance, a model that postulates the availability of wage-goods (say, food) as the constraint on increased investment and growth (in an overpopulated economy with surplus labour) has prompted in practice a trade policy characterized by imported food/grains and focuses sharply on the role of PL480 variety

[1] Ethical arguments are also current. For instance, some free traders claim to be 'internationalists' and object to the optimum tariff argument as purely 'nationalistic' and of the 'beggar-my-neighbour' variety. At the purely ethical level, of course, no argument can be refuted. In this instance, however, one can point out that free trade is optimal internationally only in the situation sense, so that the problem of income distribution does remain with the 'internationalists'. Moreover, the free-trade case does not take cognisance of non-economic objectives *or* dynamic welfare complications.

of foreign aid to developing countries [136]. On the other hand, a two-sector model, with two different investment and consumption goods, helps to highlight the role of developing an adequate capital-goods production base in supporting the targeted rate of investment at some future date (if the economy is faced with a shortfall in exchange earnings currently and prospectively) and hence has resulted in the utilization of exchange to build up capacity in heavy industries [141].[1]

The central limitation of these models, however, is that they can be treacherous in ignoring *other* equally important factors: as in most economic problems, planning is necessarily a complex process. Hence, more detailed, inter-industry models which *permit* the introduction of much other information, have come to be extensively employed in framing developmental plans. Among the operational models actually used, the formulations have generally been limited in being both static and centred on just consistency [140]. Using the Leontief, static-exercise approach, the analyst takes an autonomous export vector and *either* uses the concept of an *import-structure* (involving an import-coefficients matrix analogous to the input-coefficients matrix [142]) to derive the import pattern and total corresponding to the assigned bill of goods *or* derives *imports as residuals* by taking an assigned set of production targets and setting them off against the requirements worked out from the assigned bill of goods. The former approach, using the notion of an import structure, is clearly inappropriate to a planning model which, in looking ahead, need not be tied down to an arbitrary, base-year import structure and, indeed, in doing so, rejects out of hand the important choice (available to the planner) between domestic production and imports. In this respect, the imports-as-residuals approach, used for instance in the Indian planning framework [140], is superior.[2]

[1] While these simple models do often serve to make an important point clear, as for instance the necessity to have a capital-goods industry, they fail in giving a clear guide line on the *magnitudes* with which the planners should work. For the latter, more detailed work, involving also other constraints in the system, will be necessary. Reliance on the former alone, therefore, may do far more harm than good. For a discussion of some of the fallacies which have actually sprung from over-reliance on such simplified modes of reasoning, the reader may refer to my paper [97].

[2] Of course, in choosing the assigned domestic production targets themselves, the planner may have *implicitly* made a choice on some sort of 'optimizing' lines. More usually, however, the domestic production targets are in varying degrees 'arbitrary'.

It is possible, however, to introduce explicit optimization into these procedures, at varying levels. The most interesting innovation, from the present viewpoint, is the operational determination of the *shadow* exchange rate, as outlined by Chenery [139] in his Survey and claimed to have been used to determine the choice between imports and domestic production of commodities for Israel by him and Bruno [138] in an excellent paper which develops a useful way of framing *alternative* programmes from which the planner may make his ultimate choice. While the objectives in these exercises are to achieve partial optimization (in limited areas of the economy) and the frameworks are essentially static, the principle of optimization used merely reflects the basic insights of the theory of trade and welfare, and there is every prospect that further work in this area will clear the way for an operational and empirically meaningful use of trade theory in developmental planning.[1]

9. Concluding Remarks

The overwhelming impression that this survey leaves is one of an area of inquiry which has been unusually active and is witnessing the emergence of many new trends. A growing concern with empirical verification, an explicit introduction of dynamic modes of analysis, the recognition of the importance of intermediates and capital goods, a policy orientation in welfare economics leading to interest in measurement and the attempts at the operational use of trade theory in developmental planning represent, as of today, the gravitational centres towards which the analytical interests of the profession are moving. In some of these respects trade theory is merely modernizing itself, 'catching up' with the advances in theory generally. But in others, as for instance in the measurement of welfare changes, trade theory is the innovator. Indeed, this is the way the subject has always

[1] For instance, if there are no distortions of any sort, either internally or externally, a static (traditionalist) optimization procedure, in a programming framework, would yield the equality of FP and DP, and of FRT and DRT. In this sense, the programming approach merely reflects the insights of trade theory. This is, after all, what one would expect, since the proposition that free trade is superior to a tariff (under standard first-best assumptions) is a statement *merely* about the relationship between FP and DP, and *not* about the institutions by which this equality is brought about. The unwary reader, therefore, should note that nothing of what may have been said in favour of *free trade*, for instance, is an argument in favour of *laissez faire*.

grown: in a two-way flow of ideas with the general theory of value and welfare.

ADDENDUM

The preceding Survey was written during 1962, revised during 1963 and published in 1964. Much has been written in the five years since the completion of the Survey: this is inevitable in a rapidly developing field. While the Survey stands intact in the main, certain interesting developments have occurred which require to be noted. This Addendum has been written, therefore, to note briefly, selectively and synoptically the main writings that have appeared since the Survey. In addition to the literature referred to in the text, other recent material has been organized by Sections as in the Survey. The references have been numbered consecutively, beginning (at 143) where the Survey bibliography terminates.

A. Among the major areas in which trade theory has developed recently are precisely those where the Survey had pointed to serious limitations of the existing theories. The Survey had noted the general neglect of dynamic analysis as also the traditional deployment of models which considered trade only in consumer goods produced with primary factors of production. In both these respects, analytical contributions have been accelerated recently. Dynamic models, analysing the pattern of trade involving trade in produced capital goods, have been produced in a series of capital-theoretic, growth models by Uzawa and Oniki [185] and Bardhan [180] [181]. An important capital-theoretic model has been built also by Kenen [154] who has used it to examine familiar issues such as factor price equalization and the pattern of trade. The welfare theory of trade has also been enriched by the extension of the Ramsey analysis to an open economy by Bardhan [179].

Tariff theory has further been extended to consideration of trade in intermediate goods by Corden [188], Travis [192], Balassa [186] and Johnson [189] in a series of papers which look at the effective tariff on processes rather than on products. Among the interesting theoretical analyses, deploying models with trade in intermediates, are McKinnon's [190] examination of the Lerner theorem on the symmetry of export and import taxes and Ramaswami and Srinivasan's [191] analysis of second-best trade policies under additional constraints such as specified levels of importable production and revenue collection.

B. Another set of interesting developments relates to the exploration of models involving the international mobility of factors. Kemp [174] and Jones [173] have recently analysed in depth the question of the optimal policy intervention when monopoly power in trade combines with factor mobility.

C. Finally, a considerable amount of work has continued to be stimulated by Leontief's [25] original test of the Heckscher–Ohlin hypothesis for United States foreign trade. Since, in some respects, this work has qualified the findings reviewed in the Survey besides also opening up new lines of analysis, we treat this set of developments somewhat more fully in this Addendum.

Three areas of analysis, in particular, need to be noted: (1) the seminal and original work of Minhas [33] had demonstrated that factor intensities were reversible in reality within observable ranges of factor price ratios; these results have now been challenged, at both conceptual and empirical levels; (2) the notion of 'human capital' has been deployed to re-estimate the direct and indirect labour and capital coefficients in exports and imports (as also the CES production functions which were estimated by Minhas to demonstrate the empirical possibility of factor intensity reversals); and (3) the role of research and developmental expenditure in determining the US pattern of trade has been systematically investigated.

A. *Factor-Intensity Reversals*

Minhas seemed to have shown that factor intensities were reversible because the CES production functions fitted by him to international data showed elasticities of substitution both significantly different from unity and zero as also from one another; he also had shown, by estimating the production functions, that the reversals were likely to take place within observable ranges of factor endowments internationally. However, the following qualifications must now be listed, on statistical and analytical grounds, to these results.

(i) To begin with, Leontief [159] has pointed out that Minhas inexplicably left much of his data untouched when it came to finding out whether the reversals would take place within observable ranges of factor endowments. On completing the unfinished empirical analysis, using the primary data collected by Minhas himself, Leontief finds that:

> Of the theoreticaly possible 210 crossover points between the 21 lines entered on the graph, only 17 are found to locate within the wide range of

factor price ratios, spanned on the one end by those observed in the United States and on the other by those reported from India. Moreover, most of these crossovers occur between industries whose curves run so close together throughout the entire range that for all practical purposes their capital-labor intensities would be considered identical. With two or three exceptions, each one of the twenty-one industries represented can be characterized as capital-intensive, labor-intensive, or as belonging to an intermediate group.

Thus, the evidence from Minhas' work points to a confirmation, rather than a rejection, of the strong factor-intensity hypothesis which rules out intensity-reversals.

(ii) Secondly, the results are derived from an estimating procedure which renders them, in effect, arbitrary and dependent on the choice of the exchange rate or 'conversion factor' assumed for converting local-currency values to a common-dollar basis. The side-relation from which an unbiased estimate of the elasticity of substitution 'σ' would be derived, as Minhas derived it, is:

$$\log \frac{X}{L} = a + b \log \frac{w}{P_x} \quad . \quad . \quad . \quad . \quad (1)$$

where X is output, L is labour, w is the money wage rate and P_x is the unit price of output, the wage and price being in domestic currency units. However, since the data which are used are in value and do not permit breakdown of output value into unit price and quantity, the actual relation used for estimation is:

$$\log \gamma \, . \, \frac{P_x X}{L} = a + b \log \gamma w + [(1 - b) \log \gamma P_x] \quad . \quad (2)$$

from which the last term is again omitted as P_x is not available, with γ being the conversion factor which reduces domestic-currency prices to 'common values'. Now, if we make *either* the assumption that γP_x and γw are uncorrelated *or* the assumption that γP_x is constant (which means that the conversion factor γ is so chosen as to equalize converted prices internationally), then it is true that we will get an unbiased estimate of 'b', which is the elasticity of substitution 'σ'. But, *precisely because P* is not available, neither of these assumptions is verifiable *in practice*.

The upshot, strictly speaking, is that when Minhas chooses his γ's, in general, so as to correspond to IMF parities and then assumes (what is unverifiable in absence of information on P_x) that, at these γ's, γP_x and γw are uncorrelated, his procedure becomes essentially arbitrary. Thus, an alternative estimator of 'σ', from the *same* data in domestic currency units, could choose an alternative set of γ's, say from random numbers, and assert equally that, at *these* (different) γ's, γP_x and γw are uncorrelated and that therefore the alternative resulting estimate of 'σ' is the true estimate. Whose estimate of 'σ' are we then to choose (when the data on P_x are not available to enable us to choose between the two rival claims of lack of correlation between γP_x and γw) as the true estimate? In fact, there are an infinite number of estimates of 'σ' which can be produced, each generated by an alternative set of γ's, and each prefaced by an (unverifiable) assertion-cum-assumption that, at the γ's chosen, γP_x and γw are uncorrelated. Clearly, therefore, the Minhas estimates must be treated as arbitrary and rejected as evidence in support of the hypothesis that factor intensities are reversible.[1]

(iii) Thirdly, following on Mrs Joan Robinson's [163] earlier lead, Harcourt has pointed out that the elasticity of substitution which Minhas seeks to estimate is that of a

> production function which is characterized by disembodied technical progress and *ex-post* variability of factor proportions, so that, at any moment of time, the machines in the capital stock can be treated as if they have been moulded into the form of the latest vintage. But, clearly, the figures for value added relate to the current total production, and those for labour to total employment on machines of *different* vintages in the respective industries of the countries examined, that is, they are observations taken from the *short-run* production functions of the industries in the countries concerned. Moreover, these short-run production functions are likely to be characterized by embodied technical progress and, if not zero, at least extremely limited possibilities of *ex post* substitution.[152, page 227].

This criticism may not be considered serious insofar as economic analysis necessarily proceeds by abstraction; it may be contended that the very fact that the CES production function is fitted significantly indicates that it 'works'. But insofar as direct observation indicates that different countries do have capital equipments of altogether different vintages, and the *ex post* substitution is limited, this counter-argument in defence of Minhas' estimates would appear to rely on a methodological position of the Friedman variety.

(iv) Finally, the observed relationship between labour productivity

[1] This point has emerged as a result of correspondence initiated by the author with Robert Solow, B. S. Minhas and T. N. Srinivasan. The judgment that the estimates presented by Minhas then become arbitrary is, however, entirely mine.

and wage rates, in the same industry across countries, could well run, *not* from the latter to the former but the other way around, and thus may signify merely that, on macro grounds, the real wages are higher where the labour productivity is higher. In fact, this hypothesis is equally consistent with the facts, as Gupta [151] has shown by demonstrating an equally significant linear relationship between wage rates (as the dependent variable) and labour productivity (as the independent variable), even though the data to which this relation was fitted were taken from a different industry for each country. For those who consider the Minhas procedure untenable on grounds such as (iii) preceding, this alternative, macro-type explanation of the observed statistics may appear more persuasive.

Aside from these four points of major importance, there are two others which may be surveyed prior to concluding this area of analysis.

(1) Fuchs [149], who analysed the ACMS data, has argued that separating out the developed and the underdeveloped countries, and introducing a dummy variable, yields estimates of elasticities of substitution which are very close to unity – in contrast to the ACMS results. Fuchs has argued that, with his dummy variable significantly different from zero in most of the industries, the probable explanation is a systematic understatement of wages to labour in the payroll data of one set of countries as against the other. On the other hand, the explanation may well be that labour is not homogeneous between the two sets of countries, in which case we would revert to the original suggestion of Leontief (concerning the 'superiority' of labour in the USA).

(2) Merle Yahr [166], in an interesting recent dissertation, has explored this aspect further, by estimating the CES production function, from international data, with amendment for the possibility that labour is not homogeneous across countries but reflects different levels of training and education. This is done essentially by making the parameters attached to capital and labour in the CES production function dependant, in turn, on an index of human capital, Q. This leads to a modified estimating equation of the following type (if we follow the ACMS procedure):

$$\log \frac{P_x \cdot X}{L} = a + b_1 \log w + b_2 \log Q$$

The resulting estimates of the 'true' elasticity of substitution between labour and capital are close to unity, for 37 three-digit industries,

19 two-digit industries, and 13 industrial categories used by the UN Statistical Office. Thus again the results indicate the non-reversibility of factor-intensities internationally.

While this attempt at differentiating between different types of labour is extremely important, this may not be the best way to set about analysing the problem. The view implicit in the Yahr-formation of the problem is that an Indian structural engineer, for example, is less efficient than a US structural engineer; and the proxy taken for human capital, Q, in the estimation involves elements such as the educational level of the population measured by indices such as the mean level of education of males aged fifteen and over.

The real trouble with this kind of argument is that there is no reason why a lower position for India on such an index should mean that an Indian structural engineer is less efficient than a corresponding US engineer. All that it means is that, while a US and an Indian engineer will be equivalent in quality (as firms operating internationally often testify), the *relative number* of such qualified people will be less, for a country such as India.[1] It seems more sensible to argue that the problem is created, not by the fact that people are less efficient in one country than in another because some such index as used by Yahr is supposed to show it, but that the number of qualified people in some countries is less, in relation to total working population, than elsewhere. Once the problem is posed this way, it may be more fruitful to analyse it directly by introducing a multi-factor production function, distinguishing between different classes of skills as different factors. This could be done even within the framework of CES production functions (although, as Uzawa [165] and Mukerjee [162] have recently pointed out, certain difficulties arise); in which case, the elasticity of substitution among alternative pairs of a multi-factor production function could be measured.

Minhas' pioneering and stimulating work on estimating CES production functions and thereby arguing the possibility of reversals of factor intensity has thus been shown to be subject to important

[1] Moreover, lumping all education together, regardless of its quality and content, is surely meaningless for the purpose at hand. More education of the liberal arts variety need not lead to greater industrial efficiency; it may lead to less. Further, unless there is matching capital accumulation, more graduates and hence a higher index of education, *ceteris paribus*, will mean urban unrest and/or work-sharing arrangements, both of which are likely to impair rather than contribute to industrial efficiency.

drawbacks. At the same time, his alternative (and more direct) test of such reversals by examining the rank correlation between two arrays of twenty-four industries for the USA and Japan, each array containing (direct and indirect) capital/labour ratios in descending order, which had shown that factor-intensity rankings were significantly different, has also been re-examined.

Thus, for example, Ball [147] has argued that the Minhas tests are defective because he should not have included primary, agricultural and food-processing industries on the grounds that (i) because of natural resources, they need not have identical production functions; (ii) the categories are so large and broad that the covered items may be strongly dissimilar between countries; and (iii) the measurements of factor use may be defective in these industries. On performing the rank correlation tests, by excluding such industries, Ball finds that the hypothesis of factor intensity reversals is no longer refuted by Minhas' data.

However, Minhas must be defended against such a criticism. While there is something to Ball's last point (to which the correct response should have been to try alternative estimates rather than to drop the industries from the analysis altogether), the first two points are certainly not the distinguishing marks of the industries described as agricultural and food-processing. Within the same finely-defined industry, for example, it is customary to find (within the same country) plants using quite different inputs and processes, even in strictly manufacturing industries such as chemicals. Nor is it possible to argue that the categories in the manufactures left in by Ball are significantly homogeneous as compared to the ones he has chosen to leave out; his choice of what to include and what to exclude is arbitrary in the absence of more detailed empirical analysis. Besides, it is difficult to see why the fact that these industries rely more on natural resources (even were it true, in some sense) should make them subject to different production functions any more than would other primary or produced factors (whose incidence internationally may also be quite diverse, thanks to transport costs and natural endowments) make the other industries subject to different production functions.

Hal Lary's [158] recent examination of international data on thirteen main groups for nine countries (as also three summary groups for twenty countries, for broadly comparable years), has also tended to support the rejection of the reversibility hypothesis.[1] Lary uses value

[1] Lary also undertakes detailed bilateral comparisons for the United States with the United Kingdom, Japan and India.

added per employee data as proxy for capital/labour data, arguing that this is an adequate way of dealing with human capital as well:

This procedure assumes that there is no such thing in reality as completely 'unskilled labour,' and that, if average earnings are the same in two industries, the average level of human capital per worker is also equal, even though the dispersion around the average is much wider in one case than in the other. For purpose of analysis, however, it is helpful to think of the labour force as if it were composed of units of completely unskilled labour to each of which is added, according to the industry, varying amounts of skill or human capital . . . and of machinery and other physical assets. . . . The higher the value added per employee, the more capital-intensive the industry on both accounts combined; the lower the value added per employee, the more labour-intensive the industry.[1]

While Lary's method represents a rough and interesting way of adjusting for the fact of human capital, there may be difficulties in accepting this index of capital intensity if one remembers that value added may reflect varying rates of monopoly profits and rents which arise from severe controls on imports and entry in less developed countries (such as India). Furthermore, the entire group of tests which seeks to test reversibility of factor intensities by comparison of actual capital-intensity rankings of different industries internationally, requires the assumption that factor price ratios, though they may differ among countries, are everywhere the same within a given country. For, if this is not so, the international comparisons of observed rankings of industries by capital-intensity could demonstrate reversibility which arises, not from reversibility resulting from production function properties, but from the mere fact that factor price ratios facing entrepreneurs are different among industries in a manner which is not similar internationally. This problem may be of some significance in less developed countries where the use of discriminatory taxes between industries and accelerated depreciation or investment allowances (which discriminate *de facto* in favour of capital-intensive processes) are likely to be of importance.[2] Finally, we may note that Lary uses

[1] Lary [158, 22].

[2] In view of these and other difficulties arising whenever the analyst has to work with factor rewards data and assume perfect competition to get anywhere, it is surprising that international trade economists, seeking to verify whether production functions can show factor-intensity reversals, have not taken to working straight from engineering data; in this connection, see the interesting paper by Manne and Kurz [160].

direct coefficients, instead of direct and indirect value added per employee data.

B. *Human Capital and Skills*

Leontief's suggestion that labour is not homogeneous across countries has also led to recalculation of the capital and labour coefficients for exports and imports of the United States by Kenen and Yudin [156], of India by Bharadwaj and Bhagwati [148] and of West Germany by Roskamp and McMeekin [164], so as to allow for 'human capital'.

The method used in the Kenen–Yudin and Bharadwaj–Bhagwati exercises is outlined in the Survey. Essentially it consists in treating the difference between skilled labour wage and the unskilled labour wage as an approximate measure of the return to human capital, capitalizing this rental (at alternative rates already computed by Becker and Mincer for the USA and by Harberger and Sahota for India) to secure alternative estimates of the human capital employed in average exports and imports, which are then added to the other capital requirements to arrive at adjusted capital/labour rankings of the US and Indian foreign trade. It is interesting to record that Kenen and Yudin, despite a very large number of alternative assumptions, failed to reverse the Leontief paradox except in a very few cases. For India, the comparative labour intensity of exports was distinctly reduced by this adjustment, but not reversed.

The method used by Roskamp and McMeekin is essentially the same as that used by Kenen–Yudin and Bharadwaj–Bhagwati. However, instead of capitalizing the rental attributed to human capital and then adding it to standard capital estimates, they directly work with the data on returns to factors of production. They treat profits and interest as returns to standard capital (while adjusting them for self-employed incomes and similar complications) and separate out the rental on human capital from wages and salaries by generally treating the average wage as return to labour and wages and salaries in excess thereof as returns to human capital. The adjusted index of comparative labour-intensity then shows a reversal of the earlier, unadjusted finding that West German exports are capital-intensive. Note that the Roskamp–McMeekin variation of the technique deployed by Kenen–Yudin and Bharadwaj–Bhagwati should, in principle, give the same results. However, in an imperfect world, where the valuations of capital in different industries are likely to bear different relationships to the profit and interest incomes observed, the results could be quite sensitive to the actual method of estimation used.[1] In view of this sensitivity, it would be useful to employ *both* methods of estimating relative capital/labour intensities in exports and imports.

Note further that, both in these exercises as also the Yahr-type modification of the estimation of CES production functions, the view taken of differences in homogeneity of labour across countries is that they are attributable to differences in education and training. On the other hand, it may well be the case that sociological factors also account for differences in factor efficiency, as between countries. Thus, for example, Kreinin [157], who undertook a direct examination of Leontief's conjecture (that US labour was thrice as efficient as elsewhere) by asking firms engaged in international operations, found that such differences could indeed be observed, although at a much smaller factor of around 1·4, and were attributed by firms to, not merely inferior training and lack of adequate experience and skills, but also 'lack of motivation and drive', 'union rules' and even 'climate'.[2]

C. *Research and Development*

Another area of research, pursued by Keesing [153] and by Gruber, Mehta and Vernon [150], involves examination of possible relationships between the pattern of trade and intensiveness in 'research and development' (R & D) expenditures. Such an explanation would be, in principle, compatible with two alternative 'theories': (i) that technical progress, induced by this expenditure, lowers costs, pulls resources into these industries, and confers comparative advantage on them; (ii) that such R & D expenditures lead to new products and thus confer temporary 'availability' advantage of the Kravis-type, discussed in the Survey, which leads to comparative advantage.

A considerable amount of evidence in support of the R & D hypothesis, as the relevant explanation of the United States pattern of foreign trade, has been turned up by Keesing and Gruber–Mehta–Vernon. Both use essentially the same data and even similar

[1] Quite aside from factor market imperfections, which the Heckscher–Ohlin theory eschews, there could also be simply problems in estimating employed capital correctly.

[2] It may even be argued that Yahr's results are attributable, not to human capital, but to such sociological factors as listed above: that her proxy indices for human capital are themselves correlated with the incidence of such factors, and both in turn to differences in *per capita* incomes. Inefficient work habits and what appear to Western observers as 'lack of drive' are typically related to low income levels, as are low levels of education and literacy.

techniques. Keesing has correlated the 1962 share of US exports in the Group-of-Ten exports for eighteen industries with the January 1961 ratio of R & D scientists and engineers in total employment in each industry, turning up a linear correlation of 0·88 and a Spearman coefficient of rank correlation of 0·94. For twenty-two product-fields, but taking this time the ratio of R & D *expenditures* to value added in 1960, he finds a linear correlation of 0·66 and a Spearman coefficient of 0·78. He further finds that these correlations are stronger than when he substitutes, for R & D factors, indices such as skilled labour, (direct) capital intensity, natural resources and value added per establishment (as a proxy for economies of scale). Using direct coefficients, he also finds that scientists and engineers in R & D represented 2·87 per cent of the labour required to produce US exports but only 1·21 per cent for US imports in 1961. The Gruber–Mehta–Vernon results are broadly similar. They take nineteen industries, using 1962 data. They correlate successfully their two R & D indices, the ratio of R & D expenditure to sales and the ratio of scientists and engineers in R & D to total employment, with alternative indices of US export performance in each industry: the ratio of exports to sales, the ratio of exports minus imports to sales, the ratio of US world exports as a percentage to the exports of OECD countries (including Japan), the UK, West Germany and France, and finally the first two ratios broken down by the trade of the US industries with Europe and non-Europe. As with Keesing, their results generally support the conclusion that, except when other countries with similar R & D orientation (such as UK and Germany) are concerned, the R & D indices correlate pretty well with the different indices of export performance by US industries.

These results are extremely suggestive and are likely to stimulate fresh attempts at relevant theoretical formulations which would incorporate induced technological change as an endogeneous factor. It is probably relevant to note, however, that these empirical exercises still fall short of investigation of the R & D indices of partner countries. Furthermore, as these authors recognize, the indices of R & D are crude: for example, the industrywise attribution is made 'according to the main industry of the company performing the task, though firms that perform R & D characteristically spread their efforts over many product fields' [153, page 39].

REFERENCES

The references have been classified into separate groups corresponding to the Sections in the text, while the numbering is consecutive for the groups together. The correspondence between the Sections and the groups is naturally not precise. The works listed do not constitute an exhaustive bibliography; the necessary and sufficient criterion for a work to be cited is that it should have been referred to in the text.

INTRODUCTION

1 Bhagwati, J., 'Some Recent Trends in the Pure Theory of International Trade', Ch. 1, *International Trade Theory in a Developing World* (Ed. Harrod and Hague; London, Macmillan & Co., 1963).

2 Bhagwati, J., and Johnson, H. G., 'Notes on some Controversies in the theory of International Trade', *Economic Journal*, Vol. 70 (March 1960).

3 Caves, R. E., *Trade and Economic Structure* (Cambridge, Mass., Harvard University Press, 1960).

4 Haberler, G., *A Survey of International Trade Theory*, Special papers in International Economics, No. I (International Finance Section, Department of Economics, Princeton University, 1961).

5 Johnson, H. G., *International Trade and Economic Growth*, London (George Allen and Unwin, 1958).

6 Johnson, H. G., *Money, Trade and Growth* (London, George Allen and Unwin, 1962).

7 Lipsey, R. G., 'The Theory of Customs Unions: A General Survey', *Economic Journal*, Vol. 70 (September 1960).

8 Meade, J. E., *Trade and Welfare* (*The Theory of International Economic Policy*, Vol. II) (Oxford, Oxford University Press, 1955).

9 Meade, J. E., *Mathematical Supplement* (*Trade and Welfare*) (Oxford, Oxford University Press, 1955).

10 Meade, J. E., *A Geometry of International Trade* (London, George Allen and Unwin, 1952).

11 Mundell, R. A., 'The Pure Theory of International Trade', *American Economic Review*, Vol. 50 (March 1960).

1

12 Balogh, T., 'Factor Intensities of American Foreign Trade and Technical Progress', *Review of Economics and Statistics*, Vol. 37 (November 1955).

13 Balassa, B., 'An Empirical Demonstration of Classical Comparative Cost Theory,' *Review of Economics and Statistics*, Vol. 45 (August 1963).

14 Bhagwati, J., 'Protection, Real Wages and Real Incomes,' *Economic Journal*, Vol. 69 (December 1959).
15 Bharadwaj, R., *Structural Basis of India's Foreign Trade* (Series in Monetary and International Economics, No. 6) (University of Bombay, 1962).
16 Bharadwaj, R., 'Factor Proportions and the Structure of Indo-US Trade', *Indian Economic Journal*, Vol. 10 (October 1962).
17 Coppock, J., *International Economic Instability* (Economic Handbook Series) (McGraw Hill Book Company Inc., 1962).
18 Diab, M., *The United States Capital Position and the Structure of the Foreign Trade* (Amsterdam, North Holland Publishing Co., 1956).
19 Heckscher, E., 'The Effect of Foreign Trade on the Distribution of Income', *Readings in the Theory of International Trade*, Ed. H. S. Ellis and L. A. Metzler for the American Economic Association (Philadelphia, Blakiston, 1949).
20 Jones, R., 'Factor Proportions and the Heckscher–Ohlin Model', *Review of Economic Studies*, Vol. 24 (1956–7).
21 Kravis, I., 'Wages and Foreign Trade', *Review of Economics and Statistics*, Vol. 38 (February 1956).
22 Kravis, I., 'Availability and other Influences on the Commodity Composition of Trade', *Journal of Polictial Economy*, Vol. 64 (April 1956).
23 Lebergott, S., 'Wage Structures', *Review of Economics and Statistics*, Vol. 29 (November 1947).
24 Leontief, W., 'The Use of Indifference Curves in the Analysis of Foreign Trade', *Quarterly Journal of Economics*, Vol. 47 (May 1933).
25 Leontief, W., 'Domestic Production and Foreign Trade: The American Capital Position Re-examined', *Economia Internazionale*, Vol. 7 (1954).
26 Leontief, W., 'Factor Proportions and the Structure of American Trade: Further Theoretical and Empirical Analysis', *Review of Economics and Statistics*, Vol. 38 (November 1956).
27 Linder, S., *An Essay on Trade and Transformation* (New York, John Wiley and Sons 1961).
28 MacDougall, G. D. A., 'British and American Exports: A Study suggested by the Theory of Comparative Costs, Part I', *Economic Journal*, Vol. 61 (December 1951).
29 MacDougall, G. D. A., 'British and American Exports: A Study Suggested by the Theory of Comparative Costs, Part II', *Economic Journal*, Vol. 62 (September 1952).
30 MacDougall, G. D. A., M. Dowley, P. Fox and S. Pugh, 'British and American Productivity, Prices and Exports: An Addendum', *Oxford Economic Papers*, Vol. 14 (October 1962).
31 Michaely, M., *Concentration in World Trade* (Contributions to Economic Analysis) (Amsterdam, North Holland Publishing Co., 1962).

32 Mill, J. S., *Principles of Political Economy*, Ed. W. J. Ashley (London, Longmans, Green and Co., 1917).

33 Minhas, B. S., 'The Homohypallagic Production Function, Factor Intensity Reversals, and the Heckscher–Ohlin Theorem', *Journal of Political Economy*, Vol. 70 (April 1962).

34 Ohlin, B., *Interregional and International Trade*, Harvard Economic Studies, Vol. 39 (Cambridge, Mass., Harvard University Press, 1933).

35 Pearce, I. F., and James, S. F., 'The Factor Price Equalisation Myth', *Review of Economic Studies*, Vol. 19 (1951–2).

36 Robinson, R., 'Factor Proportions and Comparative Advantage: Part I', *Quarterly Journal of Economics*, Vol. 70 (May 1956).

37 Robinson, R., 'Factor Proportions and Comparative Advantage: Part II', *Quarterly Journal of Economics*, Vol. 70 (August 1956).

38 Samuelson, P. A., 'International Trade and Equalisation of Factor Prices', *Economic Journal*, Vol. 58 (June 1948).

39 Samuelson, P. A., 'International Factor Price Equalisation Once Again', *Economic Journal*, Vol. 59 (June 1949).

40 Stern, R., 'British and American Productivity and Comparative Costs in International Trade', *Oxford Economic Papers*, Vol. 14 (October 1962).

41 Stolper, W., and Roskamp, K., 'Input–Output Table for East Germany with Applications to Foreign Trade', *Bulletin of the Oxford University Institute of Statistics*, Vol. 23 (November 1961).

42 Tatemoto, M., and Ichimura, S., 'Factor Proportions and Foreign Trade: The Case of Japan', *Review of Economics and Statistics*, Vol. 41 (November 1959).

43 Vanek, J., 'The Natural Resource Content of Foreign Trade, 1870–1955, and the Relative Abundance of Natural Resources in the United States', *Review of Economics and Statistics*, Vol. 41 (May 1959).

44 Viner, J., *Studies in the Theory of International Trade* (New York, Harper and Bros., 1937).

45 Wahl, D. F., 'Capital and Labour Requirements for Canada's Foreign Trade', *Canadian Journal of Economics and Political Science*, Vol. 27 (August 1961).

2

46 Harrod, R. F., 'Factor–Price Relations under Free Trade', *Economic Journal*, Vol. 68 (June 1958).

47 Kuhn, H. W., 'Factor Endowments and Factor Prices: Mathematical Appendix,' *Economica*, N.S., Vol. 26 (May 1959).

48 Laing, N., 'Factor Price Equalization in International Trade and Returns to Scale', *Economic Record*, Vol. 37 (September 1961).

49 McKenzie, L., 'Equality of Factor Price in World Trade', *Econometrica*, Vol. 23 (July 1955).

50 Meade, J. E., 'The Equalisation of Factor Prices: the Two-Good, Two-Country Three-product Case', *Metroeconomica*, Vol. 2 (December 1950).
51 Pearce, I. F., 'A Further Note on Factor–Commodity Price Relationships', *Economic Journal*, Vol. 69 (December 1959).
52 Reiter, S., 'Efficient International Trade and Equalisation of Prices', *International Economic Review*, Vol. 2 (January 1961).
53 Samuelson, P. A., 'Prices of Factors and Goods in General Equilibrium', *Review of Economic Studies*, Vol. 21 (1953–4).
54 Samuelson, P. A., 'Equalisation by Trade of the Interest Rate along with the Real Wage', Mimeographed, 1960.
55 Vanek, J., 'Variable Factor Proportions and Inter-Industry Flows in the Theory of International Trade', *Quarterly Journal of Economics*, Vol. 77 (February 1963).

3

56 Asimakopulos, A., 'A Note on Productivity Changes and the Terms of Trade', *Oxford Economic Papers*, N.S., Vol. 9 (June 1957).
57 Baldwin, R. E., 'The Effects of Tariffs on International and Domestic Prices', *Quarterly Journal of Economics*, Vol. 74 (February 1960).
58 Balogh, T., 'The Concept of a Dollar Shortage', *Manchester School*, Vol. 17 (May 1949).
59 Black, J., 'Economic Expansion and International Trade: A Marshallian Approach', *Review of Economic Studies*, Vol. 23 (1955–6).
60 Bhagwati, J., and Johnson, H. G., 'A Generalised Theory of the Effects of Tariffs on the Terms of Trade', *Oxford Economic Papers*, N.S., Vol. 13 (October 1961).
61 Corden, W. M., 'Economic Expansion and International Trade: A Geometrical Approach', *Oxford Economic Papers*, N.S., Vol. 8 (June 1956).
62 Findlay, R., and Grubert, H., 'Factor Intensity, Technological Progress, and the Terms of Trade', *Oxford Economic Papers*, N.S., Vol. II (February 1959).
63 Graham, F. D., 'The Theory of International Values', *Quarterly Journal of Economics*, Vol. 46 (August 1932).
64 Johnson, H. G., 'Economic Development and International Trade', *National Konomick Tidsskript* (Arganj, 1959).
65 Johnson, H. G., 'Effects of Changes in Comparative Cost as Influenced by Technical Change', *Malayan Economic Review*, Vol. 6 (October 1961).
66 Johnson, H. G., 'International Trade, Income Distribution and the Offer Curve', *Manchester School*, Vol. 27 (September 1959).
67 Johnson, H. G., 'Income Distribution, the Offer Curve and the Effects of Tariffs,' *Manchester School*, Vol. 28 (September 1960).

68 Johnson, H. G., 'The Pure Theory of International Trade: Comment', *American Economic Review*, Vol. 50 (September 1960).

69 Jones, R., 'Comparative Advantage and the Theory of Tariffs: A Multi-Country, Multi-Commodity Model', *Review of Economic Studies*, Vol. 28 (June 1961).

70 Kemp, M. C., 'The Relation between Changes in International Demand and the Terms of Trade', *Econometrica*, Vol. 24 (January 1956).

71 Kemp, M. C., 'Technological Change, the Terms of Trade and Welfare', *Economic Journal*, Vol. 65 (September 1955).

72 Kemp, M. C., and Jones, R., 'Variable Labour Supply and the Theory of International Trade', *Journal of Political Economy*, Vol. 70 (February 1962).

73 Kindleberger, C. P., 'Group Behaviour and International Trade', *Journal of Political Economy*, Vol. 59 (February 1951).

74 Lerner, A. P., 'The Symmetry between Import and Export Taxes', *Economica*, N.S., Vol. 3 (August 1936).

75 MacDougall, I., 'Tariffs, Protection and the Terms of Trade', *Economic Record*, Vol. 37 (1961).

76 MacDougall, I., 'A Note on Tariffs, the Terms of Trade, and the Distribution of the National Incomes', *Journal of Political Economy*, Vol. 70 (August 1962).

77 Marshall, A., *The Pure Theory of Foreign Trade* (Reprints of scarce Tracts on Political Economy) (London, London School of Economics, 1930).

78 McKenzie, L., 'Specialization and Efficiency in World Production', *Review of Economic Studies*, Vol. 21 (1953–4).

79 Meade, J. E., *The Theory of Customs Unions* (Amsterdam, North Holland Publishing Co., 1955).

80 Metzler, L., 'Tariffs, the Terms of Trade and the Distribution of National Income', *Journal of Political Economy*, Vol. 57 (February 1949).

81 Metzler, L., 'Tariffs, International Demand and Domestic Prices', *Journal of Political Economy*, Vol. 57 (August 1949).

82 Mundell, R. A., 'International Trade and Factor Mobility', *American Economic Review*, Vol. 47 (June 1957).

83 Myint, H., 'The Classical Theory of International Trade and the Underdeveloped countries', *Economic Journal*, Vol. 68 (June 1958).

84 Oliver, F. R., 'Shifting Demand Schedules and the Terms and Volume of Trade', *Metroeconomica*, Vol. 12 (April 1960).

85 Ozga, S. A., 'An Essay in the Theory of Tariffs', *Journal of Political Economy*, Vol. 63 (December 1955).

86 Ramaswami, V. K., 'The Effects of Accumulation on the Terms of Trade', *Economic Journal*, Vol. 70 (September 1960).

87 Rybczynski, T. N., 'Factor Endowment and Relative Commodity Prices', *Economica*, N.S., Vol. 22 (November 1955).
88 Samuelson, P. A., 'The Transfer Problem and Transport Costs', *Economic Journal*, Vol. 62 (June 1952).
89 Samuelson, P. A., 'The Transfer Problem and Transport Costs', *Economic Journal*, Vol. 62 (June 1952).
90 Seton, F., 'Productivity, Trade Balance and International Structure', *Economic Journal*, Vol. 66 (December 1956).
91 Stolper, W., and Samuelson, P. A., 'Protection and Real Wages', *Review of Economic Studies*, Vol. 9 (November 1941).
92 Vanek, J., 'An Afterthought on the Real Cost–Opportunity Cost Dispute and some Aspects of General Equilibrium under Conditions of Variable Factor Supplies', *Review of Economic Studies*, Vol. 26 (June 1959).
93 Vanek, J., *International Trade: Theory and Economic Policy* (Illinois, Richard D. Irwin Inc., 1962).
94 Viner, J., *The Customs Union Issue* (New York, Carnegie Endowment for International Peace, 1950).
95 Walsh, V. C., 'Leisure and International Trade', *Economica*, N.S., Vol. 23 (August 1956).

4

96 Bensusan-Butt, D. M., 'A Model of Trade and Accumulation', *American Economic Review*, Vol. 44 (September 1954).
97 Bhagwati, J., 'The Theory of Comparative Advantage in the Context of Underdevelopment and Growth', *Pakistan Development Review*, Vol. 2 (Autumn 1962).
98 Brems, H., 'The Foreign Trade Accelerator and International Transmission of Growth', *Econometrica*, Vol. 24 (July 1956).
99 Graham, F. D., 'Some Aspects of Protection Further Considered', *Quarterly Journal of Economics*, Vol 37 (February 1923).
100 Johnson, A., 'Protection and the Formation of Capital', *Political Science Quarterly*, Vol. 23 (June 1908).
101 Kindleberger, C. P., 'Foreign Trade and Economic Growth: Lessons from Britain and France, 1850 to 1913', *Economic History Review*, Vol. 14 (1961).
102 Kitamura, H., *International Economics* (Tokyo), March 1951.
103 Kojima, K., 'A Survey of the Theories on International Economics in Japan', *Japan Science Review* (*Economic Sciences*, No. 1), Japan Union of Associations of Economic Sciences, 1953.
104 Srinivasan, T. N., 'A Two-Country, Three-Commodity, Dynamic Model of International Trade', *Metroeconomica*, forthcoming.
105 Verdoorn, P. J., 'Complementarity and Long-Range Projections', *Econometrica*, Vol. 24 (October 1956).

5

106 Akamatsu, K., 'The Theory of Supply-Multiplier in Reference to the Post-War Economic Situation in Japan', *The Annals of the Hitotsubashi Academy* (October 1950).

107 GATT, *Basic Instruments and Selected Documents, Tenth Supplement* (Geneva, March 1962).

108 McKenzie, L., 'On Equilibrium in Graham's Model of World Trade and Other Competitive Systems', *Econometrica*, Vol. 22 (April 1954).

109 Stolper, W., 'Notes on the Dollar Shortage', *American Economic Review*, Vol. 40 (June 1950).

110 Stolper, W., 'A Note on Multiplier, Flexible Exchanges and the Dollar Shortage', *Economica Internationale*, Vol. 11 (August 1950).

6

111 Bhagwati, J., 'Immiserizing Growth: A Geometrical Note', *Review o, Economic Studies*, Vol. 25 (June 1958).

112 Bhagwati, J., and Ramaswami, V. K., 'Domestic Distortions, Tariffs, and the Theory of Optimum Subsidy', *Journal of Political Economy* Vol. 71 (February 1963).

113 Dorfman, R., Samuelson, P. A., and Solow, R. M., *Linear Programming and Economic Analysis* (New York, McGraw Hill, 1958).

114 Fleming, M., 'The Optimal Tariff from an International Standpoint', *Review of Economics and Statistics*, Vol. 38 (February 1956).

115 Gorman, W. M., 'Tariffs, Retaliation and the Elasticity of Demand for Imports,' *Review of Economic Studies*, Vol. 25 (June 1958).

116 Graaff, J., 'On Optimum Tariff Structures', *Review of Economic Studies*, Vol. 17 (1949–50).

117 Haberler, G., 'Some Problems in the Pure Theory of International Trade', *Economic Journal*, Vol. 60 (June 1950).

118 Hagen, E., 'An Economic Justification of Protectionism', *Quarterly Journal of Economics*, Vol. 72 (November 1958).

119 Jasay, A. E., 'The Choice between Home and Foreign Investment', *Economic Journal*, Vol. 70 (March 1960).

120 Kemp, M. C., 'The Gain from International Trade', *Economic Journal*, Vol. 72 (December 1962).

121 Lipsey, R. G., 'The Theory of Customs Unions: Trade Diversion and Welfare', *Economica*, N.S., Vol. 24 (February 1957).

122 MacDougall, G. D. A., 'The Benefits and Costs of Private Investment from Abroad: A Theoretical Approach', *Bulletin of the Oxford University Institute of Statistics*, Vol. 22 (August 1960).

123 Matthews, R. C. O., 'Reciprocal Demand and Increasing Returns', *Review of Economic Studies*, Vol. 17 (1949–50).

124 Panchmukhi, V., 'A Theory for Optimum Tariff Policy', *Indian Economic Journal*, Vol. 9 (October 1961).

125 Samuelson, P. A., 'The Gains from International Trade', *Canadian Journal of Economics and Political Science*, Vol. 5 (May 1939).

126 Samuelson, P. A., 'The Gain from International Trade Once Again', *Economic Journal*, Vol. 62 (December 1962).

127 Tinbergen, J., *International Economic Cooperation* (Amsterdam, 1946).

7

128 Corden, W. M., 'Tariffs, Subsidies and the Terms of Trade', *Economica*, N.S., Vol. 24 (August 1957).

129 Johnson, H. G., 'Optimum Welfare and Maximum Revenue Tariffs', *Review of Economic Studies*, Vol. 19 (1951–2).

130 Johnson, H. G., 'Discriminatory Tariff Reduction: A Marshallian Analysis', *Indian Journal of Economics*, Vol. 38 (July 1957).

131 Johnson, H. G., 'The Gain from Freer Trade with Europe: An Estimate', *Manchester School*, Vol. 26 (September 1958).

132 Johnson, H. G., 'The Cost of Protection and the Scientific Tariff', *Journal of Political Economy*, Vol. 42 (October 1960).

133 Johnson, H. G., 'Optimal Trade Intervention in the Presence of Domestic Distortions', *Money, Trade and Growth: Essays in Honour of G. Haberler* (Ed. Caves, Johnson and Kenen) (Chicago, Rand-McNally, 1965).

134 Marris, R. L., 'The Purchasing Power of British Exports', *Economica*, N.S., Vol. 22 (February 1955).

135 Wemelsfelder, J., 'The Short-term Effect of the Lowering of Import Duties in Germany', *Economic Journal*, Vol. 70 (March 1960).

8

136 Brahmandand, P. R., and Vakil, C. N., *Planning for an Expanding Economy* (Bombay, Vora & Co., 1956).

137 Chakravarty, S., *The Logic of Investment Planning* (North Holland Series) (Amsterdam, North Holland Publishing Co., 1957).

138 Chenery, H., and Bruno, M., 'Development Alternatives in an Open Economy: The Case of Israel', *Economic Journal*, Vol. 72 (March 1962).

139 Chenery, H., 'Comparative Advantage and Development Policy', *American Economic Review*, Vol. 51 (March 1961).

140 Desai, P., 'The Development of the Indian Economy: An Exercise in Economic Planning', *Oxford Economic Papers*, Vol. 15 (October 1963).

141 Mahalanobis, P. C., 'Science and National Planning', *Sankhya*, Vol. 20 (1958).

142 Wonnacott, R., *Canadian–American Dependence* (Contributions to Economic Analysis) (Amsterdam, North Holland Publishing Co., 1961).

ADDENDUM REFERENCES

INTRODUCTION

143 Chipman, J. S., 'A Survey of the Theory of International Trade: Part 1: The Classical Theory; Part 2: The Neo-Classical Theory; Part 3: The Modern Theory', *Econometrica*, Vol. 33, July 1965, October and Vol. 34, January 1966.
144 Corden, W., *Recent Developments in the Theory of International Trade*, International Finance Section, Department of Economics, Princeton University, 1965.
145 Jones, R. W., 'The Structure of Simple General Equilibrium Models', *Journal of Political Economy*, Vol. 73, December 1965.
146 Kemp, M. C., *The Pure Theory of International Trade*, Prentice-Hall, Englewood Cliffs, New Jersey, 1964.

1

147 Ball, D. S., 'Factor Intensity Reversals in International Comparison of Factor Costs and Factor Use', *Journal of Political Economy*, Vol. 74, February 1966.
148 Bharadwaj, R., and Bhagwati, J., 'Human Capital and the Pattern of Foreign Trade: the Indian Case', *Indian Economic Review*, Vol. 2 (New Series), October 1967.
149 Fuchs, V., 'Capital-labor Substitution: A Note', *Review of Economics and Statistics*, Vol. 45, November 1963.
150 Gruber, W., Mehta, D., and Vernon, R., 'The R and D Factor in International Investment of United States Industries', *Journal of Political Economy*, Vol. 75, February 1967.
151 Gupta, S. B., 'Estimating CES Production Functions', *unpublished*, 1966.
152 Harcourt, G. C., 'Biases in Empirical Estimates of the Elasticities of Substitution of C.E.S. Production Functions', *Review of Economic Studies*, Vol. 33, July 1966.
153 Keesing, D., 'The Impact of Research and Development on United States Trade', *Journal of Political Economy*, Vol. 75, February 1967.
154 Kenen, P. B., 'Nature, Capital and Trade', *Journal of Political Economy*, Vol. 73, October 1965; Erratum, December 1965.
155 Kenen, P. B., 'Efficiency Differences and Factor Intensities in the C.E.S. Production Function: An Interpretation', *Journal of Political Economy*, Vol. 74, December 1965.
156 Kenen, P. B., and Yudin, E., 'Skills, Human Capital, and U.S. Foreign Trade', *International Economics Workshop*, Columbia University, December 1965.
157 Kreinin, M., 'Comparative Labor Effectiveness and the Leontief

Scarce-factor Paradox', *American Economic Review*, Vol. 55, March 1965.

158 Lary, H., *Imports of Manufactures from Less Developed Countries*, NBER, Columbia University Press, New York, 1968.

159 Leontief, W., 'An International Comparison of Factor Costs and Factor Use', *American Economic Review*, Vol. 54, June 1964.

160 Manne, A., and Kurz, M., 'Engineering Estimates of Capital-labor Substitution in Metal Machining', *American Economic Review*, Vol. 53, September 1963.

161 Moroney, J., and Walker, J. M., 'A Regional Test of the Heckscher–Ohlin Hypothesis', *Journal of Political Economy*, Vol. 74, December 1966.

162 Mukerjee, V., 'A Generalized S.M.A.C. Function with Constant Ratios of Elasticity of Substitution', *Review of Economic Studies*, Vol. 30, October 1963.

163 Robinson, J., 'International Factor Price Not Equalised', *Quarterly Journal of Economics*, Vol. 78, May 1964.

164 Roskamp, K., and McMeekin, G., 'Factor Proportions, Human Capital and Foreign Trade: The Case of West Germany Reconsidered', *Quarterly Journal of Economics*, Vol. 82, February 1968.

165 Uzawa, H., 'Production Functions with Constant Elasticities of Substitution', *Review of Economic Studies*, Vol. 29, October 1962.

166 Yahr, M., *Estimating the Elasticity of Substitution from International Manufacturing Census Data*, Ph.D. Thesis at Columbia University, 1967.

2

167 McKenzie, L. W., 'The Inversion of Cost Functions: A Counter-example', *International Economic Review*, Vol. 8, October 1967.

168 McKenzie, L. W., 'Theorem and Counter-example', *International Economic Review*, Vol. 8, October 1967.

169 Pearce, I. F., 'More about Factor Price Equalisation', *International Economic Review*, Vol. 8, October 1967.

170 Pearce, I. F., 'Rejoinder to Professor McKenzie', *International Economic Review*, Vol. 8, October 1967.

171 Pearse, I. F., 'Rejoinder to Professor Samuelson's Summary', *International Economic Review*, Vol. 8, October 1967.

172 Samuelson, P. A., 'Summary on Factor-Price Equalisation', *International Economic Review*, Vol. 8, October 1967.

3

173 Jones, R. W., 'International Capital Movements and the Theory of Tariffs and Trade', *Quarterly Journal of Economics*, Vol. 81, February 1967.

174 **Kemp, M. C.,** 'The Gain from International Trade and Investment:

A Neo-Heckscher–Ohlin Approach', *American Economic Review*, Vol. 56, September 1966.

175 Komiya, R., 'Non-traded Goods and the Pure Theory of International Trade', *International Economic Review*, Vol. 8, June 1967.

176 MacDougall, I., 'Non-traded Goods and the Transfer Problem', *Review of Economic Studies*, Vol. 32, January, 1965.

177 Södersten, B., *A Study of Economic Growth and International Trade*, Almqvist and Wiksell, Stockholm, 1964.

178 Takayama, A., 'Economic Growth and International Trade', *Review of Economic Studies*, Vol. 31, June 1964.

4

179 Bardhan, P. K., 'Optimum Accumulation and International Trade', *Review of Economic Studies*, Vol. 32, July 1965.

180 Bardhan, P. K., 'Equilibrium Growth in the International Economy', *Quarterly Journal of Economics*, Vol. 79, August 1965.

181 Bardhan, P. K., 'On Factor Accumulation and the Pattern of International Specialization', *Review of Economic Studies*, Vol. 33, January 1966.

182 Bardhan, P. K., 'Optimum Foreign Borrowing', in Shell, K., ed., *Essays on the Theory of Optimal Economic Growth*, The MIT Press, Cambridge Mass., and London, England, 1967.

183 Kemp, M. C., 'Foreign Investment and the National Advantage', *Economic Record*, Vol. 38, March 1962.

184 Negishi, T., 'Foreign Investment and the Long-run National Advantage', *Economic Record*, Vol. 41, December 1965.

185 Oniki, H., and Uzawa, H., 'Patterns of Trade and Investment in a Dynamic Model of International Trade', *Review of Economic Studies*, Vol. 32, January 1965.

5

186 Balassa, B., 'Tariff Protection in Industrial Countries: An Evaluation', *Journal of Political Economy*, Vol. 73, December 1965.

187 Basevi, G., 'The U.S. Tariff Structures: Estimate of Effective Rates of Protection of U.S. Industries and Industrial Labor', *Review of Economics and Statistics*, Vol. 48, May 1966.

188 Corden, W., 'The Structure of a Tariff System and the Effective Protective Rate', *Journal of Political Economy*, Vol. 74, June 1966.

189 Johnson, H. G., 'The Theory of Tariff Structures, with Special Reference to World Trade and Development', in *Trade and Development*, Institut des Hautes Etudes Internationales, Geneva, 1965.

190 McKinnon, R. I., 'Intermediate Products and Differential Tariffs: A Generalisation of Lerner's Symmetry Theorem', *Quarterly Journal of Economics*, Vol. 80, November 1966.

191 Ramaswami, V. K., and Srinivasan, T. N., 'Optimal Subsidies and Tariffs when Some Factors are Traded', *Journal of Political Economy*, August 1968.

192 Travis, W. P., *On the Theory of Commercial Policy*, Ph.D. Thesis submitted to Harvard University, 1961; pages 214–50.

6

193 Bhagwati, J., 'Non-economic Objectives and the Efficiency Properties of Trade', *Journal of Political Economy*, Vol. 75, October 1967.

194 Bhagwati, J., *The Theory and Practice of Commercial Policy: Departures from Unified Exchange Rates*, Special Papers in International Economics, No. 8, Princeton University, Princeton University Press, 1968.

195 Bhagwati, J., 'The Gains from Trade Once Again', *Oxford Economic Papers*, Vol. 20 (New Series), July 1968.

196 Bhagwati, J., 'Distortions and Immiserizing Growth: A Generalization', *Review of Economic Studies*, Vol. 35, October 1968.

197 Bhagwati, J., and Kemp, M. C., 'Ranking of Tariffs under Monopoly Power in Trade', *Quarterly Journal of Economics*, Vol. 83, February 1969.

198 Bhagwati, J., and Srinivasan, T. N., 'Optimal Intervention to Achieve Non-economic Objectives', *Review of Economic Studies*, Vol. 36, January 1969.

199 Kemp, M. C., 'Tariffs and the Gains from Trade', *Oxford Economic Papers*, Vol. 20 (New Series), July 1968.

200 Kreuger, A. O., and Sonnenschein, H., 'The Terms of Trade, the Gains from Trade and Price Divergence', *International Economic Review*, Vol. 8, February 1967.

7

201 Dardis, R., 'Intermediate Goods and the Gains from Trade', *Review of Economics and Statistics*, Vol. 49, November 1967.

202 Johnson, H. G., 'The Gain from Exploiting Monopoly and Monopsony Power in International Trade', *Economica*, N.S., Vol. 35, May 1968.

203 Wan, H. Y., 'Maximum Bonus – An Alternative Measure for Trading Gains', *Review of Economic Studies*, Vol. 32, January 1965.

8

204 Bruno, M., 'Optimal Patterns of Trade and Development', *Review of Economics and Statistics*, Vol. 49, November 1967.

205 Chenery, H. B., and McEwan, A., 'Optimal Patterns of Growth and Aid: The Case of Pakistan', *Pakistan Development Review*, Vol. 7, Summer 1966.

206 Chenery, H. B., and Strout, A. M., 'Foreign Assistance and Economic Development', *American Economic Review*, Vol. 76, September 1966.

207 Hansen, B., *Long and Short-term Planning in Underdeveloped Countries*, North Holland Publishing Co., Amsterdam, 1968.

208 Tinbergen, J., 'International, National, Regional and Local Industries', in Baldwin and others, *Trade, Growth and the Balance of Payments; Essays in honor of G. Haberler*, Rand McNally, Chicago, and North Holland Publishing Co., Amsterdam, 1965.

Editor's Note

The issue of human capital and the pattern of trade in the Heckscher-Ohlin model, discussed in pages 30 and following, has been analyzed empirically for the case of India by R. Bharadwaj and J. N. Bhagwati, "Human Capital and the Pattern of Foreign Trade: The Indian Case," *Indian Economic Review* 2(2) (N.S.) (October 1967): 117–142.

NOTES ON SOME CONTROVERSIES IN THE THEORY OF INTERNATIONAL TRADE

It is proposed in this paper to review four disputed problems in the theory of international trade.

(1) The first problem concerns the impact of an autonomous shift in international demand on the net barter terms of trade and the volume of trade. Graham disputed the solution that Marshall offered to this problem in *Money, Credit and Commerce.* The contradiction between their rival solutions stems from alternative meanings attached to the "increase" in demand; this is seen to emerge readily from an extension of recent developments of demand theory.

(2) The second problem concerns Edgeworth's proposition that a reduction in the cost of production of exportables in a country may lead to her impoverishment. Nicholson disputed this proposition on the ground, among others, that the model used to demonstrate the result was very restrictive. It is shown that this possibility, and the conditions under which it will obtain, can be established for less restrictive models.

(3) The third problem relates to Marshall's measure of the "net benefit" from foreign trade and Viner's objection to it. These rival measures are here evaluated with the aid of an extension of modern welfare economics to the theory of international trade.

(4) The fourth problem relates to Marshall's theorem that, where international demands are sufficiently inelastic for international equilibrium to be unstable, there exists at least one position of stable equilibrium on each side of the unstable equilibrium point.

I. Marshall *vs.* Graham on Changes in International Demand, Terms of Trade and Volume of Trade

In Chapter VIII of *Money, Credit and Commerce* Marshall discusses the problem of how far the terms of trade and the volume of trade would be changed if "trade between two countries E and G having been in equilibrium, there is a considerable increase in E's demand for G's goods, unaccompanied by any corresponding increase of demand on the part of G." [1] His solution, lucidly set out in Appendix J, is that the extent of the deterioration in E's terms of trade will vary directly with E's elasticity of demand for imports and inversely with G's elasticity of demand for imports; and the magnitude of the increase in the volume of trade will vary directly with *both* these elasticities.[2]

[1] Marshall, *Money, Credit and Commerce* (Macmillan, 1923), p. 177.
[2] *Ibid.*, p. 178.

Graham, on the other hand, has argued that deterioration in E's terms of trade will vary inversely with *both* these elasticities while the extent of the increase in the volume of trade will vary inversely with E's elasticity and directly with G's elasticity.[1]

A. *Graham's Solution*

In the following analysis we shall use the two-country (E and G), two-commodity (E-goods and G-goods) " real " model which both Marshall and Graham were using.

Starting from a position of balanced trade, assume that E's demand for G's goods has increased in the sense that, at each level of the terms of trade, the quantity of imports demanded by E from G has increased in a given proportion; this increase can be represented by an increase in the quantity of imports demanded by E at the initial terms of trade. What will be the resultant impact on the international commodity terms of trade?

Assuming that the terms of trade have been readjusted so as to restore equilibrium in trade, we can analyse the change in the quantity of G-goods imported into E into two components:

(i) The postulated increase in the quantity of G's goods demanded at the initial terms of trade: it may be denoted by $\overline{dM}$, where M refers to E's initial quantity of imports of G's goods.

(ii) The decrease in the quantity of G's goods demanded as the terms of trade move in favour of G-goods to restore equilibrium: this is measured by $M \,.\, \alpha \,.\, dp$, where $\alpha = -\dfrac{p}{M} \cdot \dfrac{dM}{dp}$ is the elasticity of E's demand for imports, and p is the terms of trade, measured as the price of G-goods divided by the price of E-goods and assumed by choice of units to be unity initially.

The total change in the quantity of G-goods imported into E may thus be measured by:

$$\overline{dM} - M \,.\, \alpha \,.\, dp \qquad (1)$$

[1] Graham, " The Theory of International Values," *Quarterly Journal of Economics*, Vol. 46, 1932, pp. 601–2. Viner supports Graham's position in his *Studies in the Theory of International Trade* (Harper & Bros., N.Y., 1937), pp. 543–6. In analysing the Marshall–Graham controversy Viner discards the use of offer curves in favour of diagrams with E-bales on the *X*-axis and the terms of trade (G-bales per E-bale) on the *Y*-axis, which leads him easily into construing " shift in demand " in the traditional, and as we shall see Graham's, sense of change in the quantity of E-bales demanded by G from E at given terms of trade. It should also be mentioned that alternative solutions of the Marshall–Graham controversy are to be found in Allen, " The Effects on Trade of Shifting Reciprocal Demand Schedules," *American Economic Review*, Vol. 42, 1952, pp. 135–40; and Kemp, " The Relation between Changes in International Demand and the Terms of Trade," *Econometrica*, Vol. 24, 1956, pp. 41–6. As contrasted with these solutions, however, our approach combines simplicity with the explicit demonstration of the significance of stability conditions, further enabling us to attack directly the Edgeworth–Nicholson controversy in Section II; we further link the problem to the general theory of value.

But it can also be measured in terms of the change in the quantity of G-goods supplied by G:

(2) $$M \, . \, r_m \, . \, dp$$

where $r_m = \frac{p}{M} \cdot \frac{dSm}{dp}$ ($Sm \equiv M$ initially) is the elasticity of G's supply of G-goods to E. In equilibrium, (1) = (2). Solving for dp, therefore, we get:

(3) $$dp = \frac{\overline{dM}}{M(r_m + \alpha)}$$

However, both Marshall and Graham couch their argument, as we have seen, in terms of G's elasticity of demand for E's goods instead of in terms of G's elasticity of supply of her goods to E as we have done. We must, therefore, recast formula (3) accordingly. Let us define G's elasticity of demand for imports of E's goods as $\eta_x = \frac{p}{X} \cdot \frac{dX}{dp}$, where X is the initial quantity of E-goods imported by G. Then, by a well-known proposition, $\eta_x - r_m = 1$. Formula (3) thus becomes:

(4) $$dp = \frac{\overline{dM}}{M(\eta_x + \alpha - 1)}$$

Concerning the change in the terms of trade, therefore, we have emerged with Graham's solution: if we confine ourselves to stable situations ($\eta_x + \alpha - 1 > 0$) the extent to which the terms of trade will become unfavourable to E varies inversely with the elasticities of *both* G and E. It may also be noticed that, provided the stability condition is fulfilled, this conclusion holds even when G's elasticity is less than unity.[1]

The change in the volume of trade is also in conformity with Graham's findings, and can be obtained readily as:

(5) $$M \, . \, r_m \, . \, dp = \frac{(\eta_x - 1)\overline{dM}}{(\eta_x + \alpha - 1)}$$

For elastic G-demand ($\eta_x > 1$), therefore, the increase in the volume of trade will be greater, the smaller is E's elasticity of demand for imports and the larger is G's elasticity, provided the stability condition is satisfied.

B. *Marshall's Solution*

It seems surprising that Marshall should, however, have reached a different result. But the puzzle is readily solved when we find that Marshall is construing the increase in E's demand for G's goods to mean that "the number *OM'* of her bales, which she will [now] give for *PM* (or *P'M'*) of

[1] Marshall explicitly confined his discussion to the case of elastic demands, although Graham did not. It is best, therefore, to regard the controversy as confined to the case of elastic demands. Cf. Viner, *op. cit.*, pp. 543–6.

G bales, is greater than OM" and that "there will be an advantage in speaking of OE [E's offer curve] *as moved to the right* by an increase in E's demand."[1] Marshall clearly means by a "given" increase in E's demand for G's goods an equi-proportional increase in the quantity of exports E will offer for each quantity of imports received from G; this is the same thing as an equi-proportional increase in the price E will offer for each given quantity of imports.

This being so, the reason for the contradiction in the solutions offered by **Marshall and Graham emerges readily. It will be remembered that $\overline{dM}$, which occurs in the earlier formulæ, represented the *given* increase in the demand for G's goods, and hence was a datum. Under Marshall's assumption, however, it varies in turn with the elasticity of E's demand for imports. If $\overline{dX}$ is the postulated increase in the quantity of exports of E-goods that E will offer for the initial quantity of G-goods imported from G, $\Delta p = \frac{\overline{dX}}{M}$ is** the increase in the price E will pay per unit. The increase in the quantity of G-goods E will demand at the initial price is approximately:

$$\overline{dM} = -\frac{M}{p} \,.\, \alpha \,.\, (-\Delta p) = \alpha \,.\, \overline{dX} \tag{6}$$

Substituting (6) into (4), we get:

$$dp = \frac{\overline{dX}}{M\left(\frac{\eta_x - 1}{\alpha} + 1\right)} \tag{7}$$

Marshall's solution follows quite readily now. For stable situations and elastic G-demand ($\eta_x > 1$), the extent to which the terms of trade will become unfavourable to E will vary inversely with G's elasticity and directly with E's elasticity. However, when G-demand is inelastic ($\eta_x < 1$)—a case which Marshall excluded by assumption[2]—and the stability condition holds, Marshall's conclusion is inadmissible and the Graham conclusion holds even under the Marshall-type change in international demand.

The change in the volume of trade again is in conformity with Marshall's conclusions and can be obtained readily as:

$$M \,.\, r_m \,.\, dp = \frac{\overline{dX}}{\left(\frac{1}{\alpha} + \frac{1}{\eta_x - 1}\right)} \tag{8}$$

For stable situations and elastic G-demand the increase in the volume of trade will be greater, the greater are *both* G's and E's elasticities of demand for imports.

[1] Marshall, *op. cit.*, p. 342, Marshall's italics.
[2] See footnote 1, p. 76.

We thus see that, where stability obtains and G-demand is elastic, the Graham conclusions hold when the change in international demand is defined in terms of a change in the quantity demanded at given terms of trade; whereas the Marshall conclusions hold when the change in international demand is defined in terms of a change in the price at which the given quantity is demanded.

C. *Generalisation of the Problem*

Our discussion points directly to a more general proposition in the theory of value, of which the Marshall–Graham controversy is an illustration. This is that the answer to the problem of how the elasticity of demand (supply) affects the extent to which a shift in demand (supply) alters the price and quantity exchanged depends on the precise way in which the shift is defined. There are two possible definitions of such a shift:

(*a*) a change in the quantity demanded (supplied) at a given price; and

(*b*) a change in the price at which a given quantity is demanded (supplied).[1]

According to which definition is chosen, the influence of the elasticity of the shifted curve on the effect of the shift will be different, as follows, if stability is assumed:

(i) An increase in demand will produce a greater increase in quantity exchanged, and a greater increase in price—

(1) on definition (*a*), the *less* elastic is the demand;
(2) on definition (*b*), the *more* elastic is the demand;

and conversely.

(ii) An increase in supply will produce a greater increase in quantity exchanged, and a greater reduction in price—

(1) on definition (*a*), the *less* elastic is the supply;
(2) on definition (*b*), the *more* elastic is the supply;

and conversely.

D. *Concluding Observations*

Both ways of construing a change in demand—change in quantity demanded at a given price, and change in price at which a given quantity is demanded—may be useful in the analysis of international trade problems. Broadly speaking, Graham's approach is likely to be more convenient when the problem is to examine the effects of some change on the volume and terms of international trade, when the conditions of international competition are

[1] Definition (*a*) is the Graham-type; definition (*b*) is the Marshall-type. The former corresponds to Hicks' *p*-theory; the latter to Hicks' *q*-theory (Hicks, *A Revision of Demand Theory* (O.U.P., 1956)).

assumed constant, since the direction of change of international equilibrium can be predicted from the effect of the change on quantity demanded at the initial price. Examples are the transfer problem and the effect of economic expansion on international trade equilibrium.[1] Marshall's approach, on the other hand, is likely to be more convenient when the problem concerns the effects of a change in a country's commercial policy on its internal equilibrium prices and quantities, since the direction of change of this equilibrium can be predicted from the effect of the tariff on the quantity of imports demanded at the initial internal price, and of the corresponding reduction of the external price on the quantity of imports the foreigner would supply. Marshall himself used this technique for the analysis of tariffs and subsidies; a more recent example of its successful application is Metzler's classic analysis of the case in which a tariff shifts production towards exports.[2]

II. Edgeworth *vs.* Nicholson on the Effect of an Improvement in Production on Foreign Trade and Welfare

Edgeworth, in the first of his three celebrated articles on " The Theory of International Values " in this Journal, argued that where there has occurred " a diminution . . . in the cost of production of an exported article," an extension of Mill's analysis indicates that " the improvement may prove detrimental to the exporting country." While claiming that his proposition is " sufficiently supported by common sense," Edgeworth demonstrated it in the context of a model of complete specialisation in production of exportables and in consumption of importables, arguing that the foreign elasticity of demand for the country's exportables should be less than unity for such impoverishment to occur in the context of his model.[3]

Nicholson, in his *Principles*, raised objection to Edgeworth's proposition on the ground that " If, however, we introduce money, this case is seen to work out differently " [4] and that Edgeworth's model was highly restrictive.

Edgeworth returned briefly to the subject in this Journal to argue that the introduction of money would not affect the proposition; and, further, that, although his proposition had been demonstrated with respect to his restrictive model, it was clearly not confined to it and should be demonstrable in the context of models of incomplete specialisation.[5]

[1] H. G. Johnson, *International Trade and Economic Growth* (Allen & Unwin Ltd., 1958), Chapters III and VII. Also J. Bhagwati, " International Trade and Economic Expansion," *American Economic Review*, Vol. 48, December 1958, pp. 941–53.

[2] Marshall, *op. cit.*, pp. 344–6. Metzler, " Tariffs, the Terms of Trade and the Distribution of National Income." *Journal of Political Economy*, Vol. 57, February 1949, pp. 1–29.

[3] Edgeworth, " The Theory of International Values," Economic Journal, Vol. 4, 1894. The argument set out in the text is from pp. 40–1.

[4] Nicholson, *The Principles of Political Economy*, Vol. II (London, 1897), p. 311.

[5] Edgeworth, " On a Point in the Theory of International Trade," Economic Journal, Vol. 9, 1899, pp. 125–8.

In his *Theory of International Trade* Bastable entered the controversy to argue in favour of Edgeworth, seeking to demonstrate Edgeworth's result, in terms of a model of incomplete specialisation in consumption along familiar classical lines, by showing how the country with the postulated improvement may, as a result of inelastic foreign demand, find herself with less of both exportables and importables than prior to the improvement. Bastable then proceeded to state the proposition that: " It is only where the benefit from improvement is smaller than the advantage of interchange that loss could result from it." [1]

A. *Edgeworth Model: Complete Specialisation in Production and in Consumption*

Edgeworth postulates that the country with the improvement in technique produces only exportables and consumes only importables. This remarkable model makes for the simplest, if not the most persuasive, demonstration of Edgeworth's proposition.

Thus, using the notation introduced in Section I, assume E to be the country with the postulated improvement. Then, the Edgeworth model amounts to arguing: (1) the Marshall-type increment in supply of exports: $\overline{dX}$; (2) that α is unity; and (3) that E's welfare varies directly with the quantity of her imports.

From formula (8) it follows then that E will be impoverished by the improvement if

$$\frac{\overline{dX}(\eta_x - 1)}{\eta_x} < 0 \tag{9}$$

which yields us the Edgeworth condition that $0 < \eta_x < 1$ for the country to be damnified by the improvement.

B. *Model of Complete Specialisation only in Production*

Where, however, consumption of both exportables and importables obtains, different and more complex analysis becomes necessary to establish Edgeworth's proposition.

What we must now discover is the condition under which, in this model, the gain directly accruing from the improvement is outweighed by the loss from the resultant deterioration in the terms of trade.[2] This can be done readily. Let K be defined as country E's productive capacity, which is always fully employed and is measured in terms of the output of exportables that E would produce at the initial terms of trade. Then $\overline{dK}$ is the increase

[1] Bastable, *The Theory of International Trade* (Macmillan, 1903), 4th edition (revised), pp. 185 and 186–7. Bastable also correctly dismisses Nicholson's contention that the introduction of money would affect the validity of the result.

[2] This argument is to be found in a rudimentary stage in Edgeworth's 1899 ECONOMIC JOURNAL note, *op. cit.*, as also in his earlier 1894 article, *op. cit.* (p. 41): " The case of an improvement in the process of manufacture of an article which is both exported and consumed at home . . . is a compound between the certain gain to the native consumer and the possible loss to the home country in the way of foreign trade."

in real income directly resulting from the postulated improvement. To measure the loss from the deterioration in the terms of trade, we must first discover the change in the terms of trade resulting from the improvement; this is found simply by substituting for $\overline{dM}$ in formula (4) the expression $m \,.\, \overline{dK}$, in which m is the marginal propensity to consume importables. The loss of real income due to this change in the terms of trade is approximately the increase in the cost of the initial volume of imports:

$$(10) \qquad M \,.\, dp = \frac{m \,.\, \overline{dK}}{(\eta_x + \alpha - 1)}$$

It follows, then, that E will be impoverished by the improvement if

$$\overline{dK} < \frac{m \,.\, \overline{dK}}{(\eta_x + \alpha - 1)}$$

i.e., if

$$(11) \qquad (\eta_x + \alpha - 1) < m$$

This condition can be fulfilled without violating the stability condition; hence Nicholson's second objection, concerning the restrictiveness of the model used by Edgeworth, is refuted.

Since α can be decomposed into $m + \varepsilon$, where ε is an expenditure-compensated elasticity of demand, the condition for impoverishment can be rewritten as

$$(12) \qquad \eta_x < 1 - \varepsilon$$

This formula shows, as might be expected, that for impoverishment to ensue both the foreign demand for exports and the domestic (expenditure-compensated) demand for imports must be inelastic.

C. *Model of Incomplete Specialisation in both Production and Consumption*

The analysis resulting in formula (11) can be easily extended to the case where the country is producing and consuming both exportables and importables. All that is required to do is (*i*) to rewrite m in equation (11) as $c - h$, the difference between the marginal propensity to consume the importable good (c) and the proportion of the increase in productive capacity that would take the form of production of importables if the terms of trade remained at the initial level (h); and (*ii*) to recognise that the elasticities of international demand η_x and α now depend on the elasticities of transformation of exportable goods into importables in domestic production, as well as on the elasticities of final demand.[1]

While the possibility of increasing domestic production of importables in

[1] The actual reworking of the formula along these lines may be found in J. Bhagwati, "Immiserizing Growth: A Geometrical Note," *Review of Economic Studies*, Vol. 25, June 1958, pp. 201–5; and in H. G. Johnson, *op. cit.*, p. 76.

response to an increase in their price introduces a factor tending to raise elasticities of international demand and so increase the restrictiveness of the conditions required for the Edgeworth case, the possibility that the improvement may lead to a decrease in domestic production of importables works in the opposite direction. Since h can be negative, m can exceed unity and impoverishment can occur even if international demands are elastic.

The theoretical analysis of the effects on production of an improvement in technique in an industry, for the standard two-good two-factor constant-returns model of international trade, may be summarised as follows.[1] Assuming initially unchanged factor prices and no change in factor employment in the other industry, technical progress in an industry has two effects: except when it is "neutral," it releases a quantity of one of the factors from the industry; and it reduces the unit cost of production. At unchanged factor prices the quantity of the factor which is released must be absorbed by an expansion of the industry which uses it relatively intensively, accompanied by a contraction of the other industry (which contraction releases the amount of the other factor required to co-operate with the released factor in the combination optimal at the given factor prices). At unchanged commodity prices the reduction of cost in the industry where the improvement has occurred must be offset by a shift of resources into that industry out of the other, which will raise the price of the factor used relatively intensively in that industry and cheapen the factor used relatively intensively in the other industry, so restoring the initial comparative cost ratio.[2]

It follows that if progress in an industry is (*a*) neutral, so that only the second adjustment is called for; (*b*) saving of the factor used relatively intensively in the industry, so that both adjustments work in the same direction; or (*c*) not sufficiently saving of the factor used relatively unintensively in the industry for the first adjustment to outweigh the second; then production in the other industry will fall. Conversely, if progress is (*d*) sufficiently saving of the factor used relatively unintensively in the industry for the first adjustment to outweigh the second, output in the other industry will rise, and in the extreme case output of the industry in which progress occurs will actually decrease.

Thus an improvement in the export industry which is neutral, or saving of the factor used intensively in that industry, will increase demand for imports by both increasing consumption and reducing domestic production of the importable good; and impoverishment may result from such an im-

[1] See H. G. Johnson, *op. cit.*, for the analysis of neutral progress and a brief indication (p. 78, n. 20) of the required line of argument on cases of biased progress; and Findlay and Grubert, "Factor Intensities, Technological Progress and the Terms of Trade," *Oxford Economic Papers*, Vol. 11, February 1959, pp. 111–21, for the analysis of the effects of biased progress.

[2] Since the factor used relatively unintensively in the progressing industry falls in price, more than the whole of the benefit of progress goes to the other factor. If the marginal propensities to consume of owners of the two factors differ, this redistribution effect may reduce consumption of one of the goods. This possibility, which could make c negative, is ignored in what follows.

provement, even if international demands are elastic.[1] But improvements in the export industry which save the factor used relatively unintensively there do not necessarily give rise to the possibility of impoverishment. On the contrary, improvements sufficiently strongly saving of the factor used relatively unintensively in the export industry may, by increasing domestic production of imports, actually reduce the country's demand for imports. In this case the country will enjoy a double gain—in total output, and through improved terms of trade—instead of a gain in output offset in whole or part by a terms of trade loss.

Edgeworth was therefore incorrect in implying that any improvement which reduced costs in the export industry might prove detrimental to the exporting country. On the other hand, modern analysis points to a possibility not mentioned by Edgeworth, that an improvement in the import-competing industry, if it is sufficiently saving of the factor used relatively intensively in the export industry, will increase the country's demand for imports and so create the possibility of a net loss of welfare from the improvement. Again, this possibility arises even if international demands are elastic.

D. *Concluding Observations*

We have shown that it is possible, contrary to Nicholson's assertion, to demonstrate the possibility of impoverishment of a country from domestic improvement in the context of models less restrictive than Edgeworth's. Moreover, in the general case of incomplete specialisation we have shown that this possibility does not require inelasticity of international demands.

Also, whereas Edgeworth, Nicholson and Bastable confined their discussion (necessarily in view of their models) to improvement in the production of exportables, our analysis of the case of incomplete specialisation in production demonstrates, on the one hand, that not all improvements in the export industry will create the possibility of impoverishment, but, on the other hand, that impoverishment is possible even if the improvement occurs in the domestic production of the importable good, and thus further generalises the scope of Edgeworth's proposition.

Further, since the maximum loss that the country may suffer from adverse terms of trade cannot be greater than her gains from trade, the Bastable proposition follows that the necessary condition for Edgeworth's possibility to arise is that the direct gain from growth is less than the initial gains from trade. Our analysis again proceeds farther and establishes conditions for such impoverishment which are both sufficient and less restrictive.

Finally, it may be noted that Edgeworth correctly argued that where the country is thus damnified by the improvement, it follows " by parity of reasoning " that it " may be benefited by a restriction of its exports." [2]

[1] This proposition, and the following ones, assume the fulfilment of the stability condition and the absence of inferior goods.

[2] Edgeworth, Economic Journal (Vol. 4, 1894), p. 40.

Whatever the model used, it is clear that where impoverishment results from domestic improvement in production, the country can restrict its trade to advantage.

III. Marshall *vs.* Viner on Measurement of the " Net Benefit " from Trade

A. *Marshall's Measure*

In *Money, Credit and Commerce* Marshall measured the " net benefit " derived by a country from its international trade as the sum of the excesses of the unit prices at which the country would have purchased successive quantities of imports, over the equilibrium " rate of interchange " established in international trade.[1] In other words, he applied his concept of consumer's surplus to the problem, measuring the gain by the area between the demand curve and the price-line; though the application of the concept to the country's offer curve required considerable geometrical ingenuity, and the prices involved, as well as the surpluses, were expressed in terms of representative bales of export goods rather than money.[2]

Since the representative bales embody unit products of labour and capital, Marshall was able to measure the aggregate gain from trade to the world as a whole in terms of unit products of labour and capital, as the sum of the surpluses of the trading countries, measured in bales of their export goods. In addition, he stated the following proposition concerning a country's (G's) net benefit from trade: " the surplus is the greater, the more urgent is G's demand for a small amount of E's goods and the more of them she can receive without any great movement of the rate of interchange in her favour " [3]—*i.e.*, the higher the price G will pay for sub-equilibrium quantities, and the more elastic her demand in the sub-equilibrium quantity range.

B. *Viner's Criticism and Amendment*

Viner's criticism of Marshall's measure, set out in his *Studies in the Theory of International Trade*,[4] runs along lines which are by now familiar. He points out that Marshall's measure assumes that the offer curve is unaffected by whether or not the importing country pays the equilibrium price or the maximum price it is willing to pay for intra-marginal increments in its imports, which in turn implies constancy of the marginal utility of exportables. On the contrary, he argues, the marginal utility of exportables is greater, and therefore the price the country will pay for a marginal increment of imports less, the more that has been paid for the previous volume

[1] Marshall, *op. cit.*, Appendix J, Section 3, pp. 338–40.
[2] *Ibid.*, p. 339.
[3] *Ibid.*, pp. 339–40.
[4] Viner, *op. cit.*, pp. 570–5.

of imports; so that Marshall's measure exaggerates the amount of the surplus the country receives in trade. Because of this exaggeration, Viner claims, Marshall's measure may lead to improbable or meaningless magnitudes of the surplus.

In place of Marshall's measure Viner suggests going behind the offer curve to the country's utility function: deriving from it the offer curve as it would be if the country paid the maximum price it was willing to pay for each successive unit, and measuring the country's benefit from trade as the sum of the excesses (or deficiencies) of the prices shown on this curve for successive quantities of imports over the equilibrium price established in international trade. The offer curve so derived is, of course, the equivalent of the marginal valuation curve in welfare theory; and the measure it leads to is the true Marshallian consumer's surplus (the excess of what the consumer would be willing to pay for the equilibrium volume of imports over what he actually pays) as contrasted with the defective, exaggerated measure of it obtained by integrating the area under the demand curve. Thus Viner's measure is a theoretically sound version of Marshall's consumer's surplus concept, in the context of international exchange.

C. *Alternative Measures of the Gains from Trade*

Both Marshall and Viner employ the analytical tool of the offer curve—the aggregative version of the demand curve—and both are concerned with measurement according to the concept of benefit from exchange associated with the demand curve: consumer's surplus. Other concepts of benefit from exchange have since been developed, requiring the use of indifference curves for their exposition. The purpose of this section is to apply these concepts to the problem of the benefits derived from international exchange and to develop alternative measures of the gains from trade.

Three alternative approaches to the problem of measuring the gains from trade are available: Marshallian surplus, compensating variation and equivalent variation. The first assumes that the advantage of trade consists in the opportunity to exchange the equilibrium quantity of exports for the equilibrium quantity of imports, and measures the gain from trade by the amount of one good that could be extracted from the country without making it worse off than it would be in the absence of trade. The second and third both assume that the advantage of trade consists in the ability to exchange exports for imports at the equilibrium price ratio; but whereas the second measures the gain from trade by the amount of one good that could be extracted from the country (while leaving it free to trade at the equilibrium price ratio) without making it worse off than it would be in the absence of trade, the third measures the gain by the amount of one good that would have to be donated to the country to make it as well off without trade as it would be when free to trade at the equilibrium price.

Each measure can be made in terms of either of the two goods, exportables and importables. Since, in the world market, the country is a net producer of the former in order to be a net consumer of the latter, measures in terms of exportable goods (the cost of consumption of importables) may be regarded as measures of the country's gain in its capacity as a consumer, while

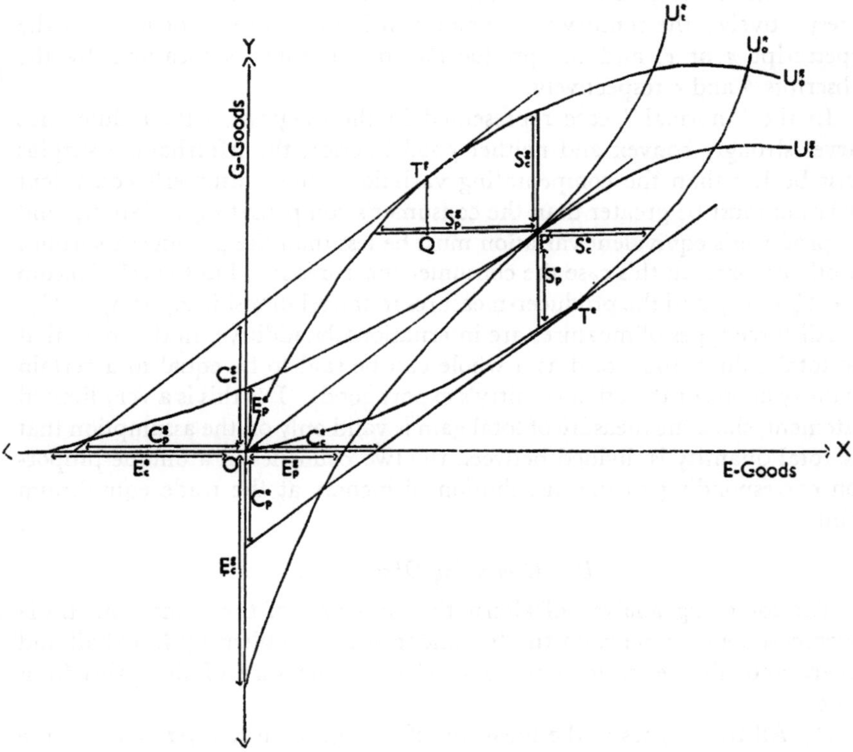

FIG. 1

measures in terms of importable goods (the reward for production of exportables) may be regarded as measures of its gain in its capacity as a producer. Consequently, the alternative measurements in terms of the exportable and importable goods may (at the risk of some confusion in the Marshallian terminology) be described as the consumer and producer measurements respectively. Thus there are six possible measures of the gains derived by a country from international trade—Marshallian consumer's and producer's surplus, consumer's and producer's compensating variation, and consumer's and producer's equivalent variation—and twelve in all for the (two-country) world as a whole.

The six measures for each country are illustrated in Fig. 1. Country E's exports are measured along OX, country G's along OY; P is the free-trade equilibrium point at which the two countries' offer curves intersect, the slope of OP representing the equilibrium terms of trade. U_o^e and U_o^g represent the no-trade indifference curves, and U_t^e and U_t^g the free-trade equilibrium indifference curves of the two countries.[1] T^e and T^g are the points on the no-trade indifference curves with slopes equal to the equilibrium terms of trade. The three measures of the gains from trade are denoted by S, C and E respectively; the country whose gain is being measured is denoted by the superscript g or e, and the producer's and consumer's measures by the subscripts p and c respectively.

In the "normal" case represented in the diagram, with indifference curves strongly convex and neither good inferior, the Marshallian surplus must be less than the compensating variation; the consumer's equivalent variation must be greater than the consumer's compensating variation; and the producer's equivalent variation must be less than the producer's surplus. In other words, in this case the consumer-measures stand in the relationship $S_c < C_c < E_c$; and the producer-measures in the relationship $E_p < S_p < C_p$.[2]

All three types of measures are internationally additive, in the sense that the total gain of the world as a whole can be said to be equal to a certain quantity of one or the other country's export good. But this is a very limited statement, since the measure of total gain is valid only on the assumption that the total quantity is divided between the two countries in a unique proportion corresponding to the distribution of income at the trade equilibrium point.

D. Concluding Observations

The foregoing analysis of alternative measures of the gains from trade suggests some comments on the treatment of the problem by Marshall and Viner, and also leads to a more satisfactory measure of the gains from trade.

(1) All three types of the measures of benefit discussed here employ the no-trade indifference curve as a basis of comparison. It follows that Marshall's proposition concerning the conditions under which the benefit is likely to be large, which runs in terms of the characteristics of the offer curve, must

[1] These are to be construed as the trade-indifference curves introduced by Meade, *A Geometry of International Trade* (G. Allen & Unwin, 1952). It is interesting to note that, as Viner records, *op. cit.*, p. 576, Edgeworth, in his "On the Application of Mathematics to Political Economy," *Journal of the Royal Statistical Society*, Vol. 52, 1889, pp. 555–60, had already introduced, for measuring the net benefit from trade, a "no-gain from trade" curve, which he called a "collective utility curve," and had measured the gain from trade (for Germany) by a method exactly identical to our own. Whereas, however, Edgeworth's indifference curve was based purely on exchange analysis, the trade-indifference curve of Meade allows us to admit production into the model.

[2] Universal non-inferiority means that the slope with reference to the import–good axis of any point on the U_o curve is steeper than that on the U_t curve for the same quantity of exports, and less steep than that on the U_o curve for the same quantity of imports. Hence the distance between the two curves in the export direction increases, and in the import direction decreases, as the point on U_o moves towards the origin.

now be reformulated in terms of the properties of the no-trade indifference curve. The revised proposition, about the size of the Marshallian consumer's surplus, must involve the marginal rate of substitution between the goods in the absence of trade, and the shape of the indifference curve between the origin and the point corresponding to the equilibrium volume of imports: the consumer's surplus derived from trade will be larger, the greater the difference between the slope of the free-trade terms of trade line (OP) and the slope of the tangent to the no-trade indifference curve at the point of origin, and the higher the elasticity of substitution between the goods (along the no-trade indifference curve). Marshall's own proposition, in terms of the offer curve, is thus clearly incorrect except when the trade-indifference curves are homothetic.

(2) Viner's criticism of Marshall's measure, that " Marshall's method . . . is capable of producing such improbable results as a surplus, measured in G-bales, many times greater than the total amount of G-bales actually exported, and—if the OG curve is inelastic—may produce such meaningless results as a surplus, measured in G-bales, greater than the total amount of G-bales which G can produce " [1] is both equally applicable to his amended version of Marshall's measure and totally irrelevant. As is easily seen from contemplation of S_c^g in Fig. 1, it is perfectly easily conceivable that the gain from trade on Viner's measure (or the other two consumer-measures, though *not* the producer-measures) might exceed the total quantity of goods exported by the country. Nor is the possibility that the gain might exceed the total amount of exportables the country could *produce* ruled out by Viner's measure. This possibility does require that the no-trade indifference curve can be drawn for regions involving exports above the country's productive capacity, implying that the country can value negative consumption of exportables combined with positive consumption of importables; but the fulfilment of this requirement is itself implied by the usual practice of drawing the offer curve through the origin, which assumes that at some finite high price of importables the country becomes a net exporter of such goods. If this possibility is ruled out by assumption, however, the defective Marshallian measure, which exaggerates the true surplus, could still produce the requisite result, so that Viner's argument is justified to that extent.

(3) All three of the measures of gain discussed in the previous section are open to a logical objection. If the quantity of the relevant good which measures the gain were actually extracted from the country the equilibrium volume and terms of trade would be different from their initial equilibrium values: if the gain were extracted in exportable goods the volume would be smaller and the terms of trade more favourable than initially, and the converse if the gain were extracted in importable goods. The measures are, therefore, in a sense logically inconsistent.

[1] Viner, *op. cit.*, p. 572.

In order to avoid such inconsistency, the gain must be measured by the quantities of the two goods which, if extracted, would leave the international trade equilibrium unchanged. The simplest such measure, illustrated for country G, is T^gQ of G-goods and QP of E-goods, which quantities might be extracted by an income tax, the proceeds of which are spent in buying these amounts of the goods. But T^g is only one point on the no-trade indifference curve, that at which the marginal rate of substitution between the goods is equal to the terms of trade; any of the other points could be reached, in principle at least,[1] by a combination of excise taxes and subsidies (remembering that an income tax is, in this model, equivalent to an excise tax at the same rate on both goods). Thus the gain can be thought of as a transformation curve between the two goods, formed by the no-trade indifference curve referred to the origin P; for simplicity, the curve could be confined to the range bounded by the two Marshallian surpluses, within which the quantity of neither good is negative. By extension of this notion, the value of the opportunity to trade can be regarded as a family of such transformation curves, one for each point on the foreign-offer curve; or as a single curve formed by points on the foreign-offer curve and the points on the no-trade indifference curve at which the marginal rate of substitution between the goods is equal to the terms of trade.

IV. Marshall's Theorem Concerning the Stability of International Equilibrium

Our fourth problem is whether, if international demands are so inelastic in the neighbourhood of an equilibrium point as to make that equilibrium unstable, this necessarily implies the existence of at least two points of stable equilibrium, one at a higher and one at a lower exchange ratio than the (unstable) equilibrium ratio. This problem is rather different from the preceding three, in that no well-recognised controversy over it is embedded in the literature of international trade, though clearly opposed views on it have been stated by different writers.

The proposition that instability of equilibrium implies an odd number of equilibrium prices, alternatively stable and unstable, was stated by Marshall as follows:[2]

> " 9. *On the extreme hypothesis that each of two imaginary countries, in exclusive trade with one another, had an urgent demand for a small quantity of the other's goods, but could find no good use for any large quantity of them, then there might be several positions, alternatively stable and unstable, of equilibrium between them.*
>
> " If OE and OG both belong to this Exceptional Demand class, they

[1] For instance, by negative purchases of goods.
[2] Marshall, *op. cit.*, Appendix J, Section 9, p. 352.

may cut one another three (or any other odd number of) times, not counting *O*. The first of these reached from *O* in either direction, will be stable, the second unstable, the third stable and so on. . . ."

As is clear from the quotation, Marshall regarded inelasticity of international demand (and therefore instability of equilibrium) as of no conceivable practical relevance. Experience in the 1930s changed opinion on this score, and the conditions required for instability were re-explored in connection with the theory of devaluation and floating exchange rates. But the classic treatments of this subject did not investigate the question of the existence of stable equilibria at all thoroughly, and in *obiter dicta* implied agreement with the Marshallian position. Joan Robinson, in "The Foreign Exchanges,"[1] asserts the existence of a stable lower equilibrium rate of exchange on the grounds that "a sufficiently violent rise in the price of imports must ultimately choke demand, and even if exports fail to react, in the flurry of the moment, the value of imports must somewhere begin to fall off." Abba Lerner, in *The Economics of Control*,[2] while arguing generally in terms of constant elasticities which may be too low for stability, implies agreement with the Marshallian proposition in the following passage:

> "One country after another is forced off the gold standard, finds its currency appreciating without this affording much relief, and is able to find a stable position only after a long fall in the value of its currency and the introduction of special restrictions on trade have so altered the situation that the elasticities are no longer so low."

On the other hand, Lloyd Metzler, in "The Theory of International Trade,"[3] does not mention the Marshallian proposition, but writes as if elasticities of international demand were the same at all levels of price, though increasing with the passage of time. The only explicit attack on the Marshallian proposition known to us is contained in Paul Samuelson's "Disparity in Postwar Exchange Rates,"[4] where it is remarked, *à propos* a restatement of the classical position in Joan Robinson's "The Pure Theory of International Trade":[5]

> "At the critical point in her argument she assumes as obvious what is not universally necessarily true. She says, 'at some point the goods become so expensive relative to world money incomes that demand

[1] J. Robinson, *Essays in the Theory of Employment* (Oxford: Blackwell, 1947), Part III, p. 201.

[2] A. P. Lerner, *The Economics of Control* (New York: Macmillan, 1944), Chapter 28, p. 380.

[3] *A Survey of Contemporary Economics*, H. S. Ellis ed. (Blakiston, 1948), Chapter 6.

[4] *Foreign Economic Policy for the United States*, Seymour Harris ed. (Harvard U.P., 1948), Chapter 22, p. 409, n. 14. In addition, Samuelson makes the theoretically far more important point that, if demand can be financed from an accumulated stock of assets as well as from income, there is no reason why devaluation of any degree should restrict demand to what can be paid for from current income. But we shall restrict our argument to the offer-curve analysis.

[5] *Review of Economic Studies*, Vol. 14, 1946–47, pp. 100–2.

turns elastic . . . and there is some level . . . at which exports fall to zero.' I grant that it is customary to draw demand curves so that at high prices they do touch the price axis and become elastic. Probably this is realistic. But it is not universally necessary as a matter of logic. It is easy to specify indifference curves such that demand is *always* inelastic."

More recently, the Marshallian proposition has been revived as part of the argument for the adoption of flexible exchange rates.[1]

The Marshallian proposition may be illustrated by reference to Figs. 2 (*a*) and 2 (*b*). In Fig. 2 (*a*), which is based on Fig. 20 of Appendix J to

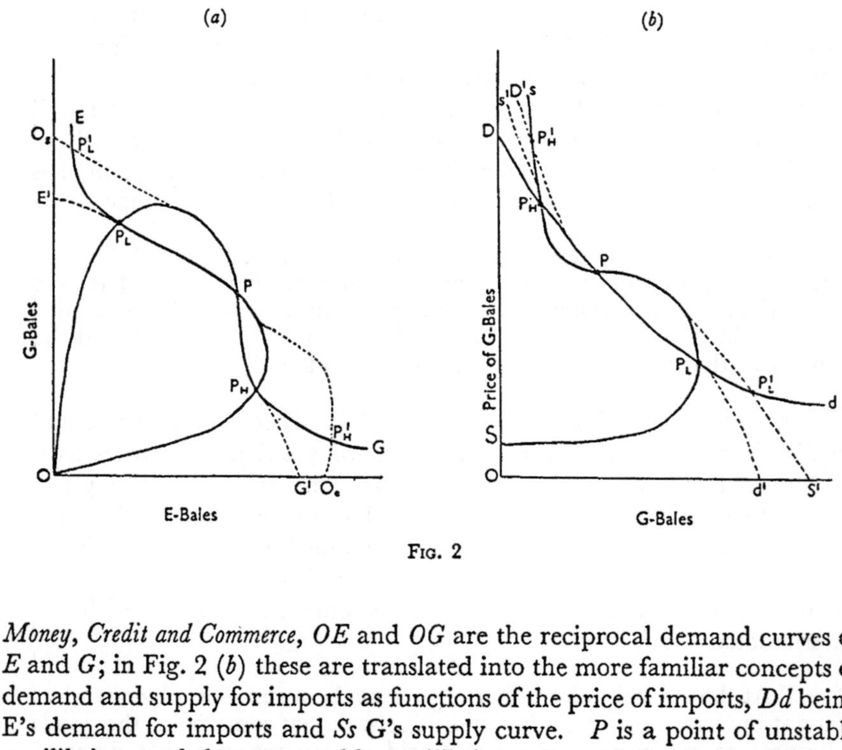

Fig. 2

Money, Credit and Commerce, *OE* and *OG* are the reciprocal demand curves of *E* and *G*; in Fig. 2 (*b*) these are translated into the more familiar concepts of demand and supply for imports as functions of the price of imports, *Dd* being E's demand for imports and *Ss* G's supply curve. *P* is a point of unstable equilibrium and there are stable equilibria at P_H and P_L, representing respectively a higher and a lower price of E's imports than the price at *P*.

It is at once apparent from the diagrams that the Marshallian proposition is a consequence of the way in which the curves are drawn. Each reciprocal demand curve has two characteristics:

(i) it passes through the origin, implying that there exists a finite

[1] Milton Friedman, "The Case for Flexible Exchange Rates," *Essays in Positive Economics* (University of Chicago Press, 1953), Chapter 6, p. 160, n. 4.

high price of imports which will choke off demand for them; *i.e.*, the demand for imports is terminable; [1]

(ii) it does not join the import-good axis as the price of imports falls, implying that the quantity of imports demanded increases indefinitely as their price falls; *i.e.*, the demand for imports is insatiable.

It is these characteristics which ensure that the reciprocal demand curves (demand and supply curves) intersect at least once above and below the (unstable) equilibrium price. But neither of these characteristics is a necessary logical consequence of demand theory: [2] on the contrary, both are empirical assumptions. Moreover, both characteristics appear inconsistent with Marshall's own assumption that each country has "an urgent demand for a small quantity of the other's goods, but could find no good use for any large quantity of them."

If neither assumption holds good for either country, the demand for imports being interminable but satiable in each country, the unstable equilibrium may be the only equilibrium possible at a finite exchange ratio; this possibility is illustrated by the curves O_eE' and O_gG' in Fig. 2 (*a*), and $D'd'$ and $S's'$ in Fig. 2 (*b*). If one country's demand for imports is satiable but not interminable, while the other country's demand for imports is interminable, there may be only one stable equilibrium possible at a finite exchange ratio, this ratio entailing a higher price for the first country's imports than the unstable equilibrium price ratio. This case is illustrated by the combination of OE' with O_gG or O_gG' and of OG' with O_eE or O_eE' in Fig. 2 (*a*), to which correspond the combinations of Dd' with $S's$ or $S's'$ and Ss' with $D'd$ or $D'd'$ in Fig. 2 (*b*). If one country's demand for imports is interminable but not satiable, while the other country's demand for imports is both satiable and interminable, there may again be only one stable equilibrium possible at a finite exchange ratio, this ratio entailing a lower price for the first country's imports than the unstable equilibrium price ratio. This case is illustrated by the combination of O_eE with O_gG' and of O_gG with O_eE' in Fig. 2 (*a*), to which correspond the combinations of $D'd$ with $S's'$ and $S's$ with $D'd'$ in Fig. 2 (*b*). But if the demand for imports is both insatiable and terminable in one country, or satiable but terminable or insatiable but interminable in both, there will be a stable equilibrium at both a higher and a lower exchange ratio than the unstable equilibrium price ratio. These cases are illustrated in Fig. 2 (*a*) respectively by the combinations involving OE or OG, the combination of OE' and OG', and the combination of O_eE and O_gG; to these correspond combinations involving Dd

[1] Each country's reciprocal demand curve must cut its export axis somewhere, as the country cannot spend more than its total national income on imports; but intersection at any other point than the origin implies that an infinitely high price is required to end demand.

[2] Consider, on the one hand, a bread-and-water economy or one relying on imports of a raw material not producible at home; on the other hand, the case of inferior goods.

or *Ss*, the combination of *Dd'* and *Ss'*, and the combination of *D'd* and *S's* in Fig. 2 (*b*).[1]

JAGDISH BHAGWATI

Nuffield College, Oxford.

HARRY G. JOHNSON

University of Manchester.

[1] Our analysis thus demonstrates the fallacy of the assertion made by Milton Friedman (*op. cit.*) and more recently alleged to be proved by Egon Sohmen (" Demand Elasticities and the Foreign Exchange Market," *Journal of Political Economy*, Vol. 65, October 1957, pp. 431–6) that an unstable foreign-exchange market equilibrium is necessarily enclosed by stable equilibrium points. Sohmen argues: " It is crucial for our purposes, however, that a stable equilibrium point exists *below* as well as above the critical unstable range. This outcome is always guaranteed, provided only that for both import demand curves the quantity demanded becomes zero at a finite price (at the upper end of the demand schedule). It is theoretically possible that a demand curve approaches the price axis asymptotically without ever reaching it. But even then its elasticity cannot forever remain below unity by more than an infinitely small amount with limited budgets, since expenditures on this commodity would otherwise have to increase without limit as its price is increased. In international trade, the limited supply of resources takes the place of the budget constraint for the single consumer " (p. 434). The first three sentences are, of course, correct; but Sohmen apparently believes, quite erroneously, that the fourth and fifth sentences add enough to the argument to dismiss the qualification expressed in the third—for he provides no further proof of his assertion.

In fact, these sentences illustrate the extent to which *non sequitur* and *ignoratio elenchi* can be accepted as valid argument if the conclusion purportedly reached is of sufficient propaganda value. In the first place, Sohmen forgets that what determines the effect of an exchange-rate change on the trade balance (on his assumption) is a weighted sum of the elasticities of demand for imports in the two countries; *and* that as the price of imports in one country rises towards infinity the price of imports in the other falls towards zero. While the budget constraint implies that the demand elasticity in the country where import prices are rising must approach infinitely close to unity, it does nothing to prevent the demand elasticity in the country where import prices are falling from approaching infinitely close to zero as imports approximate to a free good. The budget constraint therefore provides no argument in support of the contention that devaluation must improve the trade balance at sufficiently high import prices: the contrary possibility is illustrated in Fig. 2, for an increasing price of E-bales, by the offer-curve segments *PE'* and PO_g. Secondly, even were this contention established, it would not prove the existence of a stable equilibrium position. Further exchange depreciation may always reduce the amount of an adverse trade balance, without ever actually eliminating it, as is illustrated in Fig. 2, for an increasing price of G-bales, by the offer-curve segments *PG'* and PO_e. To travel hopefully is not necessarily to arrive.

Contrary to Sohmen's assertion that " the main argument of this note does not require any position on empirical questions " (p. 432), the question of the existence of stable equilibria cannot be solved by theoretical argument; it can only be deduced from empirical assumptions about the nature of demand for imports in the real world. Of the two simplest assumptions that will guarantee the result—that at some high price of imports, substitution in consumption and/or production will eliminate demand for imports, and that no finite quantity of imports could satiate the demand for them—the former is probably the more plausible. Both assumptions, however, raise the question of the time required for the adjustment of production and consumption patterns to a change in relative prices, the failure to investigate which may be the most important source of disagreement between economists about the efficacy of exchange-rate adjustments.

Erratum

Page 76, line following equation (2): "*Sm*" should read "S_m" in both occurrences.

THE PROOFS OF THE THEOREMS ON COMPARATIVE ADVANTAGE

THIS note examines critically the usual statement and proofs of the two principal theories of comparative advantage: (i) Ricardian, and (ii) Heckscher–Ohlin. While none of the analysis offered here is intrinsically novel, it is presented in a manner which has fairly important implications for a full understanding—not evident in either oral or written tradition—of the postulates underlying these theories of comparative advantage. More significantly, it is shown that (contrary to what is thought) certain restrictions on demand conditions have to be specified *even when* the Ricardian theorem and the Heckscher–Ohlin theorem (using the *price* definition of factor abundance) are to be proved.

I

The proofs of the two-country, two-commodity theories of comparative advantage relating to the pattern of trade, whether one takes the Ricardian or the Heckscher–Ohlin version, depend on two successive arguments.

Argument I

Propositions are proven, relating to the determination of the *pre-trade* commodity price ratio: thus, in the Ricardian model, the pre-trade commodity price ratio is shown to be equal to the labour productivity ratio whereas, in the Heckscher–Ohlin model, it is demonstrated that the relative, pre-trade price of the commodity using the country's abundant factor intensively will be lower than in the other country.

Argument II

(i) It is argued that a country will export that commodity whose relative, pre-trade price is lower than in the other country and will import the other commodity. (ii) *Corollary:* Also usually considered implicit is the proposition that if the pre-trade prices are identical between countries no trade will occur.

The successive Arguments I and II (i) lead to the well-known theorems of comparative advantages: (1) *Ricardian Theorem*, a country will export (import) that commodity in which her comparative factor productivity is higher (lower); and (2) *Heckscher–Ohlin Theorem*, a country will export (import) that commodity which uses her abundant (scarce) factor intensively.[1] Possible corollaries to these theorems, sometimes derived from Arguments I and II (ii), are: (1) *Ricardian Corollary*, where comparative factor productivities are identical between countries, no trade will occur; and (2) *Heckscher–Ohlin Corollary*, where factor endowments are identical between countries, no trade will take place.

In Section II, addressed to the Ricardian propositions, it is shown that the Ricardian theorem requires the specification of restrictions (albeit "reasonable") on demand *in addition* to the postulates always stated. Opportunity is also taken to note that the Ricardian corollary is invalid owing to the familiar multiplicity of production equilibria in the Ricardian model. Finally, in Section III, which discusses the Heckscher–Ohlin propositions, it is argued that while the assumption that the consumption pattern be identical between countries regardless of income levels is correctly held to be required only when the *physical* definition of factor abundance (to be discussed later) is used, it is incorrect to maintain that *no* restrictions at all need to be put on demand when the *price* definition is adopted.

II. Ricardian Propositions

(A) *Ricardian Corollary*

The Ricardian corollary, stating that where factor productivity ratios are identical between the two countries no trade will take place, is not logically true. Indeed, not merely can trade take place but, in general, the pattern of trade will be reversible as well. This follows immediately from the well-known multiplicity of production equilibria corresponding to the commodity price ratio, which is equated, under perfect competition, with the identical factor productivity ratio in each country.

[1] That the traditional proofs of both Ricardian and Heckscher–Ohlin propositions rely explicitly on Argument I and implicitly on Argument II (ii) is evident not merely from oral traditions but also from the writings of various theorists.

Thus Ohlin [7, p. 29], for example, in his famous work on *Interregional and International Trade*, leads up, *via* Argument I, to an assertion of Argument II (ii) and consequently to the Heckscher–Ohlin theorem: "The first condition of trade is that some goods can be produced more cheaply in one region than in another. In each of them the cheap goods are those containing relatively great quantities of the factors cheaper than in the other regions" (Argument I). "These cheap goods make up exports, whereas goods which can be more cheaply produced in the other regions are imported" (Argument II (ii)). "We may say, therefore, that exports are in each region composed of articles into the production of which enter large quantities of cheap factors" (Heckscher–Ohlin theorem, with price definition of factor abundance).

Similarly, a modern author such as Jones [3] on the Heckscher–Ohlin theory terminates his analysis at the point at which Argument I is proven; and implicitly assuming Argument II (ii), proceeds to the Heckscher–Ohlin theorem.

At a more general level, embracing all theories of comparative advantage, Kindleberger [4, p. 88] also assumes Argument II (ii) as valid and proceeds to discuss Argument I substantively by stating that "... the law of comparative costs says that a country exports those products which are comparatively cheap in price at home, and imports those which are comparatively expensive" (Argument II (ii)). "But economics can say more than this" (Argument I).

These examples could be readily multiplied but hardly need to be.

This is readily illustrated. In Fig. 1 (*a*) the production possibility curves of countries I and II are depicted as $R_I F_I$ and $R_{II} F_{II}$ respectively. Note that these show constant and identical rates of transformation at the margin, because of the one-factor, constant-returns technology and the assumption of identical factor productivity ratios.[1] Argument I holds in this model because the *pre-trade* commodity price ratio in each country will equal the factor productivity ratio. But the factor productivity ratios being identical in the two countries, the pre-trade price ratios in the two countries will also be equalised. Does Argument II (ii) then necessarily hold, leading to the Ricardian corollary?

It does not. In Fig. 1 (*a*) the contrary possibility is illustrated. Assuming that, at the commodity price ratio $R_{II} F_{II} = R_I F_I$, country II " chooses "

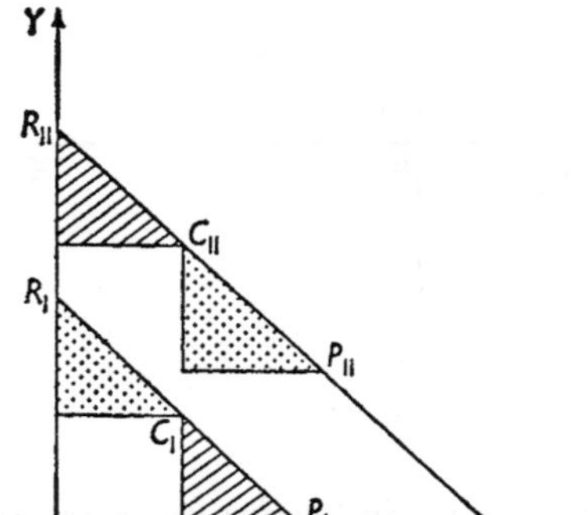

Fig. 1 (*a*)

consumption at C_{II} and country I at C_I, the production choice is still wide open for each country. Each country can have production at *any* point on its production possibility frontier. Suppose that the production then is at C_{II} in country II and at C_I in country I; in this case both Argument II (ii) and the Ricardian corollary will turn out to be valid. However, suppose that the choice of production is to the north-west of C_{II} in country II and (an identical distance, implying " matching offers " between both countries) to the south-east of C_I in country I, then trade *will* occur with II exporting *Y* and importing *X*. On the other hand, the choice of production occurring

[1] In the Ricardian model, if labour is the factor of production and x_I and x_{II} the labour productivity ratios in commodity *X* in countries I and II respectively and y_I and y_{II} in commodity *Y*, then $x_I/y_I = (P_x/P_y)_I$ (the price of *X* in terms of *Y*) and $x_{II}/y_{II} = (P_x/P_y)_{II}$ prior to trade. Therefore, any ranking of $(P_x/P_y)_I$ and $(P_x/P_y)_{II}$ prior to trade implies a corresponding, equivalent ranking of the factor productivity ratios as well. Therefore, when the factor productivity ratios x_I/y_I and x_{II}/y_{II} are identical, so will be the pre-trade commodity price ratios in the two countries.

in contrary directions, trade will again occur, but with the trade-pattern reversed. The full range of possible trade equilibria is then defined by: (i) the two identical, dotted triangles which imply export of X and import of Y by II, and (ii) the two identical, striped triangles which imply export of Y and import of X by II. The counterpart of this, in the Marshallian offer curve diagram, is shown in Fig. 1 (*b*), where the offer curves of countries I and II overlap in both quadrants, the overlap over OS (equal to $C_{II}P_{II}$ in length) representing the trade pattern involving export of X by II, and the

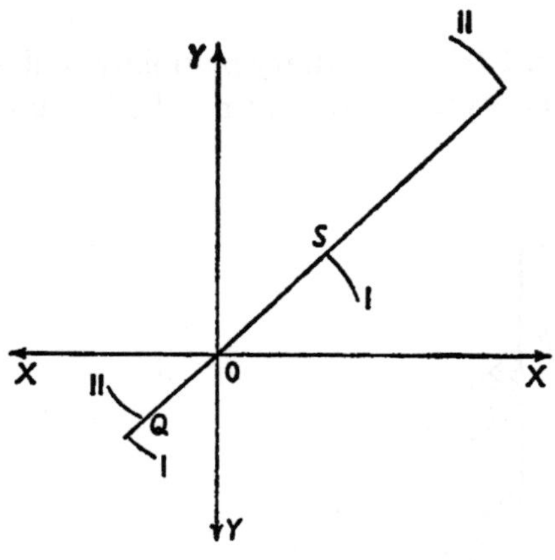

Fig. 1 (*b*)

overlap over OQ (equal to $C_{II}R_{II}$ in length) representing the opposite trade pattern.

Thus, both Argument II (ii) and, with it, the Ricardian corollary are invalid as logically true propositions. Note that this results from the multiplicity of production equilibria corresponding to the pre-trade commodity price ratio which is a direct consequence of the Ricardian one-factor, constant returns-to-scale assumption combined with perfect competition. The correct Ricardian corollary therefore is that, where comparative factor productivities are identical between countries, the volume and direction of trade are indeterminate.

(B) *Ricardian Theorem*

However, what about the case where factor productivity ratios are different between countries? In this case again, in view of Argument I retaining its validity, the pre-trade commodity price ratios will differ between the two countries. Does Argument II (i) then necessarily hold, leading to the Ricardian theorem?

It does not. The reason is that demand conditions may be such as to lead to multiple self-sufficiency equilibra. Thus in Fig. 2, OQ_IO is the offer curve of country I and $OQ_{II}O$ of country II. Note that, under self-sufficiency, each country has two possible price equilibria: OS_I and OT for country I, OS_{II} and OT for country II. If then the pre-trade equilibrium price ratios are at OS_I and OS_{II} the equilibrium price ratio will be at OT and no trade will occur, *once free trade is possible.* Argument II (i) thus collapses: although the pre-trade prices are different between the two countries, trade will *not* take place. With Argument II (i), the Ricardian theorem also collapses: the factor productivity ratio in country I equals OS_I, and thus differs from that in country II, which equals OS_{II}, and yet no trade occurs.

Suitable restrictions have to be placed therefore on demand conditions to eliminate this possibility. A sufficient restriction is to assume that societal tastes enjoy the properties of well-ordered individual taste maps—as with Samuelson's social indifference curves.[1] Since, in Ricardo's model,

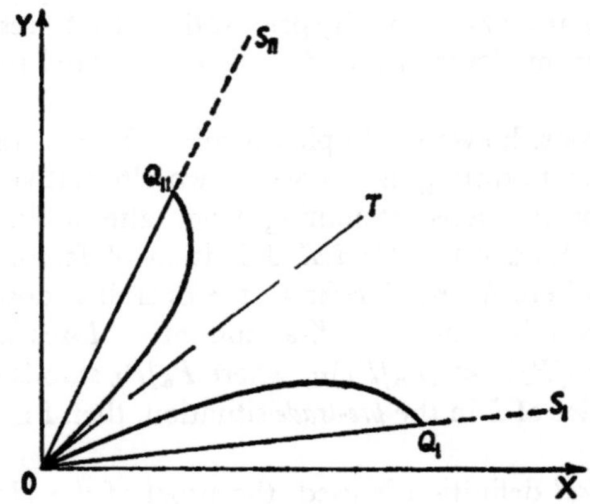

FIG. 2

there is only one factor of production and (at points of complete specialisation) the marginal product is fixed in terms of the commodity produced, the social demands will be such as to rule out the possibility of a free-trade price equilibrium involving no trade *even when* the taste map of *each* factor-owner is alternatively assumed to be well ordered. Since the latter assumption is quite reasonable, the restriction that needs to be placed on demand conditions in Ricardian analysis is not at all " significant." But it is there in any case; and some such restriction must be specified, *in addition to the*

[1] Samuelson [10] proves the following theorem: " (*a*) If each group member's demand and indifference contours have the conventional ' regular ' convexity, and (*b*) if the social welfare function is defined to have similar regular convexity properties, and (*c*) if within the group optimal lump-sum transfers are always made, then it follows: (1) there will result observable demand totals that are functions of market prices and total income alone, and (2) that these demand functions will have all the Slutsky–Hicks or revealed preference properties of any single consumer's demand, and (3) there will exist a set of indifference contours relating to the totals *X*, *Y*, . . . that has all the regular properties of any individual's contours and which we can pretend a single mind is engaged in maximising."

postulates traditionally set out in Ricardian analysis, for the proof of the Ricardian theorem to be logically tight.[1] The role of demand, which is admitted in multi-commodity or multi-country Ricardian analysis, is thus not entirely absent, even in the two-country, two-commodity case.

III. Heckscher–Ohlin Theory

The role that demand conditions can play in undermining the *traditional* proof of the Heckscher–Ohlin theory is rather more significant and not exactly parallel.

However, note first that neither Argument II (ii) nor the Heckscher–Ohlin corollary can be invalidated because of multiple production equilibria in the Heckscher–Ohlin model. This model leads to a non-strictly convex production possibilities set, and hence there is only one production equilibrium corresponding to any commodity price ratio. In *this* respect, therefore, the Heckscher–Ohlin model is at an advantage compared to the Ricardian model.

Demand conditions, however, do play a role. To discuss this role with clarity, it is necessary to distinguish between two alternative versions of the Heckscher–Ohlin propositions, stemming from alternative definitions of factor abundance. Under the *physical* definition of factor abundance, if $(K/L)_{I} > (K/L)_{II}$, where K and L refer to the overall endowments of these two factors, country I is defined as K-abundant or L-scarce. Under the *price* definition, if $(P_K/P_L)_{I} < (P_K/P_L)_{II}$, where P_K/P_L stands for the price of K in terms of the price of L in the *pre-trade* situation, then I is K-abundant or L-scarce.

Where the *physical* definition is used, the proof of the Heckscher–Ohlin theorem proceeds traditionally by: (1) showing that the K-abundant country I will have, at the *same* commodity price ratio, a higher (X/Y) ratio in production than country II, where X is the K-intensive commodity;[2] (2) assuming that the consumption pattern is identical between the two countries, in the sense that the (X/Y) ratio in consumption, at the *same* commodity price ratio, is identical between the two countries; (3) therewith deducing that, for self-sufficiency, $(P_X/P_Y)_{I} < (P_X/P_Y)_{II}$, thus completing Argument I, which requires that the K-abundant country will have its pre-trade relative price of the K-intensive commodity cheaper than the L-abundant country, and then (4) arguing, from Argument II (i), that the K-abundant country will export the K-intensive commodity and import the L-intensive commodity.

Where the *price* definition is used, the proof proceeds *directly* to Argument I, avoiding the three specific steps involved in the case of the physical definition. The assumed technology leads to a unique relationship between

[1] As H. Johnson has pointed out to me in correspondence, an alternative restriction could be to assume that some of both goods is demanded in each country at all price ratios.

[2] This proposition is valid for incomplete specialisation, of course. For proof, see Jones [3].

commodity and factor price ratios,[1] and hence $(P_X/P_Y)_I < (P_X/P_Y)_{II}$ follows immediately from $(P_K/P_L)_I < (P_K/P_L)_{II}$. Beyond that, *only* step (4), involving Argument II (i), is required. Note therefore that, in the case of the price definition, step (3) above does not have to be brought in. In view of this difference, we examine the two proofs, one for each definition, successively. Since the arguments are symmetrical for the theorem and the corollary, only the theorem is considered here to avoid tedious repetition.

(1) *Physical Definition*

Whereas steps (3) and (4) are never explicitly stated and proved, they can be shown to be valid as soon as it is assumed (as in step (2)) that the consumption pattern is identical between countries, at identical commodity

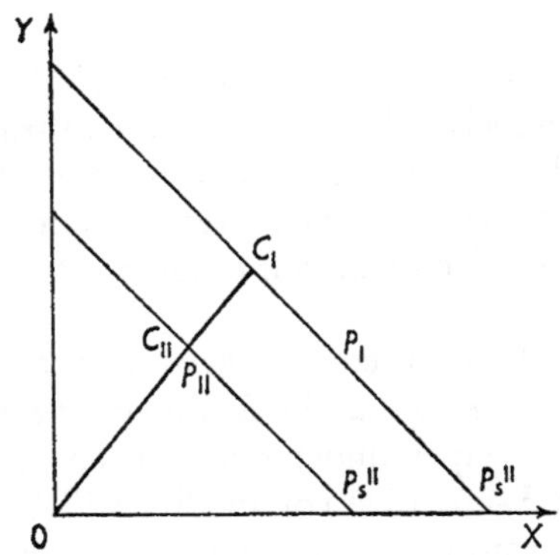

FIG. 3(*a*)

prices, regardless of income level. Note that this assumption implies non-intersecting, *homothetic* social market-demand curves, which, in conjunction with the assumption of convexity, rule out any possibility of contradicting steps (3) and (4).

Thus, for example, take step (3). P_s^{II} is the self-sufficiency price-ratio for country II in Fig. 3 (*a*), and the equilibrium consumption and production points C_{II} and P_{II} coincide. C_I and C_{II} then lie on the same ray from the origin because of the assumption in step (2); and P_I lies to the right of P_{II} by virtue of the proposition in step (1). It is then easy to see that the self-sufficiency price-ratio $(P_x/P_y) = P_s^I$ for country I will be lower than P_s^{II}. This is because a contradiction, such as shown in Fig. 3 (*b*), requires *intersecting*, social market-demand curves which are ruled out as soon as the assumption in step (2) is made. So also for step (4).

[1] This is the proposition well known to trade theorists and first proved by Samuelson [8, 9] for a two-factor, two-commodity model.

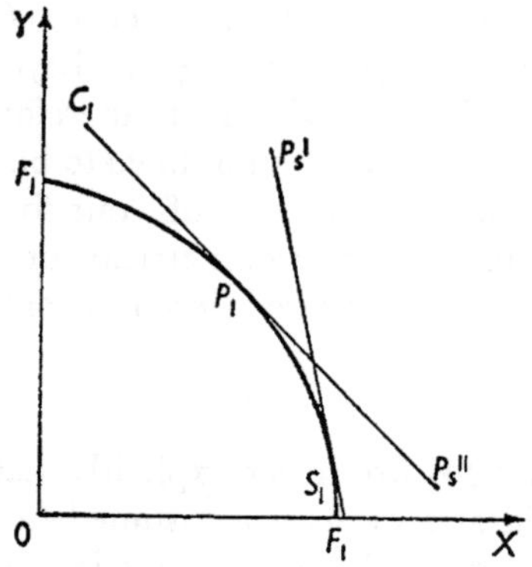

Fig. 3(*b*)

(2) *Price Definition*

While, therefore, the assumption of international identity of consumption patterns at all income levels is indeed an adequate restriction on demand for the Heckscher–Ohlin theorem to be valid when the physical definition of factor abundance is used, the customary presumption that no restriction at all is necessary when the price definition of factor abundance is used is not correct.

When the price definition is used, we have seen that we by-pass steps (2) and (3) and, in fact, infer *directly* that the *K*-abundant economy will have the *K*-intensive commodity cheaper under self-sufficiency. But *before* we can infer from this that the *K*-intensive commodity will be therefore exported (*i.e*, step (4)), we must again impose restrictions on demand.

What really happens is that the elimination of step (3) by virtue of the price definition still leaves step (4) intact in the chain of argument; and since *each* of the two steps (3) and (4) follows from the assumption of internationally identical, homothetic market-demand curves, *some* assumption with respect to demand continues to be necessary to sustain step (4), even when the price-definition of factor abundance is used.

Once again, the assumption (in step (2)) of internationally identical, homothetic demand curves can be made and will be sufficient to ensure step (4). However, this is an overly-strong assumption. It is sufficient to assume instead that the social market-demand curves, in each country, are well ordered. This is itself a " significant " restriction on demand because, in view of income-distribution being present in a two-factor model, well-ordered social market-demand curves do not follow immediately from well-ordered individual indifference curves and, as Samuelson (10) has shown, a policy of lump-sum income transfers has to be envisaged for the purpose.[1]

Hence, contrary to customary statements, demand conditions are not

[1] Note that the question of stability conditions has not been raised here. Further, the analysis has been confined to one country alone.

entirely irrelevant in the two-country, two-commodity theories of comparative advantage even when the Ricardian model or the Heckscher–Ohlin model (with *price* definition of factor abundance) is being considered.[1]

[1] The analysis in the text has accepted the framework of the Ricardian and Heckscher–Ohlin models. It is well known, however, that if either the technological or the institutional assumptions are relaxed, Arguments I and II can easily be jeopardised. For example, if increasing returns are assumed, it is known from Meade [6] and Matthews [5] that Argument II (ii) collapses: when the pre-trade prices are different between countries both patterns of trade may be possible.

Similarly, if there is a wage-differential between the two sectors it is no longer possible to sustain Argument I as logically true. This is because the equality of the commodity price-ratio with the domestic rate of transformation in production (at points of incomplete specialisation) disappears [2], so that the required ranking of the pre-trade commodity price ratios in the two countries will not necessarily emerge. On the other hand, if the wage differential operates identically in the two countries, this will be a sufficient condition for sustaining Argument I. As for Argument II (ii), it will continue to hold in the Ricardian case as also in the Heckscher–Ohlin model (with the assumption of internationally identical, homothetic market-demand curves), *despite* the wage-differential and the consequent divergence of the commodity price ratio from the (marginal) domestic rate of transformation in production.

Note finally that, although the assumption of identical wage differentials in the two countries will leave the comparative advantage theorems unscathed, it is *not* correct to argue, as Taussig [11] did. that the terms and volume of trade will also be the same as in the case where there is no wage differential at all.

JAGDISH BHAGWATI

University of Delhi.

REFERENCES

1. Bhagwati, J., and Ramaswami, V. K., " Domestic Distortions, Tariffs and the Theory of Optimum Subsidy," *Journal of Political Economy*, Vol. 71, February 1963.
2. Hagen, E., " An Economic Justification of Protectionism," *Quarterly Journal of Economics*, Vol. 72, November 1958.
3. Jones, R., " Factor Proportions and the Heckscher–Ohlin Model," *Review of Economic Studies*, Vol. 24, October 1956.
4. Kindleberger, C. P., *International Economics* (Illinois: Richard D. Irwin, Inc., 1955).
5. Matthews, R. C. O., " Reciprocal Demand and Increasing Returns," *Review of Economic Studies*, Vol. 17, February 1950.
6. Meade, J. E., *A Geometry of International Trade* (London: Allen and Unwin Ltd., 1952).
7. Ohlin, B., *Interregional and International Trade* (Cambridge: Harvard University Press, 1952).
8. Samuelson, P. A., " International Trade and the Equalisation of Factor Prices," ECONOMIC JOURNAL, June 1948.
9. Samuelson, P. A., " International Factor Price Equalisation Once Again," ECONOMIC JOURNAL, June 1949.
10. Samuelson, P. A., " Social Indifference Curves," *Quarterly Journal of Economics*, Vol. 70, February 1956.
11. Taussig, F. W., *International Trade* (New York: Macmillan Company Ltd., 1927).

The Heckscher-Ohlin Theorem in the Multi-Commodity Case

Jagdish N. Bhagwati

Massachusetts Institute of Technology

Ronald Jones, in his seminal paper (1957) on Heckscher-Ohlin theory, has argued that, for the case of two countries, two factors, and several commodities, the Heckscher-Ohlin theorem would remain valid in the following weak sense: "Ordering the commodities with respect to the capital-labor ratios employed in production is to rank them in order of comparative advantage. Demand conditions merely determine the dividing line between exports and imports; it is not possible to break the chain of comparative advantage by exporting, say, the third and fifth commodities and importing the fourth when they are ranked by factor intensity" (p. 85).

It is easy to show, however, that this proposition, although correct for the case where factor prices are *not* equalized, is untenable as literally stated. When factor-price equalization is realized, a not unimportant case, a variety of crisscrossings are possible.[1]

Thus, let there be two countries, I and II, with endowments of two factors, K and L, as shown in figure 1 by the two rays from the origin, such that Country I is K-abundant and Country II is L-abundant, in the physical sense. Let us also assume that there are four commodities, w, x, y, and z, all of them characterized by linearly homogeneous production functions with the standard restrictions. We also assume that the strong Samuelson factor-intensity rankings obtain, such that the four commodities can be ordered according to their K/L ratios unambiguously. Let the K/L ratios decline successively for commodities w, x, y, and z.

Using the Lerner-Findlay-Grubert technique, we can now take the case

Research support has been provided by the National Science Foundation. Thanks are due to Paul Samuelson and Ronald Jones for helpful comments. After finishing the final version of this note, I came across an interchange between Stewart (1971) and Melvin (1971) on the issue of the invalidity of the Heckscher-Ohlin theorem when there are three commodities and two factors. Also see Melvin's earlier paper (1968). However, the "chain" proposition is not discussed and, in consequence, the source and nature of the invalidity of the Heckscher-Ohlin theorem in the multi-commodity case are not as clearly shown as in the present note.

[1] I have long taught the Jones proposition to my graduate students, of whom only Rick Oiesen (in the fall of 1970) was certain that it was invalid and prompted me to write this note. Ronald Findlay, in his excellent Penguin text (1970, pp. 66–69) has lucidly explained the Jones proposition, without again noticing its invalidity as a general proposition.

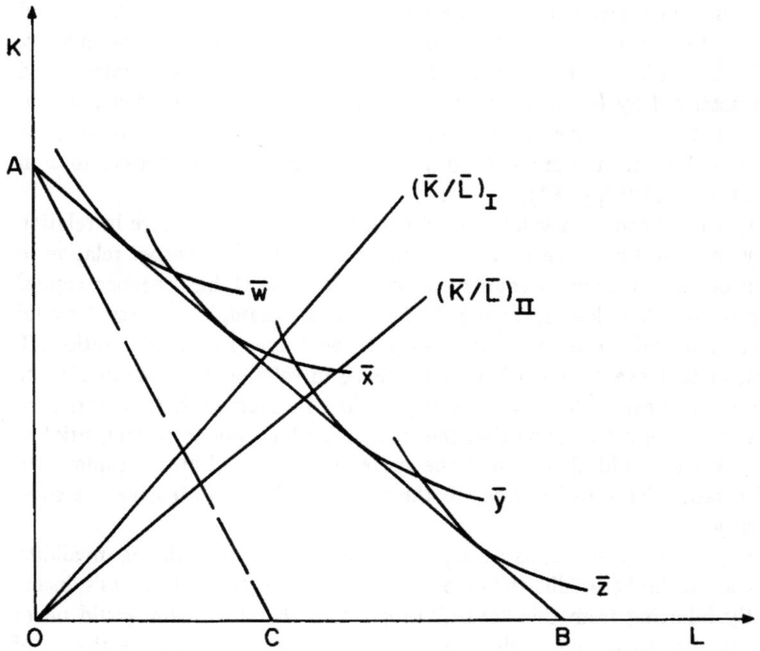

Fig. 1

where the commodity price ratio which obtains in free-trade equilibrium is one where $\bar{w}$, $\bar{x}$, $\bar{y}$, and $\bar{z}$ exchange for one another on the market. This commodity price ratio also leads, in figure 1, to factor price ratio AB. Note that, since *all* four commodities are viable at these prices in *each* country on the assumption of internationally identical production functions, we clearly have multiple production equilibria possible in each country. Readers of Tinbergen (1949) and Meade (1950) are quite familiar with this. Assume, then, that Country I produces w and y whereas Country II produces x and z; assuming further that each country consumes some of each commodity (an assumption which is consistent with identical, homothetic tastes across countries), we have Country I exporting w and y while Country II exports x and z. But commodities are ordered in a chain of K/L ratios such that $K_w/L_w > K_x/L_x > K_y/L_y > K_z/L_z$, and the Jones proposition would imply that, since $(\bar{K}/\bar{L})_{\text{I}} > (\bar{K}/\bar{L})_{\text{II}}$, with homothetic tastes, *all* of I's exports would be K-intensive in relation to all of I's imports. But this is *not* so. In short, the "comparative advantage" chain can be crisscrossed by the actual trade pattern in the Heckscher-Ohlin model. Q.E.D.

Why did Jones arrive at this erroneous proposition? A close look at his paper reveals that it was an incorrect inference from his *correct* proposition that, in a Heckscher-Ohlin model with two countries (1 and 2) and two factors (capital and labor), many commodities (x, y, z) ordered by K/L intensities, and production functions identical across countries and characterized by factor-intensity nonreversals, "regardless of demand conditions in the two countries, if commodity-x is cheaper relative to y in country 1 than in country 2, so also must y be cheaper relative to z in country 1" (1957, p. 83).

This is, of course, a valid proposition. For, if x is K-intensive in relation to y and y in turn in relation to z, commodity x can be cheaper relative to y in country 1 than in country 2 only if country 1 has cheaper capital relative to labor than country 2. In figure 1, for example, country 1 would have factor price ratio AC and country 2 would have factor price ratio AB. But, in that event, y which is K-intensive in relation to z would also be relatively cheaper than z in country 1 than in country 2. Geometrically, this can be seen by noting that the isoquants which would be tangential to AC, which would then define the corresponding equilibrium commodity price ratios, have to be closer to the origin the less K-intensive the commodity.

But this proposition, as we have seen, is compatible with the invalidity of the Heckscher-Ohlin theorem. The error came through Jones's incorrectly inferring from this "chain" proposition that the chain would never be crisscrossed in free trade—an inference by analogy with the theory of Ricardian chains, where such an inference *is* correct.

Lest the reader infer that therefore the Heckscher-Ohlin pattern of trade is extremely unlikely to occur in the multi-commodity case, let me stress that the Heckscher-Ohlin pattern of trade *can* arise even under factor price equalization and *must* arise if factor prices are not equalized.

Furthermore, as Jones has pointed out to me, if we introduce transport costs, the theorem can be revalidated. With transport costs on *every* commodity, commodity prices would no longer be equal across countries in trade, and therefore factor prices also could not be equalized via commodity price equalization. Thus, while a commodity in the middle of a chain of exportables may be priced out of the export market into being a nontraded good by high transportation costs, it is impossible for it to be turned into an imported good. Hence, the trade pattern cannot register a crisscrossing of the chain; each exportable must thus have a higher K/L ratio than each importable, in the K-abundant country (with identical homothetic tastes across countries).

Note, finally, that, as Samuelson has commented to me, we always have the truism (in the case of internationally identical, homothetic tastes) that the country with the lower endowment of one of the factors cannot have *all* its exports more intensive in that factor than *all* its imports. This is because, with homothetic and identical tastes, each country's average (identical) consumption K/L ratio must lie between the K/L endowment ratios of each country; hence the K-abundant country must be exporting a higher K/L *bundle* of exports than its bundle of imports,[2] which implies that *all* its exports cannot be L-intensive in relation to *all* of its imports.

References

Findlay, R. *Trade and Specialization.* Penguin Modern Economics Series. Harmondsworth, Middlesex: Penguin, 1970.

Jones, R. "Factor Proportions and the Heckscher-Ohlin Theorem." In *International Trade,* edited by J. Bhagwati. Penguin Modern Economics Series. Harmondsworth, Middlesex: Penguin, 1957. Reprinted from *Rev. Econ. Studies* 24 (1956): 1–10.

Meade, J. E. "The Equalization of Factor Prices: The Two Country, Two-Factor, Three-Product Case." *Metroeconomica* 2 (1950): 129–33.

Melvin, J. "Production and Trade with Two Factors and Three Goods." *A.E.R.* 58 (December 1968): 1249–68.

———. "Production Indeterminacy with Three Goods and Two Factors: Reply." *A.E.R.* 60 (March 1971): 245–46.

Stewart, D. B. "Production Indeterminacy with Three Goods and Two Factors: A Comment on the Pattern of Trade." *A.E.R.* 60 (1971): 241–44.

Tinbergen, J. "The Equalization of Factor Prices between Free Trade Areas." *Metroeconomica* 1 (1949): 39–47.

Vanek, J. "The Factor Proportions Theory: The *n*-Factor Case." *Kyklos,* vol. 4 (October).

2 This proposition was stated earlier by Melvin (1968, 1971) and is also discussed in Vanek (1968).

TRADE-DIVERTING CUSTOMS UNIONS AND WELFARE-IMPROVEMENT: A CLARIFICATION[1]

In his classic paper on trade-diverting customs unions [1957], and his later Survey in this Journal [1960], Lipsey showed how a country forming a trade-diverting customs union (*i.e.*, one where imports shift from a lower-cost to a higher-cost source of supply *à la* Viner) could none the less register welfare-improvement if substitution in consumption were allowed. He then proceeded to argue geometrically that the phenomenon of welfare-improvement had been overlooked by Viner [1950] and that this was allegedly because Viner had (implicitly) assumed consumption to be of a fixed-coefficients variety.[2]

But, as is clear now, the absence of substitution in consumption is *not* a sufficient condition for a trade-diverting customs union (as defined by Viner) to be welfare-reducing. For while this rules out consumption gain to offset the terms-of-trade loss implicit in the trade diversion, variability in *production* can also be a source of gain. Hence the Lipsey analysis, while excellent in highlighting the consumption gain, is insufficient in its treatment of the question as to why Viner overlooked the possibility that a trade-diverting customs union may none the less be welfare-improving.

In fact, as soon as we translate Lipsey's analysis into a general-equilibrium model which allows for variability in production, it is easy to see that a sufficient condition for a trade-diverting customs union to be welfare-reducing is that the level of *imports* is fixed, and *not* that the pattern of *consumption* is fixed. Indeed, an examination of Viner's own treatment of trade diversion indicates that there is probably as much support for the interpretation that Viner was assuming the level of imports to be fixed as for Lipsey's interpretation, that he was assuming the pattern of consumption to be fixed.

I

Viner is somewhat difficult to pin down on this question, although it is clear that the assumption of fixity in the level of imports is as consonant with his actual analysis as Lipsey's assumption of fixity of the consumption

[1] Thanks are due to Harry Johnson and James Melvin for comments and to Professor Champernowne who spotted an error in an earlier draft. Research support by the National Science Foundation is acknowledged.

[2] The reference here, and throughout the analysis in this paper, is to Lipsey's three-country, two-good model; Lipsey used a general-equilibrium exchange model for his analysis of trade diversion. A further simplification, retained from Lipsey's analysis, is the assumption that the external terms of trade at which the "partner" and the "outside" countries will trade are *constant*: thus the cost at which the "home" country can import the importable commodity from either of the two countries abroad is not a function of the volume of its imports from them.

pattern. This is seen by reference to Viner's relevant passages (1950, pp. 42–43):

> The analysis will be directed toward finding answers to the following questions: in so far as the establishment of the customs union results in change in the national locus of production of goods purchased, is the net change one of diversion of purchases to lower or higher money-cost sources of supply, abstracting from duty-elements in money costs: (a) for each of the customs union countries taken separately; (b) for the two combined; (c) for the outside world; (d) for the world as a whole? If the customs union is a movement in the direction of free trade, it must be predominantly a movement in the direction of goods being supplied from lower money-cost sources than before. If the customs union has the effect of diverting purchases to higher money-cost sources, it is then a device for making tariff protection more effective . . . .
>
> There will be other commodities which one of the members of the customs union will now newly import from the other whereas before the customs union it imported them from a third country, because that was the cheapest possible source of supply even after payment of duty. The shift in the locus of production is now not as between the two member countries but as between a low-cost third country and the other, high-cost, member country. This is a shift of the type which the protectionist approves, but it is not one which the free-trader who understands the logic of his own doctrine can properly approve.

It is clear that Viner was referring somewhat ambiguously to the " locus of production " being transferred from the external, non-member country to the higher-cost partner country. Thus he may well be interpreted as thinking of a given level of production being thus shifted to the partner country and hence of the level of imports into the " home " country remaining constant.[1]

II

Let us now examine Lipsey's analysis via Figs. 1(*a*) and 1(*b*). Assuming specialisation of the home country on commodity " X ", at A, he took the given, external terms of trade with the partner country as AP and with the (cheapest-cost-supplier-of-commodity X) outside country as AE.

Before customs union, with a uniform tariff applicable to the import of Y from both the partner and the outside countries, equilibrium consumption

[1] This, of course, implies that Viner implicitly was thinking of a negative income elasticity of demand for one good, and this is difficult to accept. However, it is equally difficult to imagine that, as Lipsey interprets, Viner was alternatively thinking of consumption being fixed along a ray from the origin! Aside from the intrinsic oddity of the latter assumption, it implies that the post-customs-union level of imports will have fallen (a consequence not noted by Viner) and that the level and pattern of consumption in the free-trade and pre-customs-union situations are identical: which would be a still greater oddity, as Terence Ryan has pointed out to me. The only plausible conclusion seems to be that Viner had not thought through this question very clearly, so that either interpretation may be considered to be compatible with his actual analysis.

in Fig. 1(*a*) would be at C_1 at the tariff-inclusive price-ratio DP_E, implying the import of OQ amount of commodity Y. With the customs union the tariff would be eliminated on the partner country and imports would then shift to the partner country at the internal and external price-ratio AP.

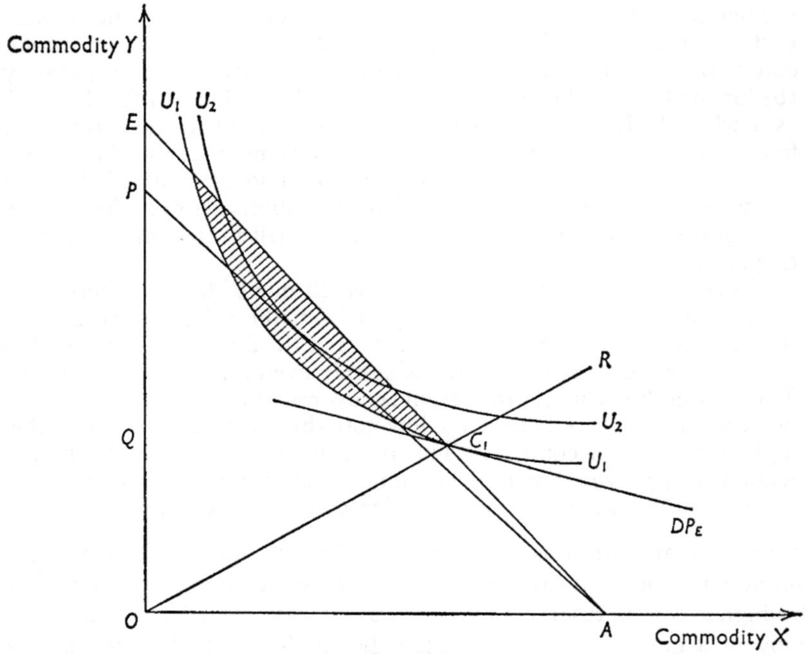

FIG. 1(*a*)

Lipsey thus showed that, if AP passed through the striped area as in Fig. 1(*a*), the customs union would raise welfare even though it was trade-diverting ($U_2 > U_1$). Lipsey then argued that Viner ruled this out by assuming that consumption would be characterised by fixed coefficients, and hence would lie along the ray OC_1R before and after the formation of the customs union, as in Fig. 1(*b*). If so, it is clear that consumption after the customs union would be at C_2 and welfare would *necessarily* be reduced ($U_1 > U_2$).

However, this interpretation of Viner implies that the level of imports is reduced (see Fig. 1(*b*)).[1] Our alternative interpretation of Viner is that the level of imports (M) should be constant ($dM = 0$), and we illustrate this in Fig. 2.

There, the post-customs union equilibrium is shown at C_2, with a reduced welfare level ($U_2 < U_1$): a result which is *inevitable* if the level of

[1] On the other hand, Viner's arithmetical example clearly keeps the level of imports, after the formation of the trade-diverting customs union, at the *same* level as before the customs union: this seems to cast doubt on the appropriateness of Lipsey's interpretation, if nothing else.

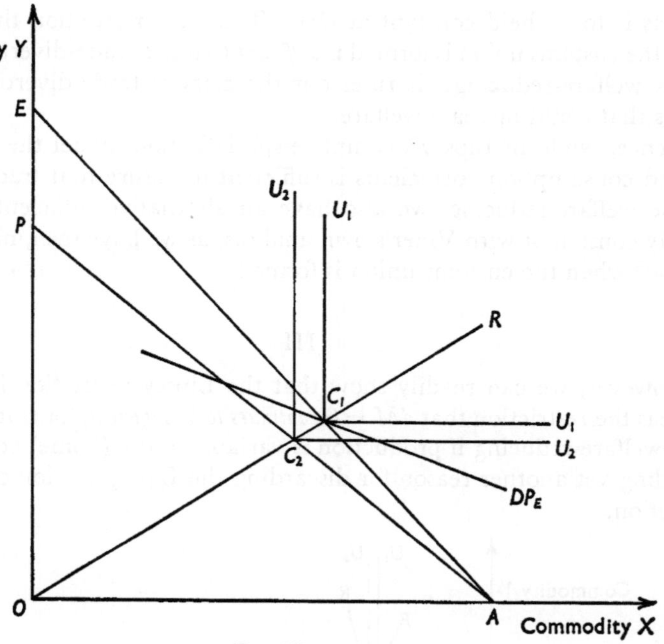
Commodity Y
E
P
U2
U1
R
C1
C2
U1
U2
DPE
O
A
Commodity X

FIG. 1(*b*)

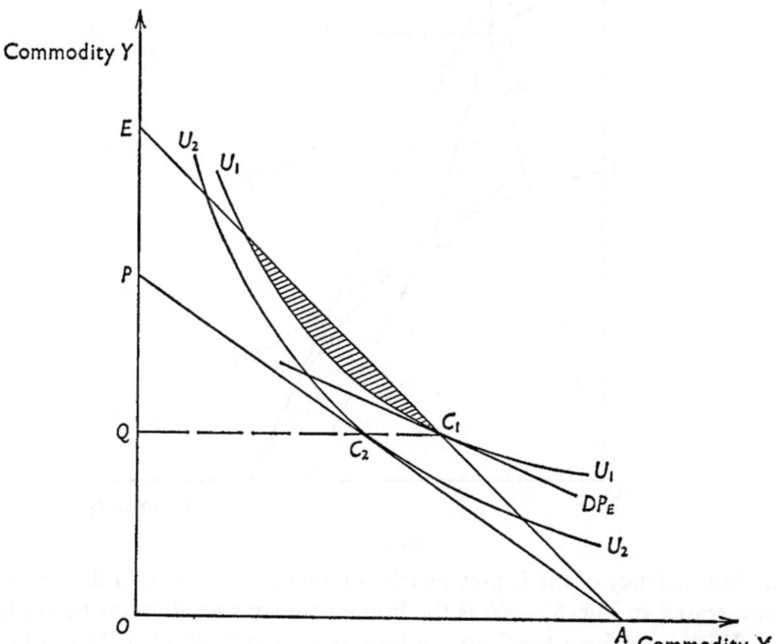
Commodity Y
E
U2
U1
P
Q
C1
C2
U1
DPE
U2
O
A
Commodity X

FIG. 2

imports is to be held constant at OQ. Thus, the restriction that $dM = 0$ when the customs union is formed is *sufficient* to make trade-diverting customs unions welfare-reducing: it rules out the class of trade-diverting customs unions that could increase welfare.

Hence, while in Lipsey's complete-specialisation model the assumption of fixed consumption coefficients is sufficient to ensure that trade diversion will be welfare-reducing, we also have an alternative sufficient condition, equally consonant with Viner's own analysis, as we have seen, namely that: $dM = 0$ when the customs union is formed.

III

However, we can readily show that the Lipsey restriction is *insufficient*, whereas the restriction that $dM = 0$ *continues to be sufficient*, for trade diversion to be welfare-reducing if production is variable in the (home) country, thus providing yet another reason for discarding the Lipsey version of the Viner restriction.

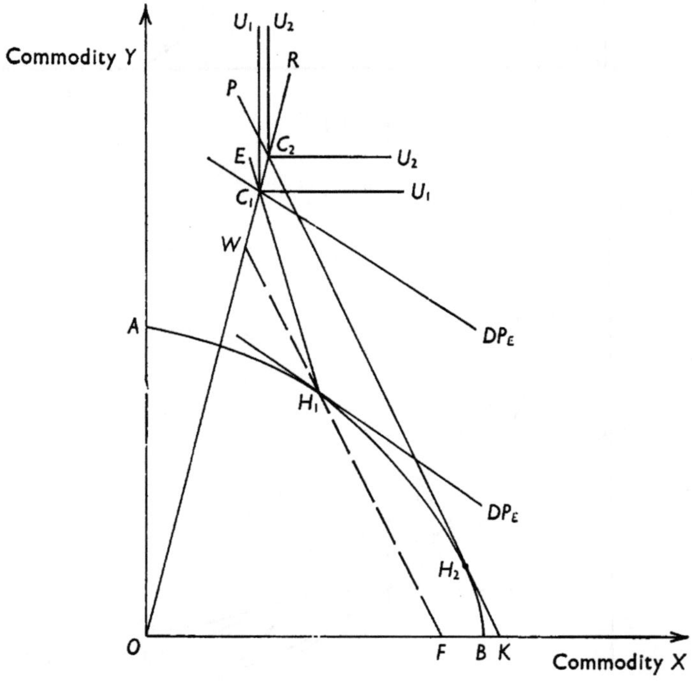

FIG. 3

The insufficiency of the Lipsey restriction on consumption, in this regard, is demonstrated in Fig. 3. AB is the home country's production possibility curve. With a uniform tariff on the import of commodity "Y" from both the external and the partner country, the home country imports from the former at international price-ratio H_1C_1E, the consumption point is C_1 (along the ray OWC_1C_2R, since fixity of the consumption pattern is assumed) and production is at the tariff-inclusive price-ratio DP_E at point H_1. On the formation of the customs union, the tariff is eliminated on partner-country imports; production shifts to H_2 at tangency of the production possibility curve AB to the partner-country price-ratio H_2C_2P. Equilibrium consumption is then at C_2, and welfare has increased ($U_2 > U_1$) despite the fixity of the consumption pattern.

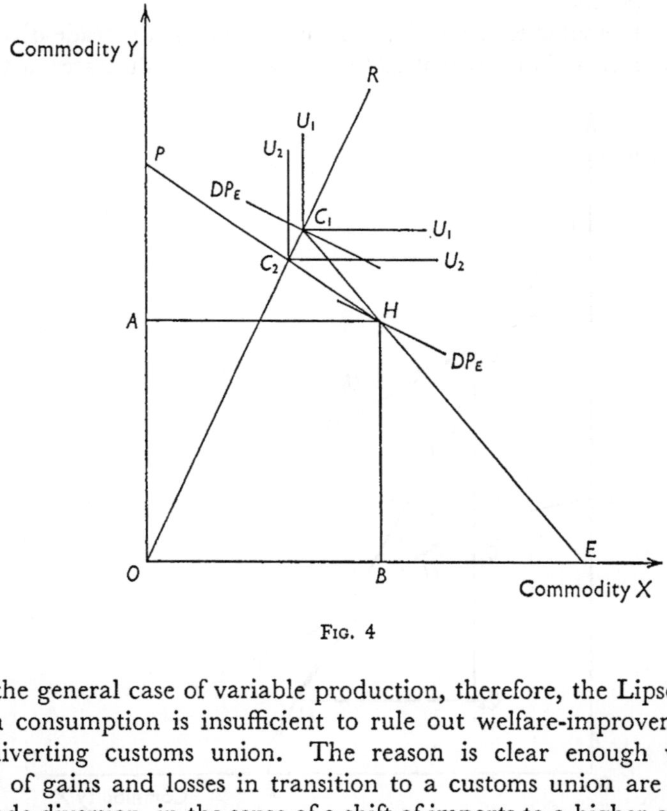

Fig. 4

In the general case of variable production, therefore, the Lipsey restriction on consumption is insufficient to rule out welfare-improvement in a trade-diverting customs union. The reason is clear enough when the sources of gains and losses in transition to a customs union are analysed. The trade diversion, in the sense of a shift of imports to a higher-cost source of supply, implies a terms of trade loss. On the other hand, the price-ratio facing domestic consumers and producers moves closer to the "true" (least-cost) international price-ratio so that there is a consumption gain and a production gain respectively. In so far as the aggregate of these gains outweighs the terms of trade loss, a trade-diverting customs union will show welfare-improvement. Lipsey's assumption of a fixed consumption pattern merely rules out the consumption gain while leaving open the accrual of a production gain which could outweigh the terms of trade loss: a possibility illustrated in Fig. 3, where the production gain, measured in X-units at the partner-country price-ratio, is FK.[1]

Fig. 4 illustrates how the ruling out of substitution possibilities in both production and in consumption ensures that a trade-diverting customs union will be welfare-reducing. The production possibility curve here is AHB, with a kink at H denoting immobility of resources therefrom (Haberler, 1950), and the consumption pattern is fixed along the ray OR. In this case the post-customs-union consumption at C_2 is necessarily below the pre-customs-union consumption at C_1 for a trade-diverting customs union, and $U_1 > U_2$ necessarily.

An alternative sufficient condition, which ensures that the trade-diverting union will worsen welfare, is that $dM = 0$. As Fig. 5 illustrates, a trade-

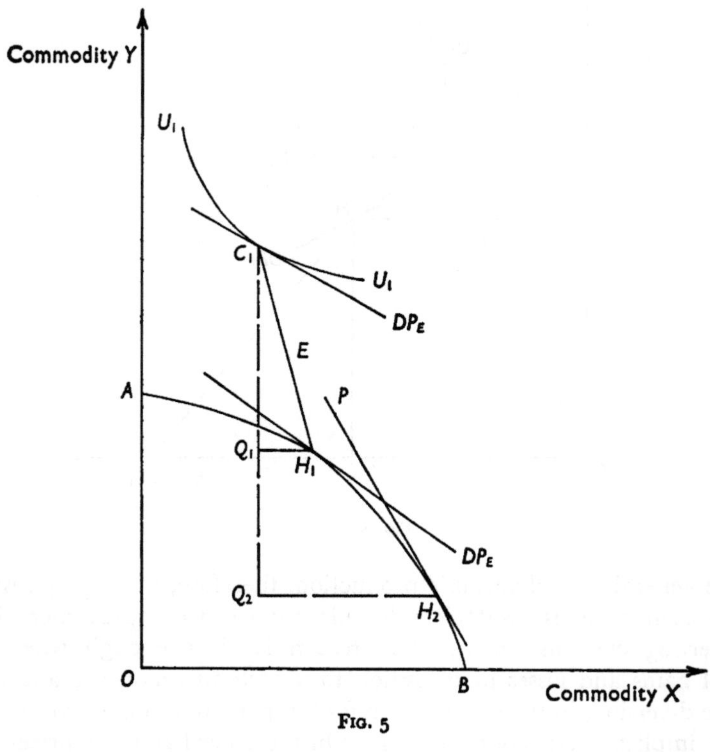

FIG. 5

diverting union would shift production from H_1 to H_2 and thus decrease domestic production of the importable good Y by Q_1Q_2: hence increasing imports, *ceteris paribus*. Therefore, to hold $dM = 0$, consumption of the importable good would have to fall by the same amount. This, however, would prevent the partner-country price-ratio H_2P from crossing over

[1] The importance of production variation has also been noted earlier by Melvin (1969), and it is clearly implicit in the cardinal analysis of James Meade (1955).

to the northeast of C_1 and being tangential to a social indifference curve higher than U_1: hence welfare-improvement would be ruled out.

On the same line of argument, it is immediately clear that a still weaker sufficient condition for ruling out welfare-improvement in a trade-diverting customs-union is that $dM \leqslant 0$.

JAGDISH BHAGWATI

Massachusetts Institute of Technology.

REFERENCES

Haberler, G. [1950] "Some Problems in the Pure Theory of International Trade," ECONOMIC JOURNAL, June 1950, pp. 223–40.

Lipsey, R. G. [1957] "The Theory of Customs Unions: Trade Diversion and Welfare," *Economica*, Vol. 24 (February 1957), pp. 40–46.

Lipsey, R. G. [1960] "The Theory of Customs Unions: A General Survey," ECONOMIC JOURNAL, September 1960, pp. 496–513.

Meade, J. E. [1955] *The Theory of Customs Unions* (Amsterdam: North-Holland).

Melvin, J. [1969] "Comments on the Theory of Customs Unions," *The Manchester School*, Vol. 37 (June 1969), pp. 161–68.

Viner, J. [1950] *The Customs Union Issue* (Carnegie Endowment for Peace).

Editor's Note

The production gain that may accompany a trade-diverting customs union, analyzed in section III of this essay, is itself a result of trade creation according to Viner's definition, that is, a shift of production from home to the lower-opportunity-cost partner country. This distinction in terminology is explicitly noted in essay 64 in this volume.

A REPLY TO PROFESSOR KIRMAN

ALAN Kirman is probably right. There is enough internal evidence in Viner's discussion to suggest that *neither* Lipsey's *nor* my interpretation, both in a general-equilibrium mould, can be reconciled with *everything* that Viner said. On the other hand, Kirman admits that his partial-equilibrium interpretation runs into difficulty by this test as well. So perhaps Viner had not thought through this question completely, as I had speculated in my paper: I am not really surprised.[1]

If, however, (i) the general-equilibrium interpretation is accepted, and (ii) the 3-country, 2-commodity Lipsey model of constant costs (or rates of transformation), implicitly at home and explicitly in trade with partner and outside countries, is considered as the equivalent of what Viner had in mind at the theoretical level, then I would maintain that I correctly argued in my paper—and this should be duly noted by those who will continue to use Lipsey's excellent paper—that:

(1) a trade-diverting customs union, defined (consistently with Viner) as one where the home country shifts from importing from the lower-cost outside country to the higher-cost partner country, can none the less improve its welfare thanks to a " consumption " effect which may outweigh the " terms of trade " effect; and, here is the novel element,

(2) this consumption effect can be ruled out in alternative ways: according to Lipsey, the sufficient restriction (allegedly Viner's) was that the consumption pattern was invariable; according to me, the sufficient restriction (allegedly Viner's again) was rather that the level of imports would not rise ($dM \leq 0$). In Fig. 1 overleaf, when a customs union shifts the home country from trade with the outside country at price-ratio HQ, unvarying production at H and consumption at C, Lipsey's restriction would shift the new equilibrium, on the partner-country trade line HP, to L, and my restriction would shift it to B: *either* would suffice to rule out welfare-improvement for the home country. So much is incontrovertible.

But I also said that my restriction ($dM \leq 0$) fitted Viner's words less unhappily than Lipsey's—I still think this is so because Viner does not appear to have been happy with the fixed-consumption pattern assumption (as he pointed out in a personal letter to Max Corden) whereas he does talk of

[1] I should emphasise, however, that I do *not* require, as does Lipsey, that the tariff be " ineffective " before the customs union is formed. I only require that $dM \leq 0$, as is explicitly stated in my paper; and this sufficient condition is perfectly compatible with the pre-customs-union tariff being " effective." Where my sufficient condition can be faulted, therefore, is *only* in its not being consistent with Viner's discussion of changing levels of imports.

shift of "national locus of production."[1] I still think I am on safe ground here.

I also went further and claimed that my restriction was *more powerful* than Lipsey's because, if home production were now permitted to be variable,

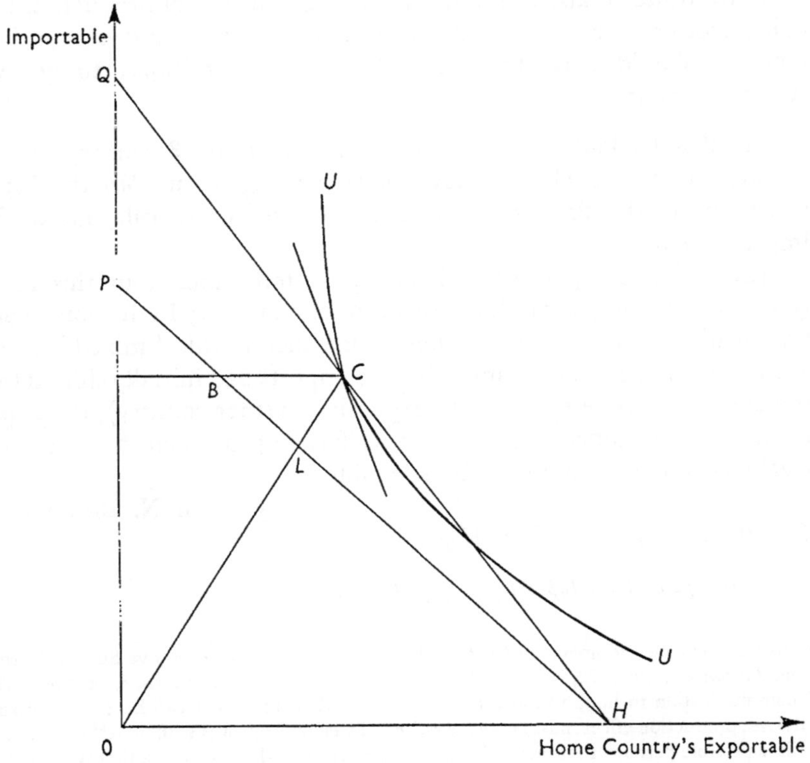

FIG. 1.

OH is the home country's unchanging production of the exportable good. Trade with the outside country takes place at price-ratio *HQ*, and with partner country at price-ratio *HP*. Before the customs union, trade is with the outside country, and consumption is at *C*, and welfare at *U*. After the union, trade shifts to the partner country. Under Lipsey's restriction of a fixed consumption pattern, consumption would now be at *L*; under Bhagwati's restriction of an unincreased import level, the new consumption point would be *B* (for unchanged import level). In either case, welfare would deteriorate.

then $dM \leq 0$ would still rule out welfare-improvement for the home country which shifted to importing from the cheaper outside to the more expensive partner country whereas Lipsey's fixed-consumption-pattern assumption would *not*. This is *also* correct.

[1] Historians of thought, however, may well put little faith in an old man's memory and accuracy of recollection: witness, for example, the controversy surrounding Einstein's retraction, in his later years, of a connection between the Michelson-Morley experiment and the formulation of the theory of relativity.

But, in demonstrating the insufficiency of Lipsey's restriction to rule out welfare improvement for the home country when the model was modified so that home production could vary, I did not note that the " production gain," the source of trouble for Lipsey in this case, was (as Spraos reminded me) of course trade creation in Viner's language: a shift of production from the higher-cost home country to the lower-cost partner country.

Hence, I should carefully reformulate my propositions, to go with Lipsey's, as follows:

(1) if a trade-diverting customs union, in the 3-country, 2-commodity Lipsey model, is purely trade-diverting, then *either* the Lipsey restriction *or* the Bhagwati restriction will suffice to rule out welfare improvement;

(2) if, however, a trade diverting customs union, in this model (modified so as to permit domestic production to vary in the home country), leads *further* to trade creation *as well*, then in this " mixed " case of a trade diverting customs union (where imports had initially shifted from the cheaper outside to the more expensive partner country), the Lipsey restriction is insufficient to rule out welfare improvement but the Bhagwati restriction continues to be adequate.[1]

Jagdish N. Bhagwati

Massachusetts Institute of Technology.

Date of receipt of final typescript: April 1973.

[1] In his " Recent Developments in Customs Union Theory: An Interpretive Survey," *Journal of Economic Literature*, June 1972, Vol. X (2), M. B. Krauss touches on this issue, on the basis of Spraos' communication to him, and asserts tautologously that, in what I call here the " mixed " case, " the net production effect must be *trade creation* " if welfare improves without a " consumption gain." It is possible perhaps that one *could* ingeniously arrive at the conclusion that when there is net trade creation, suitably defined, there follows a net gain to the home country on this account; but to assert that, *because* there is a net gain, there " must be " net trade creation as defined by Viner, is obviously to take a methodologically erroneous position. Krauss also misses altogether the distinction between the two sufficiency conditions, Lipsey's and mine, even when domestic production is not variable, this being only one of several " interpretive " lapses in this survey.

Erratum

Page 895: The chapter title, which has been corrected for this reprinting, originally read "A Reply to Professor Kirmam".

VI
AID, TRADE, AND PAYMENTS

Journal of Development Economics 2 (1975) 85–98. © North-Holland Publishing Company

FOREIGN CAPITAL, DEPENDENCE, DESTABILISATION AND FEASIBILITY OF TRANSITION TO SOCIALISM*

Jagdish N. BHAGWATI and Earl GRINOLS

Massachusetts Institute of Technology, Cambridge, Mass. 02139, U.S.A.

Received November 1974, revised version received March 1975

The paper analyses the argument that external capital inflow could create dependence and thus sabotage the possibility of a successful transition to socialism. The formal model deployed is of the Harrod–Domar variety and simulation runs are undertaken for five underdeveloped countries, using savings functions estimated by Weisskopf. The conclusions lend some support to radical concerns about the adverse effects of foreign aid on recipient countries.

1. Introduction

Foreign aid, in radical arguments, increases the dependence of the recipient LDC and hence its vulnerability to donor-country pressures to keep away from genuine socialism. There are basically two major types of arguments which we may develop to provide a rationale for this hypothesis:

(1) That aid and private capital inflow reduce domestic savings; that the achievement of a target ratio of domestic savings to income is the key to being able to sustain self-reliant growth (as in a typical Harrod–Domar model) and that the receipt of foreign capital compromises the reaching of this target by pushing off the date at which it can be reached by hurting domestic savings.

(2) That the receipt of external capital enables the expansion of consumption and investment at high levels, and that the shift of the country to a socialist regime leads to a cessation of capital inflow, even to net repayment burdens, and related declines in efficiency of resource use in consequence, thus leading to a resource-crunch and reduced consumption and investment levels, resulting in 'chaos' and discontent under which the capitalist donors can then readily and unobtrusively stage indigenous military takeovers, thus destroying the socialist regime.

*Thanks are due to the National Science Foundation for contributing to the financial support of the research underlying this paper. The stimulating environment of the Stockholm Institute for International Economic Studies during August 1974 is gratefully acknowledged. Thomas Weisskopf and a referee have provided useful comments on an earlier draft of this paper.

We have examined the former argument at some length elsewhere.[1] Here we concentrate on the latter argument, which clearly has suggestive parallels in the experience of socialist regimes in Ghana under President Nkrumah and in Chile under President Allende.

2. The basic argument

Thus, contemplate the following scenario. Assume that the aid is from the capitalist West to a recipient which is either a neutral country or a faithful ally or satellite in the cold war of either the pre-detente or the post-detente variety. Assume further that aid has enabled the recipient country to sustain increasing levels of consumption and investment. Now, the recipient country changes its political hue to socialism, getting dangerously close to implementing genuine redistributional policies (as with Allende) and/or openly expressing support for the socialist countries such as the USSR (as with Nkrumah). With this unpalatable shift to the left, the foreign private investors (who may be faced with expropriation of existing investments, as in Chile) shy away from further investments; foreign aid is cut off or, more euphemistically, 'suspended' (as with Chile); pressure is brought even on the international agencies such as the IMF and IBRD to withhold credits; and the net result is *either* an elimination of the foreign capital inflow on both official and private accounts *or*, worse still, a net repayment burden on past debts incurred by the favoured predecessors of happier political persuasions. This crunch in resource availability would further come in the face of expectations of continued growth of consumption and income generated by the past-aid-inflow-supported economic expansion, thus straining greatly the economic viability of the socialist regime.

In addition, if aid has also involved a restructuring of the economy so as to involve considerable use of imported intermediates for the industrial sector, the reduced availability of foreign exchange may also seriously affect productivity in that sector, and hence the capital–output ratio could increase (as indeed seems to have happened in Ghana). Further, if the socialist transformation generates hostility from the bourgeoisie to the point of sabotage (possibly supported by 'destabilisation' action from external agencies, as now confirmed in the case of Chile), that too would be ground for decline in productivity from investments, past and current. Finally, there may well be an element of economic mismanagement, resulting from the application of ideological but unrealistic ideas about economic policy and perhaps also from the difficulties that have been detailed above as resulting from the withdrawal of foreign capital.

The effect of the resource-crunch, including associated declines in productivity, is to generate a climate of 'chaos' and growing disenchantment and discontent with the socialist regime, under which a military takeover (as in both Ghana and

[1] Grinols and Bhagwati (1974).

Chile) is practically inevitable and the assisting hand of the CIA, like Adam Smith's, remains unseen (though, as in the case of Allende, not necessarily forever) but has proven to be extremely effective.

This scenario can doubtless be filled out, and carefully qualified, to explain the specific episodes involving Presidents Nkrumah and Allende. Here, however, our purpose is rather to work with a simple Harrod–Domar type of model and to examine whether, taking plausible behavioral functions on savings, investment, etc., and observed values of external capital flows, we can put orders of magnitude on the kind and magnitude of resource-crunch that could emerge if a recipient LDC shifted left. For, if the overall resource-crunch is significant, then the radical economist is indeed legitimately concerned about aid leading to lack of independence: right wing and centrist politicians and parties, by accepting aid, may well be mortgaging for the country its democratic right to shift its political coloring and the international affiliations that it desires.

3. The model

The model used here is a simple Harrod–Domar type, with a slightly-modified savings equation to allow for foreign inflow of capital and exports as independent variables. Thus we have:

$$Y_T = C_T+I_T+E_T-M_T, \tag{1}$$

$$S_T = Y_T-C_T, \tag{2}$$

$$F_T = M_T-E_T, \tag{3}$$

$$S_T = a+bY_T+cF_T+\delta E_T, \tag{4}$$

$$Y_T = \alpha K_{T-1}, \tag{5}$$

$$I_T = K_T-K_{T-1}, \tag{6}$$

where Y, C, I, E, M, S, K and F are real national income, consumption, investment, exports, imports, savings, capital stock and inflow of foreign capital, respectively, and T denotes the time subscript. The model, in essential respects, is too well known to require detailed spelling-out by each equation. M and E are taken as exogenously specified: i.e., given exports (E), the amount of foreign aid (F) defines the available amount of imports (M).

The model can be readily solved to give the time-paths of income (Y), savings (S), consumption (C) and investment (I), once the parameters and the exogenous variables (imports, exports and initial income level) are specified.

4. The analysis

Our procedure then is to use (i) the Weisskopf (1972) estimated savings functions for LDCs,[2] (ii) their initial-income values (Y_0), (iii) their actual exports (E) during 1961–1970, and (iv) their average, mean value of external capital inflow (F) during 1961–1970, and then to generate, for each of these countries, the time-path of Y, C, I and S for the period 1961–1970 by assuming that the country would start out with the initial income-level, and be experiencing the observed annual export values and a mean-value capital inflow (as estimated).

Then, after this 10-year inflow of capital, each economy is assumed, from 1971 onwards, to have shifted left to a degree inviting economic 'blackmail' from the West. We then work out, for the years 1971 to 1976, the time-paths of Y, C, S and I that the economy will experience under three increasingly unfavourable sets of assumptions: (1) that net aid reduces to zero (so that $M = E$, i.e., $F = 0$); (2) that the gross aid reduces to zero, leading to a net repayment burden (put conservatively at 10 percent of the exports);[3] and (3) that, in addition to this net repayment burden, the resource-crunch is accentuated by the decline in productivity that it increasingly generates and/or propels – a factor built into our model by assuming an annual reduction, beginning in 1971, of the output–capital ratio by 3 percent.[4] The rest of the parameters in the model are assumed to be identical before the end of 1970 and thereafter: however, since exports are exogenously specified, they have been assumed to expand at the same *trend* rate after 1970 as before.

We can then examine the magnitude and importance of the resource-crunch imposed by external-capital blackmail by comparing what would have happened to income and consumption *if capital inflow had continued*, with their behaviour *in the absence of such inflow*, during 1971–1975: a significant decline in the growth of consumption under the former could well be taken as disruptive, given the expectations built up by the increased resource-availability in the aid regime. Of particular interest would also be a comparison of the consumption levels during 1970 with these in 1971 and thereafter: this may well reveal an *absolute*

[2]We take the Weisskopf (1972) estimates as the most comprehensive and sophisticated ones available to date. Weisskopf's estimates have stimulated additional work and, while the specific parametric estimates are not duplicated, it is worth noting that the basic finding that $c < 0$ remains, to date, unrefuted.

[3]A referee has raised the question of whether a socialist regime would not also abrogate existing debts or at least suspend unilaterally all repayments. Neither possibility, while impossible to rule out, is, however, probable and did not transpire in the cases of Ghana and Chile.

[4]The referee has also raised the question whether the decline in productivity would not rather take the form of a 30–40 percent decline immediately, and steady recovery in succeeding years. We did consider this alternative scenario (which, of course, strongly increases the likelihood of ratchet effects transpiring), but preferred our 'progressive chaos' version for the simple reason that it seems to correspond much more closely to what happened in Ghana and Chile and, even on a priori grounds, is the more probable as destabilisation efforts, 'sabotage' by domestic bourgeoisie, etc., are likely to increase slowly over time rather than peak immediately and fall progressively thereafter.

decline in consumption such that, given the strong possibility of a 'ratchet'-effect constraint, there would be the virtual inevitability of an economic crisis and chaos.

Before we present the simulation runs in the next section, note that the direct effect of capital inflow cessation or reversal – as distinct from the indirect effect *via* decline in productivity as captured by an increased capital–output ratio–would reflect itself in our model through the reduced level of imports (as exports are exogenously given).

In turn, this reduction of imports immediately reduces consumption and increases saving (as $c < 0$), but reduces total investment by $(1+c)$ times the reduced imports. However, the reduced investment means reduced income by α times the reduced investment in the next period. This leads to a b times $\alpha(1+c)\mathrm{d}M$ amount of reduced savings and, in turn, to an α times $b\alpha(1+c)\mathrm{d}M$ reduction in income. It is thus easy to see that the reduction in income that accrues from the reduced capital inflow (and hence reduced imports) can be written as

$$\frac{\mathrm{d}Y_{T+k}}{\mathrm{d}M_{T-1}} = (1+\alpha b)^k \alpha(1+c). \tag{7}$$

This effect increases with time; besides, it is a function of, and increases with, α and b (as long as $-1 < c$). Thus, if the cessation of capital inflow also causes a decline in productivity and hence a rise in 'α', the effect will again be to accentuate the fall in income from the termination of the capital inflow.

5. Simulation results

We are now ready to examine the simulation runs. Tables 1–5 present the main results, in a form which can be easily read, for the following five countries: Ghana, India, Israel, Philippines and South Korea. These countries were chosen because they happen to be part of Weisskopf's 17 LDCs; besides, they represent an interesting cross-section of countries from different regions and with diverse political and economic experiences. Each table refers to a single country and is assembled in a form which is amenable to easy reference.

To enable the reader to make inferences without straining his calculating ability, we have turned the series under alternative simulations into indices. Thus, in table 1 for Ghana, column (2) contains the simulation run for a constant capital inflow (estimated as the average flow during 1961–1970). YZ represents the income levels for this simulation, with 1961 = 100 and the base year income being of course the observed income for 1961. Column (3), marked YZ_0, contains the values of the income levels, with 1961 = 100, for this capital inflow reduced to zero as of 1970. YM, in column (4), contains the income levels, with 1961 = 100 again, on the alternative assumption that gross capital inflow is zero and there is a net capital outflow of 10 percent of the export value in each year. YM_α, in column (5), represents the estimates on the further assumption that there is also a continuous decline in productivity such that the output-capital ratio α declines by 3 percent annually. This description holds for each country, for each of tables 1–5. Corresponding explanations clearly hold for consumption under alternative simulations in columns (6)–(9).

Columns (10)–(15) utilise the same information but with a different focus. In each of the tables, columns (10)–(12) show the proportionate decline (or rise) in income under the no-inflow simulation runs as against the capital-inflow simulation run. Columns (13)–(15) do that for consumption.[5]

In making inferences from these tables for our purposes, remember that we *are* committing the economy to behaviour according to the postulated savings function, in particular. There is of course no valid reason to assume that a sudden decline in capital inflows and/or productivity will not involve a significant shift in this function: e.g., the marginal propensity to save may be reduced drastically to meet this situation, so as to appease current demands for increased consumption by the workers (as in Chile). Doubtless such scenarios could be worked out, for specific cases, as well. Here, however, we have confined ourselves to a limited-option scenario which ties the LDC government into reacting to a resource scarcity by playing according to the same behavioral rules as before the scarcity. The results of the simulation exercise are further 'realistic' in letting the capital inflow run at *observed* (but averaged-out, annually constant) values during a longish *ten-year* period during 1960s and then building in the shift to socialism and attendant capital-inflow blackmail.

The results in the tables suggest a number of conclusions which, in varying degrees, may be taken as supportive of radical concerns.

(1) Since domestic savings will move up immediately, given $c < 0$ in the Weisskopf savings functions, we should rather focus on the effect on income. It turns out that in none of the cases considered is there an absolute decline in income with the elimination of capital inflow: the inflow is just not large enough to lead to such a substantial impact as to outweigh the growth due to investment from domestic savings. Even the disruption effect at 3 percent annually will not produce an absolute decline in income. No possibility of a ratchet effect is therefore to be found in these simulations, as far as income is concerned.

(2) However, absolute consumption does decline immediately for Israel, even in the least unfavourable run (CZ_0), and consumption declines almost by 7 percent under the most unfavourable simulation (CM_α). This contrast between the behaviour of income and consumption reflects, of course, the high level of capital inflow combined with a very high coefficient to consume from it (i.e., a high value of $|c|$): the withdrawal of aid therefore leads to a big increase

[5]Table 6 brings together the main parametric values used in the simulation runs.

Table 1
Simulation runs for Ghana: Income and consumption under alternative scenarios.

Yr.	YZ[a]	YZ_0[b]	YM[c]	YM_α[d]	CZ[e]	CZ_0[e]	CM[e]	CM_α[e]	$100\left(1-\frac{YZ_0}{YZ}\right)$	$100\left(1-\frac{YM}{YZ}\right)$	$100\left(1-\frac{YM_\alpha}{YZ}\right)$	$100\left(1-\frac{CZ_0}{CZ}\right)$	$100\left(1-\frac{CM}{CZ}\right)$	$100\left(1-\frac{CM_\alpha}{CZ}\right)$
(1)	(2)	(3)	(4)	(5)	(6)	(7)	(8)	(9)	(10)	(11)	(12)	(13)	(14)	(15)
1	100.00[f]													
2	101.35				92.81									
3	102.86				94.68									
4	104.34				96.28									
5	105.80				93.20									
6	107.76				96.95									
7	109.53				97.69									
8	111.41				97.90									
9	113.47				100.46									
10	115.48				101.09									
11	117.63	117.50	117.43	117.37	101.82	97.70	95.58	95.53	0.11	0.17	0.22	4.04	6.13	6.17
12	119.95	119.67	119.54	119.30	103.17	98.94	96.71	96.52	0.23	0.34	0.54	4.10	6.26	6.45
13	122.37	121.95	121.74	121.14	104.61	100.27	97.92	97.44	0.34	0.51	1.00	4.15	6.40	6.86
14	124.90	124.34	124.05	122.85	106.41	101.68	99.21	98.25	0.45	0.68	1.64	4.20	6.53	7.43
15	127.54	126.83	126.46	124.38	107.75	103.18	100.58	98.91	0.55	0.85	2.48	4.25	6.65	8.20
16	130.29	129.43	128.98	125.71	109.46	104.76	102.04	99.42	0.66	1.01	3.52	4.29	6.77	9.17
17	133.16	132.15	131.60	126.82	111.26	106.44	103.59	99.75	0.76	1.17	4.76	4.33	6.89	10.34
18	136.14	134.98	134.34	127.73	113.15	108.20	105.23	99.92	0.86	1.33	6.18	4.37	7.00	11.69
19	139.25	137.92	137.18	128.45	115.14	110.06	106.95	99.94	0.95	1.48	7.76	4.41	7.11	13.20

[a] YZ = income with constant capital inflow annually.
[b] YZ_0 = income with capital inflow reduced to zero.
[c] YM = income with repayments at 10 percent of exports.
[d] YM_α = income with output–capital ratio declining at 3 percent annually *and* repayments at 10 percent of exports.
[e] CZ, CZ_0, CM and CM_α refer to corresponding values for consumption.
[f] The first year for income is reduced to base = 100 for the consumption and income series. Thus both series are income deflated and have a common base.

Table 2

Simulation runs for India: Income and consumption under alternative scenarios.

Yr.	YZ[a]	YZ_0[b]	YM[c]	YM_α[d]	CZ[e]	CZ_0	CM[e]	CM_α[e]	$100\left(1-\frac{YZ_0}{YZ}\right)$	$100\left(1-\frac{YM}{YZ}\right)$	$100\left(1-\frac{YM_\alpha}{YZ}\right)$	$100\left(1-\frac{CZ_0}{CZ}\right)$	$100\left(1-\frac{CM}{CZ}\right)$	$100\left(1-\frac{CM_\alpha}{CZ}\right)$
(1)	(2)	(3)	(4)	(5)	(6)	(7)	(8)	(9)	(10)	(11)	(12)	(13)	(14)	(15)
1	100.00[f]													
2	104.34				83.04									
3	108.84				86.21									
4	113.59				89.06									
5	118.70				93.00									
6	124.04				98.08									
7	129.43				102.10									
8	135.07				106.75									
9	140.90				110.80									
10	147.08				116.13									
11	153.40	153.07	153.00	152.82	120.90	119.99	119.76	119.62	0.22	0.27	0.38	0.75	0.95	1.07
12	160.03	159.36	159.18	158.48	126.09	124.91	124.59	124.02	0.42	0.53	0.97	0.94	1.19	1.64
13	166.93	165.90	165.63	163.86	131.50	130.03	129.63	128.20	0.62	0.78	1.84	1.12	1.43	2.52
14	174.12	172.72	172.35	168.81	137.14	135.37	134.88	132.02	0.80	1.02	3.05	1.29	1.65	3.73
15	181.59	179.82	179.33	173.21	143.02	140.94	140.36	135.41	0.98	1.24	4.62	1.45	1.86	5.32
16	189.37	187.20	186.60	177.00	149.14	146.74	146.07	138.30	1.15	1.46	6.53	1.61	2.06	7.27
17	197.47	194.89	194.17	180.15	155.52	152.79	152.01	140.67	1.31	1.67	8.77	1.76	2.26	9.55
18	205.89	202.89	202.04	182.69	162.16	159.09	158.20	142.55	1.46	1.87	11.27	1.90	2.44	12.09
19	214.65	211.21	210.23	184.67	169.08	165.65	164.65	143.98	1.60	2.06	13.97	2.03	2.62	14.85

[a] YZ = income with constant capital inflow annually.
[b] YZ_0 = income with capital inflow reduced to zero.
[c] YM = income with repayments at 10 percent of exports.
[d] YM_α = income with output–capital ratio declining at 3 percent annually *and* repayments at 10 percent of exports.
[e] CZ, CZ_0, CM and CM_α refer to corresponding values for consumption.
[f] The first year for income is reduced to base = 100 for the consumption and income series.

Table 3

Simulation runs for Israel: Income and consumption under alternative scenarios.

Yr.	YZ[a]	YZ_0[b]	YM[c]	YM_α[d]	CZ[e]	CZ_0	CM[e]	CM_α[e]	$100\left(1-\frac{YZ_0}{YZ}\right)$	$100\left(1-\frac{YM}{YZ}\right)$	$100\left(1-\frac{YM_\alpha}{YZ}\right)$	$100\left(1-\frac{CZ_0}{CZ}\right)$	$100\left(1-\frac{CM}{CZ}\right)$	$100\left(1-\frac{CM_\alpha}{CZ}\right)$
(1)	(2)	(3)	(4)	(5)	(6)	(7)	(8)	(9)	(10)	(11)	(12)	(13)	(14)	(15)
1	100.00[f]													
2	109.42				106.17									
3	119.83				114.04									
4	131.02				122.05									
5	143.21				130.46									
6	156.57				139.08									
7	171.39				146.00									
8	188.67				158.84									
9	207.32				170.75									
10	228.06				179.56									
11	252.49	251.42	251.16	250.49	200.89	173.07	166.33	165.74	0.42	0.53	0.79	13.85	17.20	17.49
12	277.89	275.71	275.18	272.44	222.58	193.79	186.74	184.34	0.79	0.98	1.96	12.94	16.10	17.18
13	304.45	301.10	300.29	293.39	242.59	212.79	205.03	198.99	1.10	1.36	3.63	12.29	15.48	17.97
14	333.02	328.48	327.36	313.33	264.29	233.43	224.92	212.65	1.36	1.70	5.92	11.67	14.89	19.54
15	363.74	357.95	356.48	331.67	287.85	255.90	246.62	224.91	1.59	2.00	8.82	11.10	14.32	21.86
16	396.67	389.58	387.74	347.95	313.35	280.27	270.19	235.38	1.79	2.25	12.28	10.56	13.77	24.88
17	431.90	423.47	421.21	361.91	340.87	306.61	295.70	243.81	1.95	2.47	16.20	10.05	13.25	28.47
18	469.53	459.69	456.99	373.47	370.48	334.99	323.22	250.13	2.10	2.67	20.46	9.58	12.76	32.48
19	509.64	498.35	495.17	382.70	402.26	365.51	352.84	254.43	2.21	2.84	24.91	9.14	12.29	36.75

[a] YZ = income with constant capital inflow annually.
[b] YZ_0 = income with capital inflow reduced to zero.
[c] YM = income with repayments at 10 percent of exports.
[d] YM_α = income with output–capital ratio declining at 3 percent annually *and* repayments at 10 percent of exports.
[e] CZ, CZ_0, CM and CM_α refer to corresponding values for consumption.
[f] The first year for income is reduced to base = 100 for the consumption and income series.

Table 4

Simulation runs for Philippines: Income and consumption under alternative scenarios.

Yr.	YZ[a]	YZ_0[b]	YM[c]	YM_α[d]	CZ[e]	CZ_0[e]	CM[e]	CM_α[e]	$100\left(1-\frac{YZ_0}{YZ}\right)$	$100\left(1-\frac{YM}{YZ}\right)$	$100\left(1-\frac{YM_\alpha}{YZ}\right)$	$100\left(1-\frac{CZ_0}{CZ}\right)$	$100\left(1-\frac{CM}{CZ}\right)$	$100\left(1-\frac{CM_\alpha}{CZ}\right)$
(1)	(2)	(3)	(4)	(5)	(6)	(7)	(8)	(9)	(10)	(11)	(12)	(13)	(14)	(15)
1	100.00[f]													
2	107.14				93.38									
3	114.16				97.74									
4	122.36				104.53									
5	101.17				111.03									
6	140.97				117.81									
7	152.07				127.49									
8	163.78				138.85									
9	175.64				149.79									
10	187.89				154.76									
11	203.28	202.38	200.53	200.91	170.62	169.26	167.19	166.85	0.44	1.17	1.35	0.79	2.01	2.21
12	218.47	216.62	213.82	212.33	183.33	181.14	177.84	176.52	0.85	2.13	2.81	1.20	2.99	3.71
13	234.72	231.88	227.62	223.82	196.98	193.91	189.27	185.91	1.21	3.03	4.64	1.56	3.91	5.62
14	252.09	248.21	242.34	234.64	211.62	207.63	201.52	194.70	1.54	3.87	6.92	1.89	4.77	8.00
15	270.63	265.66	258.03	244.47	227.30	222.34	214.63	202.62	1.84	4.66	9.67	2.18	5.57	10.86
16	290.40	284.28	274.73	253.09	244.08	238.10	228.64	209.47	2.11	5.40	12.85	2.45	6.32	14.18
17	311.47	304.14	292.51	260.39	261.99	254.95	243.60	215.15	2.35	6.09	16.40	2.69	7.02	17.88
18	333.88	325.30	311.40	266.37	281.10	272.94	259.55	219.65	2.57	6.73	20.22	2.90	7.67	21.86
19	357.72	347.81	331.47	271.09	301.47	292.14	276.53	223.04	2.77	7.34	24.22	3.10	8.27	26.02

[a] YZ = income with constant capital inflow annually.
[b] YZ_0 = income with capital inflow reduced to zero.
[c] YM = income with repayments at 10 percent of exports.
[d] YM_α = income with output–capital ratio declining at 3 percent annually *and* repayments at 10 percent of exports.
[e] CZ, CZ_0, CM and CM_α refer to corresponding values for consumption.
[f] The first year for income is reduced to base = 100 for the consumption and income series.

Table 5

Simulation runs for South Korea: Income and consumption under alternative scenarios.

Yr.	YZ^a	YZ_0^b	YM^c	YM_α^d	CZ^e	CZ_0^e	CM^e	CM_α^e	$100\left(1-\frac{YZ_0}{YZ}\right)$	$100\left(1-\frac{YM}{YZ}\right)$	$100\left(1-\frac{YM_\alpha}{YZ}\right)$	$100\left(1-\frac{CZ_0}{CZ}\right)$	$100\left(1-\frac{CM}{CZ}\right)$	$100\left(1-\frac{CM_\alpha}{CZ}\right)$
(1)	(2)	(3)	(4)	(5)	(6)	(7)	(8)	(9)	(10)	(11)	(12)	(13)	(14)	(15)
1	100.00[f]													
2	114.01				85.85									
3	128.29				97.33									
4	143.40				108.24									
5	159.77				119.29									
6	177.74				118.74									
7	201.26				149.39									
8	222.65				163.29									
9	246.28				180.23									
10	271.91				197.03									
11	300.18	299.12	298.88	298.09	222.93	206.03	202.15	201.38	0.36	0.43	0.70	7.58	9.32	9.66
12	329.18	327.04	326.56	323.42	246.38	228.44	223.97	220.91	0.65	0.80	1.75	7.28	9.10	10.34
13	359.85	356.63	355.87	347.94	271.45	252.46	247.37	239.66	0.90	1.11	3.31	7.00	8.87	11.71
14	329.19	387.88	386.82	370.93	298.16	278.10	272.38	256.91	1.10	1.37	5.42	6.73	8.65	13.84
15	426.22	420.81	419.43	391.78	326.51	305.38	299.01	272.08	1.27	1.59	8.08	6.47	8.42	16.67
16	461.96	455.44	453.71	410.09	356.53	334.32	327.25	284.77	1.41	1.79	11.23	6.23	8.21	20.13
17	499.41	491.77	489.67	425.66	388.21	364.91	357.14	294.80	1.53	1.95	14.77	6.00	8.00	24.06
18	508.59	529.83	527.32	438.48	421.58	397.19	388.68	302.14	1.63	2.09	18.59	5.79	7.81	28.33
19	579.51	569.62	566.69	488.71	456.65	431.15	421.88	306.96	1.71	2.21	22.57	5.58	7.61	32.78

[a] YZ = income with constant capital inflow annually.
[b] YZ_0 = income with capital inflow reduced to zero.
[c] YM = income with repayments at 10 percent of exports.
[d] YM_α = income with output–capital ratio declining at 3 percent annually *and* repayments at 10 percent of exports.

[e] CZ, CZ_0, CM and CM_α refer to corresponding values for consumption.
[f] The first year for income is reduced to base = 100 for the consumption and income series.

Table 6

Parametric values used in simulation runs of the model for the five countries.[a,b]

Country	a	b	c	δ	α[d]	Average $(M-E)$[c] in the with-inflow run (Z)	Initial income (deflator)	Average $(M-E)$[c] as percent of initial income
Ghana	−254.5	0.197	−0.765	0.688	0.11	60.6861	1158.62	5.24
India	−4.968	0.191	−0.270	1.082	0.19	3.89582	163.5658	2.38
Israel	88.3	0.125	−0.886	0.621	0.31	2,104.85	6938.296	30.33
Philippines	−0.4150	0.114	−0.209	0.348	0.43	0.395798	14.9222	2.65
South Korea	147.6	0.026	−0.817	1.132	0.30	82.524	425.122	19.41

[a]The units in which $(M-E)$ and initial income are stated are as follows: Ghana, million cedis; India, billion rupees; Israel, million Israeli pounds; Philippines, million pesos; and South Korea, billion won.

[b]$S = a+bY+cF+\delta E$.

[c]Average $(M-E)$ figures were for the $\approx$ 10-year figures of the 1960s from IMF Financial Statistics.

[d]α was chosen so that the model tracked most closely the historical path of GNP over the decade of the 1960s.

in domestic savings (as seen in table 3) and a correspondingly big drop in consumption. This is true also for Ghana with its absolute decline in consumption.[6]

(3) While, however, the ratchet-effect possibility is not probable in the case of income, and only mildly probable for consumption, there is plenty of evidence that declines, *relative to what would have happened under continued capital inflow and what therefore may have been built into expectations from the government,* in income and consumption do occur in the short-run of one to five years, under even the most favourable (Z_0) simulations. Thus, to illustrate by reference to the Philippines simulations, by the 3rd year itself, the income decline (relative to YZ) for Philippines would have been over 1 percent for zero capital inflow (YZ_0), over 3 percent for the net repayment case (YM) and over 4.5 percent for the worst case (YM_α). If one lets the situation unfold to the 9th year (the socialist experiment will likely have ended long before that!), the declines increase, but rather mildly, except in the declining-productivity simulation (YM_α), where one gets a staggering decline of nearly 25 percent! It would appear that the capital-flow elimination, in itself, does not create a large decline in income growth; though even a 1–2 percent 'shortfall' may be critical for a democratic government.[7]

The results are broadly similar for all the countries, suggesting that the elimination of capital inflow, taking plausible values, *does* in itself reduce the growth of consumption and investment below the levels sustainable with the inflow (and thus 'expected' to be so sustained after a decade or so of such inflow-caused growth in consumption and investment). But, in general, these declines are relatively small proportions of the 'expected' values and may not create as much difficulty for transition to socialism as might be feared. However, the results of the declining-productivity simulations are much more disturbing: suggesting that the real 'crunch' of resources, and hence the stranglehold on the socialist experiments, may come from the effect of the reduced/eliminated capital inflow on the ability to sustain the productivity of investment at the customary levels. Here, the role of the domestic bourgeoisie in economic sabotage, with or without 'destabilising' aid from external forces, the underutilisation of capacity closely geared to the availability of more foreign exchange, and the difficulty of managing an economy already under strain from the direct effect of reduced resources may well be the critical factors in the eventual sabotage of the socialist experiment.

In fact, our simulation exercises, in underlining the relatively small impact of

[6]South Korea should also have shown a ratchet effect for similar reasons; but the effect is clouded by the impact of the exports behavior on savings.

[7]Similar conclusions can be reached if attention is focused instead on the relative declines in consumption. Note, however, that the percentage decline in consumption under either of the three 'blackmail' simulation runs need not necessarily rise; in fact, for Israel and South Korea, the reader can observe the opposite. This paradox is readily resolved by noting that $C_0/Y_0 = [(1-b)-(a/Y_0)]-(\delta E/Y_0)$, so that if $a > 0$, as in the case of Israel and South Korea, the term $[(1-b)-(a/Y_0)]$ will *rise*, instead of fall, as Y_0 rises.

'aid blackmail' per se and the significantly larger impact of the declining-productivity effect in undermining the socialist LDC, can be taken as providing the underlying rationale of the 'destabilisation' activities in Chile that played a critical role in President Allende's overthrow by the military. We may have thus ended up by providing a sound economic explanation of the reasons why Dr. Kissinger had to resort to destabilisation, instead of relying merely on the usual forms of economic blackmail, to destroy the Allende government.

References

Grinols, E. and J. Bhagwati, 1974, Foreign capital, savings and dependence, mimeo (M.I.T., Cambridge).

Weisskopf, T., 1972, The impact of foreign capital inflow on domestic savings in underdeveloped countries, Journal of International Economics 2, no. 1, 25–38.

Reprinted from THE REVIEW OF ECONOMICS AND STATISTICS
Published by Harvard University. Copyright, 1976, by the President and Fellows of Harvard College
Vol. LVIII, No. 4, November 1976

FOREIGN CAPITAL, SAVINGS AND DEPENDENCE

Earl Grinols and Jagdish Bhagwati*

THE recent focus of radical economists such as Thomas Weisskopf (1972) and Keith Griffin (1970) on the possible reduction in domestic savings caused by aid inflow has raised an important issue: How much does this matter?[1]

A characteristic answer by orthodox economists would be that increased current consumption is also welfare-improving. Hence, the evidence of reduced domestic savings following on the influx of foreign capital — or, what is the same thing, the evidence that aid is only partially used for investment — may be dismissed as interesting but irrelevant to the discussion of the benefits of aid programmes.[2]

But, while the radical economists have not systematically spelled out an argument to sustain the thesis that a reduction of domestic savings by foreign capital is harmful, it is clear that their concern arises from the notion of "dependence": in particular, that reduced savings would somehow increase dependence on the aid-giving country (which is likely to be part of the "imperialist" or the "social-revisionist" bloc).

This "dependence" argument can indeed be formalised. Take a typical Harrod-Domar type model and define the capital-recipient country's objective as reaching a Millikan-Rosenstein-Rodan-Rostow self-reliant growth rate by raising its domestic savings rate to a target level. The radical case can then be constructed by examining whether, in reducing domestic savings, an influx of foreign capital postpones, or renders infeasible, the reaching of self-reliance. (Needless to say, "dependence" can only be one dimension out of many that would enter a complete social welfare function; but it is certainly one that has to be formalised, as here, before it can be usefully discussed.)

Two things are clear as soon as the problem of "dependence" is defined in this way. First, whether capital inflow creates dependence will depend on the assumed parameters of the model as well as the targeted level of the savings rate and the time by which it must be achieved. Contrary to the radical notions, an aid programme may achieve a targeted increase in the savings rate *earlier* than in the absence of aid, or may make an infeasible target a feasible one. Second, it is therefore useful to take estimates of the parameters involved and to examine simulation runs to see whether the radical concerns are worth bothering about. It is our intention to derive the logical implications of such savings behavior in a dynamic framework to see where it can lead.

This paper constructs a simple version of the Harrod-Domar model and discusses the simulation runs of savings and the savings ratio, with and without aid, for a number of less developed countries (LDCs). These countries are those for which Weisskopf (1972) has fitted savings functions, using time series analysis, so that we have had to add only plausible

Received for publication March 19, 1975. Revision accepted for publication November 10, 1975.

* The research underlying this paper was financed by the National Science Foundation. The facilities provided by the Institute for International Economic Studies, Stockholm, are also gratefully acknowledged. A companion paper by Bhagwati and Grinols (1975) which examines a different argument linking foreign capital inflow to dependence and hence to the feasibility of transition to socialism has been published separately in the *Journal of Development Economics*.

[1] The precise line of arguments developed below may be considered to be implicit in the concerns and writings of the radical economists, though we have not seen them carefully developed and stated. The focus in many of the radical writings is rather on the inadequacy of the early aid-requirements estimates, where the analyst assumed a Harrod-Domar model and a realistic capital-output ratio, fixed a target rate of growth to get a target rate of investment, then made a Keynesian savings assumption and came out with the estimate of aid or capital inflow required to fill the gap between the required investment and the available domestic savings. This method, along with alternative approaches, is reviewed in Bhagwati (1971). If the aid inflow itself affects domestic savings, the model is clearly specified incorrectly. To be fair, however, to the economists (such as Rosenstein-Rodan) who used the approach being criticised, they thought of the Keynesian domestic savings function as one which the economy would adhere to (via tax effort, for example) as part of its "matching effort" while receiving the capital inflow, so that it was a "policy" function rather than a "behavioral" function as implied by the radical writings.

[2] Following this line of argument, the radicals should focus on the distribution of benefits from additional consumption instead of on whether such additional consumption follows on the capital inflow.

capital-output ratios and the estimated initial-income, capital outflow and export values.[8] Section I discusses the model's analytics and derives the relationships important to the notion of dependence. In section II simulation runs are presented and, in light thereof, there follows a discussion of the characteristics of those countries most likely to reach self-reliance. Section III then concludes with remarks addressed to the problem of dependence, in light of our analysis.

I

A. *The Model*

The model used here is a simple Harrod-Domar type, with a slightly modified savings equation to allow for foreign inflow of capital and exports as independent variables. Thus we have

$$Y_T = C_T + I_T + E_T - M_T \quad (1)$$
$$S_T = Y_T - C_T \quad (2)$$
$$F_T = M_T - E_T \quad (3)$$
$$S_T = a + bY_T + cF_T + dE_T \quad (4)$$
$$Y_T = \alpha K_{T-1} \quad (5)$$
$$I_T = K_T - K_{T-1} \quad (6)$$

where Y, C, I, E, M, S, K and F are real national income, consumption, investment, exports, imports, savings, capital stock, and inflow of foreign capital, respectively, and T denotes the time subscript. M and E are taken as exogenously specified: i.e., given exports (E), the amount of foreign aid (F) defines the available amount of imports (M).

B. *Analysis*

The following properties of the model can be readily spelled out.

(1) *National Income:* The dynamic equation describing national income is

$$Y_T = (1 + \alpha b)\, Y_{T-1} + \{\alpha a + \alpha(1 + c)\, M_{T-1} + \alpha(d - c - 1)\, E_{T-1}\}. \quad (7)$$

[8] The inclusion of exports as an independent variable, by Weisskopf, in the savings function is based on the earlier work of Maizels. However, there is little evidence of any underlying rationale for this, as discussed at some length in Bhagwati (1977, chapter 11). We use Weisskopf's formulation, however, as we wish to use his estimated savings functions for our simulation runs.

Solving it recursively for Y_T, we get

$$Y_T = (1 + \alpha b)^T Y_0 + \alpha \sum_{i=0}^{T-1} (1 + \alpha b)^i \{a + (1 + c)\, M_{T-i-1} + (d - c - 1)\, E_{T-i-1}\}. \quad (8)$$

(2) *National Income with Capital Inflow:* With aid (foreign capital) inflow at level A_T, the model reacts formally as if it were given an increase in imports by that amount. National income, T years after aid begins, is therefore given from (8) by

$$Y_T^A = Y_T + \alpha(1 + c) \sum_{i=0}^{T-1} (1 + \alpha b)^i A_{T-i-1} \quad (9)$$

where the superscript A in Y_T^A refers to the with-aid value of national income.

(3) *Savings with Capital Inflow:* Similarly, while saving is given by (4), the saving with capital inflow is given as

$$S_T^A = S_T + cA_T + b\alpha(1 + c) \sum_{i=0}^{T-1} (1 + \alpha b)^i A_{T-i-1}. \quad (10)$$

(4) *Income and Savings with Constant Capital Inflow:* While the above results allow for varying levels of capital inflow (A_T), nothing substantive is gained by retaining this freedom. We have therefore simplified by assuming that aid is received at a constant level (A) in each period. With this assumption,

$$Y_T^A = Y_T + \frac{A(1 + c)}{b} [(1 + \alpha b)^T - 1] \quad (11)$$

and

$$S_T^A = S_T + A(1 + c)\, [(1 + \alpha b)^T - 1] + cA. \quad (12)$$

Having thus derived Y_T, Y_T^A, S_T and S_T^A, we can address ourselves to a number of questions.

(5) *"Recovery" Period Analysis for (absolute) Savings:* We may first investigate the problem of the time taken to recover (absolute) savings, with capital inflow, to the level that would have been reached without capital inflow. It is easy to see from (12) that the value of $[S_T^A - S_T]$ will be negative for small T as long as $c < 0$. I.e., the immediate impact of the capital inflow is to reduce domestic savings. Since the expression is a monotonically rising function in T, we wish to know when it reaches zero (i.e., savings, with capital inflow, recovers

to the level that would be reached without the inflow). Using equation (12) one gets

$$T_0 = -\frac{\log(1+c)}{\log(1+\alpha b)} \quad (13)$$

where T_0 is the time period over which $[S_T^A - S_T] = 0$. Values for T_0 will be computed in section II.

(6) *"Recovery" Period Analysis for Savings Ratio:* Reverting to our original focus on the savings ratio, as one would expect, we find its behavior not as straightforward.

Using the definition of savings one has

$$\frac{S_T^A}{Y_T^A} = b + [a + cM_T + (d-c)E_T] \cdot \frac{1}{Y_T^A} + \frac{cA}{Y_T^A} \quad (14)$$

and similarly

$$\frac{S_T}{Y_T} = b + [a + cM_T + (d-c)E_T] \cdot \frac{1}{Y_T}. \quad (15)$$

Therefore, we can write

$$\frac{S_T^A}{Y_T^A} - \frac{S_T}{Y_T} = \frac{cA}{Y_T^A} - [a + cM_T + (d-c)E_T]\left[\frac{1}{Y_T} - \frac{1}{Y_T^A}\right] \quad (16)$$

and

$$R_T \equiv \frac{S_T^A}{Y_T^A} \Big/ \frac{S_T}{Y_T} = \frac{b + \dfrac{[a + cM_T + (d-c)E_T]}{Y_T^A} + \dfrac{cA}{Y_T^A}}{b + \dfrac{[a + cM_T + (d-c)E_T]}{Y_T}}. \quad (17)$$

Given $-1 < c < 0$, $d > 0$ and $b > 0$ there are five possible time paths for the savings ratio. Three correspond to a marginal propensity to save (MPS) *greater* than the average propensity to save (APS) and two correspond to the marginal propensity to save *less* than the average propensity to save.

These five variations give rise to only three outcomes for the ratio R_T. They are labeled as cases I, II and III in figure 1, which serves also to give their taxonomy. In all cases R_T approaches unity asymptotically.

Case I: Let the marginal propensity to save exceed the average propensity to save (i.e., $b > S/Y$ or equivalently $[a + cM + (d-c)E] < 0$).

It might be thought that aid, causing higher GNP, would cause higher savings which, because the marginal savings rate is above the average, would eventually cause the average with-aid savings rate to exceed the savings rate without aid.

This is indeed what happens in case I. The influx of capital initially makes the value of (16) negative by depressing $(S^A/Y^A) = (S^A/Y)$ by the amount cA/Y. As $[(1/Y_T) - (1/Y_T^A)]$ increases with time and cA/Y_T^A diminishes (in absolute value), $[(S_T^A/Y_T^A) - (S_T/Y_T)]$ goes from an initial negative value to a positive enough value to outweigh the other terms and cause the ratio R_T to exceed 1.

The above situation need not always occur, however, since $[(S_T^A/Y_T^A) - (S_T/Y_T)]$ may never reach a sufficient value to outweigh the other terms. As an example of this, consider the higher GNP-higher savings argument given above. While moving *along* the savings-income curve, the curve itself shifts with changes in M_T and E_T. The shift can be enough so that the savings ratio actually declines over time. Aid would accentuate the drop and overtaking would never occur.

If we impose the condition that M_T and E_T are constant over time, this will yield a constant intercept of the savings-income line and we can revert to the normal conclusion that S_T/Y_T and S_T^A/Y_T^A will be a monotonically increasing (decreasing) function of time if $b > (<)\ S_T/Y_T$ and S_T^A/Y_T^A, respectively. But the constancy of M_T and E_T does not insure the case I argument, as will be seen below.

Cases II, III: Cases II and III are characterized by R_T forever below 1 but approaching it asymptotically. In case II, $R_T \to 1$ monotonically, whereas in case III it drops away from 1 initially before resuming its climb. The reader is referred to figure 1.

An examination of equation (16) shows that cA/Y_T^A is necessarily negative and $(1/Y_T) - (1/Y_T^A)$ is necessarily positive. Therefore, if the marginal propensity to save is below the average propensity to save (i.e., $b < S/Y$ or equivalently $[a + cM_T + (d-c)E_T] > 0$), $(S_T^A/Y_T^A) - (S_T/Y_T)$ will necessarily be nega-

FIGURE 1.—ALTERNATIVE TIME-PATHS OF SAVINGS/INCOME RATIO WITH AND WITHOUT AID

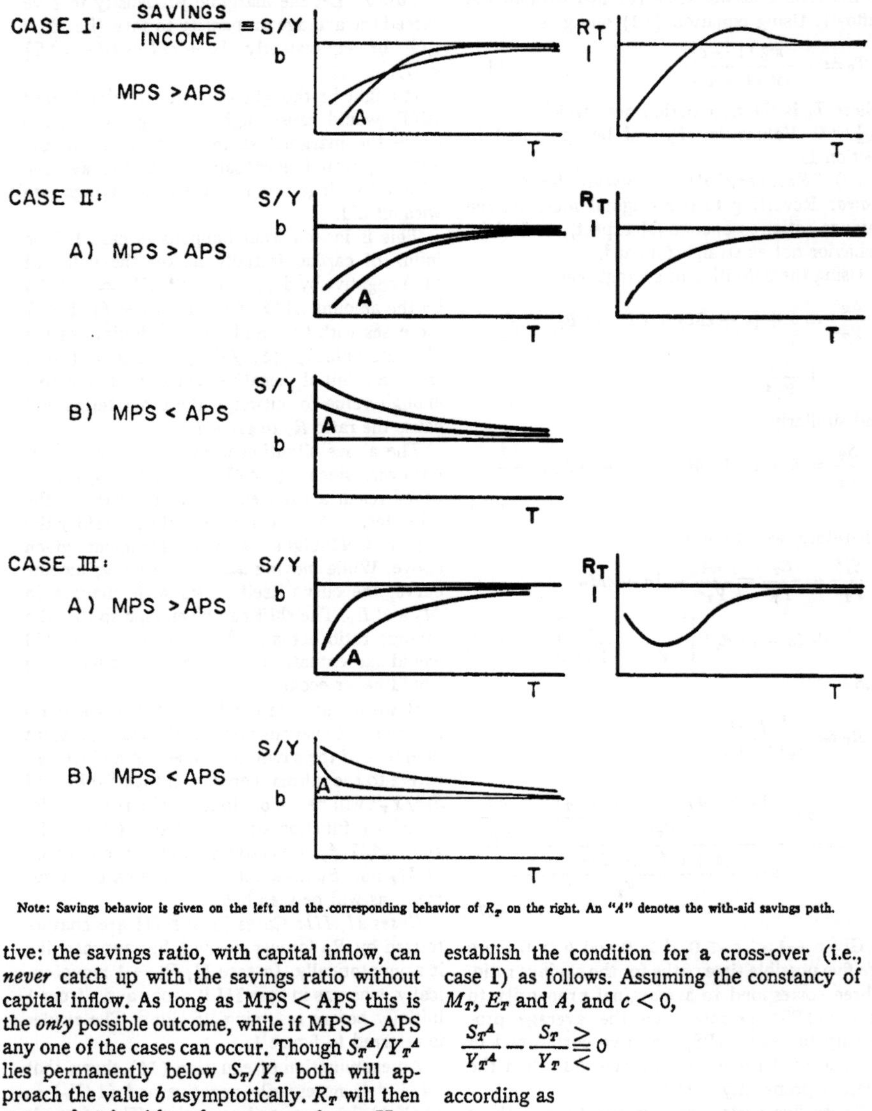

Note: Savings behavior is given on the left and the corresponding behavior of R_T on the right. An "A" denotes the with-aid savings path.

tive: the savings ratio, with capital inflow, can *never* catch up with the savings ratio without capital inflow. As long as MPS < APS this is the *only* possible outcome, while if MPS > APS any one of the cases can occur. Though S_T^A/Y_T^A lies permanently below S_T/Y_T both will approach the value b asymptotically. R_T will then approach 1 in either the manner of case II or case III.

The foregoing analysis of the three possibilities can be carried a little further and we can establish the condition for a cross-over (i.e., case I) as follows. Assuming the constancy of M_T, E_T and A, and $c < 0$,

$$\frac{S_T^A}{Y_T^A} - \frac{S_T}{Y_T} \gtreqless 0$$

according as

$$Y_T \lesseqgtr \frac{(1+c)\,[(1+\alpha b)^T - 1]}{bc}\,[a + c\bar{M} + (d-c)\,\bar{E}]. \qquad (18)$$

Now, we know that

$$Y_T = (1+\alpha b)^T Y_0 + \{a + (1+c)\,M + (d-c-1)\,\bar{E}\}\left\{\frac{(1+\alpha b)^T - 1}{b}\right\}$$

so that, substituting this into (18), we get the condition according as

$$\frac{(1+\alpha b)^T}{(1+\alpha b)^T - 1}\,Y_0 \lesseqgtr \frac{a}{bc} + \frac{d}{bc}\cdot\bar{E}. \quad (19)$$

Now, since $(S_T^A/Y_T^A) - (S_T/Y_T) < 0$ for small T the condition implying no cross-over is that the LHS in (19) exceed the RHS. If we choose $\bar{E} > (bcY_0 - a)/d$, this implies that $(a + d\bar{E})/bc < Y_0$ where Y_0 is the initial income level. It then follows that

$$\frac{(1+\alpha b)^T}{(1+\alpha b)^T - 1}\,Y_0 > Y_0 > \frac{a + d\bar{E}}{bc}$$

for all T. Hence a sufficient condition for no cross-over is that

$$\frac{\bar{E}}{Y_0} > \left[\frac{bc}{d} - \frac{a}{dY_0}\right] \quad (20)$$

(after rewriting it as a condition on the size of the export sector relative to the economy when aid is initiated), where bc/d is negative while $-(a/dY_0)$ is positive (for a negative a).[4] Thus, even with the import and export sectors constant in absolute size, there are three possible paths which R_T can take; and one purpose of our simulation runs will be to get some indication of which behavior is most common.

C. *Diagrammatic Analysis*

The foregoing discussion of the behavior of savings and the savings ratio with and without capital inflow may be illuminated by illustration in terms of the standard savings-income diagram as in figure 2. Assuming that the marginal propensity to save is greater than the average — the opposite case can be illustrated equally easily — we can see that the savings ratio rises over time. Hence, in order for the lowered savings ratio in an economy with capital inflow to catch up with the savings ratio when there is no capital inflow, national income in the inflow-situation must rise faster by the amounts shown on the income-axis in thick lines. If the conditions are not sufficient to warrant such a growth in Y_T^A so that $(Y_T^A - Y_T)$ rises over time by as much as the thick lengths in figure 2, the savings ratio in the inflow situation will *never* overtake that for the no-inflow situation. If the growth in Y_A^T is faster than indicated by the thick lengths, the cross-over in the savings ratios will occur. The conditions for such a cross-over to occur or not are, of course, already established in (19) and (20).

FIGURE 2. — EXCESS GROWTH OF INCOME NECESSARY FOR SAVINGS/INCOME RATIO TO CATCH-UP (i.e., for R_T to reach unity)

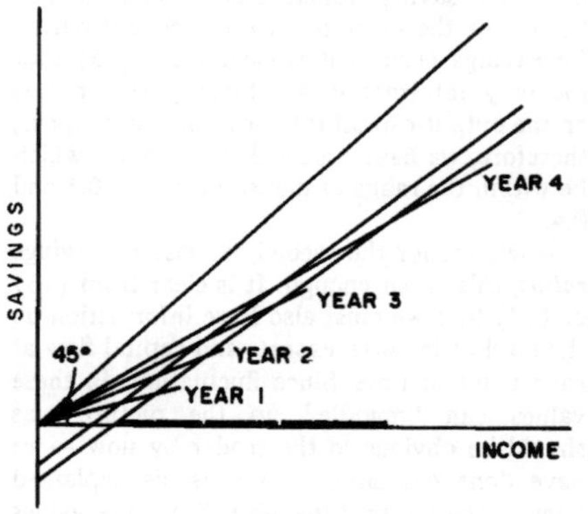

Note: The thick lines represent $(Y_T^A - Y_T)$.

II

We are now in a position to discuss the simulation runs for 17 LDCs with the greater insight earned by the preceding analysis. Note, of course, that it is not possible, in the absence of knowledge of the desired savings levels or ratios and the time over which they are sought to be attained by the LDC in question, to attack the problem of dependence as earlier defined in this paper.

However, it is possible to answer certain related questions.

(i) What is the number of years (T_0) that it would take the capital-receiving LDC in question to recover the level of savings that would

[4] This condition, and the sufficiency condition earlier established for absence of cross-over (i.e., that $a + cM + (d-c)E > 0$), are readily seen to be consistent with each other. Since α, b, $-c$ are positive, the sign of the RHS of (18) will be negative. Y_T is positive, so that it will exceed this value. Both conditions therefore ensure that the LHS of (18) will exceed its RHS.

have been reached in the absence of capital inflow A? If the savings level recovers, in this sense, only after a protracted period, the radical concerns may be held to have some empirical support.

(ii) What is the number of years that it would take for the savings ratio with capital inflow to cross-over the savings ratio without the inflow — when such a cross-over is possible? And for how many LDCs analysed will the cross-over be ruled out altogether, so that the savings ratio with the inflow will remain—except asymptotically — permanently lower?

For both exercises we use a common set of estimated parameters and Weisskopf's savings functions for 17 LDCs (for which he has argued that the savings-constraint operates and hence the savings function is correctly identified). For the exercise on the recovery period for savings (level), it is clear from (13) that the only information additionally required is on the output-capital ratio, α. For this purpose, therefore, we have assumed three values which lie within the range of plausibility: 0.2, 0.3 and 0.4.

However, for the second exercise on savings *ratios*, this is not enough. It is clear from (16) or (17) that we must also have information on the level of imports, exports and capital flow at each point of time. Since fluctuations in these values can "muddle" up the picture — as should be obvious to the reader by now — we have done our simulation runs, as explained later in the paper, "smoothing" out the values of these variables.[6]

Recovery Period for Savings Levels

The results of our calculations on the recovery time for savings levels, using the above-detailed procedures, are presented in table 1. As one would expect, the catching-up time falls as the output-capital ratio rises: the growth in income (and hence savings) from capital-inflow-increased investment is larger, the larger the output-capital ratio.

[6] We might clarify to the reader that our data base could have been updated and the Weisskopf equations also correspondingly re-estimated. However, this would have required a massive research effort while our purpose here was only to indicate broad orders of magnitude. It is particularly important, therefore, not to attach great significance to the runs for any *specific* country.

TABLE 1. — YEARS REQUIRED FOR SAVINGS LEVEL WITH CAPITAL INFLOW TO CATCH-UP WITH SAVINGS LEVEL IN ABSENCE OF CAPITAL INFLOW

Country	Catching-up Time (α = output-capital ratio)		
	$\alpha = 0.2$	$\alpha = 0.3$	$\alpha = 0.4$
(1)	(2)	(3)	(4)
Burma	174.45	116.41	87.39
Colombia	3.09	2.07	1.56
Costa Rica	13.26	8.99	6.84
Ghana	31.48	25.22	19.09
Guiana	1.38	4.99	3.80
Honduras	159.29	106.53	80.16
India	8.39	5.65	4.21
Israel	87.94	58.99	44.51
Jordan	137.56	92.22	69.55
Malta	10.04	6.75	5.10
Mexico	2.29	1.54	1.16
Philippines	10.40	6.97	5.26
Portugal	26.50	17.90	13.60
Puerto Rico	15.54	10.49	7.96
S. Korea	327.44	218.58	164.14
Taiwan	15.58	10.46	7.91
Uruguay	0.34	0.24	0.18

The interesting result is that there is, in fact, a very large spread in the catching-up period. For the middle-valued α at 0.3, the range is from a low of 0.24 years for Uruguay to a high of 218.58 for S. Korea. Even if we lop off two extreme values at each end, we get a range from 2.07 years for Colombia to 92.22 for Jordan. If we take an unweighted mean, it comes to just over 40 years! It is clear that time considerations make the implications for savings very sensitive to the parameters.

If the radicals are worried about savings levels being depressed below the levels reached in the absence of the capital inflow, the results of our exercise can be viewed as moderately encouraging to their thesis. On the other hand, it should be emphasized that even though the savings level with capital inflow will not catch up for many years with the levels reached, at each point of time, without the inflow, savings will be increasing through time. Moreover, if there is a target level of savings, the *additional* time necessary to reach it may be substantially smaller than several of the numbers in table 1 may suggest.

Recovery Period for Savings Ratios

The results for the savings ratio exercise are somewhat more encouraging for the radicals, as it appears, under plausible assumptions, that the ratio R_T ($\equiv (S_T^A/Y_T^A)/(S_T/Y_T)$) flips over in excess of unity for only 2 out of the 12 LDCs which we retained for our simulations (the others being eliminated because they resulted in extreme values, e.g., persisting negative savings).

The results of our simulations are tabulated in table 2. The LDCs were all normalized to initial income at 100, capital inflow maintained throughout at 5, output-capital ratio at 0.3, and the only differences among the LDCs were in the parameters of the savings function and in the values of E and M assumed.[6] Two alternative assumptions were made for exports and imports over time: (I) that they remained constant; and (II) that they remained a constant proportion of income. In *both* cases $\lim_{T\to\infty} R_T$ is unity so that the only real differences between countries under each assumption (I or II) relate to whether R_T, having fallen initially, will rise and flip over beyond unity *or* rise while remaining below unity (though it may continue to fall temporarily as in the case of Burma and Colombia).[7]

The radicals may note from table 2 that the flip-over possibility arises in only two cases; and moreover, in some cases (i.e., Burma and Honduras) the ratio remains significantly depressed below unity even at the end of 30 years. We should also note that, depending on the economy's savings ratio before aid is instituted, aid even at the level of 5% of GNP may or may not significantly reduce that ratio (com-

[6] These values were set at their historical average percentage of GNP based on the sample period for which the corresponding savings function was estimated. A table setting forth these values is available from the authors on request.

[7] The assumption that the import and export sectors remain a constant proportion of GNP in the presence of aid changes the analysis slightly from that done in equations (7)–(9) since it implies that aid enlarges the import and export sectors over time to keep them growing as fast as GNP does.

If one assumes $E_T = \beta_2 Y_{T-1}$, $M_T = \beta_1 Y_{T-1}$ where β_1, β_2 are constants between zero and one, while retaining the equations (1)–(6), the dynamic equations for the new system can be written:

$$Y_T = (1 + \alpha\Phi)\, Y_{T-1} + \alpha K \qquad (21)$$

$$Y_T^A = (1 + \alpha\Phi)\, Y_{T-1}^A + \alpha K + \alpha A(1 + c) \qquad (22)$$

where $\Phi = b + (1 + c)\, \beta_1 + (d - c - 1)\, \beta_2$ and $K = a$. The dynamic equation (7) for constant $M_T = M$, $E_T = E$ can also be put in the above form where $\Phi = b$, $K = a + (1 + c)\, M + (d - c - 1)\, E$ so that analysis of the two regimes is formally similar and differs only in the values of K and Φ.

TABLE 2. — VALUE OF $R_T \equiv (S_T^A/Y_T^A/S_T/Y_T) \cdot 100$ FOR NORMALIZED LDCs, WITH INITIAL INCOME = 100 AND CAPITAL INFLOW = 5

Period (year)	Burma[a] I[c]	Burma[a] II[d]	Colombia[a] I	Colombia[a] II	Costa Rica I	Costa Rica II	Ghana I	Ghana II	Honduras I	Honduras II	Israel I	Israel II
1	79.38	79.89	98.59	98.65	91.55	91.52	64.79	66.01	66.23	66.77	59.50	57.76
2	79.05	80.57	98.09	98.84	92.51	92.46	67.17	70.50	66.91	68.02	63.08	60.02
3	78.76	81.22	97.67	99.01	93.35	93.28	69.79	74.51	67.51	69.23	66.19	62.18
4	78.50	81.84	97.34	99.14	94.09	94.02	72.17	77.86	68.22	70.39	68.91	64.25
5	78.27	82.44	97.01	99.26	94.73	94.66	74.33	80.72	68.86	71.50	71.30	66.23
10	77.46	85.11	96.39	99.61	96.97	96.96	82.61	90.05	71.87	76.44	79.95	74.80
20	76.92	89.20	96.54	99.85	98.93	98.98	91.54	96.89	77.04	83.85	88.85	86.44
30	77.13	92.10	97.21	99.92	99.60	99.65	95.65	98.88	81.26	88.89	93.21	92.91

Period (year)	Mexico I	Mexico II	Philippines I	Philippines II	Puerto Rico[b] I	Puerto Rico[b] II	Portugal I	Portugal II	Taiwan I	Taiwan II	Uruguay I	Uruguay II
1	97.69	97.82	91.75	91.87	—	—	83.65	83.51	90.35	90.46	99.68	99.68
2	97.92	99.33	92.06	92.68	27.81	—	85.23	85.05	90.81	91.16	99.89	99.95
3	98.12	100.6	92.36	93.39	54.95	32.78	86.74	86.44	91.26	91.80	100.03	100.10
4	98.30	101.6	92.64	94.04	68.98	52.89	88.02	87.69	91.68	92.40	100.11	100.18
5	98.46	102.3	92.91	94.61	77.42	65.16	89.15	88.82	92.08	92.94	100.15	100.21
10	99.08	104.0	94.12	96.71	93.30	88.65	93.26	93.02	93.80	95.41	100.12	100.14
20	99.70	102.9	95.90	98.64	98.94	97.39	97.21	97.20	96.16	97.53	100.02	100.02
30	99.94	101.4	97.12	99.32	99.80	99.11	98.78	98.85	97.59	98.74	100.00	100.00

Notes: Several countries are omitted because of negative savings which would yield time data incommensurable with the positive ratios given elsewhere in the table. The output-capital ratio is taken as 0.3 for all economies start out with the same GNP and the same capital stock.
[a] Time path descends before ascending towards 1 again.
[b] Savings are negative initially.
[c] I refers to simulation with export, import sectors fixed in absolute size.
[d] II refers to simulation with export, import sectors fixed in ratio to GNP.

pare Israel and Mexico, for example). Moreover, if the country is a low saver initially and aid does reduce its savings ratio significantly, again the economy may or may not *quickly* be able to attain the aid ratio which would have prevailed without aid (compare Ghana, Honduras, and Israel after 30 years). On the other hand, recovery to near-unity can be rather quick; 5 years for Colombia, Costa Rica and Mexico, for example, where the initial effect of the aid was less drastic.

The above observations led us to examine more systematically what type of economy is most likely to be relatively immune from this radical dilemma with regard to domestic savings. To do this, we had to analyse the impact that shifts in the coefficients *a, b, c, d* of equation (4) and changes in the output-capital ratio would have on the comparison of with-aid to no-aid savings. (For this purpose, the time shapes of R_T given in figure 1 become relevant.) The following observations may be of interest.

In the early periods after aid is given, an economy that was initially saving a larger fraction of its GNP will be less affected by a given amount of aid, so that unambiguously in the immediate years following aid, any economy which is a high saver will fare better (i.e., have a higher R_T) than an economy which is a low saver. The same is true asymptotically as $T \rightarrow \infty$. In the intermediate period, however, if (and only if) growing GNP causes R_T to *dip further* before resuming its climb towards unity, for *those intermediate* years changes in parameters causing *increased* saving may actually *reduce* R_T relative to what it would have been. In only 2 of 15 cases (i.e., including 3 others not given in table 2) did R_T exhibit such a dip, so that it is likely in practice that anything that will increase the savings effort of the LDC will unambiguously, *for all subsequent time periods,* reduce the negative impact on savings.

We also gave attention to *b*, the marginal propensity to consume, and α, the output-capital ratio. An increase in *b* of 10% was found *in every case* to raise R_T unambiguously for all *T* so that the "dip effect" mentioned above, where present, was not large enough to outweigh the intermediate-term favorable aspects of increased *b*. The effect of an increase in α from 0.3 to 0.4 was also tabulated and it was found that short-run effects were not enough to outweigh the positive effects of an increase in α of this magnitude. However, in those countries where R_T took an initial dip before trending towards one, an increase in α *accentuated* this drop. The two cases are shown in figures 3.1 and 3.2.

FIGURE 3. — EFFECT OF CHANGE IN α (output-capital ratio) ON R_T

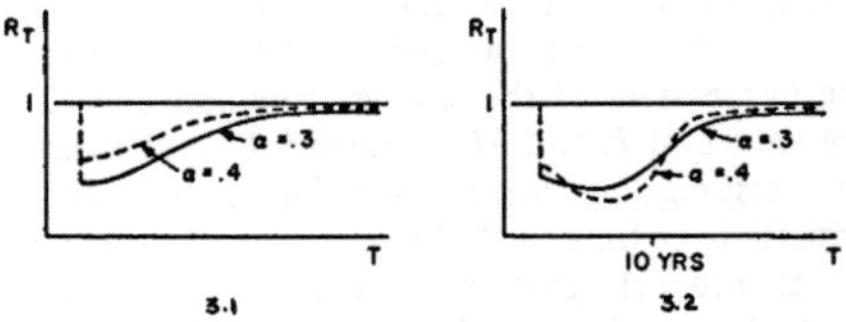

It should therefore be clear that any parametric change that will increase savings will work to lessen the negative effect of capital inflow on domestic savings. This is always true in the initial period (of 1 to 2 years) and also in the limit at $T \rightarrow \infty$. In the intermediate period, say, of $T = 3$, 15 years, there can be secondary effects which cancel out the initial impact; our simulations however suggest that this is unimportant.

III

In conclusion, it is indeed surprising that we have a rather large variety of possible outcomes even in our highly-simplified dynamic model. What does emerge, however, in relation to the radical economists' worry about the possibly adverse effects of capital inflows on domestic savings (and hence on "self-reliance") is that our analysis and simulation runs lend *some* support to this concern. At the same time, it is necessary to note that against this (mildly) negative aspect of capital inflows we must weigh the positive effects: for example, the increased levels of investment and income in the presence of the inflows. Thus no overall judgment on whether foreign aid has been beneficial or not to recipient countries can be reached without adding several other relevant dimensions of a social welfare function.

Finally, even if one wishes to confine oneself to the effects of foreign aid on domestic savings, our analysis makes it clear that it is necessary to look at the problem of the impact of foreign inflow on domestic savings in a dynamic framework as it is certainly possible for the usual, static, adverse impact of external capital to be eliminated quickly by a growing economy receiving the capital inflow.

REFERENCES

Bhagwati, J., *Amount and Sharing of Aid* (Washington, D.C.: Overseas Development Council, 1971).

———, *Foreign Trade Regimes and Economic Development: Anatomy and Consequences of Exchange Controls*, National Bureau of Economic Research, mimeographed, 1975; forthcoming from Columbia University Press, 1977.

Bhagwati, J., and E. Grinols, "Foreign Capital, Dependence, Destabilisation and Feasibility of Transition to Socialism," *Journal of Development Economics* (June 1975).

Griffin, K. B., "Foreign Capital, Domestic Savings and Economic Development," *Bulletin of the Oxford University Institute of Economics and Statistics* (May 1970).

Weisskopf, T., "The Impact of Foreign Capital Inflow on Domestic Savings in Underdeveloped Countries," *Journal of International Economics* (Feb. 1972).

Errata

Page 418, column 1, line 3: "over which" should read "at which".

Page 423, column 2, paragraph 2, line 7: "3, 15" should read "3 to 15".

Editor's Note

See also chapter 6 in J. N. Bhagwati, *Anatomy and Consequences of Exchange Control Regimes*, Cambridge, MA: Ballinger, 1978, for further analysis of the issue of foreign capital and domestic savings.

Reprinted from The Review of Economics and Statistics
Published for Harvard University. Copyright, 1979, by North-Holland Publishing Company
Vol. LXI, No. 1, February, 1979

FOREIGN CAPITAL, SAVINGS AND DEPENDENCE: A REPLY TO MR. WASOW*

Earl Grinols and Jagdish Bhagwati*

In essence, Mr. Wasow extends our basic exercise in two directions: (i) our assumption regarding the aid inflow is changed; and (ii) some measures of "dependence," which are related in no direct fashion to the effect of foreign aid on domestic savings (which was the focal point of our analysis) are presented and discussed in the framework of our Harrod-Domar type of model. It is difficult for us, however, to be enthusiastic about these extensions or to be alarmed by the occasional presentation of them as criticisms of our analysis.

I.

While we had assumed, in our detailed analysis, that the aid inflow was a constant value, Wasow thinks that we ought to have allowed for return outflows and that, if we had done so, the "savings recovery period" would have been greater with the aid inflow: see his argumentation based on his equation (15).

Now, it should have been evident from our analysis that we assumed that aid would be maintained at a constant "net" level. Focusing on net values is common practice, not merely in the analysis of aid but also in donor-recipient negotiations. Moreover, if we were to analyze outflows seriously, we would have to take into account varying terms and conditions on amortisation and interest payments, so that a simplistic relationship such as the one assumed by Wasow (see his equation (5)) may be objected to as adding little that is helpful to the analysis we had undertaken.

However, the conclusion that repayments would necessarily lengthen the savings recovery period in the Grinols-Bhagwati (1976) model is reached by Wasow with the aid of assumptions that are not carefully stated or examined so that the reader is likely to be mystified and misled.[1] In particular, we should note that his treatment of outflows affects our analysis at *two* levels. First, he assumes his repayments θ are specified by $\dot{\theta} = iF$ (equation (5)) so that augmenting F by the constant increment A (cases (i) and (ii) just before equation (12)) means a *growing* repayment (relative to repayment if A were zero), and $A - \Delta\theta$ (A less the induced additional repayment) is a declining function which becomes negative in finite time. Second, he assumes, by writing $S = a + b\,GDP + cF - b\theta$ and $I = S + F$ (equations (3) and (4)), that the marginal propensity to save out of reduced repayments is different from the marginal propensity to save out of F, but does not give any justification. (The usual forms that were estimated in the literature are $S = a + b\,GDP + c(F - \theta)$ and $I + \theta = S + F$.) His "comparison" therefore involves changing savings behavior *as well as* the net inflow profile.

To understand the full implications of this twofold amendment, consider the formulation where we modify our model (perfectly generally to account for Wasow's *and* other amendments as special cases) to write $S = a + bY + cF - d\theta$ and $I = S + (F - \theta)$. Solving for this amended Grinols-Bhagwati model, we find that the difference in savings due to a gross inflow change $\Delta F_T \equiv A_T$ coincident with a repayment change $\Delta\theta_T$ is now given by

$$S_T^A - S_T = c(A_T - \Delta\theta_T) + (c - d)\Delta\theta_T + b\sum_{i=0}^{T-1}(1 + \alpha b)^i \{\alpha(1 + c) \times (A_{T-i-1} - \Delta\theta_{T-i-1}) + \alpha(c - d)\Delta\theta_{T-i-1}\} \quad (1)$$

Received for publication April 3, 1978. Revision accepted for publication May 22, 1978.

* Cornell University and Massachusetts Institute of Technology, respectively.

Thanks are due to the National Science Foundation for partial financial support and to Richard Freeman for helpful conversations.

[1] Wasow's confusions arise from the fact that the inclusion of repayments, *in itself*, need not influence the effect of aid on domestic savings and that the treatment of outflows will affect our conclusions only insofar as it alters the system at the two different levels which we have distinguished in the text.

rather than by our original equation (10), with net inflows now being represented by $(A_T - \Delta\theta_T)$.

Now, it is easy to see that if $c = d$, i.e., the savings coefficient for repayments is identical with that for gross inflows, equation (1) above *does* reduce quite simply to our original equation (10), which has already been analyzed by us. And it also follows that, in this case, if we make the simple assumption that repayments are a constant fraction of the gross inflow so that the aid is kept at a constant net level, the absolute-savings recovery period will not change at all as a result of the introduction of the repayments. For, in this case, the effect on the absolute-savings recovery period is derivable merely by differentiating equation (13) in our original paper with respect to A. Hence, contrary to what the reader may infer from Wasow's argumentation, the inclusion of repayments in the Grinols-Bhagwati model does *not* necessarily imply a lengthening of the recovery period.

It appears that Wasow gets his specific conclusion, therefore, by assuming instead that $d = (b - 1)(\neq c)$ and that $\Delta\theta > 0$ for all T and is growing. In this case, equation (1) is replaced by

$$S_T^A - S_T = cA_T - b\Delta\theta_T + b\sum_{i=0}^{T-1}(1 + \alpha b)^i \times \{\alpha(1 + c)A_{T-i-1} - \alpha b\Delta\theta_{T-i-1}\}. \quad (2)$$

It is then easy to see that, *relative to equation (1) with* $\Delta\theta = 0$, equation (2) with $\Delta\theta$ contributing necessarily negatively implies that increments in repayments will necessarily keep $(S_T^A - S_T)$ below zero longer and hence extend the absolute-savings recovery time.

However, it is now clear that Wasow gets his result only because net inflows are declining in one case and constant in the other *and* simultaneously a different savings propensity has been imposed on repayments. If we were to compare like with like by assuming a common, given net aid profile, the only contribution that repayments make in equation (1), apart from their appearance in the net-inflows term, is through the terms $(c - d)\Delta\theta$. If, as we believe, it is proper to put $c = d$, this effect vanishes. If it is not, the effect will surely vary with the size and sign of $\Delta\theta$ and whether c is greater or smaller than d. As it happens, in the Wasow case where $d = (b - 1)$, c exceeds d for 14 out of 17 countries in our original paper and is positive in Wasow's own example of Puerto Rico. The effect of repayments in these cases, therefore, is to *shorten* the absolute-savings recovery time, if the net inflow profile is held constant!

It should be clear at this point why simulation runs are necessary. While analytical solutions can be worked out for a variety of values (our original paper shows the qualitative properties that any such solution must have), only the calculations for a *number* of countries can show which qualitative outcomes are likely to be relevant in practice and what numerical magnitudes are likely to be involved. Thus Wasow's strictures against our simulations are totally groundless.

So much for the introduction of outflows. However, Wasow would also like to replace the constant increment-of-aid assumption by three alternative, exponentially growing forms of aid inflow. His main reason for this preference is that our assumption is not "dynamic" since, in the steady state, the constant-aid assumption (naturally, and as must have been obvious from our mathematics, if not from the asymptotic curves in our diagrams) rules out any effect on the savings rate from the inflow of the additional aid. But this objection is hardly persuasive. One makes assumptions that make economic sense, not those that give results to one's taste. It would be marvelous if aid inflows were indeed growing exponentially; but they are not. And, steady state analysis, while interesting to Wasow, did not interest us at all since the problem of the effect of savings in the model, as formulated, ceases to be economically meaningful in the steady state: can one seriously believe that the savings and investment parameters in the model are sensibly assumed constant until the steady state is reached? A mere glance at our simulations, with particular reference to the time periods, would disabuse the reader of any doubts on this score.

The reader may further note that table 1 of Wasow shows d_1, the savings ratio as a measure of "dependence," at less than unity in the limit as long as the marginal propensity to save out of aid is less than unity and furthermore that this type of dependence can exist even when outflows are zero ($i = 0$). This strange result needs to be understood and seems to be explained as follows. In each of the three cases for which Wasow calculates d_1, borrowing is required to grow exponentially in the steady state. Since Wasow continues to use our "short-term" assumption of a fixed savings function for his steady state analysis, quite unjustifiably as we have just argued, he is therefore saddled with the fact that, with exponentially growing borrowing and constant trade balance as $\dot{Y}/Y$ approaches its steady state growth rate γ, borrowings as a percentage of $Y(B/Y)$ and hence total debt as a percentage of $Y(D/Y)$ and $\dot{D}/Y$ will also approach a positive constant.[2] Since the difference between B/Y

[2] Let F denote foreign capital inflows, G aid, B borrowings and E, M exports and imports. Then $F = (M - E) = G + B$. Setting $G = 0$ or an arbitrary constant (i.e., treating all additional inflows as if they were borrowed) does not affect steady state values. Hence from system dynamics we have

$$\gamma(t) \equiv \dot{Y}/Y = \alpha b + \alpha a/Y + [\alpha(1 + c) - i]B/Y$$

and a constant aid level divided by Y will be non-zero in the limit, holding savings to the fixed functional form will *always* imply a savings ratio (our R_T or Wasow's d_1) different from one so long as the difference in γ and the economy's natural growth rate αb *must* be made up by the production from borrowed funds!

In fact, we deliberately focused on analysis prior to the steady state because it makes little sense to consider the savings function as invariant in the "long run."[3] Therefore, rather than play around with Wasow-type variations in our model, we think it more meaningful to consider other "short-term" questions within the framework of our model. Thus, in a different exercise, Bhagwati and Grinols (1975), we have considered within the framework of the same basic Harrod-Domar type of model a different and possibly more meaningful type of vulnerability that may arise from the receipt of foreign aid: namely, that the economy, having adjusted to higher levels of consumption and/or investment during the periods of aid inflow, could be "disrupted" by suspension of such inflow for political reasons, as in the case of Chile under Allende.

(see Wasow's equation (6)). In the limit γ is a constant, $\alpha a/Y$ is zero and B/Y can be solved for.

[3] Since the borrowing country's capacity for servicing debt bounds its ability to borrow, aggregate debt in the long run will be less than its service capacity (SC) divided by the one period interest rate. Making a simplistic steady state assumption that SC grows at the same rate as the economy ($SC = \delta Y$ for small δ between zero and one) implies only that $0 \leq D \leq \delta/i\ Y$ in the limit. To argue further that D/Y approaches some specific value in $[0, \delta/i]$ for any country (based solely on a fixed borrowing and repayment rule) and that we should calculate this number for policy purposes is not persuasive to us.

II.

Finally, Wasow's additional measures of dependence, d_2 through d_5, must be treated with skepticism. A close inspection will reveal that they are related to the productivity of foreign aid relative to its interest cost. In fact, for measure d_5 in Wasow's cases (i) and (iii), c does not even enter the formula.[4] Dependence defined in terms of d_2 through d_5 thus merely reveals the true but obvious proposition that if a borrower does not pay back more than interest costs, continued borrowing will leave him with a growing debt position regardless of what fraction between zero and one is put to productive use.[5]

REFERENCES

Bhagwati, Jagdish, and Earl Grinols, "Foreign Capital, Dependence, Destabilization and Feasibility of Transition to Socialism," *Journal of Development Economics* 2 (June 1975), 85–98.

Grinols, Earl, and Jagdish Bhagwati, "Foreign Capital, Savings and Dependence," this REVIEW (Nov. 1976).

Wasow, Bernard, "Savings and Dependence with Externally Financed Growth," this REVIEW, this issue (Feb. 1979).

[4] The meaning of d_2 and d_3 as measures of dependence is also unclear since even with costless borrowing ($i = 0$) and full investment of proceeds ($c = 0$) they show non-zero levels of dependence. At best there is a problem of choosing the origin to better relate them to true measures of dependence.

[5] $\theta = iF$ implies that repayments grow only as fast as the interest on new borrowings so that $\dot{D} = F$. Of course, even though everything in a steady state grows at the same exponential rate and one can therefore predict a priori a growing debt position at the rate of net borrowing, one needs a model to calculate relative magnitudes.

Journal of International Economics 13 (1982) 353–364. North-Holland Publishing Company

IMMISERIZING TRANSFERS FROM ABROAD

Richard A. BRECHER

Carleton University, Ottawa, Ontario K1S 5B6, Canada

Jagdish N. BHAGWATI*

Columbia University, New York, NY 10027, USA

Received November 1981, revised version received July 1982

This paper shows that an international transfer payment may paradoxically immiserize the recipient country (or increase the donor country's welfare), even when world markets are stable, despite the traditional view that such a paradox theoretically requires market instability. To demonstrate this paradoxical possibility, the paper extends the conventional trade-theoretic analysis to admit exogenous distortions created by tax-cum-subsidies in domestic production, or endogenous distortions due to 'additionality' requirements imposed by the donor on the recipient. This analysis of immiserizing transfers from abroad immediately suggests significant implications for important policy issues, including the evaluation of real benefits from foreign aid.

1. Introduction

It is well known from Leontief (1936), Mundell (1960), and Samuelson (1947, p. 29; 1952) that immiserizing transfers from abroad require market instability, unlike Bhagwati's (1958) case of immiserizing growth. Should one therefore discard the immiserizing-transfer paradox as a curiosum?

The instability implied by this paradox has been demonstrated in the case of free trade with no domestic distortions. In reality, however, the analyst must confront two other possibilities: (1) transfers may take place in the presence of (exogenously given) distortions, as in Samuelson's (1954) positive analysis of transfer-induced changes in the terms of trade in the presence of tariffs;[1] and (2) acceptance of the transfers itself may impose distortions in the transferee (i.e. transfer-receiving country), as when aid from the transferor (i.e. transfer-providing country) is accompanied by 'additionality' requirements which interfere with efficient allocation of domestic resources.

Once these realistic possibilities are admitted, we can show that market

*Comments and suggestions from Tatsuo Hatta, J. Peter Neary, Paul A. Samuelson, and anonymous referees are gratefully acknowledged. Thanks are due to the National Science Foundation Grant No. 5-24718 for partial financial support of the research underlying this paper.

[1]**Interestingly, Samuelson does not extend this analysis to the welfare impact of transfers in the presence of tariffs in this second paper of his pioneering two-paper investigation of the transfer problem.**

instability is not required for the paradox of immiserizing transfers from abroad. Section 2 reviews the welfare effects of transfers in the standard (distortion-free) case. In section 3, immiserizing transfers are considered in the presence of exogenously given distortions. Section 4 analyzes the possibility of immiserization by distortion-inducing transfers from abroad. Concluding remarks are offered in section 5.

2. Distortion-free transfers reviewed

Consider the standard model of a two-commodity world, with two countries engaging in free international trade, in the absence of domestic distortions. Throughout the analysis, for simplicity of exposition, each country is assumed to be incompletely specialized in both production and consumption of commodities 1 and 2.

The initial (pre-transfer) equilibrium is illustrated in fig. 1. The home country produces at point P on the production-possibility frontier HH', consumes at point C on the community-indifference curve hh', and trades from point P to point C at the (domestic and international) commodity–price

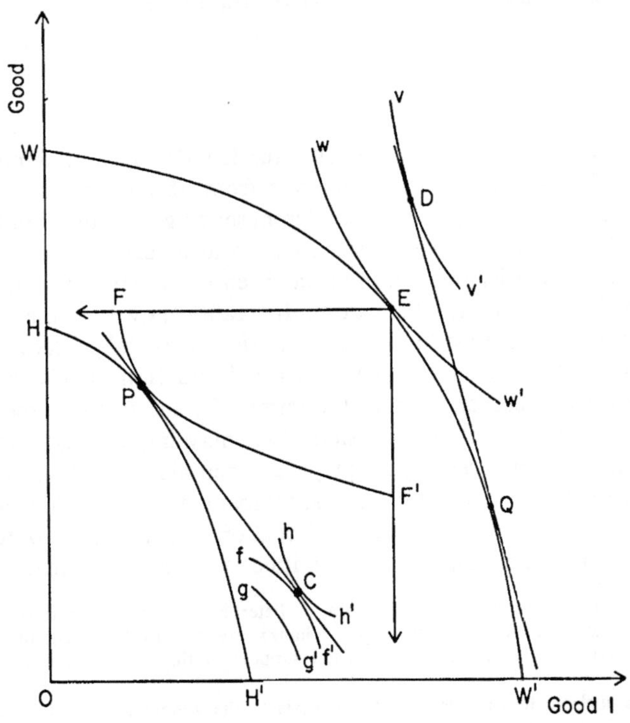

Fig. 1

ratio given by the slope of line *PC*. The foreign country also respectively produces and consumes at points *P* and *C* — on production-possibility frontier *FF′* and community-indifference curve *ff′* — and trades between these two points.

For the world as a whole, production initially takes place at point *E*, on the world's production-possibility frontier *WW′*. Following a well-known procedure, this frontier is traced by the origin (*E*) of the quadrant *FEF′* as this quadrant is moved to make curve *FF′* slide continuously along curve *HH′*, while curves *FF′* and *HH′* are kept always tangent to each other (as at point *P*) with their corresponding axes parallel.[2] As a result of this construction, each point (say *E*) on curve *WW′* has the same slope as the corresponding point (*P*) on curves *FF′* and *HH′*, within the region of incomplete specialization for both countries.

World consumption also occurs initially at point *E*, on the curve *ww′*, which is a Scitovsky frontier[3] for the world as a whole. This frontier is traced by the origin (*E*) of quadrant *FEF′* as this quadrant is moved to make curve *ff′* slide continuously along curve *hh′*, while curves *ff′* and *hh′* are kept always tangent to each other (as at point *C*) with their corresponding axes parallel. As a consequence of this construction, each point (say *E*) on curve *ww′* has the same slope as the corresponding point (*C*) on the curves *ff′* and *hh′*. Curve *ww′* is a type of indifference curve for the world as a whole.

An entire map of (non-intersecting) Scitovsky frontiers (including curve *vv′*) can be constructed by repeating the foregoing procedure for alternative indifference curves (such as *gg′*) of the foreign country, given always the same indifference curve (*hh′*) of the home country. Thus, in moving to successively higher frontiers (say from *ww′* to *vv′*), foreign welfare correspondingly increases, while home welfare remains constant.

Suppose now that the foreign country makes an international transfer which worsens the home terms of trade. Imagine hypothetically what would happen if the net effect on home welfare was nil. In fig. 1 this situation can be represented for the world as a whole by having production and consumption shift respectively to points *Q* and *D*, with the new world–price ratio given by line *DQ*. Notice, however, that the world must now have an excess supply of good 1, the home importable.

Therefore, given stability of equilibrium, the home terms of trade must utlimately improve toward (without actually reaching) their initial value (defined by the slope at *E*). This improvement must then raise home welfare above the pre-transfer level.[4] By similar reasoning, the equilibrium level of

[2]See Graaff (1957, ch. II).

[3]For details of this frontier and its derivation, see Scitovsky (1942) and Graaff (1957, ch. III).

[4]The final equilibrium for the world as a whole occurs where a Scitovsky frontier from an entirely new map (corresponding to the higher level of home welfare) is tangent to curve *WW′* between points *E* and *Q*.

foreign welfare must be reduced by the transfer. As suggested by the discussion in fig. 1, the present analysis applies equally well for 'large' as well as 'small' transfers.

3. Transfers in the presence of distortions

In this section, the example of an ad valorem tax-cum-subsidy in home production is analyzed explicitly. Without diminishing the main thrust of the argument, however, the analysis can be extended readily to any case in which the marginal rate of substitution in production and/or consumption differs between countries.

The initial equilibrium is illustrated in fig. 2, which has been labeled similarly to fig. 1 to enable their straightforward comparison. The essential difference arises from the home tax-cum-subsidy, which causes a divergence between the home producer–price ratio (given by the slope of curve HH' at point P) and the world–price ratio (given by the common slope of line PC and curve FF' at point P) in fig. 2. Consequently, in deriving curve WW', the

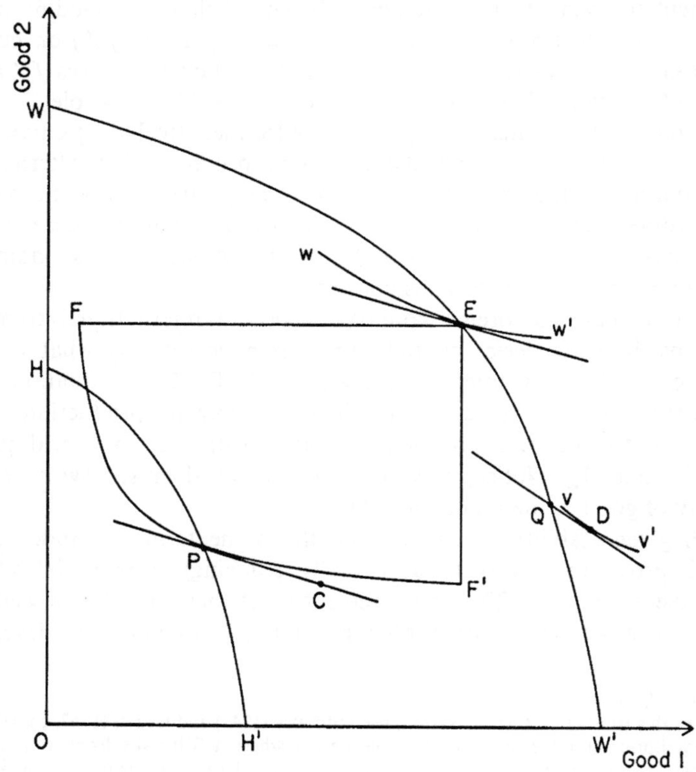

Fig. 2

method described in section 2 must now be modified, to keep a constant proportional wedge between the slopes of curves FF' and HH'. For this reason, the slope at each point (say E) on curve WW' clearly lies between the slopes at the corresponding point (P) on curves FF' and HH'.[5] For the world as a whole, production and consumption take place at point E, where curve WW' is cut by a Scitovsky frontier (ww') with a slope equaling the world-price ratio. To avoid cluttering the diagram, the indifference curves ff' and hh' tangent to line PC at point C are not shown in fig. 2.

Once again, suppose that the foreign country makes an international transfer that worsens the home terms of trade,[6] and imagine hypothetically what would happen if home welfare remains constant. In fig. 2, world production and consumption correspondingly move to (say) points Q and D, respectively. If point D lies southeast of point Q, as drawn, there is now a world excess demand for good 1. Thus, world markets ultimately clear by causing a further deterioration in the home terms of trade, and home welfare hence must fall below the pre-transfer level.

For this possibility to occur, it is clear from a comparison of points D and E in fig. 2 that the home importable must be an inferior good for the world as a whole. In fact, this inferiority must exist specifically in the foreign country, since the home country remains on its same indifference curve (by construction) as world consumption moves from point E to point D. The fact that this move creates an excess world demand for the home importable is not inconsistent with stability of equilibrium, because the rise in the relative price of this good is accompanied by the international purchasing-power transfer.[7] By similar reasoning, the foreign country can raise its own welfare by making a transfer to the home country, provided that the foreign exportable is inferior in home consumption.

There is an intuitively plausible explanation for the immiserizing-transfer paradox in fig. 2. A deterioration in the home terms of trade leads (as usual)

[5]Also, curve WW' now might fail to be strictly concave to the origin, despite the strict concavity assumed for curves FF' and HH' individually. Such failure, however, would not qualitatively affect the present analysis.

[6]As long as the relative price of the home importable is greater for home producers than for international transactions, a rise in the relative price of this good in world markets will unambiguously tend (ceteris paribus) to reduce home welfare. For conditions determining the direction of transfer-induced changes in the international terms of trade, see Mundell (1960) and Samuelson (1952, 1954).

[7]For example, assuming a 'small' transfer in an initially transfer-free situation (although the analysis in fig. 2 is not restricted to this simple case), it is well known that stability requires $e+e^{*}>1$, where e and e^{*} denote the total elasticity of import demand with respect to price for the home and foreign countries, respectively. Given no domestic distortions in the foreign country, a standard decomposition of e^{*} allows the stability condition to be written as $e+\varepsilon^{*}+m^{*}>1$, where ε^{*} (>0) and m^{*} denote the compensated (constant-utility) elasticity of import demand with respect to price and the marginal propensity to consume the importable, respectively, for the foreign country. If $m^{*}>1$ because the home importable is inferior in foreign consumption, then stability is ensured if e is either positive (as usually assumed) or not too negative. For further details see the appendix.

to an increased output of the home importable. This commodity, however, is already 'overproduced' at home, because of the distortive tax-cum-subsidy. Thus, the change in relative prices has the additional effect of exacerbating the existing 'overproduction'. This extra cost may be enough to ensure a decline in welfare for the transfer-receiving country.

Since the foregoing possibilities of paradoxical changes in welfare require inferiority in national consumption,[8] three additional remarks are in order. Because certain products (say food items) may well be inferior even for individual consumers, inferiority at the national level cannot be automatically dismissed as implausible. Furthermore, even when each good is normal for every individual, national consumption may still exhibit inferiority if the construction of community-indifference curves involves redistribution of income among individuals (with possibly different tastes) along the lines of (say) Samuelson (1956). Thus, the welfare paradoxes of the present section are more than simply curiosa.

4. Distortion-inducing transfers

A classic instance where transfers *create* distortions arises when aid is given. For example, the concern that food aid may adversely affect the transferee's production of food — as contended by Schultz (1960) in a classic contribution — has led donors to press for governmental reallocation of investment in favor of agriculture. Also, donor countries have sought to impose additionality requirements on imports, in response to balance-of-payments concerns or pressure from exporters.

Thus, we distinguish between two central ways in which the country receiving the transfer may be faced with a transfer-induced distortion in the Mundell–Samuelson analysis. In particular, this country may have to (1) shift production away from its efficient allocation, and (2) increase the level of imports to meet an additionality requirement. Although we assume a 'small' country for simplicity of exposition, the analysis readily extends to the large-country case.

4.1. Production distortion

Suppose, in fig. 3, that a small country, with production-possibility frontier HH', faces a fixed world–price ratio given by the slope of line AP (parallel to lines BK, MN, and RP'). Efficiency will imply home production at point P.

[8]Similarly, if the production tax-cum-subsidy were altered to let the relative price of the second good be larger (rather than smaller) for home producers than for world consumers and international transactions in a modified version of fig. 2, the transfer could have a paradoxical effect on welfare in each country only if good 2 is inferior in the other country, as confirmed by the appendix.

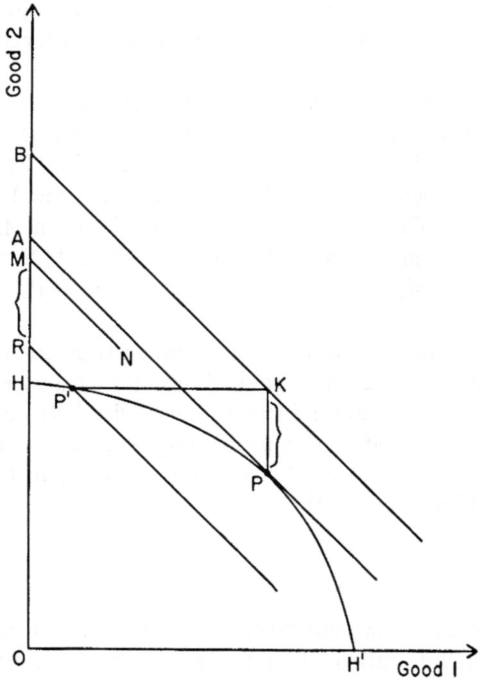

Fig. 3

To this situation, add now a transfer receipt represented by the length AB ($=PK=MR$) in terms of commodity 2 (say food). If this transfer were unconstrained, national expenditure would exceed national income by the length AB, and evidently the augmented social budget line (BK) would rule out immiserization of the home country.

Suppose, however, that the foreign country (say a food-aid donor) which provides the transfer is concerned about home output of good 2, and the condition for receiving the transfer is that production of this good be raised in the transferee. This condition can be satisfied at least cost by a production subsidy for good 2, according to the theory of non-economic objectives [e.g. Johnson (1965)]. Evidently, then, it is easy to imagine the cost of the production distortion (imposed by the transferor on the transferee) possibly outweighing the gain that would occur without the simultaneous imposition of this distortion. Thus, in principle, immiserization due to distortion-inducing transfers from abroad cannot be ruled out, and is consistent with stability (which is guaranteed by the small-country assumption).

But would such a conclusion still be valid if we were to impose the restriction that the increment in domestic production not exceed the transfer (e.g. that the food-production increase demanded by the donor not exceed the food supplied as aid)? This would seem to be a natural restriction to impose.[9]

Even with this restriction, we can easily establish that the transferee may be immiserized by the transfer. In fig. 3 the economy is forced by the conditions imposed by the transferor to shift production from point P to point P', so that production of good 2 increases by the length PK, the amount of the transfer. The national income line falls from AP to RP', and the national expenditure line is raised by the transfer to MN. Since line MN lies below the pre-transfer national-expenditure line AP, immiserization ensues.

A little reflection will demonstrate that this immiserization is caused by the production loss outweighing the gain from the transfer. Hence, the probability of such immiserization increases with the loss imposed by any given shift in production. That is, this probability will vary inversely with the ease with which production can be shifted from one good to the other along the production-possibility frontier.[10]

4.1. Trade distortion

However, consider now the case where the transferor imposes an *import* additionality requirement, rather than the production additionality of the foregoing subsection. In the present case, the theory of non-economic objectives dictates that the least-cost way of meeting the new target is to use an import subsidy. Again, it should be possible for the distortive cost of such a transfer-induced subsidy to exceed the gain from the transfer, leaving the transferee immiserized, if the additionality is not constrained to the value of the transfer.

But if this constraint is imposed so that the additional import level must not exceed the transfer, then we can show that the transferee *cannot* be immiserized, unlike in the production-additionality case. In fig. 4 the home economy can retain productive efficiency (at point P), absorb the transfer represented by the length BA in terms of good 2, and raise imports by the required increment (equal to length CC') by simply adopting a consumption subsidy in favor of the importable good 2. As the home consumption point moves from C to C' in this way, the transferee necessarily reaches a higher community-indifference curve despite the distortive cost of the subsidy,

[9]It could be appropriately expressed in terms of present discounted values if the transfer must eventually be repaid.

[10]In the present case, the likelihood of transfer-induced immiserization would be less for a large country than for a small one, because the requirement to increase production of the importable would tend to lessen the deterioration (or augment the improvement) in the transferee's terms of trade.

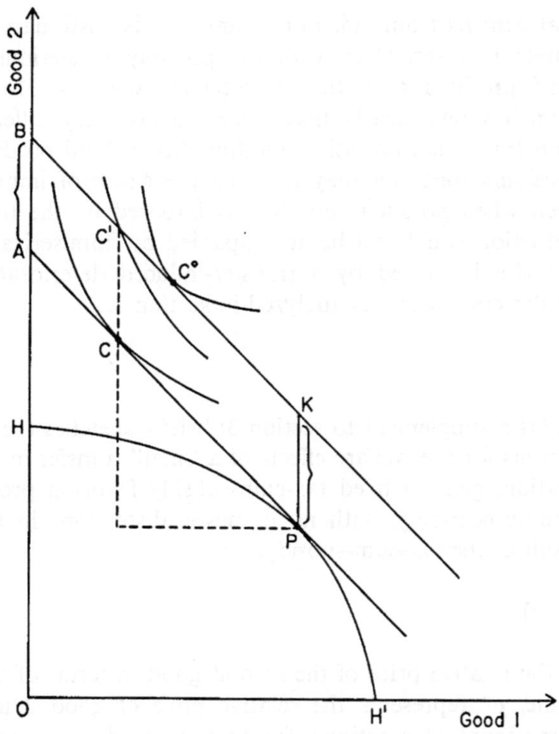

Fig. 4

although home welfare would be still greater at point C^0 which is achievable only with a distortion-free transfer.

Recall, however, that a consumption subsidy is not even the best method for achieving the additionality requirement in terms of imports. As noted already, the least-cost policy for satisfying this requirement is an import subsidy. Thus, since a (sub-optimal) consumption subsidy to achieve the import-additionality target cannot leave the transferee immiserized, then surely an (optimal) import subsidy to attain the same target must also preclude the possibility of transfer-induced immiserization.[11]

5. Concluding remarks

While this paper has focused on the possibility of immiserizing transfers from abroad, the analysis has immediate implications for issues such as the

[11]This possibility could arise, however, in the large-country case, because the import subsidy would augment the deterioration (or lessen the improvement) in the transferee's terms of trade.

evaluation of real benefits from aid. For example, it is customary in the aid literature to equate immiserization with the possibly deleterious effects of food aid on food production in the aid-receiving country. However, our analysis in section 4 shows clearly that these are two very different issues, and in fact demonstrates that imposing additionality in food production as a condition for receiving food aid may itself be the cause of immiserization. Furthermore, even when no such condition is imposed by the transferor, a rise in food production could still be accompanied by immiserization of the transferee, if this rise is caused by a transfer-induced deterioration of the terms of trade under circumstances analyzed in section 3.

Appendix

This appendix (as a supplement to section 3) briefly sketches the derivation of precise expressions for the welfare effects of a 'small' transfer in an initially transfer-free situation, given a fixed tax-cum-subsidy favoring production of good 1 in the home economy, with no domestic distortions in the foreign country. As a result of the tax-cum-subsidy,

$$p=p^*(1-\tau), \tag{A1}$$

where p denotes the relative price of the second good in terms of the first for producers at home; p^* represents the relative price of good 2 in terms of good 1 for international transactions, for foreign producers, and (in both countries) for all consumers; while τ is a constant, with $0<\tau<1$.

Balanced international trade implies

$$C_1+p^*C_2=X_1+p^*X_2+T, \tag{A2}$$

where C_i and X_i, respectively, denote home consumption and home production of good i for $i=1,2$; and T (initially equal to zero) represents the real value of the transfer in terms of the first good. Using eqs. (A1) and (A2), given a social welfare function $U(C_1,C_2)$ with the usual properties for the home country, we have:

$$\mathrm{d}U/\mathrm{d}T=1+[E_2+p^*\tau(1-\tau)(\mathrm{d}X_2/\mathrm{d}p)]\,\mathrm{d}p^*/\mathrm{d}T, \tag{A3}$$

where $E_2 \equiv X_2-C_2>0$; $\mathrm{d}X_1/\mathrm{d}p+p\mathrm{d}X_2/\mathrm{d}p=0$ by profit maximization (with $\mathrm{d}X_2/\mathrm{d}p>0$ as usual); $p^*=U_2/U_1$ (with $U_i \equiv \partial U/\partial C_i>0$ for $i=1,2$) by welfare maximization; and, without loss of generality, $U_1=1$ initially.

According to a well-known result [see Mundell (1960)],

$$\mathrm{d}p^*/\mathrm{d}T=(1-m_1-m_2^*)/(e_1+e_2^*-1)E_2, \tag{A4}$$

where e_1 and m_1 denote the total price elasticity of demand for imports of good 1 and the marginal propensity to consume the first good, respectively, for the home country; e_2^* and m_2^* represent (for good 2) the corresponding variables of the foreign country; and, as usual, $e_1+e_2^*-1>0$ for stability. An equivalent way of writing this stability condition is

$$\varepsilon_1+\varepsilon_2^*-m_1^*+m_1[1+p^*\tau(1-\tau)(\mathrm{d}X_2/\mathrm{d}p)/E_2]>0, \tag{A5}$$

where, as a well-known result, $1-m_2^*=m_1^*$, which denotes the foreign marginal propensity to consume good 1; ε_1 (>0) and ε_2^* (>0) represent the compensated elasticity of import demand with respect to price for the home and foreign countries, respectively; $\varepsilon_2^*+m_2^*=e_2^*$ by a well-known decomposition; and, by a similar decomposition (which could be readily verified):

$$e_1=\varepsilon_1+m_1[1+p^*\tau(1-\tau)(\mathrm{d}X_2/\mathrm{d}p)/E_2].$$

Using these decompositions with eqs. (A3) and (A4), we get:

$$\mathrm{d}U/\mathrm{d}T=[\varepsilon_1+\varepsilon_2^*+m_1^*p^*\tau(1-\tau)(\mathrm{d}X_2/\mathrm{d}p)/E_2]/(e_1+e_2^*-1). \tag{A6}$$

Similarly, it is straightforward to derive

$$\mathrm{d}U^*/\mathrm{d}T=-[\varepsilon_1+\varepsilon_2^*+m_1p^*\tau(1-\tau)(dX_2/\mathrm{d}p)/E_2]/(e_1+e_2^*-1), \tag{A7}$$

where U^* denotes social welfare of the foreign country.

From eq. (A6), it is clear that $\mathrm{d}U/\mathrm{d}T$ can be negative if and only if m_1^* is sufficiently negative (i.e. the home importable is sufficiently inferior in foreign consumption). Similarly, from eq. (A7), $\mathrm{d}U^*/\mathrm{d}T>0$ if and only if m_1 is sufficiently negative. To see that these paradoxical changes in welfare can both hold simultaneously under stable conditions, start by setting m_1 at a level that is sufficiently negative to guarantee $\mathrm{d}U^*/\mathrm{d}T>0$. Given the chosen value of m_1, next let m_1^* be sufficiently negative to both ensure $\mathrm{d}U/\mathrm{d}T<0$ and satisfy the stability condition (A5).

If instead $\tau<0$, the welfare paradoxes require inferiority of the second (rather than the first) good. This result emerges readily when eqs. (A6) and (A7), respectively, are manipulated to yield:

$$\mathrm{d}U/\mathrm{d}T=[\varepsilon_1^c C_1/p^*+p(\mathrm{d}X_2/\mathrm{d}p)(1-m_2^*\tau)]/(e_1+e_2^*-1)E_2, \tag{A6'}$$

$$\mathrm{d}U^*/\mathrm{d}T=-[\varepsilon_1^c C_1/p^*+p(\mathrm{d}X_2/\mathrm{d}p)(1-m_2\tau)]/(e_1+e_2^*-1)E_2, \tag{A7'}$$

using the straightforward decomposition which states that $\varepsilon_1=\varepsilon_1^c C_1/(C_1-X_1)$

$+\varepsilon_1^x X_1/(C_1-X_1)$ where ε_1^c (>0) and ε_1^x (>0) denote the compensated elasticity of C_1 and the total elasticity of X_1, respectively, with respect to price. When $\tau<0$, $\mathrm{d}U/\mathrm{d}T<0$ in eq. (A6′) implies $m_2^*<0$, whereas $m_2<0$ in eq. (A7′) if $\mathrm{d}U^*/\mathrm{d}T>0$.

References

Bhagwati, Jagdish N., 1958, Immiserizing growth: A geometrical note, Review of Economic Studies 25, 201–205.

Graaff, J. de V., 1957, Theoretical welfare economics (Cambridge University Press).

Johnson, Harry G., 1965, Optimal trade intervention in the presence of domestic distortions, in: Robert E. Baldwin et al., eds., Trade, growth and the balance of payments: Essays in honor of Gottfried Haberler (Rand McNally, Chicago, Illinois).

Leontief, Wassily, 1936, Note on the pure theory of capital transfer, in: Explorations in economics: Notes and essays contributed in honor of F.W. Taussig (McGraw-Hill, New York).

Mundell, Robert A., 1960, The pure theory of international trade, American Economic Review 50, 67–110.

Samuelson, Paul A., 1947, Foundations of economic analysis (Harvard University Press, Cambridge, Mass).

Samuelson, Paul, A., 1952, The transfer problem and transport costs: The terms of trade when impediments are absent, Economic Journal 62, 278–304.

Samuelson, Paul A., 1954, The transfer problem and transport costs, II: Analysis of effects of trade impediments, Economic Journal 64, 264–289.

Samuelson, Paul A., 1956, Social indifference curves, Quarterly Journal of Economics 70, 1–22.

Schultz, T.W., 1960, Value of U.S. farm surpluses to underdeveloped countries, Journal of Farm Economics 42, 1019–1030.

Scitovsky, Tibor de, 1942, A reconsideration of the theory of tariffs, Review of Economic Studies 9, 89–110.

Editor's Note

For an analysis of international transfers under foreign ownership of factors see essay 54 in this volume (coauthored by R. A. Brecher) and also the more recent papers cited in the editor's note to this essay.

Sankhyā : The Indian Journal of Statistics
1978, Volume 40, Series D, Pt. 2, pp. 99–117.

DEVALUATION IN A SMALL ECONOMY WITH FLEXIBLE AND RIGID, REAL AND NOMINAL, PRICES*

By JAGDISH N. BHAGWATI
Massachusetts Institute of Technology

0. Introduction

In this paper, we plan to discuss the impact of a devaluation in a small economy with given international prices of the traded goods. The model used, however, permits the two traded goods to be treated throughout the analysis *as if* they were one good : their relative prices do not shift and their factor-ratios remain equal[1]. There is a third, non-traded good, so that this is a strong version of the so-called Salter model, popularised by many theorists such as Trevor Swan and Ivor Pearce (cf. Swan, 1963; Pearce, 1961).

In the analysis that follows, we distinguish two steps. First, under alternative assumptions, the "primary" impact of the devaluation in such an economy on the excess demand for tradeables (i.e. a deficit or a surplus in balance of payments) and for nontradeables is worked out and reported in Section 1. Next, the analysis of the elimination of such disequilibrium is carried out in Section 2.

Section 1 distinguishes among two basic assumptions subject to which the impact-disequilibrium effects of a devaluation are worked out :

Assumption I : that, as devaluation raises the (absolute) domestic price of the tradeables, the domestic price of the nontradeables remains fixed or rises but by less than the devaluation, so that the initial impact of the devaluation is to raise the domestic, *relative* price of the tradeables in terms of non tradeables; and

Assumption II : that, as devaluation raises the (absolute) domestic price of the tradeables, the money wages in the tradeables sector remain fixed or rise but by less than the price of the tradeables.

---

*The author is Ford International Professor of Economics at the Massachusetts Institute of Technology. Research on the paper has been supported by the National Science Foundation. This paper is a revised version of MIT Economics Working Paper No. 157, December 1975, and has profited from the comments of David Richardson, Richard Brecher and a referee.

[1]The complications introduced by the presence of three goods and two factors, if the two traded goods are not effectively reduced to one, have been considered in Berglas and Razin (1973).

Under each of Assumptions I and II, one can work out the impact of this change on the excess demands for tradeables and nontradeables, by assuming that the economy adjusts production and consumption to the price changes implied by the assumption made. Under Assumption I, where devaluation implies a rise in the domestic, relative price of the tradeables, the usual convexity and competitive assumptions will thus produce an excess demand for nontradeables and an excess supply of tradeables, with wages and rentals to factors adjusting to the changed commodity prices. Under Assumption II, where the devaluation-induced change in money wages is instead predetermined, the production and consumption effects of the devaluation will be determined *along with* the change in the commodity price-ratio (which should itself be a consequence of the adjustments initiated by the devaluation) : and the latter may turn out to imply either a rise *or* a fall in the relative price of the tradeables and hence an excess supply of tradeables *or* of nontradeables.

Once the primary impact on commodity and factor prices, and the consequence for excess demands for the commodities is worked out under either of the two basic assumptions in Section I, the analysis turns in Section 2 to eliminating these excess demands and examining the property of the equilibrium reached. This analysis, in turn, can be carried out by assuming *either* that all money wages and prices are fully flexible at this stage *or* that the (absolute) price of nontradeables (Assumption I) or the money wage (Assumption II) will be rigid at the level defined for analyzing the primary impact *or* most plausibly, that money wages and prices will be flexible upwards but *not* downwards. Further, we will distinguish between equilibria reached under assumptions of active and passive governmental policy.

Before we begin the analysis, let us introduce some notation. Let P_T and P_{NT} be the domestic prices of the tradeables and the nontradeables, π the exchange rate, and P_T^F the foreign prices of the tradeables so that $P_T^F.\pi = P_T$. The two factors of production, when explicitly considered, will be K and L. The money wage will be w_m, and the money rental r_m.

1. Primary impact of devaluation on excess demands for commodities

We consider each of Assumptions I and II, in turn.

A : *Assumption* I. Recall that, given the international terms of trade and the exchange rate devaluation, the domestic price of the tradeables (P_T) must rise by the amount of the devaluation. By Assumption I, the primary induced-effect of this price-rise in the tradeables sector is, *not* on money wages or rentals, but on the price of the nontradeables. But this induced rise in the price of the nontradeables is less than proportionate to that of the tradeables; and, in the limiting case, the nontradeable price may be assumed constant. Then the primary effect of the devaluation is to raise the domestic relative price of the tradeables (P_T/P_{NT}).

1. *"Normal" case.* If we now make the standard convexity assumptions on production plus the assumption of a social utility function, the increase in P_T/P_{NT} from its value at (Q, C) to Q^1C^1 will raise the production of tradeables to Q^1 and reduce their consumption-unless nontradeables are strongly inferior in consumption-to C^1 in Figure 1. The primary impact of the

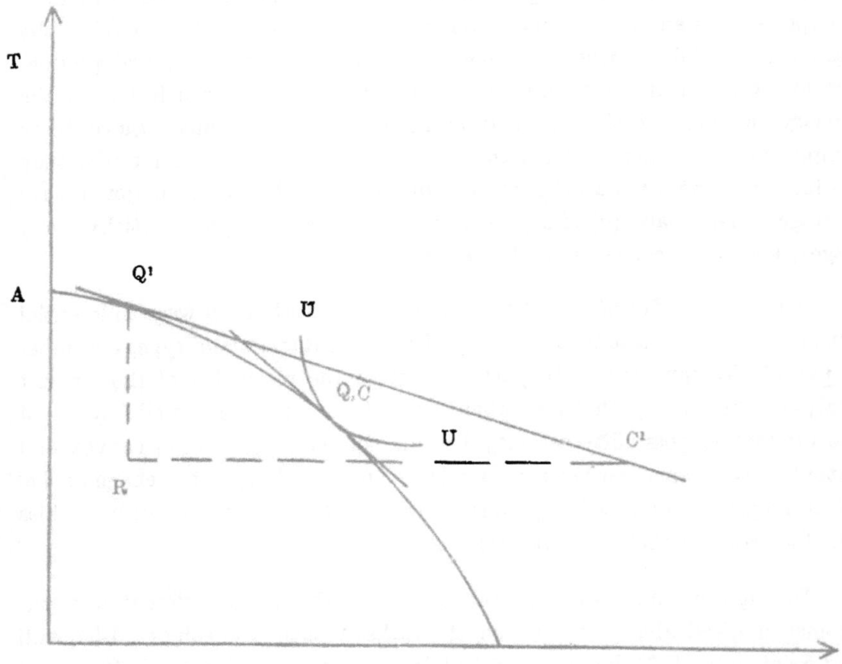

Figure 1

devaluation, with production and consumption adjusting to the primary change in the relative commodity price-ratio (P_T/P_{NT}), is then to create an excess supply of tradeables (Q^1R) and excess demand for nontradeables (C^1R) or, in other words, a trade surplus (Q^1R) and domestic inflationary pressure.

The *ultimate* outcome, as distinct from the primary impact stated here on Assumption I, will be analyzed in Section 2. Note here, however, that this primary impact does imply that the *average* domestic price-*level* has gone up and hence, if we assume that the domestic money supply must increase so as to accommodate this, we must correspondingly assume that it is so increased by active policy : this is however a complication that needs to be considered fully only when we consider the return to full equilibrium in Section 2 under alternative assumptions.

2. *Factor market rigidities and income-distributional issues.* Prior to doing that, however, for this "normal" case of the primary impact of a devaluation, we must note that, in a typical developing country, there may be a number of imperfections and distortions in the economy, as also inability to affect the market-imputed distribution of income, so as to give rise to "perverse" production and consumption responses which would reverse the conclusion on the primary outcome of the devaluation in our small economy. Since these complications are familiar from the pure theory of international trade, they are illustrated here *via* a brief analysis of only the following major cases : (i) wage differentials; (ii) sticky real wages; (iii) sector-specific sticky, real wages; and (iv) income-distributional effects.

(i) *Wage differentials.* Where there is a distortionary wage differential between the two sectors, of a Hagen-Bhagwati-Ramaswami type, a number of pathologies can arise.[2] In particular, from the viewpoint of the present analysis, the two pathologies that interest us are the possibility that the production possibility set may become concave rather than convex and output may change perversely to relative (commodity) price change : i.e. when the production possibility set is convex (concave), the output of tradeables will fall (rise) as their relative price rises.

Distinguish now two possibilities : where the wage differential works against nontradeables; and where it works against tradeables. Bhagwati and Srinivasan (1971) have established the conditions under which the wage differential will lead to convex or concave production possibility sets, and to normal or perverse (in the sense just discussed) production responses to commodity price change (see Bhagwati and Srinivason, 1971 for these conditions). Here, we merely consider the possibilities, assuming throughout that demand can be inferred from a social utility function.

---

[2]Hagen (1958); Bhagwati and Ramaswani (1963); Bhagwati and Srinivasan (1971). For a valuable survey of the vast literature on wage differentials, see Magee (1973).

Case (1) : *Wage differential against nontradeables, convex production possibility set and normal production response.* Starting with equilibrium at (Q, C), devaluation implies a rise in P_T/P_{NT} to $Q^1C^1 = Q^2C^2$ in Figure 2.

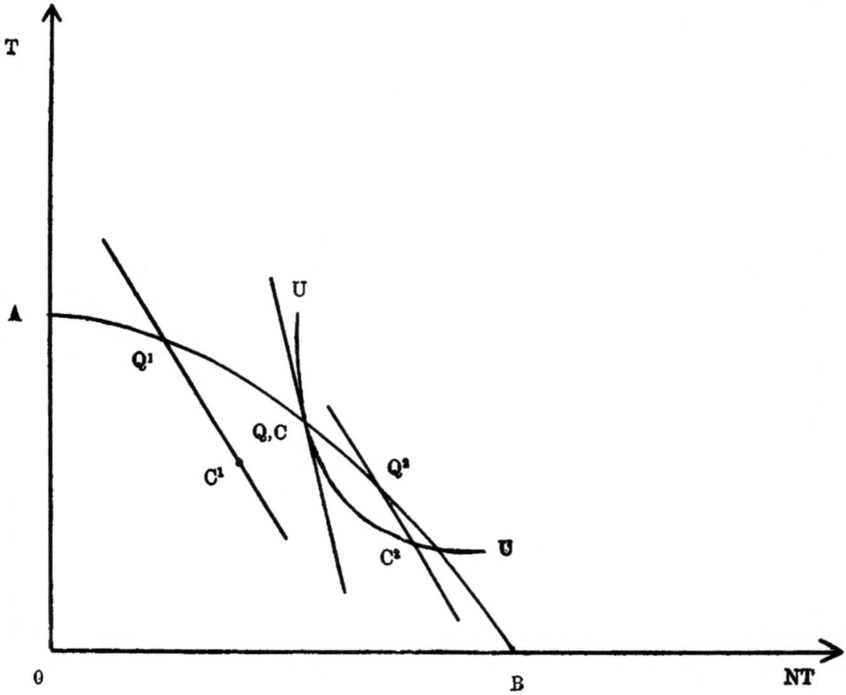

Figure 2

With a normal production response, production shifts to Q^1. We can then conclude that (a) ruling out inferiority of tradeables in social consumption, the primary impact of the devaluation is to create an external *surplus* (i.e. excess supply of tradeables) and corresponding excess demand for nontradeables; but (b) if inferiority is not ruled out, a devaluation *could* lead to an external *deficit* and corresponding excess supply of nontradeables.

Case (2) : *Wage differential against nontradeables, convex production possibility set and perverse production response.* In Figure 2, this implies shift with devaluation to Q^2 and C^2. It is readily seen then that, *even if inferiority in consumption is ruled out* for either good, the devaluation may cause a primary *deficit* in the balance of payments.

Case (3) : *Wage differential against nontradeables, concave production possibility set and normal production response.* Shift now to Figure 3, where

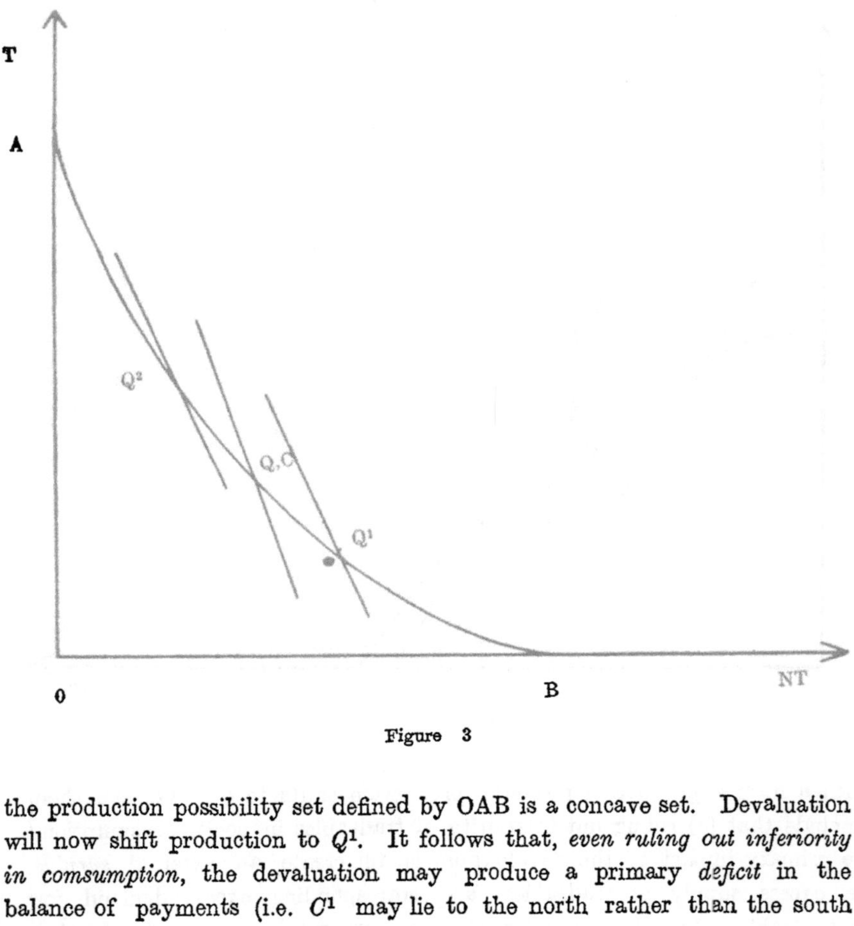

Figure 3

the production possibility set defined by OAB is a concave set. Devaluation will now shift production to Q^1. It follows that, *even ruling out inferiority in comsumption*, the devaluation may produce a primary *deficit* in the balance of payments (i.e. C^1 may lie to the north rather than the south of Q^1).

Case (4) : *Wage differential against nontradeables, concave production possibility set and perverse production response.* Now, in Figure 3, devaluation shifts production to Q^2. It follows that (a) ruling out inferiority in consumption, (C^2 must lie to the south of Q^2 and therefore) devaluation will create a primary *surplus* in the balance of payments; and (b) if inferiority in consumption is permitted, (C^2 could lie to the north of Q^2 and therefore) a *deficit* could arise.

The results do not change if the differential operates against the tradeables : the possibility of a "counter-intuitive" creation of a primary deficit in the balance of payments with a devaluation arises in the same manner as in the four cases considered above. This identity of results, regardless of whether the differential operates against tradeables or non-tradeables, is in contrast to the results for welfare analysis where the ranking of policies such as free trade and autarky depends critically on which sector has to pay to the higher cost for the same factor of production.

(ii) *Sticky wages* : Next, consider the case where wages are identical between sectors but sticky so that the actual wage is different from the shadow wage.[3] For simplicity, assume that factors are also immobile between sectors. Also, assume that the real wage of labour is sticky in terms of the tradeables.

Then, as in Figure 4, devaluation raises P_T/P_{NT} to Q^1C^1, the equilibrium at (Q, C) must give way to a production point such as Q^1 because the rise in P_T/P_{NT} must create unemployment in the nontradeables sector until the marginal physical product of labour therein rises sufficiently to yield the required real wage (in terms of the tradeables at the increased P_T/P_{NT}.

It is then easy to see that (a) if inferiority in consumption of the tradeables is ruled out, a *surplus* in balance of payments must result from the devaluation; but (b) if inferiority in consumption of the tradeables is permitted, then a *deficit* could emerge.

If, on the other hand, the real wage is fixed in this model in terms of the nontradeable (which may well be a "wage good") then it is easily seen that inferiority in consumption can be admitted and nonetheless a primary surplus would necessarily follow a devaluation.

(iii) *Sector-specific sticky, real wages*. The best-known model for analyzing the effects of a sticky wage in *one* sector (alone) is the Harris-Todaro model and its marginally-modified variants (cf. Harris and Todaro 1970; Bhagwati and Srinivasan, 1973, 1974). The model allows for only one factor, L, to be mobile between sectors, sector-specific "other" factors leading then to declining marginal products to increasing labour input in each sector. If tradeables and nontradeables are the two sectors, and real wage in the

[3] This is a factor market inperfection first analyzed by Gottfried Haberler (1950) and subsequently analyzed by Harry Johnson (1965), Bhagwati (1967) and most fully, in both its positive and welfare aspects, in two excellent articles by Richard Brecher (1974).

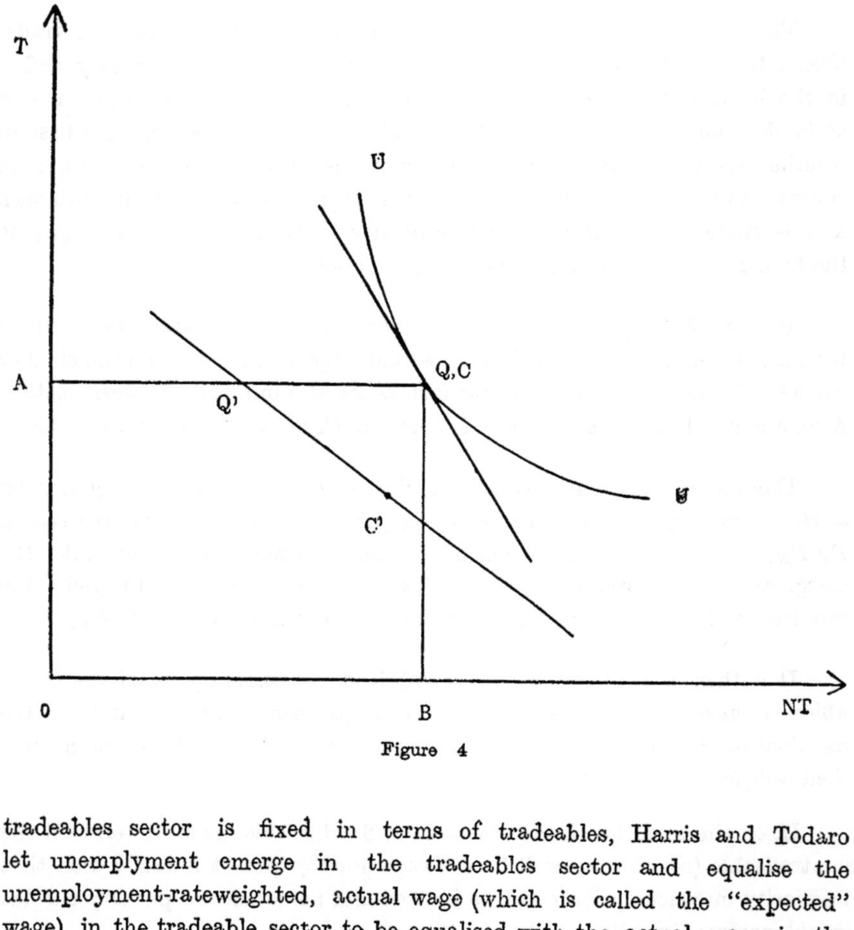

Figure 4

tradeables sector is fixed in terms of tradeables, Harris and Todaro let unemplyment emerge in the tradeables sector and equalise the unemployment-rateweighted, actual wage (which is called the "expected" wage) in the tradeable sector to be equalised with the actual wage in the nontradeable sector.

Assume, in Figure 5, that *AB* represents the technological production possibility curve and *BSM* the curve that would be feasible given the real wage constraint-a move beyond *S* on *SA* is infeasible because the increased labour input in tradeables beyond *S* reduces its marginal product therein, and hence its real wage, below the floor specified. Equilibrium production and consumption, prior to devaluation, are at (*Q*, *C*). The devaluation-induced rise in P_T/P_{NT} shifts production (along the "feasible" stretch *SM*) to Q^1. For details of this argument, see Bhagwati and Srinivassan (1973).

It is then easy to see that (a) if inferiority in consumption is ruled out, (C^1 must lie below Q^1 and therefore) a *surplus* in the balance of payments will follow; but (b) if inferiority in the consumption of tradeables is admitted, a *deficit* could emerge (as C^1 could lie to the north of Q^1).

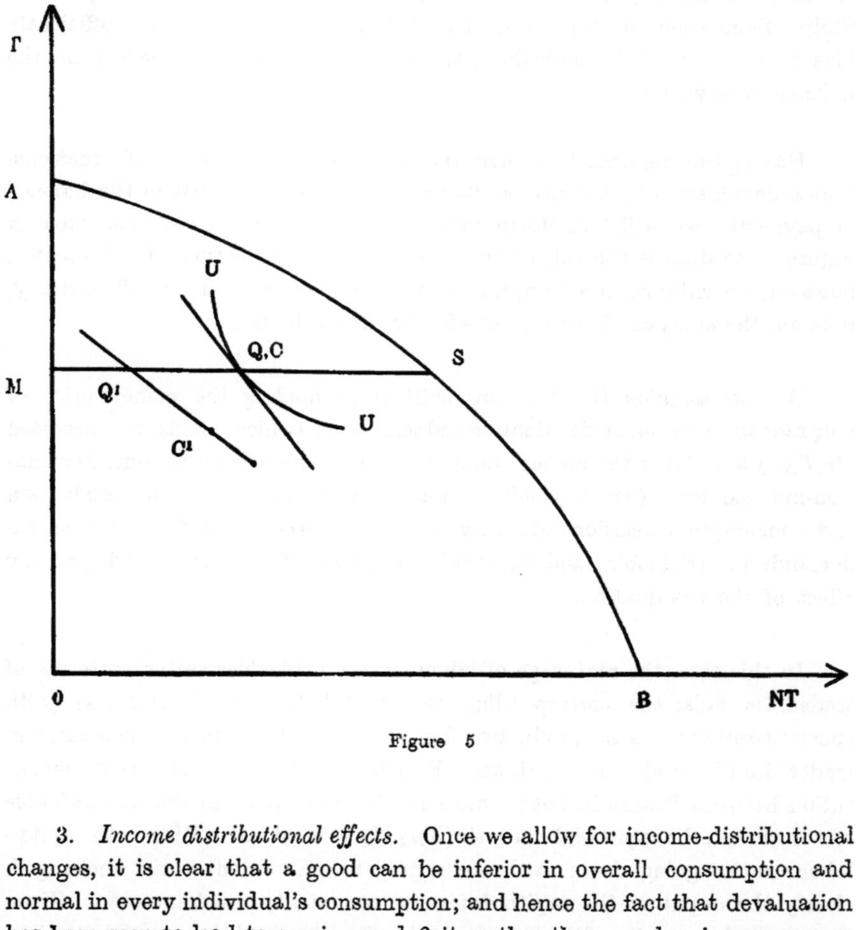

Figure 5

3. *Income distributional effects.* Once we allow for income-distributional changes, it is clear that a good can be inferior in overall consumption and normal in every individual's consumption; and hence the fact that devaluation has been seen to lead to a primary deficit, rather than surplus, in many cases when tradeables are inferior goods is more disturbing than would otherwise appear to be.

At the same time, we cannot rely on the usual inequality arguments for well-behaved social utility functions (with non-intersecting indifference curves) for the consumption change following a price change to be constrained in a specific way. Thus, in Figure 1, C^1 could well lie to the west of Q^1 on Q^1C^1, leading to a devaluation-induced *deficit*, rather than surplus, in the balance of payments. To demonstrate this, note that as the production of tradeables rises with their (relative) price, the absolute and relative share of the factor intensively used in their production will also rise (as per the Stolper-Samuelson theorem); and if that factor's consumption is sufficiently biased in favour of the tradeables, the net result would be a deficit in the balance of payments.

Having thus reminded ourselves that it is possible, in a variety of situations, that a devaluation may cause, as its primary impact, a deficit in the balance of payments, we will henceforth focus on the "normal" case, illustrated in Figure 1, to discuss the full return to equilibrium in Section II. Presently, however, we will turn to Assumption II, to examine how it affects differentially, if at all, the analysis of the impact effect of a devaluation.

B : *Assumption* II. We now shift from holding the money price of nontradeables to some devaluation-induced level (which yields an increased P_T/P_{NT}) to holding the money wage in the tradeables sector to some devaluation-induced level (which yields an increased P_T/w_m) : and the production and consumption decisions are now to be reworked, yielding the excess demands for tradeables and non-tradeables, subject to this altered primary effect of the devaluation.

In this case, the real wage of labour in the tradeables sector, in terms of tradeables, falls; the corresponding real rental *to capital must rise* (with constant-returns-to-scale production functions); and the capital-labour ratio in tradeables (K_T/L_T) must go down. Equality of the marginal rate of substitution between factors in both sectors implies then that, in the nontradeable sector as well, the capital-labour ratio (K_{NT}/L_{NT}) must fall. With both capital-labour ratios going down, and the aggregate endowment ratio unchanged, clearly the ouput of the capital-intensive commodity must increase. Given the assumed convexity of the transformation function, and absence of distortions in a competitive economy, it follows simply that the relative (domestic) price of the capital-intensive commodity must then rise. If therefore the non-tradeables are capital-intensive, devaluation will have led to a "perverse" increase in *their* relative price and hence to a deficit in balance of payments; if they are labour-intensive, the effect of the devaluation on the relative price of nontradeables will be normal and a primary-impact surplus will result from the devaluation.[4]

Before we proceed to the "elimination-of-primary-disequilibrium" analysis of Section 2, two observations on the analysis so far are warranted. First, it is clear that one can get strikingly different results on the (primary) impact of a devaluation, depending on which prices are assumed to be "sluggish" and therefore which markets and prices are assumed to adjust to the devaluation in the first round, as it were. Thus, when it is postulated (Assumption I) that the price of the nontradeable is quasi-sticky at the outset so that the devaluation leads to increased relative price of the tradeables and then the production and consumption decisions, as also all other prices (including money wages) in the system, adjust to it, we "normally" get a primary surplus in the balance of trade. But if we instead postulate (Assumption II) that the money wage in the tradeables sector is quasi-sticky at the outset so that the devaluation leads to a reduced real wage in terms of tradeables, and then production, consumption and all other prices (including the price of the nontradeables) adjust to it, we can get a primary *deficit* in the balance of trade : and, this contrast obtains in the *same* real model, with identical parameteric values for factor endowments and production functions. Our analysis therefore underlines well the critical fact, missing from non-dynamic

[4] In either case, whether the relative price of nontradeables rises or falls, their absolute price will increase, given the general increase in money wage and the unambiguous decrease in the real wage (in terms of both goods). Note also that a special case of the above analysis, where the money wage is totally fixed, has been analyzed independently by Jones and Corden (1976), using a different form of argument from that deployed in the text above. They also consider the case of fixed money wages in the context of a model where labour is mobile but two "capitals" are immobile with one capital specific to one sector. This model, very similar to Harris-Todaro in its assumption of only one mobile factor, was analyzed by Jones earlier in 1971. This simple model leads to a simple conclusion readily. With P_T/w_m rising with the devaluation, the marginal product of labor in tradeables will fall, implying that labor is attracted therein and the output of tradeables therefore increases. Nontradeables correspondingly lose labor and their output falls. Since the production possibility curve is obviously convex (because of diminishing returns to labor input in each sector), the relative increase in the output of tradeables also implies that their relative price increases. Thus devaluation necessarily leads, in this "essentially" one-factor model, to a rise in the relative price and output of the tradeables : a "normal" result. (Note also that, if the money wage (w_m) is *totally* rigid in response to the devaluation, as Jones-Corden assume, the absolute price of nontradeables (P_{NT}) will also fall because the reduced labor input in nontradeables implies increased marginal product of labor (MPP_L^{NT}) therein : for, $w_m = MPP_L^{NT}.P_{NT}$.] Credit for considering the impact of nominal wage rigidity in the context of balance of payments analysis, to the best of my knowledge, belongs to Dornbusch (1974).

analyses that the impact of a devaluation can depend crucially on the postulated sequence of adjustment in different markets in response to the initial disturbance implied by the devaluation.

Second, note that the primary impact, under Assumptions I and II, would be identical in the limiting case of no impact on the balance of trade. Under Assumption I, this would be the case where P_{NT} rises fully by the amount of the devaluation as well, leaving P_T/P_{NT} unchanged. Under Assumption II, this would be the case where w_m rises fully by the amount of the devaluation as well, leaving P_T/w_m unchanged. In both cases, the relative commodity and factor prices would be unchanged after the devaluation, and the average price and wage level would have risen by the full amount of the devaluation.

2. The full impact of devaluation

So far we have considered only the primary impact of a devaluation in our small economy, starting from a position of initial equilibrium with zero trade deficit and assuming that the production and consumption adjustments are carried out in response to the changed prices initially assumed to be resulting (under two alternative assumptions) from the devaluation. But clearly the analysis cannot be left there; we have to examine further how the resulting imbalances in disequilibrium are eliminated and equilibrium restored; only then would we have the full answer to the question of the impact of a devaluation. To undertake this analysis, we need to make some important distinctions

(1) We may assume that the prices initially set for the analysis of the impact effect of the devaluation continue to be so set (i.e. P_{NT} is held rigid at the devaluation-induced level under Assumption I and w_m is kept frozen at the devaluation-induced level under Assumption II) *or* we may totally unfreeze them and work out the return to equilibrium on the assumption of full price and wage flexibility, *or* we may assume that these prices are rigid downwards but not upwards; and (2) we may assume either that the economy is left to adjust with a passive government or we may assume that the government, in a Meade-like world, intervenes actively with fiscal and monetary policy. In the analysis that follows, we work with these alternative possibilities. We begin with analysis under Assumption I, but considering only the "normal" case where the devaluation creates a primary surplus in the balance of trade. We then turn to analysis under Assumption II, considering only the case of a primary surplus following the devaluation.

A: *Assumption* I. We can distinguish among four cases and now proceed to analyze them, in turn.

Case (1): *Policy equilibrium: active government with P_{NT} flexible or rigid.* We now consider the standard analysis of policy equilibrium, where the price of nontradeables may be *rigid or flexible* at the level defined to derive the primary impact of the devaluation. In Figure 6, based on Figure 1, this equilibrium, resulting from a governmental policy of sufficient deflation to eliminate the excess demand for nontradeables (at Q^1, C^1), leads to a shift in the national expenditure line below the income line and the equilibrium consumption shifts then to C^2. The associated surplus in the balance of trade then is Q^1C^2.

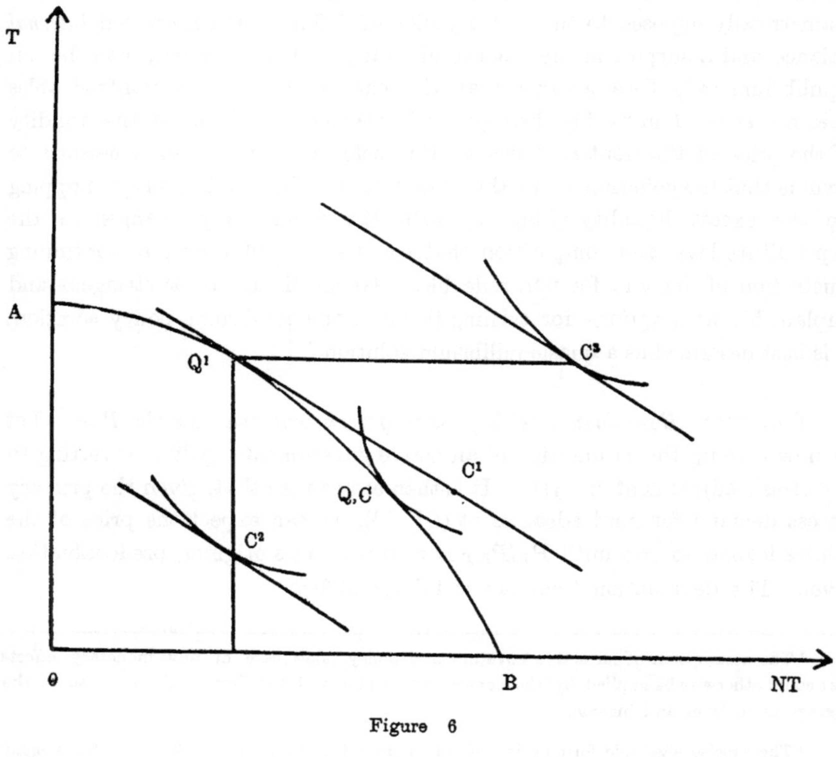

Figure 6

This represents the final, full equilibrium as long as we assume that the government pursues an active policy to maintain total expenditure below the total income level and that the rest of the world which registers the deficit is willing to put up with it.[5] We can then argue that, in this policy equilibrium involving a policy of sustained deflation, the effect of a devaluation will be to create a continuing surplus in the balance of trade.[6] Note also that this equilibrium can be reached whether the absolute price of the nontradeables is rigid at the level defined in the primary-impact analysis or fully flexible; for, the primary-impact level of P_T/P_{NT} remains constant in the analysis (at Q^1C^1). Hence this particular policy equilibrium applies *equally* to the cases where P_{NT} is flexible or rigid.

Case (2) : *Policy quasi-equilibrium : active government with P_{NT} altogether rigid.* We can also consider a different outcome, under a policy of givernment *inflation*, rather than deflation. In Figure 6, this leads the economy to *external* balance but excess demand for nontradeables at C^3 : a result diametrically opposed to the earlier policy of deflation which created *internal* balance and a surplus in the balance of trade. This, however, can be an equilibrium *only* if we assume that the excess demand for nontradeables does not succeed in raising their price : hence the critical role of the rigidity of the price of the nontradeables to this solution. It is also necessary to assume that the government further counters (e.g. by continuously mopping up the excess liquidity piling up with the public) any changes in the expenditure level and composition that could ensue from such a continuing frustration of demand for nontradeables. Given these rather stringent and implausible assumptions for turning this into an equilibrium, policy solution, it is best described as a quasiequilibrium solution.[7]

Case (3) : *Equilibrium with passive government and flexible P_{NT}.* Let us now give up the assumption of an active governmental policy, reverting to the classic adjustment analysis. It is then easy to see that, given the primary excess demand for nontradeables at (Q^1, C^1), we can expect the price of the nontradeables to rise until P_T/P_{NT} is restored to its original, predevaluation level. The devaluation therefore is fully nullified.

[5] The assumption of an active governmental policy takes care of any monetary effects that could otherwise be implied by the continuing surplus and the fact of the increase in the average price level and income.

[6] The precise algebraic formulation of this model has been undertaken in the elegant paper of Berglas and Razin (1973).

[7] Brecher has suggested that a way out of the difficulty would be to assume the existence of buffer stocks of nontradeables which are used to meet the demand for nontradeables instead of frustrating it.

This conclusion, however, does require further modification because, with the devaluation, the restoration of the original P_T/P_{NT} does mean that the average price level and money income have gone up. Hence, if the government is totally passive, and the money supply is therefore construed as being held constant, there will be a cash balance effect leading to a decline in national expenditure below national income—as noted by Sidney Alexander in his classic and seminal analysis of devaluation in 1952 that initiated the absorption approach. The surplus will imply an increment in money supply; and the surplus will thus continue until the integral of the associated increment in money supply adds up to the required increment in money supply that is assumed to go with the increased money income.[8] Thus, in the *ultimate*, long-run equilibrium, we can argue that the economy will reach the predevaluation equilibrium at (Q, C) under a passive governmental policy; but that, until this equilibrium is reached, the devaluation will be generating a balance of trade surplus.

Case (4) : *Equilibrium with passive government and rigid* P_{NT}. Finally, let us consider the analysis of devaluation under the assumption of a rigid price of nontradeables, so that the restoration of the predevaluation *relative* prices (as at Q, C) is not feasible. In this case, we cannot have the equilibrium solution discussed in the preceding subsection. For equilibrium to be reached in this case, with external balance (without which equilibrium cannot be achieved, for it would imply a continuing injection or withdrawal of money supply corresponding to a surplus or a deficit and, with a passive government, this cannot be part of a long-run equilibrium situation), it is clear that we have to find some degree of freedom to accommodate the changed commodity price-ratio. This is available in our model only through the forced unemployment of one of the factors of production.

Thus, if tradeables are capital-intensive, and we start at the production point Q^1 (reached under the rigid, devaluation-changed price-ratio P_T/P_{NT}), we can trace out the Rybczynski locus Q^1G for increasing unemployment of capital and the Rybczynski locus Q^1F for growing unemployment of labour. Equilibrium will lie on Q^1G, at a point such as Q^2C^2, which has both external balance and internal clearance of the market for nontradeables : if we rule out inferior goods. If we do not rule them out, such an equilibrium could well lie on Q^1F where the other factor, labour, is unemployed.

Neither of these possible equilibria is fully satisfactory, however, as the unemployment of the factor will have to occur in the face of positive factor

[8] This point has been neatly spelled out in recent papers by Mussa (1976) and Dornbusch (1974).

rewards : unless we can postulate *also* that factor rewards are inflexible downwards at the levels defined by the devaluation-changed commodity price-ratio. The equilibrium solution presented here for the case of rigid P_{NT} then makes total sense only if we add to it a further assumption about factor price inflexibility at the required stage. Furthermore, note that while the average price level has gone up, it is just conceivable that the average money income may have fallen from the predevaluation level because of the move along the Rybczynski line : hence the "required" money supply may actually fall, in which case we would have to envisage a period of continuing *deficit* in the balance of payments as necessary for "mopping up" the excess money supply for the *ultimate* equilibrium to be reached at Q^2C^2.

Thus, the assumption of price rigidity, under a passive governmental policy, manages to undermine the firmness of the conclusions reached under the assumption of totally flexible prices. We should add however that the kind of price rigidity posed here (which is in the upward direction) may be quite unimportant, unless of course the government has a policy of holding down prices by fiat while it is passive on the macroeconomic management front.

Before we turn to the analysis of full equilibrium under Assumption II, however, we should note that the analysis under Assumption I so far can be readily extended to the case where the domestic price of nontradeables, on devaluation, rises by *more than* the devaluation, so that the primary impact of the devaluation is to create a *deficit* rather than a surplus. The analysis just finished can be readily adapted by the reader to this case of a primary deficit. Thus, Case (1) would now show the government *inflating*, rather than deflating, to create enough demand for nontradeables to eliminate the excess demand for nontradeables, and there would be a *deficit* in the balance of trade. Under Case (3), the economy would return ultimately to the predevaluation equilibrium with P_{NT} falling back to the level commensurate with the devaluation. The only new, interesting wrinkle now is that if we assume that prices are inflexible *downwards*—not as implausible an assumption as that they are rigid—we cannot admit Case (3) into our analysis; hence, we transit to Cases (2) and (4), without having to assume that P_{NT} is totally rigid but by merely assuming, far more plausibly, that it is inflexible *downwards*. Since empirical observation suggests that the prices of nontradeables do rise in induced-response to devaluation, and that a devaluation is occasionally taken as a signal for triggering a rise in a number of prices which were held down hitherto, it is perhaps not unreasonable to consider this case of an "excessive" price rise in P_{NT} (so that P_T/P_{NT} actually falls with devaluation) as more than a theoretical curiosum.

B. *Assumption* II : From Section I, we know that, under Assumpt/on II, the primary effect of a devaluation could be to create a surplus or a deficit in the balance of trade. We consider here the surplus situaton; the reader can readily extend the analysis to the case of a primary deficit. For brevity, we distinguish now among three cases.

Case (1) : *Policy equilibrium : active government with w_n flexible or rigid.* This case is identical with Case (1) analyzed under Assumption I. The money wage, subject to which the primary-impact surplus is worked out, will remain unchanged in this policy equilibrium : hence it may be assumed flexible or rigid at that level and either assumption will be consistent with the policy equilibrium analyzed.

Case (2) : *Equilibrium with passive government and flexible w_m.* This case is identical with Case (3) analyzed under Assumption I. The excess demand for nontradeables under the primary-impact will lead to their price rising until the ratio P_T/P_{NT} is restored to the predevaluation level and the money wage (w_m) has risen commensurately with the devaluation. As before, we should envisage a transient surplus to increase the money supply to the level required to accomodate the increased money income at (Q, C) after the devaluation.

Case (3) : *Equilibrium with passive government and rigid w_m.* In this case, the rigidity of the money wave (w_m) implies that the excess demand for nontradeables in the initial-impact situation (Q^1, C^1) cannot be eliminated by a rise in the relative price of nontradeables : the capital-labour ratio in tradeables, and hence in nontradeables, and hence the commodity price-ratio as well are determined, given the real wage P_T/w_m. Therefore, as in Case (4) under Assumption I, we must adjust the economy to this situation by creating unemployment of a factor and shifting production down a Rybczynski line from Q^1 and having it coincide with consumption at the same point.

Thus, in Figure 7, assuming now that the analysis applies for a money wage rigid at some devaluation-induced level, if nontradeables are labour-intensive, a primary surplus will have been created after devaluation, with Q^1 as production and C^1 as consumption. With a passive government, equilibrium would be restored at (Q^2, C^2) on the Rybczynski line Q^1G where capital gets unemployed. As before, we must assume that a transient surplus or

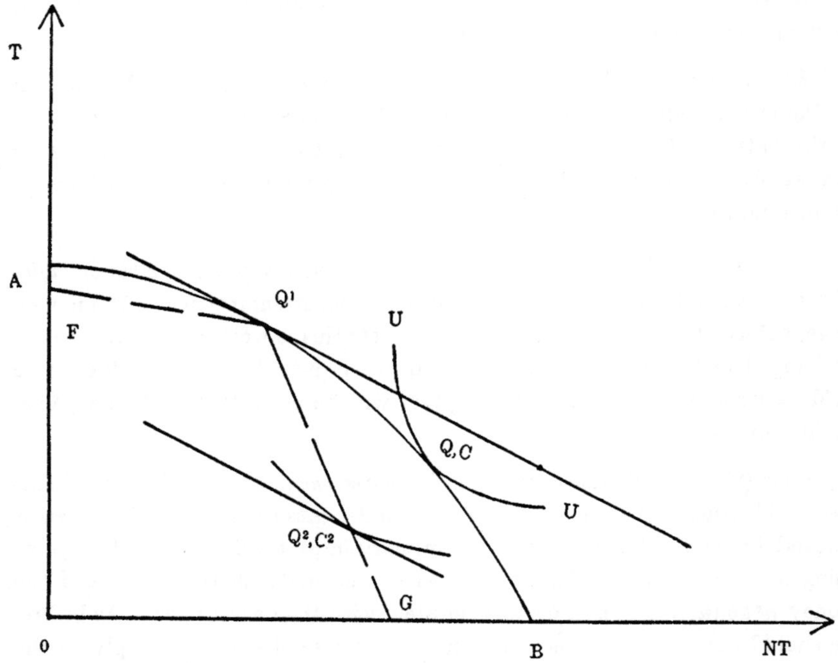

Figure 7

deficit will have to arise to create or destroy the difference between the actual and the required money supply, depending on whether the money income rises or falls given the increased price-level and the possible reduction in income (measured in terms of either good) as a result of the forced unemployment of capital in the economy.

3. Concluding remarks

It is thus clear that the consequences of devaluation, in the Salter model, can depend critically on the assumptions made concerning the commodity and factor price rigidities, nominal and real, in the system. Once these are taken into account, it is not possible to conclude that either the primary or the full impact of a devaluation is necessarily to generate a trade surplus.

References

Berglas, E. and Razin, A. (1973): Real exchange rate and devaluation. *Jour. International Economics*, **3, 2, 179-192-**

Bhagwati, J. (1968): *The Theory and Practice of Commercial Policy, Departure from Unified Exchange Rates*, Princeton University Press, Princeton,

BHAGWATI, J. and RAMASWAMY, V. K. (1963): Domestic distortions, tariffs and the theory of optimum subsidy. *Jour. of Political Economy*, **71**, 44-52.

BHAGWATI, J. and SRINIVASAN, T. N. (1971): The theory of wage differentials: production response and factor price equalisation. *Jour. International Economics*, **1**, No. (1), 19-36.

——— (1973): The ranking of policy interventions under factor market imperfection: the case of sector-specific sticky wages and unemployment. *Sankhyā*, Series B, **35**, 405-420.

——— (1974): On reanalysing the Harris-Todaro Model: policy rankings in the case of sector-specific sticky wages. *American Economic Review*, **64**, No. (3) 502-508.

BRECHER, RICHARD (1974a): Minimum wage rates and the pure theory of international trade. *Quarterly Journal of Economics*, **88**, No. (1) 86-97.

——— (1974b): Optimal commercial policy for a minimum-wage economy. *Jour. International Economics*, **4**, No. (2) 139-149.

DORNBUSCH, R. (1973): Devaluation money, and non-traded goods. *American Economic Review* **63**, 871-880.

——— (1974): Real and monetary aspects of the effects of exchange rate changes, in R. Aliber (ed.) *National Monetary and Policies and the International Financial System*, University of Chicago Press.

HAGEN, E. (1958): An economic justification of protectionism. *Quarterly journal of Economics*, **72**, 496-514.

HABARLER, GOTTFRIED (1950): Some problems in the pure theory of international trade. *Economic Journal*, **60**, 496-514.

HARRIS, JOHN and TODARO, MICHAEL (1970): Migration, unemployment and development: a two-sector analysis. *American Economic Review*, **60**, 26-142.

JOHNSON, HARRY (1965): Optimal trade intervention in the presence of domestic distortions, in P. Kenen *et al.* (ed.), *Trade, Growth and the Balance of Payments*, Rand Mc. Mally & Co, Chicago.

JONES, R. (1971): A three factor model in theory, trade and history, in J. Bhagwati *et al* (ed.) *Trade, Balance of Payments and Growth*, North Holland Publishing Company.

JONES, R. and CORDEN, W. M. (1976): Devaluation, non-flexible prices, and the trade balance for a small country. *Canadian Journal of Economics*, **9**, 150-161.

MAGEE, S. (1973): Factor market distortions, production and trade: a survey. *Oxford Economic Papers*, **25**, 1-43.

MUSSA, M. (1976): Tariffs and the balance of payments: a monetary approach, in J. A. Frenkel and H. G. JOHNSON (ed.), *The Monetary Approach to the Balance of Payments*, George Allen & Unwing Ltd. London.

PEARCE, I. F. (1961): The problem of the balance of payments. *International Economic Review*, **2**, 1-28.

SWAN, T. (1963): Longer-run problems of the balance of payments, in H. Arndt and W. M. Corden (ed.), *The Australian Economy : a volume of Readings*, F. W. Cheshire, Australia.

Paper received : October, 1978.

Three Alternative Concepts of Foreign Exchange Difficulties in Centrally Planned Economies

Padma Desai and Jagdish N. Bhagwati

I Introduction

The recent entry of the Soviet economy into the world economy, in regard to trade, credit, and technology, has prompted much popular and some scientific discussion of the foreign exchange problems confronting the Soviet Union.[1] However, the analysts of these problems have deployed, and the generalist discussions have occasionally confused, what are quite distinct concepts of the foreign exchange problems.

It is necessary, therefore, to distinguish among three alternative concepts, which are in reality quite different from one another. These are (1) Foreign Exchange Bottleneck; (2) Open Payments Deficit; and (3) Suppressed Payments Deficit. These are considered in sections II–IV, respectively.

II Foreign Exchange Bottleneck

The concept of a foreign exchange bottleneck is a simple *ex ante* planning concept and has no intrinsic relationship (as we will shortly demonstrate) to the *ex post* payments deficit concepts. As developed in the planning literature, it essentially amounts to arguing that, given the objective function and domestic resources-cum-technology of the planners, their inability to transform available into demanded goods is the effective constraint on increasing the value of this objective function.

The classic statement of a foreign exchange bottleneck is in a simple corn-tractor model. The economy produces corn, saves and exports corn to import tractors which constitute investment and produce the corn. In this economy, let the current objective be to increase investment. This means buying more tractors from abroad. Now, if the finance minister

This paper was originally published in *Oxford Economic Papers*, November 1979.

cannot tax the economy into saving more corn, to purchase more tractors by exporting this corn, then the economy has a *savings* bottleneck. However, if the economy can be coaxed or taxed into more saving, but the economy faces a unitary price elasticity of demand in the world markets for its corn, foreign exchange receipts will not increase. Tractor imports and therefore investment will not increase; we then have a transformation or *foreign exchange* bottleneck.[2]

It will be evident to the reader that a necessary, though not sufficient condition for a foreign exchange bottleneck to exist is the absence of the economy's ability to transform goods into one another in world markets at the initial world prices. That is, a "small" country, which is atomistic in world markets, cannot have a foreign exchange bottleneck. (It follows equally that, compared to the free trade situation, such an economy will, for a more general class of objective functions (than merely maximizing the volume of investment), do *better* by *restricting* its trade, as is well known from the theory of optimal tariff in the presence of monopoly power in trade.)

In the Soviet context it can be argued that the foreign exchange bottleneck operates *not* with respect to growth of income, but rather with respect to a shift towards greater availability of consumer goods in total and in composition.

This argument of foreign resource inflow being a contraint on the growth and diversification of consumption .levels is best illustrated by reference to the classical and idealized demonstration of the foreign exchange bottleneck for developing countries in figure 1.

Assume there that the economy, at the relevant point of time, has a production possibility vector, $\bar{P}$, that is, resources cannot be transferred from one sector to another.[3] Let the two sectors be producing capital and consumer goods respectively *a la* the standard two-sector model. For the developing countries traditionally, the argument of the developmental planners during the 1950s and 1960s was that a foreign exchange bottleneck existed for raising investment (that is, availability of capital goods) and growth of income. For, starting from $\bar{P}$, the foreign offer curve facing them was $\bar{P}$QR and if the developing countries could save more than $\bar{P}$W, say $\bar{P}$N, the incremental *ex ante* savings worth NW would not yield any incremental imports of capital goods and hence there would be no increase in *ex post* investment. NW worth of consumer goods, saved by the developing countries, would only accure to foreigners *via* terms of trade loss from $\bar{P}$Q to $\bar{P}$V.[4]

The Soviet Union's present situation, on the other hand, may be

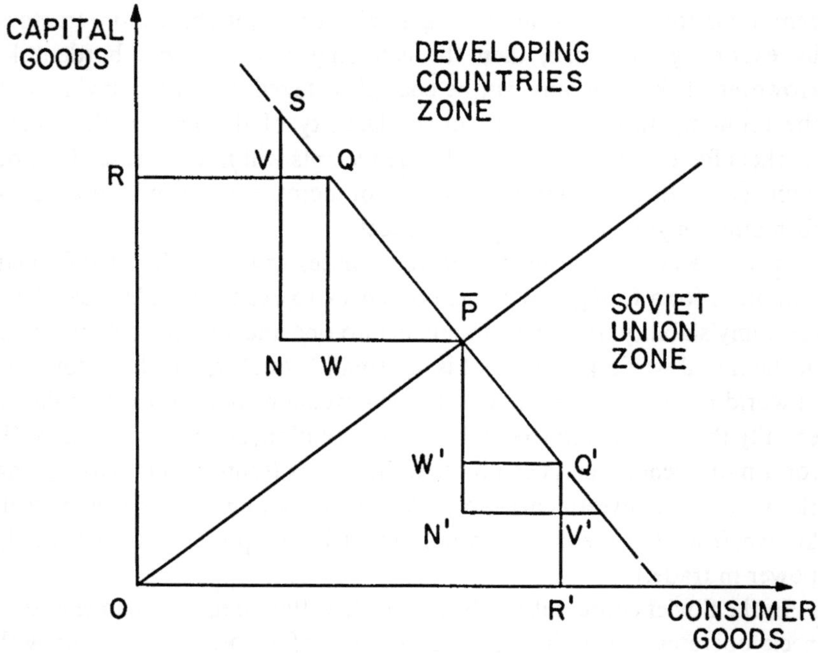

Figure 1

idealized in this illustration by turning the dilemma on its head. With its objective of shifting availabilities in favor of consumer goods, the foreign exchange constraint for the Soviet Union would seem to imply a willingness, but not the ability (beyond $\bar{P}W'$ of capital goods), to transform capital goods[5] into consumer goods through foreign exchange earnings with foreign offer curve $\bar{P}Q'R'$. The foreign exchange constraint of the Soviet Union, therefore, is indeed, as with developing countries, on shifting the availabilities between investment and consumption through trade. However, in the case of the developing countries, this is translated into a constraint on growth of income; in the case of the Soviet Union, it amounts rather to a constraint on the composition of the growing income.[6]

III Open Payments Deficit

In constrast to the *ex ante* planning concept of the foreign exchange bottleneck, the payments deficit concepts relate to the *ex post* macroeconomic situation.

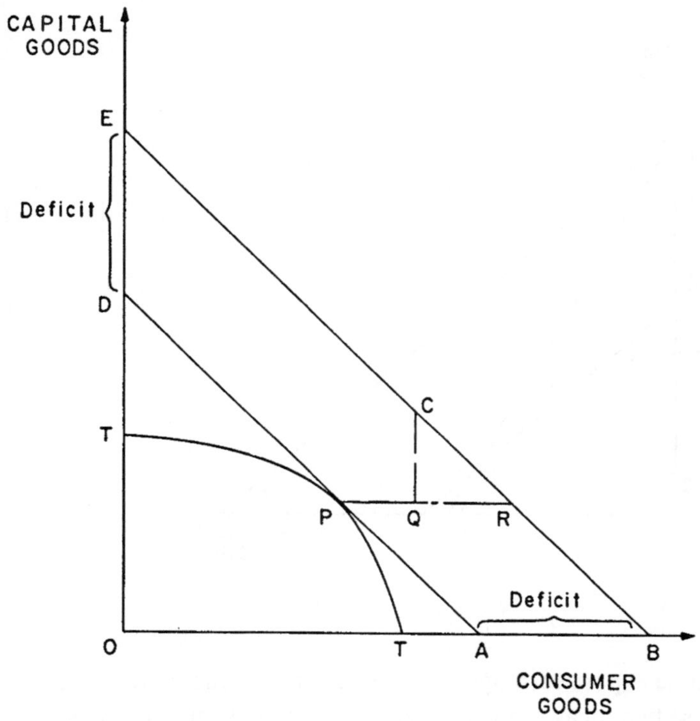

Figure 2

For "flow" current-account deficits, it is evident that an open payments deficit means that imports exceed exports *ex post*. Therefore we can amend the illustration in figure 1 to portray an open deficit simply as in figure 2. There, the production possibility curve is TT; production is at P; the world price line, identical with the domestic price line, is APD; the domestic expenditure line is BCE and the national income line is APD, so that the open deficit is AB (if measured in units of consumer goods) or equivalently DE (if measured in units of capital goods).[7] With the consumption vector chosen at C, the deficit is "absorbed" as PQ of consumer goods and CQ of capital goods.

Note two things. First, unlike the foreign exchange bottleneck concept which hinges critically on the assumption of monopoly power in trade, an open payments deficit can arise obviously regardless of whether the country is atomistic in world markets. Second, it is possible for such an open payments deficit to arise in several alternative ways. Holzman's (1978) interesting recent paper in fact argues that CPEs have a built-in tendency to get into payments difficulties because they systematically

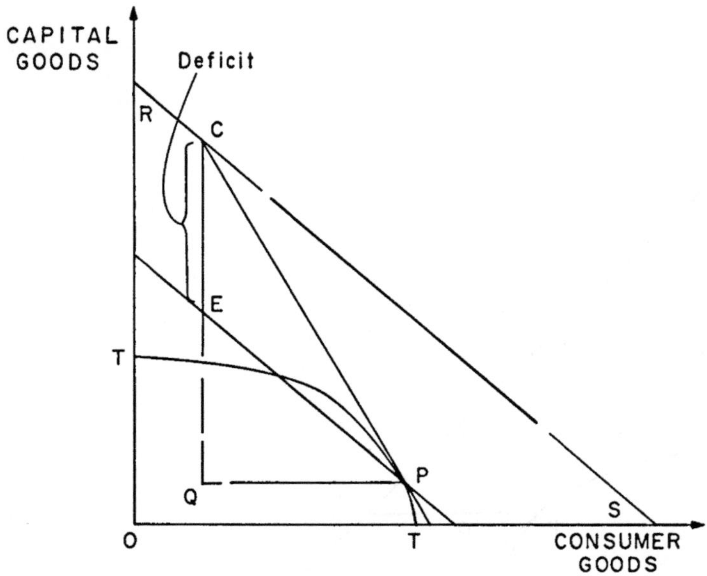

Figure 3a

either overestimate export earnings or overestimate production/income. Drawing on these two ideas, we will illustrate precisely some (but by no means all) of the ways in which CPEs may actually experience open payments deficits.

Demand-Determined Open Deficit

First, consider cases where the CPE overestimates export performance, not because of supply difficulties but because of unduly optimistic assessment of world demand for its exports, but sticks to its import targets instead of revising them downwards. The resulting (world-) demand-determined open deficit may be illustrated for two polar cases: (i) where the export quantity is forecast accurately but the price is overestimated; and (ii) where the export price is forecast accurately, but the quantity is overestimated.

In figure 3a, the first case is illustrated. The CPE plans *ex ante* for PQ exports in exchange for QC imports. However, the terms of trade turn out to be PE instead of PC. Thus the planned and actual exports PQ pay for only QE imports. With planned imports sticky at QC, the CPE then has to run an open payments deficit of CE. The effective social budget line then is RCS and exceeds the income line PE by the deficit.

Note that the "adjustment mechanism" postulated here allows for the

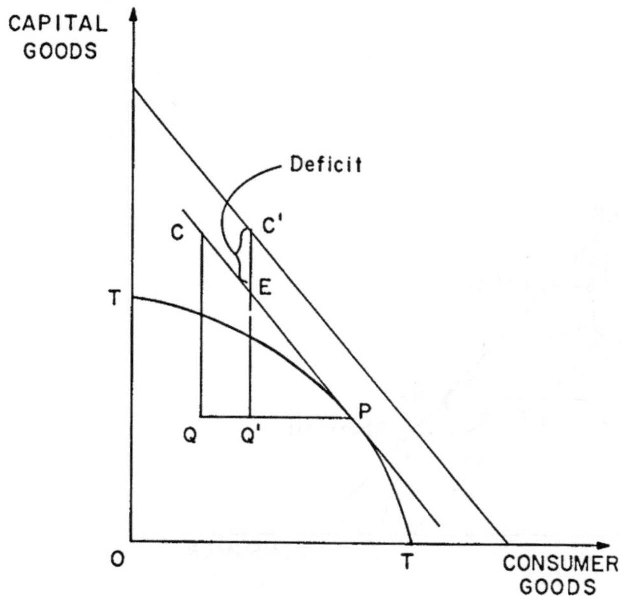

Figure 3b

disequilibrium resulting from the *ex post* deterioration in export prices relative to *ex ante* expectations to be eliminated by external borrowing or running down of reserves *and* without permitting reallocation of consumption and production decisions so as to maximize some objective function subject to the constraints constituted by domestic transformation and *ex post* foreign transformation possibilities and borrowing stipulated at CE.[8]

In figure 3b, we illustrate the other polar case where the quantity of exports is overestimated and falls short of PQ by QQ′, whereas their price and hence the terms of trade are correctly anticipated as PEC. Exporting PQ′ however will pay only for Q′E imports, thus leaving a payments deficit of C′E to pay for the planned and actual imports CQ = C′Q′.[9]

Supply-Determined Open Deficit

Consider next a situation where the failure in export performance comes from an overly optimistic assessment of production of exportables.

Then, assuming that the CPE is atomistic in world markets and can trade as much as it wants to, let P_e be the *expected* production vector and P_a the actual *ex post* production vector, so that P_aP_e measures the shortfall in exportable production. P_eQ and QS represent the planned exports and

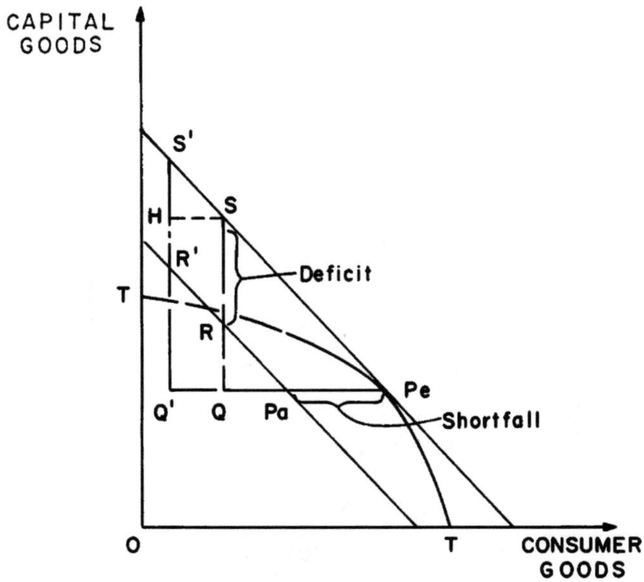

Figure 4

imports respectively. If expenditure is not revised downwards *a la* Holzman (1978), expenditure and income will diverge by SR, which will constitute the open deficit. However, depending on what the planners choose to export in face of the production shortfall, the import level (but not the deficit) will vary; and it can differ from the *ex ante* level QS. In figure 4, if the shortfall in exportable production leads the planners to a fully offsetting reduction in (total) exports from P_eQ to P_aQ, the CPE will wind up importing altogether SQ, the planned level of imports. On the other hand, if part of the shortfall in exportable production is accommodated through reduced *domestic* availability, exports will not be reduced as much. Thus, if they fall, not to P_aQ but to P_aQ', the payments deficit will remain the same (for it equals the postulated excess of expenditure over income) but the actual import level will rise to Q′S′ (> QS).

But we can tell an altogether different story, reflecting a different "adjustment mechanism". So far, we have argued with Holzman (1978) that the excess of expenditure over income is fixed by the assumption that anticipated expenditure is necessarily *ex post* expenditure while *ex post* income falls below anticipated income, and therefore that the trade decisions must accommodate to yield consistency with this. Rather, assume now that it is domestic expenditure that will adjust to accommodate the trade decisions.

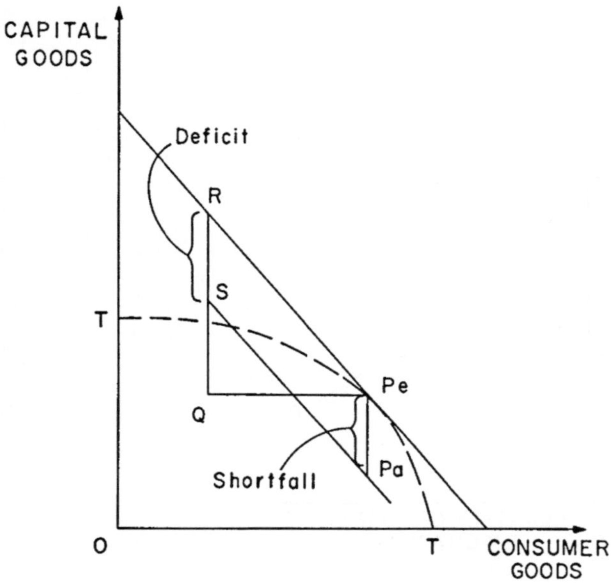

Figure 5

Thus, in figure 4, assume that the planners react to the shortfall in exportable production by reducing exports from P_eQ to P_aQ'. The planned level of imports is sticky at SQ. Then R′H is clearly the level of imports that cannot be financed from export earnings. These imports then imply a corresponding, open payments deficit, a deficit in this instance that is smaller than under the Holzman (1978) assumptions: $HR' < S'R' (= SR)$.

In conclusion, note that the supply-determined open payments deficit can equally arise from shortfall in importable production. Thus the planned exports QP_e, when effected, will yield in figure 5 the anticipated imports QR. But P_eP_a, the shortfall in importable production, implies a shortfall then in domestic availability of RS importables which may lead to an open payments deficit of identical magnitude to eliminate this shortfall.

IV Suppressed Payments Deficit

In contrast to the open payments deficit, no matter what precise circumstances cause and shape it, the suppressed payments deficit characterizes a situation where these same circumstances are not permitted to "spill over" into the balance of payments in the shape of an excess of imports over exports.

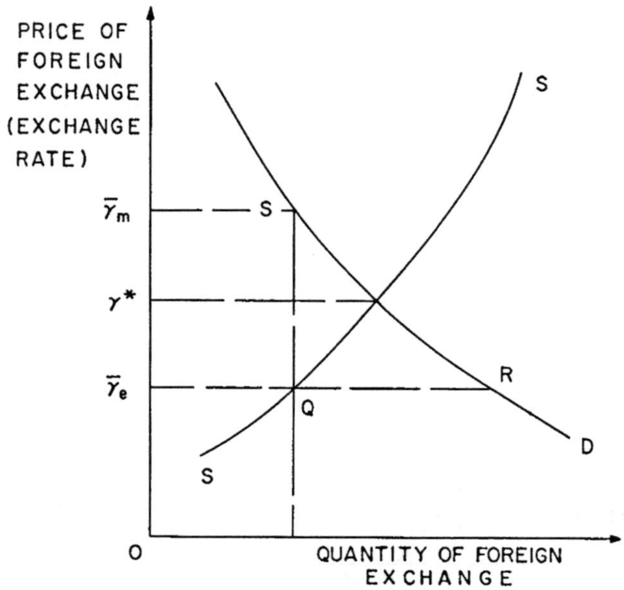

Figure 6

In the case of market economies, this distinction between open and suppressed payments deficits is quite important for analytical purposes. For, a suppressed deficit implies essentially that, instead of maintaining the balance between expenditure and income by a suitable mix of macroeconomic policies which preserves unified exchange rates, and similarly in contrast to the open deficit situation which also permits the preservation of unified exchange rates, the suppressed deficit situation typically implies differential, effective exchange rates on foreign transactions. This is seen in the traditional foreign-exchange-market diagram in figure 6. There, the exchange rate r* corresponds to an equilibrium, unified exchange rate that clears the market. The exchange rate $\bar{r}_e$ leads to an excess demand for foreign exchange that could be met by an open deficit, financed by borrowing or use of reserves, of amount QR; this situation also yields identical, unified exchange rates for export and import transactions (which underlie the supply and demand curves respectively). However, when the open deficit is suppressed, the exchange rate $\bar{r}_e$ gencrates supply of foreign exchange $\bar{r}_e$Q which is cleared in the market at the "premium-inclusive" price, or effective exchange rate, $\bar{r}_m$; and therefore the effective exchange rates on exports ($\bar{r}_e$) and on imports ($\bar{r}_m$) are unequal in this suppressed-deficit situation.

The general-equilibrium "real" counterpart of these distinctions in the traditional two-sector model of trade theory is usually demonstrated as the free-trade solution for the equilibrium unified exchange rate, the free-trade-with-transfer (equal to the deficit) solution for the open deficit case, and a tariff (implying a higher effective exchange rate on imports than on exports) solution for the suppressed deficit case.

The "suppressed deficit" concept therefore permits us to examine explicitly the allocational implications of managing the balance of payments, not by adjusting the exchange rate (and therewith the domestic and foreign residents' transactions), but by pegging the exchange rate and using exchange controls to equate import payments to exchange earnings.

Thus, aside from the obvious fact that an open payments deficit and a suppressed deficit differ because the open deficit implies increased current availability of resources to the economy, the open deficit also is characterized by an adjustment mechanism that ensures, *ceteris paribus*, unified exchange rates whereas the suppressed deficit does not. For CPEs, however, the latter distinction is not particularly relevant in view of the general delinking of the foreign payments situation from domestic production and consumption decisions. Thus, for the case illustrated in figure 3a, the open deficit situation was not based on either steady-state optimality or even short-run optimality (given the production decision). The corresponding suppressed deficit situation again, if shown by winding up at E (implying that the imports take the entire adjustment burden), would not generally represent an optimal situation either. The distinction between open and suppressed deficits is therefore unlikely to be of the same significance for CPEs as it is regarded for the analysis of market economies: the welfare implications for resource allocation of these alternative situations are not as clear for the CPEs as they are for the market economies.[10,11]

Thanks are due to the National Science Foundation Grants No. SOC77-07254 and No. SOC77-07188 for financial support of the first and second authors, respectively, in writing this paper. Thanks are due to Franklyn Holzman and Peter Neary for extremely helpful comments on an earlier draft of this paper.

References

1. Bhagwati, Jagdish N. 1978. *The Anatomy and Consequences of Exchange Control Regimes*. Cambridge, Massachusetts: NBER, Ballinger and Co.

2. Bhagwati, Jagdish N. "The Nature of Balance of Payments Difficulties in Developing Countries." In *Measures for Trade Expansion of Developing Countries*, October 1966. Japan Economic Research Center, Center Paper No. 5.

3. Chenery, Hollis, and Michael Bruno. 1962. "Development Alternatives for an Open Economy: The Case of Israel," *Economic Journal*, volume 72.

4. Desai, Padma. 1978. "The Productivity of Foreign Resource Inflow to Soviet Economy," *Harvard Russian Research Center*, 1978. Paper presented at the *American Economic Association* Meetings, Chicago (1978). Also in *American Economic Review*, May 1979.

5. Findlay, Ronald. 1971. "The Foreign Exchange Gap and Growth in Developing Economies." In J. Bhagwati et al., editors, *Trade, Balance of Payments and Growth*. Amsterdam: North Holland Co.

6. Holzman, Franklyn, 1978, "Foreign Exchange Problems of Centrally Planned Economies," *American Review*, May 1979. Paper presented at the *AEA* Meetings, Chicago.

Editor's Note

Also see Jagdish N. Bhagwati, "The Case for Devaluation," *The Economic Weekly (Bombay)* 14(31) (1962). This article notes the possibility of a contractionary devaluation in the context of the discussions in India immediately preceding the June 1966 devaluation and the fears that it would be inflationary. The large current-account deficit, reflecting the absorption of foreign aid, is cited as a major factor resulting in this contractionary effect. Richard Cooper and Paul Krugman and Lance Taylor, among others, have recently written on the contractionary possibility: see Richard Cooper, "Devaluation and Aggregate Demand in Aid-Receiving Countries," in J. N. Bhagwati, R. W. Jones, R. A. Mundell, and J. Vanek, eds. *Trade, Balance of Payments and Growth: Papers in International Economics in Honor of Charles P. Kindleberger*, Amsterdam: North-Holland, chapter 16, pp. 355–376; and Paul Krugman and Lance Taylor, "Contractionary Effects of Devaluation," *Journal of International Economics* 8:445–460.

CONTENTS

Volume 1
The Theory of Commercial Policy

III
Tariffs, Quotas, and Subsidies

IV
Directly Unproductive Profit-Seeking (DUP) Activities: Illegal Trade and Lobbying

ACKNOWLEDGMENTS

The author, editor, and The MIT Press wish to thank the publishers of the following essays for permission to reprint them here.

42 "International Factor Movements and National Advantage," *Indian Economic Review* 14(2) (N.S.) (October 1979):73–100. Copyright 1979 by Allied Publishers.

43 "On the Choice between Capital and Labour Mobility" (with T. N. Srinivasan), *Journal of International Economics* 15 (1983). Copyright 1983 by North-Holland Publishing Company.

45 "International Migration of the Highly Skilled: Economics, Ethics and Taxes," *Third World Quarterly* 1(3) (July 1979):17–30. Copyright 1979 by New Zealand House.

46 "Welfare-Theoretical Analyses of the Brain Drain" (with Carlos Rodriguez), *Journal of Development Economics* 2 (1975):195–221. Copyright 1975 by North-Holland Publishing Company.

47 "The Brain Drain, International Integration of Markets for Professionals and Unemployment: A Theoretical Analysis" (with Koichi Hamada), *Journal of Development Economics* 1 (1974):19–42. Copyright 1974 by North-Holland Publishing Company.

48 "Domestic Distortions, Imperfect Information and the Brain Drain" (with Koichi Hamada) in J. N. Bhagwati, ed., *The Brain Drain and Taxation*, Vol. II: *Theory and Empirical Analysis*, Amsterdam: North-Holland, 1976, chapter 7, pp. 139–153. Copyright 1976 by North-Holland Publishing Company.

49 "Education in a 'Job Ladder' Model and the Fairness-in-Hiring Rule" (with T. N. Srinivasan), *Journal of Public Economics* 7 (1977):1–22. Copyright 1977 by North-Holland Publishing Company.

50 "Introduction," *Journal of Public Economics* 18 (Symposium on the Exercise of Income Tax Jurisdiction over Citizens Abroad) (1982):285–289. Copyright 1982 by North-Holland Publishing Company.

51 "Tax Policy in the Presence of Emigration" (with Koichi Hamada), *Journal of Public Economics* 18 (1982):291–317. Copyright 1982 by North-Holland Publishing Company.

52 "Tariff Change, Foreign Capital and Immiserization" (with Ernesto Tironi), *Journal of Development Economics* 7 (1980):71–83. Copyright 1980 by North-Holland Publishing Company.

53 "National Welfare in an Open Economy in the Presence of Foreign-Owned Factors of Production" (with Richard A. Brecher), *Journal of International Economics* 10 (1980):103–115. Copyright 1980 by North-Holland Publishing Company.

54 "Foreign Ownership and the Theory of Trade and Welfare" (with Richard A. Brecher), *Journal of Political Economy* 89(3) (June 1981):497–511. Copyright 1981 by The University of Chicago Press.

55 Review of *Sovereignty at Bay: The Multinational Spread of U.S. Enterprises* (New York: Basic Books, 1971) by Raymond Vernon, *Journal of International Economics* 2 (1972):455–459. Copyright 1972 by North-Holland Publishing Company.

56 Review of *The International Operations of National Firms: A Study of Direct Foreign Investment* (Cambridge, MA: MIT Press, 1976) by Stephen H. Hymer, *Journal of Development Economics* 4 (1977):391–395. Copyright 1977 by North-Holland Publishing Company.

57 "Shifting Comparative Advantage, Protectionist Demands, and Policy Response" (with appendix by Robert C. Feenstra), in J. N. Bhagwati, ed., *Import Competition and Response*, Chicago: University of Chicago Press, 1982, pp. 153–195. Copyright 1982 by The National Bureau of Economic Research.

58 "Oligopoly, Theory, Entry-Prevention, and Growth," *Oxford Economic Papers* 22(3) (N.S.) (November 1970):297–310. Copyright 1970 by Oxford University Press. [Reprinted in R. E. Neel, ed., *Readings in Price Theory*, Cincinnati: South-Western Publishing, 1973, chapter 21, pp. 365–378.]

59 "The Pure Theory of International Trade: A Survey," *Economic Journal* 74 (March 1964):1–84. Copyright 1964 by Macmillan and Co. Ltd. [Reprinted with addendum, in J. N. Bhagwati, *Trade, Tariffs and Growth*, Cambridge, MA: MIT Press, 1969, chapter 1, pp. 3–122.]

60 "Notes on Some Controversies in the Theory of International Trade" (with Harry G. Johnson), *Economic Journal* 70 (March 1960):74–93. Copyright 1960 by Macmillan and Co. Ltd.

61 "The Proofs of the Theorems on Comparative Advantage," *Economic Journal* 77 (March 1967):75–83. Copyright 1967 by Macmillan and Co. Ltd.

62 "The Heckscher-Ohlin Theorem in the Multi-Commodity Case," *Journal of Political Economy* 80(5) (September/October 1972):1052–1055. Copyright 1972 by The University of Chicago Press.

63 "Trade-Diverting Customs Unions and Welfare-Improvement: A Clarification," *Economic Journal* 81 (September 1971):580–587. Copyright 1971 by Macmillan and Co. Ltd.

64 "A Reply to Professor Kirman," *Economic Journal* 83 (September 1973):895–897. Copyright 1973 by Macmillan and Co. Ltd.

65 "Foreign Capital, Dependence, Destabilisation and Feasibility of Transition to Socialism" (with Earl Grinols), *Journal of Development Economics* 2 (1975):85–98. Copyright 1975 by North-Holland Publishing Company.

66 "Foreign Capital, Savings and Dependence" (with Earl Grinols), *Review of Economics and Statistics* 58(4) (November 1976):416–424. Copyright 1976 by North-Holland Publishing Company.

67 "Foreign Capital, Savings and Dependence: A Reply to Mr. Wasow" (with Earl Grinols), *Review of Economics and Statistics* 61(1) (February 1979):154–156. Copyright 1979 by North-Holland Publishing Company.

68 "Immiserizing Transfers from Abroad" (with Richard A. Brecher), *Journal of International Economics* 13 (1982):353–364. Copyright 1982 by North-Holland Publishing Company.

69 "Devaluation in a Small Economy with Flexible and Rigid, Real and Nominal, Prices," *Sankhya* 40(2) (Series D) (1978):99–117. Copyright 1978 by the Indian Statistical Institute.

70 "Three Alternative Concepts of Foreign Exchange Difficulties in Centrally Planned Economies" (with Padma Desai), *Oxford Economic Papers* 31(3) (N.S.) (November 1979). Copyright 1979 by Oxford University Press. [Reprinted in J. N. Bhagwati, ed., *International Trade: Selected Readings*, Cambridge, MA: MIT Press, chapter 27, pp. 349–359.]

AUTHOR INDEX

SUBJECT INDEX

9 780262 521215

Printed by Libri Plureos GmbH in Hamburg,
Germany